FORTUNE

DIGEST

FORTUNE
DIGEST

Oxmoor
House®

FORTUNE Digest
Senior Editor: Clark Scott
Editors: David Dunbar, Noel Rae
Editorial Assistants: Stacey Harmis, L. Amanda Owens
Production Manager: Jerry Higdon
Designer: Joe Freedman, The Sarabande Press

Special thanks to Ann Morrison, Assistant Managing Editor, *Fortune*, for her
patience and guidance throughout the development of this book.

To order *Fortune* magazine, write to: *Fortune*, Subscription Service Dept. P.O. Box
60001, Tampa, Florida 33660-0001

— CONTENTS —

FOREWORD

A well-known writer recently received a call from a reader who liked the writer's first book but complained that the second was too difficult. "I asked him what he meant by *too difficult*," the writer explains, "and he said there were too many words on a page."

While I don't know the easy solution to that reader's problem, his complaint echoes a frustration we've all experienced: sometimes it seems there are too many words out there for us to absorb. Author Richard Wurman has coined a term for the 20th century affliction that comes from overexposure to information and the resulting sense of underassimilation; he calls it "Information Anxiety." That anxiety builds as we contemplate the pile of information we have to read at work, then the books we want to read at home. Which brings me to the mission of *FORTUNE Digest*.

In this crisp volume, we give you a big quantity of information—five of the most stimulating business books on the market, each carefully condensed to make the assimilation of information easier and less time consuming. By honing each of these books to its essential message, *FORTUNE* is doing its part to ease the information crunch while keeping you informed.

The books chosen for this first edition of *FORTUNE Digest* do not represent any single editorial point of view, and we don't necessarily agree with everything the authors say. Our intent is to bring you books that offer informed, provocative, useful discussions of important business topics or, at the very least, a unique treatment of some aspect of management. We looked, too, for popular books because sometimes a book is important simply because everybody else is reading it.

Leadership Secrets Of Attila The Hun falls into the latter category. A manual for maneuvering in a highly politicized office, it has won praise from an impressive list of top executives, including H. Ross Perot, founder of Electronic Data Systems, and Robert L. Crandall of American Airlines. At the opposite end of the spectrum from *Attila* is *A Great Place To Work*, which argues for depoliticizing the workplace and analyzes successful businesses to show how they have profited from treating their employees right.

We chose *The Enigma Of Japanese Power* because it deals so persuasively with a subject that affects every American business, the economic rivalry that the author calls "The Japan Problem." A journalist who has covered Japan for 25 years, Karel van Wolferen gives a detailed analysis of life in that country to support his surprising thesis that Japan is a place where no one is really in control.

The ITT Wars is an inside look into the age of runaway buyouts. The author, ITT's CEO Rand Araskog, defended his company in one of the nastiest, most complicated takeover battles of the decade. Araskog tells readers about the high-stakes games and huge egos that can destroy financially solid corporations.

The fifth book, *One Up On Wall Street*, offers investment insights from one of the best mutual fund managers in the country, Peter Lynch. Over the past decade his fund, Fidelity Magellan, has returned an astounding 1,251 percent profit to its investors.

With these books, *FORTUNE Digest* brings you a well-rounded collection of some of the most fascinating ideas, trends, and personalities in the business world today. We have not sacrificed readability in the condensing process; what we have given you is world enough and time. And that's even better than fewer words on a page.

ONE UP ON WALL STREET

How to Use What You Already Know to Make Money in the Market

Peter Lynch
with John Rothchild

Condensed from *One Up On Wall Street*, © 1989 by Peter Lynch. Published by Simon & Schuster, Inc. Printed by permission.

Editor's Note

You would expect the portfolio manager of America's top-performing mutual fund over the past decade to have a special system of buying and selling stocks that eludes the ordinary guy on the street. In fact, Fidelity Magellan's Peter Lynch, who has led his fund to a phenomenal 10-year 1,251 percent gain, relies on just the opposite: he succeeds by doing the obvious.

He bought Taco Bell because he liked the taste of its burritos; La Quinta Motor Inns because somebody at rival Holiday Inn recommended it; and Apple Computer because his kids had one at home. His wife, Carolyn, introduced him to L'eggs and its then manufacturer, Hanes. Over the years, Fidelity Magellan rode each of these companies to impressive gains. Most were "ten-baggers," stocks that appreciated tenfold or better.

Obviously, there's more to picking a good stock than finding a good burrito. But Lynch maintains that liking a company's product is the first step—one that too many investors ignore but one that gives amateur stockpickers an edge over professional managers.

In One Up On Wall Street, *Lynch tells fascinating stories about some of his bargains. He also explains how to research a stock and how to recognize which numbers count and which don't. Lynch offers easy directions for determining a company's potential and some rules for investing in cyclicals, turnarounds, fast growers, and other types of companies. Most important, he recommends that you buy a stock as you would buy a piece of a business, asking yourself, "Is this something I would be comfortable owning?"*

Lynch's formula for success—pick a growing business at a low price—is not a new concept. But it's amazing how few investors follow it. One Up On Wall Street *shows you how to use this approach to design your own personal portfolio. What sets this book apart is its pure readability, insights, and unexpected wit.*

From beginning to end, Peter Lynch offers sensible advice for every potential investor. As he says: "It is personal preparation, as much as knowledge and research, that distinguishes the successful stockpicker from the chronic loser. Ultimately, it is not the stock market nor even the companies themselves that determine an investor's fate. It is the investor."

THE ADVANTAGES OF DUMB MONEY

his is where the author, a professional investor, promises the reader that he'll share the secrets of his success. But rule number one, in my book, is: Stop listening to professionals! Twenty years in this business convinces me that any normal person using the customary three percent of the brain can pick stocks just as well, if not better, than the average Wall Street expert.

I know you don't expect the plastic surgeon to advise you to do your own facelift, or the plumber to tell you to install your own hot-water tank, but this isn't surgery or plumbing. This is investing, where the smart money isn't so smart, and the dumb money isn't really as dumb as it thinks.

The amateur investor has numerous advantages that, if exploited, should result in his or her outperforming the experts and the market in general. When you pick your own stocks, you ought to outperform the experts. Otherwise, why bother?

I'm not going to get carried away and advise you to sell all your mutual funds. If that started to happen on any large scale, I'd be out of a job. Besides, there's nothing wrong with profitable mutual funds. Honesty and not immodesty compels me to report that millions of amateur investors have been well-rewarded for investing in Fidelity Magellan, which is why I was invited to write this book. The mutual fund is a wonderful invention for people who have neither the time nor the inclination to test their wits against the stock market, as well as for people with small amounts of money to invest who seek diversification.

It's when you decide to invest on your own that you ought to try going it alone. That means ignoring the hot tips, the recommendations from brokerage houses, and the latest "can't miss" suggestion from your favorite newsletter—in favor of your own research. If you stay half-alert, you can pick the spectacular performers right from your place of business or out of the neighborhood shopping mall long before Wall Street discovers them. It's impossible to be a credit-card-carrying American consumer without having done a lot of fundamental analysis on dozens of companies—and if you work in the industry, so much the better. This is where you'll find the tenbaggers.

THOSE WONDERFUL TENBAGGERS

In Wall Street parlance a "tenbagger" is a stock in which you make ten times your money. I suspect this highly technical term has been borrowed from baseball, which only goes up to a fourbagger, or home run. In my business a fourbagger is nice, but a tenbagger is the fiscal equivalent of two home runs and a double.

I developed a passion for making ten times my money early in my investing career. The first stock I ever bought, Flying Tiger Airlines, turned out to be a multibagger that put me through graduate school. In the last decade the occasional five- and tenbagger, and the rarer twentybagger, have helped my fund outgain the competition—and I own 1,400 stocks. In a small portfolio even one of these remarkable performers can transform a lost cause into a profitable one.

APPLES AND DONUTS

You may have thought that a tenbagger can only happen with some wild penny stock in some weird company like Braino Biofeedback or Cosmic R and D. Actually there are numerous tenbaggers in companies you'll recognize: Dunkin' Donuts, Wal-Mart, Toys "R" Us, Stop & Shop, and Subaru, to mention a few. These are companies whose products you've admired and enjoyed, but who would have suspected that if you'd bought the Subaru stock along with the Subaru car, you'd be a millionaire today?

This serendipitous calculation is based on several assumptions: first, that you bought the stock at its low of $2 a share in 1977; second, that you sold at the high in 1986, which would have amounted to $312 a share, unadjusted for an 8-for-1 split. That's a 156-bagger, and the fiscal equivalent of 39 home runs, so if you'd invested $6,410 in the stock (certainly in the price range of a car), you'd come out with $1 million exactly. (Throughout this book we're going to be faced with the complication that occurs when companies split their shares—two-for-one, three-for-one, etc. If you invest $1,000 in 100 shares of Company X, a $10 stock, and there's a two-for-one split, then suddenly you own 200 shares of a $5 stock. In the case of Subaru the stock never actually sold for $312. There had been an eight-for-one split just before the high, so the stock was actually at $39 [$312 divided by 8] at the time. To conform with this price, all presplit levels must be divided by 8. The $2 low in 1977 is now a "split-adjusted" 25 cents per share [$2 divided by 8 equals $0.25], although the stock never actually sold for 25 cents. Companies generally prefer not to have their share prices too high in absolute dollar terms, which is one reason why stock splits are declared.)

THE POWER OF COMMON KNOWLEDGE

To get these spectacular terms you had to buy and sell at exactly the right time. But even if you missed the highs or the lows, you would have done better to have invested in any of the familiar companies mentioned above than in some esoteric enterprise.

There's a famous story about a fireman from New England. Apparently back in the 1950s he couldn't help noticing that a local Tambrands plant (then the company was called Tampax) was expanding at a furious pace. It occurred to him that they wouldn't be expanding so fast unless they were prospering, and on that assumption he and his family invested $2,000. Not only that, they put in another $2,000 each year for the next five years. By 1972 the fireman was a millionaire—and he hadn't even bought any Subaru.

I get many of my best investment ideas the way the fireman got his. I talk to hundreds of companies a year and spend hour after hour in heady powwows with CEOs, financial analysts, and my colleagues in the mutual-fund business, but I stumble onto the big winners the same way you could:

Taco Bell, I was impressed with the burrito on a trip to California; La Quinta Motor Inns, somebody at the rival Holiday Inn told me about it; Volvo, my family and friends drive this car; Apple Computer, my kids had one at home and then the systems manager bought several for the office; Dunkin' Donuts, I loved the coffee; and recently the revamped Pier 1 Imports, recommended by my wife. In fact, Carolyn is one of my best sources. She's the one who discovered L'eggs.

L'eggs is the perfect example of the power of common knowledge. It turned out to be one of the two most successful consumer products of the seventies. In the early part of that decade, before I took over Fidelity Magellan, I was a securities analyst at the firm. I knew the textile business from having traveled the country visiting textile plants, calculating profit margins, price/earnings ratios, and the esoterica of warps and woofs. But I didn't find L'eggs in my research; Carolyn found it at the grocery store.

Right there in a freestanding metal rack near the checkout counter was a new display of women's panty hose, packaged in colorful plastic eggs. The company, Hanes, was test-marketing L'eggs at several sites around the country, including suburban Boston. Carolyn didn't need to be a textile analyst to realize that L'eggs was a superior product. All she had to do was buy a pair and try them on. These stockings had what they call a heavier denier, which made them less likely to develop a run than normal stockings. They also fit very well, but the main attraction was convenience. You could pick up L'eggs right next to the bubble gum and the razor blades, without having to make a special trip to the department store.

Hanes already sold its regular brand of stockings in department and specialty stores. However, the company had determined that women customarily visit one or the other every six weeks, on average, whereas they go to the grocery store twice a week, which gives them twelve chances to buy L'eggs for every one chance to buy the regular brand. Selling stockings in the grocery store was an immensely popular idea. How many women who bought panty hose, store clerks who saw the women buying panty hose, and husbands who saw the women coming home with the panty hose knew about the success of L'eggs? Millions. Two or three years after the product was introduced, you could have walked into any one of thousands of supermarkets and realized that this was a best-seller. From there, it was easy enough to find out that L'eggs was made by Hanes and that Hanes was listed on the New York Stock Exchange.

Once Carolyn alerted me to Hanes, I did the customary research into the story. The story was even better than I'd thought, so with the same confidence as the fireman who bought Tambrands, I recommended the stock to Fidelity's portfolio managers. Hanes turned out to be a sixbagger before it was taken over by Consolidated Foods, now Sara Lee. L'eggs still makes a lot of money for Sara Lee and has grown consistently over the past decade. I'm convinced Hanes would have been a 50-bagger if it hadn't been bought out.

IS THIS A PUBLIC COMPANY?

Despite my winner with Hanes, I could go on for several pages about tenbaggers I've missed. When it comes to ignoring promising opportunities, I'm as adept as the next person. Once I was standing on the greatest asset play of the century, the Pebble Beach golf course, and it never occurred to me to ask if it was a public company. I was too busy asking about the distance between the tees and the greens.

Luckily there are enough tenbaggers around so that both of us could fail to notice the majority and we'll still hit our share. Moreover, the nice thing about investing in familiar companies such as L'eggs or Dunkin' Donuts is that when you try on the stockings or sip the coffee, you're already doing the kind of fundamental analysis that Wall Street analysts are paid to do.

During a lifetime of buying cars or cameras, you develop a sense of what's good and what's bad, what sells and what doesn't. If it's not cars you know something about, you know something about something else, and the most important part is, you know it before Wall Street knows it. Why wait for the Merrill Lynch restaurant expert to recommend Dunkin' Donuts when you've already seen eight new franchises opening up in your area? The Merrill Lynch restaurant analyst isn't going to notice Dunkin' Donuts (for reasons I'll soon explain) until the stock has quintupled from $2 to $10, and you noticed it when the stock was at $2.

GIGGING THE GIGAHERTZ

For some reason, amateur investors don't equate driving around town eating donuts with research into equities. People seem more comfortable investing in something about which they are entirely ignorant. There seems to be an unwritten rule on Wall Street: If you don't understand it, then put your life savings into it. Shun the enterprise around the corner, which can at least be observed, and seek out the one that manufactures an incomprehensible product.

I heard about one such opportunity just the other day. According to a report somebody left on my desk, this was a fantastic chance to invest in a company that makes "one megabit S-Ram, C-mos (complementary metal oxide semiconductor); bipolar risc (reduced instructive set computer), floating point, data I/O array processor, optimizing compiler, 16-bytes dual port memory, unix operating system, whetstone megaflop polysilicon emitter, high band width, six gigahertz, double metalization communication protocol, asynchronous backward compatibility, peripheral bus architecture, four-way interleaved memory and 15 nanoseconds capability."

Gig my gigahertz and whetstone my megaflop; if you couldn't tell if that was a racehorse or a memory chip stay away from it, even though your broker recommends it as the opportunity of the decade to make countless nanobucks.

A POX ON THE CABBAGE PATCH

Does that mean you ought to buy shares in every new public company that opens an outlet in the local mall? If it were that simple, I wouldn't have lost money on Bildner's, the yuppie 7-Eleven right across the street from my office.

And how about Coleco? Just because the Cabbage Patch doll was the best-selling toy of this century, it couldn't save a mediocre company with a bad balance sheet. The stock dropped from a high of $65 in 1983 to a recent $1¾ as the company went into Chapter 11, filing for bankruptcy in 1988.

Finding the promising company is only the first step. The next step is doing the research. The research is what helps you to sort out Toys "R" Us from Coleco, Apple Computer from Televideo, or Piedmont Airlines from People Express. All my failures notwithstanding, during the twelve years I've managed Fidelity Magellan, it has risen over twentyfold per share—partly thanks to some of the little-known and out-of-favor stocks I've discovered and researched on my own. Any investor can benefit from the same tactics.

— 1 —

THE MAKING OF A
STOCKPICKER

There's no such thing as a hereditary knack for picking stocks. Though many would like to blame their losses on some inbred tragic flaw, believing somehow that others are just born to invest, my own history refutes it. There was no ticker tape above my cradle, nor did I teethe on the stock pages. As far as I know, my father never left the pacing area to check the price of General Motors, nor did my mother ask about the ATT dividend between contractions.

Only in hindsight can I report that the Dow Jones industrial average was down on January 14, 1944, the day I was born, and declined further the week I was in the hospital. Though I couldn't have suspected it then, this was the earliest example of the Lynch Law at work. The Lynch Law states: Whenever Lynch advances, the market declines. (The latest proof came in the summer of 1987, when just after the publisher and I reached an agreement to produce this book, a high point in my career, the market lost 1,000 points in two months. I'll think twice before attempting to sell the movie rights.)

Most of my relatives distrusted the stock market, and with good reason. My mother was the youngest of seven children, which meant that my aunts and uncles were old enough to have reached adulthood during the Great Depression, and to have had firsthand knowledge of the Crash of '29. Nobody was recommending stocks around our household.

The only stock purchase I ever heard about was the time my grandfather, Gene Griffin, bought Cities Service. He was a very conservative investor, and he chose Cities Service because he thought it was a water utility. When he took a trip to New York and discovered it

was an oil company, he sold immediately. Cities Service went up
fiftyfold after that.

Distrust of stocks was the prevailing American attitude throughout
the 1950s and into the 1960s, when the market tripled and then doubled
again. This period of my childhood, and not the recent 1980s, was truly
the greatest bull market in history, but to hear it from my uncles, you'd
have thought it was the craps game behind the pool hall. "Never get
involved in the market," people warned. "It's too risky. You'll lose all
your money."

Looking back on it, I realize there was less risk of losing all one's
money in the stock market of the 1950s than at any time before or since.
This taught me not only that it's difficult to predict markets, but also
that small investors tend to be pessimistic and optimistic at precisely the
wrong times, so it's self-defeating to try to invest in good markets and
get out of bad ones.

My father, an industrious man and former mathematics professor
who left academia to become the youngest senior auditor at John
Hancock, got sick when I was seven and died of brain cancer when I was
ten. My mother had to go to work, and I decided to help out by getting a
part-time job. On July 7, 1955, at the age of eleven, I was hired as a
caddy. That day the Dow Jones fell from 467 to 460.

To an eleven-year-old who'd already discovered golf, caddying was
an ideal occupation. They paid me for walking around a golf course. In
one afternoon I would outearn delivery boys who tossed newspapers
onto lawns at six a.m. for seven days in a row. What could be better than
that?

In high school I began to understand the subtler and more important advantages of caddying, especially at an exclusive club such as Brae
Burn, outside of Boston. My clients were the presidents and CEOs of
major corporations: Gillette, Polaroid, and more to the point, Fidelity.
In helping D. George Sullivan find his ball, I was helping myself find a
career. I'm not the only caddy who learned that the quickest route to the
boardroom was through the locker room of a club like Brae Burn.

If you wanted an education in stocks, the golf course was the next
best thing to being on the floor of a major exchange. Especially after
they'd sliced or hooked a drive, club members enthusiastically described their latest triumphant investment. In a single round of play I
might give out five golf tips and get back five stock tips in return.

Though I had no funds to invest in stock tips, the happy stories I
heard on the fairways made me rethink the family position that the stock

market was a place to lose money. Many of my clients actually seemed to have made money in the stock market. I continued to caddy throughout high school and into Boston College, where the Francis Ouimet Caddy Scholarship helped pay the bills. In college, except for the obligatory courses, I avoided science, math, and accounting—all the normal preparations for business. I was on the arts side of school, and along with the usual history, psychology, and political science, I also studied metaphysics, epistemology, logic, religion, and the philosophy of the ancient Greeks.

As I look back on it now, studying history and philosophy was much better preparation for the stock market than, say, studying statistics. Investing in stocks is an art, not a science, and people who've been trained to rigidly quantify everything have a big disadvantage. If stockpicking could be quantified, you could rent time on the nearest Cray computer and make a fortune. But it doesn't work that way. All the math you need in the stock market you get in the fourth grade.

Logic is the subject that's helped me the most in picking stocks, because it taught me to identify the peculiar illogic of Wall Street. Wall Street thinks just as the Greeks did. The early Greeks used to sit around for days and debate how many teeth a horse has, instead of checking the horse. A lot of investors sit around and debate whether a stock is going up, as if the financial muse will give them the answer, instead of checking the company. In 1963, my sophomore year in college, I bought my first stock—Flying Tiger Airlines for $7 a share. Between the caddying and a scholarship I'd covered my tuition, living at home reduced my other expenses, and I had already upgraded myself from an $85 car to a $150 car. I finally was rich enough to invest!

Flying Tiger was no wild guess. I picked it on the basis of some dogged research into a faulty premise. In one of my classes I'd read an article on the promising future of air freight, and it said that Flying Tiger was an air freight company. That's why I bought the stock, but that's not why the stock went up. It went up because we got into the Vietnam War and Flying Tiger made a fortune shunting troops and cargo in and out of the Pacific. In less than two years Flying Tiger hit $32 ¾ and I had my first fivebagger. Little by little I sold it off to pay for graduate school. I went to Wharton on a partial Flying Tiger scholarship.

If your first stock is as important to your future in finance as your first love is to your future in romance, then the Flying Tiger pick was a very lucky thing. It proved to me that the big-baggers existed, and I was sure there were more of them from where this one had come.

During my senior year at Boston College I applied for a summer job at Fidelity, at the suggestion of Mr. Sullivan, the president—the hapless golfer, great guy, and good tipper for whom I'd caddied. Fidelity was the New York Yacht Club, the August National, the Kentucky Derby. It was the Cluny of investment houses, and like that great medieval abbey to which monks were flattered to be called, what devotee of balance sheets didn't dream of working here? There were one hundred applications for three summer positions.

Fidelity had done such a good job selling America on mutual funds that even my mother was putting $100 a month into Fidelity Capital. That fund, run by Gerry Tsai, was one of the two famous go-go funds of this famous go-go era. The other was Fidelity Trend, run by Edward C. Johnson III, also known as Ned, the son of the fabled company founder Edward C. Johnson II, also known as Mister Johnson.

Ned Johnson's Fidelity Trend and Gerry Tsai's Fidelity Capital outperformed the competition by a big margin and were the envy of the industry over the period from 1958 to 1965. With these sorts of people training and supporting me, I felt as if I understood what Isaac Newton was talking about when he said: "If I have seen further . . . it is by standing upon the shoulders of Giants."

Long before Ned's great successes, his father, Mister Johnson, had changed America's mind about investing in stocks. Mister Johnson believed that you invest in stocks not to preserve capital, but to make money. Then you take your profits and invest in more stocks, and make even more money. "Stocks you trade, it's wives you're stuck with," said the always quotable Mister Johnson. He wouldn't have won any awards from *Ms.* magazine.

I was thrilled to be hired at Fidelity, and also to be installed in Gerry Tsai's office, after Tsai had departed for the Manhattan Fund in New York. The Dow Jones industrials, at 925 when I reported for work the first week of May, 1966, had fallen below 800 by the time I headed off to graduate school in September.

QUANTUM ANALYSIS AND RANDOM WALK

Summer interns were put to work researching companies and writing reports, the same as the regular analysts. The whole intimidating business was suddenly demystified—even liberal arts majors could analyze a stock. I was assigned to the paper and publishing industry and set out across the country to visit companies such as Sorg Paper and International Textbook.

After that interlude at Fidelity, I returned to Wharton for my second year of graduate school more skeptical than ever about the value of academic stock-market theory. It seemed to me that most of what I learned at Wharton, which was supposed to help you succeed in the investment business, could only help you fail. I studied statistics, advanced calculus, and quantitative analysis. The latter taught me that the things I saw happening at Fidelity couldn't really be happening.

I also found it difficult to integrate the efficient-market hypothesis (that everything in the stock market is "known" and prices are always "rational") with the random-walk hypothesis (that the ups and downs of the market are irrational and entirely unpredictable). Already I'd seen enough odd fluctuations to doubt the rational part, yet the success of the great Fidelity fund managers was hardly unpredictable.

It also was obvious that Wharton professors who believed in quantum analysis and random walk weren't doing nearly as well as my new colleagues at Fidelity, so between theory and practice, I cast my lot with the practitioners. My distrust of theorizers and prognosticators continues to the present day.

Some Wharton courses were rewarding, but even if they'd all been worthless, the experience would have been worth it, because I met Carolyn on the campus. (We got married while I was in the Army, on May 11, 1968, a Saturday when the market was closed, and we had a week-long honeymoon during which the Dow Jones lost 13.93 points— not that I was paying attention. This is something I looked up later.)

After finishing that second year at Wharton, I reported to the Army to serve my two-year hitch required under the ROTC program. From 1967 to 1969, I was a lieutenant in the artillery, sent first to Texas and later to Korea—a comforting assignment considering the alternative. Lieutenants in the artillery mostly wound up in Vietnam. The only drawback to Korea was that it was far away from the stock exchange. By this time I was suffering from Wall Street withdrawal. I returned from Korea in 1969, rejoined Fidelity as a permanent employee and research analyst, and the stock market promptly plummeted. In June 1974, I was promoted from assistant director of research to director of research, and the Dow Jones lost 250 points in the next three months. In May 1977, I took over the Fidelity Magellan fund. The market stood at 899 and promptly began a five-month slide to 801.

Fidelity Magellan had $20 million in assets. There were only 40

stocks in the portfolio, and Ned Johnson, Fidelity's head man, recommended that I reduce the number to 25. I listened politely and then went
out and soon raised the number to 150 stocks. I didn't do it to be
contrary. I did it because when I saw a bargain I couldn't resist buying
it, and in those days there were bargains everywhere.

The open-minded Ned Johnson watched me from a distance and
cheered me on. Our methods were different, but that didn't stop him
from accepting mine—at least as long as I was getting good results.

My portfolio continued to grow, to the point that I once owned 150
S&L stocks alone. Instead of settling for a couple of savings-and-loans, I
bought them across the board (after determining, of course, that each
was a promising investment in itself). It wasn't enough to invest in one
convenience store. Along with Southland, the parent company of
7-Eleven, I couldn't resist buying Circle K, National Convenience,
Shop and Go, Hop-In Foods, Fairmont Foods, and Sunshine Junior, to
mention a few. I became known as the Will Rogers of equities, the man
who never saw a stock he didn't like.

Meanwhile, the assets in Fidelity Magellan have grown to $9 billion,
which makes this fund half as large as the gross national product of
Greece. As for Will Rogers, he may have given the best bit of advice ever
uttered about stocks: "Don't gamble; take all your savings and buy some
good stock and hold it till it goes up, then sell it. If it don't go up, don't
buy it."

— 2 —

THE WALL STREET OXYMORONS

To the list of famous oxymorons—military intelligence, deafening silence, and jumbo shrimp—I'd add professional investing. It's important for amateurs to view the profession with a properly skeptical eye. Since 70 percent of the shares in major companies are controlled by institutions, it's likely that you're competing against oxymorons whenever you buy or sell shares. This is a lucky break for you. Given the numerous cultural, legal, and social barriers that restrain professional investors, it's amazing that we've done as well as we have, as a group.

Of course, not all professionals are oxymoronic. There are great fund managers, innovative fund managers, and maverick fund managers who invest as they please. John Templeton is a pioneer in the global market, one of the first to make money all around the world. His shareholders avoided the 1972-74 collapse in the U.S. because he had cleverly placed most of his fund's assets in Canadian and Japanese stocks. Michael Price buys asset-rich companies at fifty cents on the dollar, then waits for the marketplace to pay the full amount. John Neff is constantly sticking his neck out in out-of-favor stocks. Ken Heebner at Loomis-Sayles sticks his neck out, too, and the results have been remarkable. Peter deRoeth, a Harvard Law School graduate who developed an incurable passion for equities, gave me Toys "R" Us.

These notable exceptions are entirely outnumbered by the run-of-the-mill fund managers, dull fund managers, comatose fund managers, sycophantic fund managers, timid fund managers, plus other assorted camp followers hemmed in by the rules.

STREET LAG

With every spectacular stock I've managed to ferret out, the virtues seemed so obvious that if 100 professionals had been free to add it to their portfolios, I'm convinced that 99 would have done so. But they couldn't. There are simply too many obstacles between them and the tenbaggers.

Under the current system, a stock isn't truly attractive until a number of large institutions have recognized its suitability and an equal number of respected Wall Street analysts have put it on the recommended list. With so many people waiting for others to make the first move, it's amazing that anything gets bought.

The Limited is a good example of what I call Street lag. When the company went public in 1969, it was all but unknown to large institutions and big-time analysts. The underwriter of the offering was a small firm called Vercoe & Co., located in Columbus, Ohio, where the headquarters of The Limited can also be found. Peter Halliday, a high school classmate of Limited chairman Leslie Wexner, was Vercoe's sales manager back then. Halliday attributed the disinterest of Wall Street to the fact that Columbus, Ohio, isn't exactly a corporate Mecca.

A lone analyst (Susie Holmes of White, Weld) followed the company for a couple of years before a second analyst, Maggie Gilliam of First Boston, took official notice of The Limited in 1974. Maggie Gilliam stumbled onto The Limited store at Chicago's Woodfield Mall during a snow emergency at O'Hare airport. To her credit, she paid attention to her amateur's edge.

The first institution which bought shares in The Limited was T. Rowe Price New Horizons Fund in 1975. By then there were one hundred Limited stores across the country. Thousands of observant shoppers could have initiated their own coverage during this period. Still, by 1979, only two institutions owned Limited stock, accounting for 0.6 percent of the outstanding shares. Employees and executives in the company were heavy owners—usually a good sign, as we'll discuss later.

In 1981, seven years after Ms. Gilliam's discovery, four hundred Limited stores were doing a thriving business and only six analysts followed the stock. By 1983, when the stock hit its intermittent high of $9, long-term investors were up eighteenfold from 1979, when the shares had sold for 50 cents, adjusted for splits.

The price fell to $5 a share in 1984, but the company was still doing well, so that gave investors another chance to buy in. (As I'll explain in later chapters, if a stock is down but the fundamentals are positive, it's best to hold on and even better to buy more). It wasn't until 1985, with the stock back up to $15, that analysts joined the celebration. In fact, they were falling all over one another to put The Limited on their buy lists, and aggressive institutional buying helped send the shares on a ride all the way up to $52 ⅞—way beyond what the fundamentals would have justified. By then, there were more than thirty analysts on the trail (thirty-seven as of this writing), and many had arrived just in time to see The Limited drop off the edge.

My favorite funeral home company, Service Corporation International, had its first public offering in 1969. Not a single analyst paid the slightest heed for the next ten years! The company made great efforts to get Wall Street's attention, and finally it got noticed by a small investment outfit called Underwood, Neuhaus. Shearson was the first major brokerage firm to show an interest, and that was in 1982. By then the stock was a fivebagger.

Thousands of people had to be familiar with this company if for no other reason than they'd been to a funeral, and the fundamentals were good all along. It turns out that the Wall Street oxymorons overlooked SCI because funeral services didn't fall into any of the standard industry classifications. It wasn't exactly a leisure business and it wasn't a consumer durable, either.

Throughout the decade of the 1970s, when Subaru was making its biggest moves, only three or four major analysts kept tabs on it. Dunkin' Donuts was a 25-bagger between 1977 and 1986, yet only two major firms follow it even today. Pep Boys sold for less than $1 a share in 1981 and hit $9 ½ in 1985 before it caught the attention of three analysts. Stop & Shop soared from $5 to $50 as the ranks of its analysts swelled from one to four.

Contrast the above with the fifty-six analysts who cover IBM or the forty-four who cover Exxon.

INSPECTED BY 4

Whoever imagines that the average Wall Street professional is looking for reasons to buy exciting stocks hasn't spent much time on Wall Street. It's the rare fund manager who has the guts to traffic in the unknown. Most mutual-fund managers, pension-fund managers, or corporate-portfolio managers would rather lose only a small amount on an established company than to take a chance on making an unusually large profit on an unknown company. Success is one thing, but it's more important not to look bad if you fail. There's an unwritten rule on Wall Street: "You'll never lose your job losing your client's money in IBM."

If IBM goes bad and you bought it, clients and bosses ask: "What's wrong with that damn IBM lately?" But if La Quinta Motor Inns goes bad, they ask: "What's wrong with you?" That's why security-conscious portfolio managers don't buy La Quinta Motor Inns when two analysts cover the stock and it sells for $3 a share. They don't buy Wal-Mart when the stock sells for $4, and it's a dinky store in a dinky little town in Arkansas, but soon to expand. They buy Wal-Mart when there's an outlet in every large population center in America, fifty analysts follow the company, and the chairman of Wal-Mart is featured in *People* magazine as the eccentric billionaire who drives a pickup truck to work. By then the stock sells for $40.

The worst of the camp-following takes place in the bank pension-fund departments and in the insurance companies, where stocks are bought and sold from preapproved lists. Nine out of ten pension managers work from such lists as a form of self-protection from the ruination of "diverse performance." "Diverse performance" can cause a great deal of trouble, as the following example illustrates.

Two company presidents, Smith and Jones, both of whom have pension accounts managed by the National Bank of River City, are playing golf. While waiting to tee off, they chat about pension accounts, and soon they discover that while Smith's account is up 40 percent for the year, Jones's account is up 28 percent. Both men ought to be satisfied, but Jones is livid. Early Monday morning he's on the phone with an officer of the bank, demanding to know why his money has underperformed Smith's money, when both accounts are handled by the same pension department. "If it happens again," Jones blusters, "we're pulling our money out."

This unpleasant problem for the pension department is soon avoided if the managers of various accounts pick stocks from the same approved batch. That way, it's very likely that both Smith and Jones will enjoy the same result, or at least the difference will not be great enough to make either of them mad. Almost by definition the result will be mediocre, but acceptable mediocrity is far more comfortable than diverse performance.

It would be one thing if an approved list were made up of, say, thirty ingenious selections, each chosen via the independent thinking of a different analyst or fund manager. Then you might have a dynamic portfolio. But the way it usually works is that each stock on the list has to be acceptable to all thirty managers, and if no great book or symphony was ever written by committee, no great portfolio has ever been selected by one, either.

I am reminded here of the little slips of paper that say "Inspected by 4" stuck inside the pockets of new shirts. The "Inspected by 4" method is how stocks are selected from the lists. The would-be decision-makers don't travel around visiting companies or researching new products, they just take what they're given and pass it along.

It's no wonder that portfolio managers and fund managers tend to be squeamish in their stock selections. There's about as much job security in portfolio management as there is in go-go dancing and football coaching. Coaches can at least relax between seasons. Fund managers can never relax because the game is played year-round. The wins and losses are reviewed after every third month, by clients and bosses who demand immediate results.

Whenever fund managers do decide to buy something exciting (against all the social and political obstacles), they may be held back by rules and regulations. Some bank trust departments simply won't allow the buying of stocks in companies with unions. Others won't invest in nongrowth industries or in specific industry groups, such as electric utilities or oil or steel. If it's not the bank or the mutual fund making up rules, then it's the SEC. For instance, the SEC says a mutual fund such as mine cannot own more than ten percent of the shares in any given company, nor can we invest more than five percent of the fund's assets in any given stock.

The various restrictions are well-intentioned, and they protect against a fund's putting all its eggs in one basket (more on this later) and also against a fund's taking over a company a la Carl Icahn (more on that later, too). The secondary result is that the bigger funds are forced to limit themselves to the top 90 to 100 companies, out of the 10,000 or so that are publicly traded.

Let's say you manage a $1-billion pension fund, and to guard against diverse performance, you're required to choose from a list of 40 approved stocks, via the Inspected by 4 method. Since you're only allowed to invest five percent of your total stake in each stock, the most you can have is 40 stocks, with $25 million in each. Then you have to find companies where $25 million will buy less than ten percent of the outstanding shares. That cuts out a lot of opportunities, especially in the small fast-growing enterprises that tend to be the tenbaggers. For instance, you couldn't have bought Dunkin' Donuts under these rules.

Some funds are further restricted with a market-capitalization rule: they don't own stock in any company below, say, a $100-million size. (Size is measured by multiplying the number of outstanding shares by the current stock price.) A company with 20 million shares outstanding that sell for $1.75 a share has a market cap of $35 million and must be avoided. But once the stock price has tripled to $5.25, that same company has a market cap of $105 million and suddenly it's suitable for purchase. This results in a strange phenomenon: large funds are allowed to buy shares in small companies only when the shares are no bargain.

By definition, then, the pension portfolios are wedded to the ten-percent gainers, the plodders, and the regular Fortune 500 bigshots that offer few pleasant surprises. They almost have to buy the IBMs, the Xeroxes, and the Chryslers, but they'll probably wait to buy Chrysler until it's fully recovered and priced accordingly. No wonder so many pension-fund managers fail to beat the market averages. When you ask a bank to handle your investments, mediocrity is all you're going to get in a majority of the cases.

It's a bit more comfortable on my side of the business, working for the general public, than it is for the managers who pick stocks for their fellow professionals. Shareholders at Fidelity Magellan tend to be smaller investors who are perfectly free to sell out at any time, but they don't review my portfolio stock-by-stock to second-guess my selections. That's not to say that my bosses and overseers at Fidelity don't monitor my progress, ask me challenging questions, and periodically review my results. It's just that nobody tells me I must own Xerox, or that I can't own Dunkin' Donuts.

My biggest disadvantage is size. The bigger the equity fund, the harder it gets for it to outperform the competition. Expecting a $9-billion fund to compete successfully against an $800-million fund is the same as expecting Larry Bird to star in basketball games with a five-pound weight strapped to his waist. Big funds have the same built-in handicaps as big anythings—the bigger it is, the more energy it takes to move it.

Yet even at $9 billion, Fidelity Magellan has continued to compete successfully. Since June 1985, when Magellan became the country's largest fund, it has outperformed 98 percent of general equity mutual funds. For this, I have to thank Chrysler, Taco Bell, Pep Boys, and all the other fast growers, turnaround opportunities, and out-of-favor enterprises I've found. The stocks I try to buy are the very stocks that traditional fund managers try to overlook. *In other words, I continue to think like an amateur as frequently as possible.*

GOING IT ALONE

You don't have to invest like an institution. Nor do you have to force yourself to think like an amateur if you already are one. If you're a surfer, a trucker, or an eccentric retiree, then you've got an edge already. That's where the tenbaggers come from, beyond the boundaries of accepted Wall Street cogitation.

When you invest, there's no one around to criticize your quarterly results or your semiannual results, or to grill you as to why you bought Agency Rent-A-Car instead of IBM. Well, maybe there's a spouse and perhaps a stockbroker with whom you are forced to converse, but a stockbroker isn't going to fire you for your odd choices—as long as you're paying the commissions. And hasn't your spouse already proven a faith in your investment schemes by allowing you to continue to make mistakes? You don't have to spend a quarter of your waking hours explaining to a colleague why you are buying what you are buying. There's no rule prohibiting you from buying a stock that costs less than $6, or a stock in a company that's connected to the Teamsters. There's nobody to gripe, "I never heard of Wal-Mart" or "Dunkin' Donuts sounds silly—John D. Rockefeller wouldn't have invested in donuts." There's nobody to chide you for buying back a stock at $19 that you earlier sold at $11—which may be a perfectly sensible move.

You're free to own one stock, four stocks, or ten stocks. If no company seems attractive on the fundamentals, you can avoid stocks altogether and wait for a better opportunity. Equity fund managers do not have that luxury, either. We can't sell everything, and when we try, it's always all at once, and then there's nobody buying at decent prices. Then again, maybe you shouldn't have anything to do with the stock market, ever. That's an issue worth discussing in some detail, because the stock market rewards conviction as surely as it victimizes the unconvinced.

— 3 —

IS THIS GAMBLING,
OR WHAT?

After major upsets such as the Hiccup of October 1987, some investors have taken refuge in bonds. This issue of stocks versus bonds is worth resolving right up front, and in a calm and dignified manner, or else it will come up again at the most frantic moments, when the stock market is dropping and people rush to the banks to sign up for CDs.

Investing in bonds, money-markets, or CDs are all different forms of investing in debt—for which one is paid interest. There's nothing wrong with getting paid interest, especially if it is compounded. Consider the Indians of Manhattan, who in 1626 sold all their real estate to a group of immigrants for $24 in trinkets and beads. For 362 years the Indians have been the subjects of cruel jokes because of it—but it turns out they may have made a better deal than the buyers who got the island.

At 8 percent interest on $24 (let's suspend our disbelief and assume they converted the trinkets to cash) compounded over all those years, the Indians would have built up a net worth just short of $30 trillion, while the latest tax records from the Borough of Manhattan show the real estate to be worth only $28.1 billion. Give Manhattan the benefit of the doubt: that $28.1 billion is the assessed value, and for all anybody knows it may be worth twice that on the open market. So Manhattan's worth $56.2 billion. Either way, the Indians could be ahead by $29 trillion and change without having to maintain any property or mow Central Park. There's something to be said for the supposed dupes in this transaction. Investing in debt isn't bad.

Bonds have been especially attractive in the last twenty years. Historically, interest rates never strayed far from 4 percent, but in the last decade we've seen long-term rates rise to 16 percent then fall to 8 percent, creating remarkable opportunities. People who bought U.S. Treasury bonds with 20-year maturities in 1980 have seen the face value of their bonds nearly double, and meanwhile they've still been collecting the 16 percent interest on their original investment. If you were smart enough to have bought 20-year T-bonds then, you've beaten the stock market by a sizable margin, even in this latest bull phase. Moreover, you've done it without having to read a single research report or having to pay a single tribute to a stockbroker.

Long-term T-bonds are the best way to play interest rates because they aren't "callable"—until five years prior to maturity. Many corporate and municipal bonds are callable much sooner, which means the debtors buy them back the minute it's advantageous to do so. Bondholders have no more choice in the matter than property owners who face a condemnation. As soon as interest rates begin to fall, causing bond investors to realize they've struck a shrewd bargain, the deal is canceled and they get their money back in the mail. On the other hand, if interest rates go in a direction that works against the bondholders, the bondholders are stuck with the bonds. Since there's very little in the corporate bond business that isn't callable, you're advised to buy Treasuries if you hope to profit from a fall in interest rates.

LIBERATING THE PASSBOOKS

Traditionally bonds were sold in large denominations—too large for the small investor, who could only invest in debt via the savings account, or the boring U.S. savings bonds. Then the bond funds were invented, and regular people could invest in debt right along with tycoons. After that, the money-market fund liberated millions of former passbook savers from the captivity of banks, once and for all. There ought to be a monument to Bruce Bent and Harry Browne, who dreamed up the money-market account and dared to lead the great exodus out of the Scroogian thrifts. They started it with the Reserve Fund in 1971.

My own boss, Ned Johnson, took the idea a thought further and added the check-writing feature. Prior to that, the money-market was most useful as a place where small corporations could park their weekly payroll funds. The check-writing feature gave the money-market fund universal appeal as a savings account and a checking account.

It's one thing to prefer stocks to a stodgy savings account that yields 5 percent forever, and quite another to prefer them to a money-market

that offers the best short-term rates, and where the yields rise right away
if the prevailing interest rates go higher.

If your money has stayed in a money-market fund since 1978, you've
missed a couple of major stock market declines. The worst you've ever
collected is 6 percent interest, and you've never lost a penny of your
principal. When short-term interest rates rose to 17 percent in 1981 and
the stock market dropped 5 percent, you made a 22 percent relative gain
by staying in cash.

During the stock market's incredible surge from Dow 1775 on
September 29, 1986, to Dow 2722 on August 25, 1987, let's say you
never bought a single stock, and you felt dumber and dumber for having
missed this once-in-a-lifetime opportunity. After a while you wouldn't
even tell your friends you had all your money in a money-market—
admitting to shoplifting would have been less mortifying.

But the morning after the October 1987 crash, with the Dow beaten
back to 1738, you felt vindicated. You avoided the whole trauma of
October 19. With stock prices so drastically reduced, the money-market
actually had outperformed the stock market over the entire year—6.12
percent for the money-market to 5.25 percent for the S&P 500.

THE STOCKS REBUT

But two months later the stock market had rebounded, and once again
stocks were outperforming both money-market funds and long-term
bonds. Over the long haul they always do. Historically, investing in
stocks is undeniably more profitable than investing in debt. In fact,
since 1927, common stocks have recorded gains of 9.8 percent a year on
average, as compared to 5 percent for corporate bonds, 4.4 percent for
government bonds, and 3.4 percent for Treasury bills.

The long-term inflation rate, as measured by the Consumer Price
Index, is 3 percent a year, which gives common stocks a real return of
6.8 percent a year. The real return on Treasury bills, known as the most
conservative and sensible of all places to put money, has been nil. That's
right. Zippo.

The advantage of a 9.8 percent return from stocks over a 5 percent
return from bonds may sound piddling to some, but consider this
financial fable. If at the end of 1927 a modern Rip Van Winkle had gone
to sleep for 60 years on $20,000 worth of corporate bonds, paying 5
percent compounded, he would have awakened with $373,584, whereas
if he'd invested in stocks, which returned 9.8 percent a year, he'd have

$5,459,720. (Since Rip was asleep, neither the Crash of '29 nor the ripple of '87 would have scared him out of the market.)

In 1927, if you had put $1,000 in each of the four investments listed below, and the money had compounded tax-free, then 60 years later you'd have had these amounts:

Treasury bills	$ 7,400
Government bonds	13,200
Corporate bonds	17,600
Common stocks	272,000

In spite of crashes, depressions, wars, recessions, and ten different presidential administrations, stocks in general have paid off fifteen times as well as corporate bonds, and well over thirty times better than Treasury bills!

There's a logical explanation for this. In stocks you've got the company's growth on your side. You're a partner in a prosperous and expanding business. In bonds, you're nothing more than the nearest source of spare change. When you lend money to somebody, the best you can hope for is to get it back, plus interest. You'll never get a tenbagger bond—unless you're a debt sleuth who specializes in bonds in default.

WHAT ABOUT THE RISKS?

"Ah, yes," you say to yourself, especially after drops in stock prices, "but what about the risks? Aren't stocks riskier than bonds?" Of course stocks are risky. Nowhere is it written that a stock owes us anything, as it's been proven to me on hundreds of sorry occasions.

Even blue-chip stocks held long term, supposedly the safest of all propositions, can be risky. RCA was a famous prudent investment, suitable for widows and orphans, yet it was bought out by GE in 1986 for $66.50 a share, about the same price that it traded in 1967, and only 74 percent above its 1929 high of $38.25 (adjusted for splits). Less than one percent worth of annual appreciation is all you got in 57 years of sticking with a solid, world-famous, and successful company. Bethlehem Steel continues to sell far belows its high of $60 a share reached in 1958.

Buy the right stocks—even blue chips—at the wrong price at the wrong time and you'll suffer great losses. Look what happened in the

1972-74 market break, when conservative issues such as Bristol-Myers fell from $9 to $4, Teledyne from $11 to $3, and McDonald's from $15 to $4. These aren't exactly fly-by-night companies. Buy the wrong stocks at the right time and you'll suffer more of the same. During certain periods it seems to take forever for the theoretical 9.8 percent annual gain from stocks to show up in practice. The Dow Jones industrials reached an all-time high of 995.15 in 1966 and bounced along below that point until 1972. In turn, the high of 1972-73 wasn't exceeded until 1982.

But with the possible exception of the very short-term bonds and bond funds, bonds can be risky, too. Here, rising interest rates will force you to accept one of two unpleasant choices: suffer with the low yield until the bonds mature, or sell the bonds at a substantial discount to face value. If you are truly risk-averse, then the money-market fund or the bank is the place for you. Otherwise, there are risks wherever you turn.

Municipal bonds are thought to be as secure as cash in a strongbox, but on the rare occasion of a default, don't tell the losers that bonds are safe. (The best-known default is that of the Washington Public Power Supply System, and their infamous "Whoops" bonds.) Yes, I know bonds pay off in 99.9 percent of the cases, but there are other ways to lose money on bonds besides a default. Try holding on to a 30-year bond with a 6 percent coupon during a period of raging inflation, and see what happens to the value of the bond.

A lot of people have invested in funds that buy Government National Mortgage Association bonds (Ginnie Maes) without realizing how volatile the bond market has become. They are reassured by the ads—"100 percent government-guaranteed"—and they're right, the interest will be paid. But that doesn't protect the value of their shares in the bond fund when interest rates rise and the bond market collapses. Open the business page and look at what happens to such funds on a day that interest rates rise half a percent and you'll see what I mean. These days, bond funds fluctuate just as wildly as stock funds. The same volatility in interest rates that enables clever investors to make big profits from bonds also makes holding bonds more of a gamble.

STOCKS AND STUD POKER

Frankly, there is no absolute division between safe and rash places to store money. It was in the late 1920s that common stocks finally reached the status of "prudent investments," whereas previously they were dismissed as barroom wagers—and this was precisely the moment at which the overvalued market made buying stocks more wager than investment.

For two decades after the Crash, stocks were regarded as gambling by a majority of the population, and this impression wasn't fully revised until the late 1960s when stocks once again were embraced as investments, but in an overvalued market that made most stocks very risky. Historically, stocks are embraced as investments or dismissed as gambles in routine and circular fashion, and usually at the wrong times. *Stocks are most likely to be accepted as prudent at the moment they're not.*

For years, stocks in large companies were considered "investments" and stocks in small companies "speculations," but lately small stocks have become investments and the speculating is done in futures and options. We're forever redrawing this line.

I'm always amused when people describe their investments as "conservative speculations" or else claim that they are "prudently speculating." Usually that means they hope they're investing but they're worried that they're gambling.

Once the unsettling fact of the risk in money is accepted, we can begin to separate gambling from investing not by the type of activity (buying bonds, buying stocks, betting on the horses, etc.) but by the skill, dedication, and enterprise of the participant. To a veteran handicapper with the discipline to stick to a system, betting on horses offers a relatively secure long-term return, which to him has been as reliable as shares in General Electric. Meanwhile, to the rash and impetuous stockpicker who chases hot tips and rushes in and out of his equities, an "investment" in stocks is no more reliable than throwing away paychecks on the horse with the prettiest mane, or the jockey with the purple silks.

(In fact, to the rash and impetuous stock player, my advice is: Forget Wall Street and take your made money to Hialeah, Monte Carlo, Saratoga, Nassau, Santa Anita, or Baden-Baden. At least in those pleasant surroundings, when you lose, you'll be able to say you had a great time doing it. If you lose on stocks, there's no consolation in watching your broker pace around the office.

Also, when you lose mad money at the horses you simply throw your worthless tickets on the floor and you're done with it, but in stocks, options, and so forth you have to relive the painful episodes with the tax accountant every spring.)

To me, an investment is simply a gamble in which you've managed to tilt the odds in your favor. It doesn't matter whether it's Atlantic City or the S&P 500 or the bond market. In fact, the stock market most reminds me of a stud poker game.

Betting on seven-card stud can provide a very consistent long-term return to people who know how to manage their cards. Four of the cards are dealt faceup, and you not only can see all of your hand but most of your opponents' hands. After the third or fourth card is dealt, it's pretty obvious who is likely to win and who is likely to lose, or else it's obvious there is no likely winner. It's the same on Wall Street. There's a lot of information in the open hands, if you know where to look for it.

By asking some basic questions about companies, you can learn which are likely to grow and prosper. You can never be certain what will happen, but each new occurrence—a jump in earnings, the sale of an unprofitable subsidiary, the expansion into new markets—is like turning up another card. As long as the cards suggest favorable odds of success, you stay in the hand.

Anyone who plays regularly in a monthly stud poker game soon realizes that the same "lucky stiffs" always come out ahead. These are the players who undertake to maximize their return on investment by carefully calculating and recalculating their chances as the hand unfolds. Consistent winners raise their bet as their position strengthens, and they exit the game when the odds are against them, while consistent losers hang on to the bitter end of every expensive pot, hoping for miracles and enjoying the thrill of defeat. In stud poker and on Wall Street, miracles happen just often enough to keep the losers losing.

Consistent winners also resign themselves to the fact that they'll occasionally be dealt three aces and bet the limit, only to lose to a hidden royal flush. They accept their fate and go on to the next hand, confident that their basic method will reward them over time. People who succeed in the stock market also accept periodic losses, setbacks, and unexpected occurrences. Calamitous drops do not scare them out of the game. They realize the stock market is not pure science, and not like chess, where the superior position always wins. If seven out of ten of my stocks perform as expected, then I'm delighted. If six out of ten of my stocks perform as expected, then I'm thankful. *Six out of ten is all it takes to produce an enviable record on Wall Street*.

The greatest advantage to investing in stocks, to one who accepts the uncertainties, is the extraordinary reward for being right. This is borne out in the mutual fund returns calculated by the Johnson Chart Service of Buffalo, New York. There's a very interesting correlation here: the "riskier" the fund, the better the payoff. If you'd put $10,000 into the average bond fund in 1963, fifteen years later you'd come out with $31,338. The same $10,000 in a balanced fund (stocks and bonds) would have produced $44,343; in a growth and income fund (all stocks), $53,157; and in an aggressive growth fund (also all stocks), $76,556.

Clearly the stock market has been a gamble worth taking—as long as you know how to play the game. And as long as you own stocks, new cards keep turning up. Now that I think of it, investing in stocks isn't really like playing a seven-card stud-poker hand. It's more like playing a 70-card stud-poker hand, or if you own ten stocks, it's like playing ten 70-card hands at once.

— 4 —

PASSING THE
MIRROR TEST

66 I s General Electric a good investment?" isn't the first thing I'd
inquire about a stock. Even if General Electric is a good investment, it still doesn't mean you ought to own it. There's no point
in studying the financial section until you've looked into the nearest
mirror. Before you buy a share of anything, three personal issues ought
to be addressed: (1) Do I own a house? (2) Do I need the money? and (3)
Do I have the personal qualities that will bring me success in stocks?
Whether stocks make good or bad investments depends more on your
responses to these three questions than on anything you'll read in the
Wall Street Journal.

(1) Do I Own a House?

As they might say on Wall Street, "A house, what a deal!" Before
investing in stocks, consider buying a house, since a house, after all, is
the one good investment that almost everyone makes. Millions of real
estate amateurs have invested brilliantly in their houses. Sometimes
families must move quickly and are forced to sell at a loss, but it's the
rare individual who manages to lose money on a string of residences one
after another, the way it routinely happens with stocks. It's a rarer
individual yet who gets wiped out on a house, waking up one morning to
discover that the premises have declared bankruptcy or turned belly up,
which is the sad fate of many equities.

A house is entirely rigged in the homeowner's favor. The banks let
you acquire it for 20 percent down and in some cases less, giving you the

remarkable power of leverage. True, you can buy stocks with 50 percent cash down, which is known in the trade as "buying on margin," but every time a stock bought on margin drops in price, you have to put up more cash. You never have to put up more cash if the market value of your house goes down. The real estate agent never calls at midnight to announce: "You'll have to come up with twenty thousand dollars by eleven a.m. tomorrow or else sell off two bedrooms," which frequently happens to stockholders forced to sell their shares bought on margin.

Because of leverage, if you buy a $100,000 house for 20 percent down and the value of the house increases by five percent a year, you are making a 25 percent return on your down payment, and the interest on the loan is tax-deductible. As a bonus you get a federal tax deduction on the local real estate tax on the house, plus the house is a perfect hedge against inflation and a great place to hide out during a recession, not to mention the roof over your head.

The customary progression in houses is as follows: You buy a small house (a starter house), then a medium-sized house, then a larger house. After the children move away, you sell the big house and revert to a smaller house, making a sizable profit in the transition. This windfall isn't taxed, because the government gives you a once-in-a-lifetime house windfall exemption. That never happens in stocks, which are taxed as frequently and as heavily as possible.

There are important secondary reasons you'll do better in houses than in stocks. It's not likely you'll get scared out of your house by reading a headline in the Sunday real estate section: "Home Prices Take Dive." They don't publish the Friday afternoon closing market price of your home address in the classifieds. Newscasters do not list the ten most active houses—"100 Orchard Lane is down ten percent today. Neighbors saw nothing unusual to account for this unexpected decline."

Finally, you're a good investor in houses because you poke around from the attic to the basement and ask the right questions. You check into the public services, the schools, the taxes. You remember rules such as "Don't buy the highest-priced property on the block." You drive through neighborhoods and see what's being fixed up, what's run-down, how many houses are left to renovate. Then, before you close the deal on a house, you hire experts to search for termites, roof leaks, dry rot, rusty pipes, faulty wiring, and cracks in the foundation.

No wonder people make money in the real estate market and lose money in the stock market. They spend months choosing their houses, and minutes choosing their stocks.

(2) Do I Need the Money?

This brings us to question two. Review the family budget before you buy stocks. Maybe you're a widow (there are always a few widows in these stock market books) and your son Dexter, now a sophomore in high school, has a chance to get into Harvard — but not on a scholarship. Since you can scarcely afford the tuition as it is, you're tempted to increase your net worth with conservative blue-chip stocks.

In this instance, even buying blue-chip stocks would be too risky. Stocks are relatively predictable over ten to twenty years. As to whether they're going to be higher or lower in two or three years, you might as well flip a coin to decide. Blue chips can fall down and stay down over a three-year period or even a five-year period, so if the market hits a banana peel, then Dexter's going to night school.

There are all kinds of complicated formulas for figuring out what percentage of your assets should be put into stocks, but I have a simple one, and it's the same for Wall Street as it is for the racetrack. *Only invest what you could afford to lose without that loss having any effect on your daily life in the foreseeable future.*

(3) Do I Have the Personal Qualities It Takes to Succeed?

This is the most important question. The list of qualities ought to include patience, self-reliance, common sense, a tolerance for pain, open-mindedness, detachment, persistence, humility, flexibility, a willingness to do independent research, an equal willingness to admit to mistakes, and the ability to ignore general panic. It's also important to be able to make decisions without complete or perfect information. Things are almost never clear on Wall Street, or when they are, then it's too late to profit from them. The scientific mind that needs to know all the data will be thwarted here.

And finally, it's crucial to be able to resist your human nature and your "gut feelings." It's the rare investor who doesn't secretly harbor the conviction that he or she has a knack for divining stock prices or gold prices or interest rates. It's uncanny how often people feel most strongly that stocks are going to go up or the economy is going to improve just when the opposite occurs. This is borne out by the popular investment-advisory newsletter services, which themselves tend to turn bullish and bearish at inopportune moments.

According to information published by Investor's Intelligence, which tracks investor sentiment via the newsletters, at the end of 1972, when stocks were about to tumble, optimism was at an all-time high, with only 15 percent of the advisors bearish. At the beginning of the stock market rebound in 1974, investor sentiment was at an all-time low, with 65 percent of the advisors fearing the worst was yet to come. Before the market turned downward in 1977, once again the newsletter writers were optimistic, with only 10 percent bears. At the start of the 1982 sendoff into a great bull market, 55 percent of the advisors were bears, and just prior to the big gulp of October 19, 1987, 80 percent of the advisors were bulls again.

The problem isn't that investors and their advisors are chronically stupid or imperceptive. It's that by the time the signal is received, the message may already have changed. When enough positive general financial news filters down so that the majority of investors feel truly confident in the short-term prospects, the economy is soon to get hammered.

Things inside humans make them terrible stock market timers. The unwary investor continually passes in and out of three emotional states: concern, complacency, and capitulation. He's concerned after the market has dropped or when the economy seems to falter, which keeps him from buying good companies at bargain prices. Then after he buys at higher prices, he gets complacent because his stocks are going up. This is precisely the time he ought to check the fundamentals, but he doesn't. Then finally, when his stocks fall on hard times and the prices fall to below what he paid, he capitulates and sells in a snit.

Some have fancied themselves "long-term investors," but only until the next big drop (or tiny gain), at which point they quickly become short-term investors and sell out for huge losses or the occasional minuscule profit. It's easy to panic in this volatile business. Since I've run Magellan, the fund has declined from 10 to 35 percent during eight bearish episodes, and in 1987 alone the fund was up 40 percent in August, down 11 percent by December. We finished the year with a 1 percent gain, thus barely preserving my record of never having had a down year—knock on wood. Recently I read that the price of an average stock fluctuates 50 percent in an average year. If that's true, and apparently it's been true throughout this century, then any share currently selling for $50 is likely to hit $60 and/or fall to $40 sometime in the next twelve months. In other words, the high for the year ($60) is 50 percent higher than the low ($40). If you're the kind of buyer who can't resist getting in at $50, buying more at $60 ("See, I was right, that sucker *is* going up"), and then selling out in despair at $40 ("I guess I was wrong. That sucker's going *down*"), then no shelf of how-to books is going to help you.

Some have fancied themselves contrarians, believing that they can profit by zigging when the rest of the world is zagging, but it didn't occur to them to become contrarian until that idea had already gotten so popular that contrarianism became the accepted view. The true contrarian is not the investor who takes the opposite side of a popular hot issue (i.e., shorting a stock that everyone else is buying). The true contrarian waits for things to cool down and buys stocks that nobody cares about, and especially those that make Wall Street yawn.

When E. F. Hutton talks, everybody is supposed to be listening, but that's just the problem. Everybody ought to be trying to fall asleep. When it comes to predicting the market, the important skill here is not listening, it's snoring. The trick is not to learn to trust your gut feelings, but rather to discipline yourself to ignore them. Stand by your stocks as long as the fundamental story of the company hasn't changed. If not, your only hope for increasing your net worth may be to adopt J. Paul Getty's surefire formula for financial success: "Rise early, work hard, strike oil."

Is This a Good
Market? Please
Don't Ask

During every question-and-answer period after I give a speech, somebody stands up and asks me if we're in a good market or a bad market. I always tell them the only thing I know about predicting markets is that every time I get promoted, the market goes down. As soon as those words are launched from my lips, somebody else stands up and asks me when I'm due for another promotion.

Obviously you don't have to be able to predict the stock market to make money in stocks, or else I wouldn't have made any money. I've sat right here at my Quotron through some of the most terrible drops, and I couldn't have figured them out before hand if my life had depended on it. In the middle of 1987, I didn't warn anybody about the imminent 1,000-point decline. In fact, if ignorance loves company, then I was surrounded by an impressive mob of famous seers, prognosticators, and other experts who failed to see it, too. "If you must forecast," an intelligent forecaster once said, "forecast often."

Every year I talk to the executives of a thousand companies, and I can't avoid hearing from the various gold bugs, interest-rate disciples, Federal Reserve watchers, and fiscal mystics quoted in the newspapers. Thousands of experts study overbought indicators, oversold indicators, head-and-shoulder patterns, put-call ratios, the Fed's policy on money supply, foreign investment, the movement of the constellations through the heavens, and the moss on oak trees, and they can't predict markets with any useful consistency any more than the gizzard squeezers could tell the Roman emperors when the Huns would attack.

Since the stock market is in some way related to the general economy, some people try to predict inflation and recessions, booms and busts, and the direction of interest rates. True, there is a wonderful correlation between interest rates and the stock market, but who can foretell interest rates with bankable regularity? Many of the 60,000 economists in the U.S. are employed full-time trying to forecast recessions and interest rates, and if they could do it successfully twice in a row, they'd all be millionaires by now.

PENULTIMATE PREPAREDNESS

No matter how we arrive at the latest financial conclusion, we always seem to be preparing ourselves for the *last* thing that's happened, as opposed to what's going to happen next. This "penultimate preparedness" is our way of making up for the fact that we didn't see the last thing coming along.

The day after the market crashed on October 19, 1987, people began to worry that the market was *going* to crash. It had already crashed and we'd survived it (in spite of our not having predicted it), and now we were petrified there'd be a replay. Those who got out of the market to ensure that they wouldn't be fooled the next time were fooled again as the market went up.

The next time is never like the last time, and yet we can't help readying ourselves for it anyway. This all reminds me of the Mayan conception of the universe.

In Mayan mythology the universe was destroyed four times, and every time the Mayans learned a sad lesson and vowed to be better protected—first there was a flood and the survivors remembered it and moved to higher ground into the woods, built dikes and retaining walls, and put their houses in the trees. The next time the world was destroyed by fire. The survivors came down out of the trees and built new houses out of stone, particularly along a craggy fissure as far away from woods as possible. Soon enough, the world was destroyed by an earthquake. I don't remember the fourth bad thing that happened—maybe a recession—but whatever it was, the Mayans were going to miss it. They were too busy building shelters for the next earthquake.

Two thousand years later we're still looking backward for signs of the upcoming menace. Not long ago, people were worried that oil prices would drop to $5 a barrel and we'd have a depression. Two years before that, those same people were worried that oil prices would rise to $100 a barrel and we'd have a depression.

Someday there will be another recession, which will be very bad for the stock market, as opposed to the inflation that is also very bad for the stock market. Maybe there will already have been a recession between now and the time this is published. Maybe we won't get one until 1994. You're asking me?

THE COCKTAIL THEORY

If the professionals can't predict economies and markets, then what chance does the amateur investor have? This brings me to my own "cocktail party" theory of market forecasting, developed over years of standing in the middle of living rooms, near punch bowls, listening to what the nearest ten people said about stocks.

In the first stage of an upward market—one that has been down awhile and that nobody expects to rise again—people aren't talking about stocks. If they ask me what I do for a living, and I answer, "I manage an equity mutual fund," they nod politely and wander away, or change the subject to the Celtics game. Soon they are talking to a nearby dentist about plaque.

When ten people would rather talk to a dentist about plaque than to the manager of an equity mutual fund about stocks, it's likely that the market is about to turn up.

In stage two, after I've confessed what I do for a living, the new acquaintances linger a bit longer—perhaps long enough to tell me how risky the stock market is—before they move over to talk to the dentist. The cocktail party talk is still more about plaque than about stocks. The market's up 15 percent from stage one, but few are paying attention.

In stage three, with the market up 30 percent from stage one, a crowd of interested parties ignores the dentist and circles around me all evening. A succession of enthusiastic individuals takes me aside to ask what stocks they should buy. Everybody at the party has put money into one issue or another, and they're all discussing what's happened.

In stage four, once again they're crowded around me—but this time it's to tell *me* what stock I should buy. Even the dentist has three or four tips, and in the next few days I look up his recommendations in the newspaper and they've all gone up. When the neighbors tell me what to buy and then I wish I had taken their advice, it's a sure sign that the market has reached a top and is due for a tumble.

Do what you want with this, but don't expect me to bet on the cocktail party theory. I don't believe in predicting markets. I believe in buying great companies—especially companies that are undervalued, and/or underappreciated. Whether the Dow Jones industrial average was at 1,000 or 2,000 or 3,000 points today, you'd be better off having owned Marriott, Merck, and McDonald's than having owned Avon Products, Bethlehem Steel, and Xerox over the last ten years. You'd also be better off having owned Marriott, Merck, or McDonald's than if you'd put the money into bonds or money-market funds over the same period.

If you had bought stocks in great companies back in 1925 and held on to them through the Crash and into the Depression (admittedly this wouldn't have been easy), by 1936 you would have been very pleased at the results.

WHAT STOCK MARKET?

The market ought to be irrelevant. If I could convince you of this, I'd feel this book had done its job. And if you don't believe me, believe Warren Buffett. "As far as I'm concerned," Buffett has written, "the stock market doesn't exist. It is there only as a reference to see if anybody is offering to do anything foolish."

Buffett has turned his Berkshire Hathaway into an extraordinarily profitable enterprise. In the early 1960s it cost $7 to buy a share in his great company, and that same share is worth $4,900 today. A $2,000 investment in Berkshire Hathaway back then has resulted in a 700-bagger that's worth $1.4 million today. That makes Buffett a wonderful investor. What makes him the greatest investor of all time is that during a certain period when he thought stocks were grossly overpriced, he sold everything and returned all the money to his partners at a sizable profit to them. The voluntary returning of money that others would gladly pay you to continue to manage is, in my experience, unique in the history of finance.

Like Buffett, search out profitable companies, even in lousy markets. Several of my favorite tenbaggers made their biggest moves during bad markets. Taco Bell soared through the last two recessions. The only down year in the stock market in the eighties was 1981, and yet it was the perfect time to buy Dreyfus, which began its fantastic march from $2 to $40, the twentybagger that yours truly managed to miss.

Just for the sake of argument, let's say you could predict the next economic boom with absolute certainty, and you wanted to profit from your foresight by picking a few high-flying stocks. You still have to pick the right stocks, just the same as if you had no foresight.

If you knew there was going to be a Florida real estate boom and you picked Radice out of a hat, you would have lost 95 percent of your investment. If you knew there was a computer boom and you picked Fortune Systems, you'd have seen it fall from $22 in 1983 to $1⅞ in 1984. If you knew the early 1980s was bullish for airlines, what good would it have done if you'd invested in Pan Am, which declined from $9 in 1983 to $4 thanks to inept management?

In case after case the proper picking of markets would have resulted in your losing half your assets because you'd picked the wrong stocks. If you rely on the market to drag your stock along, then you might as well take the bus to Atlantic City and bet on red or black. You're relying on the market to bail you out, and chances are, it won't. Pick the right stocks and the market will take care of itself.

That's not to say there isn't such a thing as an overvalued market, but there's no point in worrying about it. The way you'll know when the market is overvalued is when you can't find a single company that's reasonably priced or that meets your other criteria for investment. The reason Buffett returned his partners' money was that he said he couldn't find any stocks worth owning. He'd looked over hundreds of individual companies and found not one he'd buy on the fundamental merits.

The only buy signal I need is to find a company I like. In that case, it's never too soon nor too late to buy shares.

— 6 —

STALKING THE
TENBAGGER

The best place to begin looking for the tenbagger is close to home—if not in the backyard then down at the shopping mall, and especially where you work. With most of the tenbaggers already mentioned—Dunkin' Donuts, The Limited, Subaru, Dreyfus, McDonald's, Tambrands, and Pep Boys—the first signs of success were apparent at hundreds of locations across the country long before Wall Street got its original clue.

The average person comes across a likely prospect two or three times a year—sometimes more. Executives at Pep Boys, clerks at Pep Boys, lawyers and accountants, suppliers of Pep Boys, the firm that did the advertising, sign painters, building contractors for the new stores, and even the people who washed the floors all must have observed Pep Boys' success. Thousands of potential investors got this "tip," and that doesn't even count the hundreds of thousands of customers.

At the same time, the Pep Boys employee who buys insurance for the company could have noticed that insurance prices were going up—which is a good sign that the insurance industry is about to turn around—and so maybe he'd consider investing in the insurance suppliers. Or maybe the Pep Boys building contractors noticed that cement prices had firmed, which is good news for the companies that supply cement.

All along the retail and wholesale chains, people who make things, sell things, clean things, or analyze things encounter numerous stock-picking opportunities. You don't have to work in Kodak's main office to learn that the new generation of inexpensive, easy-to-use, high-quality 35mm cameras from Japan is reviving the photo industry, and that film sales are up. You could be a film salesman, the owner of a camera store, or a clerk in a camera store. You don't have to be Steven Spielberg to know that some new blockbuster, or string of blockbusters, is going to give a significant boost to the earnings of Paramount or Orion Pictures. You could be an actor, an extra, a stuntman, or the usher at a local cinema, where the standing-room-only crowds six weeks in a row inspire you to investigate Orion's stock.

How about Automatic Data Processing, which processes nine million paychecks a week for 180,000 small and medium-sized companies? The company went public in 1961 and the worst it ever did was to earn 11 percent more than the previous year. That was during the 1982-83 recession when many companies reported losses.

Automatic Data Processing sounds like the sort of high-tech enterprise I try to avoid, but it's not a computer company. It uses computers to process paychecks, and users of technology are the biggest beneficiaries of high-tech. As competition drives down the price of computers, a firm such as Automatic Data can buy the cheaper equipment, so its costs are continually reduced. This only adds to profits. Without fanfare, this mundane enterprise that came public at six cents a share (adjusted for splits) now sells for $40—a 600-bagger long-term.

The officers and employees of 180,000 client firms could certainly have known about the success of Automatic Data Processing, and since many of Automatic Data's biggest and best customers are major brokerage houses, so could half of Wall Street.

So often we struggle to pick a winning stock, when all the while a winning stock has been struggling to pick us.

THE TENBAGGER IN ULCERS

Can't think of any such opportunity in your own life? What if you're retired, live ten miles from the nearest traffic light, grow your own food, and don't have a television set? Well, maybe one day you have to go to a doctor. The rural existence has given you ulcers, which is the perfect introduction to SmithKline Beckman.

Hundreds of doctors, thousands of patients, and millions of friends and relatives of patients heard about the wonder drug Tagamet, which came on the market in 1976. So did the pharmacist who dispensed the pills and the delivery boy who spent half his workday delivering them. Tagamet was a boon for the afflicted, and a bonanza for investors.

A great patient's drug is one that cures an affliction once and for all, but a great investor's drug is one that the patient has to keep buying. Tagamet was one of the latter. It provided fantastic relief from the suffering from ulcers, and the direct beneficiaries had to keep taking it again and again, making indirect beneficiaries out of the shareholders of SmithKline Beckman, the makers of Tagamet. Thanks largely to Tagamet, the stock rose from $7 ½ a share in 1977 to $72 a share at the 1987 high.

These users and prescribers had a big lead on the Wall Street talent. No doubt some of the oxymorons suffered from ulcers themselves—this is an anxious business—but SmithKline must not have been included on their buy lists, because it was a year before the stock began its ascent. During the testing period for the drug, 1974-76, the price climbed from around $4 to $7, and when the government approved Tagamet in 1977, the stock sold for $11. From there it shot up to $72.

Did the doctors who prescribed Tagamet buy shares in SmithKline? Somehow I doubt that many did. It's more likely that the doctors were fully invested in oil stocks. Perhaps they heard that Union Oil of California was a takeover candidate. Meanwhile, the Union Oil executives were probably buying drug stocks, especially the hot issues like American Surgery Centers, which sold for $18.50 in 1982 and fell to 5 cents.

In general, if you polled doctors, I'd bet only a small percentage would turn out to be invested in medical stocks, and more would be invested in oil; and if you polled the shoe-store owners, more would be invested in aerospace than in shoes, while the aerospace engineers are more likely to dabble in shoe stocks. Why is it that stock certificates, like grasses, are always greener in somebody else's pasture?

You don't necessarily have to know anything about a company for its stock to go up. But the important points are that (1) the oil experts, on average, are in a better position than doctors to decide when to buy or to sell Schlumberger, an oil-service company; and (2) the doctors, on average, know better than oil experts when to invest in a successful drug. The person with the edge is always in a position to outguess the person without an edge—who after all will be the last to learn of important changes in a given industry.

Though people who buy stocks about which they are ignorant may get lucky and enjoy great rewards, it seems to me they are competing under unnecessary handicaps, just like the marathon runner who decides to stake his reputation on a bobsled race.

THE DOUBLE EDGE

Of course it's absurd to contend that the knowledge of an oil executive is equal to the knowledge of customers in the checkout line at Pep Boys. One is a professional's understanding of the workings of an industry; the other is a consumer's awareness of a likable product. Both are useful in picking stocks, but in different ways.

The professional's edge is especially helpful in knowing when to buy shares in companies that have been around awhile, especially those in the so-called cyclical industries. If you own a Goodyear tire store and after three years of sluggish sales you suddenly can't keep up with new orders, you've just received a strong signal that Goodyear may be on the rise. You already know that Goodyear's new high-performance tire is the best. You call up your broker and ask for the latest background information on the tire company, instead of waiting for the broker to call to tell you about Wang Laboratories.

Unless you work in some job that's related to computers, what good is a Wang tip to you? What could you possibly know that thousands of other people don't know a lot better? If the answer is "nada," then you haven't got an edge in Wang. But if you sell tires, make tires, or distribute tires, you've got an edge in Goodyear. All along the supply lines of the manufacturing industry, people who make things and sell things encounter numerous stockpicking opportunities. In most endeavors the grassroots observer can spot a turnaround six to twelve months ahead of the financial analysts. This gives an incredible head start in anticipating an improvement in earnings—and earnings, as you'll see, make stock prices go higher.

It doesn't have to be a turnaround in sales that gets your attention. It may be incredible hidden assets that don't show up on the balance sheet. If you work in real estate, maybe you know that a department store chain owns four city blocks in downtown Atlanta, carried on the books at pre-Civil War prices. This is a definite hidden asset, and similar opportunities might be found in gold, oil, timberland, and TV stations.

You're looking for a situation where the value of the assets per share exceeds the price per share of the stock. In such delightful instances you can truly buy a great deal of something for nothing. I've done it myself numerous times. The exciting part about the edge that being in a business gives the average stockpicker is that you can develop your own stock detection system outside the normal channels of Wall Street, where you'll always get the news late.

MY WONDERFUL EDGE

Who could have had a greater advantage than yours truly, sitting in an office at Fidelity during the boom in financial services and in the mutual funds? I'd been coming to work here for nearly two decades, I know half the officers in the major financial-service companies, I follow the daily ups and downs, and I could notice important trends months before the analysts on Wall Street. You couldn't have been more strategically placed to cash in on the bonanza of the early 1980s.

Fidelity isn't a public company, so you couldn't invest in the rush here. But what about Dreyfus? The stock sold for 40 cents a share in 1977, then nearly $40 a share in 1986, a 100-bagger in nine years, and much of that during a lousy stock market. Franklin was a 138-bagger, and Federated was up 50-fold before it was bought out by Aetna.

How much did I make from all this? Zippo. I didn't buy a single share of any of the financial services companies. I missed the whole deal. I guess I was too busy thinking about Union Oil of California, just like the doctors.

Every time I think of Dreyfus, it reminds me of the advice I've been trying to give you all along: Invest in things you know about. Neither of us should let an opportunity like this one pass us by again, and I didn't. The 1987 market break gave me another chance with Dreyfus, and I made the most of it.

— 7 —

I'VE GOT IT, I'VE GOT IT — WHAT IS IT?

Whether a stock has come to your attention via the office, the shopping mall, or something you heard from Ivan Boesky's parole officer, the discovery is not a buy signal. Just because Dunkin' Donuts is always crowded doesn't mean you ought to own the stock. What you've got so far is simply a lead to a story that has to be developed.

Treat the initial information as if it were an anonymous and intriguing tip, mysteriously shoved into your mailbox. This will keep you from buying a stock just because you've seen something you like, or worse, because of the reputation of the tipper, as in: "Uncle Harry's buying it, and he's rich, so he must know what he's talking about."

Developing the story is not difficult: at most it will take a couple of hours. This homework phase is just as important to your success in stocks as your previous vow to ignore the market's short-term gyrations. Perhaps some people make money in stocks without doing research, but why take unnecessary chances? *Investing without research is like playing stud poker without looking at the cards.*

For some reason the whole business of analyzing stocks has been made to seem so esoteric and technical that normally careful consumers invest their life savings on a whim. The same couple that spends the weekend searching for the best airfares to London buys 500 shares of KLM without spending five minutes learning about the company.

All you have to do is put as much effort into picking your stocks as you do into buying your groceries. Even if you already own stocks, it's useful to go through the exercise, because it's possible that some of these stocks will not and cannot live up to your expectations. That's because there are limits to how different kinds of stocks can perform. In developing the story you have to make certain initial distinctions.

WHAT'S THE BOTTOM LINE?

Remember I mentioned that L'eggs was one of the two most profitable new products of the 1970s. The other was Pampers. Any friend or relative of a baby could have realized how popular Pampers were, and right on the box it says that Pampers are made by Procter and Gamble.

Should you have rushed out to buy the stock? Not if you'd begun to develop the story. You would have noticed that Procter and Gamble is a huge company and that Pampers sales contribute only a small part of the earnings. Pampers made some difference to Procter and Gamble, but it wasn't nearly as consequential as what L'eggs did for a smaller outfit such as Hanes.

If you're considering a stock on the strength of a specific product first find out: What effect will the success of the product have on the company's bottom line? In February 1988, investors got very enthused about Retin-A, a skin cream made by Johnson & Johnson. Since 1971 this cream had been sold as an acne medicine, but a recent doctors' study suggested it might also fight skin blots and blemishes caused by the sun. The newspapers loved this story, and headline writers called it the anti-aging cream, and the "wrinkle-fighter." You would have thought that Johnson & Johnson had discovered the Fountain of Youth.

So what happens? Johnson & Johnson stock jumps $8 a share in two days (January 21-22, 1988), which adds $1.4 billion in extra market value to the company. In all this hoopla the buyers must have forgotten to notice that the previous year's sales of Retin-A brought in only $30 million a year to Johnson & Johnson, and the company still faced further FDA review on the new claims.

In another case, which happened about the same time, investors did better homework. A new medical study reported that an aspirin every other day might reduce the risk of men getting heart attacks. The study used the Bufferin brand of aspirin made by Bristol-Myers, but Bristol-Myers stock hardly budged, moving up just 50 cents per share to $42 ⅞. A lot of people must have realized that domestic Bufferin sales last year were $75 million, less than 1.5 percent of Bristol-Myers's total revenues of $5.3 billion.

A somewhat better aspirin play was Sterling Drug, maker of Bayer aspirin, before it was bought out by Eastman Kodak. Sterling's aspirin sales were 6.5 percent of its total revenues, but close to 15 percent of the company's profits—aspirin was Sterling's most profitable product.

BIG COMPANIES, SMALL MOVES

The size of a company has a great deal to do with what you can expect to get out of the stock. Big companies don't have big stock moves. Don't buy stock in a giant such as Coca-Cola expecting to quadruple your money in two years. If you buy Coca-Cola at the right price, you might triple your money in six years, but you're not going to hit the jackpot in two.

Sometimes a series of misfortunes drives a big company into desperate straits, and as it recovers, the stock will make a big move. Chrysler had a big move, as did Ford and Bethlehem Steel. When Burlington Northern got depressed, the stock dropped from $12 to $6 and then climbed back to $70. But these are extraordinary situations that fall into the category of turnarounds. In the normal course of business, multibillion-dollar enterprises such as Chrysler or Burlington Northern, DuPont or Dow Chemical, Procter and Gamble or Coca-Cola, simply cannot grow fast enough to become tenbaggers.

For a General Electric to double or triple in size in the foreseeable future is mathematically impossible. GE already has gotten so big that it represents nearly one percent of the entire U.S. gross national product. Think of that. Every time you spend a dollar, GE gets almost a penny of it. The stock can't help but inch along since it's attached to such a huge enterprise.

GE has 900 million shares outstanding, and a total market value of $39 billion. The annual profit, more than $3 billion, is enough to qualify as a Fortune 500 company on its own. There is simply no way that GE could accelerate its growth very much without taking over the world. And since fast growth propels stock prices, it's no surprise that GE moves slowly as La Quinta soars.

Everything else being equal, you'll do better with the smaller companies. In the last decade you'd have made more money on Pic 'N' Save than on Sears, although both are retail chains. Now that Waste Management is a multibillion-dollar conglomerate, it will probably lag behind the speedy new entries in the waste-removal field. In the recent comeback of the steel industry, shareholders in the smaller Nucor have fared better than shareholders in U.S. Steel (now USX).

THE SIX CATEGORIES

Once I've established the size of the company, I place it into one of six categories: slow growers, stalwarts, fast growers, cyclicals, asset plays, and turnarounds. There are almost as many ways to classify stocks as there are stockbrokers—but I've found that these six categories cover all of the useful distinctions that any investor has to make.

Countries have a growth rate (the GNP), industries have a growth rate, and so does an individual company. Whatever the entity, "growth" means that it does more of whatever it does this year (make cars, shine shoes, sell hamburgers) than it did last year. With individual companies, growth can be measured in various ways: growth in sales, growth in profits, growth in earnings, etc. But when you hear about a "growth company," you can assume that it's expanding: more sales, more production, and more profits in each successive year.

The growth of an individual company is measured against the growth of the economy at large. Slow-growing companies grow more or less in line with the nation's GNP, which lately has averaged about three percent a year. Fast-growing companies sometimes grow as much as 20 to 30 percent a year. That's where you find the most explosive stocks.

Three of my six categories have to do with growth stocks. I separate the growth stocks into slow growers (sluggards), medium growers (stalwarts), and then the fast growers—the superstocks that deserve the most attention.

The Slow Growers

Usually these large and aging companies are expected to grow slightly faster than the gross national product. Slow growers started out as fast growers and eventually pooped out, either because they had gone as far as they could, or else they got too tired to make the most of their chances. When an industry at large slows down (as they always seem to do), most of the companies within the industry lose momentum as well.

Electric utilities are today's most popular slow growers, but throughout the 1950s and into the 1960s the utilities were fast growers, expanding at over twice the rate of GNP. As people installed central air conditioning, bought big refrigerator/freezers, and generally ran up their electric bills, electricity consumption became a high-growth industry, and the major utilities, particularly in the Sunbelt, expanded at double-digit rates. In the 1970s, as the cost of power rose sharply, consumers learned to conserve electricity, and the utilities lost their momentum.

There's always a tendency to think that things will never change, but sooner or later every fast-growing industry becomes a slow-growing industry. Alcoa once had the same kind of go-go reputation that Apple Computer has today, because aluminum was a fast-growth industry. In the twenties the railroads were the great growth companies, and when Walter Chrysler left the railroads to run an automobile plant, he had to take a cut in pay. "This isn't the railroad, Mr. Chrysler," he was told.

Then cars became the fast-growth industry, then steel, chemicals, electric utilities, computers. Now even computers are slowing down, at least in the mainframe and minicomputer parts of the business. IBM and Digital may be the slow growers of tomorrow.

It's easy enough to spot a slow-grower in the books of stock charts that your broker can provide, or that you can find at the local library. The chart of a slow grower such as Houston Industries resembles the topographical map of Delaware, which, as you probably know, has no hills. Compare this to the chart of Wal-Mart, which looks like a rocket launch, and you'll see that Wal-Mart is definitely not a slow grower.

Another sign of a slow grower is that it pays a generous and regular dividend. In many cases it may be the best use to which the company's earnings can be put (see Chapter 13), but often companies pay generous dividends when they can't dream up new ways to use the money to expand the business. Corporate managers would much prefer to expand the business, an effort that always enhances their prestige, than to pay a dividend, an effort that is mechanical and requires no imagination.

You won't find a lot of two to four percent growers in my portfolio, because if companies aren't going anywhere fast, neither will the price of their stocks. If growth in earnings is what enriches a company, then what's the sense of wasting time on sluggards?

The Stalwarts

Stalwarts are companies such as Coca-Cola, Bristol-Myers, Procter and Gamble, the Bell telephone sisters, Hershey's, Ralston Purina, and Colgate-Palmolive. These multibillion-dollar hulks are not exactly agile climbers, but they're faster than slow growers. When you traffic in stalwarts, you're more or less in the foothills: 10 to 12 percent annual growth in earnings.

Depending on when you buy them and at what price, you can make a sizable profit in stalwarts. Procter and Gamble has performed well throughout the 1980s. However, if you'd bought it back in 1963, you only made fourfold on your money. Holding a stock for twenty-five years for that kind of return isn't a very exciting prospect—since you're no better off then if you'd bought a bond or stuck with a cash fund.

In fact, when anyone brags about doubling or tripling his money on a stalwart (or on any company, for that matter), your next question ought to be: "And how long did you own it?" In many instances the risk of ownership has not resulted in any advantage to the owner, who therefore took chances for nothing. I generally buy stalwarts for a 30 to 50 percent gain, then sell and repeat the process with similar issues that haven't yet appreciated.

I always keep some stalwarts in my portfolio because they offer pretty good protection during recessions. You know Bristol-Myers and Kellogg, Coca-Cola and MMM, Ralston Purina and Procter and Gamble won't go bankrupt, and soon enough they will be reassessed and their value will be restored. Bristol-Myers has had only one down quarter in twenty years, and Kellogg hasn't had a down quarter for thirty. When things get bad, people may take fewer trips, postpone the purchase of new cars, buy fewer clothes, and order fewer lobster dinners at restaurants, but they eat just as many cornflakes as ever.

The Fast Growers

These are among my favorite investments: small, aggressive new enterprises that grow at 20 to 25 percent a year. This is the land of the 10- to 40-baggers, and even the 200-baggers. With a small portfolio, one or two of these can make a career.

A fast-growing company doesn't necessarily have to belong to a fast-growing industry. As a matter of fact, I'd rather it didn't as you'll see in Chapter 8. All it needs is the room to expand within a slow-growing industry. Beer is a slow-growing industry, but Anheuser-Busch has been a fast grower by taking over market share, and enticing drinkers of rival brands to switch to theirs. The same thing happened to Taco Bell in the fast-food business, Wal-Mart in the general store business, and The Gap in the retail clothing business. These upstart enterprises learned to succeed in one place, and then to duplicate the winning formula over and over, mall by mall, city by city. The expansion into new markets results in the phenomenal acceleration in earnings that drives the stock price to giddy heights.

There's plenty of risk in fast growers, especially in the younger companies that tend to be overzealous and underfinanced. When an underfinanced company has headaches, it usually ends up in Chapter 11. Larger fast growers risk rapid devaluation when they begin to falter. Aluminum was a great growth industry even into the 1960s and so was carpets, but when these industries matured, the companies within them became GNP-type growers, and the stock market yawned. Once a fast grower gets too big, it faces the same dilemma as Gulliver in Lilliput: There's simply no place for it to stretch out.

But for as long as they can keep it up, fast growers are the big winners in the stock market. I look for the ones that have good balance sheets and are making substantial profits. The trick is figuring out when they'll stop growing, and how much to pay for the growth.

The Cyclicals

A cyclical is a company whose sales and profits rise and fall in regular if not completely predictable fashion. In a growth industry, business just keeps expanding, but in a cyclical industry it expands and contracts.

The autos and the airlines, the tire companies, steel companies, and chemical companies are all cyclicals. Even defense companies behave like cyclicals, since their profits' rise and fall depends on the policies of various administrations. Charts of the cyclicals look like the polygraphs of liars, or the maps of the Alps, as opposed to the maps of Delaware you get with the slow growers.

Coming out of a recession and into a vigorous economy, the cyclicals flourish, and their stock prices tend to rise much faster than the prices of the stalwarts. This is understandable, since people buy new cars and take more airplane trips in a vigorous economy, and there's greater demand for steel, chemicals, etc. But going the other direction, the cyclicals suffer, and so do the pocketbooks of the shareholders. You can lose more than fifty percent of your investment very quickly if you buy cyclicals in the wrong part of the cycle, and it may be years before you'll see another upswing.

Cyclicals are the most misunderstood of all the types of stocks. It is here that the unwary stockpicker is most easily parted from his money, and in stocks that he considers safe. Because the major cyclicals are large and well-known companies, they are naturally lumped together with the trusty stalwarts. Since Ford is a blue chip, one might assume that it will behave the same as Bristol-Myers, another blue chip. But Ford's stock fluctuates wildly as the company alternately loses billions of dollars in recessions and makes billions of dollars in prosperous stretches. A stalwart such as Bristol-Myers can lose half its value in a sorry market and/or a national economic slump; a cyclical such as Ford can lose 80 percent. That's just what happened to Ford in the early 1980s.

Timing is everything in cyclicals, and you have to be able to detect the early signs that business is falling off or picking up. If you work in some profession that's connected to steel, aluminum, airlines, automobiles, etc., then you've got your edge, and nowhere is it more important than in this kind of investment.

Turnarounds

Turnaround candidates have been battered, depressed, and often can barely drag themselves into Chapter 11. These aren't slow growers; these are no growers. These aren't cyclicals that rebound; these are potential fatalities, such as Chrysler. Actually Chrysler once was a cyclical that went so far down in a down cycle that people thought it would never come back up.

The Penn Central bankruptcy was one of the most traumatic events that ever happened to Wall Street. That this blue chip, this grand old company, could collapse was as startling and as unexpected as the collapse of the George Washington Bridge would be. An entire generation of investors had its faith shaken—and yet once again there was opportunity in this crisis. Penn Central has been a marvelous turnaround play.

Turnaround stocks make up lost ground very quickly, as Chrysler, Ford, Penn Central, General Public Utilities, and numerous others have proven. The best thing about investing in successful turnarounds is that of all the categories of stocks, their ups and downs are related to the general market.

I started buying Chrysler at $6 (unadjusted for later splits) in early 1982 and watched it go up fifteenfold in five years. And I didn't even buy Chrysler at the bottom! Other more daring Chrysler fans bought in at $1.50 and made a 32-bagger out of it. Lockheed, another happy occurrence, sold for $1 in 1973. Even after the government bailed out the company you could have bought the stock for $4 in 1977 and sold it for $60 in 1986. Lockheed was one I missed.

There are several types of turnarounds, and I've owned all of them at one time or another. There's the bail-us-out-or-else kind of turnaround such as Chrysler or Lockheed, which depend on a government loan guarantee. There's the who-would-have-thunk-it kind of turnaround, such as Con Edison. Who would ever have believed you could make this much money in a utility, as the stock price rebounded from $3 in 1974 to $52 in 1987?

There's the little-problem-we-didn't-anticipate kind of turnaround, such as Three Mile Island. This was a minor tragedy perceived to be worse than it was, and in minor tragedy there's major opportunity. I made a lot of money in General Public Utilities, the owner of Three Mile Island. Anybody could have. You just had to keep up with the news, and read it with dispassion.

After the meltdown of the nuclear unit in 1979, the situation eventually stabilized. In 1985 GPU announced it was going to start up the sister reactor that had been turned off for years after the crisis but was unaffected by it. It was a good sign for the stock that they got that sister plant back on line, and an even better sign when other utilities agreed to share in the costs of the Three Mile Island cleanup. You had almost seven years to buy the stock after the place calmed down and all this good news had come out. The low of 3 ⅜ was reached in 1980, but you could still have gotten in for $15 a share in late 1985 and watched the stock hit $38 in October 1988.

There's the perfectly-good-company-inside-a-bankrupt-company kind of turnaround, such as Toys "R" Us. Once Toys "R" Us was spun out on its own, away from its less successful parent, Interstate Department Stores, the result was 57 bags.

There's the restructuring-to-maximize-shareholder-values kind of turnaround, such as Penn Central. Restructuring is a company's way of ridding itself of certain unprofitable subsidiaries it should never have acquired in the first place. The earlier buying of these ill-fated subsidiaries is called diversification. I call it *diworseification*.

I'll have more to say about diworseification later—most of it unflattering. The only positive aspect is that some companies that diworseify themselves into sorry shape are future candidates for turnarounds. Goodyear, for example, is coming back right now. It's gotten out of the oil business, sold off some sluggish subsidiaries, and rededicated itself to the thing it does best: making tires.

The Asset Plays

An asset play is any company that's sitting on something valuable that you know about, but that the Wall Street crowd has overlooked. The asset play is where the local edge can be used to greatest advantage.

The asset may be as simple as a pile of cash. Sometimes it's real estate. I've already mentioned Pebble Beach as a great asset play. Here's why: At the end of 1976 the stock was selling for 14 ½ per share, which, with 1.7 million shares outstanding, meant that the whole company was valued at only $25 million. Less than three years later (May 1979), Twentieth Century-Fox bought Pebble Beach for $72 million, or 42 ½ per share. What's more, a day after buying the company, Twentieth Century sold Pebble Beach's gravel pit—just one of the company's many assets—for $30 million. In other words, the gravel pit alone was worth more than what investors in 1976 paid for the whole company. Those investors got all the adjacent land, the 2,700 acres in Del Monte Forest and the Monterey Peninsula, the 300-year-old trees, the hotel, and the two golf courses for nothing.

I once visited a mundane little Florida cattle company called Alico, run out of La Belle, a small town at the edge of the Everglades. All I saw there was scrub pine and palmetto brush, a few cows grazing around, and perhaps twenty Alico employees trying unsuccessfully to look busy. It wasn't very exciting, until you figured out that you could have bought Alico for under $20 a share, and ten years later the land alone turned out to be worth more than $200 a share. A smart codger named Ben Hill Griffin, Jr., kept buying up the stock and waiting for Wall Street to notice Alico. He must have made a fortune by now.

Many of the publicly traded railroads such as Burlington Northern, Union Pacific, and Santa Fe Southern Pacific are land rich, dating back to the nineteenth century when the government gave away half the country as a sop to the railroad tycoons. These companies have the oil and gas rights, the mineral rights, and the timber rights as well.

There are asset plays in metals and in oil, in newspapers and in TV stations, in patented drugs and even sometimes in a company's losses. After Penn Central came out of bankruptcy, it had a huge tax-loss carryforward, which meant that when it started making money again, it wouldn't have to pay taxes. In those years the corporate tax rate was 50 percent, so Penn Central was reborn with a 50 percent advantage up front.

Actually Penn Central might have been the ultimate asset play. The company had everything: tax-loss carryforward, cash, extensive land holdings in Florida, other land elsewhere, coal in West Virginia, and air rights in Manhattan. Penn Central stock went up eightfold.

Regrettably, I never took more than a piddling position in the cable industry, despite the urging of Fidelity's Morris Smith, who periodically pounded on my table to convince me to buy more. He definitely was right—for the following important reason. Fifteen years ago, each cable subscriber was worth about $200 to the buyer of a cable franchise, ten years ago it was $400, five years ago $1,000, and now it's as high as $2,200. The millions of subscribers are a huge asset to Telecommunications, Inc.

I think I missed all of this because cable TV didn't arrive in my town until 1986 and in my house until 1987. So I had no firsthand appreciation of worth of the industry in general. If I'd seen how my youngest daughter, Beth, loves the Disney channel, how much Annie looks forward to watching Nickelodeon, how my oldest daughter Mary appreciates MTV, how Carolyn takes to the old Bette Davis movies and I take to CNN news and cable sports, I would have understood that cable is as much of a fixture as water or electricity—the video utility. It's impossible to say enough about the value of personal experience in analyzing companies and trends.

HIGHFLIERS TO LOW RIDERS

Companies don't stay in the same category forever. Fast growers can't maintain double-digit growth forever, and sooner or later they settle into the comfortable single digits of sluggards and stalwarts. From Dow Chemical to Tampa Electric, the highfliers of one decade become the groundhogs of the next. Stop & Shop went from being a slow grower to a fast grower, an unusual reversal.

Growth companies that can't stand prosperity foolishly diworseify and fall out of favor, which makes them into turnarounds. A fast grower such as Holiday Inn inevitably slows down, and the stock is depressed until some smart investors realize that it owns so much real estate that it's a great asset play. Look what's happened to retailers such as Federated and Allied Stores—because of the department stores they built in prime locations, and because of the shopping centers they own, they've been taken over for their assets. McDonald's is a classic fast grower, but because of the thousands of outlets it either owns or is repurchasing from the franchisees, it could be a great future asset play in real estate.

Disney, over its lifetime, has been in every major category: years ago it had the momentum of a fast grower, which led to the size and financial strength of a stalwart, followed by a period when all those great assets in real estate, old movies, and cartoons were significant. Then, in the mid-1980s, when Disney was in a slump, you could have bought it as a turnaround.

SEPARATING THE DIGITALS
FROM THE WAL-MARTS

If you can't figure out what category your stocks are in, ask your broker. Are you looking for slow growth, fast growth, recession protection, a turnaround, a cyclical bounce, or assets? Basing a strategy on general maxims, such as "Sell when you double your money," "Sell after two years," or "Cut your losses by selling when the price falls ten percent," is absolute folly. It's simply impossible to find a generic formula that sensibly applies to all the different kinds of stocks.

You have to separate the Procter and Gambles from the Bethlehem Steels, and the Digital Equipments from the Alicos. Unless it's a turnaround, there's no point in owning a utility and expecting it to do as well as Philip Morris. There's no point in treating a young company with the potential of a Wal-Mart like a stalwart, and selling for a 50 percent gain, when there's a good chance that your fast grower will give you a 1,000-percent gain.

Putting stocks in categories is the first step in developing the story. Now at least you know what kind of story it's supposed to be. The next step is filling in the details that will help you guess how the story is going to turn out.

— 8 —

THE PERFECT STOCK,
WHAT A DEAL!

etting the story on a company is a lot easier if you understand the basic business. That's why I'd rather invest in panty hose than in communications satellites, or in motel chains than in fiber optics. The simpler it is, the better I like it. When somebody says, "Any idiot could run this joint," that's a plus as far as I'm concerned, because sooner or later any idiot probably is going to be running it.

If it's a choice between owning stock in a fine company with excellent management in a highly competitive and complex industry, or a humdrum company with mediocre management in a simpleminded industry with no competition, I'd take the latter. For one thing, it's easier to follow. During a lifetime of eating donuts or buying tires, I've developed a feel for the product line that I'll never have with laser beams or microprocessors.

"Any idiot can run this business" is one characteristic of the perfect company, the kind of stock I dream about. You never find the perfect company, but if you can imagine it, then you'll know how to recognize favorable attributes, the most important thirteen of which are as follows:

(1) It Sounds Dull—or, Even Better, Ridiculous

The perfect company has to be engaged in a perfectly simple business with a perfectly boring name. Automatic Data Processing is good, but even better is Bob Evans Farms. What could be duller than a stock named Bob Evans? It puts you to sleep just thinking about it. But even Bob Evans Farms won't win the prize for the best stock name, and neither will Shoney's or Crown, Cork, and Seal. None of these has a chance against Pep Boys—Manny, Moe, & Jack.

Pep Boys—Manny, Moe, and Jack is the most promising name I've ever heard. It's better than dull, it's ridiculous. What Wall Street analyst or portfolio manager in his right mind would want to put money into a company that sounds like the Three Stooges? Blurting out that you own Pep Boys won't get you much of an audience at a cocktail party, but whisper "GeneSplice International" and everybody listens. Meanwhile, GeneSplice International is going nowhere but down, while Pep Boys— Manny, Moe, and Jack just keeps going higher.

If you discover an opportunity early enough, you probably get a few dollars off the price just for the dull or odd name, which is why I'm always on the lookout for the Pep Boys or the Bob Evanses, or the occasional Consolidated Rock. Too bad that wonderful aggregate company changed its name to Conrock and then the trendier Calmat. As long as it was Consolidated Rock, nobody paid attention to it.

(2) It Does Something Dull

I get even more excited when a company with a boring name, terrific earnings, and a strong balance sheet also does something boring. It gives you a lot of time to purchase the stock at a discount. Then when it becomes trendy and overpriced, you can sell your shares to the trend-followers. Crown, Cork, and Seal makes cans and bottle caps. What could be duller than that? You won't see an interview with the CEO of Crown, Cork, and Seal in *Time* magazine alongside an interview with Lee Iacocca, but that's a plus. There's nothing boring about what's happened to the shares of Crown, Cork, and Seal.

(3) It Does Something Disagreeable

Better than boring is a stock that's boring *and* disgusting. Something that makes people shrug, retch, or turn away in disgust is ideal. Take Safety-Kleen. That's a name with promise to begin with—any company that uses a *k* where there ought to be a *c* is worth investigating. The fact that Safety-Kleen was once related to Chicago Rawhide is also favorable (see "It's a Spinoff" below).

Safety-Kleen provides gas stations with a machine that washes greasy auto parts. This saves auto mechanics the time and trouble of scrubbing the parts by hand in a pail of gasoline, and gas stations gladly pay for the service. Periodically the Safety-Kleen people come around to remove the dirty sludge and oil from the machine, and they carry the sludge back to the refinery to be recycled. You'll never see a miniseries about it on network TV.

Safety-Kleen hasn't rested on the spoils of greasy auto parts. It has since branched out into restaurant grease traps and other sorts of messes. What analyst would want to write about this, and what portfolio manager would want to have Safety-Kleen on his buy list? There aren't many, which is precisely what's endearing about Safety-Kleen. Like Automatic Data Processing, this company has had an unbroken run of increased earnings. Profits have gone up every quarter, and so has the stock.

(4) It's a Spinoff

Spinoffs of divisions or parts of companies into separate, freestanding entities—such as Safety-Kleen out of Chicago Rawhide or Toys "R" Us out of Interstate Department Stores—often result in astoundingly lucrative investments. Dart & Kraft, which merged years ago, eventually separated so that Kraft could become a pure food company again. Dart (which owns Tupperware) was spun off as Premark International and has been a great investment on its own. So has Kraft, which was bought out by Philip Morris in 1988.

Large parent companies do not want to spin off divisions and then see those spinoffs get into trouble, because that would bring embarrassing publicity that would reflect back on the parents. Therefore, the spinoffs normally have strong balance sheets and are well-prepared to succeed as independent entities. And once these companies are granted their independence, the new management, free to run its own show, can cut costs and take creative measures that improve the near-term and long-term earnings.

Spinoff stocks offer great opportunities for the amateur shareholder, especially in the recent frenzy of mergers and acquisitions. Companies that are targets of hostile takeovers frequently fight off raiders by selling or spinning off divisions that then become publicly traded issues on their own. When a company is taken over, the parts are often sold off for cash, and they, too, become separate entities in which to invest. If you hear about a spinoff, begin an immediate investigation. A month or two after the spinoff is completed, check to see if there is heavy insider buying among the new officers and directors. This will confirm that they, too, believe in the company's prospects.

The greatest spinoffs of all were the "Baby Bell" companies that were created in the breakup of ATT: Ameritech, Bell Atlantic, Bell South, Nynex, Pacific Telesis, Southwestern Bell, and US West. The seven regional companies got all the local and regional telephone business, the yellow pages, along with 50 cents for every $1 of long-distance business generated by ATT. While the parent has been an uninspiring performer, the average gain from stock in the newly created companies was 114 percent from November 1983 to October 1988. Add in the dividends and the total return is more like 170 percent. This beats the market twice around, and it eats the majority of all known mutual funds, including the one run by yours truly.

Investors who owned the old ATT stock had eighteen months to decide whether to sell ATT and be done with the whole complicated mess, keep ATT plus the shares and fractions of shares in the new Baby Bells that they received, or sell the parent and keep the Baby Bells. If they did their homework, they sold ATT, kept the Baby Bells, and added to their position with as many more shares as they could afford.

Pounds of material were sent out to the 2.96 million ATT share-holders explaining the Baby Bells' plans. A million employees of ATT and countless suppliers could have seen what was going on. So much for the amateur's edge being restricted to a lucky few. For that matter, anyone who had a phone knew that there were big changes going on. I participated in the rally, but only in a modest way — I never dreamed that conservative companies such as these could do so well so quickly.

(5) The Institutions Don't Own It, and the Analysts Don't Follow It

If you find a stock with little or no institutional ownership, you've found a potential winner. Find a company that no analyst has ever visited, and you've got a double winner. When I talk to a company that tells me the last analyst showed up three years ago, I can hardly contain my enthusiasm. It frequently happens with banks, savings-and-loans, and insurance companies, since there are thousands of these and Wall Street only keeps up with fifty to one hundred.

I'm equally enthusiastic about once-popular stocks the professionals have abandoned, as many abandoned Chrysler and Exxon at the bottom, just before both began to rebound.

Data on institutional ownership are available from the following sources: *Vicker's Institutional Holdings Guide*, *Nelson's Directory of Investment Research*, and the *Spectrum Surveys*, a publication of CDA Investment Technologies. Although these publications are not always easy to find, you can get similar information from the *Value Line Investment Survey* and from the S&P stock sheets, also called tear sheets. Both are routinely provided by regular stockbrokers.

(6) The Rumors Abound: It's Involved with Toxic Waste and/or the Mafia

It's hard to think of a more perfect industry than waste management. If there's anything that disturbs people more than grease and dirty oil, it's sewage and toxic waste dumps. That's why I got very excited one day when the solid waste executives showed up in my office. They had come to town for a solid waste convention complete with booths and slides— imagine how attractive that must have been. Anyway, instead of the usual blue cotton button-down shirts that I see day after day, they were wearing polo shirts that said "Solid Waste." These are the kind of executives you dream about.

As you already know if you were fortunate enough to have bought some, Waste Management, Inc. is up about a hundredfold.

Waste Management actually has two unthinkables going for it: toxic waste itself, and also the Mafia. Everyone who fantasizes that the Mafia runs all the Italian restaurants, the newsstands, the dry cleaners, the construction sites, and the olive presses also probably thinks that the Mafia controls the garbage business. This fantastic assertion was a great advantage to the earliest buyers of underpriced shares in Waste Management.

Maybe the rumors of the Mafia in waste management kept away the same investors who worried about the Mafia in hotel/casino management. Remember the dreaded casino stocks that are now on everybody's buylist? Respectable investors weren't supposed to touch them because the casinos allegedly were all Mafia. Then the earnings exploded and the profits exploded, and the Mafia faded into the background. When Holiday Inn and Hilton got into the casino business, it suddenly was all right to own casino stocks.

(7) There's Something Depressing About It

In this category my favorite all-time pick is Service Corporation International (SCI), which also has a boring name. Now, if there's anything Wall Street would rather ignore besides toxic waste, it's mortality. And SCI does burials.

For several years this Houston-based enterprise has been going around the country buying up local funeral homes, just as Gannett did with small-town newspapers. SCI has become a sort of McBurial. At last count the company owned 461 funeral parlors, 121 cemeteries, 76 flower shops, 21 funeral product-and-supply manufacturing centers, and 3 casket distribution centers, so they're vertically integrated. They broke into the big-time when they buried Howard Hughes.

They also pioneered the pre-need policy, a popular layaway plan. It enables you to pay off your funeral service and your casket right now while you can still afford it, so your family won't have to pay for it later. Even if the cost has tripled by the time you require a funeral service, you're locked in at the old prices. This is a great deal for the family of the deceased, and an even greater deal for the company.

SCI gets the money from its pre-need sales right away, and the cash just keeps compounding. If they sell $50 million worth of these policies each year, it will add up to billions by the time they've had all the funerals. Lately they've gone beyond their own operations to offer the pre-need policies to other funeral homes. Over the past five years the sales of prearranged funerals have been climbing at 40 percent a year.

Once in a while a positive story is topped off by an extraordinary kicker, an unexpected valuable card that turns up. In SCI's case it happened when the company struck a very lucrative bargain with another company (American General) that wanted to buy the real estate under one of SCI's Houston locations. In return for the rights to this land, American General, which owned 20 percent of SCI's stock, gave all their stock back to SCI. Not only did SCI retrieve 20 percent of its shares at no cost, but it was allowed to continue to operate the funeral home at the old location for two years, until it could open a new home at a different site in Houston.

(8) It's a No-Growth Industry

Many people prefer to invest in a high-growth industry, where there's a lot of sound and fury. I prefer to invest in a low-growth industry like plastic knives and forks, but only if I can't find a no-growth industry like funerals. That's where the biggest winners are developed.

There's nothing thrilling about high-growth industry, except watching the stocks go down. Carpets in the 1950s, electronics in the 1960s, computers in the 1980s, were all exciting high-growth industries, in which numerous companies unerringly failed to prosper for long. That's because for every product in a hot industry, there are a thousand MIT graduates trying to figure out how to make it cheaper in Taiwan. As soon as a computer company designs the best word-processor in the world, ten other competitors are spending $100 million to design a better one, and it will be on the market in eight months. This doesn't happen with bottle caps, oil-drum retrieval, or motel chains.

(9) It's Got a Niche

I'd rather own a local rock pit than Twentieth Century-Fox, because a movie company competes with other movie companies, and the rock pit has a niche. Twentieth Century-Fox understood that when it bought up Pebble Beach, and the rock pit with it.

If you're in the jewelry business, you're competing with other jewelers from across town, across the state, and even abroad, since vacationers can buy jewelry anywhere and bring it home. But if you've got the only gravel pit in Brooklyn, you've got a virtual monopoly, plus the added protection of the unpopularity of rock pits. The nearest rival owner from two towns over isn't going to haul his rocks into your territory because the trucking bills would eat up all his profit. No matter how good the rocks are in Chicago, no Chicago rock-pit owner can ever invade your territory in Brooklyn or Detroit.

I always look for niches. The perfect company would have to have one. Warren Buffett started out by acquiring a textile mill in New Bedford, Massachusetts, which he quickly realized was not a niche business. He did poorly in textiles but went on to make billions for his shareholders by investing in niches. He was one of the first to see the value in newspapers and TV stations that dominated major markets, beginning with the *Washington Post*. Thinking along the same lines, I bought as much stock as I could in Affiliated Publications, which owns the local *Boston Globe*. Since the *Globe* gets over 90 percent of the print ad revenues in Boston, how could the *Globe* lose?

The Times Mirror Company has several niches, including the *Los Angeles Times*, *Newsday*, the *Hartford Courant*, and the *Baltimore Sun*.

Gannett owns 90 daily newspapers, and most of them are the only major dailies in town. Investors who discovered the advantages of exclusive newspaper and cable franchises in the early 1970s were rewarded with a number of tenbaggers as the cable stocks and media stocks got popular on Wall Street.

Drug companies have niches—products that no one else is allowed to make. It took years for SmithKline to get the patent for Tagamet. Once a patent is approved, all the rival companies with their billions in research dollars can't invade the territory. They have to invent a different drug, prove it is different, and then go through three years of clinical trials before the government will let them sell it.

Brand names such as Robitussin, Tylenol, or Coca-Cola are almost as good as niches. It costs a fortune to develop public confidence in a soft drink or a cough medicine. The whole process takes years.

(10) People Have to Keep Buying

I'd rather invest in a company that makes drugs, soft drinks, razor blades, or cigarettes than in a toy company. Somebody can make a wonderful doll that every child has to have, but every child gets only one each. Eight months later that product is taken off the shelves to make room for the newest doll the children have to have—manufactured by somebody else.

Why take chances on fickle purchases when there's so much steady business around?

(11) It's a User of Technology

Instead of investing in computer companies that struggle to survive in an endless price war, why not invest in a company that benefits from the price war—such as Automatic Data Processing? As computers get cheaper, Automatic Data can do its job cheaper and thus increase its own profits. Or instead of investing in a company that makes automatic scanners, why not invest in the supermarkets that install the scanners? If a scanner helps a supermarket company cut costs just three percent, that alone might double the company's earnings.

(12) The Insiders are Buyers

There's no better tip-off to the probable success of a stock than that people in the company are putting their own money into it. In general, corporate insiders normally sell 2.3 shares to every one share that they buy. After the 1,000-point drop from August to October 1987, it was reassuring to discover that there were four shares bought to every one share sold by insiders across the board. At least they hadn't lost their faith.

Long term, there's another important benefit. When management owns stock, then rewarding the shareholders becomes a first priority, whereas when management simply collects a paycheck, then increasing salaries becomes a first priority. Since bigger companies tend to pay bigger salaries to executives, there's a natural tendency for corporate wage-earners to expand the business at any cost, often to the detriment of shareholders. This happens less often when management is heavily invested in shares.

It's simple to keep track of insider purchases. Every time an officer or a director buys or sells shares, he or she has to declare it on Form 4 and send the form to the Securities and Exchange Commission. Several newsletter services, including *Vicker's Weekly Insider Report* and *The Insiders*, keep track of these filings. *Barron's*, *The Wall Street Journal*, and *Investor's Daily* also carry the information. Many local business newspapers report on insider trading on local companies—I know the *Boston Business Journal* has such a column. Your broker may also be able to provide the information, or you may find that your local library subscribes to the newsletters. There's also a tabulation of insider buying and selling in the *Value Line* publication.

Insider selling usually means nothing. Officers may need the money to pay their children's tuition or to buy a new house or to satisfy a debt. They may have decided to diversify into other stocks. But there's only one reason that insiders buy: They think the stock price is undervalued and will eventually go up.

(13) The Company is Buying Back Shares

Buying back shares is the simplest and best way a company can reward its investors. If a company has faith in its own future, then why shouldn't it invest in itself, just as the shareholders do? On October 20, 1987, the announcement of massive share buybacks by company after company broke the fall of many stocks, and stabilized the market at the height of its panic. Long term, these buybacks can't help but reward investors.

When stock is bought by the company, it is taken out of circulation, therefore shrinking the number of outstanding shares. This can have a magical effect on earnings per share, which in turn has a magical effect on the stock price. If a company buys back half its shares and its overall earnings stay the same, the earnings per share have just doubled. Few companies could get that kind of result by cutting costs or selling more widgets.

Exxon has been buying in shares because it's cheaper than drilling for oil. It might cost Exxon $6 a barrel to find new oil, but if each of its shares represents $3 a barrel in oil assets, then retiring shares has the same effect as discovering $3 oil on the floor of the New York Stock Exchange.

This sensible practice was almost unheard of until quite recently. In the 1960s, International Dairy Queen was one of the pioneers in share buybacks, but there were few others who followed suit. At the delightful Crown, Cork, and Seal they've bought back shares every year for the last twenty. They never pay a dividend, and they never make unprofitable acquisitions, but by shrinking shares they've gotten the maximum impact from the earnings. If this keeps up, someday there will be a thousand shares of Crown, Cork, and Seal—worth $10 million apiece.

The common alternatives to buying back shares are (1) raising the dividend, (2) developing new products, (3) starting new operations, and (4) making acquisitions. Gillette tried to do all four, with emphasis on the final three. Gillette has a spectacularly profitable razor business, which it gradually reduced in relative size as it acquired less profitable operations. If the company had regularly bought back its shares and raised its dividend instead of diverting its capital to cosmetics, toiletries, office products, and lots of other diversions, the stock might well be worth over $100 instead of the current $35. In the last five years, Gillette has gotten back on track by eliminating losing operations and emphasizing its core shaving business, where it dominates the market.

THE GREATEST COMPANY OF ALL

If I could dream up a single glorious enterprise that combines all of the worst elements of Waste Management, Pep Boys, Safety-Kleen, rock pits, and bottle caps it would be Cajun Cleansers. Cajun Cleansers, a recent spinoff from Louisiana BayouFeedback, is engaged in the boring business of removing mildew stains from furniture, rare books, draperies, and other victims of subtropical humidity.

Its headquarters is in the bayous of Louisiana, and to get there you have to change planes twice, then hire a pickup truck to take you from the airport. Not one analyst from New York or Boston has ever visited Cajun Cleansers, nor has any institution bought a solitary share.

While expanding quickly through the bayous and the Ozarks, Cajun Cleansers has had incredible sales. These sales will soon accelerate because the company just developed a niche: a patent on a new gel that removes all sorts of stains from clothes, furniture, carpets, bathroom tiles, and even aluminum siding.

The company is also planning to offer lifetime prestain insurance to millions of Americans, who will pay in advance for a guaranteed removal of all the future stains they ever cause. A fortune in off-balance-sheet revenue will soon be pouring in.

No popular magazines except the ones that think Elvis is alive have mentioned Cajun and its new patent. The stock opened at $8 in a public offering seven years ago and soon rose to $10. At that price the important corporate directors bought as many shares as they could afford.

I hear about Cajun from a distant relative who swears it's the only way to get mildew off leather jackets left too long in dank closets. I do some research and discover that Cajun has had a 20 percent growth rate in earnings for the past four years, it's never had a down quarter, there's no debt on the balance sheet, and it did well in the last recession. I visit the company and find out that any trained crustacean could oversee the making of the gel.

The day before I decide to buy Cajun Cleansers, the noted economist Henry Kaufman predicts that interest rates are going up, and then the head of the Federal Reserve slips on the lane at a bowling alley and injures his back, both of which combine to send the market down 15 percent, and Cajun Cleansers with it. I get in at $7.50, which is $2.50 less than the directors paid.

That's the situation at Cajun Cleansers. Don't pinch me. I'm dreaming.

— 9 —

STOCKS I'D AVOID

I f I could avoid a single stock, it would be the hottest stock in the hottest industry, the one that gets the most favorable publicity, the one that every investor hears about in the car pool or on the commuter train—and succumbing to the social pressure, often buys.

Hot stocks can go up fast, usually out of sight of any of the known landmarks of value, but since there's nothing but hope and thin air to support them, they fall just as quickly. If you aren't clever at selling hot stocks (and the fact that you've bought them is a clue that you won't be), you'll soon see your profits turn into losses, because when the price falls, it's not going to fall slowly, nor is it likely to stop at the level where you jumped on.

Consider Home Shopping Network, a recent hot stock in the hot teleshop industry, which in 16 months went from $3 to $47 back to $3½ (adjusted for splits). That was terrific for the people who said good-bye at $47, but what about the people who said hello at $47? Where were the earnings, the profits, the future prospects? This investment had all the underlying security of a roulette spin. The balance sheet was deteriorating rapidly (the company was taking on debt to buy television stations), there were problems with the telephones, and competitors had begun to appear. How many zirconium necklaces can people wear?

High growth and hot industries attract a very smart crowd that wants to get into the business. Entrepreneurs and venture capitalists stay awake nights trying to figure out how to get into the act as quickly as possible. If you have a can't-fail idea but no way of protecting it with a patent or a niche, as soon as you succeed, you'll be warding off the imitators.

There's never been a hotter stock than Xerox in the 1960s. Copying was a fabulous industry, and Xerox had control of the entire process. "To xerox" became a verb, which should have been a positive develop-

78

ment. Many analysts assumed that Xerox would keep growing to infinity when the stock was selling for $170 a share in 1972. But then the Japanese, IBM, and Eastman Kodak all got into it. Soon there were twenty firms that made nice dry copies, as opposed to the original wet ones. Xerox got frightened and bought some unrelated businesses it didn't know how to run, and the stock lost 84 percent of its value. Several competitors didn't fare much better. Copying has been a respectable industry for two decades and there's never been a slowdown in demand, yet the copy machine companies can't make a decent living.

BEWARE THE NEXT SOMETHING

Another stock I'd avoid is that in a company that's been touted as the next IBM, the next McDonald's, the next Disney, etc. The next of something almost never is—on Broadway, the best-seller list, or the National Basketball Association.

When people tout a stock as the next of something, it often marks the end of prosperity not only for the imitator but also for the original to which it is being compared. When other computer companies were called the "next IBM," you could have guessed that IBM would go through some terrible times, and it has. The next Toys "R" Us was Child World, which also stumbled; and the next Price Club was the Warehouse Club, which fared no better.

AVOID DIWORSEIFICATIONS

Instead of buying back shares or raising dividends, profitable companies often prefer to blow the money on foolish acquisitions. Every second decade the corporations seem to alternate between rampant diworseification (when billions are spent on exciting acquisitions) and rampant restructuring (when those no-longer-exciting acquisitions are sold off for less than the original purchase price). Some corporations, like some individuals, just can't stand prosperity.

From an investor's point of view, the only two good things about diworseification are owning shares in the company that's being acquired, or in finding turnaround opportunities among the victims of diworseification that have decided to restructure.

The 1960s was the greatest decade for diworseification since the Roman Empire diworseified all over Europe and northern Africa. There are so many examples I hardly know where to begin. As discussed, Gillette not only bought the medicine chest, it diworseified into digital watches and then announced a write-off of the whole fiasco. It's the only time in my memory that a major company got out of a losing business before anybody realized it had gotten into the business in the first place. General Mills owned Chinese restaurants, Italian restaurants, steak houses, Parker Brothers toys, Izod shirts, coins, stamps, travel companies, Eddie Bauer retail outlets, and Footjoy products. Allied Chemical bought everything but the kitchen sink, and probably somewhere in there it actually took over a company that made kitchen sinks. U.S. Industries made 300 acquisitions in a single year. They should have called themselves one-a-day. Beatrice Foods expanded from edibles into inedibles, and after that anything was possible.

This great acquisitive era ended in the market collapse of 1973-74, when Wall Street finally realized that the best and the brightest could not manage one business as well as the next, and even the most charming of corporate directors could not turn all those toads they bought into princes.

That's not to say it's always foolish to make acquisitions. It's a good strategy in situations where the basic business is terrible. We would never have heard of Warren Buffett or his Berkshire Hathaway if Buffett had stuck to textiles. The Tisches started out with a chain of movie theaters (Loew's) and used the proceeds to buy a tobacco company (Lorillard), which in turn helped them acquire an insurance company (CNA), which led to their taking a huge position in CBS. The trick is to make the right acquisitions and then manage them successfully.

BEWARE THE WHISPER STOCK

I get calls all the time from people who recommend solid companies for Magellan, and then, usually after they've lowered their voices as if to confide something personal, they add: "There's this great stock I want to tell you about. It's too small for your fund, but you ought to look at it for your own account. It's a fascinating idea, and it could be a big winner."

These are the longshots, also known as whisper stocks, and the whizbang stories. They probably reach your neighborhood about the same time they reach mine: the company that sells papaya juice derivative as a cure for slipped-disc pain (Smiths Labs); jungle remedies in general; high-tech stuff; monoclonal antibodies extracted from cows (Bioresponse); miracle additives; and energy breakthroughs that violate the laws of physics. Often the whisper companies are on the brink of solving the latest national problem: the oil shortage, drug addiction, AIDS. The solution is either (a) very imaginative, or (b) impressively complicated. The stockpicker is relieved of the burden of checking earnings because usually there are no earnings. Understanding the p/e ratio? No problem. There is no p/e ratio. But there's no shortage of microscopes, Ph.D.'s, high hopes, and cash from the stock sale.

Whisper stocks have a hypnotic effect, and usually the stories have emotional appeal. This is where the sizzle is so delectable that you forget to notice there's no steak. As long-term propositions, I've lost money on every single one I've ever bought.

What I try to remind myself (and obviously I'm not always successful) is that if the prospects of these long shots are so phenomenal, then this will be a fine investment next year and the year after that. Why not put off buying the stock until later, when the company has established a record? Wait for the earnings. You can get tenbaggers in companies that have already proven themselves. When in doubt, tune in later.

BEWARE THE MIDDLEMAN

The company that sells 25 to 50 percent of its wares to a single customer is in a precarious situation. SCI Systems (not to be confused with the funeral-home firm) is a well-managed company and a major supplier of computer parts to IBM, but you never know when IBM will decide to make its own parts, or do without the parts, and then cancel the SCI contract. The big customer also has incredible leverage in extracting price cuts and other concessions that will reduce the supplier's profits. If the loss of one customer would be catastrophic to a supplier, I'd be wary of investing in the supplier.

— 10 —

EARNINGS, EARNINGS, EARNINGS

L et's say you've reviewed your portfolio and you've found two stalwarts and three cyclicals. What possible assurance do you have that the stocks will go up in price? And if you're buying, how much should you pay? What you're asking here is what makes a company valuable, and why it will be more valuable tomorrow than it is today. There are many theories, but to me, it always comes down to earnings and assets. Especially earnings. Sometimes it takes years for the stock price to catch up to a company's value, and the down periods last so long that investors begin to doubt that will ever happen. But value always wins out—or at least in enough cases that it's worthwhile to believe it.

Analyzing a company's stock on the basis of earnings and assets is no different from analyzing a local laundromat, drugstore, or apartment building that you might want to buy. *A share of stock is not a lottery ticket. It's part ownership of a business.*

Here's another way of thinking about earnings and assets. If you were a stock, your earnings and assets would determine how much an investor would be willing to pay for a percentage of your action. Evaluating yourself as you might evaluate General Motors is an instructive exercise.

Your assets would include your real estate, cars, furniture, clothes, rugs, boats, tools, jewelry, golf clubs, and everything else that would go in a giant garage sale if you decided to liquidate yourself and go out of business. Of course, you'd have to subtract outstanding mortgages, liens, car loans, other loans from banks, relatives, or neighbors, unpaid bills, IOUs, poker debts, and so forth. The result would be your positive bottom line, or book value, or net economic worth as a tangible asset. (If the result is negative, then you're a human candidate for Chapter 11.)

As long as you're not liquidated and sold off to the creditors, you also represent the other kind of value: the capacity to earn income. Over your working life you may bring home either thousands or millions of dollars, depending on how much you're paid and how hard you work.

Now that you're thinking about it, put yourself in one of the six categories of stocks we've already gone over. This could be a halfway decent party game:

People who work in secure jobs that pay low salaries and modest raises are slow growers, the human equivalents of the electric utilities. Librarians, schoolteachers, and policemen are slow growers.

People who command good salaries and get predictable raises, such as the middle-level managers of corporations, are stalwarts: the Coca-Cola and Ralston Purinas of the work force.

Farmers, hotel and resort employees, jai alai players, and Christmas tree sales-lot operators who make all their money in short bursts and then try to budget it through long, unprofitable stretches are cyclicals. Writers and actors may also be cyclicals, with the potential to be fast growers.

Trust-fund men and women and others who live off family fortunes but contribute nothing from their own labor are asset plays, the gold-mining stocks and railroads of our analogy.

Guttersnipes, drifters, down-and-outers, bankrupts, laid-off workers, and others in the unemployment lines are all potential turnarounds, as long as there's any energy and enterprise left in them.

Investors, real estate developers, small businessmen, athletes, musicians, and criminals are all potential fast growers, the human equivalents of Taco Bell or Stop & Shop.

When you buy a stock in a fast-growing company, you're really betting on its chances to earn more money in the future. Consider the decision to invest in a young Dunkin' Donuts such as Harrison Ford, as opposed to a Coca-Cola type such as a corporate lawyer. Investing in the Coca-Cola type seems a lot more sensible while Harrison Ford is working as an itinerant carpenter in Los Angeles, but look what happens to earnings when Mr. Ford makes a hit movie such as *Star Wars*. That's why investors seek out promising fast growers and bid the stock up, even when the companies are earning nothing at present—or when the earnings are paltry as compared to the price per share.

You can see the importance of earnings on any chart that has an earnings line running alongside the stock price. Books of stock charts are available from most brokerage firms, and it's instructive to flip through them. On chart after chart the two lines will move in tandem, or if the stock price strays away from the earnings line, sooner or later it will come back to the earnings. Consider Dow Chemical. When earnings are up the stock is up. That's what happened during the period from 1971 to 1975 and again from 1985 through 1988. In between, from 1975 through 1985, earnings were erratic and so was the stock price.

And how about Masco Corporation, which developed the single-handle ball faucet? Between 1958 and 1987, through war and peace, inflation and recession, earnings rose 800-fold and the stock increased in value 1,300-fold. It's probably the greatest stock in the history of capitalism. As long as the earnings continued to increase, there was nothing to stop it.

Look at Shoney's, a restaurant chain that has had 116 consecutive quarters (twenty-nine years) of higher revenues—a record few companies could match. Sure enough, the stock price has steadily moved up. In those few spots where the price got ahead of the earnings, it promptly fell back to reality.

A quick way to tell if a stock is overpriced is to compare the price line to the earnings line on the stock's chart. If you bought familiar growth companies—such as Shoney's, The Limited, or Marriott—when the stock price fell well below the earnings line, and sold them when the stock price rose dramatically above it, the chances are you'd do pretty well. I'm not necessarily advocating this practice, but I can think of worse strategies.

THE FAMOUS P/E RATIO

Any serious discussion of earnings involves the price/earnings ratio—also known as the p/e ratio, the price/earnings multiple, or simply, the multiple. This ratio is a numerical shorthand for the relationship between the stock price and the earnings of the company. The p/e ratio for each stock is listed in the daily stock tables of most major newspapers, as shown here.

THE WALL STREET JOURNAL
(Tuesday, September 13, 1988)

52 Weeks				Yld	P-E	Sales				Net
High	Low	Stock	Div.	%	Ratio	100s	High	Low	Close	Chg.
43¼	21⅝	K mart	1.32	3.8	10	4696	35⅛	34½	35	+ ⅜

Like the earnings line, the p/e ratio is often a useful measure of whether any stock is fairly priced relative to a company's money-making potential.

In a few cases the p/e ratio listed in the newspaper may be abnormally high, often because a company has written off some long-term losses against the current short-term earnings, thus "punishing" those earnings. If the p/e seems out of line, ask your broker for an explanation.

In today's *Wall Street Journal*, for instance, I see that K mart has a p/e ratio of 10. This was derived by taking the current price of the stock ($35 a share) and dividing it by the company's earnings for the prior 12 months or fiscal year (in this case, $3.50 a share). The $35 divided by the $3.50 results in the p/e of 10.

The p/e ratio can be thought of as the number of years it will take the company to earn back the amount of your initial investment—assuming, of course, that the company's earnings stay constant. Let's say you buy 100 shares of K mart for $3,500. Current earnings are $3.50 per share, so your 100 shares will earn $350 in one year, and the original investment of $3,500 will be earned back in ten years. However, you don't have to go through this exercise because the p/e ratio of 10 tells you it's ten years.

If you buy shares in a company selling at two times earnings (a p/e of 2), you will earn back your initial investment in two years, but in a company selling at 40 times earnings (a p/e of 40) it would take forty years to accomplish the same thing. Why would anybody buy a stock with a high p/e? Because they're looking for Harrison Ford at the lumber yard. The fact that some stocks have p/e's of 40 and other have p/e's of 3 tells you that investors are willing to take substantial gambles on the improved future earnings of some companies, while they're quite skeptical about the future of others. You'll be amazed at the range of p/e's that you see in the newspaper.

The p/e levels tend to be lowest for slow growers and highest for fast growers, with cyclicals vacillating in between. That's as it should be, if you follow the logic of the discussion above. An average p/e for a utility (7 to 9 these days) will be lower than the average p/e for a stalwart (10 to

14 these days), and that in turn will be lower than the average p/e of a fast grower (14-20).

MORE ON THE P/E

A full discussion of p/e ratios of various industries and different types of companies would take an entire book that nobody would want to read. Ask your broker whether the p/e ratios of various stocks you own are low, high, or average, relative to industry norms. Sometimes you'll hear things like "this company is selling at a discount to the industry"— meaning that its p/e is at a bargain level.

A broker can also give you the historical record of a company's p/e— and the same information can be found on the S&P reports also available from the brokerage firm. Before you buy a stock, track its p/e ratio back through several years to get a sense of its normal levels. (New companies, of course, haven't been around long enough to have such records.) If you buy Coca-Cola, for instance, it's useful to know whether what you're paying for the earnings is in line with what others have paid for the earnings in the past.

The *Value Line Investment Survey*, available in most large libraries and also from most brokers, is another good source for p/e histories. In fact, *Value Line* is a good source for all the pertinent data that amateur investors need to know. It's the next best thing to having your own private securities analyst.

If you remember nothing else about p/e ratios, remember to avoid stocks with excessively high ones. It's usually a handicap to a stock, in the same way that extra weight in the saddle is a handicap to a racehorse. A company with a high p/e must have incredible earnings growth to justify the high price that's been put on the stock.

I couldn't believe it when I saw a brokerage report on Ross Perot's company, Electronic Data Systems (EDS), a hot stock in the late 1960s. This company had a p/e of 500! It would take five centuries to make back your investment in EDS if earnings stayed constant. Not only that, but the analyst who wrote the report suggested that EDS ought to have a p/e of 1,000.

If you had invested in a company with a p/e of 1,000 when King Arthur roamed England, and earnings stayed constant, you'd just be breaking even today.

I wish I had saved this report and had it framed for my office wall, to put alongside one that was sent to me from another brokerage firm that read: "Due to the recent bankruptcy, we're removing this stock from our buy list."

In the years that followed, EDS the company performed very well. EDS the stock is another story. The price declined from $40 to $3 in 1974, not because there was anything amiss at headquarters, but because the stock was the most overpriced of any I've ever seen before or since. You often hear about companies whose future performance is "discounted" in the stock price. If that's the case, then EDS investors were discounting the Hereafter.

THE P/E OF THE MARKET

Company p/e ratios do not exist in a vacuum. The stock market as a whole has its own collective p/e ratio, which is a good indicator of whether the market at large is overvalued or undervalued. I know I've already advised you to ignore the market, but when you find that a few stocks are selling at inflated prices relative to earnings, it's likely that most stocks are selling at inflated prices relative to earnings. That's what happened before the big drop in 1973-74, and once again (although not to the same extent) before the big drop of 1987.

During the five years of the latest bull market, from 1982 to 1987, you could see the market's overall p/e ratio creep gradually higher, from about 8 to 16. This meant that investors in 1987 were willing to pay twice what they paid in 1982 for the same corporate earnings—which should have been a warning that most stocks were overvalued.

Interest rates have a large effect on the prevailing p/e ratios, since investors pay more for stocks when interest rates are low and bonds are less attractive. But interest rates aside, the incredible optimism that develops in bull markets can drive p/e ratios to ridiculous levels, as it did in the case of EDS. In that period, the fast growers commanded p/e ratios that belonged somewhere in Wonderland, the slow growers were commanding p/e ratios normally reserved for fast growers, and the p/e of the market itself hit a peak of 20 in 1971.

Any student of the p/e ratio could have seen that this was lunacy, and I wish one of them had told me. In 1973-74 the market had its most brutal correction since the 1930s.

FUTURE EARNINGS

Future earnings—there's the rub. How do you predict those? The best you can get from current earnings is an educated guess whether a stock is fairly priced. However, what you'd really like to know is what's going to happen to earnings in the next month, the next year, or the next decade.

Earnings, after all, are supposed to grow, and every stock price carries with it a built-in growth assumption.

Battalions of analysts and statisticians are launched against the questions of future growth and future earnings, and you can pick up the nearest financial magazine to see for yourself how often they get the wrong answer (the word most frequently seen with "earnings" is "surprise"). I'm not about to suggest that you can begin to predict earnings, or growth in earnings, successfully on your own.

Once you got into this game seriously, you'd be boggled by the examples of stocks that go down even though the earnings are up, because professional analysts and their institutional clients expected the earnings to be higher, or stocks that go up even though earnings are down, because that same cheering section expected the earnings to be lower. These are short-term anomalies, but nonetheless frustrating to the shareholder who notices them.

If you can't predict future earnings, at least you can find out *how* a company plans to increase its earnings. Then you can check periodically to see if the plans are working out.

Some people confuse dividends with the earnings we've been discussing in this chapter. A company's earnings is what it makes every year after all expenses and taxes are taken out. A dividend is what it pays out to stockholders on a regular basis as their share of the profits. A company may have terrific earnings and yet pay no dividend at all. The five basic ways a company can increase earnings are to reduce costs; raise prices; expand into new markets; sell more of its product in the old markets; or revitalize, close, or otherwise dispose of a losing operation. These are the factors to investigate as you develop the story. If you have an edge, this is where it's going to be most helpful.

— II —

THE TWO-MINUTE DRILL

You've found out whether you're dealing with a slow grower, a stalwart, a fast grower, a turnaround, an asset play, or a cyclical. The p/e ratio has given you a rough idea of whether the stock is undervalued or overvalued relative to its immediate prospects. The next step is to learn what the company is doing to bring about the added prosperity, the growth spurt, or whatever happy event is expected to occur. This is known as the "story."

With the possible exception of the asset play (where you can sit back and wait for the value of the real estate or the oil reserves or the TV stations to be recognized by others), something dynamic has to happen to improve earnings. The more certain you are about what that something is, the better you'll be able to follow the script.

The analyst's reports on the company you get from your broker, and the short essays in the *Value Line* give you the professional version of the story, but if you've got an edge in the company or in the industry, you'll be able to develop your own script in useful detail.

Before buying stock, I like to be able to give a two-minute monologue that covers the reasons I'm interested in it, what has to happen for the company to succeed, and the pitfalls that stand in its path. Once you're able to tell the story of a stock to your family, your friends, or the dog (and I don't mean "a guy on the bus says Caesars World is a takeover"), and so that even a child could understand it, then you have a proper grasp of the situation.

Here are some of the topics that might be addressed in the monologue:

If it's a slow-growing company, then presumably you're in it for the dividend (why else own this kind of stock?). Therefore, the important elements of the script would be: "This company has increased earnings every year for the last ten, it offers an attractive yield, it's never reduced or suspended a dividend, and in fact it's raised the dividend during good times and bad, including the last three recessions. It's a telephone utility, and the new cellular operations may add a substantial kicker to the growth rate."

If it's a cyclical company, then your script revolves around business conditions, inventories, and prices. "There has been a three-year business slump in the auto industry, but this year things have turned around. I know that because car sales are up across the board for the first time in recent memory. I notice that GM's new models are selling well, and in the last eighteen months the company has closed five inefficient plants, cut twenty percent off labor costs, and earnings are about to turn sharply higher."

If it's an asset play, then what are the assets, how much are they worth? "The stock sells for $8, but the videocassette division alone is worth $4 a share and the real estate is worth $7. That's a bargain in itself, and I'm getting the rest of the company for a minus $3. Insiders are buying and the company has steady earnings and there's no debt to speak of."

If it's a turnaround, then has the company gone about improving its fortunes? "General Mills has made great progress in curing its diworseification. It's gone from eleven basic businesses to two. By selling off Eddie Bauer, Talbot's Kenner, and Parker Brothers and getting top dollar for these excellent companies, General Mills has returned to doing what it does best: restaurants and packaged foods. The company has been buying back millions of its shares. The seafood subsidiary, Gortons, has grown from 7 percent of the seafood market to 25 percent. They are coming out with low-cal yogurt, no-cholesterol Bisquick, and microwave brownies. Earnings are up sharply."

If it's a stalwart, then the key issues are the p/e ratio, whether the stock already has had a dramatic run-up in price in recent months, and what, if anything, is happening to accelerate the growth rate. You might say to yourself: "Coca-Cola is selling at the low end of its p/e range. The stock hasn't gone anywhere for two years. The company has improved itself in several ways. It sold half its interest in Columbia Pictures to the public. Diet drinks have sped up the growth rate dramatically. Foreign sales are excellent in general. Through a separate stock offering, Coca-Cola Enterprises, the company has bought out many of its independent regional distributors. Now the company has better control over distribution and domestic sales. Because of these factors, Coca-Cola may do better than people think."

If it is a fast grower, then where and how can it continue to grow fast? "La Quinta was a very profitable motel chain in Texas. The company successfully duplicated its formula in Arkansas and Louisiana. Last year it added 20 percent more motel units. Earnings have increased every quarter. The company plans rapid future expansion. The debt is not excessive. Motels are a low-growth industry, and very competitive, but La Quinta has found something of a niche. It has a long way to go before it has saturated the market."

Those are some basic themes for the story, and you can fill in as much detail as you want. The more you know the better. I often devote several hours to developing a script, though that's not always necessary. Let me give you two examples, one a situation that I checked out properly, and the other where there was something I forgot to ask. The first was La Quinta, which has been a fifteenbagger, and the second was Bildner's, a fifteenbagger in reverse.

CHECKING OUT LA QUINTA

At one point I'd decided the motel industry was due for a cyclical turnaround. I'd already invested in United Inns, the largest franchiser of Holiday Inns, and I was keeping my ears open for other opportunities. During a telephone interview with a vice president at United Inns, I asked which company was Holiday Inn's most successful competitor.

Asking about the competition is one of my favorite techniques for finding promising new stocks. Muckamucks speak negatively about the competition ninety-five percent of the time, and it doesn't mean much. But when an executive of one company admits he's impressed by another company, you can bet that company is doing something right. Nothing could be more bullish than begrudging admiration from a rival.

"La Quinta Motor Inn," the vice president of United Inns enthused. "They're doing a great job. They're killing us in Houston and in Dallas."

As soon as I got off the phone, I got back on the phone with Walter Biegler at La Quinta headquarters in San Antonio to find out what the story was. Mr. Biegler told me that in two days he'd be coming to Boston for a business conference at Harvard, at which time he'd be glad to tell me the story in person.

Between the United Inn man's dropping the hint and five minutes later the La Quinta man's mentioning that he just happened to be traveling to Boston, the whole thing sounded like a set-up job. But as soon as I heard Biegler's presentation, I knew the best way to have gotten suckered would have been not to have bought this wonderful stock.

The concept was simple. La Quinta offered rooms of Holiday Inn quality, but at prices that were 30 percent cheaper. How was that possible? Biegler went on to explain.

La Quinta had eliminated the wedding area, the conference rooms, the large reception area, the kitchen area, and the restaurant — all excess space that contributed nothing to the profits but added substantially to the costs. La Quinta'a idea was to install a Denny's or some similar 24-hour place next door to every one of its motels. La Quinta didn't even have to own the Denny's. Somebody else could worry about the food. Holiday Inn isn't famous for its cuisine, so it's not as if La Quinta was giving up a major selling point. Right here, La Quinta avoided a big capital investment and sidestepped some big trouble. It turns out that most hotels and motels lose money on their restaurants, and the restaurants cause 95 percent of the complaints.

From Mr. Biegler I learned that hotel and motel customers routinely pay one one-thousandth of the value of a room for each night's lodging. If the Plaza Hotel in New York is worth $400,000 a room, you're probably going to pay $400 a night to stay there, and if the No-Tell Motel is built for $20,000 a room, then you'll be paying $20 a night. Because it cost 30 percent less to build a La Quinta than it did to build a Holiday Inn, I could see how La Quinta could rent out rooms at a 30-percent discount and still make the same profit as a Holiday Inn.

Where was the niche? There were hundreds of motel rooms at every fork in the road already. Mr. Biegler said they had a specific target: the small businessman who didn't care for the budget motel, and if he had the choice, he'd rather pay less for the equivalent luxury of a Holiday Inn.

Nobody else had captured this part of the market, the middle ground between the Hilton hotels above and the budget inn below. Also, there was no way that some newer competitor could sneak up on La Quinta. The prototypes of would-be hotel and restaurant chains have to show up someplace — you simply can't build 100 of them overnight, and if they are in a different part of the country, they wouldn't affect you anyway.

What about the costs? When small and new companies undertake expensive projects like hotel construction, the burden of debt can weigh them down for years. Biegler reassured me on this point as well. He said that La Quinta had kept costs low by building 120-room inns instead of 250-room inns, by supervising the construction in-house, and by following a cookie-cutter blueprint. Furthermore, a 120-room operation could be managed by a live-in retired couple, which saved on overhead. And most impressive, La Quinta had struck a deal with major insurance companies who were providing all the financing at favorable terms, in exchange for a small share in the profits.

As partners in La Quinta's success or failure, insurance companies weren't likely to make loan demands that would drive the company into bankruptcy if a shortfall ever occurred. In fact, this access to insurance-company money is what enabled La Quinta to grow rapidly in a capital-incentive business without incurring the dreaded bank debt (see Chapter 13).

Soon enough, I was satisfied that Biegler and his employers had thought of everything. La Quinta had already been operating for four or five years at that time. The original motor inn had been duplicated several times and in several different locations. The company was growing at an astounding 50 percent a year, and the stock was selling at ten times earnings, which made it an incredible bargain. I knew how many new units La Quinta was proposing to build, so I could keep track of future progress.

To top it all off, only three brokerage firms covered La Quinta in 1978, and less than 20 percent of the stock was held by the big institutions. The only thing wrong with La Quinta that I could see was it wasn't boring enough.

I followed up on this conversation by spending three nights in three different La Quintas while I was on the road talking to other companies. I bounced on the beds, tugged at the curtains, squeezed the towels, and satisfied myself that La Quinta was the equal of Holiday Inn.

The La Quinta story checked out in every detail. I bought as much La Quinta as possible for Magellan fund. I made elevenfold on it over a ten-year period before it suffered a downturn due to declining fortunes in the energy-producing states. Recently the company has become an exciting combination of asset play and turnaround.

BILDNER'S, ALAS

Investing in Bildner's is a perfect example of what happens when you get so caught up in the euphoria of an enterprise that you ask all the questions except a most important one, and that turns out to be the fatal flaw.

Bildner's is a specialty food store located right across the street from my office in Boston. There was also a Bildner's out in the town where I live—although it's gone now. Among other things, Bildner's sells gourmet sandwiches and prepared hot foods, a sort of happy compromise between a convenience store and a three-star restaurant. I'm well-acquainted with their sandwiches, since I've been eating them for lunch for several years. That was my edge on Bildner's: I had firsthand information that they had the best bread and the best sandwiches in Boston. The company had carved out a perfect niche—the millions of white-collar types who had no tolerance for microwave sandwiches in plastic wrappers, and yet who also refused to cook.

I'd fully researched the operation by wandering into the store across the street. One of the original Bildner's, it was clean, efficient, and full of satisfied customers, a regular yuppie 7-Eleven. I also discovered it was a fabulous money-maker. When I heard that Bildner's was planning to sell stock and use the proceeds to open more stores, I was understandably excited.

From the prospectus of the stock offering, I learned that the company was not going to burden itself with excessive bank debt. This was a plus. It was going to lease space for its new stores, as opposed to buying the real estate. This, too, was a plus. Without further investigation I bought Bildner's at the initial offering price of $13 in September 1986.

Soon after this sale of stock, Bildner's opened two new outlets in Boston department stores, and these flopped. Then it opened three new outlets in the center of Manhattan, and these got killed by the delis. It expanded into more distant cities, including Atlanta. By quickly spending more than the proceeds from the public offering, Bildner's had overextended itself financially. One or two mistakes at a time might not have been so damaging, but instead of moving cautiously, Bildner's suffered multiple and simultaneous failures. The company no doubt learned from these mistakes, and Jim Bildner was a bright, hardworking, and dedicated man, but after the money ran out, there was no second chance. It's too bad, because I thought Bildner's could have been the next Taco Bell. (Did I really say the "next Taco Bell"? That probably doomed it from the start.)

The stock eventually bottomed out at $⅛, and the management retreated to its original stores, including the one across the street. Bildner's optimistic new goal was to avoid bankruptcy, but recently it's bought The Chapter. I gradually unloaded my shares at losses ranging from 50 percent to 95 percent.

I continue to eat sandwiches from Bildner's, and every time I take a bite of one it reminds me of what I did wrong. I didn't wait to see if this good idea from the neighborhood would actually succeed someplace else. Successful cloning is what turns a local taco joint into a Taco Bell or a local clothing store into The Limited, but there's no point buying the stock until the company has proven that the cloning works.

That's what I forgot to ask Bildner's: Does the idea work elsewhere? I should have worried about a shortage of skilled store managers, its limited financial resources, and its ability to survive those initial mistakes.

It's never too late *not* to invest in an unproven enterprise. If I'd waited to buy Bildner's until later, I wouldn't have bought it at all. I should also have sold sooner. It was clear from the two department-store flops and the New York flops that Bildner's had a problem, and it was time to fold the hand right then, before the cards got worse. I must have been asleep at the table.

Great sandwiches, though.

— 12 —

GETTING THE FACTS

Although there are various drawbacks to being a fund manager, there's the advantage that companies will talk to us—several times a week if we'd like. It's amazing how popular you feel when people want you to buy a million shares of their stock. I get to travel from coast to coast, visiting one opportunity after another. Chairmen, presidents, vice presidents, and analysts fill me in on capital spending, expansion plans, cost-cutting programs. Fellow portfolio managers pass along what they've heard. And if I can't visit the company, the company will come to me.

On the other hand, I can't imagine anything that's useful to know that the amateur investor can't find out. All the pertinent facts are just waiting to be picked up. These days, companies are required to tell nearly all in their prospectuses, their quarterlies, and their annual reports. Trade associations report on the general industry outlook in their publications. (Companies are also happy to send you the company newsletter. Sometimes you can find useful information in these chatty highlights.)

Rumors, I know, are still more exciting than public information, which is why a snippet of conversation overheard in a restaurant— "Goodyear is on the move"—carries more weight than Goodyear's own literature. It's the old oracle rule at work: the more mysterious the source, the more persuasive the advice. Perhaps if they stamped the annual and quarterly reports "classified," more recipients would browse through them.

What you can't get from the annual report you can get by asking your broker, by calling the company, by visiting the company, or by doing some grassroots research, also known as kicking the tires.

GETTING THE MOST OUT OF A BROKER

If you buy and sell stocks through a full-service brokerage firm instead of a discount house, you're probably paying an extra 30 cents a share in commissions. That's not a lot, but it ought to be worth something besides a Christmas card and the firm's latest ideas. Remember, it only takes a broker about four seconds to fill out a buy or sell order, and another fifteen seconds to walk it to the order desk.

Why is it that people who wouldn't dream of paying for gas at the full-service pump without getting the oil checked and the windows washed demand nothing from the full-service broker? As information gatherers, brokers can be the stockpicker's best friend. They can provide the S&P reports and the investment newsletters, the annuals, quarterlies and prospectuses and proxy statements, the *Value Line* survey and the research from the firm's analysts. Let them get the data on p/e ratios and growth rates, on insider buying and ownership by institutions. They'll be happy to do it, once they realize that you're serious.

If you use the broker as an advisor (a foolhardy practice generally, but sometimes worthwhile), then ask the broker to give you the two-minute speech on the recommended stocks. Prompt the broker with some of the questions I've listed, and a typical dialogue that now goes—

BROKER: "We're recommending Zayre. It's a special situation."
YOU: "Do you really think it's good?"
BROKER: "We really think it's good."
YOU: "Great. I'll buy it."
—would be transformed into something like this:
BROKER: "We're recommending La Quinta Motor Inns. It just made our buy list."
YOU: "How would you classify this stock? Cyclical, slow grower, faster grower, or what?"
BROKER: "Definitely a fast grower."
YOU: "How fast? What's the recent growth in earnings?"
BROKER: "Offhand, I don't know. I can check into it."
YOU: "I'd appreciate that. And while you're at it, could you get me the p/e ratio relative to historic levels."
BROKER: "Sure."
YOU: "What is it about La Quinta that makes it a good buy now? Where is the market? Are the existing La Quintas making a

profit? Where's the explanation coming from? What's the debt situation? How will they finance growth without selling lots of new shares and diluting the earnings? Are insiders buying?"

BROKER: "I think a lot of that will be covered in our analyst's report."

YOU: "Send me a copy. I'll read it and get back to you. Meanwhile, I'd also like a chart of the stock price versus the earnings for the last five years. I want to know about dividends, if any, and whether they've always been paid. While you are at it, find out what percentage of the shares is owned by institutions. Also, how long has your firm's analyst been covering this stock?"

BROKER: "Is that all?"

YOU: "I'll let you know after I read the report. Then maybe I'll call the company . . ."

BROKER: "Don't delay too long. It's a great time to buy."

YOU: "Right now in October? You know what Mark Twain says: 'October is one of the peculiarly dangerous months to speculate in stocks. The others are July, January, September, April, November, May, March, June, December, August, and February.'"

CALLING THE COMPANY

Professionals call companies all the time, yet amateurs never think of it. If you have specific questions, the investor relations office is a good place to get the answers. That's one more thing the broker can do: get you the phone number. In the unlikely event that investor relations gives you the cold shoulder, you can tell them that you own 20,000 shares and are trying to decide whether to double your position. Then casually mention that your shares are held in "street name." That ought to warm things up. Actually I'm not recommending fibbing, but the odds of your being caught are nil. The company has to take your word for the 20,000 shares, because shares held in street name are lumped together by the brokerage firms and stored in an undifferentiated mass.

Before you call the company, prepare your questions, and you needn't lead off with "Why is the stock going down?" That immediately brands you as a neophyte undeserving of serious response. In most cases a company has no idea why the stock in going down.

Earnings are a good topic, but for some reason it's not regarded as proper etiquette to ask the company "How much are you going to make?" The accepted form of the question is subtle and indirect: "What are the Wall Street estimates of your company's earnings for the upcoming year?"

As you already know, future earnings are hard to predict. The people at Procter and Gamble have a pretty good idea, since that company makes 82 different products in 100 different brands and sells them in 107 different countries, so everything tends to even out. But the people at Reynolds Metals couldn't possibly tell you, because it all depends on aluminum prices. If you ask Phelps Dodge what it will earn next year, Phelps Dodge will turn around and ask you what the price of copper is going to be.

What you really want from investor relations is the company's reaction to the script you've been developing. Does it make sense? If you wonder if the drug Tagamet will have a significant effect on SmithKline's fortunes, the company can tell you that—and they can also give you the latest figures for Tagamet sales.

Is there really a two-month backlog on orders for Goodyear tires, and have tire prices really gone up as you've concluded from local evidence? How many new Taco Bells are being built this year? How much market share has Budweiser added? Are the Bethlehem Steel plants running at full capacity? If your story line is well-defined, you'll know what points to check.

Better that you lead off with a question that shows you've done some research on your own, such as: "I see in the last annual report that you reduced debt by $500 million. What are the plans for further debt reduction?" This will get you a more serious answer than if you ask: "What are you guys doing about debt?"

Even if you have no script, you can learn something by asking "What are the positives this year?" and "What are the negatives?" Maybe they'll tell you that they closed down the plant in Georgia that lost $10 million last year. Maybe some new product has come along to speed up the growth rate. On the negative side, you'll learn there's been an increase in labor costs, that demand for a major product has slipped or that there's a new competitor in the business. At the end, you can sum up the conversation: three negatives, four positives. In most cases you'll hear something that confirms what you suspected—especially if you understand the business. But once in a while you'll learn something unexpected—that things are either better or worse than they appear. The unexpected can be very profitable if you're buying or selling stocks.

CAN YOU BELIEVE IT?

For the most part, companies are honest and forthright in their conversations with investors. They all realize that the truth is going to come out sooner rather than later in the next quarterly report, so there's nothing to be gained by covering things up the way they sometimes do in Washington. In all my years of listening to thousands of corporate representatives tell their side of the story — as terrible as business might have gotten — I can only remember a few instances when I was misled deliberately. So when you call investor relations, you can have full confidence that the facts you'll be hearing are correct. The adjectives, though, will vary widely. Different kinds of companies have different ways of describing the same scene.

Take textiles. Textile companies have been around since the nineteenth century. JP Stevens got started in 1899, West Point-Pepperell in 1866 — these are the corporate equivalents of the Daughters of the American Revolution. When you've been through six wars, ten booms, fifteen busts, and thirty recessions, you tend not to get excited. You're also strong enough to admit to adversity.

The investor relations people in textiles manage to sound unenthusiastic when business is terrific, and absolutely downcast when business is good. And if business is poor, you'd think that the executives were hanging themselves by their percale sheets. The wool-worsted business? "Mediocre," they say. Polyester-blend shirts? "Not so hot." "Denim?" "Ah, it's been better." But you realize from the actual numbers that the company is doing great. *When looking at the same sky, people in mature industries see clouds where people in immature industries see pie.*

Take apparel companies, which make the finished products from textiles. These companies have a tenuous existence and are forever disappearing from financial life. For the number of times they've declared Chapter 11, you'd think it was an amendment to the Constitution. Yet you'll never hear the word "mediocre" from an apparel person, even when sales are disastrous. And when things are basically okay, you'll hear that the situation is "fantastic," "unbelievable," "fabulous," and "out of this world."

The technology people and the software people are equally Pollyannaish. You can almost assume that the more tenuous the enterprise, the more optimistic the rhetoric is going to be. Why shouldn't they be upbeat? With so many competitors, you have to sound upbeat. If you appear to lack confidence, some other sweet-talker will win all the contracts.

Don't waste time deciphering the corporate vocabulary; it's simpler to ignore all the adjectives.

VISITING HEADQUARTERS

One of the greatest joys of being a shareholder is visiting the headquarters of the companies you own. When I visit a headquarters, what I'm really after is a feel for the place. I got positive feelings when I saw Taco Bell's headquarters behind a bowling alley. When I saw those executives operating out of that grim little bunker, I was thrilled. Obviously, they weren't wasting money on landscaping the office.

(The first thing I ask, by the way, is: "When is the last time a fund manager or an analyst visited here?" If the answer is "two years ago, I think," then I'm ecstatic. That was the case at Meridian Bank—22 years of up earnings, a great record of raising dividends, and they'd forgotten what an analyst looked like.)

Seek out the headquarters with the hope that if it's not stuck behind a bowling alley, then it will be located in some seedy neighborhood where financial analysts wouldn't want to be seen. The summer intern I sent to visit Pep Boys—Manny, Moe, & Jack reported that the Philadelphia cab drivers didn't want to take him there. I was as impressed with that as almost anything else he found out.

At Crown, Cork, and Seal, I noticed that the president's office had a scenic view of the can lines, the floors were faded linoleum, and the office furniture was shabbier than stuff I sat on in the Army. Now there's a company with the right priorities—and you know what's happened to the stock? It's gone up 280-fold in the last thirty years. Rich earnings and a cheap headquarters is a great combination.

So what do you make of Uniroyal, perched on a Connecticut hillside like all the fancy prep schools? Sure enough, the company went downhill. Other bad signs include fine antique furniture, trompe l'oeil drapes, and polished-walnut walls. When they bring the rubber trees indoors, it's time to fear for the earnings.

KICKING THE TIRES

From the time Carolyn discovered L'eggs in the supermarket, and I discovered Taco Bell via the burrito, I've continued to believe that wandering through stores and tasting things is a fundamental investment strategy. It's certainly no substitute for asking key questions, as the

Bildner's case proves. But when you're developing a story, it's reassuring to be able to check out the practical end of it.

One trip to the nearest local outlet of Toys "R" Us convinced me that this company knew how to sell toys. Before I bought La Quinta, I spent those three nights in their motor inns. Before I bought Pic 'N' Save, I stopped in at one of their stores in California and was impressed with the bargains. When I visited a Pep Boys outlet at a new location in California, I only wanted to look the place over, but a salesman there was so enthusiastic that I almost had four new tires shipped home with me on the airplane. I figured with personnel like that, Pep Boys could sell anything. Sure enough, they have.

The more homogeneous the country gets, the more likely that what's popular in one shopping center will also be popular in all the other shopping centers. Think of all the brand names and products whose success or failure you've correctly predicted.

Why then didn't I buy OshKosh B'Gosh when our children have grown up in those wonderful OshKosh bib overalls? Why did I talk myself out of investing in Reebok because one of my wife's friends complained that the shoes hurt her feet? Imagine missing a fivebagger because the neighbor gave a pair of sneakers a bad review. Nothing is ever easy in this business.

READING THE REPORTS

It's no surprise why so many annual reports end up in the garbage can. The text on the glossy pages is the understandable part, and that's generally useless, and the numbers in the back are incomprehensible, and that's supposed to be important. But there's a way to get something out of an annual report in a few minutes, which is all the time I spend with one.

Consider the 1987 annual report of Ford. It has a nice cover shot of the back end of a Lincoln Continental, and inside there's a flattering tribute to Henry Ford II and a photograph of him standing in front of a portrait of his grandfather, Henry I. There's a friendly message to stockholders, a treatise on a corporate culture, and mention of the fact that Ford sponsored an exhibition of the works of Beatrix Potter, creator of Peter Rabbit.

I flip past all that and turn directly to the Consolidated Balance Sheet printed on the cheaper paper on page 27 of the report. (That's a rule with annuals and perhaps with publications in general—the cheaper the paper the more valuable the information.) The balance sheet lists the assets and then the liabilities. That's critical to me.

In the top column marked Current Assets, I notice that the company has $5.672 billion in cash and cash items, plus $4.424 billion in marketable securities. Adding these two items together, I get the company's current overall cash position, which I round off to $10.1 billion. Comparing the 1987 cash to the 1986 cash in the right-hand column, I see that Ford is socking away cash, a sure sign of prosperity.

The other half of the balance sheet has an entry that says "long-term debt." Here I see that the 1987 long-term debt is $1.75 billion, considerably reduced from last year. Debt reduction is another sign of prosperity. When cash increases relative to debt, it's an improving balance sheet. When it's the other way around, it's a deteriorating balance sheet.

Subtracting the long-term debt from the cash, I arrive at $8.35 billion, Ford's "net cash" position. The cash and cash assets alone exceed the debt by $8.35 billion. When cash exceeds debt it's very favorable. No matter what happens, Ford isn't about to go out of business. I ignore Ford's short-term debt of $1.8 billion. I simply assume that the company's other assets (inventories and so forth) are valuable enough to cover the short-term debt, and I leave it at that.

Next, I look at the 10-Year Financial Summary, where I discover that there are 511 million shares outstanding. That number has been reduced in each of the past two years. This means that Ford has been buying back its own shares, another positive step.

Dividing the $8.35 billion in cash and cash assets by the 511 million shares outstanding, I conclude that there's $16.30 in net cash to go along with every share of Ford. Why this is important will be apparent in the next chapter.

Value Line is easier to read than a balance sheet, so if you've never looked at any of this, start there. It tells you about cash and debt, summarizes the long-term record so you can see what happened during the last recession, whether earnings are on the upswing, whether dividends have always been paid, etc. Finally, it rates companies for financial strength on a simple scale of 1 to 5, giving you a rough idea of a company's ability to withstand adversity. (There's also a rating system for the "timeliness" of stocks, but I don't pay attention to that.)

I'm putting aside the annual report for now. Let's instead consider the important numbers one by one on their own.

— 13 —

SOME FAMOUS NUMBERS

Here, in no particular order of importance, are the various numbers worth noticing:

PERCENT OF SALES

When I'm interested in a company because of a particular product—such as L'eggs, Pampers, or Bufferin—the first thing I want to know is what percent of sales does it represent to the company in question? L'eggs sent Hanes stock soaring because Hanes was a relatively small company. Pampers was more profitable than L'eggs, but it didn't mean as much to the huge Procter and Gamble.

THE PRICE/EARNINGS RATIO

We've gone on about this already, but here's a useful refinement: The p/e ratio of any company that's fairly priced will equal its growth rate of earnings. If the p/e of Coca-Cola is 15, you'd expect the company to be growing at about 15 percent a year, etc. But if the p/e ratio is less than the growth rate, you may have found yourself a bargain. In general, a p/e ratio that's half the growth rate is very positive, and one that's twice the growth rate is very negative. Ask your broker for a company's growth rate. You can also figure it out by taking the annual earnings from *Value Line* or an S&P report and calculating the percent increase in earnings from one year to the next.

A slightly more complicated formula enables us to compare growth rates to earnings, while also taking the dividends into account. Find the long-term growth rate (say, Company X's is 12 percent), add the dividend yield (Company X pays 3 percent), and divide by the p/e ratio (Company X's is 10). 12 plus 3 divided by 10 is 1.5.

Less than a 1 is poor, and 1.5 is okay, but what you're really looking for is a 2 or better.

THE CASH POSITION

We just went over Ford's $8.35 billion in cash net of long-term debt. When a company is sitting on billions in cash, it's definitely something you want to know about. Here's why:

Ford's stock had moved from $4 a share in 1982 to $38 a share in early 1988 (adjusted for splits). Along the way I'd bought my 5 million shares. At $38 a share I'd already made a huge profit in Ford, and the Wall Street chorus had been sounding off for almost two years about Ford's being overvalued. Numerous advisors said that this cyclical auto company had had its last hurrah and the next move was down. I almost cashed in the stock on several occasions.

But by glancing at the annual report I'd noticed that Ford had accumulated the $16.30 a share in cash beyond debt—as mentioned in the previous chapter. For every share of Ford I owned, there was this $16.30 bonus sitting there on paper like some delightful hidden rebate.

The $16.30 bonus changed everything. It meant that I was buying the auto company not for $38 a share, the stock price at the time, but for 21.70 a share ($38 minus the $16.30 in cash). Analysts were expecting Ford to earn $7 a share from its auto operations, which at the $38 price gave it a p/e of 5.4, but at the $21.70 price it has a p/e of 3.1, a tantalizing number, cycles or no cycles. The cash factor helped convince me to hold on to Ford, and it rose another 40 percent.

I also knew (and you could have found out on page 5 of the annual report—still in the readable glossy section) that Ford's financial services group—Ford Credit, First Nationwide, U.S. Leasing, and others—earned $1.66 per share on their own in 1987. For Ford Credit, which alone contributed $1.33 per share, it was "its 13th consecutive year of earnings growth." Assigning a hypothetical p/e ratio of 10 to the earnings of Ford's financial businesses (finance companies commonly have p/e ratios of 10) I estimated the value of these subsidiaries to be 10 times the $1.66, or $16.60 a share.

So with Ford selling for $38, you were getting the $16.30 in net cash and another $16.60 in the value of the finance companies, so the automobile business was costing you a grand total of $5.10 per share. And this same automobile business was expected to earn $7 a share. Was Ford a risky pick? At $5.10 per share it was an absolute steal, in spite of the fact that the stock was up almost tenfold already since 1982.

Cash doesn't always make a difference. More often than not, there isn't enough of it to worry about. Schlumberger has a lot of cash, but not an impressive amount per share. Bristol-Myers has $1.6 billion in cash and only $200 million in long-term debt, which produces an impressive ratio, but with 280 million shares outstanding, $1.4 billion net cash (after subtracting debt) works out to $5 per share. The $5 doesn't count for much with the stock selling for over $40. If the stock dropped to $15, it would be a big deal.

THE DEBT FACTOR

How much does the company owe, and how much does it own? Debt versus equity. It's just the kind of thing a loan officer would want to know about you in deciding if you are a good credit risk.

A normal corporate balance sheet has two sides. On the left side are the assets (inventories, receivables, plant and equipment, etc.). The right side shows how the assets are financed. One quick way to determine the financial strength of a company is to compare the equity to the debt on the right side of the balance sheet.

This debt-to-equity ratio is easy to determine. Looking at Ford's balance sheet from the 1987 annual report, you see that the total stockholder's equity is $18.492 billion. A few lines above that, you see that the long-term debt is $1.7 billion. (There's also short-term debt, but in these thumbnail evaluations I ignore that, as I've said. If there's enough cash to cover short-term debt, then you don't have to worry about short-term debt.)

A normal corporate balance sheet has 75 percent equity and 25 percent debt. Ford's equity-to-debt ratio is a whopping $18 billion to $1.7 billion, or 91 percent equity and less than 10 percent debt. That's a very strong balance sheet. Among turnarounds and troubled companies, I pay special attention to debt. More than anything else, it's debt that determines which companies will survive and which will go bankrupt in a crisis. Young companies with heavy debts are always at risk.

It's the kind of debt, as much as the actual amount, that separates the winners from the losers in a crisis. Bank debt (the worse kind) doesn't have to come from a bank. It can also take the form of commercial paper, which is loaned from one company to another for short periods of time. The important thing is that it's due on demand. That means that the lender can ask for his money back at the first sign of trouble. If the borrower can't pay back the money, it's off to Chapter 11. Creditors strip the company, and there's nothing left for the shareholders.

Funded debt (the best kind, from the shareholder's point of view) can never be called in no matter how bleak the situation, as long as the borrower continues to pay the interest. The principal may not be due for 15, 20, or 30 years. Funded debt usually takes the form of regular corporate bonds with long maturities. Corporate bonds may be upgraded or downgraded by the rating agencies depending on the financial health of the company, but whatever happens, the bondholders cannot demand immediate repayment of principal the way a bank can. Sometimes even the interest payments can be deferred. Funded debt gives companies time to wiggle out of trouble. (In one of the footnotes of a typical annual report, the company gives a breakdown of its long-term debt, the interest that is being paid, and the dates that the debt is due.)

I pay particular attention to the debt structure, as well as to the amount of the debt, when I'm evaluating a turnaround like Chrysler. In the famous bailout arrangement, the key element was that the government guaranteed a $1.4-billion loan in return for some stock options. Later the government sold these stock options for a big profit, but at the time you couldn't have predicted that. What you could have realized, though, was that Chrysler's loan arrangement gave the company room to maneuver.

I also saw that Chrysler had $1 billion in cash, and that it had recently sold off its tank division to General Dynamics for another $336 million. True, Chrysler was losing a small amount of money at the time, but the cash and the structure of the government loan told you that the bankers weren't going to shut the place down for at least a year or two.

So if you believed the auto industry was coming back, as I did, and you knew that Chrysler had made major improvements and had become a low-cost producer in the industry, then you could have had some confidence in Chrysler's survival. It wasn't as risky as it looked from the newspapers.

DIVIDENDS

Stocks that pay dividends are often favored over stocks that don't pay dividends by investors who desire the extra income. There's nothing wrong with that. A check in the mail always comes in handy, even for John D. Rockefeller. But the real issue, as I see it, is how the dividend, or the lack of a dividend, affects the value of a company and the price of its stock over time.

The basic conflict between corporate directors and shareholders over dividends is similar to the conflict between children and their parents over trust funds. The children prefer a quick distribution, and the parents prefer to control the money for the children's greater benefit.

One strong argument in favor of companies that pay dividends is that companies that don't pay dividends have a sorry history of blowing the money on a string of stupid diworseifications. I've seen this happen enough times to begin to believe in the bladder theory of corporate finance, as propounded by Hugh Liedtke of Pennzoil: The more cash that builds up in the treasury, the greater the pressure to piss it away.

Another argument in favor of dividend-paying stocks is that the presence of the dividend can keep the stock price from falling as far as it would if there were no dividend. In the wipeout of 1987, the high-dividend payers fared better than the nondividend payers and suffered less than half the decline of the general market. This is one reason I like to keep some stalwarts and even slow growers in my portfolio. When a stock sells for $20, a $2 per share dividend results in a 10 percent yield, but drop the stock price to $10, and suddenly you've got a 20 percent yield. If investors are sure that the high yield will hold up, they'll buy the stock just for that. This will put a floor under the stock price. Blue chips with long records of paying and raising dividends are the stocks people flock to in any sort of crisis.

Then again, the smaller companies that don't pay dividends are likely to grow much faster because of it. They're plowing the money into expansion. The reason that companies issue stock in the first place is so they can finance their expansion without having to burden themselves with debt from the bank. I'll take an aggressive grower over a stodgy old dividend-payer any day.

Electric utilities and telephone utilities are the major dividend-payers. In periods of slow growth they don't need to build plants or expand their equipment, and the cash piles up. In periods of fast growth the dividends are lures to attract the enormous amounts of capital that plant construction requires. Consolidated Edison has discovered it can buy extra power from Canada, so why should it waste money on expensive new generators and all the expense of getting them approved and constructed? Because it has no major expenses these days, Con Ed is amassing hundreds of millions in cash, buying back stock in above-average fashion, and continually raising the dividend.

DOES IT PAY?

If you plan to buy a stock for its dividend, find out if the company is going to be able to pay it during recessions and bad times. If a slow grower omits a dividend, you're stuck with a sluggish enterprise that has little going for it.

A company with a 20- or 30-year record of regularly raising the dividend is your best bet. How about Fleet-Norstar, formerly Industrial National Bank, which has paid uninterrupted dividends since 1791? Kellogg and Ralston Purina haven't reduced dividends—much less eliminated them—through the last three wars and eight recessions. Cyclicals are not always reliable dividend-payers: Ford omitted its dividend back in 1982 and the stock price declined to under $4 per share (adjusted for splits)—a 25-year low. As long as Ford doesn't blow all its cash, nobody has to worry about their omitting dividends today.

BOOK VALUE

Book value gets a lot of attention these days—perhaps because you see it reported everywhere. Popular computer programs can tell you instantly how many stocks are selling for less than the stated book value. People invest in these on the theory that if the book value is $20 a share and the stock sells for $10, they're getting something for half price.

The flaw is that the stated book value often understates or overstates reality by a large margin. Penn Central had a book value of more than $60 a share when it went bankrupt!

At the end of 1976, Alan Wood Steel had a stated book value of $32 million, or $40 per share. In spite of that, the company filed for Chapter 11 bankruptcy six months later. The problem was that its new steel-making facility, worth perhaps $30 million on paper, was ineptly planned and practically useless. To pay off some of the debt, the steel-plate mill was sold to Lukens Corp. for about $5 million, and the rest of the plant was presumably sold for scrap.

A textile company may have a warehouse full of fabric that nobody wants, carried on the books at $4 a yard. In reality, they couldn't give the stuff away for 10 cents. There's another unwritten rule here: The closer you get to a finished product, the less predictable the resale value. You know how much cotton is worth, but who can be sure about an orange cotton shirt?

Overvalued assets on the left side of the balance sheet are especially treacherous when there's a lot of debt on the right. Let's say that a company shows $400 million in assets and $300 million in debts, resulting in a positive book value of $100 million. You know the debt part is a real number. But if the $400 million in assets bring only $200 million in a bankruptcy sale, then the actual book value is a negative $100 million. The company is less than worthless. When you buy a stock for its book value, you have to have a detailed understanding of what the assets really are. At Penn Central, tunnels through mountains and useless rail cars counted as assets.

MORE HIDDEN ASSETS

Just as often as book value overstates true worth, it can understate true worth. This is where you get the greatest asset plays.

Companies that own natural resources—such as land, timber, oil, or precious metals—carry those assets on their book at a fraction of the true value. Sometimes you'll find an oil company or a refiner that's kept inventory in the ground for forty years, and at the original cost of acquisition from the days of the Teddy Roosevelt administration. The oil alone is worth more than the current price of all the shares of stock. They could scrap the refinery, fire all the employees, and make a fortune for the shareholders in forty-five seconds by peddling the oil. It's no trouble to sell oil. It's not like selling dresses—nobody cares if it's this year's oil or last year's oil, or whether it's fuchsia or magenta.

Brand names such as Coca-Cola or Robitussin have tremendous value that isn't reflected on the books. So do patented drugs, cable franchises, TV and radio stations—all are carried at original cost, then depreciated until they, too, disappear from the asset side of the balance sheet.

A couple of years ago Channel 5 in Boston sold for $450 million— that was the fair market price. However, when that station was originally awarded its license, it probably paid $25,000 to file the proper papers, maybe $1 million for the tower, and another $1 million or $2 million for the studio. The whole shebang was worth $2.5 million on paper to begin with, and the $2.5 million was depreciated. At the time it was sold, this enterprise probably had a book value that was 300 times too low.

Now that the station has changed owners, the new book value will be based on the $450-million sale price, so the anomaly will disappear. If you pay $450 million for a TV station worth $2.5 million on the books, the accounts call the extra $447.5 million "goodwill." Goodwill is carried on the new books as an asset, and eventually it, too, will be written off. This in turn will create another potential asset play. When Monsanto bought Searle, it picked up NutraSweet. NutraSweet comes off patent in four years and will continue to be valuable even then, but Monsanto is writing the whole thing off against earnings. In four years NutraSweet will show up as a zero on Monsanto's balance sheet.

When Monsanto writes something off against earnings, the real earnings are understated. If the company actually makes $10 per share in profits, but has to devote $2 of that to "pay" to write things off such as NutraSweet, when it stops writing off NutraSweet the earnings will rise by $2 a share.

In addition, Monsanto is expensing all its research and development in the same fashion, and someday when the expenses stop and the new products come onto the market, the earnings will explode. If you understand this, you have a big edge.

There can be hidden assets in the subsidiary businesses owned wholly or in part by a large parent company. We've already gone over Ford's. There are also hidden assets when one company owns shares of a separate company—as Raymond Industries did with Teleco Oilfield Services. People close to either situation realized that Raymond was selling for $12 a share, and each share represented $18 worth of Teleco. By buying Raymond you were getting Teleco for minus $6. Investors who did their homework bought Raymond and got Teleco for minus $6, and investors who didn't bought Teleco for $18. This sort of thing happens all the time.

Sometimes the best way to invest in a company is to find its foreign owner. I realize this is easier said than done, but if you have any access to European companies, you can stumble onto some unbelievable situations. European companies in general are not well-analyzed, and in many cases they're not analyzed at all. I discovered this on a fact-finding trip to Sweden, where Volvo and several other giants of Swedish industry were covered by one person who didn't even have a computer.

When Esselte Business Systems came public in the U.S., I bought the stock and kept up with the fundamentals, which were positive. George Noble, who manages Fidelity's Overseas Fund, suggested that I visit the parent company in Sweden. It was there that I discovered you could buy the parent company for less than the value of its U.S. subsidiary, plus pick up numerous other attractive businesses—not to mention real estate—as part of the deal. While the U.S. stock went up only slightly, the price of the parent company's stock doubled in two years.

If you followed the Food Lion Supermarkets story, you might have discovered that Del Haize of Belgium owned 25 percent of the stock, and the Food Lion holdings alone were worth a lot more than the price of a share of Del Haize. Again, when you bought Del Haize, you were getting valuable European operations for nothing. I purchased the European stock for Magellan and it rose from $30 to $120, while Food Lion gained a relatively unexciting 50 percent.

Finally, tax breaks turn out to be a wonderful hidden asset in turnaround companies. Because of its tax-loss carryforward, when Penn Central came out of bankruptcy it didn't have to pay any taxes on millions in profits from the new operations it was about to acquire. Bethlehem Steel currently has $1 billion in operating-loss carryforwards, an extremely valuable asset if the company continues to recover. It means that the next $1 billion that Bethlehem earns in the U.S. will be tax-free.

CASH FLOW

Cash flow is the amount of money a company takes in as a result of doing business. All companies take in cash, but some have to spend more than others to get it. This is a critical difference that makes a Philip Morris such a wonderfully reliable investment, and a steel company such a shaky one.

Let's say Pig Iron, Inc. sells out its entire inventory of ingots and makes $100 million dollars. That's good. Then again, Pig Iron, Inc. has to spend $80 million to keep the furnaces up-to-date. That's bad. The first year Pig Iron doesn't spend $80 million on furnace improvements, it loses business to more efficient competitors. In cases where you have to spend cash to make cash, you aren't going to get very far.

Philip Morris doesn't have this problem, and neither does Pep Boys or McDonald's. That's why I prefer to invest in companies that don't depend on capital spending. The cash that comes in doesn't have to struggle against the cash that goes out. It's simply easier for Philip Morris to earn money than it is for Pig Iron, Inc.

A lot of people use the cash flow numbers to evaluate stocks. For instance, a $20 stock with $2 per share in annual cash flow has a 10-to-1 ratio, which is standard. A ten percent return on cash corresponds nicely with the ten percent that one expects as a minimum reward for owning stocks long term. A $20 stock with a $4-per-share cash flow gives you a 20 percent return on cash, which is terrific. And if you find a $20 stock with a sustainable $10-per-share cash flow, mortgage your house and buy all the shares you can find.

If cash flow is ever mentioned as a reason to buy a stock, make sure that it's "free cash flow" left over after the usual capital spending. Pig Iron, Inc. will have a lot less free cash flow than Philip Morris.

Occasionally, I find a company that has modest earnings and yet is a great investment because of the free cash flow. Usually it's a company with a huge depreciation allowance for old equipment that doesn't need to be replaced in the immediate future. The company continues to enjoy the tax breaks (the depreciation on equipment is tax deductible) as it spends as little as possible to modernize and renovate.

Coastal Corporation is a good example. The company was fairly priced at $20 a share. Its earnings of $2.50 a share gave it a p/e of 8, which was standard for a gas producer and a diversified pipeline company at the time. But beneath this humdrum opportunity, something wonderful was going on. Coastal had borrowed $2.45 billion to acquire a major pipeline company, American Natural Resources. The beauty of the pipeline was that they didn't have to spend much to maintain it. A pipeline, after all, mostly just sits there. Maybe they'd dig down to patch a few holes, but otherwise they'd leave it alone in the ground. Meanwhile they'd depreciate it.

Coastal had $10-$11 per share in total cash flow in a depressed gas environment, and $7 was left over after capital spending. That $7 a share was free cash flow. On the books this company could earn nothing for the next ten years, and shareholders would get the benefit of the $7-a-share annual influx, resulting in a $70 return on their $20 investment. This stock had great upside potential on cash flow alone.

Dedicated asset buyers look for this situation: a mundane company going nowhere, a lot of free cash flow, and owners who aren't trying to build up the business. It might be a leasing company with a bunch of railroad containers that have a 12-year life. All the company wants to do is contract the old container business and squeeze as much cash out of it as possible. In the upcoming decade, management will shrink the plant, phase out the containers, and pile up cash. From a $10 million operation, they might be able to generate $40 million this way. (It wouldn't work in the computer business, because the prices drop so fast that old inventory doesn't hold its value long enough for anybody to squeeze anything out of it.)

INVENTORIES

There's a detailed note on inventories in the section called "management's discussion of earnings" in the annual report. I always check to see if inventories are piling up. When a manufacturer or a retailer's inventories grow faster than sales, it's a red flag.

A company may brag that sales are up 10 percent, but if inventories are up 30 percent, you have to say to yourself: "Wait a second. Maybe they should have marked that stuff down and gotten rid of it. The new stuff they make will compete with the old stuff, and inventories will pile up even higher until they're forced to cut prices, and that means less profit."

In an auto company an inventory buildup isn't so disturbing because a new car is always worth something, and the manufacturer doesn't have to drop the price very far to sell it. A $35,000 Jaguar isn't going to be marked down to $3,500. But a $300 purple miniskirt that's out of style might not sell for $3. It's hard for amateurs and neophytes to have any feel for inventories and what they mean, but investors with an edge in a particular business will know how to figure this out. Companies must now publish balance sheets in their quarterly reports, so that the inventory numbers can be regularly monitored.

PENSION PLANS

As more companies reward their employees with stock options and pension benefits, investors are well-advised to consider the consequences. Companies don't have to have pension plans, but if they do, the plans must comply with federal regulations. These plans are absolute obligations to pay—like bonds.

Even if a company goes bankrupt, it must continue to support the pension plan. Before I invest in a turnaround, I always check to make sure the company doesn't have a pension obligation that it can't meet. I specifically look to see if pension fund assets exceed the vested benefit liabilities. USX shows pension plan assets of $8.5 billion and vested benefits of $7.3 billion, so that's not worrisome. Bethlehem Steel, on the other hand, reports pension assets of $2.3 billion and vested benefits of $3.8 billion, or a $1.5 billion deficit. This is a big negative if Bethlehem Steel gets into deeper financial trouble. It would mean that investors would put a lower value on the stock until the pension problem was cleared up.

This used to be a guessing game, but now the pension situation is laid out in the annual report.

GROWTH RATE

That "growth" is synonymous with "expansion" is one of the most popular misconceptions on Wall Street, leading people to overlook the really great growth companies such as Philip Morris. You wouldn't see it from the industry—cigarette consumption in the U.S. is growing at about a minus two percent a year. True, foreign smokers have taken up where the U.S. smokers left off. One out of four Germans now smokes Marlboros made by Philip Morris, and the company sends 747s full of Marlboros to Japan every week. But even the foreign sales can't account for Philip Morris's phenomenal success. The key to it is that Philip Morris can increase earnings by lowering costs and especially by raising prices. That's the only growth rate that really counts: earnings.

Philip Morris has lowered costs by installing more efficient cigarette-rolling machinery. Meanwhile, the industry raises prices every year. If the company's costs increase 4 percent, it can raise prices 6 percent, adding 2 percent to its profit margin. This may not seem like much, but if your profit margin is 10 percent (about what Philip Morris's is) a 2-percentage-point rise in the profit margin means a 20 percent gain in earnings. If you find a business that can get away with raising prices year after year without losing customers (an addictive product such as cigarettes fills the bill), you've got a terrific investment.

One more thing about growth rate: all else being equal, a 20-percent grower selling at 20 times earnings (a p/e of 20) is a much better buy than a 10 percent grower selling at 10 times earnings (a p/e of 10). This may sound like an esoteric point, but look at the widening gap in earnings between a 20-percent grower and a 10-percent grower that both start off with the same $1 a share in earnings:

	Company A (20% earnings growth)	Company B (10% earnings growth)
Base Year	$1.00 a share	$1.00 a share
Year 1	$1.20	$1.10
Year 2	$1.44	$1.21
Year 3	$1.73	$1.33
Year 4	$2.07	$1.46
Year 5	$2.49	$1.61
Year 7	$3.58	$1.95
Year 10	$6.19	$2.59

At the beginning of our exercise, Company A is selling for $20 a share (20 times earnings of $1), and by the end, it sells for $123.80 (20 times earnings of $6.19). Company B starts out selling for $10 a share (10 times earnings of $1) and ends up selling for $26 (10 times earnings of $2.60).

Even if the p/e ratio of Company A is reduced from 20 to 15 because investors don't believe it can keep up its fast growth, the stock would still be selling for $92.85 at the end of the exercise. Either way, you'd rather own Company A than Company B.

This in a nutshell is the key to the bigbaggers, and why stocks of 20-percent growers produce huge gains in the market, especially over a number of years. It's no accident that the Wal-Marts and The Limiteds can go up so much in a decade. It's all based on the arithmetic of compounded earnings.

THE BOTTOM LINE

Everywhere you turn these days you hear some reference to the "bottom line." "What's the bottom line?" is a common refrain in sports, business deals, and even courtship. So what is the real bottom line? It's the final number at the end of an income statement: profit after taxes.

Corporate profitability tends to be misunderstood. In a survey I once saw, college students and other young adults were asked to guess the average profit margin on the corporate dollar. Most guessed 20-40 percent. In the last few decades the actual answer has been closer to 5 percent.

Profit before taxes, also known as the pretax profit margin, is a tool I use in analyzing companies. That's what's left of a company's annual sales dollar after all the costs, including depreciation and interest expenses, have been deducted. In 1987, Ford Motor had sales of $71.6 billion and earned $7.38 billion pretax, for a pretax profit margin of 10.3 percent. Retailers have lower profit margins than manufacturers—an outstanding supermarket and drugstore chain such as Albertson's still earns only 3.6 percent pretax. On the other hand, companies that make highly profitable drugs, such as Merck, routinely make 25 percent pretax.

There's not much to be gained in comparing pretax profit margins across industries, since the generic numbers vary so widely. Where it comes in handy is in comparing companies within the same industry. The company with the highest profit margin is by definition the lower-cost operator, and the low-cost operator has a better chance of surviving if business conditions deteriorate.

Let's say that Company A earns 12 percent pretax and Company B earns only 2 percent. Suppose there's a business slowdown and both companies are forced to slash prices 10 percent to sell their merchandise. Sales drop by the same 10 percent. Company A is now earning 2 percent pretax and is still profitable, while Company B has fallen into the red with an 8 percent loss. It's headed for the endangered species list.

The technicalities of pretax profit margin get very tricky, because as business improves, the companies with the lowest profit margins are the biggest beneficiaries. Consider what happens to $100 in sales to our two companies in these two hypothetical situations:

Company A

Status Quo	Business Improves
$100 in sales	$110.00 in sales (prices up 10%)
$88 in costs	$92.40 in costs (up 5%)
$12 pretax profit	$17.60 pretax profit

Company B

$100 in sales	$110.00 in sales (up 10%)
$98 in costs	$102.90 in costs (up 5%)
$2 pretax profit	$7.10 pretax profit

In the recovery, Company A's profits have increased almost 50 percent, while Company B's profits have more than tripled. This explains why depressed enterprises on the edge of disaster can become very big winners on the rebound. It happens again and again in the auto, chemical, paper, airline, steel, electronics, and nonferrous metals industries. The same potential exists in such currently depressed industries as nursing homes, natural gas producers, and many retailers.

What you want, then, is a relatively high profit-margin in a long-term stock that you plan to hold through good times and bad, and a relatively low profit-margin in a successful turnaround.

— 14 —

RECHECKING THE
STORY

Every few months it's worthwhile to recheck the company story. This may involve reading the latest *Value Line*, or the quarterly report, and inquiring about whether the earnings are holding up as expected. It may involve checking the stores to see that the merchandise is still attractive, and that there's an aura of prosperity. Have any new cards turned over? With fast growers, especially, you have to ask yourself what will keep them growing.

There are three phases to a growth company's life: the start-up phase, during which it works out the kinks in the basic business; the rapid expansion phase, during which it moves into new markets; and the mature phase, also known as the saturation phase, when there's no easy way to continue to expand. Each of these phases may last several years. The first phase is the riskiest for the investor, because the success of the enterprise isn't yet established. The second phase is the safest, and also where the most money is made, because the company is growing simply by duplicating its successful formula. The third phase is the most problematic, because the company runs into its limitations. Other ways must be found to increase earnings.

As you periodically recheck the stock, you'll want to determine whether the company seems to be moving from one phase into another. Automatic Data Processing, the company that processes paychecks, is still in phase two. They haven't even begun to saturate the market.

When Sensormatic was expanding its shoplifting detections system into store after store (the second phase), the stock went from $2 to $40, but eventually it reached the limit—no new stores to approach. The company was unable to think of new ways to maintain its momentum, and the stock fell from $42½ in 1983 to a low of $5⅝ in 1984. As you saw this time approaching, you needed to find out what the new plan was, and whether it had a realistic chance to succeed.

When The Limited had positioned itself in 670 of the 700 most popular malls in the country, then The Limited finally was. At that point the company could only grow by luring more customers to its existing stores. As soon as there's a Wendy's next door to every McDonald's, the only way Wendy's can grow is by winning over the McDonald's customers. Where can Anheuser-Busch grow if it already has captured 40 percent of the beer-drinking market? Even Spuds McKenzie the party dog can't convince 100 percent of the nation to drink Bud, and at least a minority of brave souls is going to refuse to order Bud Light. Sooner or later Anheuser-Busch is going to slow down, and the stock price and the p/e multiple will both shrink accordingly.

Or perhaps Anheuser-Busch will think of new ways to grow, the way McDonald's has. First, they installed the drive-in windows, which now account for over one-third of the business. Then there was breakfast, which expanded sales by over 20 percent at very low cost. Then there were salads, and chicken, both of which added to earnings and also ended the company's dependence on the beef market. McDonald's is in foreign countries, and it will be decades before there's a McDonald's on every street corner in England or in Germany. In spite of the lower p/e ratio, it's not all over for McDonald's.

Texas Air is an example of a story that got worse, then better, then worse again in a matter of five years. I took a small position in the stock in mid-1983, only to watch the company's principal asset, Continental Air, deteriorate and file for Chapter 11. Texas Air stock fell from $12 to $4¾, and Continental stock, in which Texas Air held the majority position, fell to $3. I kept a close eye on the situation as a potential turnaround. Texas Air cut costs; Continental won back its customers and returned from the accountant's graveyard. On the strength of their improvement, I built up a large holding in both companies. By 1986 both stocks had tripled.

In February 1986, Texas Air announced it had purchased a large share of Eastern Airlines — also viewed as a favorable development. In a single year Texas Air stock tripled once again to a high of $51½, making it a tenbagger since it solved its problems in 1983.

At this point my concern over the company's outlook unfortunately turned to complacency, and because the potential earning power of

Eastern and Texas Air was so terrific, I forgot to pay attention to the near-term realities. When Texas Air bought out the remaining Continental stock, I was forced to cash in over half of my position in Continental stock and some bonds convertible to Continental stock. It was a stroke of fortune, and I made a tidy profit. But instead of selling my remaining Texas Air shares and making a happy exit, I bought more shares at $48¼ in February 1987. Given Texas Air's mediocre balance sheet in a precarious cyclical industry, why was I buying and not selling? I fell for the latest, improved Texas Air story even when the fundamentals were falling apart.

The new, improved story was as follows: Texas Air was benefiting from a leaner operation and sharply reduced labor costs. In addition to its interest in Eastern, it had just bought Frontier Air and People Express and planned to revive them in the same way it had revived Continental. The concept was great: acquire failed airlines, cut costs, and big profits would naturally follow.

What happened? Like Don Quixote, I was so enamored of the promise that I forgot to notice I was riding a nag. I focused on the predictions of $15 per share earnings for Texas Air in 1988, ignoring the warning signs that appeared every day in the newspaper: lost bags, botched schedules, delayed arrivals, angry customers, and disgruntled employees at Eastern.

Earnings at Texas Air started to deteriorate early in 1987. The idea was to cut $400 million out of Eastern's operating costs, but I should have reminded myself that there was a substantial likelihood that it would never occur. The existing labor contract didn't expire for several months, and meanwhile both sides were at loggerheads. Finally I came to my senses and started selling the stock at $17-$18 a share. It fell to $9 by the end of 1987. I still own some shares, and I'm going to stay tuned.

Not only did I make a mistake by not cutting back on Texas Air in the summer of 1987, when the severe problems with Eastern became obvious, but I should also have used this fundamental information to pick another winner: Delta Airlines. Delta was Eastern's main competitor and the greatest beneficiary of Eastern's operating problems and plans to reduce the size of Eastern on a permanent basis. I had a modest position in Delta, but I should have made it one of my top ten holdings. The stock went from $48 to $55 from mid-1987 to mid-1988. Thousands of people who flew Eastern and Delta could have seen the same things I saw and used their amateurs' edge.

THE FINAL CHECKLIST

All of this research takes a couple of hours, at most, for each stock. The more you know the better, but it isn't imperative that you call the company. Nor do you have to study the annual report with the concentration of a Dead Sea scroll scholar. Some of the "famous numbers" apply only to specific categories of stocks.

What follows is a summary of the things you'd like to learn about stocks in each of the six categories:

Stocks in General

- The p/e ratio. Is it high or low for this particular company and for similar companies in the same industry.
- The percentage of institutional ownership. The lower the better.
- Whether insiders are buying and whether the company itself is buying back its own shares. Both are positive signs.
- The record of earnings growth to date and whether the earnings are sporadic or consistent. (The only category where earnings may not be important is an asset play.)
- The company's balance sheet (debt-to-equity ratio) and how it's rated for financial strength.
- The cash position. With $16 in net cash, I know Ford is unlikely to drop below $16 a share. That's the floor on the stock.

Slow Growers

- Since you buy these for the dividends (Why else would you own them?) you want to check to see if dividends have always been paid, and whether they are routinely raised.

- When possible, find out what percentage of the earnings are being paid out as dividends. If it's a low percentage, then the company has a cushion in hard times. It can earn less money and still retain the dividend. If it's a high percentage, then the dividend is riskier.

Stalwarts

- The key issue is price, and the p/e ratio will tell you whether you are paying too much for these big companies.
- Check for possible diworseification that may reduce future earnings.
- Check the company's long-term growth rate, and whether it has kept up the same momentum in recent years.
- If you plan to hold the stock forever, see how the company has fared during previous recessions and market drops.

Cyclicals

- Keep a close watch on inventories, and the supply-demand relationship. Watch for new entrants into the market, which is usually a dangerous development.
- Anticipate a shrinking p/e multiple over time as business recovers and investors look ahead to the end of the cycle, when peak earnings are achieved.
- If you know your cyclical, you have an advantage in figuring out the cycles. (For instance, everyone knows eventually there are going to be three or four up years in the auto industry to follow three or four down years. Older cars have to be replaced. Sooner or later people are back to the dealerships. Lately we've had five years of good car sales, so we are in the middle, and perhaps somewhere close to the end, of a prosperous cycle. But it's much easier to predict an upturn in a cyclical industry than it is to predict a downturn.)

Fast Growers

- Investigate whether the product that's supposed to enrich the company is a major part of the company's business.
- What is the recent growth rate in earnings? (My favorites are the

ones in the 20 to 25 percent range. I'm wary of companies that seem to be growing faster than 25 percent. Those 50 percenters usually are found in hot industries, and you know what that means.)

- That the company has duplicated its successes in more than one city or town, to prove that expansion will work.
- That the company still has room to grow. When I first visited Pic 'N' Save, they were established in southern California and were just beginning to talk about expanding into northern California. There were forty-nine other states to go. Sears, on the other hand, is everywhere.
- Whether the stock is selling at a p/e ratio at or near the growth rate.
- Whether the expansion is speeding up (three new motels last year and five new motels this year) or slowing down (five last year and three this year). For stocks of companies such as Sensormatic Electronics, whose sales are primarily "one-shot" deals—as opposed to razor blades, which customers have to keep on buying—a slowdown in growth can be devastating.
- That few institutions own the stock and only a handful of analysts have ever heard of it. With fast growers on the rise this is a big plus.

Turnarounds

- Most important, can the company survive a raid by its creditors? How much cash does the company have? How much debt? What is the debt structure, and how long can it operate in the red while working out its problems without going bankrupt?
- If it's bankrupt already, then what's left for the shareholders?
- How is the company supposed to be turning around? Has it rid itself of unprofitable divisions? This can make a big difference in earnings. In 1980 Lockheed earned $8.04 per share from its defense business, but it lost $6.54 per share in its commercial aviation division because of its L-1011 TriStar passenger jet. The L-1011 was a great airplane, but it suffered from competition with McDonnell Douglas's DC10 in a relatively small market. And in the long-distance market, it was getting killed by the 747. These losses were persistent, and in December 1981, the company announced that it would phase out the

L-1011. This resulted in a large write-off in 1981 ($26 per share), but it was a one-time loss. In 1982, when Lockheed earned $10.78 per share from defense, there were no more losses to deal with. Earnings had gone from $1.50 to $10.78 per share in two years! You could have bought Lockheed for $15 at the time of the L-1011 announcement. Within four years it hit $60, for a fourbagger.

- Is business coming back? (This is what's happening at Eastman Kodak, which has benefited from the new boom in film sales.)
- Are costs being cut? If so, what will the effect be? (Chrysler cut costs drastically by closing plants. It also began to farm out the making of a lot of the parts it used to make itself, saving hundreds of millions in the process. It went from being one of the highest-cost producers of automobiles to one of the lowest.)

Asset Plays

- What's the value of the assets? Are there any hidden assets?
- How much debt is there to detract from these assets? (Creditors are first in line.)
- Is the company taking on new debt, making the assets less valuable?
- Is there a raider in the wings to help shareholders reap the benefits of the assets?

— 16 —

DESIGNING A
PORTFOLIO

I've heard people say they'd be satisfied with a 25 or 30 percent annual return from the stock market! Satisfied? At that rate they'd soon own half the country along with the Japanese and the Bass brothers. Even the tycoons of the twenties couldn't guarantee themselves 30 percent forever, and Wall Street was rigged in their favor.

If 25 to 30 percent isn't a realistic return, then what is? Certainly you ought to do better in stocks than you'd do in bonds, so to make 4, 5, or 6 percent on your stocks over a long period of time is terrible. If you review your long-term record and find that your stocks have scarcely outperformed your savings account, then you know your technique is flawed. (When you are figuring out how you're doing in stocks, don't forget to include all the costs of subscriptions to newsletters, financial magazines, commissions, investment seminars, and long-distance calls to brokers.)

Nine to ten percent a year is the generic long-term return for stocks, the historic market average. You can get ten percent, over time, by investing in a no-load mutual fund that buys all 500 stocks in the S&P 500 Index, thus duplicating the average automatically. This return can be achieved without any homework, so it's a useful benchmark against which you can measure your own performance, and also the performance of the managed equity funds such as Magellan.

If professionals who are employed to pick stocks can't outdo the index funds that buy everything at large, then we aren't earning our keep. But give us a chance. First consider the kind of fund you've invested in. The best managers in the world won't do well with a gold-stock fund when gold prices are dropping. Nor is it fair to judge a fund for a single year's performance. But if after three to five years or so you find that you'd be just as well off if you'd invested in the S&P 500, then either buy the S&P 500 or look for a managed equity fund with a better record.

Given all these convenient alternatives, to be able to say that picking your own stocks is worth the effort, you ought to be getting 12-15 percent return, compounded over time. That's after all the costs and commissions have been subtracted, and all dividends and other bonuses have been added.

Here's another place where the person who holds on to stocks is far ahead of the person who frequently trades in and out. It costs the small investor a lot of money to trade in and out. Trading is cheaper than it used to be, thanks to the discount commissions and also to a modification in the so-called odd-lot surcharge—the extra fee tacked on to transactions of less than 100 shares. (Now if you put in your odd-lot order before the market opens, your shares are pooled with those of other odd-lotters and you all avoid the surcharge.) Even so, it still costs between one and two percent to buy or sell a stock.

Turn over the portfolio once a year, and you've lost as much as four percent to commissions. This means you're four percent in the hole before you start. So to get 12-15 percent after expenses, you'll have to make 16-19 percent. And the more you trade, the harder it's going to be to outperform the index funds or any other funds. (The newer "families" of funds may charge a 3-8½ percent fee to join, but from then on you can switch from stocks to bonds to money-market funds and back again without ever paying another commission.)

All these pitfalls notwithstanding, the individual investor who manages to make, say, 15 percent over ten years when the market average is 10 percent has done himself a considerable favor. If he started with $10,000, a 15 percent return will bring a $40,455 result, and a 10 percent return only $25,937.

HOW MANY STOCKS IS TOO MANY?

How do you design a portfolio to get that 12-15 percent return? How many stocks should you own? In my view it's best to own as many stocks as there are situations in which: (a) you've got an edge; and (b) you've uncovered an exciting prospect that passes all the tests of research. Maybe that's a single stock, or maybe it's a dozen stocks. Maybe you've decided to specialize in turnarounds or asset plays and you buy several of those; or perhaps you happen to know something special about a single turnaround or a single asset play. There's no use diversifying into unknown companies just for the sake of diversity. A foolish diversity is the hobgoblin of small investors.

That said, it isn't safe to own just one stock, because in spite of your best efforts, the one you choose might be the victim of unforeseen circumstances. In small portfolios I'd be comfortable owning between three and ten stocks. There are several possible benefits:

(1) If you are looking for tenbaggers, the more stocks you own the more likely that one of them will become a tenbagger. Among several fast growers that exhibit promising characteristics, the one that actually goes the furthest may be a surprise. You increase your odds of benefiting from one by owning several stocks.

(2) The more stocks you own, the more flexibility you have to rotate funds between them. This is an important part of my strategy.

Some people ascribe my success to my having specialized in growth stocks, although I never put more than 30-40 percent of my fund's assets into growth stocks. The rest I spread out among the other categories described in this book. Normally I keep about 10-20 percent or so in the stalwarts, another 10-20 percent or so in the cyclicals, and the rest in the turnarounds. Although I own 1,400 stocks in all, half of my fund's assets are invested in 100 stocks, and two-thirds in 200 stocks. One percent of the money is spread out among 500 secondary opportunities I'm monitoring periodically, with the possibility of tuning in later. I'm constantly looking for values in all areas, and if I find more opportunities in turnarounds than in fast-growth companies, then I'll end up owning a higher percentage of turnarounds. If something happens to one of the secondaries to bolster my confidence, then I'll promote it to a primary selection.

SPREADING IT AROUND

Spreading your money among several categories of stocks is another way to minimize downside risk. Assuming that you've done all the proper research and have bought companies that are fairly priced, then you've already minimized the risk to an important degree, but beyond that, it's worth considering the following:

Slow growers are low-risk, low-gain because they're not expected to do much and the stocks are usually priced accordingly. Stalwarts are low-risk, moderate gain. If you own Coca-Cola and everything goes right next year, you could make 50 percent; and if everything goes wrong, you could lose 20 percent. Asset plays are low-risk and high-gain if you're sure of the value of the assets. If you are wrong on an asset play, you probably won't lose much, and if you are right, you could make a fivebagger.

Cyclicals may be low-risk and high-gain or high-risk and low-gain, depending on how adept you are at anticipating cycles. If you are right, you can get your tenbaggers here, and if you are wrong, you can lose 80-90 percent.

Meanwhile, additional tenbaggers are likely to come from fast growers or from turnarounds—both high-risk, high-gain categories. The higher the potential upside, the greater the potential downside, and if a fast grower falters or the troubled old turnaround has a relapse, the downside can be losing all your money. At the time I bought Chrysler, if everything went right, I thought I could make 400 percent, and if everything went wrong, I could lose 100 percent. As it turned out, I was pleasantly surprised and made fifteenfold on it.

There's no pat way to quantify these risks and rewards, but in designing your portfolio you might throw in a couple of stalwarts just to moderate the thrills and chills of owning four fast growers and four turnarounds. Again, the key is knowledgeable buying.

Finally, your portfolio may change as you get older. Younger investors with a lifetime of wage-earning ahead of them can afford to take more chances on tenbaggers than older investors who must live off the income from their investments. Younger investors have more years in which they can experiment and make mistakes before they find the great stocks that make investing careers. The circumstances vary so widely from person to person that any further analysis of this point will have to come from you.

WATERING THE WEEDS

In the next chapter I'll explain when to sell a stock, but here I want to discuss selling as it relates to portfolio management. I'm constantly rechecking stocks and rechecking stories, adding and subtracting to my investments as things change. But I don't go into cash—except to have enough of it around to cover anticipated redemptions. Going into cash would be getting out of the market. My idea is to stay in the Market forever, and to rotate stocks depending on the fundamental situations. If you decide that a certain amount of your money will always be invested in the stock market, you'll save yourself a lot of mistimed moves and general agony.

Some people automatically sell the "winners"—stocks that go up— and hold on to their "losers"—stocks that go down—which is about as sensible as pulling out the flowers and watering the weeds. Others automatically sell their losers and hold on to their winners, which doesn't work out much better. Both strategies fail because they're tied to the current movement of the stock price as an indicator of the company's fundamental value. As we've seen, the current stock price tells us absolutely nothing about the future prospects of a company, and it occasionally moves in the direction of the fundamentals.

A better strategy, it seems to me, is to rotate in and out of stocks depending on what has happened to the price as it relates to the story. For instance, if a stalwart has gone up 40 percent—which is all I expected to get out of it—and nothing wonderful has happened with the company to make me think there are pleasant surprises ahead, I sell the stock and replace it with another attractive stalwart that hasn't gone up.

Successfully rotating in and out of several stalwarts for modest gains, yields the same result as a single big winner: six 25-percent moves compounded is nearly a fourbagger.

The fast growers I keep as long as the earnings are growing and the expansion is continuing, and no impediments have come up. Every few months I check the story just as if I were hearing it for the first time. If between two fast growers I find that the price of one has increased 50 percent and the story begins to sound dubious, I'll rotate out of that one and add to my position in the second fast grower whose price has declined or stayed the same, and where the story is sounding better.

Ditto for cyclicals and turnarounds. Get out of situations in which the fundamentals are worse and the price has increased, and into situations in which the fundamentals are better and the price is down. A price drop in a good stock is only a tragedy if you sell at that price and never buy more.

If you can't convince yourself, "When I'm down 25 percent, I'm a buyer," and banish forever the fatal thought, "When I'm down 25 percent, I'm a seller," then you'll never make a decent profit in stocks.

For reasons that should by now be obvious, I've always detested "stop orders," those automatic bailouts at a predetermined price, usually 10 percent below the price at which a stock is purchased. True, when you put in a "stop order" you've limited your losses to 10 percent, but with the volatility in today's market, a stock almost always hits the stop. You would have lost Taco Bell ten times over with stop orders!

Show me a portfolio with 10 percent stops, and I'll show you a portfolio that's destined to lose exactly that amount. When you put in a stop, you're admitting that you're going to sell the stock for less than it's worth today.

It's equally uncanny how stocks seem to shoot straight up after the stop is hit, and the would-be cautious investor has been sold out. There's simply no way to rely on stops as protection on the downside, or on artificial objectives as goals on the upside. If I'd believed in "Sell when it's a double," I would never have benefited from a single big winner, and I wouldn't have been given the opportunity to write a book. Stick around to see what happens—as long as the original story continues to make sense, or gets better—and you'll be amazed at the results in several years.

— 17 —

THE BEST TIME TO BUY AND SELL

fter all that's been said, I don't want to sound like a market timer and tell you that there's a certain best time to buy stocks. The best time to buy stocks will always be the day you've convinced yourself you've found solid merchandise at a good price—the same as at the department store. However, there are two particular periods when great bargains are likely to be found.

The first is during the peculiar annual ritual of end-of-the-year tax selling. It's no accident that the most severe drops have occurred between October and December. It's the holiday period, after all, and brokers need spending money like the rest of us, so there's extra incentive for them to call and ask what you might want to sell to get the tax loss. For some reason investors are delighted to get the tax loss, as if it's a gift of some kind—I can't think of another situation in which failure makes people so happy.

Institutional investors also like to jettison the losers at the end of the year so their portfolios are cleaned up for the upcoming evaluations. All this compound selling drives stock prices down, and especially in the lower-priced issues, because once the $6-per-share threshold is reached, stocks do not count as collateral for people who buy on credit in margin accounts. Margin players sell their cheap stocks, and so do the institutions, who cannot own them without violating one stricture or another. This selling begets more selling and drives perfectly good issues to crazy levels.

If you have a list of companies that you'd like to own if only the stock price were reduced, the end of the year is a likely time to find the deals you've been waiting for.

The second is during the collapses, drops, burps, hiccups, and freefalls that occur in the stock market every few years. If you can summon the courage and presence of mind to buy during these scary episodes when your stomach says "sell," you'll find opportunities that you wouldn't have thought you'd ever see again.

The 1987 Break

The sell-off of October 1987 was a chance to buy many of the companies I've mentioned throughout this book. The 1,000-point drop between summer and fall took everything with it, but in the real world all the companies listed below were healthy, profitable, and never missed a beat. Many of them recovered in quick fashion, and I took advantage whenever I could. I missed Dreyfus the first time around, but not this time (fool me once, shame on you; fool me twice, shame on me). Dreyfus was beaten down to $16 and the company had $15 in cash after debt, so what was the risk? In addition to the cash, Dreyfus actually profited from the crisis, as many investors switched out of stocks and into money-market funds that Dreyfus manages.

The 1987 Break	1987 High	1987 Low	October 1988
Wal-Mart	$41	$20	$31⅛
Dreyfus	45	16	25⅝
Albertson's	34	21	36⅛
Home Depot	28	12½	28⅜
Student Loan Marketing	88	62	83⅞
Toys "R" Us	42	22	38¼
Coca-Cola	53	28	43⅛
Pier 1	14	5	11¼
Inco	24	14	28⅝
Envirodyne	29¼	10⅞	26

WHEN TO SELL

Even the most thoughtful and steadfast investor is susceptible to the influence of skeptics who yell "sell" before it's time to sell. I ought to know. I've been talked out of a few tenbaggers myself.

Soon after I started Magellan in May 1977, I was attracted to Warner Communications, a promising turnaround from a conglomerate that had diworseified. Confident of the fundamentals, I invested three percent of my fund in Warner at $26.

A few days later I got a call from a technical analyst who follows Warner. I don't pay much attention to that science of wiggles, but just to be polite I asked him what he thought. Without hesitation he announced that the stock was "extremely extended." I've never forgotten those words. One of the biggest troubles with stock market advice is that good or bad it sticks in your brain. You can't get it out of there, and someday, sometime, you may find yourself reacting to it.

Six months or so had passed, and Warner had risen from $26 to $32. Already I was beginning to worry. "If Warner was extremely extended at $26," I argued to myself, "then it must be hyperextended at $32." I checked the fundamentals, and nothing there had changed enough to diminish my enthusiasm, so I held on. Then the stock hit $38. For no conscious reason I began a major sell program. I must have decided that whatever was extended at $26 and hyperextended at $32 has surely been stretched into three prefixes at $38.

Of course after I sold, the stock continued its ascent to $50, $60, $70, and over $180. Even after it suffered the consequences of the Atari fiasco, and the price declined by 60 percent in 1983-84, it was still twice my exit price of $38. I hope I learned my lesson.

Another time I made a premature exit from Toys "R" Us, that nifty fast grower that I've already bragged about. By 1978, when Toys "R" Us was liberated from Interstate Department Stores (a woeful dog) in that company's bankruptcy action (creditors were paid off in new Toys "R" Us shares), this was already a proven and profitable enterprise, expanding into one mall after another. It had passed the tests of success in one location, and then of duplication. I did my homework, visited the stores, and took a big position at an adjusted price of $1 per share. By 1985, when Toys "R" Us hit $25, it was a 25-bagger for some. Unfortunately, those some didn't include me, because I sold too soon. I sold too soon because somewhere along the line I'd read that a smart investor named Milton Petrie, one of the deans of retailing, had bought 20 percent of Toys "R" Us and that his buying was making the stock go up. The logical conclusion, I thought, was then when Petrie stopped buying, the stock would go down. Petrie stopped buying at $5.

I got in at $1 and out at $5 for a fivebagger, so how can I complain? We've all been taught the same adages: "Take profits when you can," and

"A sure gain is always better than a possible loss." But when you've found the right stock and bought it, all the evidence tells you it's going higher, and everything is working in your direction, then it's a shame if you sell. A fivefold gain turns $10,000 into $50,000, but the next five folds turn $10,000 into $250,000. Investing in a 25-bagger is not a regular occurrence even among fund managers, and for the individual it may happen only once or twice in a lifetime. When you've got one, you might as well enjoy the full benefit.

WHEN TO REALLY SELL

Over the years I've learned to think about when to sell the same way I think about when to buy. I pay no attention to external economic conditions, except in the few obvious instances. When oil prices go down, it obviously has an effect on oil-service companies, but not on ethical drug companies. In 1986-87, I sold my Jaguar, Honda, Subaru, and Volvo holdings because I was convinced that the falling dollar would hurt the earnings of foreign automakers that sell a high percentage of their cars in the U.S. But in nine cases out of ten, I sell if company 380 has a better story than company 212, and especially when the latter story begins to sound unlikely.

As it turns out, if you know why you bought a stock in the first place, you'll automatically have a better idea of when to say good-bye to it. Let's review some of the sell signs, category by category.

When to Sell a Slow Grower

The few slow growers I buy, I sell when there's been a 30-50 percent appreciation or when the fundamentals have deteriorated, even if the stock has declined in price. Here are some other signs:
- The company has lost market share for two consecutive years and is hiring another advertising agency.
- No new products are being developed, and spending on research and development is curtailed.
- Two recent acquisitions of unrelated businesses look like diworseifications, and the company announces it is looking for further acquisitions "at the leading edge of technology."
- The company has paid so much for its acquisitions that the balance sheet has deteriorated. There are no surplus funds to buy back stock, even if the price falls sharply.

- Even at a lower stock price the dividend yield will not be high enough to attract much interest from investors.

When to Sell a Stalwart

These are the stocks that I frequently replace with others in the category. If the price gets above the earnings line, or if the p/e strays too far beyond the normal range, think about selling the stock and waiting to buy it back later at a lower price—or buying something else, as I do.

Other sell signs:
- New products introduced in the last two years have had mixed results, and others still in the testing stage are a year away from the marketplace.
- No officers or directors have bought shares in the last year.
- A major division that contributes 25 percent of earnings is vulnerable to a current economic slump (in housing starts, oil drilling, etc.).
- The company's growth rate has been slowing down, and though it's been maintaining profits by cutting costs, future cost-cutting opportunities are limited.

When to Sell a Cyclical

The best time to sell is toward the end of the cycle, but who knows when that is? Sometimes the knowledgeable vanguard begins to sell cyclicals a year before there's a single sign of a company's decline. The stock price starts to fall for no earthly reason.

Other than at the end of the cycle, the best time to sell a cyclical is when something has actually started to go wrong. Costs have started to rise. Existing plants are operating at full capacity and the company begins to spend money to add to capacity. Inventories are building up and the company can't get rid of them, which means lower prices and lower profits down the road.

Falling commodity prices is another harbinger. Usually prices of oil, steel, etc., will turn down several months before the troubles show up in the earnings. Another useful sign is when the future price of a commodity is lower than the current, or spot, price.

Other signs:
- Two key union contracts expire in the next twelve months, and

labor leaders are asking for a full restoration of the wages and benefits they gave up in the last contract.
* The company has tried to cut costs but still can't compete with foreign producers.

When to Sell a Fast Grower

Here, the trick is not to lose the potential tenbagger. On the other hand, if the company falls apart and the earnings shrink, then so will the p/e multiple that investors have bid up on the stock. This is a very expensive double whammy for loyal shareholders.

The main thing to watch for is the end of the second phase of rapid growth, as explained earlier. If The Gap has stopped building new stores, and the old stores are beginning to look shabby, and your children complain that The Gap doesn't carry the current rage, then it's probably time to think about selling.

Unlike the cyclical where the p/e ratio gets smaller near the end, in a growth company the p/e usually gets bigger, and it may reach absurd and illogical dimensions. When Holiday Inn hit 40 times earnings, you could have sold confident that the party was over there. You would have been right. When you saw a Holiday Inn franchise every twenty miles along every major U.S. highway, and then you traveled to Gibraltar and saw a Holiday Inn at the base of the rock, it had to be time to worry. Where else could they expand? Mars?

Other signs:
* Same store sales are down 3 percent in the last quarter.
* New store results are disappointing.
* Two top executives and several key employees leave to join a rival firm.
* The company recently returned from a "dog and pony" show, selling an extremely positive story to institutional investors in twelve cities in two weeks.
* The stock is selling at a p/e of 30, while the most optimistic projections of earnings growth are 15-20 percent for the next two years.

When to Sell a Turnaround

The best time to sell a turnaround is after it's turned around. All the troubles are over and everybody knows it. The company has become the old self it was before it fell apart: growth company or cyclical or whatever. The shareholders aren't embarrassed to own it again. If the turnaround has been successful, you have to reclassify the stock.

Chrysler was a turnaround play at $2 a share, at $5, and even at $10 (adjusted for splits), but not at $48 in mid-1987. By then the debt was paid and the rot was cleaned out, and Chrysler was back to being a solid, cyclical auto company. The stock may go higher, but it's unlikely to see a tenfold rise. It has to be judged the same way that General Motors, Ford, or other prosperous companies are judged.

General Public Utilities was a turnaround at $4 a share, at $8, and at $12, but after the second nuclear unit was returned to service, and other utilities agreed to help pay the costs of the Three Mile Island cleanup, GPU became a quality electric utility again. The stock, now at $38, may hit $45, but it certainly isn't going to hit $400.

Other signs:

- Debt, which has declined for five straight quarters, just rose by $25 million in the latest quarterly report.
- Inventories are rising at twice the rate of sales growth.
- The p/e is inflated relative to earnings prospects.
- The company's strongest division sells 50 percent of its output to one leading customer, and that leading customer is suffering from a slowdown in its own sales.

When to Sell an Asset Play

Lately, the best idea is to wait for the raider. If there are really hidden assets there, Saul Steinberg, the Hafts, or the Reichmanns will figure it out. As long as the company isn't going on a debt binge, thus reducing the value of the assets, then you'll want to hold on.

Alexander and Baldwin owns 96,000 acres of Hawaiian real estate in addition to its exclusive shipping rights into the island plus other assets. A lot of people estimated that this $5 stock (adjusted for splits) was worth much more. They tried to be patient, but nothing happened for several years. Then a Mr. Harry Weinberg showed up and bought 5 percent, then 9 percent, and finally 15 percent of the shares. That inspired other investors to buy shares because Mr. Weinberg was buying, and the stock hit a high of $32 before it was marked down to $16 in the October 1987 sell-off. Seven months later it was back up to $30.

The same thing happened at Disney, a sleepy company that didn't know its own worth until Mr. Steinberg came along to goad management into "enhancing shareholder values." The company was making progress anyway. It's done a brilliant job moving away from animated movies to appeal to a broader and more adult audience. It's been successful with the Disney channel and the Japanese theme park, and the upcoming European theme park is promising. With its irreplaceable film library and its Florida and California real estate, Disney is an asset play, a turnaround, and a growth company all at once.

With so many raiders around, it's harder for the amateur to find a good asset stock, but it's a cinch to know when to sell. You don't sell until the Bass brothers show up, and if it's not the Bass brothers, then it's certain to be Steinberg, Icahn, the Belzbergs, the Pritzkers, Irwin Jacobs, Sir James Goldsmith, Donald Trump, Boone Pickens, or maybe even Merv Griffin. After that, there could be a takeover, a bidding war, or a leveraged buyout to double, triple or quadruple the stock price.

Other sell signs:

- Although the shares sell at a discount to real market value, management has announced it will issue 10 percent more shares to help finance a diversification program.
- The division that was expected to be sold for $20 million only brings $12 million in the actual sale.
- The reduction in the corporate tax rate considerably reduces the value of the company's tax-loss carryforward.
- Institutional ownership has risen from 25 percent five years ago to 60 percent today—with several Boston fund groups being major purchasers.

— 18 —

THE TWELVE SILLIEST
(AND MOST DANGEROUS)
THINGS PEOPLE SAY
ABOUT STOCK PRICES

I 'm constantly amazed at popular explanations of why stocks behave the way they do volunteered by amateurs and professionals alike. We've made great advances in eliminating ignorance and superstition in medicine and in weather reports, we laugh at our ancestors for blaming bad harvests on corn gods, and we wonder, "How could a smart man like Pythagoras think that evil spirits hide in rumpled bedsheets?" However, we're perfectly willing to believe that who wins the Super Bowl might have something to do with stock prices.

The myths and misconceptions are numerous, but I've noted the Silliest Things People Say About Stock Prices hoping that you dismiss them from your mind.

If It's Gone Down This Much Already, It Can't Go Much Lower

I'd bet the owners of Polaroid shares were repeating this very phrase just after the stock had fallen a third of the way along its long drop from a high of $143½. Polaroid had been a solid company with a blue-chip reputation, so when the earnings collapsed and the sales collapsed, a lot of people didn't pay attention to how overpriced Polaroid really was. Instead they continued to reassure themselves that, "If it's gone down this much already, it can't go much lower," and probably also threw in, "Good companies always come back," and, "There's no sense getting scared out of a good thing."

These phrases were no doubt heard again and again as Polaroid stock sank to $100, then to $90, and then $80. As the stock broke below $75, the "can't go much lower" faction must have grown into a small mob, and at $50 you could have heard the phrase repeated by every other Polaroid owner who held on.

Newer owners were buying Polaroid all the way down on the theory that it couldn't go much lower, and many of them must have regretted that decision, because in fact Polaroid did go much lower. This great stock fell from $143½ to $14⅞ in less than a year, and only then did "it can't go much lower" turn out to be true. So much for the it-can't-go-lower theory.

You Can Always Tell When a Stock's Hit Bottom

Bottom fishing is a popular investor pastime, but it's usually the fisherman who gets hooked. Trying to catch a stock at the bottom of its fall is like trying to catch a falling knife. It's normally a good idea to wait until the knife hits the ground and sticks before you try to grab it.

If you buy a turnaround, it ought to be for a more sensible reason than the stock's gone down so far it looks like up to you. Maybe you realize that business is picking up, and you check the balance sheet and you see that the company has $11 per share in cash and the stock is selling for $14. Even so, you aren't going to be able to pick the bottom on the price. What usually happens is that a stock sort of vibrates itself out before it starts up again. Generally this process takes two or three years, sometimes longer.

If It's Gone This High Already, How Can It Possibly Go Higher?

Right you are, unless of course you are talking about Philip Morris. That Philip Morris is one of the greatest stocks of all time is obvious. If you bought Philip Morris in the 1950s for the equivalent of 75 cents a share, then you might have been tempted to sell it for $2.50 a share in 1961, on the theory that this stock couldn't go much higher. Eleven years later, with the stock selling at seven times the 1961 price and 23 times the 1950s price, you might once again have concluded that Philip Morris couldn't go higher. But if you sold it then, you would have missed the next sevenbagger on top of the last 23-bagger.

Whoever managed to ride Philip Morris all the way would have seen their 75-cent shares blossom into $124.50 shares, and a $1,000 investment end up as a $166,000 result. And that doesn't even include the $23,000 in dividends you picked up along the way. The point is, there's no arbitrary limit to how high a stock can go, and if the story is still good, the earnings continue to improve, and the fundamentals haven't changed, "can't go much higher" is a terrible reason to snub a stock. Shame on all those experts who advise clients to sell automatically after they double their money. You'll never get a tenbagger doing that.

It's Only $3 a Share: What Can I Lose?

I put in twenty years in the business before it finally dawned on me that whether a stock costs $50 a share or $1 a share, if it goes to zero you still lose everything. If it goes to 50 cents a share, the results are slightly different. The investor who bought in at $50 a share loses 99 percent of his investment, and the investor who bought in at $3 a share loses 83 percent, but what's the consolation in that?

A lousy cheap stock is just as risky as a lousy expensive stock if it goes down. If you invest $1,000 in a $43 stock or a $3 stock and each falls to zero, you lose exactly the same amount. No matter where you buy in, the ultimate downside of picking the wrong stock is always 100 percent.

Eventually They Always Come Back

So will the Visigoths and the Picts. People said world-famous RCA would come back, and after 65 years it never did. Johns-Manville is another world-famous company that hasn't come back, and with all the asbestos lawsuits filed against it, the possibilities are too open-ended to measure. By printing hundreds of millions of new shares, the company has also diluted its earnings.

When you consider the thousands of bankrupt companies, plus the solvent companies that never regain their former prosperity, plus the companies that get bought out at prices far below the all-time highs, you can begin to see the weakness in the "they always come back" argument.

It's Always Darkest Before the Dawn

There's a very human tendency to believe that things that have gotten a little bad can't get any worse. In 1981 there were 4,520 active oil-drilling rigs in the U.S., and by 1984 the number had fallen to 2,200. At that point many people bought oil-service stocks, believing that the worst was over. But two years after that, there were only 686 active rigs, and today there are still fewer than 1,000. Sometimes it's always darkest before the dawn, but then again, other times it's always darkest before pitch black.

When It Rebounds to $10, I'll Sell

In my experience no downtrodden stock ever returns to the level at which you've decided you'd sell. In fact, the minute you say, "If it gets back to $10, I'll sell," you've probably doomed the stock to several years of teetering around just below $9.75 before it keels over to $4, on its way to falling flat on its face at $1. This whole painful process may take a decade, and all the while you're tolerating an investment you don't even like, and only because some inner voice tells you to get $10 for it.

Whenever I'm tempted to fall for this one, I remind myself that unless I'm confident enough in the company to buy more shares, I ought to sell immediately.

What, Me Worry? Conservative Stocks Don't Fluctuate Much

Two generations of conservative investors grew up on the idea that you couldn't go wrong with utility stocks. You could just put these worry-free issues in the safety-deposit box and cash the dividend checks. Then suddenly there were nuclear problems and rate-base problems, and stocks such as Consolidated Edison lost 80 percent of their value. Then, just as suddenly, Con Edison gained back more than it had lost.

With the economic and regulatory troubles caused by expensive nuclear plants, the so-called stable utility sector has become just as volatile and treacherous as the savings-and-loan industry or the computer stocks. There are now electric companies that were or can be tenbaggers up and tenbaggers down. You can win big or lose big, depending on how lucky or careful you are at choosing the right utility.

Companies are dynamic, and prospects change. There simply isn't a stock you can own that you can afford to ignore.

It's Taking Too Long for Anything to Ever Happen

Here's something else that's certain to occur: If you give up on a stock because you're tired of waiting for something wonderful to happen, then something wonderful will begin to happen the day after you get rid of it. I call this the postdivestiture flourish.

Merck tested everybody's patience. This stock went nowhere from 1972 to 1981, even though earnings grew steadily at an average of 14 percent a year. Then what happened? It shot up fourfold in the next five years. Who knows how many unhappy investors got out of Merck because they were tired of waiting, or because they yearned for more "action." If they had kept up to date on the story, they wouldn't have sold.

Most of the money I make is in the third or fourth year that I've owned something—only with Merck it took a little longer. If all's right with the company, and whatever attracted me in the first place hasn't changed, then I'm confident that sooner or later my patience will be rewarded.

Look at All the Money I've Lost: I Didn't Buy It!

We'd all be much richer today if we'd put all our money into Crown, Cork, and Seal at 50 cents a share (split-adjusted)! But now that you know this, open your wallet and check your latest bank statement. You'll notice that money's still there. In fact, you aren't a cent poorer than you were a second ago, when you found out about the great fortune you missed in Crown, Cork, and Seal.

This may sound like a ridiculous thing to mention, but I know that some of my fellow investors torture themselves every day by perusing the "ten biggest winners on the New York Stock Exchange" and imagining how much money they've lost by not having owned them.

Regarding somebody else's gains as your own personal losses is not a productive attitude for investing in the stock market. The more stocks you learn about, the more winners you realize that you've missed, and soon enough you're blaming yourself for losses in the billions and trillions. If you get out of stocks entirely and the market goes up 100 points in a day, you'll be waking up and muttering: "I've just suffered a $110 billion setback."

The worse part about this kind of thinking is that it leads people to try to play catch up by buying stocks they shouldn't buy, if only to protect themselves from losing more than they've already "lost." This usually results in real losses.

I Missed That One, I'll Catch the Next One

The trouble is, the "next" one rarely works, as we've already shown. If you missed Toys "R" Us, then bought Greenman Brothers, a mediocre company that went down, you've compounded your error. You've taken a mistake that cost you nothing (remember, you didn't lose anything by not buying Toys "R" Us) and turned it into a mistake that cost you plenty. In most cases it's better to buy the original good company at a high price than it is to jump on the "next one" at a bargain price.

The Stock's Gone Up, So I Must Be Right, or... The Stock's Gone Down So I Must Be Wrong

If I had to choose a great single fallacy of investing, it's believing that when a stock's price goes up, then you've made a good investment. Nothing could be further from the truth. Of course, if you sell quickly at the higher price, then you've made a fine profit, but most people don't sell in these favorable circumstances. Instead they convince themselves that the higher price proves that the investment is worthwhile, and they hold on to the stock until the lower price convinces them the investment is no good. If it's a choice, they hold on to the stock that's risen from $10 to $12, and they get rid of the one that's dropped from $10 to $8, while telling themselves that they have "kept the winner and dumped the loser."

So when people say, "Look, in two months it's up 20 percent, so I really picked a winner," or "Terrible, in two months it's down 20 percent, so I really picked a loser," they're confusing prices with prospects. Unless they are short-term traders who are looking for 20-percent gains, the short-term fanfare means absolutely nothing.

A stock's going up and down after you buy it only tells you that there was somebody who was willing to pay more—or less—for the identical merchandise.

— 19 —

OPTIONS, FUTURES, AND SHORTS

I 've never bought a future or an option in my entire investing career. It's hard enough to make money in regular stocks without getting distracted by these side bets, which are nearly impossible to win unless you're a professional trader. Reports out of Chicago and New York, the twin capitals of futures and options, suggest that between 80 and 95 percent of the amateur players lose. Those odds are worse than the worst odds at the casino or at the racetrack.

That's not to say that futures don't serve a useful purpose in the commodity business, where a farmer can lock in a price for wheat or corn at harvest and know he can sell for that amount when the crops are delivered. But stocks are not commodities, and there is no relationship between producer and consumer that makes such price insurance necessary to the functioning of a stock market.

There's no point describing how futures and options really work, because (1) it requires long and tedious exposition, after which you'd still be confused, (2) knowing more about them might get you interested in buying some, and (3) I don't understand futures and options myself.

Actually I do know a few things about options. I know that the large potential return is attractive to many small investors who are dissatisfied with getting rich slowly. Instead, they opt for getting poor quickly. That's because an option is a contract that's only good for a month or two, and unlike most stocks, it regularly expires worthless—after which the options player must buy another option. A string of these, and you're in deep kimchee.

And consider the situation when you're absolutely sure that something wonderful is about to happen to Sure Thing, Inc., and the good news will send the stock price higher. You've found the perfect company, the nearest thing to a royal flush you'll ever encounter.

You check your assets, and there's only $3,000 in your savings account to invest in Sure Thing. It will only get you 150 shares at $20 a share. Then you remember hearing about the remarkable leverage of options. You talk to your broker, who confirms that the April $20 call option in Sure Thing, now selling for $1, may be worth $15 if the stock goes to $35. A $3,000 investment here would give you a $45,000 payoff.

So you buy the options, and every day you open the paper, anxiously awaiting the moment the stock begins to rise. By mid-March there's still no movement, and the options you bought for $3,000 already have lost half their value. You're tempted to sell and get some of your money back, but you hold on because there's still a month to go before they expire worthless. A month later, that is exactly what happens.

Insult is added to injury when a few weeks later, Sure Thing makes its move. Not only have you lost all your money, you've done it while being right about the stock. You did your homework, and instead of being rewarded for it, you've been wiped out. It's an absolute waste of time, money, and talent when this happens.

The worst thing of all is that buying an option has nothing to do with owning a share of the company. When a company grows and prospers, all the shareholders benefit, but options are a zero-sum game. For every dollar that's won in the market there's a dollar that's lost, and a tiny minority does all the winning.

When you buy a share of stock, even a very risky stock, you are contributing something to the growth of the country. That's what stocks are for. In previous generations, when it was considered dangerous to speculate in stocks of small companies, at least the "speculators" were providing the capital to enable the IBMs and the McDonald'ses and the Wal-Marts to get started. In the multibillion-dollar futures and options market, not a bit of the money is put to any constructive use. It doesn't finance anything, except cars, planes, and houses purchased by the brokers and the handful of winners. What we're witnessing here is a giant transfer payment from the unwary to the wary.

Warren Buffett thinks that stock futures and options ought to be outlawed, and I agree with him.

SHORTING A STOCK

You've no doubt heard of this ancient and strange practice, which enables you to profit from a stock that's going down. (Some people get interested in this idea by looking at their portfolios and realizing that if they'd been short instead of long all these years, they'd be rich.)

Shorting is the same thing as borrowing something from the neighbors (in this case you don't know their names), then selling the item and pocketing the money. Sooner or later you go out and buy the identical item at a lower price and return it to the neighbors. You keep the difference. It works best with stocks that are inflated in price. For instance, if you figured out that Polaroid was overpriced at $140 a share, you could have shorted 1,000 shares for an immediate $140,000 credit to your account. Then you could have waited for the price to drop to $14, jumped in and bought back the same 1,000 shares for $14,000, and gone home $126,000 richer.

The person from whom you borrowed the shares originally will never have known the difference. These transactions are all done on paper and handled by stockbrokers. It's as easy to go short as it is to go long.

Before we get too excited about this, there are some serious drawbacks to going short. During all the time you borrow the shares, the rightful owner gets all the dividends and other benefits, so you're out some money there. Also, you can't actually spend the proceeds you get from shorting a stock until you've paid the shares back and closed out the transaction. In the Polaroid example, you couldn't simply take the $140,000 and run off to France for a long vacation. You are required to maintain a sufficient balance in your brokerage account to cover the value of the shorted stock. As the price of Polaroid dropped, you could have taken some of the money out, but what if the price of Polaroid had gone up? Then you would have had to add more money to cover your position.

The scary part about shorting stock is that even if you're convinced that the company's in lousy shape, other investors might not realize it and might even send the stock price higher. Though Polaroid had already reached a ridiculous plateau, what if it had doubled once more to an even more ridiculous $300 a share? If you were short then, you were very nervous. The prospect of spending $300,000 to replace a $140,000 item that you've borrowed can be disturbing. If you don't have the extra hundred thousand or so to put into your account to hold your position, you may be forced to liquidate at a huge loss.

None of us is immune to the panic that we feel when a normal stock drops in price, but that panic is restrained somewhat by our understanding that the normal stock cannot go lower than zero. If you've shorted something that's going up, you begin to realize that there's nothing to stop it from going to infinity, because there's no ceiling on a stock price. Infinity is where a shorted stock always appears to be heading.

Among all the folk tales of successful short sellers are the horror stories of shorters who watched helplessly as their favorite lousy stocks soared higher and higher, against all reason and logic, forcing them into the poorhouse. One such unfortunate was Robert Wilson, a smart man and a good investor, who a decade or so ago shorted Resorts International. He was right, eventually—most shorters are right, eventually— didn't John Maynard Keynes say, in the long run, that "We all are dead"? In the meantime, however, the stock advanced from 70 cents to $70, a modest 100-bagger, leaving Mr. Wilson with a modest $20 million or $30 million loss.

This tale is useful to remember if you're contemplating shorting something. Before you short a stock, you have to have more than a conviction that the company is falling apart. You have to have the patience, the courage, and the resources to hold on if the stock price doesn't go down—or worse, goes up. Stocks that are supposed to go down but don't remind me of the cartoon characters who walk off cliffs into thin air. As long as they don't recognize their predicament, they can just hang out there forever.

— 20 —

50,000 FRENCHMEN
CAN BE WRONG

Thinking back over my tenure as a stockpicker, I remember several major new events and their effects on the prices of stocks, beginning with President Kennedy's election in 1960. Even at the tender age of sixteen, I'd heard that a Democratic presidency was always bad for stocks, so I was surprised that the day after the election, November 9, 1960, the market rose slightly.

During the Cuban missile crisis and our naval blockade of the Russian ships—the one and only time America has faced the immediate prospect of nuclear war—I feared for myself, my family, and my country. Yet the stock market fell less than 3 percent that day. Seven months later, when President Kennedy berated U.S. Steel and forced the industry to roll back prices, I feared for nothing, yet the market had one of its largest declines in history—7 percent. I was mystified that the potential of nuclear holocaust was less terrifying to Wall Street than the president's meddling in business.

On November 22, 1963, I was about to take an exam at Boston College when the news that President Kennedy had been shot spread across the campus. Along with my classmates I went to St. Mary's Hall to pray. The next day I saw in the newspaper that the stock market had fallen less than 3 percent, though trading was halted once the news of the assassination became official. Three days later the market recovered its losses of November 22, and then some.

In April 1968, after President Johnson announced that he wouldn't seek a second term, that he would halt the bombing raids in Southeast Asia, and that he favored peace talks, the market rose 2½ percent.

Throughout the 1970s I was totally involved in stocks and dedicated to my job at Fidelity. During that period the great events, and the market reactions to them, were as follows: President Nixon imposes price controls (market up 3 percent); President Nixon resigns (market down 1 percent); President Ford's Whip Inflation Now buttons are introduced (market up 4.6 percent); IBM wins a big antitrust case (market up 3.3 percent); Yom Kippur War breaks out (market up slightly). The decade of the 1970s was the poorest for stocks of any of the five since the 1930s, and yet the major-percentage one-day changes were all up—on the days just mentioned.

The event of most lasting consequence was OPEC's oil embargo, October 1973 (another lucky October 19!), which helped take the market down 16 percent in three months and 39 percent in twelve months. It's interesting to note that the market did not respond to the significance of the embargo, actually rising 4 points that day and climbing an additional 14 points in the five following sessions before starting its dramatic decline. *This demonstrates that the market, like individual stocks, can move in the opposite direction of the fundamentals over the short term*, which, in the case of the embargo, involved rising gasoline prices, long gas lines, escalating inflation, and sharply higher interest rates.

The 1980s has had more days of exceptional gains and losses than were seen in all the other decades combined. In the big picture, most of them are meaningless. I'd rank the 508-point drop in October 1987 far below the meeting of economic ministers on September 22, 1985, for its importance to long-term investors. It was at this so-called G7 conference that the major industrial nations agreed to coordinate economic policy and to allow the value of the dollar to decline. After that decision was announced, the general market rose 38 percent over six months. It had a more dramatic impact on specific companies that benefited from the lower dollar, and whose stocks doubled and tripled in price in the following two years.

Trends and gradual changes stick in my mind:

The period of conglomeration in the mid-to-late 1960s resulted in many major companies diworseifying, falling apart, and then not recovering for another fifteen years. Many have never come back, and others, such as Gulf and Western, ITT, and Ogden, have reemerged as turnarounds.

There was a great love affair with high-quality blue chips in the 1970s. These were known as the "nifty fifty" or "the one decision" stocks that you could buy and hold forever. This brief serendipity of overrated and overpriced issues was followed by the devastating market decline of 1973-74 (the Dow hit 1050 in 1973 and had regressed all the way back to 578 in December 1974) with blue chips falling 50 to 90 percent.

The popular romance with small technology companies in mid-1982 to mid-1983 led to another collapse (60-98 percent) of the similarly beloved issues that could do no wrong. Small may be beautiful, but it's not necessarily profitable.

The rise of the Japanese market from 1966 to 1988 has taken the Nikkei Dow Jones up seventeenfold as our Dow Jones has only doubled. The total market value of all Japanese stocks actually passed that of U.S. stocks in April 1987, and the gap has widened since. The Japanese have their own way of thinking about stocks, and I don't understand it yet. Every time I go over there to study the situation, I conclude that all the stocks are grossly overpriced, but they keep going higher, anyway.

Nowadays the change in trading hours makes it harder to pay attention to fundamentals and keep your eye off the Quotron. For eighty years until 1952 the New York Stock Exchange opened at 10 a.m. and closed at 3 p.m., giving the newspapers time to print up the results for the afternoon editions so investors could check their stocks on the ride home. In 1952, Saturday trading was eliminated, but the daily closing hour was advanced to 3:30, and in 1985, the opening hour was moved to 9:30, and now the market closes at 4:00. Personally, I'd prefer a much shorter market. It would give us all more time to devote to analyzing companies, or even to visiting museums, both of which are more useful than watching stock prices go up and down.

Institutions have emerged from their minor role in the 1960s to dominate the stock market in the 1980s.

The legal status of major brokerage firms has changed from partnerships, where the individuals' personal wealth was on the line, to corporations, where the individual liability is limited. Theoretically this was supposed to strengthen the brokerage firms, since as corporations they could raise capital by selling stock to the public. I'm convinced it has been a net negative.

The rise of the over-the-counter exchange has brought thousands of secondary issues that were once traded by the obscure "pink sheet" method—where you never knew if you were getting a fair price—into a reliable and efficient computerized marketplace.

The nation is preoccupied with up-to-the-minute financial news, which twenty years ago was scarcely mentioned on television. The incredible success of *Wall Street Week, with Louis Rukeyser,* from its debut on November 20, 1970, has proven that a financial news show can actually be popular. It was Rukeyser's achievement that inspired the regular networks to expand their financial coverage, and that in turn led to the establishment of the Financial News Network, which has brought the ticker tape into millions of American homes. Amateur investors can now check their holdings all day.

Other changes seen in the eighties include:

The boom and then bust in tax shelters: farm land, oil wells, oil rigs, barges, low-rent housing syndicates, graveyards, movie productions, shopping centers, sports teams, computer leasing, and almost anything else that can be bought, financed, or rented.

The emergence of merger and acquisition groups, and other buyout groups, that are willing and able to finance $20-billion purchases. Between the domestic buyout groups (Kohlberg, Kravis, and Roberts; Kelso; Coniston Partners; Odyssey Partners; and Wesray), the European firms and buyout groups (Hanson Trust, Imperial Chemical, Electrolux, Unilever, Nestle, etc.), and the individual corporate raiders with sizable bankrolls (David Murdock, Donald Trump, Sam Hyman, Paul Bilzerian, the Bass brothers, the Reichmanns, the Hafts, Rupert Murdoch, Boone Pickens, Carl Icahn, Asher Edelman, et al.) any company, large or small, is up for grabs.

The popularity of the leveraged buyout, LBO, through which entire companies or divisions are "taken private"—purchased by outsiders or by current management with money that's borrowed from banks or raised via junk bonds.

The phenomenal popularity of these junk bonds, as first invented by Drexel Burnham Lambert and now copied everywhere.

The advent of futures and options trading, especially of the stock indexes, enabling "program traders" to buy or sell bushels of stocks in the regular stock markets and then reverse their positions in the so-called futures markets, throwing around billions of dollars for tiny incremental profits.

And throughout all this tumult, SS Kresge, a moribund five-and-dime company, develops the K mart formula and the stock goes up 40-fold in ten years; Masco develops its one-handle faucet and goes up 1,000-fold, becoming the greatest stock in forty years—and who would have guessed it from a faucet company? The successful fast growers turn into tenbaggers, the whisper stocks go bankrupt, and investors receive their "Baby Bell" shares from the breakup of ATT and double their money in four years.

If you ask me what's been the most important development in the stock market, the breakup of ATT ranks near the top (this affected 2.96 million shareholders), and the Wobble of October 1987 probably wouldn't rank in my top three.

Some things I've been hearing lately:

I've been hearing that the small investor has no chance in this dangerous environment and ought to get out. But small investors are capable of handling all sorts of markets, as long as they own good merchandise. If anyone should worry, it's some of the oxymorons. After all, the losses of October 1987 were only losses to people who took the losses. That wasn't the long-term investor. It was the margin player, the risk arbitrageur, the options player, and the portfolio manager whose computer signaled "sell" who took the losses. Like a cat who sees himself in the mirror, the sellers spooked themselves.

I'm hearing that the era of professional management has brought new sophistication, prudence, and intelligence to the stock market. There are 50,000 stockpickers who dominate the show, and like the 50,000 Frenchmen, they can't possibly be wrong.

From where I sit, I'd say that the 50,000 stockpickers are usually right, but only for the last 20 percent of a typical stock move. It's that last 20 percent that Wall Street studies for, clamors for, and then lines up for—all the while with a sharp eye on the exits. The idea is to make a quick gain and then stampede out the door.

Small investors don't have to fight this mob. They can calmly walk in the entrance when there's a crowd at the exit, and walk out the exit when there's a crowd at the entrance. Here's a short list of stocks that were the favorites of large institutions in mid-1987 but sold at sharply lower prices ten months later, in spite of higher earnings, exciting prospects, and good cash flows. The companies hadn't changed, but the institutions had lost interest: Automatic Data Processing, Coca-Cola, Dunkin' Donuts, General Electric, Genuine Parts, Philip Morris, Primerica, Rite Aid, Squibb, and Waste Management.

I've been hearing that the 200-million share day is a great improvement over the 100-million share day, and there's great advantage in a liquid market. But not if you're drowning in it—and we are. Last year 87 percent of all the shares listed on the NYSE changed owners at least once. In the early 1960s a six- to seven-million share trading day was normal, and the turnover rate in stocks was 12 percent a year. In the 1970s a forty- to sixty-million share day was normal, and in the 1980s it became 100-120 million shares. Now if we don't have 150-million-share days, people think something is wrong. I know I do my part to contribute to the cause, because I buy and sell every day. But my biggest winners continue to be stocks I've held for three and even four years.

The rapid turnover has been accelerated by the popular index funds, which buy and sell billions of shares without regard to the individual characteristics of the companies involved, and also by the "switch funds," which enable investors to pull out of stocks and into cash, or out of cash and into stocks, without delay or penalty.

Soon enough we'll have a 100 percent annual turnover in stocks. If it's Tuesday, then I must own General Motors! How do these poor companies keep up with where to send the annual reports? A new book called *What's Wrong with Wall Street* reports that we spend $25 billion to $30 billion annually to maintain the various exchanges and pay the commissions and fees for trading stocks, futures, and options. That means we spend as much money on passing old shares back and forth as we raise for new issues. After all, the raising of money for new ventures is the reason we have stocks in the first place. And when the trading is finished, come every December, the big portfolios of 50,000 stock-pickers look about the same as they did the previous January.

The large investors who've caught this trading habit are fast becoming the short-term churning suckers that neighborhood brokers used to love. Some have called it the "rent-a-stock market." Now it's the amateurs who are prudent and the professionals who are flighty. The public is the comforting and stabilizing factor.

The flightiness of trust departments, the Wall Street establishment, and the Boston financial district may be an opportunity for you. You can wait for out-of-favor stocks to hit the crazy low prices, then buy them.

I've been hearing that the October 19, 1987 drop, which happened on a Monday, was only one of several historic declines that have taken place on Mondays, and researchers have spent entire careers studying the Monday effect. They were even talking about the Monday effect back when I went to Wharton.

After looking this up, I've discovered that there seems to be something to it: from 1953 through 1984 the stock market gained 919.6 points overall, but lost 1,565 points on Mondays. If there is a Monday effect, I think I know why. Investors can't talk to companies for two days over the weekend. All of the usual sources of fundamental news are shut down, giving people sixty hours to worry about the yen sell-off, the yen bid-up, the flooding in the Nile River, or other horrors and cataclysms reported in the Sunday papers. The weekend is also when people have time to read the gloomy long-term forecasts of economists who write guest columns on the op-ed page.

Unless you're careful to sleep late and ignore the general business news, so many fears and suspicions can build up on weekends that by Monday morning you're ready to sell all your stocks. That, it seems to me, is the principal cause of the Monday effect. (By late Monday you've had a chance to call a company or two and find out that they haven't gone out of business, which is why stocks rebound the rest of the week.)

I've been hearing that the 1987-88 market was a rerun of the 1929-30 market and we're about to enter another great depression. The 1987-88 market behaved quite similarly to the 1929-30 market, but so what? If we have another depression, it won't be because the stock market crashed, any more than the earlier depression happened because the stock market crashed. In those days, only one percent of Americans owned stocks.

The earlier depression was caused by an economic slowdown in a country in which 66 percent of the work force was in manufacturing, 22 percent was in farming, and there was no Social Security, unemployment compensation, pension plans, welfare and medicare payments, guaranteed student loans, or government-insured bank accounts. Today, manufacturing represents only 27 percent of the work force, agriculture accounts for a mere 3 percent, and the service sector, which was 12 percent in 1930, has grown steadily through recession and boom and now accounts for 70 percent of the U.S. work force. Unlike the thirties, today a large percentage of people own their own homes; many own them free and clear or have watched their equity grow substantially as property values have soared. Today, the average household has two wage earners instead of one, and that provides an economic cushion that didn't exist sixty years ago. If we have a depression, it won't be like the last one!

On weekends and weekdays I've been hearing that the country is falling apart. Our money used to be as good as gold, and now it's as cheap as dirt. We can't win wars anymore. We're losing jobs to the Koreans. We're losing cars to the Japanese. We're losing basketball to the Russians. We're losing oil to the Saudis. We're losing face to Iran. If you believe the old investment adage that the stock market climbs a "wall of worry," take note that the worry is fairly good-sized now and growing every day.

I hear every day that major companies are going out of business.

Certainly some of them are. But what about the thousands of smaller companies that are coming into business and providing millions of new jobs? As I make my usual rounds of various headquarters, I'm amazed to discover that many companies are still going strong. Some are actually earning money. If we've lost all sense of enterprise and will to work, then who are those people who seem to be stuck in the rush hour?

I've even seen evidence that hundreds of these same companies have cut costs and learned to make things more efficiently. It appears to me that many of them are better off than they were in the late 1960s, when investors were more optimistic. CEOs are brighter and more heavily pressured to perform. Managers and workers understand that they have to compete.

I've been hearing that investors ought to be delighted when companies in which they've invested are bought out by corporate raiders, or taken private by management, sometimes doubling the stock price overnight.

When a raider comes in to buy out a solid and prosperous enterprise, it's the shareholders who get robbed. Maybe it looks like a good deal to the shareholders today, but they're giving away their stake in future growth. Investors were only too happy to tender their shares in Taco Bell when Pepsi-Cola bought in the shares for $40 apiece. But this fast grower continued to grow fast, and on the strength of the earnings an independent Taco Bell might be worth $150 a share by now. Let's say a depressed company is on its way back up from $10, and some deep pocket offers to take it private for $20. It seems terrific when it happens. But the rest of the rise to $100 is cut off to all but the private entrepreneur.

More than a few potential tenbaggers have been taken out of play by recent mergers and acquisitions.

I've been hearing that we're rapidly becoming a nation of useless debt-mongering, cappuccino-drinking, vacation-taking, croissant eaters. Sadly, it's true that America has one of the lowest savings rates in the developed world. Part of the blame goes to the government, which continues to punish savings by taxing capital gains and dividends, while rewarding debt with tax deductions on interest payments. The Individual Retirement Account was one of the most beneficial inventions of the last decade—finally Americans were encouraged to save something free of tax—so what does the government do? It cancels the deduction for all but the modest wage earner.

Frequent follies notwithstanding, I continue to be optimistic about

America, Americans, and investing in general. When you invest in stocks, you have to have a basic faith in human nature, in capitalism, in the country at large, and in future prosperity in general. So far, nothing's been strong enough to shake me out of it.

I'm told that the Japanese started out making little party favors and paper umbrellas to decorate Hawaiian cocktails, while we started out making cars and TVs; and now they make the cars and the TVs, and we make the party favors and the little umbrellas to decorate Hawaiian cocktails. If so, there's got to be a fast-growing company that makes party favors somewhere in the U.S. that ought to be looked into. It could be the next Stop & Shop.

LEADERSHIP SECRETS OF ATTILA THE HUN

―――

WESS ROBERTS

Condensed from *Leadership Secrets Of Attila The Hun*, © 1987 by Wess Roberts. Published by Warner Books, Inc. Printed by permission.

EDITOR'S NOTE

Just before Edwin Artzt was named CEO of Procter & Gamble, a colleague gave him a plaque that read: "It is not enough that I win; all others must lose." The quote came from a book Artzt was reading, Leadership Secrets Of Attila The Hun. Fortune *related the incident to show Artzt's competitive drive. But the anecdote also demonstrates the competitive drive of author Wess Roberts, who was determined to get his book published.* Attila *is now a bestseller, kindling the enthusiasm of an astonishingly diverse and high-powered list of readers:*

Tom Peters, co-author of In Search of Excellence, *called it, "Fantastic!"*

Pat Riley, coach of the Los Angeles Lakers, said, "It's a great point of view about another way to show leadership . . . I will be using many of the author's ideas in my own work."

Robert L. Crandall, chairman and president, American Airlines, described the book as, "packed with insights . . . marvelously creative! I highly recommend it."

Sound like book blurbs? They are. The list of Attila *fans reads like a Who's Who in American business: William Coors, chairman of Adolph Coors; James Patterson, CEO of J. Walter Thompson; Victor Kiam, CEO of Remington Products; and Kenneth Blanchard, co-author of* The One Minute Manager.

H. Ross Perot, the former head of Electronic Data Systems and one-time General Motors board member, indirectly brought Attila *to the public's attention. In 1984, after several unsuccessful attempts to get the book published, Wess Roberts, then vice president for human resources of Fireman's Fund Insurance, paid to bring the book out himself. Perot read* Attila *and liked it so much he bought 700 copies. Ultimately* Attila *came to the attention of Warner Books, which distributed it widely.*

To be honest, Attila *falls into a category of books that you either love or hate. It delivers advice in an aphoristic style that is motivating, entertaining, and occasionally enraging. For example: What should you do if your rival in the next office already has read* Attila *and is expert in the tactics it suggests? Says Attila: "Let him think of you as weak. Let him act prematurely. And never tell him anything."*

— PREFACE —

Attila the Hun is a dubious character upon whom to base a metaphor on leadership. He's been portrayed throughout history as a barbaric, ugly little tyrant whose hordes, in total disregard of accepted principles of conservation, ruthlessly destroyed the beautiful and tranquil countryside, then went on to plunder and pillage numerous cities and villages inhabited by more civilized citizens of European nations.

Void of any characterization as a brilliant leader, a genius civilizer or a compassionate and adept king, the sinister Attila is commonly used as a referent for entertaining satire and serves as a universally agreed upon example of those qualities and attributes dreadfully abhorred in leaders of any generation, organization or cause.

Typically, leadership books are based on the lives and accomplishments of socially acceptable men and women who have reached the pinnacle of achievement in business, athletics, medicine, entertainment, education, religion or the military. Many of these writings prove to be worthwhile study; in them are valuable lessons for our own leadership development.

It is, however, sometimes a painstaking challenge to extract from these books the essence of the leadership principles contained in them. Even more challenging is the application of the thoughts in these books to our own lives.

Leadership is the privilege to have the responsibility to direct the actions of others in carrying out the purposes of the organization, at varying levels of authority and with accountability for both successful and failed endeavors. It does not constitute a model or system. No model or system of leadership behavior can anticipate the circumstances, conditions and situations in which the leaders must influence the actions of others. An evaluation of leadership principles is an effective base upon which to build other skills that may be important to success in specialized fields.

For this very reason I have chosen Attila as the central figure for this book. His nation has long since vanished, nomadic Huns no longer roam, and he is a most unlikely role model for anyone to emulate. But as I will show, his career presents a compelling and opportune forum for a primer on leadership.

Individually, the Huns were a spirited, perfidious people without common purpose other than to establish their next campsite. Commodities for internal trade didn't exist, so they sought out villages to lay waste to in order to obtain booty that would later be used as barter for food and other supplies necessary for their survival.

There could be no greater leadership challenge than faced the young Attila as he forged these barbaric hordes into a nation of Huns. He was met with the perils, trials and tribulations of masterful deceit not only from the tribes and clans but also from his own brother and uncles. His army marched against more-disciplined, better-trained and -supplied forces.

Few, if any, of his subordinate chieftains shared Attila's dreams of world conquest and a Hunnish homeland. These chieftains had to be convinced, their objections listened to and overcome. Their loyalty was assured out of fear for their lives, awe of Attila's superior logic and greed at the prospect of more bountiful booty than could be obtained by other means.

As a condition of a peace treaty, Attila once secured tribute payments from Theodosius II, emperor of the Eastern Roman Empire. And, perhaps as a tired and aging king, Attila turned his army homeward at the behest of the pope.

Seen in perspectives different from those who wrote his history — much of which must be to some degree apocryphal, if not biased by political preferences — Attila might today be characterized as an entrepreneur, diplomat, social reformer, statesman, civilizer, brilliant field marshal and host of some terrific parties.

But I didn't choose Attila as the metaphoric character of this book for any of these plausible labels or for the purpose of making him a cult hero in a modern age. Rather, Attila's robust life and controversial image as a determined, tough, rugged and intriguing leader — who dared to accomplish difficult tasks and performed challenging feats against "seemingly" insurmountable odds — provides a compelling opportunity for relating leadership fundamentals to a new generation of leaders who have no fear of him and who might enjoy a novel pedagogic treatment of what can otherwise be very mundane, unexciting reading.

For those who have little knowledge of who Attila was and for the purpose of establishing a basis for my metaphor, I have included a brief history of his life and legend in the book's introduction. It is essential to point out to the reader that even the most reputable historians disagree on the size of Attila's army as well as the total population of the Hunnish confederacy. In any case, their numbers have most likely been exaggerated in both this and other sources. It also seems reasonable to me that, if noted historians have had difficulty estimating the size of his army, much of what else has been recorded is subject to question and interpretation as well. And, while I have attempted to be objective in establishing Attila as my metaphorical leader, I have given him and his Huns a slightly more positive image than can perhaps be found elsewhere.

Each chapter begins with a vignette based on accounts of Attila's life, which serves to establish the referent situation and experience from which he lectures on various leadership principles to his chieftains and Huns in campfire settings. Having no direct relationship to familiar headlines and events in this day, these vignettes provide the reader with an opportunity to visualize his own situation and prepare himself for some aphorisms that relate to leadership success in any age, society, organization or situation.

The aphorisms spoken by Attila in this book have no basis of authenticity as ever having been said by the King of Huns. They are, rather, ones that I have written based upon my own experiences, research and observations. They have been reviewed and tested by some demanding critics and were only incorporated after having survived considerable scrutiny.

In any work of this nature, one is bound to identify some poignant thoughts that remain after the writing is completed. A few of my finest remnants are provided under theme headings I have collectively coined "Attilaisms." They conclude this leadership primer.

There has been no attempt in this effort to identify any past, present or future leaders as "Attilas." Similarly, no attempt has been made to identify "Attila" organizations. This would only distract from the book's intended message and result in a tireless, moot debate.

There is no magical formula for developing leadership abilities contained in this book. Any extraordinary method for accelerating the acquisition of leadership skills, attitudes and attributes is yet to be discovered. For the time being, as in centuries past, it seems to be the nature of the human being to acquire leadership traits a little at a time — building upon previously learned precepts.

I do not consider the precepts and concepts in this book as the definitive statements of all that is known about leading people. This is, however, a comprehensive, fundamental beginning to an understanding of what we commonly refer to as leadership.

INTRODUCTION

IN SEARCH OF ATTILA

The Huns were a loosely bound nation of nomadic, multiracial and multilingual tribes. Whether they originated on the European side of the Urals, in Turkey or elsewhere in Asia is left unanswered in their rarely transcribed and sometimes confused oral history.

Clad in skins and furs, the Huns were characterized by yellowish skin, long arms, large chests and narrow, slanted eyes. The skulls of warriors were deformed in childhood by a wooden apparatus held fast by leather thongs; their cheeks were seared with hot irons to retard the growth of facial hair.

Even in their own time, the weapons of the horde were considered unsophisticated and outlandish.

They ate raw meat toughened by having been carried in pouches between their thighs or between the flanks of their horses. A portion of their nutrition came from drinking mares' milk.

Warriors rode ahead of the women, who made their homes in skin-covered chariots overflowing with children and the pillage of victory.

Known for their respect for women, elders and ancestors, the Huns had a conservative moral philosophy. They rejected secular or religious doctrines and practices that made man subordinate to abstract concepts of a philosophical, political or social nature. Their guilelessness and naive faith in human goodness frequently caused them to fall prey to the intricacies of more skilled practitioners of diplomacy.

Their songs were simple tales of nostalgic utterances filled with love for nature. In all tribes was a strong interest in romantic history and also humor filled with political satire.

Huns believed strongly in miracles, held beautiful but useless ideals and were a people of optimism and flexibility. Their love of the hunt was well-established in their tradition. It was, perhaps, the Huns who began the custom of the "stag party."

To the civilized world the Huns were barbarians not far removed from wild animals in both appearance and life-style.

Out of this perplexing and barbaric past rose one of the most formidable leaders the world has known: Attila, King of Huns.

He was born in a chariot somewhere in the valley of the Danube around the year A.D. 395. Attila was the son of King Mundzuk and could trace his ancestry some thirty-two generations to Cham. His family maintained the integrity of the horde's bloodline and its distinctly Mongol characteristics.

Learning first to ride on the back of sheep, Attila later became an extraordinary horseman. He was also talented in the use of the bow, lance, lariat, sword and whip, traditional skills among his people and essential for one of noble rank.

He developed a strong sense of pride in his personal strength and a great disdain for the weak. His strength was often publicly displayed on adventurous hunting expeditions. He would capture wolves and bears in nets, then disembowel them with a short dagger.

His strong bond with his father was prematurely severed when King Mundzuk died while Attila was still a lad. Thereafter, he fell victim to vicious uncles, particularly Rugila, King Mundzuk's successor.

Attila's open criticisms of Rugila's policy of entering the horde into the service of foreign nations, whom Attila thought the Huns could easily defeat, changed the course of his youth.

At the age of twelve, Attila was sent as a child hostage to the Roman court of Honorius. In return, Rugila received a youth by the name of Aetius, in fulfillment of a clever arrangement perpetuated by the Romans.

It was a masterful exercise in subversive diplomacy. Foreign countries were infiltrated at their highest levels by youthful spies for the empire, who reported vital information back to Rome while gaining personal knowledge of the customs, courtesies and traditions of their hosts. Meanwhile, the empire tutored the hostages sent to its court in the luxuries of life in order to influence the politics and culture of less-civilized nations when the matured hostages returned to their native land. Rugila thought such tutelage would make Attila a more compatible member of the Huns' royal family.

Attila rejected the fancy robes, pompous hairstyles, rich foods and perfumed quarters offered to him as a hostage, though such trappings intrigued his unsophisticated comrades. Attila attempted, but was unable, to ignite their spirit to resist this and other beguiling propaganda imposed by the empire. On at least two occasions, Attila tried to escape. Failing to gain freedom, he prowled the palace as if he were a caged animal. His hatred for the empire's policies and practices grew stronger day by day.

It was a time of despair for the young Attila. He had been betrayed by Rugila. He was lonely for the Hunnish homeland and customs more familiar to him.

Unable to escape, Attila turned his attention to an intense study of the empire while outwardly ceasing to struggle against his hostage status. He studied the Romans' internal and foreign policies. He often secretly observed them in diplomatic conference with foreign ministers. He studied the empire's military, observing its strengths and vulnerabilities. He learned about leadership, protocol and other essential skills for future diplomats and rulers. It was in the Roman court that Attila conceived his strategy to rule the world.

While Attila was in the court of Honorius, Aetius was serving similar time in the court of King Rugila.

Aetius was born into the family of Gaudentius, a German from Pannonia who had married into a wealthy Roman family. Gaudentius, a battlefield captain of high regard known as "Master of the Horse" and "Count of Africa," was murdered by his own soldiers during a revolt in Gaul while Aetius was still a boy. His relationship with his father was, as was Attila's, abbreviated.

While a child hostage, Aetius became a scholar of the Huns—learning their customs, traditions and motives. They schooled him in the mastery of their weapons, taught him to hunt and to ride, providing the foundation from which Aetius would later fight Attila at the Battle of Chalons.

His relationship with King Rugila grew into a strong bond. Later, he would convince Rugila to unite the armies of the Huns and ally them with John the Usurper, a Vandal who had risen to become Master of Soldiers—a man Aetius thought capable of reuniting Rome and Constantinople.

On his return to Rome, Aetius wed the daughter of the patrician Carpilio. Always remaining on the best of terms with Rugila, Aetius became "Count of Domestics" and "Mayor of the Palace of Rome."

On Attila's return to the valley of the Danube, the tribes remained independent from political or military control by a central throne.

Attila began his rise to power by renewing and developing relationships with tribal chieftains. Much of this familiarization came through Attila's many hunting expeditions throughout the Hunnish territories. He gained the loyalty of these chieftains through emotional appeal, arousing their warrior instincts and whetting their appetites for glory and pillage.

How Attila became king over the tribe in the valley of the Danube is said to be the result of his brother's death during a hunt. A more romantic legend among the Huns gives his rise another origin.

According to this legend, on the death of Bleda, tribal leaders gathered in mourning and argued over who would become their king. During this council a lad reported a flaming sword had just appeared in a nearby meadow. Following the lad to the meadow, the tribal chieftains watched in awe as the flaming sword jumped into Attila's outstretched hand. It was an omen. Surely, "The Sword of God," was sent to end this quarrel and to confirm Attila as their king.

Once he became king over the royal tribe, Attila began his unification of the other fiercely independent tribes into a Hunnish nation.

He is said to have spent days in front of his tent in conference with tribal chieftains to confirm their loyalties to his unification plan. Attila summarily executed rebellious chieftains. The fear of resistance to him became so manifest that one aging chieftain excused himself from a personal audience with King Attila by saying, "My eyes, too weak to behold the sun, could assuredly not look upon the brilliance of the conqueror."

Although he leveraged its power, Attila was not seduced by the trappings of his new office. Drinking and eating from wooden implements, Attila sat on a wooden throne in a wooden palace. His dress showed none of the elegance of the Roman rulers. Rather, he wore a coat of black fur and a black leather cap pulled down over his eyes.

Attila was held in high regard by the horde. His entry into their camps was something to behold. Women, children and warriors lined his path shouting praises. Women presented food to him as he rode by. Attila accepted these gestures with dignity, hastily eating the food while still remaining on the back of his gallant black charger, Villam.

His rule as King of Huns was marked by swift yet considerate justice. He did not act in haste. He gave the Huns a national goal—to bring under their control the Germanic and Slavic nations, to conquer

Rome and Constantinople, to march against all of Asia, then on to Africa. Thus, the Huns would reign over all the world.

Attila's plan was ambitious, fired by boyhood dreams. He aimed to realize it step by step. His method was tempered by patience and unrelenting tenacity born of Asiatic virtues and by the political insight mastered by one who listens and watches while he waits for the precise moment to act.

The conquests of the Huns under his rule are legendary. His army, an estimated 700,000-strong, was a conglomeration of barbarians. Yet it became single in purpose, well disciplined and filled with esprit de corps.

Even though the Huns proceeded with difficulty at times, victory was often theirs without local resistance. Villages were, at times, abandoned upon hearing of the Hunnish army's approach. Yet the Huns would be frustrated by Aetius, the lifelong rival of their ruler.

In A.D. 451, on the Catalaunian Plains near Chalons, in northern France, under Attila's personal command the Huns massed their chariots in preparation for battle. The Romans were led by Aetius.

Using tactics gained from his experience among the Huns, Aetius neutralized the Hunnish army's bows and cavalry by engaging them in hand-to-hand combat. Bronze helmets and body armament shielded the Roman soldiers from the stone axes of the barbarians, who were unskilled in infantry tactics. The swords of the Romans prevailed over the lariats and long lances of the Huns. The battle was savage, neither side took prisoners, and few of the wounded survived. It is believed that by nightfall, as many as 300,000 Hunnish warriors lay dead on the Catalaunian Plains.

Realizing the futility of continuing the battle, Attila ordered a retreat, leaving the Romans somewhat astonished to see the Hunnish horde's backside in Attila's first, and only, defeat. Something in Attila's plan had gone wrong and, for a moment, his confidence, unrelenting energy and will seemed to desert him. His desire to conquer the world dwindled.

Returning with his battered army to the familiar valley of the Danube, Attila turned his energy to military science and the reorganization of his army. He would have to implement radical changes to overcome the tactics of Aetius, changes that would profoundly alter customs held by generation upon generation of Huns.

Leather armor bordered with metal plates replaced the fur garments of his army. The Huns' capital city, Etzelburg, was fortified to withstand long sieges. The Huns' nomadic existence was laid aside; now they would become deeply rooted in the soil of a homeland. Catapults were prepared. Warriors were drilled in infantry tactics—learning to maneuver on foot, their protection no longer being the safety provided by accuracy with the bow but in the use of long shields.

Developing allegiances between the Persians and the Romans prematurely halted Attila's plans to restructure the Hunnish army. Immediate action was necessary to prevent the consequences of this alliance. Attila gathered his tribal chieftains and, in a few words, laid out their route of march and order of battle.

The return of the Huns to battle was not perceived by many Romans as any great peril to their safety. They had not witnessed the Hunnish army's savage ability to devastate what lay before them. They were shortly to become more familiar with the fury of the barbaric swarm.

After a swift and unobstructed entry into Italy, the Huns laid siege to Aquileia. Set high on a hillside, surrounded by a water obstacle, its walls high and thick, its city gates reinforced, Aquileia was a bastion of Italy. Over the years, it had held against the Germans and various Asiatic tribes.

Inside was a well-trained garrison. Its food reserves and magazines were sufficient to withstand long sieges. Its people were resolved not to surrender their vast treasures to any invaders—no matter how imposing.

The Aquileians were inexperienced with the Huns. The terror with which they regarded the horde was largely the result of the tales of the Huns' devastating attacks on other villages and lands. Attila's army was great in number. It consumed the countryside as though it were a swarm of locusts.

Coming off, as they were, two previous swift victories against other fortified cities, the Huns became impatient with their siege of Aquileia. Food for man and beast became scarce. The horde was restless—ready to march on to greater Italy. The conquest of Aquileia, however, was essential to Attila's plan to crush the empire.

Morale became low. The tribal chieftains challenged Attila's tactics. Dead horses were eaten and rations reduced—the Huns' situation became more desperate with each passing day.

Attila called his battle captains together in an evening council. He announced that the cost of the siege had become too great. They would bypass Aquileia the next morning. At daybreak, the Huns would begin preparing for their march.

On the following day, taking a final look at the city, Attila saw a stork flying out of Aquileia, driving a young brood before her. It was an omen that would change the course of events.

Announcing that animals could sense things before men, Attila ordered his army to attack. With catapults and tall ladders, the disciplined Hunnish horde executed a masterful, swift victory. Aquileia was left in flames, its vast treasures added to the booty already overflowing Attila's chariots.

The horde set off in a fresh fighting spirit, renewed by this major triumph. Aquileian survivors told the empire of Attila's vast army, now advancing ferociously, methodically, on Rome. The empire was terrified of this seemingly unstoppable force.

In the Roman court, Valentinian ignored the counsel of Aetius, who had fallen from favor. After questioning his generals and senators, Valentinian judged the Roman army to be incapable of a victorious engagement with Attila's newly reorganized army.

At first, the Roman leaders thought of offering gold for ransom, but decided this would not satisfy a horde that could just as easily add all of Italy's treasure to the booty that already overflowed their chariots.

In desperation, the Emperor Valentinian thought of another tactic. Why not offer Honoria, his sister, to Attila as a wife? Had this not even been promised in a treaty of long ago? This plan was put aside when it was suggested that perhaps the King of Huns was content with his more than 300 wives. Suing for peace seemed the only hope for the survival of Rome.

But who could Valentinian send to negotiate with the mighty Attila? For whom did Attila hold enough respect that the petition for peace would even be considered?

The Christian world revered Pope Leo I. He was a man of God, of eloquence and culture, and had even been consulted by the Emperor Valentinian in times of difficulty.

Valentinian called upon the aging pope to gather a cortege, then to proceed to Attila's camp and sue for peace and the sparing of Rome — the last stronghold of the empire. The emperor hoped that perhaps through respect for the clergy, the Scourge of God would show mercy as he had one year earlier in Gaul when he acceded to Bishop Lupus' request and spared the city of Troyes.

The tactic dumbfounded Aetius. He knew Attila's army would fall as it had at Chalons if the empire would but stall. Aetius, however, was not consulted, and Valentinian's plan was put into action.

On the other side of the impending battle, Attila was hesitant. He feared another defeat by the Romans. Yet his fury was fired by the humiliations he had suffered in his youth in Rome. His oath, taken silently as a child, was to someday destroy the palace, triumphal arches and churches of Rome, a city he detested.

A scout returned to Attila's camp and, bewildered, reported that a procession of priests and monks approached led by an old man with a white beard, dressed in white, upon a white steed. Attila, atop the gallant black charger Villam, rode forward with a few warriors to inquire as to the nature of this unexpected delegation.

Halting his warriors on the banks of a river, Attila challenged the stranger as to his name. "Leo" was the reply.

It was Attila who rode through the stream to approach this unusual emissary of the Roman court.

What transpired between the frail pope and the King of Huns remains a mystery. But, after their meeting, Attila turned his army northward, sparing Rome, and returned to his homeland.

Trouble was brewing for Attila in the valley of the Danube. His six favored sons were impatient at not having received their own kingdoms as promised earlier by their father. They were frustrated that he had returned without conquering lands for them.

Perhaps it was his advancing age that tempered his ambitions of world conquest. Possibly it was Attila's diminished self-confidence, or satisfaction in having willingly spared Rome. World conquest was no longer an unfulfilled need. The warrior in him was now turning more toward diplomacy. He resumed negotiations with the Romans. These actions, unfamiliar during his rule, made it necessary for disciplinary reasons that Attila reconfirm himself as King of Huns. Again, as in earlier years, he executed chieftains who rebelled against him.

The beautiful young daughter of one such rebel chieftain implored Attila to spare her father, who was, nevertheless, executed. Attila was, however, touched by the daughter's beauty and decided to take the girl, Ildico, as his wife. The marriage was considered to be a good omen by the Huns—Attila would forget his old age, his disappointments and troubles and return to his pursuit of world conquest with new vigor. Thus, his sons would be given territories over which they could rule.

After a wedding ceremony, which is still held in legendary awe, the royal couple retired to their nuptial chamber. On the following day, in the midst of an unaccustomed silence from their king, warriors smashed open the door of the nuptial chamber. There, lying naked on a white fur, was Attila, dead, his body motionless in a pool of blood!

Some say his bride slew him to avenge the death of her father; however, no wounds were discovered. Some say perhaps his sons, impatient with their father, killed him. The romantic and legendary version of Attila's death is that he died from natural causes—hemorrhage brought on by the excessive festiveness of his wedding.

Although still in shock, the high priests prepared for the burial ceremony. As Attila lay on a high bier in the main square of Etzelburg, a black horse was offered in sacrifice as the sightless high priest Kama asked the departed Hunnish spirits how their king should be buried. The answer directed that Attila be buried in a triple coffin: the first of gold like the sun; the second of silver, as the tail of a comet; the third of iron, for Attila was of iron. To prevent any threat of disturbance of the beloved king in his final rest, Kama was told by the spirits to bury Attila at the bottom of the Tisza River. A dam was constructed to divert a small channel of the river, and a grave was prepared in the riverbed.

As thousands sang mournful songs, the funeral wagon was led to the grave site by twelve black horses, preceded by a riderless Villam saddled and draped with black cloth. The royal family, nobles, chief warriors and bareheaded Hun grandees followed the coffin on foot.

Joined by people from allied nations, some having traveled as long as three days, the sea of mourners carried thousands of torches as the sun descended in the western sky. Then, with a roll of drums and final blasts of tribute from his army's bugles, Attila was laid to rest. The dam was broken, and the waters rushed to protect the site from all future evil.

Western history, in which Attila is described as cruel and ruthless, holds no reverence for him. He has been scorned by authors as prominent as Dante in *The Divine Comedy, Inferno, Canto IXX:* "There Heaven's stern justice lays chastising hand on Attila, who was the scourge of earth."

Yet, Attila is proudly remembered by many of his remnant people, the Hungarians. Perhaps the German Nibelungen-Lied said it best when he wrote, "There was a mighty king in the land of the Huns whose goodness and wisdom had no equal."

Attila is an example of a leader who is never satisfied—preferring to take the initiative, acting rather than doing nothing.

Attila was less savage than the Romans, who cast thousands of Christians to wild animals for mere entertainment. In comparison, he was less cruel than Ivan the Terrible, Cortes or Pizarro. In his sparing of Rome, he showed more mercy than did Genserich, Belizar, the Norsemen, the Germans and the Spanish mercenaries, who all pillaged it without regard.

Attila's legacy is generally unfamiliar to us in the Western World. We are naive about his historical importance as a genius civilizer, his open-mindedness and richness of views, in all of which he far exceeded Alexander the Great or Caesar.

The controversy surrounding Attila will perhaps never be resolved, but his "leadership secrets" present insightful opportunity to learn, by way of metaphor, age-old characteristics, values and principles that separate those who lead from those who follow.

After all, he became Attila, King of Huns!

IN THE ROMAN COURT

"LEADERSHIP QUALITIES"

L ife in the Roman court was a tremendous hardship for Attila. He was lonely for his people, for his family, and yearned to free them from the service of a strange and foreign nation that the Huns, once united, could surely defeat.

The boy who was sent as a hostage to the court of Honorius profited from his Asiatic virtue of patience. His attitude was one of stoicism and certitude. He learned that pushing events to happen before their time was less important than their ultimate achievement. He, therefore, set out to develop the personal abilities that would ensure his success when the time came for him to pursue the throne of the Huns.

ATTILA ON: "LEADERSHIP QUALITIES"

As we gather in this counsel, I, Attila, have prepared my innermost thoughts regarding leadership qualities so you and your subordinates might be better prepared to lead the Huns.

It is essential to the Hunnish nation that we have in our service leaders at every level who possess the abilities that will enable them to carry out the responsibilities of their office.

There is no quick way to develop leaders. Huns must learn through-out their lives—always students gaining new insights into innovative procedures or methods—whatever the source.

We must teach our young warriors early in their service certain basic qualities if they are to develop into able chieftains. Instruction in horsemanship, with the lariat, bow and lance, is sufficient for warriors but not for those who lead them. Chieftains must possess the following essential qualities, which through experience become mastered skills:

- Above all things, a Hun must be loyal. Disagreement is not necessarily disloyalty. A Hun who, in the best interest of the tribe, disagrees, should be heeded. On the other hand, a Hun who actively participates in or encourages actions that are counter to the good of the tribe is disloyal. These Huns, whether warrior or chieftain, must be expeditiously removed. Their disloyalty is contagious.
- Hun chieftains must have courage. They must be fearless and have the fortitude to carry out assignments—the gallantry to accept the risks of leadership. They must not balk at obstacles, or become bewildered by adversity. The role of a chieftain has inherent periods of loneliness, despair, ridicule and rejection. Chieftains must be long-suffering in their duties—they must have the courage to act with confidence and to excel in times of uncertainty or danger as well as in times of prosperity.
- Each succeedingly higher level of leadership places increasing demands on the emotions of chieftains. Leaders at every level must have the stamina to recover rapidly from disappointment.
- Hun chieftains must endure the physical demands of their duties. Chieftains must nurture their bodies with the basic, healthful staples. Chieftains cannot lead from their bedside. Too much food or drink saps energy. The distorting potions of the Romans only confuse minds.
- Young chieftains must learn to be decisive, knowing when to act and when not to act. Vacillation and procrastination confuse and discourage subordinates, peers and superiors, and serve the enemy well.
- Learning by observation and through instincts sharpened by experience, our chieftains must anticipate thoughts, actions and consequences. Anticipation bears a level of risk that is willingly accepted by chieftains who excel.
- Timing is essential to all acts of leadership. There is no magic formula for developing a sense of timing. One often gains this leadership skill by applying the lessons learned from failure.
- An essential quality of leadership is competitiveness. It is not

necessary to win all the time; however, it is necessary to win the important contests. Chieftains must understand that competition inside and outside our nation is strong. A sense of competitive anger drives those who win on the battlefield, in negotiations and in situations of internal strife. A leader without a sense of competitiveness is weak and easily overcome by the slightest challenge.

- Proper training and experience develops self-confident chieftains. Those who lack assurance in their abilities give signs to their subordinates, peers and superiors that these duties are beyond their capabilities. They become, therefore, weak leaders and useless chieftains.

- Accountability for personal actions and those of subordinates is fundamental to leadership. Chieftains must never praise or blame others for what they themselves achieve or fail to accomplish, no matter how glorious or grave the consequences.

- No king, chieftain or subordinate leader should ever be allowed to serve without accepting full responsibility for his actions.

- Chieftains must be credible. Their words and actions must be believable to both friend and foe. They must be trusted to have the intelligence and integrity to provide correct information. Leaders lacking credibility will not gain proper influence and are to be hastily removed from positions of responsibility, for they cannot be trusted.

- Tenacity is an essential quality of leadership. The weak persist only when things go their way. The strong persist through discouragement, deception and even personal abandonment.

- If a chieftain cannot be depended upon to carry out his responsibilities, relieve him of them. A king cannot observe each and every action of his subordinate chieftains; therefore, he must depend upon them to get things done.

- Leaders must have the essential quality of stewardship, a caretaker quality. They must serve in a manner that encourages confidence, trust and loyalty. Subordinates are not to be abused; they are to be guided and developed. Punishment is to be reserved as a consequence of last resort and sparingly applied only when all other attempts have failed to encourage the rebellious to comply. Without a flock there can be no shepherd. Leaders are, therefore, caretakers of the interest and well-being of those they serve.

Those of you who are overly ambitious may attempt to acquire these qualities of leadership over a short period. As I, Attila, have found in my own life, these qualities simply take time, learning and experience to develop. There are few shortcuts. Without paying the price, no matter how great or small, none will become prepared to lead the Huns in our pursuit of world conquest.

— 2 —

THE LUST FOR
LEADERSHIP

"YOU'VE GOT TO WANT TO
BE IN CHARGE"

While a Roman hostage, Attila turned his anger, distaste and contempt for the empire into an energetic study to learn the ways of leadership and diplomacy. His mind was fueled by the fires burning deep in his heart to unite the Huns and conquer the Romans.

Instead of immediately attempting to gain control on his return to his homeland, Attila was patient, his every step planned. He knew his knowledge of leadership must mature no matter how strong his desire to take charge. Attila traveled and hunted, using the time to focus his ambition into a plan that would succeed.

When the moment came, Attila was ready! He took charge! He was prepared to face the challenges and opposition he would encounter as king. He would not be discouraged! He would not deviate from his objective! He was ready to take risks, ready to spur the Huns to excel through unity of action. His dogged perseverance and lust to assume a position of responsibility had held—his destiny had arrived! Attila had become King of Huns.

ATTILA ON: "YOU'VE GOT TO WANT TO BE IN CHARGE"

There is little more unsettling to Huns than a king or chieftain who shows a lack of commitment in his role as leader.

Too often, the leadership of many nations falls to princes who lack ambition. Such disinterest, cowardice and incompetence discourages and bewilders subordinates, and strengthens the enemy.

It is the responsibility of all Huns to choose and follow only those chieftains who demonstrate a desire to lead. Such leaders will be as different from one another as one Hun is different from another. They will not be laden with all human virtues, nor will they possess a flawless character.

Committed leaders with a lust for leadership and a willingness to serve will, however, be distinguishable by their wisdom, sincerity, benevolence, authority and courage. They will have a human quality and a strong commitment to the cause of those they serve.

Huns who aspire to become chieftains often do not have such motives from the time they leave the comfort of the chariot. Now perhaps you Huns would ask of me, "How, Attila, might I know if I possess sufficient desire to be a chieftain?" To those who wish my counsel, I offer these thoughts:

- Above all other traits, one who desires to lead must seek personal recognition.
- You must have the courage, creativity and stamina to focus on achieving your goals through the directed, delegated efforts of subordinates.
- You must recognize and accept that your greatness will be made possible through the extremes of your personality—the very extremes that sometimes make for campfire satire and legendary stories.
- You must not be overeager. You must temper your lust to lead with preparation and experience and wait for your opportunity.
- You must remember that success will depend largely on your sustained willingness to work hard. Sweat rules over inspiration!
- You must not be threatened by capable contemporaries or subordinates. Rather, you must be wise in selecting capable

captains to achieve those things a chieftain can attain only through strong subordinates.

- You must be willing to make unrecognized and thankless personal sacrifice for those you serve and those you lead. This sacrifice may take the form of absence from a tribal hunt, spending extraordinary energies and patience to develop subordinates and tending to the needs of these subordinates at times when your own needs go unfulfilled. You must be willing to bypass a festival in your own camp if another camp requires your presence.
- You must have a passion to succeed—a passion that drives you and your Huns to excel.
- You must be willing to remain your natural self and not succumb to false pride.
- You must accept that you have flaws and will need to work every day to become a better chieftain than you were yesterday.

— 3 —

BECOMING A HUN

"CUSTOMS"

T he Huns were a collection of fiercely independent tribes, a people with no observable religion but talented in military and political matters and marked by a common thread of mercurial instability and emotional heroism. Yet they were tempered by their nomadic qualities, which for centuries led them on constant migrations in search of a peaceful, pastoral existence.

The Huns had a certain magical magnetism that affected both friend and foe. They could assimilate foreigners into their tribes as well as they could integrate themselves into foreign nations. They were a unique people of a complex culture, the synthesis of all they'd encountered. Although the Huns were feared, thousands of foreigners joined them and even died for their cause.

In all, they were a nation with basic attitudes toward life and mankind, yet their love of freedom, excessive pride and volatile tempers often caused them to reject both military and political discipline.

The Huns were a constituency of vast differences who, nevertheless, held common virtues, and it was perhaps their strong sense of honor and loyalty, paired with Attila's intense personal appeal, that united them into a nation that for a short time was a powerful military and diplomatic force.

ATTILA ON: "CUSTOMS"

All Huns and those who seek to become Huns must learn and adhere to our customs. It is not essential that a Hun compromise those charac-

184

teristics that make him a unique warrior. Every Hun, however, must be willing to conform to those things that distinguish us as a nation of strong, unified tribes. We must be single in purpose, yet individuality that does not distract from the tribe or nation must be preserved.

What is good for the Hun must be good for the tribe and nation. Conversely, what is good for the tribe and nation must be good for the Hun; otherwise, he will desert to the Romans.

When we prescribe dress for battle, celebration, ceremony or other occasions, Huns will see to it that they wear that which is customary.

Hunnish methods must be taught to our young so they will know what is expected of them in every situation. If Huns do not learn the rules, their chieftains cannot expect them to be followed.

Our songs and dances must be unique in the celebration of our noble heritage. We must not introduce into them elements that may contaminate our heritage.

We must modify our customs when the situation warrants. We cannot, however, distill those customs that remain crucial to the success of the Hunnish nation. We cannot permit strong chieftains or groups of young Huns to establish customs that serve only their purpose. Customs are of nations, not of individuals.

Being a Hun requires dedication and devotion to the cause of our nation. Following our customs is a tribute to our heritage—and to our present and future.

Huns are required to make oaths of lasting obligation to the nation. We, in turn, as leaders, must ensure that we have customs—strong traditions—worthy of such lasting conviction and must welcome into our tribes and nation all who adhere to those principles.

To a nation of such robust and independent heritage, I, Attila, give counsel as to those things we admonish all to honor as our customs:

- The cardinal virtue of all Huns is personal and national honor. One's word must prevail over all other considerations, including political expediency.
- We must value the capable Hun, whether of lowly or of noble birth. We must appoint our chieftains from among those most qualified to lead, regardless of ancestry.
- We must not retaliate against the innocent, use unscrupulous tactics or kill unsuspecting or trapped enemies. We must be fierce in the eyes of all we seek to influence, yet the use of unnecessary terror is ignoble.

- A nation of one ancestry and race is weak. We must hold strong our custom of welcoming all foreigners who seek to join our cause, treating them with dignity and respect and teaching them our language and customs.
- Our accepted differences and diversities must be pooled into a common purpose worthy of our efforts as tribes and as a nation.
- We must never build pyramids in our own honor. While we hold strong the custom of individual and national pride, we must not fall victim to self-serving practices that weaken our moral fiber.
- We must hold fast to our custom of high ideals and optimism— never being discouraged by those who oppose us.
- Our songs, dances, games, jests and celebrations must always renew our allegiance and identity as Huns.

You chieftains have the responsibility to teach and to practice the customs that make our diverse people and tribes a strong and powerful Hunnish nation, lest we falter for lack of an identity.

— 4 —

PEACE IN THE CAMP

"MORALE AND DISCIPLINE"

The camps of the Huns enjoyed a spirited life with pronounced fluctuations in joy and sorrow. Victory brought joy and celebration. The death of warriors, periods of diminished supplies and tribal struggles brought sorrow and despair.

Hunnish morale and discipline was either very high or very low. Ambitious Huns could undermine the rule of weak chieftains and throw the camp into confusion. The absence of a national cause contributed to the mixed patterns of morale and discipline.

The Huns' ways were more attuned to an uncertain life, to a morale that was fired by battle, booty or caravaning into a new home. They were in fact disciplined only by the bounds of nature and the whims of fortune.

Attila's task as King of Huns was to instill a new sense of morale and discipline that would provide unity in and among the barbaric tribes. Their greater destiny was served only by setting aside past individual customs as smaller, independent, undisciplined bands of nomads. Peace in the camps would only result from a new spirit of nationalism. Attila's was not a simple chore!

ATTILA ON: "MORALE AND DISCIPLINE"

The traditions of our nomadic life have given little concern to our morale and discipline as a nation.

We have had passing moments of unity among our tribes, but this unity has been set aside when tribal loyalties have been purchased by foreign nations.

Our people need the constancy of knowing what it means to be a Hun. Our spirit as Huns has been betrayed each time we've been subjected to an alliance with a nation we could surely conquer.

Morale and discipline are utmost if we are to be a unified nation.

I have called you together at this time to teach you the ways of morale and discipline, through which we may have peace in our camps.

Listen and learn from my counsel.

- Morale and discipline are central to unity.
- The conclusive test of the morale of your Huns is the disciplined manner in which they bear the burdens of trial.
- Discipline is not suppression. It is the teaching of correct ways expected of Huns.
- Without discipline, Huns cannot behave with common action.
- Morale is the spirit by which Huns submit their services to the tribe. It is not uncontrolled celebration and romping around the campfire.
- Discipline is not always welcomed by Huns.
- Discipline does not mean a loss of individuality.
- Discipline never allows deviation from order or from principles we hold important among our tribes or nation.
- Discipline builds the confidence of Huns. Thus, discipline builds morale.
- Huns seek discipline in their lives. They more willingly follow chieftains who are themselves disciplined.
- Lack of morale and discipline is the most contagious and destructive disease that can ever enter your camp.
- Wise chieftains frequently test the discipline of Huns by challenging their physical and emotional stamina. However, chieftains should never test Huns beyond reasonable capacity.
- Discipline should be expected only at those levels of order and conformity that serve the good of the tribe or nation. Demanding more than is required is an abuse of power and gives rise to rebellion.
- Wise chieftains realize that unduly harsh or unnecessarily lax discipline will undo the morale of their Huns.

Peace and harmony in your camps will come from reasonable expectation of disciplined action and purpose. Morale will accompany such reasonable exacting of discipline. There is no simple pattern by which morale and discipline can be attained. These critical secrets to your success as leaders are rather an awareness—an attitude—by which you carry out the charge of your office.

The morale and discipline of your camps bear fruit on the battlefield or in diplomatic encounters.

Now, having the benefit of my counsel, go forth to your camps and instill, even demand, new purpose of unity, new pride in being a Hun. The loyalty, dedication and spirit of your Huns will instill in all our camps confidence, comfort and peace, without which we will continue to have widespread discontent and will return to a life of aimless wandering.

— 5 —

THE FURY OF
INTERNAL BATTLES

"CUNNING IN THE TRIBES"

The Huns, long divided into independent tribes, obeyed the precepts of nomadic life. They were still not a nation but small tribes bound together solely by their customs.

As a political matter, the king who reigned on the banks of the Danube held no authority over the Huns of Asia or Russia. Chieftains ruled their tribes as they wished, pillaged on their own accord and migrated whenever resources were exhausted. Never did they trouble to plan what their next destination might be.

Intermarriages with conquered races were common. Without the powerful forces of unification, the Huns would have slowly been assimilated into the medley of European peoples.

Attila, son of Mundzuk and a descendant of an ancient imperial family, faced little opposition so long as he did not seek to force his authority over chieftains not directly subject to him.

Thus it happened that the Huns were often under orders of different nations. Their chieftains often sold themselves and their warriors as dearly as possible, showing no reluctance to fight against even men of their own race.

No national sentiment could exist in a people so fragmented, no concerted action was possible when everyone played his own hand. Uprooted, driven hither and thither by caprice or need, the Huns wasted their strength in battles from which they gained no profit.

Attila comprehended that, once knit together, the Huns could easily become a mighty power. At a time when the Huns had nothing to fear either from Rome or Constantinople, he devoted himself to the task of forging the instrument necessary for the conquest of the world—an invincible Hunnish army.

But first the army had to be assembled and the independent tribes consolidated, and in these labors there would be no lack of obstacles. The first presented themselves in his own family.

ATTILA ON: "CUNNING IN THE TRIBES"

The Hunnish nation is comprised not only of those who have long ridden on our many journeys but of all the tribes who seek the fulfillment that comes with being a Hun. The worth of a Hun is not determined by tenure. A Hun's value rests solely upon his demonstrated desire to support those goals we seek as a nation of unified tribes.

Among our tribes we have suffered ills brought on by chieftains and Huns who prefer their own ambitions to those of the nation. These are clearly those who, openly or secretly, pledge their support even to the enemy solely for personal gain. There are those among our own tribes who indulge in pointless bickering and other forms of rebellion. Their interests are served at the cost of loyalty to the tribe or nation.

Now, if we are to become and remain a powerful nation, we must make radical changes in our ways of independence as tribes, as chieftains or as Huns who fail to make a contribution toward the unification that I, Attila, am bound by destiny to achieve.

Let it be known that I will no longer tolerate any cunning among our Huns, chieftains or tribes that undermines the unification of our nation. He who attempts such cunning and becomes known to me, or to any chieftain exercising authority over him, will hastily conform to our values or will be subjected to the most extreme reprimand.

While the coals of our campfires would long become dust before I could pronounce guidance and caution for all the evils a cunning Hun would bring upon us, I shall provide you with counsel that is sufficient for your learning and understanding at this time.

- Beware of the treacherous Hun who pledges loyalty in public then spreads discontent in private. Make every effort to identify and remove these ignoble characters, be they chieftains or your best warriors.

- Be wise and anticipate the Brutus of your camp. Caesar paid fatally for his unfailing loyalty to Brutus.
- Never expect your Huns always to be compatible. But expect their differences to be resolvable without the spread of discontent to other Huns.
- Never allow your Huns too many idle moments. These give rise to discontent.
- Never cast blame for failure upon the guiltless.
- Never allow your Huns to gain fame for the deeds of others.
- Never threaten the security or esteem of another Hun unless you are prepared to deal with the consequences.
- Be approachable; listen to both good and bad news from your Huns. Otherwise, you will provide reason for murmurings.
- Be principled, not inflexible.
- Reward Huns of character and integrity—they are rare.
- The spirit of unity must be a cardinal principle in the ways and attitudes of all Huns. Once divided, we are easily made subject to foreign nations.

In imparting these secrets of success, I, Attila, charge to you, as leaders of Huns, to be forthright in your demonstration of unity and to hold in contempt any who spread discontent among our tribes.

The unification of our tribes into a strong and formidable nation can only be realized through loyalty to our cause and to those who reign responsibly over the destiny of our mighty horde.

— 6 —

THE TRIBUTE

"PAYING AND RECEIVING
DEFERENCE"

Attila was well-schooled in the power of rumor. He knew that advantageous rumor in the hearts and minds of ten could result in thousands becoming his victims. Thus, through rumor, many obstacles to his "great conquest" were removed.

He considered himself above the reproach of the masses; therefore, his reputation was important to him alone. He knew who he was, what he could achieve; his reputation was not as important to his feelings of self-worth as it was to influencing the outcome of battles and negotiations. Thus, Attila turned a nickname that in certain circles might have been considered unflattering into an advantage and, in doing so, gained riches for his treasury and tribute from untold thousands.

As the story goes, a Gallic monk, provoked either by the horror of Attila's ambition or by a taste for martyrdom, created a new title for him. The monk hailed Attila not as "King of Huns" but as "The Scourge of God."

Attila, sensing the power this newly acquired title would yield on the battlefield and in negotiations, was quick to adopt it, for he knew the sobriquet would have the influence of an army of 100,000.

Attila pressed the advantage of his reputation as "The Scourge of God," counting on the fear inspired by rumor to guarantee the success of a well-planned tactic to obtain needed moneys for his march on the Roman Empire. So, in the year A.D. 446, Attila invaded Thessaly. His goal was to ransom money from Theodosius II.

Attila ordered the most vicious and ferocious-looking warriors from his army to wear garb of rough fur and leather, to eat only raw meat and to inflict the most horrible tortures on their prisoners. All of this planned fury was for the sake of perpetuating a legend.

Resolved to fight the Huns that he mistakenly believed he had conquered five years earlier when the horde halted within reach of the capital, and with the audacity and determination of a weakling annoyed at the disruption of his pleasure, Theodosius allowed the utter destruction of more than seventy villages before he sought to make a truce at Thermopylae.

Because of Theodosius' earlier resistance and now his meek submission of the Eastern Roman Empire, Attila raised the price of peace. Roman prisoners were to be freed at a new cost of twelve pieces of gold instead of the usual eight.

Attila could have demanded much more. However, he knew the Romans would simply slap their subjects with new taxes to recoup the moneys. Attila had no wish to burden the peasants, merchants, artisans, plebeians, and other subjects of the empire; he simply sought to conquer its corrupt leaders.

ATTILA ON:
"PAYING AND RECEIVING DEFERENCE"

It is noble to accord the proper courtesy and recognition of stature to one in an office over you. And it is wise to pay deference to your peers and subordinates as well.

If a chieftain does not command the respect of his Huns and that of his foes, he is weak and undeserving of his title.

Respect may be born of fear, real or perceived, as in my notoriety as "The Scourge of God." When deference is born of fear, however, it results in passive resistance to authority and purpose. It further leads to subversion, to sabotage and to generally low morale.

Real deference results in unyielding loyalty—a tribe full of spirit and willing to follow their chieftain into the mouth of hell, if necessary, for the cause of the nation.

A chieftain's office is accepted by all as a position of greater privileges because of increased responsibilities. Who would aspire to such an office if it brought no greater merit or privilege than that of an ordinary Hun?

Our system of deference prescribes rewards for effort, enterprise and accomplishment. The Hunnish people will acknowledge the privilege attending our various offices of leadership only so long as the demanded deference is reasonable and poses no harm to them. They are willing to grant such deference to those brave enough to lead the way. For they themselves see such respect as a cheap price to pay someone else to take on the responsibilities of leadership.

I must caution you, however; there are subtle aspects of paying and receiving deference that will make the deciding difference in one who leads by notoriety and one who leads with nobility. My words of counsel are:

- Never exercise your authority to the disadvantage of your subordinates. Never exact more privilege from your office than your subordinates are willing to grant.
- You are your reputation! If people speak evil of you, erroneously attribute misdeeds to you and will not serve a greater purpose, you must do away with those adversaries or you must behave in a manner that will encourage them to amend their judgments. It isn't easy being the Scourge of God, but it has its advantages in dealing with the enemy. Among my own people, however, I seek no such reputation. For if they perceived me as having such a wicked intent, I would not long serve as their king.
- The king may use his fury and power to gain tribute from the enemy; however, a chieftain has no such privilege. Although, as king, I must rely on my chieftains to use their power wisely to influence the actions of their Huns, I, Attila, will hastily remove any chieftain who supposes similar influence over me.
- Never should a chieftain fret over privilege. The responsibilities of office should always prevail. Deference comes to the chieftain who does not seek it.
- The deference that attends any office of leadership is confirmed by custom, yet it is modified by circumstance. What stands as privilege in the court or palace seldom has importance on the battlefield or in foreign territory. Be aware of where you are and whom you are with when exercising the privileges of your leadership position.
- Any promotion will require an adjustment on your part as well as on the part of those who remember you in your former role. Have patience with yourself and others. Dignity of person and title is a noteworthy attribute in this situation.

- Always pay proper courtesy to your subordinate leaders. Should you fail to accord them respect, so will their subordinates.
- Paying deference to your adversaries is essential. Once you fail to recognize their abilities, influence and potential, they may gain advantage over you. Even as I was underestimated by Theodosius, it was I, Attila, who exacted tribute from his kingdom. With this counsel, I share with you chieftains the duty of seeing to it that every position of leadership is paid appropriate deference and that this deference is acceptable to those Huns whom we serve.

— 7 —

BATTLE DRESS AND ARMAMENT

"CHIEFTAINS ARE AS THEY APPEAR TO THEIR HUNS"

Attila's presence was felt wherever he rode or rested. He was not only a Hun, he was the most distinguished Hun of all.

Scorning the garb of noble Romans, Attila attired himself in the simple, crude skins of animals, which was the custom of his people. Even his crown, as king, was a simple leather helmet adorned by only a single feather. It was headgear similar to that of his warriors.

He rode upon the mighty and gallant black charger Villam ("Lightning"). So majestic an animal was Villam, it is said that grass never grew again on the path he trod. Villam was stronger and swifter than the mount of any other Hun. This was a necessity, for Attila had to ride first into battle, at the front of the horde. He was, after all, their leader.

In battle, Attila was armed with the customary bow, lance and lariat of the Huns. His sword was another matter. Legend had it that it was the Sword of God.

The Huns identified with Attila; his appearance was not markedly different from theirs. Yet, Villam and his mystical Sword of God were sufficient to distinguish him as one destined to lead, to be followed and to be respected.

ATTILA ON: "CHIEFTAINS ARE AS THEY APPEAR TO THEIR HUNS"

Life in the Roman court taught me how essential it is for a chieftain or king to appear as is expected and acceptable to those he serves and those he chooses to impress.

Roman leaders adorn themselves in a manner that is pompous, one that is unnatural to their constituency and repulsive to their allies.

It is the custom of all followers to expect their leaders to be marked at times with armament that distinguishes them from the masses in the court or on the battlefield.

It is wise, however, that such distinction not be offensive to warriors and not fuel the destructive spirit of the opposition.

Therefore, as we chat around this campfire, I will share my observations concerning the appearance of chieftains.

- A chieftain neither dresses nor arms himself at the expense of his Huns. His dress and weaponry may be of subtle distinction as is accepted by custom. Yet it must never be ostentatious, or project ignoble superiority lest his men scorn him for it.
- A sword is the mark of a chieftain. It should be well-made, not glittering with jewels and gold but honed to a sharp edge and made of the finest material in the land. A chieftain should dress in fine skins and furs, and not be draped with gold and silver adornments. Pompous appearance breeds hate and gives rise to contempt and laughter among the ranks.
- If it is necessary to appear as ferocious savages in order to project courage, then Huns and chieftains should wear the most barbaric of all furs, robes and other apparel. Such appearance further serves to destroy the will of the enemy.
- If it is appropriate to dress as peaceful, pastoral peoples for daily life in your camp or in negotiations with strangers, clothe yourself in furs and robes fitting the occasion.
- A chieftain who appears to be noble will be treated as such.
- One who appears as a jester of the courts will receive deference as the same.

These observations have served me well as your king. Insignificant as they may seem, dress and armament are important to a chieftain and will be counted in the measure of your success or failure.

— 8 —

AETIUS

"PICKING YOUR ENEMIES WISELY"

S ent to a foreign court as a child hostage, Aetius was received with honor by the Hunnish court of King Rugila in exchange for Attila.

In the court of Rugila, Aetius learned the ways of the Huns, their traditions, and gained insight into their collective personality. This learning would serve him and the empire well in future dealings with the Huns—particularly with Attila.

A man of unwavering principle, Aetius was physically strong, an expert in the art of war—a formidable warrior in every aspect. He mastered the intellect of both Hun and Roman and learned well the strengths and vulnerabilities of both nations.

Aetius knew hardship and was subjected to great personal and professional challenges throughout his life. On more than one occasion, he was the target of hired cutthroats and escaped seemingly by a miracle.

The corruption of the empire affected Aetius to the point that he contemplated, more than once, changing his allegiance to the Huns. It was, however, his strong sense of duty and his oath to serve that harnessed his anxieties. Thus, he always remained true to the empire.

In time, the corruption of the Roman leaders overcame Aetius. His advice was not sought when Attila began his final campaign against Italy. The price of neglecting Aetius' counsel was the defeat of the empire in many battles.

Although he remained loyal to the end, Aetius, in his old age, was reluctant to lead the Roman army against Attila, whom he considered a worthy opponent and a man in pursuit of a great destiny.

In the end, Aetius was the victim of an assassination ordered by the emperor, Valentinian, he had so loyally served. The ignominious death of Aetius marked the end of a great general and the only man in the empire whom Attila held in high regard.

ATTILA ON: "PICKING YOUR ENEMIES WISELY"

Now, you chieftains and Huns, I, Attila, have need to counsel you on how to choose your enemies.

Most conflicts in our lives lie within the Hunnish nation, between our tribes, our chieftains or among the people. Seldom is our real enemy a Roman. Only infrequently will an external enemy have the stature and skill of an Aetius to defeat us on the battlefield or in diplomacy, for we are Huns.

Being somewhat wise in the ways of Huns, yet naive about the sources of conflict, most of you are totally unaware when you make enemies. In dealing with other Huns and particularly with the Romans, we must be cunning insofar as we should make enemies only with purpose. As I reflect on my observations and experience, it has served me well to be aware of a few dangers in making enemies without intent.

These pitfalls are perils to your effectiveness as chieftains and warriors. Learn these, my secrets, well.

- Do not expect everyone to agree with you—even if you are king.
- Do not waste stamina trying to negotiate with implacable, uncooperative enemies—conquer them by more effective means.
- Not all opponents are enemies. You may have productive, friendly confrontations inside and outside your tribe.
- Do not delegate an assignment and then attempt to manage it yourself—you will make an enemy of the overruled subordinate.
- Do not lose your temper without reason.
- Do not underestimate the power of an enemy, no matter how great or small, to rise against you on another day.
- Do not neglect the opportunity to deceive your enemy. Make him think of you as a friend. Let him think of you as weak. Let him act prematurely. And never tell him anything.

- Do not make enemies who are not worthy of you.
- Do not fail to use an enemy's weakness to your advantage. On the other hand, when it becomes apparent that an enemy is too formidable, retreat and return another day when you can conquer him.
- Do not insult unless you mean it.

It should be sufficient for all Huns to recognize that when they exercise unbridled antagonism and create useless jealousy and hatred, their actions may serve to persuade even friends to become foes. A chieftain will not be followed long by Huns who despise him.

— 9 —

LEADING THE CHARGE

"RESPONSIBILITIES OF A CHIEFTAIN"

The Hunnish horde adapted a new spirit of unity during the reign of Attila, for he had applied seemingly simple principles to unite the tribes into a strong nation.

No longer would chieftains have the option to pledge their loyalty to other than the Hunnish nation. Should they choose to do so, Attila would remove them from their office.

No longer would the Huns be tribes of nomads rambling through the countryside in search of booty. They had a new direction! They would rule the world.

Now, under Attila, the barbarians so dreaded by the empire and even nations of afar had a strategy for their wanderings.

When possible, Attila exploited his influence through diplomatic relations, skills learned as a boy in the Roman court. But if he failed to gain his objectives by peaceful means, Attila would unleash the fury of his horde, then attempt new negotiations to bring villages and nations under his control.

Attila, with his magnetic personality and, perhaps, charm, was so awe-inspiring to his warriors and chieftains that he was worshipped by them—even as a god by some.

His power became so prevalent during his reign that chieftains, not wishing to offend him and face his fury, would simply yield to him without the slightest resistance.

By way of fulfilling the obligations of his title, Attila exhibited patience—not haste—and prudent judgment; his plan had been formulated over years. It was a calculated scheme of sequenced events that resulted in Attila's short-lived but complete leadership over a nation of barbarians whom, for a time, the world held in fear.

ATTILA ON: "RESPONSIBILITIES OF A CHIEFTAIN"

It has been my observation over the years that nations, tribes and lesser bands rise and fall on the strength of their leaders and on the ability with which their leaders carry out their responsibilities of office—seeking first the good of the people.

The corruption of the empire is largely a result of the glamorous yet empty life of its leaders. They have lost their sense of national purpose and employ foreign armies to carry out the responsibilities incumbent on the Roman Legion.

They seek to gain office and stature by political maneuverings, casting aside personal standards of excellence. Their leadership is, therefore, based on weakened foundations and shallow loyalties.

While we are a young nation, we have strong traditions that tie us mystically together. We must use this delicate alliance as a basis for powerful, lasting bonds that better serve our collective destiny.

Our leaders—you chieftains and valued warriors, gathered here this night—must learn the responsibilities of office.

As many of you are unschooled in what I, Attila, consider to be the responsibilities of leadership, I now grant you my counsel on this subject.

- Chieftains and leaders in every subordinate office are responsible for establishing the atmosphere in which they lead. This atmosphere may have periods of change even as the seasons change. Nonetheless, unlike our lack of influence over the weather, our leaders can and must influence and control the spirit of our tribes.
- Leaders are bound by the traditions of office to establish and follow the order under which their Huns are judged, rewarded, punished and constrained. Without such order, all Huns will live in chaos.
- By their own actions, not their words, leaders establish the morale, integrity and sense of justice of their subordinate commanders. They cannot say one thing and do another.

- Leaders must establish a high spirit of mutual trust among subordinates and with their peers and superiors.
- Leaders must value high standards of performance and not tolerate the uncommitted.
- Leaders must expect continual improvement in their subordinates.
- Leaders must encourage creativity and innovation among their subordinates, so long as these efforts are consistent with the goals of the tribe or nation.
- Chieftains realize greater recognition and booty than their Huns. I, Attila, expect, therefore, more from them than from their people.
- Chieftains should never misuse power. Such action causes great friction and leads to rebellion.
- Chieftains make great personal sacrifice for the good of their Huns.
- Chieftains must not favor themselves over their Huns when supplies are short.
- Chieftains must encourage healthy competition among their people, but must contain it when such becomes a detriment to tribal or national goals.
- Chieftains must understand that the spirit of the law is greater than its letter.
- Chieftains must never shed the cloak of honor, morality and dignity.
- Chieftains must never form selfish relationships and, therefore, take advantage of their subordinates, peers or superiors.
- Chieftains must hold a profound conviction of duty above all other ambitions.

You must leave this campfire counsel with one thought and one thought only. That is, success is the result of hard work that overcomes disappointment and discouragement. Success is not achieved through complex strategies; it is achieved only through conscientiously carrying out the duties of your office and exercising the responsibilities of leadership—nothing else will prevail.

Now, go to your Huns and arise tomorrow with a new determination to follow your leaders, to support your peers and to lead your subordinates; otherwise we are destined to be slaves of the empire.

— 10 —

THE OMEN OF
AQUILEIA

"THE ESSENTIALS OF
DECISIVENESS"

The siege of Aquileia was long, rations became scarce, and morale threatened to fade. But when the disciplined Hunnish warriors attacked upon the sighting of a good omen—that of a stork and its brood leaving the city's towers—victory was instant! The walls crumbled, and the city was set in flames.

Destiny had been fulfilled through patience and the ability to sense the precise moment to act.

ATTILA ON: "THE ESSENTIALS OF DECISIVENESS"

Our seasoned chieftains have become wise through experience as to when it is right to act and when it remains best to contemplate further. On the other hand, our young, ambitious Huns, anxious to demonstrate their deftness, will often precipitate actions that result in loss for them, their tribe and perhaps the nation.

Such rashness is unacceptable. All chieftains must learn that victory comes to those who know not only what to do, but when to do it.

Young Huns are taught skill in weaponry—mastering the bow, the lance, the lariat—and in horsemanship. They learn the advantage of swift action on the battlefield.

As their mentors, we teach them to take the initiative, to have the moral courage and force that make the difference between followers and leaders. We must, however, demonstrate for them the main points possessed by the leader who travels the determining mile from sporadic accomplishment to resolute performance in all things. One of these points is decisiveness.

Now, I give you chieftains counsel for acquiring skill in decisiveness.

- Noble resolve to do the right thing is characteristic of prudent decision making.
- Wise is the chieftain who never makes a decision when he doesn't understand the issue.
- A chieftain should allow his subordinates the privilege of making decisions appropriate to their level of responsibility. Weak is the chieftain who reserves every decision for himself out of fear that he might lose control.
- The circumstances of a given moment are not to be used as an excuse for being unprepared to make decisions. Indecisiveness is bred by failure to accept the responsibility of office.
- A chieftain who fails to accept full decision-making responsibility—or who blames others for his own bad decisions—lacks an essential quality of leadership.
- Rarely are there perfect decisions. The best decisions are usually the more prudent of the logical alternatives. When you must be overly persuasive in gaining support for your decision, it's usually a sign of a bad one.
- Next to the importance of knowing when to make a decision stands the insight to know when to forgo making one. Impatient chieftains often precipitate premature action.
- Perhaps the most critical element of decision making is timing. Prompt determination after appropriate deliberation is a worthy principle of decisiveness.
- Chieftains are to be cautioned against rushing to conclusions when there is time and opportunity to improve upon the basic decision.
- Wise chieftains often extract from obscure places the critical elements for making the right decision. The key is learning to find the obscure places and to recognize the critical elements.
- Skepticism has value in that it delays premature decision mak-

ing. When a chieftain can't make up his mind, it's worthwhile to restate the problem.

- Initiative in decision making is not sufficient when it occurs only in relation to easy assignments. It must be exhibited for difficult and high-risk tasks as well.
- Doubt and delay are the signs of chieftains promoted beyond their capacities.
- Paradoxical as it may seem, sometimes the best decisions are made void of the emotions evoked by the facts bearing on the problem.

You chieftains must make the extra effort and demonstrate rigor in developing a sense of decisiveness. Knowing by instinct or by fact when the time is right for action will yield a high measure of success. Decisiveness in leadership action carries a heavy burden. Often it means victory or defeat.

— II —

HORSE HOLDERS

"THE ART OF DELEGATION"

E ven as a warrior who dismounts and expects to return to his fiery steed requires a horse holder, so too Attila relied on his chieftains. Early in his efforts to unify the tribes, Attila sought to gain loyalty from easily allied chieftains. Thus, he would have the formidable power of numbers when he challenged more powerful chieftains.

As king, he would not be capable of overseeing every action of his nation, its tribes and its chieftains. He would require the loyalty of trusted chieftains to whom he could delegate responsibility.

The chieftains and their tribes had lost some deference for Attila as a member of the Hunnish royal family for he had not been long in their camps, as his childhood had been spent in the court of the Romans as a hostage.

Waiting patiently, as a spider waits for its prey, Attila used his time to develop loyalties and a following that would yield him chieftains to whom he could delegate national unification responsibilities. This he could do with a minimum of risk that they would cast their lots once again with other chieftains or with foreign leaders.

Risk in delegation was high; however, without accepting such a risk Attila would, alas, have been destined to rule over only the tribe of his royal family, and his greater ambition to unify the tribes into a powerful nation would have been lost.

ATTILA ON: "THE ART OF DELEGATION"

Our nation cannot prevail as the dominant world power if its leadership is restricted to one man. Even I, Attila, cannot accomplish for you what you are not willing to accomplish for yourselves. You must be willing to accept the responsibilities that I delegate to you. At the same time, your charters are too great for you to accomplish alone. You must trust to your subordinates responsibilities that fit their office.

This gathering is for the purpose of imparting my counsel regarding the leadership principle of delegation, which is central to your success as chieftains.

Learn these precepts well, or your burden will be too great to accomplish those responsibilities in your charge.

- Chieftains should never delegate responsibilities necessitating their direct attention.
- Wise chieftains grant both authority and responsibility to those they have delegated assignments.
- Wise chieftains always hold their subordinates accountable for delegated assignments.
- Worthy chieftains accept full responsibility for all assignments—even those they have delegated to their subordinates.
- Once a chieftain has delegated responsibilities, he should never interfere, lest his subordinates come to believe that the duties are not truly theirs. Such superficial delegation yields fury in the hearts of subordinates.
- A competent chieftain will delegate important assignments to inexperienced subordinates in order that he might develop his subordinates' skills and demonstrate his trust in them.
- A chieftain should never punish a subordinate who has failed if he did his best to carry out a delegated responsibility.
- Chieftains should encourage subordinates to use creativity to fulfill delegated responsibilities.
- Subordinates will never develop skills if their chieftain precisely directs them how to accomplish their delegated assignments.

— 12 —

BOOTY

"REWARDING YOUR HUNS"

L ong a collection of nomadic peoples, the Huns were inspired by the glory and spoils of their exploits as intrepid warriors. Many tribes depended on booty for their survival. Often, their appetites for pillage made them forget their gods and heroes, and national goals. Looting was, for the Huns, simply a part of postbattle etiquette.

Attila understood these customs. He knew the Huns were driven by intrinsic desires so strong that, simply to enjoy the spoils of war, the tribes would often become mercenaries for foreign nations and march in campaigns, even against other Hunnish tribes.

His role was to harness this desire for short-term gain—to use discipline in the distribution of booty as reward for energies spent for the good of the Hunnish nation—as he set out to realize his people's formidable potential.

ATTILA ON: "REWARDING YOUR HUNS"

Booty is a powerful force that ignites the spirit of our warriors, driving them to commit their talents to any nation that bribes them into service.

You, as leaders of your tribes, and I, Attila, as King of Huns, must turn this lust for booty into a more disciplined distribution of rewards to Huns who willingly give their services to our nation either in or out of battle.

Booty, as such, is most often a short-lived benefit to which our Huns have become accustomed as their wages of war. We must continue to grant our warriors their rights of pillage and at the same time provide rewards for acts off the battlefield that we endorse.

Controlling the undisciplined desire for booty among our horde is necessary for our civilization to triumph over barbaric customs. For this purpose I, Attila, issue guidance on rewarding your Huns.

- Never reward a Hun for doing less than is expected of him. Otherwise, he will doubt your sincerity in rewarding appropriate acts and, even worse, expect reward for performing deeds for which you hold no approval.
- Never reward a Hun for every act completed correctly. Otherwise, he will not act in the absence of your presence or without the certainty of recognition.
- Grant small rewards for light tasks. Reserve heaps of booty for dangerous, gallant, substantial effort and worthy accomplishment.
- Praise those who are simply good Huns. Their need for gratification tends to parallel their level of ambition. Security is utmost for those who risk not. Give them, therefore, assurance—not great booty—lest they learn large value is given to those who just get by.
- Teach your Huns that booty is nothing more than wages for their service. Heaps of booty, promotion through the ranks and recognition as being a mighty warrior are reserved for those who go beyond the call of duty.
- Grant your Huns the benefit of your interest in the welfare of their families and the condition of their stores; share your riches with those who are loyal and stand in need. They will be certain to willingly follow you into the mouth of hell.
- Care more for the rewarding of your Huns than for rewarding yourself. Your own rewards will then far exceed even your greatest hopes and dreams.
- Never give a Hun a reward that holds no value for yourself.
- Never underestimate the ability of the empire or other foes to gain the support and loyalty of Huns you fail to heed and rightfully reward.
- Be generous with small tokens of appreciation—they will multiply in returned loyalty and service.

— 13 —

ATTILA AND THE POPE

"THE ART OF NEGOTIATION"

S parse rations, contaminated water, intense heat, illness and general listlessness took their toll on the Hunnish horde in the year A.D. 452. The Italian campaign, though unexpectedly successful, was taxing the Huns' endurance.

Still, Rome was ripe for the taking. The Emperor Valentinian sent Pope Leo I to negotiate with Attila. On the banks above, Attila and the pope held a counsel whose content was never revealed.

For whatever reasons history or legend may give, Rome was spared. For, after a time, Attila returned to his mighty horde and turned its march first north and then east to their homeland in the valley of the Danube.

ATTILA ON: "THE ART OF NEGOTIATION"

The techniques of negotiation are not easily taught. Both Hun and chieftain master skills useful in negotiation only through experience.

My negotiations at a time when victory seemed so apparent to my chieftains and warriors, anxious to pillage Rome, were a mystery to them. But it was to our advantage to grant respite.

Your naivete about the ways of negotiation prevents you from understanding my actions with the pope and the subsequent withdrawal of our army from Italy. For this reason, I, Attila, gather you in this council to enlighten you as to how to conduct yourself at those times when you will be required to negotiate for the good of your tribes and perhaps our nation.

- Always maintain the initiative in all negotiations. Be on the offense always—never lose contact with your enemy.
- Always negotiate at the lowest level possible. This will serve to resolve small points of contention before they grow out of proportion and make negotiating impossible.
- Enter negotiations armed with knowledge of the enemy's strengths and weaknesses; knowing his secrets makes you strong and allows you to better deceive him as to your ultimate goals.
- Keep negotiations secret! They must be conducted in private—even as I did with Pope Leo. Only the policies should become public knowledge. How they were negotiated should remain confidential, to avoid loss of face.
- Never rush into negotiations. Time is your ally. It calms temperaments and gives rise to less emotional perspectives.
- Be keenly aware of time. Present appealing alternatives appropriate to your opponent's situation at the moment of your negotiations. Otherwise, he will dismiss your propositions.
- Never arbitrate. Arbitration allows a third party to determine your destiny. It is a tactic of the weak.
- Never make negotiations difficult on immediate, lesser points, at the cost of a greater outcome. Acquiescence on lesser issues softens the spirit of your adversary.
- In negotiation you must take calculated risks. Try to foresee all possible outcomes to determine those that will yield favorable results.
- Be aware of the temperament in your foe's camp. Take advantage of troubles and turmoils that arise during negotiations.
- Never intimidate.
- Honor all commitments made during negotiations lest your enemy fail to trust your word in the future.
- Remember, agreement in principle does not dictate agreement in practice. It does, however, serve to save face at the moment.
- Be bold in facing the inevitable. Acquiesce when resistance would be pointless or when your victory can be gained only at too high a cost.

Now, you mighty chieftains must come to an understanding of a final simple fact. Never gain by battle what may be gained through negotiation. Reserve your warriors for great causes not attainable without waging war.

SURVIVING DEFEAT

"THERE IS ANOTHER DAY"

Though not unfamiliar with toil, struggle, deception and other challenges that regularly attend leaders, Attila was unprepared for defeat on the battlefield.

It was Aetius, his lifelong foe, who had so skillfully led the Roman Legion at the Battle of Chalons, who tore Attila's mighty horde apart.

Attila's will snapped! His confidence in his destiny deserted him! He turned within, ignoring for a time the confusion, shouting and wailing that accompanied the shaken horde as they retreated.

Wandering about his camp, contemplating the errors of the day, Attila was demoralized. It was the darkest moment of his reign. Would he never become master of the world?

Experiencing all of the inner turmoil concomitant with great disappointments, Attila was suffering as all responsible leaders do on such occasions.

Yet, drawing upon his extraordinary inner strengths, Attila marshaled his emotions and regained control of himself.

He would not be distracted from his ambitions! He would reorganize his armies! Introduce new customs to his nation! The Huns would rise again! There would be another day!

ATTILA ON: "THERE IS ANOTHER DAY"

I, Attila, King of Huns, have called this assembly of chieftains and mighty warriors together to kindle the fires of your emotions so that you may not become hopeless in the face of disappointment.

It has been sad for me to suffer so great a defeat. I was simply not prepared for the anguish of so paramount a loss—and my consequent bewilderment—as met me on the Catalaunian Plains.

It is, therefore, incumbent on my office that I prepare you chieftains and future chieftains to deal with disappointment and discouragement.

I will provide you with specific counsel that may become useful in dealing with your own future adversity, for only I can deal with my own defeat.

Therefore, let these guiding principles be known among you.

- No chieftain ever wins every encounter, regardless of how well prepared he is to win.
- If defeat is imminent, don't deny it. Face it and take immediate action to minimize the opponent's gain.
- Retreat is noble when continuance of the battle would result in further losses or total annihilation. In order to return on another day, you must salvage all the warriors and materials possible.
- Momentary loss of self-worth, self-confidence and self-determination are normal emotions that accompany defeat. You must pass through this misery to rid your Hunnish spirit of its depression. Lament, if necessary, but do not dwell too long on your bad moments lest they rise to rule your emotions forever.
- Learn from defeat! If you fail to sharpen your leadership skills after confronting unconquered obstacles, your suffering will be for naught.
- Remember that worthy causes meet with the most resistance—even internal withholding of support and loyalty. If victory is easily gained, you must reconsider the worthiness of your ambitions.
- It is a simple truth that the greater your accomplishments—your victories—the greater the obstacles your enemies throw in your path. Expect it! Don't become a victim of it.
- Reserve a portion of your emotional stamina for those times when to overcome obstacles requires your last resources. Never expend all your energies in the charge when there is the slightest chance you'll have to retreat and regroup.

Alas, the campfire has dwindled. Learn from my agonies. Let these insights fuel your determination to fight another day. For as long as a Hun breathes, all is not lost.

— 15 —

THE BONES OF
CARAVANS PAST

"LESSONS LEARNED"

By nightfall, the Catalaunian Plains were heaped with slain Huns, the aftermath of the Battle of Chalons. Attila's lifelong nemesis, Aetius, had dealt the Hunnish army its only defeat.

Aetius had employed delay tactics at the start of the battle, which he knew would irritate Attila and weaken his army's morale.

Frustrated by the delay in battle, the Huns finally charged in mid-afternoon. The earth shook as thousands upon thousands of Hunnish chargers pounded the ground, tearing headlong into battle.

The shields of the Roman army turned aside the avalanche of arrows that Aetius knew would precede the axes and javelins of the horde.

The fury continued as the Huns, now dismounted, began hand-to-hand combat with the well-trained infantry under Aetius' command.

The Romans' bronze helmets and body armor rendered the stone-headed axes of the horde useless. Their long lances and lariats served only to encumber the horde as the fighting turned savage.

Aetius had used his knowledge of Attila's tactics to the victorious advantage of the Latin and Frankish soldiers who composed his army.

The dazzling brilliance of his horde's accomplishments on battlefields past had not served Attila in his quest to annihilate Aetius' powerful army. Attila, unlike Aetius, had prepared neither himself nor his horde for the struggle on the Catalaunian Plains.

ATTILA ON: "LESSONS LEARNED"

The dreaded enemy led by Aetius used tactics unfamiliar to our noble warriors on the Catalaunian Plains. Many of our brave Huns were lost in a battle for which I simply had not prepared them to fight.

We have held too long to a strategy marked by swift movement, dealing death from horseback with long lances and dragging the enemy to his end by our lariats. Our battle dress and armament has been designed to serve us only under such conditions. They are not suited for infantry warfare against soldiers equipped with shields, helmets and suits of armor. The swords of the enemy have proven superior to our stone axes.

Alas, ours was a plan more aligned with past victories. Our discipline and patience wore thin under the provocation of Aetius' stalling tactics. Our fury was prematurely unleashed, which led to our suffering defeat. We are unaccustomed to losing. We are winners. We must examine the now sun-bleached bones of our lost warriors.

As we howl for our lost ones and ponder our sufferings, we must likewise learn the mighty lessons in them if we are to rise up with the strength of spirited warriors who want not to be at the mercy of the Romans!

Now, I, Attila, must relay to you the learning I accumulated in my study of the bones of caravans past.

- Our army must become more commandable in battle. We must create a new battle plan with a better arrangement of our chieftains and Huns.
- We must refrain from charging prematurely and furiously into unfamiliar situations.
- We must be prepared for new tactics employed by the enemy. We must watch him closely, using our intelligence to detect and assess his likely methods.
- We must never engage an enemy when we are outfitted in inferior battle dress and armament. Future battles with the Romans demand us to cover our leather helmets with metal, to protect our bodies with metal breastplates and to carry shields to turn away the blows of swords. We must use newly forged swords and cast aside our obsolete stone axes.
- Our adroitness as cavalrymen must be supplemented by infan-

try skills. Training in these tactics will balance our abilities to wage war.

- We must add catapults to our arsenal. We cannot expect the high walls of Roman bastions to crumble at the simple beating of our chargers' hoofs.
- We cannot rule the Romans and conquer the world as wandering tribes. We must build fortified cities from which we will send out well-trained armies supplied with the new weapons of a superior arsenal.
- We cannot expect to change our long-held traditions, to reorganize our army and to create great cities without internal opposition. Among you chieftains and Huns will be those whose spirits cling to our past ways. We will show patience with you unenlightened ones. Yet, if you choose not our new course and cause dissension, you will be stricken from our ranks.
- Our vision of the future must build on the strength of the past. Yet, we must anticipate new challenges and opportunities. Suffering another Battle of Chalons is unacceptable.
- We must analyze the past. No bleached bone of a battle-lost Hun can be forgotten as we prepare for the future with new policies and practices. We must plan to once again and forever excel against all enemies and overcome obstacles that stand in the way of our conquering the world.

Now, in ending my counsel on lessons learned from the study of bones of caravans past, I leave you with a parting bit of wisdom. Radical change is only necessary when we fail to learn from our past in anticipating the future. The greatest adversary to abandoning the ineffectiveness of our past is a reluctance among yourselves to support your king, who seeks a new trail to achieving things good for all Huns.

— 16 —

ASHES TO ASHES

"DEPARTING WITH NOBILITY"

His death came unexpectedly. It happened at a time when he was about to lead his reorganized army into a new quest to conquer the empire.

Attila was dead! His warriors and chieftains were stunned! Women wept! Children feared! Their noble king was gone forever! The Hunnish nation had prematurely lost its central figure of unity, pride and leadership.

A legend was gone, but he would long be remembered for his deeds as Attila, King of Huns.

ATTILA ON: "DEPARTING WITH NOBILITY"

Being assigned to any position of leadership over our Huns or tribes is gratifying. It is soon after a new chieftain is appointed that he will either grow or diminish in the eyes of his subordinates, peers and superiors. If he is prudent in the application of his authority, demonstrates a spirit of commitment and sees that all obligations are met, the chieftain will enlarge his stature. Then, he will have gained personal loyalty, trust, confidence and respect from all Huns. Some truly outstanding chieftains may even stir up jealousy in less capable leaders.

Nonetheless, a strong bond will develop between a true chieftain and his Huns. They will begin to emulate him, perhaps speak of him in their casual conversation. They may make him the subject of tales reflecting his courage, persona and accomplishments. In the end, they will ride into the mouth of hell for him, for he becomes more than an ordinary chieftain—he becomes their chieftain, one they are proud to serve.

Old age or death will eventually remove even the most tenured and greatest chieftain from his office. It is a tender moment in the lives of all who have developed strong bonds of loyalty when the former chieftain passes on and a new one is appointed in his place. This transition must be made with adroitness, diplomacy and protocol. For this purpose, I provide this counsel regarding departure with nobility.

- It is the wise chieftain who prepares himself for the time when a new chieftain will take charge. This preparation should be made over time, to avoid precipitating insecurity or loss of commitment.
- It is noble for the departing chieftain to express gratitude to all who have served him well, especially recognizing ways in which they have made him stronger.
- It is noble for Huns to honor their departing chieftain, giving recognition and appreciation for his service.
- It is noble for the departing chieftain to voice his confidence that the new chieftain will serve his Huns well, perhaps even improving their conditions. This reduces insecurity for the Huns who remain.
- It is noble for the departing chieftain to leave his command forever, never attempting to return, lest he subvert the authority of the new chieftain. Such action by the old chieftain would be destructive, even if invited by seemingly innocent appeal from Huns who once trusted his counsel. Every appeal of this nature should be denied, and the former chieftain should reaffirm his commitment to the new one by directing the Huns to seek counsel from their rightful leader.
- Regardless of the conditions under which a former chieftain departs his camp—no matter how distasteful or dishonorable— the new leaders should neither encourage nor tolerate disrespectful talk of him. Speaking ill will most certainly tarnish the stature of the new leader.
- If the old chieftain should depart prematurely, without warning or preparation, confusion will reign in the camp. Those who rank highest, the senior Huns and chieftains, must quickly form a council and choose a new leader. For, in dire circumstances,

our Huns look to their chieftain for strength, courage and direction.

Even as I, Attila, King of Huns, must someday be succeeded in my reign, my reflections and memories will be sweet only if I feel I have prepared the nation for this inevitable moment. And, if I have prepared you well, you will continue to be a nation of united tribes who seek to improve life for the Huns. For loyalty should not be solely placed in a man—no matter how great his personal magnetism. Loyalty of the Huns should have balance in the commitment of all to serve as a unified nation of Huns without hesitation, no matter who reigns over you.

ATTILAISMS: SELECTED THOUGHTS OF ATTILA

ADVICE AND COUNSEL

- Written reports have purpose only if read by the king.
- A king with chieftains who always agree with him reaps the counsel of mediocrity.
- A wise chieftain never kills the Hun bearing bad news. Rather, the wise chieftain kills the Hun who fails to deliver bad news.
- A chieftain who asks the wrong questions always hears the wrong answers.
- A wise chieftain never asks a question for which he doesn't want to hear the answer.

CHARACTER

- The greatness of a Hun is measured by the sacrifices he is willing to make for the good of the nation.
- A chieftain does not have to be brilliant to be successful, but he must have an insatiable hunger for victory, absolute belief in his cause and an invincible courage that enables him to resist those who would otherwise discourage him.
- Seldom are self-centered, conceited and self-admiring chieftains great leaders, but they are great idolizers of themselves.
- Great chieftains never take themselves too seriously.

- A wise chieftain adapts—he doesn't compromise.
- Chieftains who drink with their Huns become one with them and are no longer their chieftain.
- Weak chieftains surround themselves with weak Huns.
- Strong chieftains surround themselves with strong Huns.
- As a chieftain achieves greater success, the jealousy others feel for him intensifies.

COURAGE

- Huns must learn early that working through a hardship is an experience that influences them all the days of their lives.
- Successful Huns learn to deal with adversity and to overcome mistakes.
- A Hun can achieve anything, if he is willing to pay the price. Competition thins out at the top of the ranks.

DECISION MAKING

- Every decision involves some risk.
- Time does not always improve a situation for a king or his Huns.
- Fundamental errors are inescapable when the unqualified are allowed to exercise judgment and make decisions.
- Quick decisions are not always the best decisions. On the other hand, unhurried decisions are not always the best decisions.
- It is unfortunate when final decisions are made by chieftains headquartered miles away from the front, where they can only guess at conditions and potentialities known only to the captain on the battlefield.
- The ability to make difficult decisions separates chieftains from Huns.

DELEGATION

- Wise chieftains never place their Huns in situations where their weaknesses will prevail over their strengths.
- Good Huns normally achieve what their chieftain expects from them.

- A wise chieftain never expects his Huns to act beyond their wisdom and understanding.
- A wise chieftain always gives tough assignments to Huns who can rise to the occasion.
- Abdication is not delegation. Abdication is a sign of weakness. Delegation is a sign of strength.

DEVELOPING CHIEFTAINS

- Strong chieftains always have strong weaknesses. A king's duty is to make a chieftain's strengths prevail.
- Huns learn less from success than they do from failure.
- Huns learn much faster when faced with adversity.
- A good chieftain takes risks by delegating responsibilities to an inexperienced Hun in order to strengthen his leadership abilities.
- Huns are best prepared to become chieftains when given appropriate challenges at successively higher levels of responsibility.
- If it were easy to be a chieftain, everyone would be one.
- Without challenge, a Hun's potential is never realized.
- Appropriate stress is essential in developing chieftains.

DIPLOMACY AND POLITICS

- When in a political war, a Hun must always keep an eye to the rear.
- The essence of Hunnish victory lies in the answers to the questions Where? and When?
- Huns should engage only in wars they can win.
- Huns may enter war as the result of failed diplomacy; however, war may be necessary for diplomacy to begin.
- For Huns, conflict is a natural state.
- Huns only make enemies on purpose.

GOALS

- A Hun's goals should always be worthy of his efforts.
- Superficial goals lead to superficial results.

- As a nation, we would accomplish more if Huns behaved as though national goals were as important to them as personal goals.
- Critical to a Hun's success is a clear understanding of what the king wants.
- Chieftains should always aim high, going after things that will make a difference rather than seeking the safe path of mediocrity.

LEADERS AND LEADERSHIP

- Kings should appoint their best Huns as chieftains, no matter how much they are needed in their current position.
- Never appoint acting chieftains. Put the most capable Hun in charge, give him both responsibility and authority, then hold him accountable.
- A wise chieftain never depends on luck. Rather, he always trusts his future to hard work, stamina, tenacity and a positive attitude.
- Shared risk-taking will weld the relationship of a chieftain and his Huns.
- Strong chieftains stimulate and inspire the performance of their Huns.
- A chieftain can never be in charge if he rides in the rear.

PERCEPTIONS AND PUBLICITY

- In tough times, the nation will always call the meanest chieftain to lead.
- A Hun's perception is reality for him.
- Huns who appear to be busy are not always working.
- It is best if your friends and foes speak well of you; however, it is better for them to speak poorly of you than not at all. When nothing can be said of a Hun, he has probably accomplished nothing very well.
- Contrary to what most chieftains think, you're not remembered by what you did in the past, but by what most Huns think you did.

PERSONAL ACHIEVEMENT

- There is more nobility in being a good Hun than in being a poor chieftain.
- If all Huns were blind, a one-eyed warrior would be king.
- Great chieftains accept failure at some things in order to excel in more important ones.
- Every Hun is responsible for shaping his life's circumstances and experiences into success—no other Hun, and certainly no Roman, can do for a Hun what he neglects to do for himself.

PROBLEMS AND SOLUTIONS

- Huns should be taught to focus on opportunities rather than on problems.
- Some Huns have solutions for which there are no problems.

REWARD AND PUNISHMENT

- If an incompetent chieftain is removed, seldom do we appoint his highest-ranking subordinate to his place. For when a chieftain has failed, so likewise have his subordinate leaders.
- If you tell a Hun he is doing a good job when he isn't, he will not listen long and, worse, will not believe praise when it is justified.

TOLERANCE

- Every Hun has value—even if only to serve as a bad example.
- To benefit from the strength of chieftains we must tolerate some of their weaknesses.
- Suffer long for mediocre but loyal Huns. Suffer not for competent but disloyal Huns.

TRAINING

- Adequate training of Huns is essential to war and cannot be disregarded by chieftains during times of peace.
- Teachable skills are for developing Huns. Learnable skills are reserved for chieftains.

THE ENIGMA
OF
JAPANESE
POWER

PEOPLE AND POLITICS IN A
STATELESS NATION

———

KAREL VAN WOLFEREN

EDITOR'S NOTE

A correspondent for the Dutch newspaper NRC Handelsblad *and a 25-year resident of Japan, Karel van Wolferen presents a startling thesis in* The Enigma Of Japanese Power. *He maintains that the problem with Japan is that no one is in charge. According to van Wolferen, Japan's economy is in the hands of a ruling class of bureaucrats, top businessmen, and one section of the dominant Liberal Democratic Party—components of a political entity he calls the "System." Here the power is "diffused over a number of semi-self-contained, semi-mutually dependent bodies which are neither responsible to an electorate nor, ultimately, subservient to one another." He shows that the System is inexorably programmed to a post-war policy of industrial expansion that it has no power to alter. His description of the System goes a long way toward explaining why the rest of the world cannot persuade Japan to moderate its one-sided economic policies.*

To support his argument, van Wolferen shows how the System dominates everyday life from the regimentation of school children to the high-pressure tactics used by companies to control every aspect of their employees' lives. In the course of explaining the interworkings of the System, van Wolferen shatters many myths that have long dominated Western thinking about the Japanese.

Van Wolferen urges Westerners to recognize that the Japanese operate simultaneously on two levels: the way things are and the way they seem. One reason there are so many misunderstandings between Japan and other countries is that Westerners mistakenly accept what the Japanese say at face value, while the Japanese are forever trying to figure out what Westerners really mean.

The Enigma Of Japanese Power *does not engage in Japan bashing. It is an intelligent analysis of the conditions underlying Japan's difficulties with the West. The book's benefit to American business people is a simple explanation of what they are up against. According to van Wolferen: "The greatest apparent international advantage the Japanese System has enjoyed so far lies in Western misconceptions concerning the nature of the Japanese challenge. The United States has been especially vulnerable to Japan's industrial onslaught in that the U.S. government agencies overseeing interests in this respect have no institutional memory. Every two years or so U.S. officials must learn afresh that the Japanese economy does not operate in the same way as their own."*

I

THE JAPAN PROBLEM

J apan perplexes the world. It has become a major world power, yet it does not behave the way most of the world expects a world power to behave. Its formidable economic presence has made it a source of apprehension both to the Western countries and to some of its Asian neighbours. Its relationship with the United States and Europe is in serious trouble. In the late 1980s, the West is beginning to harbour doubts about Japan as a responsible partner in politics and trade. In Japan, it has become common for officials and commentators to suggest that their country has fallen victim to widespread international ill-will and to dismiss unfavourable analyses as "Japan-bashing."

For almost two decades Westerners have been advised to have patience with Japan. It was argued that the Japanese understood the necessity of adjustments and were speeding up their efforts at internationalisation. A sustained publicity campaign, with the appropriate slogans popping up in innumerable speeches and articles, seemed to confirm this. But in the late 1980s, an awareness is gradually taking hold in the West that the long-promised changes are not forthcoming. In the meantime, increased criticism, the first retaliatory measures and other forms of pressure from frustrated trading partners, particularly the United States, have changed the disposition of officials and commentators on the Japanese side. Their friendly counselling of patience has begun to change into a more belligerent message: the USA should put its own house in order, and Europe should stop being lazy and recognise its "advanced nation disease" for what it is. Both sides have expressed a firm resolve to avoid an economic war, but around 1987 some people on both sides began to realise that they were in the middle of one.

For most observers the Japan Problem, as the conflicts have collectively become known, is summed up in Japan's annual record-breaking trade surpluses: $44 billion in 1984, $56 billion in 1985, $93 billion in

1986. The near doubling of the exchange rate of the yen against the dollar caused a lower surplus of some $76 billion in 1987.

But the essence of the Japan Problem lies beyond such figures. Not only does Japan export more than it imports, but its exports, in combination with its inhospitality to foreign products, undermine Western industries. The term "adversarial trade" was coined by Peter Drucker to distinguish the Japanese method from competitive trade, in which a country imports products of the same kind as it exports. West Germany's trade surpluses are also very large, but West Germany practices competitive trade, as does the USA. With sectors such as consumer electronics and semiconductors—the bases for more specialised industries—being taken over almost completely by Japanese firms, Westerners fear they may suffer a gradual de-industrialisation. Once it has obtained the required technology, Japanese industry appears capable of taking over from the original inventors and developers in any field.

Having hitherto focused almost exclusively on the trade surpluses, in 1988 the West was coming to suspect that other astonishing developments might form part of an overall pattern of Japanese pursuits, a significant national endeavour, which is hardly understood at all. Months after the New York and London stock-market crash of October 1987—which hardly seemed to affect Tokyo's stock market at all—prices of Japanese stock reached new, and by Western standards astonishing, heights when measured against corporate earnings. Land prices in many areas of Tokyo doubled, tripled or even quadrupled within the space of one year. And from around 1986, Japanese firms, often spending significantly more than warranted by market value, suddenly began to invest very heavily in foreign real estate and to buy foreign banks and corporations. Somewhat belatedly, it began to dawn on a few anxious US and European observers that Japan, far from beating the West at its own game, might not be playing the Western game at all; and that for the West, conversely, to emulate Japan would eventually lead to the collapse of the non-communist international economic order.

Europe and the United States are, to say the least, disturbed by this entity in the Pacific Ocean that appears to be single-mindedly pursuing some obscure aim of its own. One can understand the Japanese wanting to make money, but their conquest of ever greater foreign market shares does not translate into more rewarding lives. Urban housing is cramped and extraordinarily costly. The cost of living is exorbitantly high. Only about one-third of Japanese homes are connected with sewers. Commuter trains are extremely overcrowded. The road system is ridiculously inadequate. These and other deficiencies leave average Japanese city dwellers with a lower standard of comfort than that enjoyed by their counterparts in less wealthy European countries. Nor has the flourishing of trade and industry been accompanied by any flourishing of the arts.

A number of thoughtful Japanese have concluded that something is amiss. A nationalistic anthropologist laments the fact that his country is like a black hole in space, receiving culture but not transmitting any. A respected intellect and former vice-minister diagnoses his compatriots as suffering from a Peter Pan Syndrome, refusing to grow up, asking each other what the world can do for them.

The question of what drives the Japanese has thus become something of an international conundrum. For what ultimate purpose do they deprive themselves of comfort and risk the enmity of the world?

It is usually explained that the Japanese are driven by collective concerns. As far as outsiders can tell, most Japanese accept with equanimity the daily demands that they subordinate their individual desires and interests to those of the community. This striking communalism is, however, the result of political arrangements made by a ruling elite over three centuries ago, and the Japanese are today given little or no choice in accepting these arrangements. A Japanese individual must accept as inevitable that his intellectual and psychological growth is restrained by the will of the collectivity. To sugar the pill, this supposedly collective will is presented by most of his superiors as benevolent and wholly determined by a unique culture.

But this explanation does not answer the question of where this political force comes from. The power that systematically suppresses individualism in Japan does not emanate from a harsh central regime. Japan differs as much from the collectivist communist states in Eastern Europe and Asia as it does from the free-market states of the West.

Much of the bafflement over Japan is due to a relative lack of interest on the part of Western intellectuals and people of affairs. Certainly, Japan is visited by many Westerners, but to a large extent it is still treated as a curiosity. One-sided ignorance is particularly striking in the case of the United States, considering that its relationship with Japan is among the strategically most important in the world. In fact, the view of Japanese politics apparent between the lines of statements and articles by US officials is often so faulty as to appall observers who believe that nobody in the non-communist world is served by a serious deterioration in the US-Japan relationship.

The uncommon manner in which power is exercised in Japan and the workings of the Japanese institutions responsible for the country's non-dictatorial collectivism and national motivation have received scant attention. Japan is often lumped together with Europe and the United States in discussions of the supposed "post-industrial," "technetronic" or "post-capitalistic" society, while the question of how Japan is actually ruled remains neglected.

It is curious that this should be so. Japan was the first non-Western country in modern times to play a major international role. It defeated Russia shortly after the turn of the century, became the only country ever to attack the United States, has since produced the second largest and, in terms of per capita income, most prosperous economy, has wiped out or is threatening with extinction a number of its trading partners' industries and is gaining important financial leverage over the world economy. Moreover, two other non-Western countries, South Korea and Taiwan, have become significant industrial presences by following the Japanese, instead of the Western, example of industrialisation.

Inattention to the question of how power is exercised in Japan and how this determines its international relationships is becoming dangerous. Japan has been much praised since the 1960s, but it has also been much vilified, and from the perspective of Tokyo in 1988, the antipathy appears to have overtaken the praise. Western criticism may well reawaken xenophobic sentiments in Japan and strengthen the old suspicion that, in essence, the world does not want to make room for it. The resulting strengthened nationalism, of which the first signs are already appearing, could mean political instability in Japan and undesirable developments for everyone. Under such circumstances, a better understanding of the nature and uses of power in Japan is no luxury.

CONFUSING FICTIONS

The factor most corrosive of international trust is perhaps the confusion that exists on many levels of communication between Japan and its supposed allies and friends—the apparent impossibility, even, of reaching a point at which both sides can agree to disagree. Several commonly cherished fictions cloud the perception of outsiders, two of them being central to their seeming inability to come to grips with Japan.

The Fiction of Responsible Central Government

First, there is the fiction that Japan is a sovereign state like any other, a state with central organs of government that can bear ultimate responsibility for national decision-making. This is an illusion that is very difficult to dispel.

Nevertheless, unless the relative lack of governmental responsibility in Japan, the fundamental cause of mutual frustration, is recognised, relations with Japan are bound to deteriorate further. Statecraft in Japan is quite different from in Europe and America. For centuries it has entailed a balance between semi-autonomous groups that share in power. Today, the most powerful groups include certain ministry officials, some political cliques and clusters of bureaucrat-businessmen. There are many lesser ones, such as the agricultural cooperatives, the police, the press and the gangsters. All are components of what we may call the System in order to distinguish it, for reasons to be discussed later, from the state. No one is ultimately in charge. These semi-autonomous components, each endowed with discretionary powers, are not represented by any central body that rules the roost.

It is important to distinguish this situation from others where governments are besieged by special interest groups, or are unable to make up their minds because of inter-departmental disputes. We are dealing not with lobbies but with a structural phenomenon. There is, to be sure, a hierarchy or, rather, a complex of overlapping hierarchies. But it has no peak; it is a truncated pyramid. There is no place where, as Harry Truman would have said, the buck stops.

If Japan seems to be in the world but not of it, this is because its prime minister and other power-holders are incapable of delivering on promises that may require important adjustments by one of the components of the System. The field of domestic power normally leaves no room for an accommodation to foreign wishes. Such accommodation is made only with great reluctance and very late in the day, when angry outsiders resort to coercion.

The Free-Market Fiction

The second of the central fictions that have determined Western attitudes since shortly after the Second World War is that Japan belongs in that loose category known as "capitalist, free-market" economies.

Defining the Japanese economy causes trouble to foreigners and to

Japanese alike. Japanese officials are usually indignant at any hint that Japan does not belong in the club of free-market nations. Japan is obviously not a centrally controlled, Soviet-type economy. Does it, then, belong to a category of its own? The rise of South Korea and Taiwan as industrial states, apparently driven by an extraordinary force similar to that of Japan, suggests that the Japanese economic miracle, even minus its cultural and psychological specifics, can provide a model for certain other countries.

The Japanese, Korean and Taiwanese experiences show that a third category of political economy can exist, beside the Western and communist types. US political scientist Chalmers Johnson has labelled this category of industrial nations "capitalist developmental states" (CDSs). The strength of the CDS lies in its partnership between bureaucrats and industrialists; it is a variant that traditional political and economic theory has overlooked.

Some economists question the viability of government interference in the economy. Friedrich von Hayek argues that planners at the centre can never know enough about the many ramifications of social and economic life to make the right decisions. Yet if this theory is true, how have Japan, South Korea and Taiwan, whose governments consider manufacturing and trade very much their business, managed to improve their national wealth?

The manner in which Japan, South Korea and Taiwan have found a way around the Hayekian obstacle is crucial to an understanding of their political economies. To begin with, their governments have never considered private enterprise antagonistic. Unlike the communist approach, which equates entrepreneurship with original sin, or the socialist approach of the European welfare state, where regulations obstruct the entrepreneur, the capitalist developmental state encourages the private sector. The bureaucrats never attempt to gain full power over non-governmental corporations. They guide the economy, using businessmen as their antennae. They get to know what is happening far from the centre by constantly monitoring capitalists as they try to find new ways of expanding their businesses.

The mistakes these officials undoubtedly make are more than compensated for by the unifying force they bring to bear on industrial development. The economy prospers because areas of industry that show promise are stimulated by fiscal policies favouring investment. Industries considered of strategic importance are protected against genuine foreign competition. Those that are in trouble are temporarily protected to give them an opportunity to diversify, while those that have reached a dead end are more easily abandoned by policies forcing reorganisations. In other words, this is a partnership sealed by a shared industrial policy and trade strategy. Market freedom is not considered a goal desirable in itself but one of several instruments for achieving the paramount aim of industrial expansion.

Japan pioneered the CDS model a century or so ago, during the Meiji period. It further experimented with it during the forced industrial development of Manchuria, from the early 1930s until 1945. In its post-war form this economic model is structurally protectionist. It has to stay so if it wants to continue enjoying its proven benefits.

Malleable Realities

The question of whether or not Japan represents a largely unchartered economic and social-political category generates much controversy. Clarifications from the Japanese side do not help settle the controversy. Journalists and academics, moreover, wrongly apply Western concepts in discussing their society, with the result that the unsuspecting observer is nearly always misled as to how things actually work.

It is not at all difficult for the Japanese to maintain such fictions, because it is socially acceptable in Japan for reality to consist not of the results of objective observations but of the way things are supposed to be. How things are supposed to be tends to coincide with the immediate interests of one's group. For the past four centuries the Japanese people have been told to consider socio-political loyalty as the supreme virtue. The result, as one anthropologist has put it, is that truth is socially constituted. Here we arrive at the first conceptual problem Japan has in store for the outside observer.

In the West, reality is not seen as depending on arbitrary ideas of how things *should* be. Indeed, Western philosophy — as well as Western horse sense — decrees that the human capacity for self-deceit be countered by a constant watchfulness against illusions and delusions. If there is one single command that has reverberated throughout Western intellectual development, it is: Thou shalt not cherish contradictions.

Heirs to various Asian traditions of thought may be less uncomfortable with the idea of multiple and contradictory truth, but nowhere does one find as much management of reality as in Japan. This has important political consequences. Japanese show great agility in moving from one reality to another as they seek to explain facts and motives.

A rationally argued claim made by the other side may be countered by arguments belonging to an altogether different frame of reference. In international exchanges these tactics sometimes exasperate logically reasoning Westerners. One must be prepared for the skilful use of red herrings. Occasionally these are too crude to be effective, as when new regulations threatening the import of European skis were defended with the argument that Japanese snow tends to be constituted differently from snow in the West.

In Japan the flexible approach to reality goes far beyond the bounds within which other societies tolerate lame excuses and self-serving untruths. For instance, when a Western businessman appeals to a contract or an international agreement, he may be told that Japanese society is guided not so much by cold rules as by warm human feelings responding to each situation as it occurs. Yet should the foreigner, at the next opportunity, appeal to this extra-legal tradition, he may well hear that democratic Japan is governed by laws. Both these arguments—that Japanese society is humanly flexible, and that it sticks to what the law says—are uttered with great conviction, and Japanese third parties are hardly ever inclined to point out the contradiction.

The Crucial Factor

The tolerance of contradiction is closely connected with a characteristic that, in the final analysis, is the most crucial factor determining Japan's socio-political reality. It is the near absence of any idea that there can be truths, rules, principles or morals that always apply, no matter what the circumstances.

Concepts of independent, universal truths or immutable religious beliefs, transcending the worldly reality of social dictates and the decrees of power-holders, have of course found their way into Japan, but they have never taken root. Political arrangements and social practices were originally sanctioned by Shinto, a religion of nature and ancestor-worship that tolerated contradiction and ambiguity. This indigenous Japanese religion (not to be confused with the "state Shinto" that provided the ideological underpinnings of the Japanese empire from the late nineteenth century until 1945) never developed philosophical or moral doctrines. Even when such philosophical and moral teachings were imported from China, they did not displace domestic sanctions and assumptions that supported the power-holders of the day.

The notions transcending the here-and-now of socio-political expediency that are inherent in the original teachings of Confucianism and Buddhism have always been unwelcome to Japan's ruling elite. Christianity and, later, Marxism, which both threatened to introduce transcendental concepts, were either proscribed or forced to compromise their essential tenets. The accepted view that Japan has always displayed great religious tolerance applies only where new religions or belief-systems have not been deemed a threat to existing political arrangements.

To grasp the essence of a political culture that does not recognise transcendental truths demands an unusual intellectual effort for Westerners. The Occidental intellectual and moral traditions are so deeply rooted in assumptions of the universal validity of certain beliefs that the possibility of a culture without such assumptions is hardly ever contemplated. Westerners take it for granted that all advanced civilizations develop concepts of universal validity, and they are therefore not prompted to examine the effects of their absence.

True, the fact that the Japanese have situational instead of general moral rules is routinely noticed in writing on Japan. But most authors, having dutifully mentioned that the Japanese continually adjust their beliefs to the situation they find themselves in, move on to other topics as though totally unaware of the momentousness of this observation.

Buffers and Propagandists

Two important phenomena complicate the communication-gap aspect of the Japan Problem. One is Japan's use of "buffers." The second is its monumental propaganda effort.

By "buffer" I refer to someone entrusted with the task of making contacts with foreigners as smooth as possible. Foreign diplomats and businessmen deal with Japan through an intermediary community of English-speaking buffers who are expected to absorb the shocks that an unpredictable outside world might deliver.

These buffers can convey a genuine understanding of the foreigner's difficulties and often create an impression of reasonableness with which the institutions they represent consider the foreigner's problems. Japan has a handful of super-buffers who spend much of their time travelling the globe, trouble-shooting and explaining the Japanese case at international conferences. Some of them were made ministers for external economic affairs, in which roles they only increased the confusion, because in spite of their title they had no mandate to decide anything.

Sometimes leaders of economic federations or the prime minister himself play the buffer role when speaking with foreign trade envoys. Foreign negotiators who arrive home with the news that this time they have really talked with the proper authorities, who are ready to take effective actions, are deceiving themselves. People with such broad authority do not exist in Japan.

Overlapping with the buffer category is a class of informants who are constantly being interviewed by visiting dignitaries and journalists. The rest of the world learns about Japan via the accounts of a much smaller group than is generally appreciated. Visitors who have met a "good source" in the shape of one of these informants are often under the impression that they have heard an interesting personal opinion. Most are unaware that these informants tend to regurgitate currently circulating platitudes that convey an official reality to which they routinely defer.

It often seems as if all Japanese spokesmen are hooked up to the same prompter with the same loop of tape. The predictable message may include criticism of certain points of government policy or of business attitudes. But they practically always support the System's larger contentions: that Japan is a pluralist democracy with a free-market economy, that progress is being made in opening the market, that the growth of individualism must be stimulated, that most Japanese are beginning to see the need to become more cosmopolitan, that foreigners do not try hard enough to compete and that conflict with Japan arises mainly from foreign misunderstanding.

Japan's buffers and informants constitute a propaganda effort that is not recognised for what it is, because it comes almost entirely in the guise of sincere efforts to explain Japan to the world. The propaganda is all the more convincing because many informants believe these explanations.

Foreigners also play an important role in the dissemination of opinion favourable to the System. No country has ever spent as much on officially recorded lobbying expenses as the Japanese were spending in Washington in the mid- and late 1980s. The Japanese government and corporations hire the best lawyers and former administration officials to defend their position. A large proportion of academic research on Japan by Western scholars is funded by Japanese institutions. And access to personal contacts and institutions is a great problem for businessmen and scholars working in Japan, who are acutely aware that a genuinely critical stance may close doors. Consequently, a combination of well-spent money and the need for access, as well as political innocence, has bred large numbers of Japan specialists who are in varying degrees—however unwittingly—apologists for Japan.

Japanese propaganda is also spread, consciously as well as inadvertently, by newspaper and magazine editors mindful of the convention of telling the imagined two sides of a story. And it has had an impressive effect, as can be gathered from the fact that at the time of this writing many in the US continue to think that market forces can ultimately solve the bilateral problem with Japan, notwithstanding the systematic Japanese protectionism that has been staring them in the face for more than two decades.

The Aura of Inscrutability

The idea that there is a spiritual dimension to being Japanese, which by definition cannot be grasped by foreigners, is an important ingredient for Japanese self-esteem and therefore widely believed.

A top editor on one of Japan's five national dailies once told me that his paper could print practically anything foreigners said, no matter how devastating their criticism might be, because readers could always console themselves with their belief in the ultimate inability of foreigners to understand the more subtle aspects of what they were describing.

It is almost an article of faith among Japanese that their culture is unique, not in the way that all cultures are unique, but somehow uniquely unique, ultimately different from all others, the source of unique Japanese sensibilities. Western intellectual support for the idea of the utter strangeness of Japan, which is easily converted into the idea of uniqueness, goes back many centuries. When it was still "on the other side of the world," Marco Polo turned Zippangu (as he called Japan) into something mysterious and paradisiacal, imagining roofs of solid gold on its emperor's palace. The first Westerner to interpret Japan in modern times, Lafcadio Hearn, wrote just before the turn of the century of the immense difficulty of perceiving and comprehending what underlies the surface of Japanese life. In 1946, Ruth Benedict published an appraisal of the Japanese as "the most alien enemy the United States had ever fought in an all-out struggle."

Ruth Benedict's interpretation of Japan as a cohesive entity that can stand on its own, culturally cut off from the rest of the world and essentially different from it, has remained seductive to many serious observers. Physical isolation can no longer be blamed for this. In 1962, I was one of 202,181 foreigners entering the country, and in that year only 145,749 Japanese travelled abroad. Twenty-five years later some six and a half million Japanese went overseas, and over two million foreigners visited Japan. But despite this, much of the earlier aura of remoteness has remained.

When studying a people by comparing them to other peoples one faces the age-old choice of whether to emphasise sameness or otherness. In the case of Japan this has led to great discrepancies in the views held by commentators. No important human practices and attitudes found elsewhere in the world are entirely unknown to the Japanese. Conversely, in other countries one can recognise habits and institutions corresponding with those in Japan. But to describe the Japanese experience often requires the addition of such phrases as "much more so" or "much less so." There is a point at which differences in degree add up to a difference in kind.

At the Crossroads

Countless newspaper articles, magazine features and scholarly assessments have asserted over the past quarter-century that Japan had reached a crossroads. Perhaps no other country is so regularly examined for signs of impending change: not just the routine kind of change expected in any society, but something basic.

Implicit in most reports on the Japan-at-the-crossroads theme is the idea that Japan *must* change; the things setting Japan apart from the rest of the world are seen as anomalous and temporary. In the 1960s, it was widely believed that Japanese youth was going to change things once it had reached positions of influence. At the same time, demands by labour were going to bring about drastic changes. In the 1970s, it was thought that the many employees who went abroad for their corporations were going to internationalise Japan upon their return, and that widespread hankering after better living conditions would change Japanese priorities. Later it became fashionable to think that the internationalism of the Japanese financial market would force Japan to come to terms with the outside world's expectations of greater Japanese concern on behalf of collective international interests. In 1987, there existed a pervasive notion that the pressure of a supposed public demand for change, combined with loss of bureaucratic control over businessmen, was beginning to transform the Japanese economy into one more clearly driven by market forces.

Today, Japan is stuck at the same crossroads as twenty-five years ago: the march in the direction that many Western observers thought inevitable is just not going to take place.

In the late 1970s, Japanese officials began to fight back by contending that, if there was going to be evolution anywhere, it would be in the West. A government-sponsored publication spelled this out, saying that Japanese forms of social and economic management would become universal in all advanced industrial societies.

Around this time the idea caught on in Europe and the United States that a number of Japanese practices might profitably be adopted. This is understandable. The question of whether the West should not be moving towards a society similar to that of Japan inevitably arises in the minds of visitors who learn that Japan has next to no violent crime, no labour conflicts and an economic system that seems to weather oil crises and the like better than anyone else's. But the "learn from Japan" approach has glossed over some crucial differences. The adoption of parts of the System is not likely to work without the rest of the Japanese package, and the costs of that package in terms of social and intellectual freedom cannot be paid by the West.

There is reason to emphasise Japanese differences precisely because the crossroads view persists. Many Western analysts continue to expect large-scale change. Japanese slogans about internationalisation are taken at face value. The official Japanese line in the 1980s was that governmental guidance carries much less weight with the private sector than in the past. But even though this contention is accompanied with figures intended to show that current tariff regulations make Japan about the freest market in the world, Japan has not in fact transferred into a free-market economy. What is true on paper in Japan is often not true in practice. Foreign governments and columnists continue to expect major developments, but barring some great upheaval, it is unlikely that Japanese institutions will come to mesh more smoothly with the outside world, because this would entail the break-up of the bureaucracy-business partnership that forms the heart of the System.

The crossroads view should be discarded for yet another reason. It creates frustrations when expected changes fail to materialise, and ultimately leads to further vilification of Japan.

So we are left with the Lafcadio Hearn-Ruth Benedict thesis of cultural singularity. But this approach fails to relate Japan to any wider, universally understandable realm of human experience. It is also, on a more practical level, powerless to help foreign governments and businesses formulate a modus vivendi with Japan.

There is, however, a way out of the maze. The Japan problem appears less mysterious, and many of the puzzles are soluble, when instead of looking for cultural explanations we ask questions concerning the way power is exercised in Japan.

THE NEGLECTED ROLE OF POWER

Japanese politics is still largely portrayed (very enthusiastically so by Japan's official spokesmen) as obeying cultural dictates. Japanese authors practically always take it for granted that their world is a product of the predilections of past generations. They do not give the impression that there have been power-holders at every stage with the means to organise the lives of those they controlled. Such reductionism is all the more remarkable because, if there is one nation whose predominant social and cultural idiosyncrasies can be traced back to political decisions, it is Japan.

Looking back over its history, it is clear that Japan's relative isolation meant that the elite could control the inflow and the impact of foreign culture, picking and choosing from among what the rest of the world had to offer those techniques and attitudes best calculated to consolidate their own positions. Such wide control over culture meant a near absolute control over potentially subversive thinking.

Political Control Over Culture

It is generally acknowledged that Chinese ideas and methods have helped shape official Japanese culture to a greater extent than any other influence. Apart from the writing system and the techniques and styles of artistic production, these cultural imports primarily served political purposes. In the sixth century Japan's rulers adopted Buddhism, explaining that they did so for political reasons. The introduction of the Chinese model of state administration was obviously also a political move.

Diplomatic channels to China were subsequently closed, and were kept closed until 1401, when shogun Ashikaga Yoshimitsu established trade relations with the Ming court. In spite of the huge profits and many luxuries this brought Yoshimitsu, his successors again put a stop to the Chinese traffic.

From the middle of the sixteenth century the Portuguese were allowed to bring their firearms, medicine, astronomy, clocks and, most significantly, their religion. But this hospitality was reversed not long after the turn of the century, when the shogun began to fear the potential threat posed by a Lord beyond the clouds towards whom his underlings could redirect their sense of loyalty. The result of this political insight was a policy of almost hermetic seclusion until the middle of the nineteenth century.

The new set of rulers that came in with the Meiji Restoration of 1868 promoted the import of practically anything their official missions to the United States and Europe considered useful for a new Japan. When this, inevitably, resulted in the spread of subversive ideas, they clamped down and began propagating an ancient tradition, which they had manufactured from bits and pieces of earlier political ideology, glorifying the emperor as head of the Japanese family state.

Until 1945, Japanese power-holders had a special police force with the task of eliminating "dangerous thoughts." Former officers of that police force became ministers of education, justice, labour, home affairs and welfare after the war. And the essential character of Japanese nationalism in the 1990s is still determined by notions incorporated in the mythology fabricated by the Meiji oligarchy.

No intellectual leverage over the power of the political elite was possible, since the notion of a universal or transcendental truth was never permitted to embed itself in Japanese thought. The power-holders could control even this; indeed, no law ever restrained their power. It is, thus, no exaggeration to say that political arrangements have been crucial in determining the limits on Japanese religious life and thought.

Power patterns have both directed and inhibited Japanese intellectual pursuits. Ideas of justice and the place of law in society have been fashioned by rules in terms of expediency and have not influenced the attitudes and methods of those rulers in any critical way. Supposedly typical aspects of Japanese society and culture, such as group life, company loyalty, the love of harmony, the lack of individualism, and the near absence of litigation, ultimately originate in political arrangements and are sustained for political purposes.

So long as Japan is considered primarily in social and cultural terms, one always runs up against a basic question: what is the origin of the great differences between the Japanese and other peoples? Part of the answer lies in Japan's historical isolation. But it is the political approach that can answer the question most satisfyingly, since it makes it possible to recognise the strong forces behind the shaping of Japanese society.

Exposing Political Motives

By recognising Japanese power where we should, we see things we would otherwise not be aware of. One is that the System as such is in better shape than at any other time in this century. The defeat in the Second World War and the Occupation represent less of a watershed in Japanese political life than has generally been thought. The pre-war and wartime bureaucratic power system, minus its components, consolidated its power after the war, and is in the process of consolidating it even further.

The political perspective also affords a fresh view of Japanese international business dealings. It has long been agreed that the priority of the large Japanese corporations is the expansion of market shares rather than medium-term profits. And it has often been noticed that, in order to achieve their strategic aims, they will forgo profits for much longer periods than Western firms could possibly afford. Enlarging one's market share, like enlarging the territory one controls, depends on the desire for greater power, a political motive. Making maximum profits depends on a desire for money, an economic motive. The two approaches are, of course, related and mixed in both Western and Japanese corporations, but the results of the difference in emphasis are momentous. The bureaucratisation of Japanese business in the post-war period via increased controls and protection, as well as the replacement of entrepreneurs by ministry-friendly administrators, is directly related to the politically motivated drive for ever greater international market shares.

The history of Japan's drive in the 1970s to carve out niches of power in foreign markets without reciprocity is repeating itself in the 1990s in the financial world. Japanese firms are investing their massive profits not at home, where it would solve quite a few domestic and international problems, but abroad, where there are still opportunities to carve up market shares. The effect of the much publicised "liberalisation" of financial and capital markets by the Ministry of Finance has been to foster the international emancipation of the Japanese banks, security houses and insurance firms, enabling them to compete better in the money markets of the world, and to give the trading companies a large new field for foreign investment. The possibility of counteracting Japan's unilateral economic conquests will be greatly limited if Tokyo gains the kind of leverage over the world's financial markets that its current drive appears to be heading for.

THE JAPAN PROBLEM FOR THE JAPANESE

As a nation, Japan is a problem for itself because the way Japanese power is exercised results in conflicts with, and isolation from, other countries. But Japan is also a problem for Japanese individuals. Discussions with many of them over the past quarter-century have convinced me that they are adversely affected by the way that power is exercised in their country. They are less free than they should be. Japanese are treated by their school system and their superiors in the way a landscape gardener treats a hedge; protruding bits of the personality are regularly snipped off.

I believe that the Japanese are individuals, all 120 million of them. Not all may want to assert their individuality; most, having been so conditioned, do not. But I have met quite a few who want to be taken for distinct persons, rather than as indistinct members of a group. These independent thinkers are disturbed. In many cases they have withdrawn into the private world of their own mind. Individualistic Japanese are generally non-political because they would burn their fingers if they were to challenge the existing power arrangements.

In recent decades it has become common, in referring to Japan, to dismiss the ideal of personal growth as a manifestation of Western ethnocentrism, and to surmise that Japanese have their own way of individual differentiation. Yet there are criteria for personal growth that are not culture-bound. Just as it is in the bud to become a rose, and in the cub to become a tiger, the growing human being has the built-in purpose of becoming a mature, well-integrated individual.

Many commentators on Japan have studiously avoided statements that could be labelled as value judgements. However, my position is that it is an illusion to think that meaningful discourse on political matters can be kept free of judgements. Many things may be relative, but standards for a desirable way of organising life do exist, and choices should be made.

— 2 —

THE ELUSIVE STATE

At the most basic level of political life, Japan is, of course, no different from anywhere else. Some Japanese love power, and some achieve it. The vast majority, as everywhere, submit to the exercise of power for fear of personal punishment or social chaos. The Japanese have laws, legislators, a parliament, political parties, labour unions, a prime minister, interest groups and stockholders. But one should not be misled by these familiar labels into hasty conclusions as to how power is exercised in Japan.

The Japanese prime minister is not expected to show much leadership; labour unions organise strikes to be held during lunch breaks; the legislature does not in fact legislate; stockholders never demand dividends; consumer interest groups advocate protectionism; laws are enforced only if they don't conflict too much with the interests of the powerful, and the ruling Liberal Democratic Party is, if anything, conservative and authoritarian, and is not really a party and does not in fact rule.

Why not, one might ask, simply rename things? But that would be too simple. The familiar labels sometimes indicate familiar functions. At other times they stand, in varying degrees, for something different.

Formally, and in accordance with Japan's status as a parliamentary democracy, sovereignty resides with the people and legislative power with the elected bodies of the two houses of the Diet. But these representatives of the people cannot truly be considered the final arbiter of what is permitted to go on in Japan. This should not in itself be startling; there are quite a few other countries where power does not reside in the institutions in which it is supposed to reside. In such cases, however, one expects to be able to point to an alternative institution, or set of people, in de facto charge. In Japan there is no such clearly demarcated group of power-holders.

The only other institutions that present themselves are the bureau-cracy and big business, but ultimate power rests in neither of these. One will find many obvious bosses, but no one boss among bosses. Japan is highly centralised in the sense that its capital is the economic and cultural hub of the country. Tokyo, no less than Paris or London, is the city where "everything happens." Large companies must maintain important (if not main) offices there. The most important educational institutions are concentrated there. Local governments must wait on the central bureaucrats in order to plead for budget funds. Outside Tokyo there are hardly any important publishing or entertainment industries. Yet there is no political core to this geographical centre.

To grasp the reality of the state is not easy in any country, but in Japan it is like groping in the proverbial bucket of eels.

Kings Without Power

In the tenth and eleventh centuries Japan had a well-defined group of power-holders in the form of the Fujiwara, a cunning family that usurped control over the country, legitimising its position by marrying its daughters to successive emperors. For roughly a century following the decline of the Fujiwara, the real power behind the throne lay with retired emperors. Finally, after a transitional period, *de facto* rule passed to the warrior dynasties that were to control Japan until the industrial era. In 1185 the general Minamoto no Yoritomo gained formal permis-sion from the court to police all sixty-six provinces of Japan. Seven years later he was granted the title of *seii tai shogun*, "barbarian-subduing generalissimo"—an office that, after further consolidation, would re-main the official focus of Japanese power until 1867.

The court as a political entity fell into neglect in the meantime. Some emperors were destitute. Ogimachi (1557-86), for instance, had to peddle his calligraphy and the palace furniture to make ends meet. There have been weak kings in the history of other countries too, but in Japan it was the institution itself that was powerless. Such an arrange-ment clearly suited the powerful men who throughout the centuries controlled their fellow Japanese. Not one of them ever made a serious attempt to grab the throne for himself. The advantages of delegated power seem to have made up for the lack of visible glory. The Fujiwara family that established the norm for this kind of rule felt no urge to destroy a system that provided its heirs with all the privileges of a ruler except the title. The tradition had, indeed, an obvious advantage for the

holders of real power. If the source of real power is unclear, it will also
be unclear how to attack it.

The Rigged One-Party System

Japan's Asian neighbours are completely familiar with this division
between the form and substance of authority. Much of the formal power
structure in Asia today is fictitious. In the West, too, informal relationships may have considerable influence on the exercise of power. Yet in
almost all Asian countries, personal connections are vastly more important than the more recent institutions. The formal governmental processes in Asia should not, however, be dismissed as pointless
pantomime. The official structures imported from the West have inter-
acted with the older political habits and radically altered them. Japan is
no exception here.

Japan has all the institutions considered indispensable for a parliamentary democracy. In the heart of Tokyo stands a Diet building, site
of meetings of a Lower House and an Upper House whose members
would be incensed at any suggestion that they took their democratic
tasks lightly. Every four years, or more frequently, the Japanese public
chooses these representatives from a wide assortment of candidates.

The odd thing is that ever since 1955 this freedom has resulted in a
one-party rule that has not been seriously challenged. If one excludes
the ten months in 1947-8 when conservatively inclined socialists participated in a confused coalition, one may say that ever since the end of the
war the same relatively small group of politicians has played musical
chairs with ministerial seats, making room only for its proteges.

This group of politicians is now called the Liberal Democratic Party
(LDP)—a total misnomer, as already seen, for a coalition of *habatsu*,
political cliques. It has no party organisation to speak of amongst the
grass roots, nor does it stand for any identifiable political principles. It
may have a membership of less than one and a half million one year,
more than three million a year later and less than one and a half again the
year after that. It is thus scarcely a political party at all in the accepted
Western sense.

Japan is rarely described as having a one-party system. Instead it is
argued that the populace has so much faith in the politicians who have
brought the nation economic success that it cannot get enough of them.
This, understandably, is how the LDP explains its unchallenged posi-

tion to the outside world. When a US president speaks to a Japanese prime minister of their shared commitment to pluralistic democracy, the latter is not going to contradict him.

But the truth is that the LDP has maintained itself in power by gerrymandering; by using money to assure itself of the roughly 48 percent of the popular vote it requires; and by hammering home the message that only by electing LDP candidates will rural districts get infrastructure improvements. Under the circumstances that it has itself helped create, this message is accurate enough: local governments are highly dependent on a system of financial supports allocated by the central bureaucracy. Politicians are needed to mediate with government officials, and LDP politicians have the best, if not the only, access to them. In election campaigns most LDP politicians stress their ties with precisely those officials who can allocate the funds for a project desired by their constituency. The LDP's absolute majorities are further guaranteed by uneven representation whereby a single rural vote is worth three votes in the cities. LDP candidates employ an exceedingly thorough style of pork-barrelling to get re-elected.

The LDP can continue to rig the system because the opposition is made up of parties that appear to believe that their proper permanent station in the scheme of things is outside the government. The second largest party, the Japan Socialist Party (JSP), makes it easy for the LDP to present itself as the only viable governing party. The JSP's advocacy of unarmed neutrality and its long-standing anti-US stance seem almost designed to make the party unattractive to the general voter. The other ideological party, the Japan Communist Party (JCP), is slightly less unrealistically doctrinaire, and attracts a large number of sympathy votes from non-communists. None the less, its earlier history as an undisguised instrument of Moscow's foreign policy, together with post-war fears of anything labelled communist, make it unacceptable even as a coalition partner to the other minority parties.

Inasmuch as the LDP would be castigated as dictatorial if it passed legislation in the absence of the opposition, boycotts of Dietary proceedings are an effective demonstration of symbolic anger. The minority parties resort to them in protest against the LDP's "high-handedness," or to call attention to "political ethics" (a polite reference to corruption on the part of LDP members). With few exceptions Diet debates are performances that are democratically reassuring but with not the slightest influence on the country's affairs.

The Japanese parliamentary opposition, in short, is like the chorus in a Greek tragedy. Its monotonous comments on the state of the nation and lamentations over the sins of the LDP are ritualistic and harmless.

Weak Ministers

The LDP is habitually referred to as the ruling party, but this too is a misnomer. Little legislation emanates from it. Some policy initiatives are traceable to powerful LDP groups, but most of the time they are of marginal importance. The LDP hardly ever establishes new administrative priorities. What distinguishes LDP parliamentarians from other Japanese is personal privileges and the ability to relay requests for favours from lobbying supporters to the bureaucrats.

Seated above a weak parliament, the Japanese prime minister, who is invariably president of the LDP, in theory has opportunities to exercise great power. But in fact his power does not permit him to do things that foreigners expect a prime minister to be able to do. If he focuses most of his energies on one goal and is given more than a couple of years in office, he may subtly effect a small shift in priorities among the administrators. If he tried to do much more, his rivals in the LDP, along with the opposition parties, would almost surely combine to bring him down.

The power of the Japanese prime minister is less than that of any head of government in the West or Asia. Proof of this was provided by the recent experiences of Nakasone Yasuhiro. As prime minister, Nakasone never allowed any doubt about his ambition to rule. He also tried harder than any of his post-war predecessors to strengthen his office. In the end, though, he failed to bring about the policy adjustments he championed—except for the break-up of the company running the largest losses in the world, the Japan National Railways.

According to the constitution, executive power is vested in the cabinet. But most Japanese cabinet ministers have little or no influence within their ministries. The almost yearly cabinet reshuffles give them no time to absorb sufficient detail to outsmart their senior bureaucrats. A strong politician can make his mark on a policy area through a certain amount of leverage in senior personnel appointments, but ministers who make significant decisions are so extraordinary that they fuel interdepartmental gossip and press comment for years afterward.

If cabinet members were to insist on exercising the kind of power the formal rules give them, they would in nearly all cases run into insurmountable bureaucratic sabotage. Cabinet meetings are, with rare exceptions, wholly ceremonial affairs, lasting between ten and fifteen minutes, for the sole purpose of endorsing the policy adjustments that the administrative vice-ministers (the top bureaucrats in each ministry) have agreed on the previous day at their own meeting. The cabinet does not discuss any new business of which the bureaucrats have no knowledge, as is common in European countries, or business that has not been worked out in all its details by the bureaucrats.

The Authoritarian Bureaucracy

Is the power of the Japanese state, then, to be found in the bureaucracy? A fair number of experienced observers have reached this conclusion. Groups of officials, especially those of the ministries of finance, international trade and industry, construction, and post and telecommunications, wield a great deal of power. They restrain, control and provide spurs for the economy. They make nearly all laws—which are almost always rubber-stamped by the Diet.

It might help solve the riddle of Japanese power, then, to consider Japan an "authoritarian bureaucratic state," but to try to pinpoint just who among the bureaucrats is in charge is to get lost again. Pressed to endorse decisions their respective ministries object to, the administrative vice-ministers will not give in to each other. Controversial issues always result in impasses, because there is simply no way to break a deadlock caused by a recalcitrant ministry.

Intense rivalry among officials has long prevented their achieving a general dominance over Japanese policy-making. By the same token, territorial jealousies among ministries and agencies obstruct the formulations of unified national policies.

The Zaikai

We are left with one main group of participants in the Japanese power game. It is the *zaikai*, the broad circle of top business functionaries, especially those who speak through the powerful business federations. Since Japan is known internationally almost exclusively through the products of its industry and the impact they have on other economies, foreigners are tempted to think that the captains of industry dominate its political decision-making. According to this interpretation both the LDP and the bureaucrats serve as proxies for the *zaikai*.

This picture is false. True, Japanese corporations operate in an extremely favourable political climate, but this has not turned the presidents and chairmen of industrial corporations into Japan's secret rulers.

Admittedly, the business federations, especially Keidanren, have extraordinary powers. Keidanren is a federation of leading industrial organisations such as the automobile manufacturers' association, the shipbuilders' association, the iron and steel federation, the petroleum association and the chemical industry association, together with trading companies, wholesale businesses, banks, insurance companies and securities companies. Second in importance, Nikkeiren (Japan Federation of Employers' Associations), has had the task of helping control the labour movement and keeping the lid on wage increases. The Keizai Doyukai (Committee for Economic Development) has provided a forum in which elite *zaikai* members can formulate a theoretical basis for business policies; it attracted attention in the mid-1950s with proposals for a Japanese-style "reformed capitalism." The fourth and oldest organisation, the Japan Chamber of Commerce and Industry, monitors the smaller corporations.

It would be a mistake to think of the founders and major leaders of the post-war federations as entrepreneurs. One of the reasons for the success of the bureaucrat-businessman partnership is that these organisations at the apex of the industrial hierarchy have been led by bureaucrats who were responsible for wartime economic mobilisations and by bureaucratised leaders of wartime cartels. These men provided the main impetus for the merger of the rival conservative parties to form the LDP in 1955. They have also had a decisive influence over post-Occupation education policies and the shaping of the school system.

In the late 1980s, the *zaikaijin*, business elders, form a gerontocracy at the top of an ever bureaucratised business world. As chairmen of the boards of their respective companies, they often continue to wield tremendous power. They enhance the reputation of their firms, as they pontificate on what is desirable for society and add their contributions to the ubiquitous platitudes regarding Japan's tasks and future role in the world. But they have no ability to steer Japan towards new priorities more consonant with those tasks and the international role.

Thus each of the three bodies described above may display surprising power at times and unexpected weakness at others. The essential fact is that none of them forms the apex of the Japanese power hierarchy.

The Truncated Pyramid

If there are no other groups that can compete for power, where then must one locate the Japanese state? Do the Japanese *need* a state? At least from the Middle Ages until the middle of the nineteenth century, the Japanese political elite apparently did not think so. But this has not always been the case.

The Meiji oligarchy that took control in 1868, largely as a result of foreign intervention, was obsessed with creating a strong state. Their attempts appeared surprisingly successful, earning the admiration of the Western powers, especially when victory in the Russo-Japanese War of 1905 demonstrated Japan's naval prowess. But the system of central rule proved to be not sturdy enough to outlast its creators. The next generation of leaders failed to form an effective oligarchy. The Naimusho (Home Ministry), the Army, the Navy, the Ministry of Foreign Affairs, the Ministry of Finance, the Privy Council and other vital institutions of the state were all led by men who identified with these institutions rather than with the centre of power they were expected to represent. They were often not even on speaking terms with each other.

In the 1930s, power progressively slid into the hands of the military. Yet even while this happened, no one knew who was in charge of them either. The Army and the Navy had its chiefs directly answerable to the emperor, and did not even consult with each other. The dissipation of central political power gave financial middle-ranking Army officers the opportunity to hijack the nation. In September 1931, elements of the Japanese Kwantung Army attacked the Chinese garrison in Mukden, thereby beginning the conquest of Manchuria. When this act of gross insubordination went uncensured by the government, the Army understood that it could have its way, and on its own initiative set up the puppet state of Manchukuo. The intimidating action of fanatical officers that followed set Japan on the course that was to lead to Pearl Harbor and from there to Hiroshima.

Attacking a country with an industrial machine ten times the size of one's own must be considered suicidal behaviour, and it is very unlikely that a consolidated leadership would have allowed it. It can be argued, indeed, that the Japanese surprise attack which brought the United States into the Second World War was a direct consequence of the rivalry between the Army and the Navy. The Army, in setting Japan on the path to war, took it for granted that the Navy would take care of defence, while the Navy, wishing to hold on to its power and its credibility as a patriotic body, refrained from directly expressing the belief, widespread among its ranks, that victory was impossible.

The war itself did little to pull the political bodies of the country together. It undoubtedly strengthened the power of the bureaucrats, but the Japanese never gave to any one person powers remotely comparable to the power held by Hitler, Mussolini, Stalin, Churchill or Roosevelt.

In the wake of the disastrous adventure of the Pacific War, no new attempt to establish genuine central control was made. General Douglas MacArthur and his political reformers arrived in 1945 to dismantle what they, along with practically everyone else, imagined to be the remnants of a solid dictatorship similar to those of Hitler and Mussolini. The idea that it could have been the absence of strong leadership which had brought Japan to attack the Western allies appears not to have occurred to anyone.

From 1945 until well into the 1970s, Japan had little need to worry about whether or not it was a state, since it was hardly ever called upon to act as a political entity. Foreign-policy requirements were simply not felt, since the USA took care of them. Japan became totally dependent on the United States, not only for its defence but also, ultimately, for its diplomacy. This extraordinary relationship has allowed Japan to deal with countries on the basis of purely economic priorities, with scant regard to political consequences.

At home, in the meantime, power is diffused over a number of semi-self-contained, semi-mutually dependent bodies. While all these bodies share aspects of government, it is impossible to find one among them that gives the others their mandate. No one has final responsibility for national policy or can decide national questions in emergencies.

The public, of course, perceives a "state" in the presence of the tax collector, the police and a vast body of regulations. But the Japanese state vanishes once one considers the questions of accountability. It is interesting that the average Japanese does not consider the puppet state of Manchukuo to have been "our colony;" it was the Army's colony, not Japan's. The Japanese tend not to see themselves as being symbolically part of a state whose responsibility they therefore share.

The state means different things to different people, but it should at least show some existential consistency. It should continue to be there from one moment to the next, and not suddenly trickle away like sand through one's fingers. The frustration of many a foreign negotiator, meeting the umpteenth mediator sent his way, can be summed up in the single cry, "Take me to your leader." Japan does not have one. It is

pushed, or pulled, or kept afloat, but not actually led, by r
holders in what I call the System.

The Public-Private Realm

Foreigners have often sensed in Japan something not genera
by the notion of state. "Japan Inc." is a term that has becon
but the metaphor is misleading in that Japan has nothing con
a chairman of the board, a president or even a board of directo
other hand, Japanese who do not like the notion of Japan
sometimes contend that since much more industry is natio
Britain or France, it is in those countries rather than in J
government and business interests have truly amalgamated.

Certainly, the size of Japan's bureaucracy is not impress
pared to the West. There are only 4.4 public-sector employee
inhabitants, which is one-third the figure for Great Britain and
half that for the USA and West Germany. But this is irreleva
context of the Japanese System. In the mixed economies of
Europe, the private and public elements are still fairly well del
State interference can be administered in measurable doses, m
and singled out for praise or protest if need be.

The mingling of the private and public domains in Japan
mysterious process. Japanese government bureaux have extrao
powers of awarding licences and other permissions for com
pursuits, and of withholding subsidies, tax privileges or low-i
loans. Ministries can resort to "administrative guidance" to
organisations to adopt "voluntary" measures. It is by such mea
the Ministry of International Trade and Industry has shaped ind
sectors to make them fit for *optimum performance*. The Minis
Finance and the Bank of Japan also exercise powerful control, tha
the once nearly exclusive dependence of Japanese corporations on
loans for capital. Even though a majority of large firms had by the
made so much profit that they are awash in self-generated capita
relationship between these bureaucratic and industrial bodies ren
close. By issuing binding instructions to the commercial banks
Bank of Japan still maintains a very large voice in allocating funds fo
really big investments.

The bureaucrats also preside over public and semi-public corp
tions serving all manner of economic and political purpose
including, incidentally, the provision of post-retirement sinecures

he bureaucrats themselves. Deriving funds largely from Japan's postal savings system (the largest financial institution in the non-communist world), the budget for these public policy companies is not subject to parliamentary approval.

Some three hundred bureaucrats annually join the business world as directors or senior advisers of corporations they monitored during their government career. Since the retirement age is fifty-five, such bureaucrats will have another twenty years or so in which to help ensure smooth communications between industry and the ministries or the central bank. This crucial phenomenon is called *amakudari*, "descent from heaven."

In the higher reaches of the System, bureaucrats, former bureaucrats in top business positions, former bureaucrats turned politician, and the former bureaucrats or bureaucratised businessmen who head the business federations are as one, as they monitor the economy and maintain social control. One has only to replace the term "bureaucrat" with "administrator," and the traditional divisions of the industrialised state disappear almost altogether.

Most post-war business bosses are best characterised as administrators rather than as entrepreneurs. The most powerful one-third of LDP Diet membership consists mostly of former ministry officials, and their methods and attitudes are those of administrators. Japan's top administrators have also been selected by the same filter: the law departments of the former imperial universities, especially the University of Tokyo (more popularly, Todai) and, to a much lesser extent, the University of Kyoto.

A good deal of antagonism exists in the higher reaches of the System, but it rarely pits the official organs of state against the industrial organisations. Groups of businessmen side with groups of bureaucrats against other groups on both domains. The rifts run diagonally through the truncated pyramid. Whereas the great rivalries and territorial wars among the different ministries are highly significant, true confrontations between bureaucrats and recalcitrant corporations are rarely heard of. Only much lower down, among the newer firms and the small subcontracting firms, can one find genuine entrepreneurs.

Harnessed Capitalists

Between the small and medium-sized enterprises at the bottom of the industrial hierarchy and the ministerial-corporate top lies the highly disciplined array of firms that has made Japan famous in the post-war world. These "private" corporations are only semi-autonomous. Most of the large firms belong—with varying degrees of closeness—to conglomerates, of which there are six colossal ones: Mitsui, Mitsubishi, Sumitomo, Fuyo, Sanwa and Dai-ichi Kangyo Bank.

These conglomerates, known as corporate groups or *gurupu*, contain highly diversified industrial companies that are clustered around their own banks, together with real-estate agencies, insurance firms and the famous trading houses. The entire structure in each case is tied together by interlocking directorates. Between 60 and 70 percent of all shares on the Japanese stock exchanges are held by Japanese corporations and financial institutions. They keep these shares within their conglomerate family, in a pattern of reciprocal shareholding. Because the shares are considered to be political shares rather than investment, they are never sold. To keep over half of a company's shares in such cross-holding deals eliminates the possibility of take-overs by outsiders.

No one is in charge of a *gurupu*, and no one is ultimately responsible for it. The *shachokai*, or presidents' council, which meets regularly, is an institution for mutual control, in that the participating presidents of all the major firms in a corporate group attend not as stockholders of their own companies, but as representatives of the stock their company holds in all the other member companies.

Another term for the corporate group is *keiretsu*, but this label was originally used for yet another type of conglomerate in which the members are even more closely related to one another. These are the hierarchically ordered systems of subsidiaries, suppliers, subcontractors and distributors associated with a particular major manufacturer. Each large member of a *gurupu* stands at the apex of a vertical *keiretsu* that may encompass several hundreds of companies.

The precise organisations and degree of control over members varies from group to group, but the obligation to extend mutual aid and to keep as much business as possible within the group is taken for granted.

The *gurupu* have succeeded the *zaibatsu*, which before 1945 were organised around holding companies and were ordered to disband by the United States Occupation authorities. The post-war groups are more effective because the Occupation purge provided an opportunity to eliminate much dead wood. More important, the substitution of the banks for the old holding companies established a network of financial pumps (their survival guaranteed by the central bank) without which the economic miracle would have been considerably less impressive.

Rather than doing away with the controlled pre-war and wartime industrial system, the Occupation actually reinvigorated it.

Individual members of the corporate groups are also organised by industrial sector in overlapping, guild-like, but again strongly hierarchical structures. Obligatory conformity to unwritten rules limits their options. The industrial collectivities have nearly complete extra-legal powers to apply sanctions whenever individual members step out of line. Ultimate sanctions such as enforced bankruptcy are rare, since a slight signal of displeasure is generally heeded.

The awesome combination of intertwined hierarchies nourishes a myriad of subcontractor firms reaching right down to the small sweatshops, at which level one may find whole families working a ten-hour day. It is at this level that one is reminded of capitalism in the sense that Westerners use the term. These small enterprises are run by entrepreneurs who shoulder formidable risks. However, they are dependent on the market only to a limited extent. Their chief function is to provide what amounts to cheap labour for the firms higher up in the hierarchy. Collectively, they serve as a shock-absorbing cushion in periods of economic downturn and help to explain Japan's high bankruptcy rate, since they regularly go under in large numbers, only to reappear in different manufacturing roles.

A Paralysed Superpower

One must be careful not to see the System as monolithic. This is no oriental despotism in modern guise, nor is there any ever-vigilant Big Brother. Indeed, any component of the System that might aspire to such a role would promptly find the other components lining up against it. The preservation of its own power is the first priority of every System component. The Japanese know from bitter experience that things can go desperately wrong when, as happened in the 1930s, this balance is upset.

For domestic purposes, this System without a core works reasonably well. Japan trundles along while officials, politicians and businessmen tinker endlessly with minor policy adjustments.

Post-war industrial reconstruction was an obvious priority that did not need to be determined by a strong political centre. The bureaucracy took it upon itself to administer this policy and the *de facto* one-party system guaranteed that there would be no interference from messy parliamentary democratic processes. But this also meant that the politicians abdicated responsibilities that are crucial for major policy adjustments. For lack of a mechanism to set new priorities, Japan is still basically acting in line with policies dating from the 1950s.

From an international perspective, the Japanese System is an anachronism. It might have fit a poor and isolated Japan, but it is unsuitable for Japan as an international partner. It has no strong leadership, yet it creates the impression abroad of a purposeful giant bent on economic conquest of the world.

— 3 —

SERVANTS OF THE SYSTEM

The absence of anyone in charge does not result in social chaos. Aside from the radical fringe, the System has been able to eliminate virtually all genuine political opposition. So marked, in fact, is the orderliness of life in Japan and the discipline of its people that one is led to suspect the existence of other forces that foster cohesion.

Japanese are brought up to accept that much of their lives will be managed for them. Their environment does not encourage them to play things by ear. Often, activities intended for relaxation and enjoyment are pursued with a display of great discipline. From school parties to cherry-blossom viewing, collective undertakings are almost always preceded by such painstaking preparations, and proceed so predictably, that to outsiders all the fun has been organised out of them.

The System's embrace is inescapable; it extends to institutions—the educational world and the press—that in other non-dictatorial societies frequently exist in more or less permanent tension, if not open hostility, with the forces of the established order.

Anti-Intellectual Schools

Japan's education system has gained a reputation as one of the best, if not *the* best, in the world. This reputation rests partly on the high (often highest) scores Japanese schoolchildren attain in international mathematics tests, and on the presumed connection with Japan's economic successes.

That Japanese pupils do well in international written tests is not surprising. To take just such tests is what Japanese pupils are trained for from elementary school to high school. However, if the tests were to evaluate the ability to draw conclusions, to connect abstractions, to organise one's thoughts in an essay, to express oneself in another language or just the ability to ask questions, they would reveal where the Japanese education system is deficient.

The aims of Japanese schools could hardly be further removed from the original sense of the English word "education": to bring forth and develop the power of the mind, rather than merely imparting information. Spontaneous reasoning, along with spontaneous behaviour, is systematically suppressed in practically all schools; there is no patience with originality. Pupils are not taught to think logically, or to ask the right questions—indeed to ask any questions at all. Instead, the emphasis is on rote memorisation. Japanese students who have done well carry vast masses of facts around in their heads; if they have been able to connect these facts and work them into a coherent view of life, they have had to do so entirely on their own.

School regulations have proliferated considerably since the end of the 1970s and in many cases have become absurdly restrictive. Most schools prescribe to the smallest detail how pupils must sit, stand and walk, and to what height and at which angle they should raise their hands. The route to be travelled from school to home is often laid down, and some schools have rules forbidding classmates to talk with each other in the street. The order in which school lunches are to be eaten is sometimes prescribed. School rules apply even at home and during vacations: it is generally forbidden to go out after six at night; it is decreed at which time the pupil must rise, even on Sundays. Only selected books may be read. The schools, and not the parents, decide which TV programmes may be watched. Some schools demand that permission be asked even for vacation trips with the family. Japanese higher education forms a hierarchy, with Todai (the University of Tokyo)—more specifically, its law department—at its apex. Todai's graduates have the best chance of gaining admission to the Ministry of Finance, the best jumping board for a try at the prime ministership or another career in the LDP. It also provides the business conglomerates with many of its future top managers. The University of Kyoto and other former imperial universities produce a smaller part of the elite, but the Todai label is venerated. For a century past, its law department has ordained almost all Japan's top administrators; a diploma from this school is practically a ticket into the ruling class.

One rung down the hierarchy, but still highly respectable and difficult to get into, come Waseda and Keio, two private universities in Tokyo. Waseda's reputation rests on graduates who became politicians and journalists, while Keio has always given access to the higher reaches of the business world. Farther down again one finds the medium-ranking universities such as Chuo, Meiji, Sophia (run by Jesuits) and Rikkyo. And beneath these is a plethora of smaller universities and colleges, women's junior colleges and specialised training institutions for subjects like art and music.

The quality of university education has never been the criteria for reaching the heights of Japan's administrative apparatus. What students actually absorb from the law course at Todai is unimpressive when compared with what students must know to graduate from the better American universities.

What students do during their four years as undergraduates is of little account, unless they do it in the faculties of medicine, engineering or the physical sciences—which mostly lead to careers outside business. Law, economics and commerce—with a nearly exclusive emphasis on what writers on the administrative aspects of these fields have said—are the favoured subjects for gaining entry to the higher levels of the System. For most students the university means pure relaxation, a brief fling at life before entering the regimented world of business organisations.

Cramming for a Career

Many Japanese think that the rest students get at the better universities is well deserved, because getting into them is an extremely nerve-racking process. Though money and parental connections sometimes play a role, in the vast majority of cases the ambitious youth must try to outscore ten, twenty or more rivals in entrance examinations. The way to accomplish this is to get into a high school with a reputation for producing a large crop of successful candidates. Japanese high schools are, in fact, ranked by this criterion. Three out of the 5,453 high schools in the country supply about 10 percent of the successful candidates for Tokyo University.

This means that at high schools considered better than average pupils spend most of their time training to pass exams. And since the professors who compose these exams are often quite arbitrary in their view of the correct answers, the object of these schools is not so much to teach a subject as to turn out experts who can read the minds of those professors.

Where English teaching is concerned, for example, high-school pupils learn to pass exams consisting only of multiple-choice questions, put together by professors who themselves are uncomfortable with the real language. After ten years studying English, which along with mathematics and Japanese is one of the three major examination sub-jects for all the universities, students are, with rare exceptions, unable to communicate in this language. Mathematics and physics are better suited to written exams, but where history or social studies are con-cerned, the examinations seem like nothing more than a giant trivia contest.

The critical importance of entrance examinations has brought a lucrative subsidiary industry into being in the form of special schools offering private tuition after normal school hours. Called *juku*, they, too, are ranked on the basis of how many of their students have passed which examinations. Some professional crammers even develop probability theories about exams, not unlike the theorists who peddle a systemic approach to gambling at Las Vegas.

To be admitted to a highly reputed high school, it is almost mandatory to have attended a highly reputed middle school. To get into one of the most promising middle schools, it helps to have passed through the right primary school. The latter's reputation in turn de-pends on the proportion of its pupils delivered to high-ranking middle and high schools. There are books on the market with special drills for children preparing for elementary school entrance exams. But often the selection begins even earlier.

A relatively smooth ride upward from elementary school to univer-sity is provided by certain expensive private institutions that consist of universities with their own attached high, middle and elementary schools and sometimes even kindergartens. Once one is on such a track, the exams at each level are largely perfunctory. This has come to be known as the "escalator" system, and the best way to get on an escalator is to attend a kindergarten leading to higher-level schools. As a conse-quence there are famous and extraordinarily expensive kindergartens that actually give entrance examinations of their own. Keio, Gakushuin, Seijo Gakuen and Aoyama Gakuin are among well-known private universities at the top of escalators that start at kindergarten. Exams typically test ability to recognise letters in the Japanese syllabaries, skills with building blocks and the like. At a crucial point in one routine test, the toddler was given a wrapped sweet; all eyes were on him to see whether he neatly folded the wrapper or threw it on the floor.

But still we are not at the beginning. Some mothers arrange private tuition for their three-year-olds so that they may stand a better chance of passing the kindergarten exam. Entry into one of the famous kindergartens of Tokyo usually requires training at a *juku* for infants.

Examination Hell

The education system is one of the most criticised elements of the System. A former vice-minister of the Ministry of International Trade and Industry (MITI) contends that the present educational system only seems to be able to turn out inferior versions of robots. The public at large habitually decries the *shiken jigoku*, literally "examination hell," and the social type it has brought into being, the *kyoiku mama*, or "education mother," who deprives her children of a normal childhood while pushing them up the educational ladder. The *kyoiku mama* is driven by powerful motives. To a great extent the mother is held responsible for the performance of her child, whose successes or failures in examinations have a great effect on her status in the neighbourhood. Failure in an exam can be psychologically devastating, and not only to the candidate. The tensions affecting the whole family in connection with *shiken jigoku* provide much of the drama of middle-class family life in Japan.

Children are expected to give up hobbies, sports and a social life in order to devote themselves totally to the approaching exam, often for two years in advance. Preparation entails cramming till very late at night. One *juku* holds cramming classes for twelve-year-olds from 9 p.m. on Saturday to 6 a.m. on Sunday. Fourteen-year-olds who are still at their desks at 1 a.m. are not unusual.

Even though practically every Japanese will agree that the exam system is cruel, most people realise that nothing will ever be done to change it. On the whole, it suits the System admirably. Even if the masses of facts pumped into their heads are largely useless, the people selected to reach the top will be very tenacious and have extremely good memories. Officialdom and the business world value persistence, dedication and memory much more highly than inventiveness.

These observations are not new. One of the first foreign teachers in Japan, the American missionary William Griffis, wrote of Japanese teachers in 1874 that their "chief duty was to stuff and cram the minds of…pupils. To expand or develop the mental powers of a boy, to enlarge his mental visions, to teach him to think for himself, would have been doing precisely what it was the teacher's business to prevent."

PRESERVING THE SYSTEM

The essential condition for the survival of the Japanese System is continued protection of the administrator class by keeping the criteria for membership and the rules governing transactions among the administrators themselves informal. The System is what it is by virtue of informal relations that have no basis in the constitution or in any *formal* rules of the ministries, the LDP, the corporations or any other institutions.

Informal Human Networks

Connections are crucial to life in Japan at all levels of society. Success depends almost entirely on who one knows. *Kone* (a Japanised abbreviation of the English word "connections") often provide the key to admission to desirable schools, and to finding good jobs. If one wants the best medical treatment, a special introduction to busy doctors is almost indispensable. Most Japanese are thoroughly indebted in this sense to numerous other Japanese, and others in turn are indebted to them; one of the main characteristics of Japanese life is an unremitting trade in favours.

In the upper levels of society, the *kone* multiply to form whole networks of relationships. These may derive from one-time favours, school ties or shared experiences, or may involve intricate mutual backscratching deals. They are referred to as *jinmyaku* — *jin* meaning "personal" and *myaku* a "vein" such as is found in mineral deposits, so that *jinmyaku* means a vein, or web, of personal connections running through the fabric of society. *Jinmyaku* are much more widespread, and of incomparably greater importance, than old-boy networks in the West.

Among top bureaucrats, politicians and businessmen, marriage facilitates the building up of informal contracts. LDP politicians marry the daughters of older, influential politicians, then match their own sons and daughters with the children of prosperous and influential businessmen. The resulting networks are known as *keibatsu* (family groupings through marriage). There are matchmakers who specialise in consolidating administrator ties. There are also private individuals whose full-time personal hobby is to find marriage partners for top politicians and bureaucrats, and who work closely with the secretariats of the elite ministries.

Without informal contacts the top administrators cannot fulfil what they are expected to accomplish. A bureaucrat without a good *jinmyaku* cannot climb to great heights. A minister without an elaborate *jinmyaku* is worthless to his ministry and his clique within the LDP. The power of Japan's top politicians is derived from a large complex of intermeshing *jinmyaku* forged with favours, money, marriage ties and political acumen. At the middle social levels, building a *jinmyaku* requires time, energy, charm, flattery and a liver strong enough to cope with large volumes of alcohol. The value of a manager to his company depends to a great extent on who he can get hold of on the telephone to fix what needs to be fixed. For these lesser administrators, a good *jinmyaku* means a good income, many people in one's debt and security after one's retirement. Graduating from the University of Tokyo (Todai), especially its law department, means being automatically hooked up to a huge network of connections. Of all the section chiefs and bureaucrats of higher rank in the Ministry of Finance, 88.6 percent are from Todai. For the Foreign Ministry the figure is 76 percent, for the National Land Agency 73.5 percent and for the Ministry of Transportation 68.5 percent. Nearly all post-war Japanese prime ministers who exercised any influence have been graduates of Todai—with the conspicuous exceptions of Tanaka Kakuei and Takeshita Noboru. In most post-war cabinets the crucial portfolios have been held by Todai graduates. Over a quarter of all parliamentarians and more than one-third of all LDP members are Todai graduates. In 1985, the presidents of 401 out of the 1,454 largest firms were Todai graduates.

When it became clear in the prime ministerial contest of 1972 that Tanaka Kakuei would be the main rival to Fukuda Takeo, a Todai graduate who had reached the apex of the Finance Ministry, the then *eminence grise* of the business world, Ishizaka Taizo, objected. "We cannot," he declared, "give the position to a man who is an ignorant labourer." Even though Tanaka was one of the most successful self-made businessmen in Japanese history, Ishizaka—as Keidanren chief, ostensibly representing a world of entrepreneurs—felt not the remotest affinity with him.

The world of the Todai law department graduates (to which one should add graduates of the law department of the University of Kyoto) is highly exclusive. Con-artists and other swindlers habitually pass themselves off as Todai graduates. And real ones are extremely valuable on the *omiai* (arranged marriage) market.

Shielded Administrators

The System protects the administrator class, whose members enjoy a significantly greater protection from the consequences of their actions than do ordinary Japanese.

Some are better protected than others. The bureaucrats are without doubt the most shielded category of all. To all intents and purposes, they are situated above their own formal administrative laws. They are also usually let off the hook in money scandals involving politicians.

The extent of the protection they enjoy can be surmised from the circumstances surrounding the sale of equipment to the Soviet Union by a Toshiba subsidiary in violation of COCOM (the international organisation that supervises certain types of Western trade with communist countries) rules—an incident of great significance to the US-Japan relationship. The administrators responded to agitation over this issue with the ritual resignation of the president of Toshiba and highly publicised personnel changes. Yet no one pointed a finger at the MITI bureaucrats, who have refused assistance from the Foreign Ministry and the Self-Defence Agency in monitoring violations of the Japanese COCOM law.

Another essential factor in Japanese politics is the never-ending strife among the administrators, especially those in government agencies and LDP cliques. But it is not strife between a public and a private realm. Government officials almost always get on better with the companies they watch over than with their colleagues in other ministries. And politicians by and large enjoy a symbolic relationship with both bureaucrats and businessmen.

As reward for a quarter-century of patiently fulfilling their duties, career bureaucrats may expect a second career as LDP Diet members, as executive of a government or semi-governmental corporation, or as executive of a large firm or bank. Their delayed rewards as *amakudari* ("descent from heaven") bureaucrats usually include at least a doubling of income.

The most important unwritten rule among the administrators is that each category must help keep the others in business. They do so in ways that are nowhere formally specified; indeed, some of the ways are distinctly against the letter or the spirit of the formal rules. The bureaucrats keep the LDP in business by buying off the public with subsidies and public works. The LDP parliamentarians keep the bureaucrats in business by not making the slightest attempt to change the policies of industrial expansion that emerged in the immediate post-war period. The LDP and the bureaucrats keep the businessmen in business by protecting them against foreign competition and underwriting their expansionist programmes.

Structural Corruption

In the wake of the 1974 Lockheed scandal, which forced Tanaka Kakuei to resign as prime minister, the newspapers became obsessed with *kinken seiji*, money politics, and *seiji rinri*, political ethics.

Money politics was universally decried. No one would defend it publicly or explain in the press that without it there would be no LDP. The money-flow from business to LDP underlines the partnership of the two. Leaders of the *zaikai*—the cream of Japan's financial, industrial and trade organisations—played a major part in the process that led to the birth of the LDP in November 1955, and it was only natural that they should keep it alive by providing the necessary funds.

Every year, at a New Year's meeting with business representatives, the three top LDP executives formally request donations, mentioning a target. In 1985, this was 10 billion yen. Which sector will donate how much is decided later by discussion among industries themselves. The director of the LDP's treasury bureau also visits several hundred industrial federations and large enterprises to encourage the flow of donations. Each time an LDP politician reaches a higher position, the donations he receives from businesses rise by between 55 and 100 percent. In 1985, Nakasone Yasuhiro received five times as much as in the year before he became prime minister.

A new method of increasing funding from corporations is for associates of an LDP politician to organise "encouragement" parties and charge between 20,000 and one million yen for tickets. Companies are sometimes forced to buy a number of these tickets through their industrial association. The hotels at which the parties are held may also sell tickets to other members of the *keiretsu* to which they belong. Such tickets do not violate the law, and the supervising Ministry of Home Affairs considers them "payment for refreshments."

Particularly in the case of the LDP, registered income is only a small part of the picture. There are many indirect ways of collecting money from the business world. One is through the stock market. Insider trading is very common in Japan, and a politician may buy stock that will subsequently shoot upwards in value through a variety of manipulations. (Insider trading is in theory, of course, not allowed. But between 1948 and 1987, only one case resulted in prosecution.) The money that LDP politicians collect in their own prefectures need only be registered with the local authorities, and no one keeps track of this. More significantly, all important LDP members have secret and very lucrative arrangements with corporations and banks, and there are "tunnel organisations" channelling money to individual *habatsu* (political cliques).

This flow of money from business to politicians is an old tradition and contemporary LDP politicians can be very open about their "secret" income. Accompanying them on routine trips through their constituencies, I have actually seem them accept tens of millions of yen in a brown paper bag. Registered income is only a fraction of what LDP politicians need to maintain their staffs and *koenkai* (support groups) in normal years, to buy votes indirectly in election years, and sometimes to bribe opposition parliamentarians as part of their intricate political manoeuvres. I estimate that in a year without elections it costs about 400 million yen (some $3 million) to maintain a presence in a constituency.

The benefits that the business community buys with the money spent on LDP politicians are fairly clear-cut. In 1984, the most generous, accounting for about a third of what businesses officially spent on the LDP, were the commercial banks. No wonder that the highly touted liberalisation of the financial sector helped only Japanese institutions. The traditionally high contributions from the protected steel and machinery sectors were followed, in third place, by the telecommunications industry. This was a year in which the United States had been pressing for the opening of the telecommunications market.

One specialist has found that the commission charged by the Tanaka machine—for example, to get a building contract out of the Ministry of Construction—was three percent of the value of the project. LDP members who mediate on behalf of city or prefectural governments for public projects paid for by the central government routinely receive 2 percent of their value.

Few post-war Japanese prime ministers have not been tainted by scandal or the suspicion of corruption owing to their symbolic relationships with businessmen. A series of scandals that came to light in the

1960s and were dubbed "the black mist" by the press, appeared to involve practically everyone who was anyone in the LDP.

Even though these and other scandals have caused outcries, corruption in Japan is in a sense legitimised by its systematic perpetration. It is so highly organised, and has become so much a part of the Japanese System on so many levels, that most citizens *accept* it. The press calls it "structural corruption," implicitly acknowledging that it is a necessary aspect of the System in its present condition.

Habatsu Politics

Political commentary in Japanese newspapers concentrates almost solely on what clique leaders are doing to keep or gain leverage over each other. When in the spring of 1987 Takeshita Noboru finally declared his intention of running for the LDP presidency, he touched off half a year of media speculation concerning Nakasone Yasuhiro's successor. Yet not once did editorial comment take up the question of who among the four contenders might make the best prime minister. Japanese political comment is for the most part focused on the perennial guessing game as to who is doing what to whom. References to policy find no place in it; there are no policy differences to refer to.

Sophisticated theories that see LDP cliques as *de facto* political parties are wrong. *Habatsu* compete with each other for the prime ministership and for unmediated access to the bureaucracy in order to deliver on pork-barrel promises. No idea or principle concerning how power ought to be exercised enters into it. *Habatsu* politics is a power game, entirely bereft of meaningful political discussion, and one over which the voters exercise no influence at all.

The number of *habatsu* fluctuates because of splits and mergers; during the 1970s and 1980s, there were from five to seven important ones at any one time. They take their names from their leaders, who are the candidates for the presidency of the LDP and thus the prime ministership. The *habatsu* are a source of never-ending friction, and sometimes of such severe tension that the LDP appears on the verge of disintegration. Cabinet posts are apportioned in accordance with the size of each *habatsu*, and if one of them is seen as receiving a portfolio too many, this prompts immediate debate over the "sensitive" or "very delicate" situation. The *habatsu* help regulate the distribution of political spoils and the disbursement of funds. Because the multi-member constituencies encourage competition among LDP candidates themselves, highly placed *habatsu* members are expected to campaign on behalf of their fellow members and against LDP candidates belonging to other *habatsu*.

Alliances between *habatsu* are needed to produce a prime minister, and successful ones are generally referred to as the mainstream of a government's support. The rival, anti-mainstream *habatsu* are still rewarded with cabinet posts, but they are also watched carefully for moves that could spell the beginning of a campaign to undermine the incumbent.

The Prime Minister

The Japanese prime minister has less real power than any head of government in the Western world or of most countries in Asia. Moves to strengthen the office of prime minister have failed because of strong opposition from both the LDP and the bureaucracy.

Yet while the prime minister cannot establish new national priorities or enforce important measures, one prime minister can still make a big difference from the next. Tanaka is, of course, the example that immediately comes to mind, though his importance in Japanese political history derives mainly from what he accomplished after he ceased to be prime minister. But that a prime minister can make a difference was dramatically illustrated by the last two prime ministers chosen by Tanaka, Suzuki Zenko and Nakasone Yasuhiro.

Suzuki Zenko had polished the Japanese skills of side-stepping decisions to an extent unprecedented among post-war Japanese prime ministers. In the years when Tanaka was prime minister, a then invisible Suzuki had helped keep order within the ranks of the LDP, thus giving Tanaka a reason for picking him as prime minister. His elevation was totally unexpected, because few people had ever noticed him before. He had no understanding whatsoever of economic or diplomatic affairs. Suzuki's paramount interest was never to incur anyone's wrath, and the way to ensure this was to do absolutely nothing. One example among many was the diplomatic crisis that developed with South Korea and China over the rewriting of colonial and wartime history in Japanese middle-school textbooks. At the peak of the crisis, he weighed in with his official solution: that the Ministry of Education and the Ministry of Foreign Affairs should settle the problem between them.

The bureaucrats despised Suzuki. His ministers ignored him to an extent previously unknown in post-war Japan. Insiders leaked the information that he was not treated with the usual deference at the short cabinet meetings. One of the nicknames that he earned as prime minister was "Tape Recorder" because for meetings that could not be avoided the bureaucrats had to train him to recite the answers by heart.

That Suzuki was an international liability became clear when he denied a statement included in a joint communique signed together with President Reagan. At the subsequent annual summit meeting, the US president was visibly uninterested in discussing anything with him. The preparations for the next summit in 1982 gave Japanese bureaucrats more than the normal headaches, for a pre-summit meeting between the US president and the Japanese prime minister had become an established opportunity to reduce the possibility of unpleasant surprises, and President Reagan had pointedly not found time to meet Suzuki.

In one sense Suzuki was the ideal Japanese prime minister, judged by standards often presented as ideally Japanese. He was self-effacing and believed above all in consensus. But the press was nearly unanimous in suggesting that over-consistent adherence to such ideals would not do.

In 1982, the serious deterioration in relations between the US president and the Japanese prime minister was halted when Kishi Nobusuke blocked the re-election of Suzuki Zenko. In the early summer of that year Tanaka Kakuei visited this elderly bureaucrat-politician at his country retreat. The upshot of whatever agreement they made was that Kishi sent a message to Suzuki explaining that he would not necessarily back his candidacy for a second term. Suzuki immediately announced that he would not be available for re-election.

The *habatsu* leader whom Tanaka and Kishi chose to become prime minister in November 1982 was Nakasone Yasuhiro. He was asked to repair the damage done to the US-Japan relationship, and from his very first statements he showed great enthusiasm for doing just that.

As early as the 1970s, political commentators had been speculating that Nakasone Yasuhiro would be a possible exception in a line of relatively featureless prime ministers. He did not disappoint them. But he had also long been considered rather unsuitable for the prime ministership for precisely the same reasons as made him colourful: his emphatic ideas, quotable pronouncements and nationalistic preoccupations. He had drawn an uncommon degree of attention as director-general of the Self-Defence Agency, which he attempted to shake up without much lasting effect. Long before this, in January 1951, he had had the audacity, as a new Diet member, to present General Douglas MacArthur with a manifesto summing up what the Japanese think. In this document he expressed concern that continued subservience to the United States would threaten Japanese sovereignty.

From the moment he became prime minister, Nakasone left no doubt that he had every intention of ruling. Any uncertainty about this was dispelled when he confronted the Ministry of Foreign Affairs with a *fait-accompli* decision to travel to South Korea, whose relations with Japan were surrounded by controversy. His leadership ambitions were equally clear in his choice of cabinet ministers. Hitherto, such choices had been determined by the *habatsu* power balance and only very rarely by the ability of the candidates themselves. All Nakasone cabinets were distinguished by an uncommonly high number of strong ministers. In 1985, Nakasone confessed to his former classmates at a school reunion that he wanted to be a president-type prime minister who could carry out strong policies the way Mrs. Thatcher did. He often chose to answer questions in parliament himself instead of leaving it to his ministers and their bureaucrats; and he drew attention with his (by Japanese standards) clear and straightforward answers.

A resolute manner and firm commitments tend to cause shudders among the administrators. Nakasone's decisiveness also made him unpopular among his fellow LDP members as he addressed himself to issues ranging beyond those immediately connected with economic growth, the pork-barrel or the need to hang on to the top post. He evinced great concern with questions connected with Japan's sovereignty, such as education and international responsibility. He invited questions in the Diet on defence matters, which, touching as they do on national pride, form a potential political platform. He could afford to do so because his tenure was guaranteed as long as Tanaka was in charge and the two did not fall out. Tanaka's machine not only dominated the LDP, but was also the best means for an enterprising prime minister to cope with the bureaucracy.

When, for the first time in twelve years, a Japanese prime minister was given the chance to stay in his position for more than two years, the significance was international. Nakasone had said that he would help Japan play a world role in keeping with its economic power. He presented Japan unambiguously as an active member of the Western alliance, and he introduced a style of direct personal diplomacy in dealing with the US president.

President Reagan was pleasantly surprised, when Nakasone first visited him, to find a leader who appeared to see the Soviet Union through the same glasses as he did. He asked the Japanese prime minister to call him "Ron," whereas Nakasone offered an abbreviation of his first name in return. The fact that even close male friends in Japan seldom call each other by their given names made the symbolism all the more significant in Japan. The "Ron-Yasu" relationship muted, for a couple of years, the strident voices from Washington taking the Japanese to task for various sins in connection with trade and defence.

The relationship was skilfully used on the Japanese side. Nakasone's popularity broke all records. Tanaka alone had been rewarded with similarly high figures, but his popularity subsequently sank to a record low. The support figures for the Nakasone government remained high; contrary to what has often been alleged, the Japanese public appreciated a prime minister who gave clear answers and made a strong impression at home and abroad.

These public feelings contrasted starkly with the aversion a majority of LDP parliamentarians felt for him. With Tanaka incapacitated by a stroke from 1985 onward, Nakasone's leadership seemed in jeopardy as he was confronted with renewed *habatsu* wrangling. The record LDP victory in the 1986 elections earned him an extra year, but popular support is the last thing that keeps a Japanese prime minister in power, and Nakasone had to select Takeshita as his successor in the autumn of 1987.

The French Comparison

Japan has been referred to fairly frequently as an administrative state. This poses the question of how the System compares with a good example of a Western administrative state such as France.

There are many similarities: French bureaucracy has long been one of the most powerful in the world. It is permanent and highly centralised, and no one in power can ignore its opinions on many issues. As in Japan, the central bureaucracy has jurisdiction over local government, most education, public works, the courts, the police and other areas that in most other Western countries are either under the control of independent local authorities or in private hands.

Like Japan, France has institutionalised the elite-forming process to a high degree. Another striking resemblance is the phenomenon of *pantouflage*, meaning the continual shift of civil servants into the private sector. Again, many French bureaucrats move into politics. They maintain important informal relations with each other across the division between the private and public realms. It would seem at first sight that France has a class of administrators akin to that of Japan, a class, moreover, that in the post-war period has been similarly preoccupied with creating optimum conditions for economic expansion.

But a closer look shows revealing differences. The higher-ranking French civil servants have had a relatively wide-ranging education at one of the five *grandes ecoles*. Good memories may be valued, but so are a liberal education, intellectual prowess and an extreme articulateness. The top bureaucrats are much more mobile than Japanese bureaucrats and can be temporarily detached to occupy leading positions in other government agencies, state enterprises, banks or the private sector. In Japan, top bureaucrats are moved from section to section to increase their versatility, but they remain in their first ministry and identify with it to an extent that is detrimental to the functioning of officialdom as a whole.

In the same context, *pantouflage* is not quite the same as *amakudari*. The Japanese companies and banks opening their doors to an *amakudari* bureaucrat expect him to ensure smooth relations with the ministry he has retired from, but not to perform the kind of leadership role expected of a French bureaucrat entering the private sector.

The crucial difference, of course, is that the French bureaucracy serves a highly centralised state. For all its expertise, it requires directives from an identifiable government to function properly. The power of a De Gaulle or a Mitterrand is beyond comparison with that of any Japanese prime minister.

— 4 —

THE SUBMISSIVE
MIDDLE CLASS

The System is preoccupied with industrial and commercial pursuits, the expansion of which is felt as essential to its survival. Although one cannot locate a political centre, there does exist a hard core of institutions that are tightly harnessed to these pursuits.

The administrators who stand at the apex of the interconnected hierarchies of manufacturing firms, banks and trading companies are concerned with something more than production or trade. Those firms exert a hold over the behaviour and thought of their employees that is far beyond anything that firms in the West aspire to or could get away with. It is the standard indoctrination that Japanese companies provide and their success in forcing a life-style on their employees that lends the System much of its solidity.

THE SALARYMAN MODEL

The human substance of the hard core of the System is provided by the *sarariiman* ("salaryman"). He was originally named for the salary he received, as distinct from the wages of factory hands and other workers lower in the occupational hierarchy. But the term "salaryman" connotes much more than office clerk or white-collar worker; it stands for a behavioural norm. The salaryman has such predictable concerns and habits that it has become common in Japanese to speak of salaryman culture. The production of books and magazines devoted to salaryman tastes (including comics as thick as telephone books) comprises one of

Japan's biggest industries. The media carry the salaryman model of life to every corner of Japan.

Becoming a Member

The salaryman world is open to roughly one-third of the young Japanese males who have passed through the school system. Yet even after all those hurdles have been cleared, acceptance by a firm is often dependent on introductions from professors, further exams given by the firm and the result of detective work. Former elementary-school and high-school teachers, as well as neighbours, may be asked about the conduct of the recruit as a teenager. Many companies will want to verify that the recruit is not descended from the "unclean" caste of *burakumin*, or that he is not a member of one of the so-called "new religions," since this might cause loyalty problems.

Acceptance is usually followed by an extended *rite de passage* which confirms and symbolises that the young man is becoming a member of the institution he has joined. This usually begins with a ceremony during which, sometimes in the company of hundreds of his fellows, the recruit, in a fresh salaryman uniform (sober grey or blue suit, with the company badge on the lapel), will hear the company philosophy from the mouth of the president or high executive. He will soon be able to recite this philosophy, and the shorter slogans that come with it in his sleep.

During subsequent training, considerable attention will be paid to an often complicated corporate etiquette. Even the angle of a bow is specified: 15 degrees for colleagues of equal rank met in the corridors; 30 degrees, with both hands held rigidly down the seams of the trousers, for superiors and important visitors; 45 degrees, accompanied by polite and apologetic phrases, when something has gone wrong or when special courtesy is called for. Offering and accepting the ubiquitous business card requires practice. The position one is to occupy with respect to superiors in reception rooms, automobiles or trains must be studied. One must walk slightly behind superiors in the corridors, but enter a lift before a guest. A recruit talking with contemporaries in the corridors indicates that he has not quite understood the seriousness of it all. The outward impression the new salaryman makes is considered extraordinarily important.

At the same time, a remodelling of the recruit's mind is undertaken. Lengthy submersions in an ice-cold river clad in only a loincloth, a 24-

hour march with soldiers and cleaning lavatories for an entire day are some of the more extreme solutions which corporations have found for breaking in a new group of university graduates. Companies view their annual intake of new employees as a disciplinary problem, because it is only through discipline that the recruits will fully appreciate the special relationship they have entered into. If the salaryman cannot feel that he is merged with his firm, or cannot at least pretend to be totally bound up in it, he can hardly be considered a full-fledged member of society.

Some companies have arrangements with Zen temples for what comes down to endurance training. Roughly two thousand send their recruits to the barracks of the Self-Defence Forces. Most companies approach the matter in a more relaxed fashion, but practically all have special training programmes which can last from two months to a year. During this period, the recruit may be required to live in a company dormitory where he is made to rise before dawn, perform all manner of communal tasks, obey a curfew and be in bed with the lights out at ten. The larger firms that own facilities in resort areas often isolate their recruits for a number of weeks for intensive practice in togetherness, mutual confessions and other exercises, some of which constitute rites of purification and initiation. The ultimate purpose can be compared with that of the drill-sargeant in a military unit: to break down individual resistance and inculcate a habit of obedience.

Loyalty in Bondage

Every year the newspapers print the results of an opinion poll in which new employees are asked whether they attach more importance to their families or their firms. Each year there is a slight increase in the percentage favouring the family, which inspires another round of articles on the changing ethics of the salarymen. In 1986, eight out of ten pollees stated that they would rate their private life above the demands of their company. But the experts at Nikkeiren, the federation of employees' associations, do not take such expressions of independence very seriously. Whenever the interests of the company and the family come into conflict, it is the family that will adjust as a matter of course. *Maihomu-shugi* or "my-home-ism"—the tendency of young salarymen to rate highly the claims of wife and children—has not proved the threat that officials and the business elite thought it might become. The prefix *mai* ("my") still has a relatively negative connotation, whatever noun it is made to precede, because in the eyes of the industrial administrators it is associated with a loss of preoccupation with the workplace. But at the same time the competition among salaryman families to stock their small homes with the latest-model refrigerators, stereo-sound colour television and labour-saving devices, and their tiny parking places with cars, is exactly what is needed to keep their firms running at full capacity.

Most companies give special consideration to the recently married salaryman. But following the birth of the first child, typically after some two years of marriage, the husband is expected to settle down to the serious business of devoting most of his energy, time and attention to his company.

Some commentators have argued that Japanese men prefer the company of fellow workers and that they are uncomfortable when they have to go out with their wives and children. But one can argue that the salarymen have little choice, and that their discomfort stems from a lack of practice. A visit to rural areas or the urban neighbourhoods where family workshops and blue-collar workers predominate, will confirm that most Japanese have no inherent difficulty with a social life centred on the family. The phenomenon of a middle class deprived to a large extent of men functioning as husbands and fathers is of relatively recent origin.

The salaryman is expected actively to demonstrate loyalty to his firm. There are various ways of doing this: he walked to work during railway strikes in the 1960s and 1970s, and he refrained from taking some or all of the holidays he was entitled to in the 1980s. His most common way to demonstrate loyalty is by working late hours or spending time after work with colleagues and business associates—which means limiting the time spent with his family to the hours between eleven at night and seven in the morning.

This bond between company and employee can only be maintained, of course, so long as the employee has nowhere else to hire out his services. In most cases he hasn't. Although in the lower reaches of the business hierarchy—among the small subcontracting firms—a steady turnover of employees is fairly common, in the world of the salaryman to change one's job is possible only in the first couple of years, if at all.

The psychological explanation of this lack of mobility has been overworked. While salarymen are undoubtedly conditioned to believe that it is proper to remain with the same employer, the more important factor is that changing companies nearly always entails a set-back in income, prestige and future prospects. It is the policy of large companies either not to accept white-collar employees from other companies, or to place them in a considerably lower position than the one they have come from.

FAMILIST IDEOLOGY

For the administrator elite, the salaryman's allegiance to his firm epitomises the ideal relationship between all Japanese and the System. It is most commonly expressed in the image of the corporation as a kind of family—an image that has made its way into numerous foreign assessments of Japanese economic life. It is widely believed that such familial relationships have evolved out of a centuries-old tradition of psychosocial preferences. But in fact the company-as-family idea is a fairly modern innovation. Business firms in the Meiji period tended to be run by fairly individualistic entrepreneurs. The flagrant exploitation of workers and the resulting industrial unrest, not to mention the very conspicuous status differences, would hardly have made the family metaphor acceptable in those days, even to the most credulous observer.

Familistic organisation in industry did not, even so, spring out of nowhere. Fictive kinship relations have been common for centuries, and a more immediate model emerged from the vigorous labour market created by rapidly expanding entrepreneurism in Meiji Japan. This market was originally formed by bands of workers controlled by bosses, who referred to each other as *oyakata* and *kokata* (literally, people who fill the role of parent and child, respectively), and were bound together by quasi-familial ties in which loyalty and obedience were exchanged for supposed benevolence. Early labour unions were often, in fact, little other than these *oyakata-kotata* groups.

As the large corporations came to require more refined skills, and their fear of labour activism increased, entrepreneurs were prodded into recruiting and training workers with the purpose of forming regular bodies of permanent employees. Even so, it was decades before familistic ideas began to catch on among the managers, and it was only in the second half of the 1930s, when the war in China led the government to focus on industrial programmes for increasing productivity, that the company-as-family notion spread all over the country.

In the ideal Japanese perspective—which survives in the negative connotation of "my-home-ism"—the workplace, the multi-generational family as distinct from the nuclear family, the schools and the clubs are not considered part of a private realm. This means that the public realm can encroach all the way up to the threshold of the individual psyche. For many Japanese, family, friends and colleagues do not constitute a buffer giving protection or moral support in the face of government or company authorities; the political world lies immediately outside one's skin.

The Politicised Household

The Japanese *ie*, or "household," denotes a social unit that, unlike its Chinese counterpart, is determined less by blood-ties than by a shared economic role. The kinship family may well, of course, overlap with the economic unit that the *ie* represents, but maids, farmhands and the like were traditionally considered participants in the Japanese *ie*, whereas family members no longer under the common roof were not. By contrast, Chinese generally continued to feel a deep sense of membership in the family even after generations of separation by, say, the Pacific Ocean.

The corporate character of the Japanese *ie* developed as a result of regulations enforced by the Tokugawa shogunate as part of its elaborate system of social control. The household was, quite consciously, transformed into a political unit some three and a half centuries ago. Individuals did not own property, the *ie* did. Individuals were registered as members of the *ie*, whose head was responsible for them. The head also had nearly unlimited legal power over the members of his household.

For power-holders this was a marvellous basic unit to work with, and the Meiji oligarchy extended the legal *ie* organisation to all layers of the population. In the twentieth century the *ie* was legally obliged until 1945 to produce moral citizens. The post-war civil code stripped the household and its head of their legal rights and duties and dropped the formal concept of *ie* altogether. But it survives in organisational ideals.

When the managers began replacing the entrepreneurs in the early part of this century, they simply re-adopted the *ie* imagery. Today many large firms have "ancestors" in the form of legendary founding presidents who frequently bequeathed a philosophy or moral code for the benefit of generations of employees. These are sometimes expounded in the glossy literature put out by Japanese companies, which often ask one to believe that commercial gain is the last thing on the mind of Japanese managers. Companies are portrayed as benefiting the people, if not the whole of humanity, and a fair number have inserted in their promotional literature a line or two about their ideal of contributing to world peace. But above all, according to accepted theory, the company exists for its employees, whose "sincere efforts" are expected in return for all that previous managers have done to bring it where it is.

Songs and Sacrifices

The salaryman's intensive involvement in his company makes necessary a reassuring symbolism, confirming that his time, energy and personal interests are being sacrificed for a worthy cause; the company must appear to be something more than an organisation established for the purpose of making a profit or providing its employees with a livelihood. Sometimes a company Shinto shrine on the roof provides a vague reminder of spiritual significance attached to the communal effort to continue the voyage of the company from past generations through the present into the future. One important symbol for the large modern company is its emblem, reminiscent of the family crests of the prominent *ie* of the past. Some firms—again like the old merchant *ie*—also have a constitution consisting of pieties and prescribed duties. And each large company is expected to have its own *shafu*, a "company spirit" derived from ideals set forth in catechism-like tracts. Whoever makes a tour of a contemporary Japanese factory is likely to end up with stacks of booklets setting out the special wisdom and traditions of the firm, interspersed with platitudes concerning the general welfare.

The shared company culture is regularly reaffirmed by the communal singing of company songs. The personnel of Victor Company of Japan Ltd. sing:

> *Geniuses of the world assembly here where music is played, Essence of culture, Pride of human technics, Victor, Victor, Our Victor, the Nation's welfare, Family harmony, We realise them both, We enjoy accomplishing our mission, Highest technology of the age, Pride of the world...The flame which makes our products is in our sincerity, Essence of culture, Pride of human technics.*

Employees of Toyota Motor Corporation confirm that they are full of:

> *Wishes for overflowing sunshine and green, We open the new age with guts and an eternally expanding human network...We keep growing*

tomorrow, with a unified mind and continuous effort, Our, Our, Our Toyota...We form our history with a worldly dream, wisdom and rich technology, Bright future, with a unified mind and new strides, Our, Our, Our Toyota.

Songs from other companies would cover roughly the same ground. Expressions like "brighter future" and "harmony" are rarely absent. The songs often mention belonging to a large family and refer to what others in the past have done to create the present, thus implying a duty to carry on the good work.

Although Japanese salarymen do not exactly begin the day with joint prayer, this is the impression given by the *choreikai*, the morning meetings held in an estimated 80 percent of Japanese firms. Employees are intensively and constantly involved in meetings, work discussion groups, quality control circles and the like. All of this helps to shape a personality susceptible to manipulation. The passionate clinging to the symbols of the firm, the founder and the corporate ideology; the singing of the company song; the joint calisthenics—all are symbolic acts designed to reassure the employee of his membership in the company and of its nurturing powers.

SUBMISSION AND ORDER

From the time they were again allowed to visit Japan a little over a century ago, Western authors have been greatly impressed by the force of Japanese loyalty and still tend to the conclusion that it is the highest value in Japanese life. This assessment, though true, can be misleading unless one makes clear what Japanese loyalty really consists of.

Piety for Superiors

To begin with, Japanese loyalty is directed at a group or person, not a belief or abstract idea. And since organisations that are potentially hostile to the System have been weeded out almost entirely, Japanese loyalty is most directly supportive of the established socio-political order.

Loyalty is frequently mentioned in the same breath as filial piety, as both values are central to the Chinese Confucianism that the Japanese aristocracy imported long ago to buttress its power. The influence of the injunction of filial piety has been considerable. B. H. Chamberlain wrote shortly after the turn of the century: "There are no greater favourites with the people of Japan than the 'Four-and-Twenty Paragons of Filial Piety,' whose quaint acts of virtue Chinese legend records." One Paragon had a cruel stepmother, who loved fish. Despite her awful treatment of him, he lay down naked on a frozen lake, melted a hole with his body heat and caught two carp that came up for air. Another slept naked so that all the mosquitoes bit him and left his parents alone. My favourite is the seventy-year-old Paragon who dressed in baby clothes and crawled on the floor, deluding his ninety-year-old parents into believing that they could not be so very old after all.

The Meiji government not only propagated filial piety to strengthen family morality and foster patriotism, but also decreed that filial piety and loyalty to the emperor were one and the same thing. Today, the obedience of Japanese towards their superiors is no longer unconditional, yet the element of choice is in most cases still lacking. When employees of large corporations feel that they have had enough of their present boss, they have no option but to remain loyal because, as we have seen, if they were to leave they would not find another job with a comparable income. Even today, loyalty to one's superiors overrules other moral considerations. A national television audience was reminded of this in 1976 when a group of executives consistently, elaborately and rather obviously committed perjury to protect their employers during parliamentary hearings in connection with the Lockheed bribery scandal. Systematic deceit in such cases where loyalty is involved is widely admired.

When it is carried to its ultimate expression, celebrated in Kabuki plays and some contemporary films, the ethic of loyalty is morally unacceptable to Westerners, as, for example, when parents murder their own child in order to save the life of the child of their lord. Most important, however, it must be understood that the Japanese ethic of loyalty is, in essence, an ethic of submission.

Loyal Subcontractors

The salaryman world and its preoccupations may set the tone of contemporary Japanese life, yet it encompasses no more than roughly one-third of the working population. Businesses with between 100 and 1,000 workers provide some 16 percent of jobs, and those with more than 1,000 another 15 percent. Outside this world, the relative job security known as lifetime employment (which generally ends between the ages of 55 and 58) does not apply. However, entrepreneurial ambitions provide a respected alternative. The dream of having a company of one's own is still widespread and is important to the survival of the so-called dual economy. Supporting the towering hierarchy of large conglomerates there exists a vast collection of medium-sized and small firms that can be squeezed when times are bad.

Almost half Japan's manufacturing workforce is engaged in factories with fewer than fifty workers. These are often no more than sweatshops in which husband and wife may work ten or more hours a day. As subcontractors these small companies—which make parts, or assemble finished products for distribution by the famous firms—provide cheap labour, and in times of economic downturn absorb much of the shock. When the yen doubled in value against the US dollar between 1985 and 1987, these small companies bore a large share of the loss in profits of companies eager to hang on to foreign market shares.

Japan has a much larger proportion of such small enterprises than the highly industrialised Western countries. Self-employed and family workers (mainly women) form 29 percent of the Japanese labour force, compared with 8 percent in Britain, 9 percent in the US, 14 percent in West Germany and 17 percent in France. The resilience of this vast segment of small firms is of vital importance to the international competitiveness of the large Japanese firms. A large number of bankruptcies among small firms is balanced by a roughly equal number of openings; the same entrepreneurs launch into another line of business. In large areas of Tokyo and Osaka back streets rarely visited by outsiders, one hears the same incessant clickety-clack of small machines behind hundreds of wooden doors as one did ten or twenty years ago; but the clickety-clack produces entirely different things today.

The freedom of the small entrepreneurs is real in that they can give their own name to their companies. But it is unreal to the extent that almost two-thirds of them are financially dependent on one of the larger firms, which can dictate the conditions under which they work. On this level, too, much is made of the family metaphor. The "parent firm" helps the subcontractor with supplies, technical assistance, and investments in machinery. It will not, under normal conditions, turn to cheaper subcontractors. But the "child firm" must accept its role as shock-absorber in periods of economic downturn.

Here too the System is at work, and its embrace is also apparent in the numerous associations of small and medium-sized businesses that support LDP candidates at election time. With the LDP behind them, the bureaucrats help preserve the dual economy by not burdening small manufacturers with stringent regulations and through tax privileges.

Keeping Women in Their Proper Place

Besides controlling the thought and behaviour of the salaryman, the Japanese business world helps preserve order by systematic discrimination against women. Women make up a very important part of the workforce. More than half of those who are married supplement the family income with full-time or part-time employment, often in sub-contracting firms. These working women furnish the System with a gigantic pool of relatively cheap labour through corporate policies which appeal to Japanese social customs and traditions and are supported by the bureaucracy. From the age of eighteen or twenty, girls work in the service sector or offices; then, in their mid-twenties, they marry and "retire." Many return to the labour force in their mid-thirties, after bringing up a child or two. Most women in offices start their career with 10 percent less pay than male colleagues, and this gap widens to about 30 percent. When they return to work, they cannot claim seniority and are typically employed on a "part-time" basis, though they may work as many hours as their male colleagues at half the pay, and with few if any fringe benefits.

In the wake of litigation by a few activist female employees in the 1970s, most large firms will not summarily dismiss young women when they reach "retirement age" or marry. But the pressure on them to leave "voluntarily" is nearly always irresistible. Unless she works for a bank, insurance firm, government office, department store or foreign company—organisations that do offer careers to women—a female employee approaching the age of twenty-nine will have to find a husband or an alternative source of income.

Since the spring of 1985, Japan has had an Equal Employment Opportunity Law, which enjoins corporate Japan to attempt to treat male and female employees equally. The law does not spell out the consequences of not making such an attempt. The law was the minimum Japan could come up with for the sake of its international image, and it was passed just in time for ratification of the UN's Convention on the Elimination of All Forms of Discrimination against Women.

The role of Japanese women in the economic process has become a problem that is only partially reflected by pressure from activist groups. The number of working married women in 1985 had doubled compared with twenty years before, the phenomenon of the "honeymoon baby" has drastically decreased, and the gradual increase in the still very low divorce rate is largely due to the initiative of wives wishing to pursue a career. To help defuse strains and tensions, the administrators actively endorse the picture of the traditional Japanese family purveyed by the mass media. From the vehement reactions in serious magazines to the activists who were bent on strengthening the equal employment law, one would conclude that the continuation of Japanese culture was at issue.

Although in reality Japanese tradition has never frowned on working women, the officially sponsored portrait of wholesome family life invariably shows that the proper place for women is at home. In a country where stereotypes are treasured, emphasis on the proper roles of women is especially noticeable. It extends to demurely polite deportment, a studied innocent cuteness, a gentle voice and a nurturing, motherly disposition. The model woman in the world of the salaryman is a cross between Florence Nightingale and the minister of finance (as women are almost always responsible for household finances). Superior intelligence is a liability and must be disguised. Women are frequently degraded in TV programmes and comic strips. Many bookstores have an SM section in which the most popular items are magazines and books with pictures of ladies tied up to look like rolled meat. In 1985, a director-general of the cultural affairs bureau of the Ministry of Education caused a small stir when he wrote in a magazine article that rape, although not gentlemanly conduct, was not so bad if practised on modern young women whose moral standards had slipped anyhow.

The picture is not entirely negative. A great step in the liberation of Japanese women was taken under the auspices of the United States occupation when adultery as a criminal offence was scrapped from the law books. Under the old code, in keeping with Confucianist practice, only the wife could ever be guilty of this crime. Also, there seems to be no doubt that behind a majority of closed doors the Japanese wife is the more powerful member of the family and that the salaryman shackled to his firm could use as much emancipation as his wife.

The Unrepresented Middle Class

Most salarymen are urban consumers, and it is they who, through relatively high amounts of savings, subsequently channelled into the *keiretsu* for capital investments, have played a crucial role in sustaining the economic miracle. It is they who in the late 1980s were still subsidising Japan's export industries by being systematically deprived of low-cost imports and by paying considerably higher prices than consumers in the Western industrialised countries for almost all daily necessities.

In most other countries the rise of the middle class has basically changed political relations. In Japan such a disturbing influence has been minimised. However important he may be to the survival of the System, the salaryman's interests are woefully under-represented. All efforts to organise his political potential, including a Salaryman Party, have failed. The claims made by the company on his total person leave him with insufficient time, energy and ideas to become a political force. The salarymen have been referred to as Japan's new middle class, but this white-collar class has never grown into a bourgeoisie that could be a threat to the traditional Japanese body politic.

PRODUCERS OF SALARYMAN CULTURE

A mammoth industry sees to it that Japanese have their circuses as well as their bread. Japanese mass culture is tailor-made to sustain the orderly world of the salaryman. The days of the serious Japanese cinema, exploring social and political issues, are long gone. Since the 1960s, the Japanese movie studios, which are very much part of the System, have churned out totally predictable fare made according to a small variety of rigid formulas. Japanese avant-garde theatre groups sometimes claim to make political statements, but their messages are abstract and imponderable.

The Hidden Media Boss

A crucial factor in Japanese popular culture is its degree of commercial organisation. Control is easily accomplished without open or direct governmental restraint. As is true of the education system, the entertainment industry abhors imagination that goes against the grain of socio-political expectations. The police are activated only by photographs and film scenes showing pubic hair. Everything else can be controlled because the "private" institutions are informally linked to a number of elite groups. They include film and television studios, as well as most of the gigantic newspaper and publishing firms. But the best example, probably, is afforded by the advertising world, and in particular Dentsu, the largest advertising agency in the world.

Dentsu does more than any single corporation, anywhere in the world, to mould popular culture, both directly and through hordes of subcontractors. It also orchestrates major events, such as expos and visits from the Pope, and it is highly active politically.

Dentsu is directly responsible for one-third of all advertising on Japanese TV and virtually monopolises the scheduling of sponsors during prime-time hours. Some 120 film production companies and more than 400 subcontracting graphic arts studios are under its wing. Advertisers wishing to insert commercials in television programmes between 7 and 11 p.m. have almost no choice but to go via Dentsu.

Nowhere in the world has the drug of TV taken such a hold as in Japan, with sets in restaurants, shops, tour buses and even taxis. Very few, if any, countries can be proud of the overall quality of their television programmes, but the global cultural desert has areas of greater and lesser misery. Sometimes NHK (comparable to the BBC) will broadcast a serious programme in which reporters are allowed to raise genuine questions about social issues. For the rest, Japanese television ranges from pseudo-scholarly and carefully uncontroversial "serious" fare on NHK, through soap operas to utterly vacuous show programmes. Quizzes and amateur song-fests are copied from foreign examples, but in Japan they reach an apotheosis of mindlessness. If television programmes in the USA are adjusted to viewers of an average mental age of eleven or twelve, those in Japan are attuned to an average age of eight or nine. Dentsu is the major instrument for determining the quality of Japan's daily entertainment, and it has managed to reduce nearly everything to the lowest common denominator.

The Closed Circuit of Dentsu Power

Dentsu handles about a quarter of all advertising budgets in Japan; it places over one-fifth of the ads in the major newspapers and close to a third of those in the more important magazines. Dentsu gets higher commissions than the smaller agencies, and can set conditions of payment. New magazines may be asked to take advertisements free of charge for a trial period before they will be considered as an outlet.

Dentsu has become unbeatable thanks to its *jinmyaku*. Its hiring policies have always been aimed at the sons and other close relatives of top-level administrators, executives in the television and publishing world, and special clients and professional backstage fixers. One Dentsu executive was quoted as characterising this as "taking hostages" to maintain favourable relations with big sponsors.

Advertising agencies in other countries are intermediaries. In Japan, Dentsu itself often decides how companies must advertise and where. In the USA, an independent rating agency determines how commercially successful the programmes are; in Japan this function remains in Dentsu's hands.

Dentsu is in a position to intimidate large firms, since it can make corporate scandals known and hush them up again. It is also able to apply enormous pressure on the media not to report, or to downplay, incidents that might harm the prestige of its clients. A famous case is Dentsu's controlling of news about the arsenic contamination of Morinaga Milk Industry's powdered milk in 1955. Another is the way Dentsu in 1964-5 censored news of deaths caused by a cold medicine produced by Taisyo Pharmaceutical.

Another major function of this media institution is the bolstering of traditional values with the aid of opinion polls, together with public-relations work for the bureaucrats and the LDP. It collects intelligence for the Prime Minister's Office and the LDP and is in charge of the more sophisticated aspects of LDP election campaigns. It handles propaganda concerning controversial issues such as the safety of nuclear power generation. It coordinated political manoeuvres to unseat a string of opposition mayors and prefectural governors in the late 1970s and has waged campaigns against politically significant local consumer and environmental movements.

— 5 —

NURSES OF THE
PEOPLE

I n its fighting spirit, its compulsory togetherness, its consciousness
of rank within the company and its proprietary treatment of the
employee as a family member, salaryman life is clearly reminiscent
of the military tradition. Indeed, most walks of Japanese life are highly
regimented. It is ironic that the only country in the world whose
constitution deprives it of the right to wage war, whose official spokesmen seriously suggest that it can teach the world to love peace, and
which formally decries the use of military power, whenever and wherever and no matter by whom, should so often remind one of a military
organisation. The flocks of high-school pupils dressed in black uniforms cut like those of Prussia at the turn of the century; the emphasis
on collective exercise; the drills continued for their own sake far beyond
the point where skill ceases to improve; the social approval given to
gambaru (not giving up, sticking with something beyond reason); the
sentimental emphasis on the purity of single-minded youthful exer-
tions; the Spartan discipline in judo, karate, kendo and aikido training—
all these represent a militarised approach to social order. The virtues of
self-control and endurance that the Japanese are taught to hold in
highest regard, along with loyalty, are among the most important that
soldiers must cultivate.

This is not surprising, when one considers that Japan was ruled by
soldiers during much of its history. The Tokugawa shogunate was a
warrior regime maintaining something akin to martial law. In time, it
evolved into a bureaucratic government, complete with ideology and a
privileged ruling class. But its ideals of social discipline remained those
of the barracks and the battlefield.

Those who today may apply naked power in the name of the state—the police and public prosecutors—have turned the habit of leniency into a kind of second nature. But a condition is attached: the recipient must in turn acknowledge the goodness of the established social order.

Nannies, Monitors and Missionaries

From the time of its formation in the 1870s it was understood that Japan's police force, unlike its sword-wielding samurai predecessors, could not merely scare the populace into submission. Kawaji Toshiyoshi, first chief of the Tokyo metropolitan police and architect of the modern Japanese police system, neatly summed it up by saying that the government should be seen as the parent, the people as the children and the policemen as the nurses of the children.

An important function of the police from the turn of the century was to monitor the potentially explosive relationships between entrepreneurs and the labourers they hired in factories and on building sites. The combined office and residence *(chuzaisho)* of the rural policemen was often established on factory land and supported by an entrepreneur. The latter sometimes even paid the salaries of those policemen, who thus became virtual factory guards.

Until 1945, the Japanese police were also, of course, in charge of suppressing political heterodoxy. This was made easier by an extremely elaborate information-gathering network, with spies throughout the civilian population. Police also called on important families and landowners once a year, people without property twice a year and unemployed or suspicious citizens three times. Yet even while clamping down severely on anything that might upset the established order, the police understood that a tranquil Japan was best achieved through leniency and accommodation. Even after the dreaded Tokko (Special Higher Police—later known as the "thought police") acquired great power in 1925, people with the "wrong thoughts" were not treated harshly once they had shown repentance. Recantation of one's beliefs would result in dropped charges and, frequently, in official assistance in finding a job for smooth reintegration into the community.

Today, the police are rarely overbearing towards individuals (as distinct from their exhortations directed to the public in general through megaphones and loudspeakers); they generally blend in with the area they patrol, and cultivate a friendly and helpful demeanor.

Every neighbourhood in the cities has its koban, or police box—

introduced in 1888 on the advice of a captain in the Berlin metropolitan police—and the countryside is dotted with the *chuzaisho* were local policemen live with their families. The *koban* is a source of information on many matters, from unfindable addresses to treatment for a sick pet. People still receive twice-yearly home visits from the *koban*-based police, who collect gossip about the neighbourhood and inquire after any unusual behaviour. Many foreigners in Tokyo are excluded from these rounds, but I, for example, received a visit from the policeman of the *chuzaisho* within a month of settling in the countryside to work on this book.

The public is not undivided in its admiration for policemen. To some extent they are still feared. But, especially in the countryside, people offer them free meals and invite them to drinking parties. In the cities, the police can rely on a large number of enthusiastic informers: people who monitor the life of the streets while selling cigarettes from tiny window-shops, or respected members of the neighbourhood such as doctors or dentists. There are in addition thousands of volunteer crime-prevention associations based on neighbourhood organisations and occupational groups, all linked by federations.

I once spent a Saturday afternoon with a small group of middle-aged housewives patrolling the streets of one of Tokyo's major entertainment districts. Their trained eyes would soon spot any teenagers from the suburbs, whom they would approach for questioning. The conversations usually ended with encouragement to return home and avoid the temptations and traps awaiting innocent youth in the city. Encounters which in many Western countries would have resulted at least in foul language produced only bowed heads and muttered thanks for the advice given by the crime-prevention ladies.

The function of nursemaid to all citizens is still cherished by the contemporary police. One detects it in the admonishing tone of instructions suddenly emanating from the loudspeaker on a police box or cruising patrol car. In the apartment-block districts of some smaller cities the police try to make people feel part of a community by wishing them good morning through a public address system at 7 a.m., and by providing music for calisthenics, uplifting talk and reminders to be careful about all manner of things.

The public, on its side, tends to obey police directions, however unnecessary. Pedestrians will wait for quite superfluous traffic lights to change on narrow streets that could be crossed in a stride or two, or even where no vehicles can pass because of a blocked-off road.

A good example of tolerance of police interference can be witnessed every year during the cherry-blossom season in Tokyo's Ueno Park, which attracts a large number of partying groups, who sit on mats beneath the blossoms, picnicking, drinking, singing and clapping their hands in unison. But the police have staked out large territories for themselves too, and use their megaphones liberally for exhortations and warnings. These go on until about 8:30 p.m. when, with the revelry in full swing, the police begin to shout that it is time to go home. Amazingly, within thirty minutes the park is nearly totally empty. Practically everyone obeys, even though the police are making arbitrary rules; in fact, the park is open twenty-four hours a day.

The Japanese, especially in the cities, are constantly made to feel like subjects rather than citizens. They live in a cajoling and exhortative environment. They are continually warned about dangers, reminded of the proper way to do things, gently chided. Kawaji's nurses of the people have stayed on as permanent instructors. The loudspeakers on cruising police cars recall a worrisome mother; something is always *abunai*, dangerous. The hint of aggrievedness in the tone emphasises further the likeness to a Japanese mother; people walking the streets are made to feel like potentially naughty children.

The Remorseful Suspect

A specialist in cross-cultural comparisons of police methods has concluded that Japan is a paradise for the cops because Japanese society polices itself. One might add that it is also a paradise, comparatively speaking, for those caught by the police, since few of them are actually punished. In the treatment of offenders the nursemaid function is clearly demonstrated. Occasionally the police will be strict, for the sake of setting an example; but generally, if people committing misdemeanours are sufficiently apologetic and promise to improve their behaviour, they have a very good chance of being let off after a perfunctory lecture.

Even where, with more serious offences, the police pursue the matter, the public prosecutor, or procurator as he is called, has nearly unlimited power to let the culprit go. The code of criminal procedure permits dropping a case in consideration of the suspect's character, age and circumstances, or the development of events following the offence. In recent decades just under half of all cases of serious violations of the criminal code were dropped for reasons unrelated to lack of evidence.

Older people and first offenders tend to be treated with leniency. This is, of course, not unusual elsewhere, but the Japanese prosecutor has considerably greater discretion than his Western counterpart.

Even if suspects are indicted and convicted, they are often not given prison sentences. In 1986, only 3.2 percent of all prosecution cases, including traffic violations, received such sentences, and 57.4 percent of these were suspended. Suspended prison sentences of two to three years for rapists are fairly common. As a result, this country of 120 million inhabitants has only about 50,000 people behind bars. One reason is the low budget for penal facilities, but there is more to it than that. The enormous discretionary autonomy of the Japanese law-enforcement authorities enables them to shift emphasis from punishing the crime to "converting" the offender to the side of society.

In practically all instances the most important factor determining the choice made by the public prosecutor is the extent to which the suspect makes a display of remorse. Police and prosecutors love apologies. Not the simple one-time kind, which rarely suffice even in normal social intercourse. What is expected from suspects is a continuous stream of apology, the intensity and profusion of which must indicate their sincerity. Some suspects may, in fact, go down on their knees. Thus the law-enforcement system does not apply punishment to fit the crime, but rather to fit the demeanour of the culprit after the crime. We must not mistake this for compassion. The decisions on what to do with suspects entails a symbolic determination as to whether they are still fit for society. And the overriding criterion for this is each suspect's thorough understanding of the required redemption ritual. The unspoken rationale behind this is that cooperative citizens are preferable to costly prisoners whose imprisonment may teach them only to become worse criminals.

Confess!

Japanese can be apologetic in a general way. They sometimes give the impression of thinking that their mere presence is a nuisance to others. Generalised apologies demonstrate "sincerity." But the really solid apologies that the nurses of the people expect must be related directly to the crime. Thus a major task for the police is to make a suspect confess. In this context the legal rights of the individual are as good as irrelevant. Police and prosecutors place a tremendous emphasis on admission of guilt, regardless of the constitutional guarantee that citizens are not obliged to testify against themselves. Confession is still considered the necessary first step for a return to normal society.

The police are at an advantage in extracting confessions. They may keep a suspect in custody upon issue of a warrant, without access to counsel or bail, for a period that can be extended up to twenty-three days. Another advantage is that Japanese society heartily approves of apologies where a non-Japanese observer would see absolutely no need for them. Thus a Japanese will sometimes ask forgiveness for an imaginary transgression simply in order to appear sincere. Being picked up by the police is, in any event, shameful, and there is comfort in converting an overwhelming sense of shame into an admission of guilt, since guilt can more easily be coped with; unlike shame, it can be expiated.

If suspects do not cooperate, subtle forms of blackmail may be brought into play. Much can be expected of the threat that the suspect's family will become involved. In a number of instances, relatively simple-minded suspects were told that their father and mother would also be arrested if they did not confess.

For those particularly reluctant to confess, there are early-morning-to-midnight interrogations for days on end. Suspects are under 24-hour surveillance, either directly or via closed-circuit television. They are forced to sleep under glaring fluorescent lights and are not allowed to pull their blankets over their faces. The food is minimal and of dismal quality. The investigators use the expression "confession for a bowl of *domburi*," referring to the dish of meat or vegetables with rice that suspects may order (and pay for themselves) as a reward for confessing.

Lest the impression be given that the nurses of the people are in fact a collection of ogres, I must emphasise that the behaviour of the police foot-soldiers in the local *koban* is, by and large, exemplary. Their general helpfulness, their willingness to listen while neighbourhood people unburden themselves and their friendly efforts to mediate in quarrels are all the more remarkable when one considers their fatiguing (18-20 hour) shifts.

Centuries of Favours

The theory of the benevolence of law-enforcement officers accords with a view of power relations assiduously promoted by Japanese power-holders. Everlasting gratitude of subjects towards their superiors has been, next to unconditional loyalty, the major command of Japanese life, and it is bound up with the officially sponsored faith in the ultimate beneficence and virtue of the existing political order.

Traditionally, benevolence in Japan was not considered to be a condition for rule, as in China, but something extra bestowed upon the people out of the goodness of their ruler's heart. Subordinates received privileges or goods because they had humane superiors, not because they had a right to anything. Whereas Chinese emperors were expected to be benevolent and maintain justice in order to keep the "mandate of Heaven," their Japanese counterparts, as direct descendants of the sun goddess, were not in need of heavenly endorsement.

While the System is no longer presented as a source of all blessings in life, Japanese are still expected to take its benevolence for granted. In actual practice, Japanese can be quite cynical about the supposed benevolence of those placed above them. A political representative whom voters have sent to the Diet is judged by whether or not he can deliver the bridge, road or other benefits he has promised the constituency. Villagers have for centuries fended for themselves, and in the process they have developed a strong sense of their right to certain customary amenities. Eavesdropping on salarymen imbibing sake will confirm that one of their favourite pastimes is grumbling about their superiors. But this cynicism has not undermined the habit of profusely apologising and expressing gratitude towards supposed benefactors. And the benevolent motives of officialdom and the large companies are taken for granted by the leaders of those institutions themselves.

A Safe Society

The nurses of the people and the self-policing people themselves have managed to make their society, industrialised, urbanised and congested as it is, safer than most other countries. One need not worry about being mugged, let alone murdered, in the small alleys of Tokyo. Japan has become the envy of the world for, next to its successful trade, its low crime statistics. Only 1.47 people per 100,000 of the population were murdered in 1984, as compared with 7.92 people in the United States, 3.24 in Britain and 4.51 in West Germany. Burglaries and petty theft are fairly common, but the statistics for robberies with assault are even more lopsided when compared with the West: 1.82 cases per 100,000 population in Japan, 205.38 cases in the USA, 50.02 cases in the UK and 45.77 cases in West Germany.

Besides the networks of police informants and crime-prevention

squads of ordinary civilians, the symbiotic relationship between the
Japanese police and organised crime must also be part of the explanation
for this great discrepancy. The strict control of hand-guns helps as well,
as does the absence of a crime-producing drug problem. Heroin addiction is rare, and the measures taken against its distribution and use are
merciless. No sympathy is shown for the suffering of the addict; if
caught, drug users go cold turkey. Marijuana is treated as a dangerous
hard drug, and suspected users—mainly in the entertainment world—
may expect pre-dawn raids on their apartments. If caught they go to
prison, and foreigners among them may be deported.

KEEPING THE LAW UNDER CONTROL

If Western democracies relied as little on law as Japan does, they would
be rocked by civil commotion. Conversely, if Japan were to use the law
as it is used in the Western democracies, and as it is supposed to be used
under its constitution, the present authority structure would collapse.

The constitution, a legacy of the Occupation, could not be more
democratic. It contains more explicit safeguards protecting the citizen
than those of Western Europe and the USA. But it in no way reflects
Japanese political priorities. The line it draws between law and administration, making the judiciary autonomous, goes against the practice of
Japan's entire history. A truly independent judiciary and a population
familiar with the possibilities of litigation would have checked consolidation of the post-war System as we know it. The consistent and non-
partisan enforcement of anti-trust laws would have checked it. Adherence to the election laws would have checked it, as would consistent
judicial investigation into the corrupt relationship between big business
and the LDP, and the various other practices that keep the System
going. Driven as it is by a myriad *jinmyaku*, the System could not
survive the consistent application of the legal process.

Minimising and Moulding the Judiciary and Bar

The role of law in the System is most effectively minimised by keeping
the number of lawyers and judges very small. Japan does not have
enough legal professionals to support even a fraction of the litigation
common to European countries, not to mention the United States.

Going to court to claim a right is an option that a Japanese is never
encouraged to consider. The number of civil suits per capita is roughly

between one-twentieth and one-tenth of the figures for common-law countries. Virtually all cases of civil conflict are settled by conciliation, either out of court or before a judicial verdict is reached. This custom goes back at least to the Tokugawa period, when the authorities forced people to settle their differences by conciliation.

The common explanation for the persistence of this method is that it is consonant with deeply rooted cultural concern with maintaining harmony. Litigation, by creating winners and losers, works against this ideal. Even lawyers and judges who are critical of contemporary Japanese justice tend to be convinced by such culturalist interpretations.

Yet there are good reasons to reject the culturalist explanation and, instead, view current judicial practice as a political legacy from the days when the Japanese were forced to settle by conciliation. The System prefers conciliation. As has been generally noticed, Japanese conciliation procedures almost always give the advantage to the more powerful disputant—thus helping maintain the status quo. A multitude of legal appeals might well break the System apart.

The judiciary and bar are kept artificially minuscule by strict controls over entry into the legal profession. The Ministry of Justice is gatekeeper to the Legal Training and Research Institute (LTRI), through which all those aspiring to become judges, prosecutors or lawyers must pass. This institute offers two years of not particularly heavy training, and graduation is almost automatic for everyone who is considered politically sound. But the annual passing rate for entry into the school is extremely low, at roughly 2 percent; 486 out of 23,855 candidates passed the entrance examination in 1985. In late 1986, eighty of the successful candidates were taking the exam for the fifth time.

The widespread idea that the Japanese are reluctant to enter the legal profession is pure myth. As one specialist has pointed out, the number of Japanese, relative to the total population, who took the judicial examination in 1975 was slightly higher than the figure for Americans staking a bar examination. And since 74 percent in the United States passed in that year, compared to 1.7 percent in Japan, the desire to become a lawyer in Japan must actually be much stronger.

The number of judges has not even doubled since 1890, whereas the population has more than trebled. Japanese courts are so overloaded with cases that even the simplest take between two and three years to resolve at the district court level. A bigger case may take ten years, if there are appeals. Final decisions that come a quarter-century after a plaintiff or defendant first faced a judge are not unusual.

Finding a lawyer is no simple matter either, and their scarcity makes them expensive. As of 1986, a mere 13,161 lawyers had been admitted to the bar. This means that Japan has one lawyer per 9,294 people, as compared with one for 360 in the USA, 872 in Britain and 1,486 in West Germany.

Even after court proceedings have started, the plaintiff is still under great pressure to switch to the conciliation procedure. The judge will almost always plead for an out-of-court settlement on the grounds that it saves time and money. If plaintiffs insist on a clear decision from the court, they may be given to understand that because of their non-cooperation the case will most likely go against them. Under such circumstances, it is not difficult to understand why very few Japanese will resort to litigation and stick it out to the end.

Given the awesome power of the System to deprive the Japanese citizen almost completely of the means to litigate, it should come as no surprise that action by the private individual against the government is virtually unthinkable. The Supreme Court refuses to use the powers of review given it by the post-war constitution as a means of safeguarding democracy. This has had the effect of almost totally insulating bureau-cratic activity from judicial review. When activists persist in countering administrative decisions with lawsuits, the officials perceive this as a radical, almost violent action.

The bureaucrats have ample opportunity to mould the judiciary via the entrance exams and training at the government-run LTRI. Trainees are carefully watched. Those considered suitable to serve as prosecutors receive special training that is kept secret from fellow trainees. They are invited to the homes of highly placed prosecutors, and automatically hooked up to the *jinmyaku* of the seniors. One result is a tightly hierarchical procuracy that remains easily controllable from above. Prospective judges are also carefully screened for their political pre-dilections, and trainees who show sympathy with liberal causes are carefully weeded out.

Socially instilled acceptance of the world as it is makes the Japanese relatively pliable in the hands of the judicial authorities. The judges themselves seem almost equally malleable and have allowed their au-thority to slip from their grasp. Post-war judges are in theory indepen-dent of administrative control and may be judged only by their colleagues. But the dividing line between judiciary and administration, so carefully drawn by the Occupation authorities, was carefully un-drawn once the Occupation ended. Since then, the bureaucracy has crept up on the judges. Their fear of bureaucratic opinion, in connection with tenure and promotions, looms almost as large now as it did before the war.

The impartiality of judges is undermined by worry about promotion and postings, which come up for review every three years. They are graded according to a secret marking system, introduced in the 1970s, that takes into account the number of cases they clear within a certain period; this includes cases dropped in favour of conciliation procedures.

A former high court judge asserts that the atmosphere at the courts is such that few judges, if they wish to stay in the good books of the bureaucrats, can afford to be guided solely by their conscience. Bureaucratic standards are applied throughout the system. Judges who meet these standards have a good chance of rising in the hierarchy. Those who listen mainly to their conscience as they conduct trials are generally not promoted.

This important shift of power was accomplished without much difficulty. The judges of the highest tribunal have been a poor match for the bureaucrats. Two-thirds of the fifteen Supreme Court judges are not career judges but, mostly, *amakudari* bureaucrats from various ministries; they serve relatively short terms, and remain fairly ignorant of judicial administrative matters. The Supreme Court has also gained a reputation for overturning decisions against the government made by lower courts. It has reversed decisions restraining police control of leftist demonstrations or granting government employees the right to strike. Sometimes the Supreme Court instructs lower courts as to the kind of decision it expects them to make, for example in the areas of labour and medicine.

THE PROSECUTOR AS JUDGE

In criminal cases, too, the courts do not offer the protection they are supposed to provide. The idyllic lenience of Japanese law enforcement described earlier has a darker side. The fate of Japanese suspects is, except in extremely rare cases, not decided at their trial at all. The real trial consists of the investigation, plus the judgement of the character of the suspect, made by the prosecutors' office. And, in line with the great importance of showing remorse, the attitude of suspects towards the representatives of the System is often more important than their guilt.

Infallible Guardians of the System

It is difficult to quarrel with a judicial system that keeps people out of prison as far as possible yet maintains a violent crime rate below that of other industrialised countries. This admirable achievement must be noted. Also, Japanese prosecutors try to be scrupulously fair within the interpretation of fairness prevalent in the judicial-bureaucratic community. Their sense of a duty to uphold the dignity of their office is beyond doubt.

The problem with the Japanese prosecutor is that, once he has decided to prosecute, he will not accept being shown in the wrong. Losing a case is much worse for them than it is for their Western counterparts. Their own authority is at stake, and by extension that of the entire bureaucratic apparatus. They need not worry much. They have a 99.8 percent chance of winning when they take a case to court. Of 63,204 people receiving their first criminal trial in 1986, only 67 were acquitted.

To all intents and purposes, then, the prosecutor is judge. But as we have seen, to judge blindfold is an alien notion and prosecutors are quite ready to tip the scales of justice out of social considerations. For all their humanity and sense of proportion, the prosecutors are also beholden to the System and, whether consciously or not, must discriminate against the ideologically motivated. The incredibly high conviction rate is usually explained by Japan's judicial authorities as the result of police and prosecutors doing their homework extremely well. In fact, however, it amounts to official endorsement of the prosecutors' infallibility. That they may have human failings is not recognised, for this would undermine the theory of the benevolent social order they represent.

In the extremely rare case of a not-guilty verdict, Japanese prosecutors forget all impulses to lenience and continue to appeal, fighting tenaciously to regain the dignity of the office. This expression has nothing to do with notions of the dignity of the law. Related to it is the dignity of fixed judgement with which the prosecutors' office has long resisted retrials.

— 6 —

THE MANAGEMENT OF
REALITY

The discrepancy between theory and practice, between how
people say they have organised their lives and the way they
actually live, belongs to the human condition. Japan stands out
amidst this ubiquitous experience, not only because the discrepancy
there is sometimes so colossal, but also because it does not seem to
bother people.

Socially Sanctioned Deceit

In a world of competing realities appearances are crucial. Politicians
who have been tainted by scandal use election campaigns to purify their
status, a process referred to as *misogi*, after the Shinto purification
ceremony. Even if they have claimed that they are not guilty they still
talk about *misogi*. In Japan, one can take responsibility for having
created a suspicion of involvement.

The phrase "correct image" *(tadashii imeeji)* is customarily used in
referring to various kinds of whitewash job. Another expression, "the
adjustment of views," means reaching agreement as to the nature of
whatever is at hand. It indicates that reality is seen as negotiable. And
much of the explaining of the true situation that Japanese representatives love doing at international conferences must be seen in this context.

In their daily lives, the Japanese are very helpful to one another in
minimising embarrassment and will often make it quite clear that what
they have just said may not refer to factual reality. All one has to do is
catch the signal. To make things easier, the Japanese have a relevant
terminology: *tatemae*, or the way things are presented, ostensible mo-

tives, the facade, the way things are supposed to be; and *honne*, or genuine motives, observed reality, the truth you know or sense.

This *honne-tatemae* dichotomy is constantly referred to, and provides a frame of reference in which many forms of deceit are socially sanctioned. The Japanese can be honest about their fakery to a degree that Westerners could not possibly be. They are allowed to pretend honesty without fear of being chided for dishonesty. To put it in the words of an anthropologically trained observer: "The Japanese tend to accept apparent contradictions as complementary facets of the same truth. They rarely insist on consistency and are inclined to refer to narrowly logical people as *rikutsuppoi*, that is, 'reason-freaks.'"

Much Maligned Logic

In any discussion of political and social circumstances, it is logic that provides both steady points of reference and consistency. Its rules are not made up on the spot, nor are they newly arrived at by monthly discussion. They are certainly not dictated by politicians. This may seem labouring the obvious, but in Japan one meets intelligent people who claim that logic is something invented in the West to allow Westerners to win discussions. Indeed, the belief is widespread that the Japanese can happily do without logic. This is of course untrue. Japanese engineers and scientists are as familiar with logical thinking as their counterparts anywhere else, and some have received Nobel prizes for it.

Yet, at least where social and political affairs are concerned, the Japanese are not driven by an overwhelming urge to perceive paradoxes and solve contradictions. Neither the three major Japanese spiritual systems (Shintoism, Buddhism, Confucianism) nor scientific thought have given the Japanese tools of leverage over their environment. Abstract thought tends to be practised as an end in itself and is not allowed to determine the nature of human exchanges, while social inquiry remains an exercise for its own sake. Comparing Japanese and Western education, one authority concludes that schooling in logic is as old as Western civilisation itself. By contrast, the Japanese tradition has long emphasised memorisation and imitation. One approach helps the internalisation of a moral and intellectual frame of reference, the second aids adjustment to the environment.

Japanese scholarly debates tend to exist in an intellectual vacuum as tiny, self-contained universes of discourse. The academics who wage them have, moreover, such a dislike of being contradicted that they tend to cloud their contentions to a degree making refutation nearly impossible. Intellectuals are rarely asked to prove or disprove their hypotheses, and consequently are not very good at critical evaluation. They adopt new ideas in rapid succession, but make no conscious effort to test the new ideas against their established convictions.

The poverty of the Japanese intellectual tradition is reflected in that unenthusiastic institution, the Japanese university. Perhaps the most striking characteristic of Japanese students is their general apathy. It should not surprise anyone. My own experience of teaching at, among other places, Waseda University suggests that if students discover the excitement of intellectual pursuits at all, they discover it on their own. Many of the more gifted students go through phases of extreme nihilism.

Some post-war Japanese intellectuals seem to be bothered by the continued refusal to apply universal principles. More nationalistically inclined Japanese may, however, consider the flexibility of Japanese thought a virtue. Prime Minister Nakasone appeared proud of it when, in an interview on national television in August 1984, he implied that it has given the Japanese a great advantage over Westerners. He used the occasion to explain that Japanese are polytheistic, since, as individuals, they can accept Buddhism simultaneously with Shinto and Christianity, which makes Japanese thinking more tolerant than that of "monotheistic Westerners." It clearly did not occur to him that simultaneous acceptance of beliefs that are ultimately incompatible is for all practical purposes the same as believing in none of them.

Some contemporary theorists on the national character proudly proclaim that Japanese prefer to live with intellectual ambiguity. The well-known populariser of Zen in the West, Suzuki Daisetz—who made a fortune with some forty books in English explaining truths "that cannot be captured in writing"—never tired of pointing out the shortcomings of Western "dualistic logic." Actually, the historical function of Japanese Zen, which thrived among the warrior class, was to lower the resistance of the individual against the blind obedience expected of him, as can be gathered from the common Zen imagery of "destroying" or "extinguishing" the mind.

Blunted Confucianism

The malleability, relativity and negotiability of truth in Japan; the claimed superfluity of logic; the absence of a strong intellectual tradition; the subservience to the administrators of law; and the acceptance of amorality—these are, of course, all causally intertwined. They reinforce what I have referred to as the crucial factor in the exercise of Japanese power: the absence of a tradition of appealing to transcendental truth or universal values. All other extant civilisations have developed religions and systems of thought that acknowledge the existence of a truth transcending socio-political concerns. Neither Shintoism nor Buddhism has been of assistance here.

It is helpful to make a comparison with intellectual and spiritual life in China. The dominating force there was Confucianism, a surrogate religion with roots in social experience, and thus very suitable for Japanese power-holders. Confucianist ethics were based on a very sophisticated understanding of human character and the dynamics of society. Metaphysics had no place in it; the Confucianist code of behaviour could hardly be more this-worldly. Significantly, though, the principles it developed were taken to be universally true and applicable under all circumstances.

This prepared the Chinese mind for conceiving of a moral order that transcended temporal authority and immediate social concerns. In this respect Chinese Confucianism resembles the transcendental traditions of Christianity, Judaism, Islam, Hinduism and Buddhism. As Confucius himself is supposed to have said: "The moral man must not be a cipher in but a cooperative member of society. Wherever the conventional practices seem to him immoral or harmful, he not only will refrain from conforming with them but will try to persuade others to change the convention."

However much the Japanese power-holders emulated the Chinese in other things, they were not interested in trying to produce moral citizens by invoking paramount abstract principles. Confucius rejected absolute loyalty to an overlord in favour of loyalty to principle, to the Way. The result was "a goodly company of martyrs, who have given their lives in defense of the Way." This tradition has given the Chinese, at the very least, the freedom to speculate on the legitimacy of rulers. The revolutions and usurpations that punctuate Chinese history were always justified by reference to the mandate of Heaven.

The place that the Chinese have given to abstract principles, the power they have granted ideology, could hardly be better illustrated than by the terrible social convulsions—the Great Leap Forward and the Cultural Revolution—which were justified by appeals to a supposed historical truth situated above society.

By contrast, the Japanese have never been encouraged to think that the force of an idea could measure up to the physical forces of a government. The key to understanding Japanese power relations is that they are unregulated by transcendental concepts. In short, Japanese political practice is a matter of might is right disguised by assurances and tokens of "benevolence."

— 7 —

THE RIGHT TO RULE

S o long as it is fairly diffuse, the exercise of informal power in Japan causes no acute anguish. The System's ubiquitous and inescapable power is subtle, vague, and rarely locatable. The exercise of official leadership, on the other hand, causes constant, severe and apparently insoluble tensions.

The Japanese who are formally in charge of the country—the prime minister and his cabinet—are in practice not allowed to exercise the power they should exercise under the constitution. Political leaders who hanker after genuine leadership will always face an elusive yet impenetrable wall of mistrust and sabotage. No one in Japan is given the unambiguous right to rule.

The widely remarked weakness of Japan's official leadership is usually explained with reference to a social tradition that discourages individualism, and *therefore does not produce individualist leaders*. But when one considers potentially strong leaders such as Nakasone Yasuhiro, Tanaka Kakuei and Ikeda Hayato, this theory does not hold. Nakasone, for example, was no less individualistic than the foreign counterparts with whom he conferred at the annual summit conferences. The related theory that the public which will not accept a strong leader is equally unconvincing. There have always been plenty of popular heroes who behaved quite individualistically and have been widely admired for that very reason.

To explain this issue in culturalist terms ignores the crucial political fact that Japanese are unremittingly ambivalent about who should have the right to rule. This extraordinary—for a modern industrial nation—characteristic is the most fundamental problem of Japanese political life. It is essentially a problem of political legitimacy.

THE LEGITIMACY PROBLEM

On the face of it, political legitimacy would appear to be no problem in Japan. Unlike in South Korea or the communist countries of Asia, it is not an issue that draws attention. Admittedly, leftist intellectuals routinely question the legitimacy of a state that is the servant of "monopoly capitalism." Affected despair about this binds them together in groups that actually serve the System by helping to ritualise emotional dissent. But outside this ritualistic Marxist frame of reference, the concept of legitimacy simply does not occur in Japanese political discourse. Nevertheless, the absence of discussion does not mean that the problem is not there. The fact that it is never raised may make it all the more insidious.

Self-Validation

Political legitimacy is a slippery concept. It is that kind of subtle attribute of a political system that is generally noticed only when it is absent, or when there seems to be not enough of it. Legitimacy implies more than acquiescence or consensus because it is bestowed upon a political arrangement through an external agency such as a system of laws, a sanctioning deity or whatever else transcends the temporal, political world. By common consent, it is perceived as ruling the rulers as well as the ruled. Seen in this light, it is immediately clear why legitimacy should be a problem in Japan. The Japanese System sets out to be self-validating. It is itself the "divinity," supplying its own closed system of faith and self-justification. And since a political system cannot legitimise itself, the Japanese System can by definition never be legitimate.

Public apathy, an important ingredient for the maintenance of established power in any country, has so far been a particularly potent factor in the preservation of Japanese political arrangements. *Shikataganai*, "It cannot be helped," is one of the daily interjections of Japanese life. It acknowledges a fact of nature, like saying, "It's hot!" or "It's freezing!" Obedience to the dictates of those in power is largely a matter of *shikataganai*, helped by the fact that no clear division is seen between the social order and the political system. But this kind of obedience rests on latent social threats of coercion and therefore has nothing to do with legitimacy.

Those who resign themselves with a sigh of *shikataganai* to the status quo are not likely to be excited by the question of who has the right to rule. But passive acceptance is a product of circumstances. Political belief does not enter into it. If the System is all around you and unbeatable, if it is supposed to contain the ultimate meaning of your life and if you do not know where else to look for such ultimate meaning, then there is little else to do but sit back and enjoy it or, alternatively, grin and bear it. To question the legitimacy of the System would be for the most ordinary Japanese like questioning the legitimacy of one's mother.

A Problem for the Ruling Class

In contrast to the average person, the individuals and groups that form the ruling class are often deeply involved in questions of who may demand obedience and cooperation. Though they do not express it in these terms, bureaucrats, LDP politicians, the administrators at the apexes of the industrial hierarchies and newspaper editors are all faced with the problem of the right to rule. The prime ministership of Nakasone Yasuhiro offers a splendid illustration of this.

Nakasone appeared fully aware that Japan's international difficulties were to a large extent due to weak national leadership, and he tried harder than any of his post-war predecessors to bring his office closer to the power that the world generally expects prime ministers to exercise. He formed a new administrative agency with the rank of ministry, tried to improve the ability of the Prime Minister's Office to react quickly to emergency situations and found new ways to break through bureaucratic deadlocks. One would think that such measures would be welcomed by bureaucrats, LDP politicians and editorial writers who routinely confirm the need for major structural adjustments, effective leadership and a more responsible global role. And there is no doubt that Japan's administrators and commentators, as well as a large segment of the public, noticed the advantage of having a prime minister who was taken seriously by other heads of government. Nevertheless, the very same voices that conceded that a decisive prime minister benefited the country also objected to the way in which Nakasone tried to be stronger and more decisive than his predecessors. As far as probably the majority of his fellow LDP Diet members were concerned, the attempt to establish a credible Japanese leadership was reason to dislike Nakasone. The bureaucrats made barely any move to accommodate the policy adjustments he pleaded for; and a pervasive sense of distrust emanated from editorials commenting on his efforts.

Interesting enough, the public at large was not at all distressed by Nakasone's trying to be a strong leader. The popularity polls indicated that he stood in higher esteem with the people than any of his post-war colleagues. It was the elite groups that were upset. The problem was that those who run the System simply did not accept unambiguous central political leadership.

Early Problems

Looking back through Japanese history, one can discern a succession of measures that were introduced to compensate for the failure to establish who has the right to rule. These incomplete solutions deserve attention because most of them continue to have a decisive influence on the manner in which Japanese power is exercised today.

The simplest method of maintaining political order is the threat of physical force. Residues of naked power, for instance the power the police exercise in the arrest of criminals, can be found in all advanced societies. But brute force has obvious drawbacks. It is not conducive to the stable situation that enables power-holders to hold on to their power. The exercise of naked power may give a ruler prestige, but will not, unless his subjects are masochists, produce positive emotions. Besides, the armed servants that the ruler must employ may, under the leadership of an ambitious captain, turn against him.

To solve these problems and make subjects, including soldiers, believe that the ruler has a right to control them, a body of theory, together with rituals and other symbolism, is necessary. Early Japanese chieftains asserted the right to rule by claiming kinship with patron deities, and underlined it with clan temples, burial mounds and chronicles. The *Nihon Shoki (Chronicles of Japan)*, the oldest official history, mentions a test, decreed in the year 415 by the Emperor Ingyo, in which clan chiefs and holders of hereditary titles had to subject their claims to their positions to divine judgement by putting their hands in tubs of boiling water. The chronicle relates that truthful claimants remained unharmed, while liars fled in terror, and that thenceforth no one told lies about his descent.

The attempts by the Yamato court in the sixth and seventh centuries to expand its sway required new and more compelling definitions of legitimacy. Hence the stress on the need for harmony and the eagerness with which Yamato rulers seized upon Buddhism and Confucianism in order to buttress their claims of legitimacy.

The rise of the warrior houses and the age of civil wars speak for themselves. Unsolved problems of legitimacy, wherever they occur, tend to bring military power to the fore. Hence the fact that Japan—most extraordinarily, considering the nearly total absence of any foreign threat—has experienced one form or another of warrior rule for much more than half of its history.

Japan's rulers could—and often had to—give massive demonstrations of military might to back up their political claims. Hideyoshi brought together more than 150,000 soldiers for the siege of Odawara. The third Tokugawa shogun, Tokugawa Iemitsu, symbolically consolidated his regime by marching 307,000 men through Kyoto. The emperor, incidentally, still lived there; he had, of course, no choice but to consent.

Tokugawa warrior rule was imposed upon a demonstrably unwilling populace. Contrary to the general impression that Japan enjoyed two and a half centuries of public peace, there were disturbances throughout the period. Despite an ideology presenting the body politic as the ultimate good, the peasantry, according to one compilation, rebelled 2,809 times and rioted approximately one thousand times.

The Nomenklatura Solution

When legitimacy is unobtainable and suppression by force cannot be sustained, there is still a middle way for retaining control: make sure that crucial groups believe that the current arrangements are the best for *them*. Their assent can be won by a system of scaled benefits for the military and civil servants. The *nomenklatura*, the upper layer with hereditary privileges, of Soviet society clearly belongs to this category.

Challenges to an established ruling order are unlikely to come from the lowest members of society unless these have the support and leadership of certain elite groups. Spartacus-type movements are rare and in the end they fail. On the other hand, those in key positions have very good reasons to hinder change; for them, change in the midst of economic scarcity—the condition in which this kind of system flourishes—is dangerous. Not to toe the line would mean losing privileges essential for a decent life.

The system that the Tokugawa regime forged closely resembled this *nomenklatura* solution. Its security depended on forcing all vassal lords to reside in the capital during alternate years, and to leave their families as hostages the rest of the time. An upper stratum of samurai with inherited privileges guaranteed political continuity. Beneath it, a layer of educated and disciplined lower samurai were entrusted with the daily management of a fairly rapidly evolving political economy and the channelling of wealth, through taxes and other levies, to the parasitic upper layer. The lower samurai became increasingly restive but they also realised that if they rocked the boat they would most likely fall overboard themselves.

The *nomenklatura* class of the Tokugawa period rested on a politically apathetic rural populace which was never won over by the ruling elite. The sudden United States demand in 1853 that Japan open itself to the world seems to have been the final shove that left the tottering apparatus of warrior power ready to collapse when the samurai of Satsuma and Choshu staged their *coup d'etat*.

Institutionalising Irresponsibility

The first thing the new rulers did, in an attempt to solve their colossal legitimacy problem, was to move the Meiji emperor from his palace in Kyoto to the shogunal castle in Edo, which was renamed Tokyo. This move was intended to suggest that the decisions of the oligarchy were being made in the emperor's name. In reality, the "restoration" of the emperor in no way restored his temporal powers. All shogunate govern-ments had theoretically been legitimised by imperial appointment. Since the sovereign was sacred, the powerless emperors had always been ideal instruments in power games, and ideal shields for political manipulation.

Following the Meiji Restoration, the impression existed that the ruling oligarchy was to be replaced by a parliamentary system which would give Japan a respected place in the ranks of modern nations. In the political debate that followed the introduction of new foreign theories, some advocated a constitutional monarchy roughly similar to those of Europe. Such an arrangement would, however, have meant the gradual removal from power of individual oligarchs, and the Meiji constitution that they finally came up with showed clearly that they had seen no advantage to themselves in a limited monarchy. On paper, all power resided in the emperor, who bestowed the constitution on the nation out of his generosity. In practice, a new political system encom-passing the exercise of informal power had begun to crystallise— informal power that kept the oligarchs on top. The Meiji constitution provided for yet another system that was legitimised by a theory of imperial rule that in fact had little connection with the exercise of real power.

The architects of the new state, who came from the class of restive lower samurai, understood that control through a hierarchy of privileges had to be replaced by control through propaganda, and they embarked on a major campaign to persuade the public of the inevitable rightness of their government. The campaign ran away with itself, resulting in the "national essence" (kokutai) mystique—a belief in the spiritual cohesiveness of the Japanese people, and by extension the state—which made a constitutional monarchy unthinkable. On a more practical level, they refrained from writing into the constitution provisions for the selection of leadership to be legitimised by the emperor, because that would have directly threatened their own positions. If they had allowed power to be concentrated in the hands of the prime minister, the coalition of groups comprising the Meiji oligarchy could not have stayed together.

Throughout the decades between then and the new constitution bestowed on the Japanese people by General MacArthur, it remained unclear who had the right to decide anything essential. Groups of elder statesmen, clustered around the emperor, made the system function; but they had no constitutional position in the state, and thus were not accountable.

Who was, then? The Army? The Privy Council? The Diet? The Naimusho? The Foreign Ministry? Whose legitimacy was to be judged? As the political theorist Maruyama Masao summed it up in a classic paragraph: "An uncertain sharing of responsibility was preferred so that no one person could be pointed out as bearing the ultimate responsibility for decisions. It is obvious that the mechanism of the Emperor-system state had inherent within it the danger of developing into a colossal system of irresponsibility."

Japanese power-holders of the Meiji period and later could be held responsible neither for misdeeds nor for flagrant misgovernment. The grave dangers of this tradition for the nation (and other nations) was amply demonstrated in the first half of the twentieth century. Authority for Japan's conquests in Asia officially resided with an emperor who had no practical say in what Japan did. The anonymous decisions of this period changed the political map of Asia, started a war with the world's largest industrial power, caused the death of roughly three million Japanese and between ten and twenty million non-Japanese and led to the communist take-over of China as well as the hastened departure of the European colonial powers from Asia. And this is to name only the major results.

The Ignorance Solution

One partial solution to the problem of who has the right to rule, introduced in the Meiji period and still vitally important today, is the cult of the knowledgeable administrator who, supposedly, has no ambition to wield power.

Traditionally, being in the know is associated in Japan with the right to administrative office, which seems understandable enough. The corollary, however, is that those who do not hold office should be kept in ignorance.

Popular ignorance and official secrecy were acknowledged by Tokugawa administrators to be essential to the preservation of order. Aizawa Seishisai (1782-1863), author of a seminal work on *kokutai* ideology, contended that the people should accept the fact that rules existed and were beneficial, but should not be told what those rules were. He was also open about the fact that the Tokugawa regime deliberately kept the commoners weak and ignorant. More than a hundred years after his death, frustrated exporters trying to break into the Japanese market frequently discover that their products are subject to regulations of which officials cannot give them any further particulars.

There are good reasons to assume that the power-holders of the Meiji and Taisho periods did not believe what they made the public swallow about a divine and infinitely benevolent emperor, or about the "family state" and all that went with it. The *kokutai* surrogate religion answered any questions about legitimacy that might arise among a public kept purposely in ignorance. Political doubts were considered dangerous only when they reached the ears of the common people. Although in the early decades of the present century the power-holders were obsessed with the threat dissidents posed, they did not attempt to stamp them out completely. Most intellectuals either worked directly for the government or supported it in some way, and it was difficult to restrict their intellectual production too severely. Academics whose speculations went against the grain of government-dictated ideology were, at least until the late 1920s, accommodated with a fair measure of tolerance.

Post-war Japanese administrators have dropped the term "dangerous thoughts"; the Japanese probably have more freedom to express critical ideas than any other people in Asia, aside from the Filipinos. But the presumption that much of what the administrators know should be kept hidden from ordinary people has definitely survived. The set phrase from Tokugawa days—"people must not be informed, but made dependent on the authority of the government"—is occasionally still used today.

Denial of Power

The most ingenious partial solution to the problem of the right to rule that Japanese power-holders have hit upon is a systematic denial that any power is exercised to begin with.

This solution, again, came in with the Tokugawas. Thus the Tokugawa shoguns and their deputies did not aspire to power, they were simply performing the right ceremonies to sustain the natural order. The Meiji oligarchy and the bureaucracy it spawned were also presented as motivated by a selfless desire to serve the emperor and thereby the nation, for the benefit of the entire Japanese family. Soldiers and sailors did the same; they served the emperor without the slightest thought of self-aggrandisement. Today, it would be very difficult to find a Japanese administrator who openly admitted to a desire to gain or hold on to—much less expand—his power, a desire that is of course his main concern.

This solution, however, puts politicians in a quandary. When talking to their constituents, they cannot avoid boasting that they have power and seek more of it. For if they did not have the clout to talk the ministries into building the bridges, roads and airports to benefit the electorate that sends them to the Diet, why should it vote for them? The problem for Japan's politicians has always been that they cannot hide their real political ambitions, a fact that has earned them much disapprobation.

Venal Politicians Versus Virtuous Bureaucrats

When the Western concept of a politician accountable to an electorate was introduced after the Meiji Restoration, it created confusion and ambivalence among Japan's leaders and intellectuals. The introduction of party politics was an inevitable concomitant of the Japanese effort to catch up with the West. That meant that something had to be done to curtail the potential for damage, since the samurai-bureaucrats found it difficult to accept the idea of a loyal opposition. Opposition was regarded as a threat not only to themselves but to the state. As a solution, the oligarchs made sure that anything associated with politics appeared as unpatriotic.

The Meiji press was only slightly less critical of the politicians than were the oligarchy and officialdom. Japan's early journalists were, or pretended to be, scandalised by bribery and other electoral irregularities, thus setting a pattern that is still followed today. Party politics was portrayed to the public as vile and directed by narrow self-interest. The idea was hammered home that loyal subjects of the emperor, such as soldiers and officials, should have nothing to do with politics. The anti-politician propaganda was successfully passed down to succeeding generations.

Selecting the Virtuous Administrators

Once the decision took shape among the oligarchs that Japan was not to be ruled by popular mandate through elected representatives, they were faced with the task of structuring a ruling class. The formula they adopted still determines the allocation of power in present-day Japan. The principle of hereditary selection was giving way at the time to meritocratic principles. Western knowledge, preferably absorbed in Europe or in the United States, became increasingly important. By the turn of the century the surest, and almost the sole, way to get into the class of those in the know that managed the country was to graduate from the law department of the University of Tokyo—a tradition that, as we have seen, determines the character of Japanese schooling to this day.

Todai acquired its pivotal position in conferring legitimacy as a result of the treaties providing for extraterritoriality that Japan had signed with the Western powers. The foreigners were ready to scrap these deeply hated stipulations only if and when legal trials could be conducted by a competent judiciary. It was the desperate need this created that launched the law department of Todai in its function of ordaining the modern samurai. By 1890 its supply of graduates was large enough to fill nearly all administrative vacancies and more than half the judicial vacancies.

So far as intellect and skill are concerned, this now firmly entrenched method of ordaining the ruling elite is fairly arbitrary. The special knowledge and thus virtue of the bureaucrat, which helps lend their role a semblance of legitimacy, comes down to membership in a class of people that has managed the art of passing the most abstruse entrance examinations. The ranks of Japan's elite have been selected mainly for stamina and dedication. Todai graduates tend to be bright, but many Japanese with very capable minds of a different cast are doomed permanently to operate on the fringes. Much capacity for original thinking is wasted. The Japanese ruling class is far more thoroughly schooled than it is educated: a fact of more than peripheral importance for the attitude of Japan's administrators towards the international world.

Depoliticising Politics

Legitimacy in post-war Japan is officially bestowed on the government by popular mandate. And elections and a parliament have, indeed, taken over to some extent from the emperor as institutions legitimising current arrangements. But the concept of the sovereignty of the people is not understood by most Japanese, and is certainly not a living principle among those who share power. The appeals to popular sovereignty in the press are purely rhetorical and never coupled to any analysis of the pervasive exercise of informal power that systematically prevents the realisation of this principle. The Diet and elections have not replaced older institutions in the popular mind, since both already existed when the emperor was formally the bestower of legitimacy, at which time they were widely castigated as diminishing the purity and moral soundness of the Japanese nation.

Before 1945, it was considered that all laws and directives issued in the name of the emperor were, by definition, for the public good. The bureaucrats were therefore, by definition, impartial and just. Politicians, by contrast, were demonstrably spurred on by political considerations, which in the Japanese context could not be differentiated from selfish motives. There is still today a strong tendency to assume that whatever is politically motivated can never be as good as what is (supposedly) motivated by considerations of the public good. Even though it is manifestly clear that they are guided by their own interests and proceed without consulting the public in any way, the bureaucrats' efforts are somehow made to appear more legitimate than anything done by the politicians, who have never been able completely to shake off their original reputation as loutish, self-seeking opportunists. The post-war press is still permeated with an unacknowledged prejudice against politicians, and routinely feeds the public a view of politics that is mostly sceptical and negative.

Nevertheless, Japan cannot do away with politicians, since in theory they form the link between society and the body politic. Without them, the strongest components of the System would consist only of bureaucrats and industrialists, and bureaucratic authoritarianism would become too blatant. Parliamentary proceedings form a facade behind which the administrators manage affairs, just as the imperial throne once did for the Meiji oligarchy.

To counter the lingering distaste for the archetypal politician with his "egotistical motives," the LDP likes to make it appear that it is nothing more nor less than a collection of benevolent administrators. Roughly one-third of its Diet members—generally the most powerful ones—have in fact travelled the elite administrator course from the Todai law department or its equivalents and on through one of the ministries. Whereas individual LDP members would not be credible if they denied an interest in power and would raise doubts about their ability to bring pork-barrel benefits to their constituencies, the LDP as a whole can more easily gloss over its *raison d'etre*.

In line with its denial of the exercise of power, the LDP likes to present a depoliticised picture of politics. It is greatly helped here by the ancient notion that those in power are more ethical than those out of power, that they are legitimate by the very fact of wielding power. The LDP—despite many a press campaign in which it is lambasted for its "money politics" and arrogance—has a certain aura of respectability that the other parties lack. It is still treated as if it belonged in a different category from groups entering the political arena with new political suggestions. The latter are easily denigrated as concerned with the interests of a very limited number of citizens rather than of the Japanese people as a whole. Their desire for some of the LDP's power automatically stigmatises them as "self-seeking politicians."

The concept of democracy in Japan is not a pragmatic concept guiding actual political processes. As one of the foremost specialists on Japanese intellectual history remarks, democracy is in Japan a radical concept, valued in an abstract, normative sense. It furnishes the Japanese with a point of reference, based on rational humanitarianism, outside existing politics and history.

Japan can be called a "democracy" by the criteria that Aristotle used in his famous classification of monarchies, aristocracies and democracies since what he called a democracy was simply an aristocracy of fairly broad membership. And Japan's 'democracy' is constitutional, but it is not constitutionalist. The democratic provisions of the constitution are ultimately unenforceable, if only because the Supreme Court is in the hands of the bureaucrats.

The Disloyalty of Institutionalised Opposition

In Western democracies, the preservation of a legal order is safeguarded by the opportunity to throw the rascals out. As long as voters can choose to transfer power to a different set of power-holders, they can prevent the political system from becoming a System. For this purpose, a political system must tolerate a loyal opposition. One of the most essential traits of the all-embracing Japanese System is that it tolerates no genuine opposition.

The concept of a loyal opposition has been particularly troublesome for countries where the exercise of power has been justified by traditional Chinese theories of government. In the Confucianist tradition, rulers are by definition virtuous; thus to oppose them automatically means to question their legitimacy.

In contemporary Japan genuine opposition with the potential to take over the reins of government, or merely to change the policy agenda, is not acceptable to the administrators in the LDP and the bureaucracy. To say that they would feel discomfort is wildly to understate the problem. A genuine opposition would nullify everything they stand for. Thus even Japan's official political system, that respectable mantle hiding the reality of jinmyaku deals, is in effect a one-party system.

The Mass Inclusionary Illusion

The very bases of pluralism in politics are regarded as morally suspect by the administrators, though they can never concede this while Japan is being presented to the world and to the Japanese as a parliamentary democracy. Certain statements coming from the LDP, however, appear to be groping towards a more satisfactory formulation of the actual state of affairs, one that can be used as a basis for future plans. A month after the July 1986 elections in which the LDP gained a record number of seats, Prime Minister Nakasone explained that this victory marked the beginning of "the 1986 political order." The birth of this order would be assisted by a new party strategy, with which the flexibly conservative urban voters would all be won over. Such additional support for the LDP, according to Nakasone, would signify the end of the "1955 political order"—which is common shorthand for the uneven rivalry between the LDP and the socialists.

This was more than mere rhetoric delivered in the flush of victory. Four years previously, LDP ideologues had published an important article whose theory of Japanese political history led to the conclusion that the LDP is destined to entice the labour unions away from the socialists, and to create a new political organisation that can directly absorb the political energies of city dwellers and consumers. What these LDP theorists, as well as Nakasone, were saying was that soon there would no longer be any need for the JSP, their only rival. Japanese political analysts have begun to refer routinely to a "mass inclusionary system," by which they understand bureaucratic control that is not open to checks from the public but is nevertheless supported by a majority.

In the final analysis, the claim of undivided support for a de-politicised, "mass inclusionary" political system is not credible. The idea that one can depoliticise a political system is an illusion. Pretending that relationships and social processes in which power plays a role are not political means that essential distinctions are not made. The most serious consequence of an ostensibly depoliticised society that denies the existence of genuine conflict, and constantly creates the illusion of unified consent, is that it does not provide the means for conflict resolution to be found in modern constitutionalist states. The effect of this is insufficiently appreciated but far-reaching, not least in the context of Japan's international relations. The absence of institutions for resolving conflict means that Japanese social relationships are shot through with unmediated power—or, to use another word for this, intimidation.

— 8 —

RITUAL AND
INTIMIDATION

J apanese are brought up with a socio-political imagery that portrays the authorities as united in an understanding of what the people want and need, an understanding deriving from Japan's essential homogeneity. This notion of a unique sameness that makes compassionate bureaucratic rule possible is also very important to the bureaucratic self-image.

Inextricably intertwined with the beliefs in homogeneity and benevolence is the concept of *wa*, which is generally translated as "harmony," but is rich in connotations. *Wa* is one of the concepts that is widely believed to be difficult or impossible for foreigners to understand. But the 'harmony' of Japanese *wa* is associated with a variety of universal human virtues such as conciliation, gentleness, accord, accommodation, mellowness, moderation, mollification, peace, pliancy, amiability, appeasement, conformity, softness, order, unison, compromise, and so on.

Wa is in fact the first political concept that Japanese children are taught in their history lessons—when they learn that Japan's first law-giver, Shotoku Taishi, began his famous constitution with the admonition, "Regard *wa* as noble, and non-contrariness as honourable."

A LESS THAN PERFECT HARMONY

A value system governed, ultimately, by social exigencies means the absence of an urge to fight over ideas. This means in turn that revolutions are ruled out. In Japanese history, there have been uprisings, peasant rebellions provoked by dire conditions and intolerable abuses, but they were not sustained and never amounted to a major revolution.

The leaders of peasant protest movements were often killed even when their complaints were admitted. They tended to be honoured afterwards; shrines were erected in their memory, at which the lords would worship along with the common people. But even great heroes may not disturb the *wa* of society. In 1937, the Ministry of Education distributed two million copies of *Kokutai no Hongi*, a booklet setting forth the ideology of the "national essence" and claiming that the spirit of harmony had, throughout history, been the source of Japan's national growth. Since the 1970s, *wa* has appeared frequently in Japanese writing seeking to explain Japanese culture to the rest of the world. Some Japanese will say that *wa* is for Japan what universal values are for the West, the central principle on which their society operates. It is frequently mentioned in the same breath as loyalty.

Where the Shoe Pinches

Striving for *wa* is advocated at many company meetings, and *wa* is often mentioned in public speeches. Certain things, such as not resorting to legal action to right wrongs, are considered essential for the preservation of *wa*. In other words, one has to work at *wa*—it does not come automatically.

All this emphasis on *wa* is a give-away that this is where the shoe pinches. Japanese are obsessed with the idea of harmony precisely because of a subliminal awareness that it is very difficult to achieve. *Wa* is not an existing harmony, but the uninterrupted readiness to sacrifice one's personal interests for the sake of a communal tranquility.

The possibility that parts of the System might be lacking in *wa* is a profound embarrassment, but Japanese society has no less conflict than other societies. The System is anything but static; it is moved by a tremendous internal dynamism, enhanced by strong competition. This competition starts with the examination system in schools, continues with the acquisition of as high a position as possible in the salaryman world or bureaucracy, and is then sublimated into group competition for market share or factional power. Where possible, competition involving large groups is controlled, but that still leaves much room for shifts of balance. The effort to keep up a surface decorum is supported by numerous subtle methods of avoiding and suppressing open conflict.

Japanese conflict and its suppression, and what happens when it finally can no longer be suppressed, are wonderfully portrayed, in an extreme and stylised form, in gangster movies. When tension mounts in these films the mobsters are hissing and puffing like pressure cookers. The protagonist who finally takes it upon himself to avenge the insult to his boss (or whatever else evil rivals have perpetrated) knows he will die, just like the leaders of peasant rebellions in the Tokugawa period. In these romanticised stories, death is the price for upsetting the social order, even if it is for the most honourable cause.

In everyday life, one may not actually hear the hissing and puffing. But a closer look at a Japanese who is upset often gives the impression that, behind a face struggling for control, this is exactly what is going on. One of the most common ways of releasing tension is communal drunkenness. Drinking parties constitute one of several escape-valves attached to the pressure cooker of Japanese society.

It is not likely that one will ever run into hissing and puffing bureaucrats. But over dinner with some sake, their language tends to take on a distinctly military-strategic quality when they describe the relations of their ministries and other ministries, or intra-agency rivalries. Task forces, formed to deal with a particular administrative problem, are forever carrying out advances, tactical retreats and decoy manoeuvres. Ministries are always trying to "colonise" other government agencies. Ministry officials seconded to some foreign posting will speak of their war potential in comparison with that of the Ministry of Foreign Affairs.

Political analysis in the Japanese press consists essentially of running commentary on the unceasing power struggle among the *habatsu* of the LDP. Japan's political crises are momentary intensifications of this power struggle; they can aptly be compared to instalments of the Japanese television serials on samurai history whose themes of loyalty and betrayal they markedly resemble.

Bureaucratic Wars

Like bureaucrats everywhere, Japanese bureaucrats have natural enemies, but they find their adversaries in rival ministries, rather than among politicians or businessmen. A major task for officials, especially in the middle reaches of a bureau, is to negotiate deals with other bureaucrats. Regarding control of an oil pipeline, for example, the Ministry of Transport will claim that this falls within the area of transportation, while the Ministry of International Trade and Industry

(MITI) will insist that it should be in charge since petroleum is a commercial product. Such squabbling can be found almost anywhere, but among Japanese bureaucrats it often grows into major conflicts that totally paralyse official decision-making. It is taken almost for granted that the interests of the ministry come before those of the country. Highly placed bureaucrats will themselves agree that the malfunctioning caused by *nawabari arasoi* ("territorial conflict") exceeds all reasonable limits.

There is no administrative method to adjudicate conflict between ministries. Hence the importance of *eminences grises*, shadowy power-brokers. Once an inter-ministry conflict is settled through the offices of an outside agent, such as the LDP, this does not mean that the conflict is solved; there is no peace among rival ministries, only armistice.

A less well known but significant conflict is that between the police and the prosecutors. Despite their mutual support on the surface and their joint role as the enemy of leftists, their mutual disdain is deep-seated. It goes back to before the war, when the police sometimes withheld vital information from prosecutors on the track of people harbouring "dangerous thoughts." Under the post-war constitution, the police were freed from their traditional hierarchic inferiority to the public prosecutors, but the Criminal Prosecution Law still stipulates that police comply with the prosecutors' instructions. The police are also riven by rivalry between criminal and security police, and between the Tokyo Metropolitan Police Agency and the National Police Agency.

Factional conflict can take on extreme, highly irrational forms in Japan. The emphasis on solidarity and the demands for identification with the group are so strong that groups are apt to go on a war footing against each other when there are no other issues to hold them together. In view of this, the jurisdictions of government agencies are made to overlap as little as possible, which heightens their discretionary powers but makes conflict all the more bitter.

This pattern in which the semi-autonomy of the parts undermines the coherence of the whole is repeated at various levels of the System. The departments of a newspaper, for example, seem to operate as if they constituted separate publications. Such sectionalism is also endemic to most ministries; conflict between bureaux is sometimes even greater than that between government agencies, and when one section views an impending decision of its bureau as threatening its interests, it may sabotage the plans of the larger group.

Despite the identification of individual bureaucrats with their bureau, the ultimate unit in conflict with other units is, as everywhere else, the single ambitious bureaucrat in rivalry with his immediate colleagues. The Finance Ministry official does not necessarily care much for the bureau that he defends at the expense of the whole; it is just that his quality as a loyal official will be judged by the success of his bureau. His further career will depend on it, as will the place he will land as an *amakudari*.

Institutional Paralysis

That the endemic conflict in Japan can be seriously detrimental to the public good was underlined by the aftermath of an air crash in August 1985, in which a record 520 people died. Instead of uniting different authorities in an attempt to minimise the tragedy for all concerned, the disaster served only to heighten mutual hostility.

To begin with, confusion about bureaucratic jurisdiction greatly delayed rescue efforts. It took fourteen hours before the first military rescue team made its way to the wreckage on a mountain-side. Four survivors of the crash report that there were more passengers who survived the initial impact and that children's voices could be heard gradually dying away as time passed.

The Japanese Air Force had witnessed the accident on its own instruments, and two Phantom fighters sent out to investigate found the crash site within four minutes, after which they returned to their base without taking further action. It was two and a half hours later that the agency with first responsibility, the civil aviation bureau of the Ministry of Transport, issued its request to the Ground Forces to begin the search. An emergency air-crash rescue team equipped with helicopters does exist in Japan, but it was never called into action. No Japanese agency reacted to the offer from two US air bases to help with equipment and personnel experienced in difficult mountain searches at night, and these experts stood by fruitlessly for some thirteen hours. Even though the location was known, the first ground troops went to the wrong mountain. Ten hours after the disaster, the helicopter of a Japanese military rescue team found the wreckage, but it took no action because orders for action had gone to another military unit. Hours before soldiers sent out from the Transport Ministry finally arrived at the site, local villagers had already reached it.

Questions about the disastrous lack of inter-agency communication were submerged in the subsequent welter of accusations directed at

Japan Airlines (JAL). These were to a large extent the result of an older conflict between the Ministry of Transport and the semi-governmental airline company. The transport minister, Yamashita Tokuo, declared in an interview that, even though he did not know about technical matters, he was sure that JAL was to blame. As a result the Japanese media developed an elaborate campaign in which JAL was portrayed as the great villain.

The International Federation of Airline Pilot Associations issued a declaration reminding all concerned that investigations into air crashes are not meant to apportion blame, but to find the cause so as to prevent similar accidents. It also asked the authorities to include experts of the manufacturer as well as the US National Transport Safety Board in their investigations. The latter specialists had been waiting for two weeks in Tokyo to be called upon, and had only once, as a courtesy gesture, been taken to the crash site.

This seemingly odd behaviour of Japan's military units and Transport Ministry becomes clearer when seen in the context of the absence of central leadership. The soldiers adhere painstakingly to the principle of civil responsibility so as to forestall comparisons to their pre-1945 predecessors. A functioning central military authority does not exist. Neither, however, does a civilian organ that can give and co-ordinate commands in times of emergency. Prime Minister Nakasone, who was on holiday some twenty minutes' distance by helicopter from the crash site, conspicuously refrained from visiting the area. To do so would have created the unwanted impressions that the government had taken symbolic responsibility for the event.

The Undigested Past

Most conspicuously contradicting the myth of Japan as one happy family are the national disputes provoked by what one might call Japan's undigested pre-1945 past: its attempt to rule Asia and the political suppression at home. In this instance, the conflicts are kept alive by groups that belong only partly or not at all to the System. The most important of these national conflicts revolve around the position of the emperor, National Foundation Day, the Yasukuni shrine, revision of the constitution, the introduction of patriotic ethics courses in schools and the status of the Self-Defense Forces. Whenever one of these issues is rekindled, the few remnants of the Japanese left, together with coteries of intellectuals and certain religious groups, can be counted on to react vehemently.

One of the best-known symbols of national disunity is National Foundation Day, or Kigensetsu. First instituted in 1872, it commemorates the day in 600 BC on which the mythical first emperor, Jimmu, allegedly established his capital in Yamato. Also known as Empire Day, it was celebrated on 11 February until the Occupation scrapped it as a dangerous vestige of militarist fanaticism. The holiday was reinstated in 1966 under a slightly different name, but not until 1985 did a prime minister, Nakasone Yasuhito, participate in the official ceremonies. A storm of indignant protest prevented him from attending in 1983, so that much preparation was required to help make his 1985 appearance half-way acceptable. Instead of the proposed three shouts of "Tennoheika banzai" (too reminiscent of the cry that charging soldiers and kamikaze pilots used when they threw themselves on the enemy), the ceremony called for three "banzais" for the founding of Japan, and a mere prayer on behalf of the emperor.

The left and the Christians criticised Nakasone for having brought the country "a step closer to the old militarism," while the nationalists attacked him for having diminished the significance of the commemoration. Some 22,000 teachers, Christians and other opponents participated in protest rallies all over Japan, but about double that number joined local celebrations, suggesting that perhaps the balance has turned in favour of the Kigensetsu advocates.

Once the focus of Japan's state religion, the emperor, or rather his position in the post-war order, remains very controversial. After 1945, Emperor Hirohito was made to personify the good conscience of a Japan that was supposedly victimised by the war. Yet some Japanese, even in the 1980s, resented the authority in whose name their fathers, husbands and sons were sacrificed. Pressed on this matter, a minority thinks that Hirohito should have resigned in 1945 in a gesture indicating awareness of the misery perpetrated by those who invoked his "will." A much larger and more vocal group is concerned that his son, Akihito, may once again be used as a political instrument by forces that have not rejected Japan's militaristic and authoritarian past.

Hirohito's role in the Second World War remains largely unknown. He is said to have made, at least formally, the decision in 1945 to accept the Allied terms for surrender, but the true sequence of events may never become known. He himself, long imprisoned by court officialdom, never made any public statement about his motives except for a formal reference in 1981, when he declared that he had not been able to prevent the declaration of war on the United States.

Despite the famous announcement of the emperor's human status on New Year's Day of 1946, rightist activists, some nationalistic intellectuals and bureaucrats, and several LDP groups promote a view of his status that is little different from when he was still officially a Shinto divinity. In the weeks when Hirohito was near death in the autumn of 1988, cabinet ministers excused themselves from international meetings, celebrities postponed scheduled weddings, TV stations and weekly magazines reduced their frivolous offerings, numerous corporations and schools cancelled festivities and the press contributed massively to creating a quasi-sacred atmosphere.

Another issue connected with the undigested past that illustrates an underlying national disunity concerns the position of the Self-Defence Forces. Article 9 of the constitution renounces the sovereign right to wage war and specifically forbids the maintenance of land, sea and air forces. This was a condition General MacArthur had to write into the constitution to make the retention of the emperor acceptable to the Allies. The irony of the controversy is that since the 1970s the United States has been pressing for increased Japanese defence efforts.

The Self-Defence Forces, the precise role of the emperor, and state support for national commemoration ceremonies all belong to a peculiar Japanese mental twilight zone characterised by simplistic taboos and unclearly formulated attacks on these taboos. The Socialist and Communist parties, the dwindling leftist labour movement and (depending on the issue) some intellectuals, Christians and representatives of the new religions, who regard themselves as guardians of the post-war constitution, can be counted on to react with yawn-inducing predictability to anything tending towards reinstatement of what the US Occupation authorities removed.

This anti-rightist opposition consists mostly of ritual slogans shouted at rallies, and only rarely of reasoned arguments. Its protests are highly coloured with the ideological utterances so typical of the Japanese left. They do not attempt to tie the separate issues together within a coherent, lucidly argued case.

For a considerable number of non-activist Japanese the route to follow is still the one mapped out by General MacArthur and his reformers: a route never properly followed, yet still recognisable by such US-lit beacons as the new role of the emperor, the ban on state Shinto and democratic education. The controversial issues connected with the undigested past tend to be associated with an uncomfortable sense that certain groups might again lead Japan astray.

ORDER THROUGH RITUAL

The prevalence of ritual—instead of substantive discussion and appeal to reason—is characteristic of Japanese conflict. *Wa* is achieved not by reason and of course not by law, but by mechanisms that, although known elsewhere, have reached their ultimate development in Japan.

To appreciate fully the importance of ritual in Japanese life, we must again consider what the world looks like to a conventional Japanese in the absence of a tradition of appealing to universal values.

Japanese are not expected to take their cues from an inner voice that reminds them of moral absolutes they came to embrace while growing up. Moral authority is not thought to reside in them as an internalised guide to life. They have no historical models encouraging them to stand up for their beliefs. They cannot repeat after Socrates that to follow one's conscience is better than to follow convention. They could, of course, do all these things. But they would risk disapproval and would rarely be rewarded. Japanese wishing to function in a purely Japanese context must give up logic, moral values and philosophical or scientific truths as ultimate means of defence or attack. It is tempting to label the Japanese pragmatists, but one would have difficulty finding Japanese so consistent in their pragmatism that it could be considered a principle.

Ritual and hierarchy substitute for an internalised set of abstractions in reducing the likelihood of open conflict. If everybody has a proper place in the scheme of things and sticks to it, upheavals can be avoided. Acceptance of hierarchical order in Japan appears to be the only alternative to festering conflict. There can be no *wa* without hierarchy. Throughout their lives Japanese are constantly reminded of where they stand with regard to their relatives, schoolmates, fellow employees and indeed to practically everybody else with whom they come into contact. They are also expected to demonstrate awareness of the rankings of organisations, of whatever kind, through the way they treat their representatives. Social status is the one sphere where they are not conditioned to be comfortable with vagueness.

Hierarchy begins at home. In schools, children's ranks can be recognised by the uniforms or tags they wear, and ranking in the classroom is plain and open. Hierarchy is very important in university sports clubs and cheer-leading societies. Ranking is even clearer in the salaryman world. When listening to a Japanese talking on the telephone, it is almost always immediately apparent whether he is talking to someone higher or lower in rank. The common notion propagated abroad of egalitarianism within Japanese work groups (Japanese corporate directors eating their lunch in the same cafeteria as the humblest workers being the often cited evidence) is nonsense. Japanese employees must not only adjust their speech to the rank of the person addressed, but must know the appropriate degree to bow. The rank of everyone in an office is usually immediately apparent from the position of desks and the quality of chairs.

Hierarchical order pervades every nook and cranny of Japanese society. The Bank of Japan zealously guards the pecking order among the large banks, to help maintain an easily controllable lending system. A sense of superiority or inferiority is also usually evident in Japanese attitudes towards other nations. Towards "models," first China and later the West, the Japanese have always displayed emotional ambivalence. The notion of a strongly hierarchical world order has exacerbated such feelings. While feeling inferior to their models, the Japanese nevertheless have asserted the basic superiority of their own nation by postulating the familiar mythical notions of a Japanese spirit.

The Done Thing

The obsession with social order has, at least since Tokugawa times, been accompanied by the understanding that much ceremony is needed to ensure its survival. Hierarchy and ritual are, of course, related, and ritual too is essential to *wa*. Infringements of the rules of etiquette or failure to sustain the prescribed rituals constitute grave sins.

If there is one important way in which the Japanese are clearly different from other people, from Westerners as well as their Asian neighbours, it is in the extent of their ritualistic behaviour. Japanese wrap themselves in rituals. The ceremonial Japanese behaviour noticed abroad gives but a slight impression of what a Japanese must go through at home. A rigid web of formulas covers areas such as sporting events, parties and honeymoons, for which spontaneity would be considered essential in other societies.

Japanese do not necessarily love ritual more than other people, but they feel lost without it. The rituals need not at all be old and venerable. A good example of a new one, dating from the 1960s, that has conquered the entire nation, is the Japanese wedding party. Commercial

interests, large hotels and wedding parlours have shaped the customs
that the majority of marrying Japanese are nowadays subjected to.
These wedding parties are extremely boring and expensive. They are
highly predictable, with their identical cake-cutting, flower-offering
and candle-lighting ceremonies, the three or four costume changes by
the bride (bridal dress, kimono, evening dress and optional honeymoon
uniform) and the long speeches by senior employees in the companies of
bride and groom in which the jokes at the expense of the couple are
almost totally interchangeable from one wedding to the next. Lacking
any kind of festive spirit or spontaneity, these wedding parties are
disliked by most people who go to them, judging by their common
comment, but the entire population puts up with them as the "done
thing."

Japanese are conditioned from childhood to believe in the done
thing, which extends to all areas of life, including leisure pursuits. A
conspicuous product of this conditioning is the highly ritualised golf
culture. For business officials golf is not a sport or pleasant pastime, but
a bitter necessity, and for the 30 percent of all salarymen who practise it
an extremely serious business. The obligatory *shain ryoko*, or company
outing, has in recent years usually consisted of a golf competition. The
golf culture offers ideal opportunities to display hierarchic status.
Memberships in newly opened courses cost an average ten million yen
in the mid-1980s—roughly $77,000. Courses with prestige charge 25
million to 50 million yen. Such memberships are traded like stocks and
bonds, and are considered excellent investments. But the main function
of the extraordinarily costly golf culture is to provide businessmen,
bureaucrats and politicians of roughly the same hierarchic level with an
opportunity to make contacts, and thus to expand their *jinmyaku*.

Hierarchy and ritual in Japan are marvellous mechanisms whereby
the weak can give in to the strong without loss of their sense of dignity.
This avoids much cause for conflict. The conciliation procedures allow
all concerned to save face, and the same is true of the mediation that, in
less formal contexts, smooths out a multitude of snags in relationships.

Thanks to the tradition of managing reality, social conflict can be
defused without any attempt to resolve contradictions. Logical reasoning is seldom allowed to disturb the all-important *wa*. In the West
arguments appealing to logic are an accepted (and expected) part of
reconciling differences of opinion. In Japan such argument is associated
with conflict itself, and, since all conflict is defined as bad, arguing and
debating are not recognised as healthy ways to settle disputes. There is

practically no scholarly debate, and most Japanese scholars would not know how to carry on such a debate. Visiting foreign academics and intellectuals are nearly always praised, rarely argued with. The risks of losing face are thereby minimised.

The bureaucracy lives in a thoroughly ritualistic world. Officials speak in code. When they say "the matter will be studied," they mean that nothing will be done. If they promise to "study it with a forward-looking posture," this means that, as far as circumstances allow, there will be some adjustment. As with the politicians, everything in the world of bureaucrats is settled out of sight, prior to the ritual event at which decisions are formally reached.

Where Hierarchy and Ritual Are Powerless

Hierarchy and ritual are amazingly effective in maintaining order, but they cannot cover all eventualities. In the absence of a formula for agreeing to disagree, conflicts may lead to emotional outbursts and sometimes even to physical violence. This can happen in such unlikely places as the assembly hall of the Diet or in company boardrooms. But even then, the gestures tend to become extremely ritualised.

Until the mid-1960s, the Diet was frequently the scene of violence when communication between the minority parties and the LDP completely broke down. These brawls were serious enough for the Diet's stenographers to demand a pledge in 1954 that parliamentarians would not walk over their table and not touch them or their notes during the fights. The pledge was reaffirmed in 1971 and at least once more after that.

It is not easy to ascertain how much potential for social chaos exists in Japanese society. Because the media believe it is their task to help defuse social conflict rather than reflect it, much remains unreported. When on one occasion in 1987 riot police clashed with protesters in front of the Ministry of Justice buildings, protesters were prevented from emerging from a nearby subway station, handled roughly and thrown on the ground. Yet there were no reports in the next day's newspapers. Japan's television news programmes did not show any of this either.

Japan received a glimpse of the potential for social disorder in 1974, when irate passengers, who had been cooped up in overcrowded commuter trains that had been purposely stalled as part of go-slow actions by government railway engineers, smashed an office on a platform of one of Tokyo's stations. Shortly after that, passengers went on the rampage at Ageo station in Saitama prefecture, close to Tokyo. Unorganised, spontaneous commuter riots spread all over the country. The outbursts died down quickly, but the authorities took them seriously enough to plead with the go-slow organisers to go on normal strikes (which are illegal for government personnel) so that the stations could be kept closed.

Myth of Consensus

The country that I have described so far does not resemble the common portrait of Japan as a society in which human relationships are based on consensus. This is because Japan's much vaunted consensus-style democracy is a myth. Not surprisingly, administrators who deal with the external world have discovered that "consensus formation" is a useful excuse for inaction.

The term "consensus" implies positive support for an idea or course of action. What is mislabelled consensus in Japan, however, is a state of affairs in which no party thinks it worth while to upset the apple-cart. Parties to a Japanese consensus may, in fact, have very negative feelings about what they agree to.

The Japanese term for the process used to arrive at consensus is *nemawashi* ("taking care of the roots"). *Nemawashi* involves talking with the concerned parties so as to prepare them to accept a plan, as one prepares the ground for planting something. Such spadework does not invite democratic objection (with the option of rejection), as a similar process would in the West. In Japanese-style consensus the members of a group are given the formal opportunity to object to a proposal that is generally presented as if emanating from the group as a whole. Where consensus has been established it means that nobody wants to resist what a stronger person or group wants to happen. When a face-saving procedure like *nemawashi* is omitted, or has been too quick, Japanese speak of "the dictatorship of the majority." The distinction is significant. The strong have justice on their side so long as they do not implement their will brutishly.

On a company level, Japanese employees have no more say in matters that affect their working lives than employees in any other industrialised society. But the illusion is maintained that dissenting views have been duly noted. To create this illusion is generally not too difficult, since individual views rarely conflict with what their holders have perceived to be the drift of the situation. Japanese have been conditioned to sense this kind of thing and adjust their thinking accordingly.

In my experience Japanese groups do not appreciate minority opinion and remind their participants of that fact in subtle ways. Minority opinion is a hindrance to the feelings of solidarity within the group and threatens the all-important show of unity. The leadership of the group must go through the motions of consulting with everyone, especially for important decisions. This process can be elaborate, but by and large it consists of mere gestures reassuring all members that they are not unimportant. The potentially recalcitrant member has little choice but to give his support. If his negative feelings are strong and he knows of others who share them, he is more likely to form a new faction than struggle within the main group.

A common decision-making method that also creates the illusion of consensus is the so-called *ringi* system. Under this system, plans drawn up by lower officials circulate among other officials at ever higher levels, receiving their seals of approval. The appearance of full participation is served, and those who are not in favour of the plan can sabotage it to a certain extent by allowing dust to gather on the *ringi-sho*, the circulated document, before affixing their seal. Officials can indicate their degree of dissatisfaction by adjusting the time they wait before passing the document on to the next person. Hence, *ringi* is also known as the "piling-up system."

The *ringi* system is a superb mechanism for diffusing and finally obfuscating all responsibility. The makers of inappropriate decisions are nowhere to be found. The system tends to hamper leadership from the top. A plan conceived by a middle-echelon official is sometimes best launched through informal discussion with a low-ranking official, who drafts an outline that percolates upwards, taking in the desk of the initiator on the way.

ORDER THROUGH INTIMIDATION

Open displays of power evoke fear in Japan. There are few checks in Japan, but very special balances. All organisations with some power constantly contain the power of others. A clique or an individual whose power grows so fast that it cannot smoothly be accommodated by the existing structure will engender a reaction reminiscent of white blood corpuscles converging on an alien substance in the body. Hence the suspicion of Nakasone when he tried to strengthen the office of prime minister.

The administrators are extraordinarily sensitive to fluctuations of the power balance in their respective realms. An astonishing example is the prosecutors' office and its attitude towards the left. When leftist activists raised a great outcry against corruption, the prosecutors saw the value of their traditional enemies as a cleansing agent. Although political corruption is "structural," and the prosecutors would not dream of trying to eliminate it, the System must be guarded against extremes; and with the gradual decline of leftist forces the prosecutors felt that they had to act as a counterbalance and bring more corruption cases to light.

The Ubiquity of Intimidation

Intimidation is used within trade associations to maintain their hierarchy. Prominent members have much power over the lesser ones and can even organise a bankruptcy through the leverage they have over subcontractors, distribution channels and creditors.

There are various ways to make firms realise their place in the scheme of things. Upstart companies may be taught a lesson for being too aggressive, or for having irritated dominant firms. One example is Kyocera, a relatively new, adventurous and very successful firm led by a true entrepreneur. It is not part of the established hierarchy of corporations and is therefore vulnerable to official displeasure. In June 1985, it was ordered by the Ministry of Health and Welfare to suspend production for thirty-five days, on the grounds that it had been selling (perfectly good) ceramic joints and bones to hospitals for five years without official permission. In fact, the Japanese bureaucracy confronts industry with such a plethora of regulations and restrictions that no firm can keep track of them. The strictness with which they are enforced depends on *jinmyaku* relations and the firm's power within the industrial hierarchy. Measures such as those against Kyocera are taken only if a lesson has to be taught. The press helps teach the lesson, and the president of the firm in question is obliged ceremonially to beg society's forgiveness.

Far from being abhorred, intimidation is accepted as inevitable. The highly valued conformity is to a large extent enforced by intimidation; until the recent outcry, teachers in many schools encouraged their pupils in bullying practices. The freedom and *de facto* support that gangsters enjoy is another example of how intimidation helps to operate the System. The fact that they exist and are strong automatically means that they are accepted. Their intimidation has made them acceptable. They may intimidate ordinary people with impunity; the police and most of the courts remain unsympathetic to the victims' plight.

Intimidation works in Japan, no matter where it originates. It worked when the Chinese government made Japanese newspaper correspondents promise never to write anything critical about Mao Tse-tung, the Cultural Revolution or other controversial subjects. It works when Arab countries ask Japanese companies not to trade with Israel. Japan is the only major country in the Western alliance that religiously observes the Arab economic boycott of Israel, while the path to the Arab countries is well trodden. No ship flying the Japanese flag has ever entered an Israeli port. Japanese banks do not extend long-term financing for exports to Israel, and Toyota has never sold a car in Israel. When former New York Mayor Ed Koch criticised this policy at a press briefing, none of the Japanese journalists present got one line about this in his newspaper. The controversy in the West over broadcasting films that could be construed as critical of Arab social practices is unthinkable in Japan, where such films are taken out of circulation at the slightest sign of Arab displeasure.

Any foreign country can participate in the Japanese political tug of war by applying *gaiatsu*, or pressure from the outside. Ministries, in their battles with other ministries, have on several occasions been known to encourage foreigners to use *gaiatsu*.

Bureaucratic Intimidation

As we have seen, the laws drafted by the bureaucratic control are purposely left vague. The threat of applying laws in instances where they are not usually applied gives government agencies great powers of intimidation. This is one reason for the vehement opposition to the anti-espionage bills that have been introduced, unsuccessfully, on a number of occasions, with vague clauses about national security that could be interpreted in a variety of ways.

The relationship between business corporations and the bureaucracy is not normally antagonistic, but in such instances of conflict as do occur—when the two parties differ on the details of policies—the companies normally have to comply with bureaucratic wishes. In fact, the bureaucratic technique of "administrative guidance" that has drawn so much attention from Western observers is itself a species of coercion by intimidation.

Administrative guidance is effective because of the leverage bureaucrats have over businesses. The power to withhold licences is an obvious one. Government officials are responsible for approval of applications for almost every conceivable business activity. If they do not like an applicant, they can hold off a decision on his applications. Businesses abide by the guidance simply because they want to continue to function. This is one of the keys to Japanese bureaucratic control. Official theory notwithstanding, administrative guidance is compulsory.

The coercion is sometimes more straightforward. A high Ministry of International Trade and Industry official told me that, since all companies have done something shady at one time or another, they fear exposure if they do not follow MITI's directions. Information useful in such blackmail comes from direct investigations, competitors, clients, the police, enemies in the business community and disgruntled employees. My informant estimates that more than half of all cases of corporate wrongdoing known to the police and MITI bureaucrats are covered up. The leverage this gives MITI is the fear, not of legal action, but of social punishment. For it is considered most damaging to a firm if its name is connected with any kind of scandal.

For the bureaucrats, it is very important that an illusion of voluntary co-operation be maintained, so officials nearly always prefer to approach a recalcitrant company informally, and offer it freedom from red tape in return for compliance with government wishes. And ministries dole out favours such as tax privileges and financial help in return for obedience to administrative guidance.

Of the three main tools that bureaucrats use to get their plans implemented—legislative measures, budgetary measures and administrative guidance—they much prefer the last, because it is effective and readily available for quick action. They could in most cases find a law to suit their purpose, but administrative guidance maintains the fiction of voluntary co-operation. When the Ministry of Finance forces the commercial banks to buy government bonds, it refers to this as cooperation. Administrative guidance also provides much greater scope for specific adjustments in consultation with the recipient.

The economic ministries have great power to harass firms that do not toe the line. Their trump card is the claim that what they suggest is less what they want than what the industry wanted all along. This approach is often used in tandem with the power that associations of firms have to enforce conformity, in a strategy whereby the recalcitrant firm is forced to fall in line by the threat of ostracism.

Intimidating the Administrators

How the bureaucrats view their own place in the System is highlighted by the way they perceive the very rare lawsuits initiated against them: such lawsuits are considered an unwarranted use of force. Legal entanglements hamper official duties, but the bureaucrats dislike litigation mainly because they feel that to give courtroom explanations of official actions conflicts with the highly treasured confidentiality of the administration. Court scrutiny undermines their dignity and, consequently, the settled benevolent state of affairs of the Japanese nation.

Intimidation can thus work both ways. Although the supposed servants of the people have the advantage, and the possibilities for court action against them are very limited, the possibility that some group or other may attempt to put bureaucrats in the dock has an intimidating effect. Officials consider such resistance a red light, and modify their attitudes to keep things from getting out of hand.

Japanese policy patterns are nearly always inflexible until a catastrophe occurs or until those who consider themselves victimised manage a chorus of protest. Opposition or complaint is at first usually ignored or suppressed. But when the realisation dawns that further suppression will only make the movement stronger, officialdom changes its attitude. Those in charge become more flexible and ready to overlook illegal action. In cases where a problem suddenly threatens to become acute, the metamorphosis from a stubborn to an accommodating stance is generally very dramatic. The intimidation we find in the Japanese System may be called "structural intimidation." Without it, the System would grind to a halt, since it furnishes the power-holders with power. Ritual and hierarchy help preserve order, but do not guarantee security. Only power provides security in Japan. Guarding one's power is best accomplished by subtly displaying and enlarging it. And because this can be done only through informal means, intimidation is an unavoidable and omnipresent characteristic of Japanese society.

— 9 —

A CENTURY OF
CONSOLIDATING
CONTROL

A major hindrance to an accurate assessment of the Japanese System is the still very common view that the jolt of defeat in the Pacific War, and the ministrations of the Supreme Commander of the Allied Powers (SCAP), brought into being a Japan that had made a definitive break with its immediate past. According to this view, the society that emerged in just a few years after 1945 was committed to different principles of governing itself and led by men themselves committed to these principles.

Acceptance of this view was made easy for many by an influential school of thought that presented the years between the late 1920s and 1945 as an aberration in Japanese history. All the elements that would have turned Japan into a respectable modern democratic society, such as a parliament and political parties, were in place when the country was temporarily derailed by nationalist fanatics.

This viewpoint has been undermined by recent scholarship which shows how Japan's empire-building and domestic repression can be seen as growing out of dominant trends in the Meiji period. Only in the 1980s did some scholars begin to point out that 1945 was not the watershed it was supposed to have been, and that authoritarian institutions and techniques dating from the first half of the twentieth century have been crucial in shaping present-day Japan.

With the benefit of hindsight we can go one step further and see the Japanese System of the late 1980s as a product of the consolidation of certain forces that have been evolving since before the turn of the century, a consolidation that was accelerated by the war.

THE FUNDAMENTAL CONTINUITY

There is no gainsaying that post-war Japan is a new Japan in many respects. The idea that military adventurism was a great mistake and that the nation should devote itself to peaceful pursuits has undoubtedly been very strong among the general populace. Standards of living, especially in rural Japan, cannot be compared with the poverty that prevailed before the war. Japanese today enjoy much personal freedom and need not worry about being arrested for what they say. The public is looked after in a way it has never been before. Nevertheless, in the context of our theme—how power is exercised in Japan—the continuities appear to be of more consequence than the changes.

Japan rose phoenix-like from the rubble of its bombed cities to become the second most powerful economy in the world. However, the mainsprings of this rebirth are not to be found in the economic and political restructuring measures of US-Occupation-inspired *demokurashii*, but in the socio-political world and disavowed feudal practices of Japan at war.

Luckiest Survivors of the War

The most momentous decision the Occupation authorities made when they set about transforming Japan was to leave practically the entire bureaucracy intact. The usual explanation for this is that SCAP had no choice but to work through the existing organs of state. But the vast majority of those involved in Occupation policies were not even aware that any significant decision had been made. They simply assumed that bureaucrats everywhere behaved as they did in the USA, that is to say, as apolitical technicians. An official in SCAP's grand democratisation programme describes how the nerve-centre of operations to reform defeated Japan's officialdom consisted of a single young lieutenant in the Transportation Corps, Milton J. Esman:

> Esman's desk was an oasis of quiet in a tumult of bustling reform activities, for he was in charge of the civil service under Kades, and it seemed that no one else was interested in the subject. No

paragraph in the Joint Chiefs' directive JCS 1380/15 even mentioned the bureaucracy. Esman really had no official mission.

The Occupation purge eliminated the defeated military organisations, removed fifteen hundred highly placed businessmen, barred a few politicians from holding public office and dissolved ultra-nationalist organisations. It did not go beyond this to tackle the mainspring of Japan's governing system. Moreover the strong incentive to preserve the tranquility of the Occupation led the US reformers to keep to a minimum interference in areas outside the military and ultra-nationalist organisations. Thus the purge of the bureaucracy was, in its details, left to the bureaucrats themselves, who soon realised that they were free to use a large variety of loopholes.

By 1950, when the return to public life of depurged bureaucrats coincided with the "Red Purge" (in which more than one thousand government officials and almost eleven thousand company employees suspected of communism or communistic-type thinking lost their jobs), the effects of the Occupation purge on Japan's officialdom had been reduced to almost nil.

Reform Bureaucrats and the New Order

SCAP's ignorance of the true power of Japanese bureaucrats gave them the opportunity to develop economic institutions they had experimented with from the early 1930s until 1945. This post-war effort was better organised; the bureaucrats had learned from experience and, more important, had been given powers by SCAP that they never had before.

Many of the most prominent figures associated with post-war industrial policy had been known in pre-war Japan as "reform bureaucrats," strongly influenced by the ideas of Hitler's Germany and by Mussolini's corporatism. This does not mean that they were converts to Nazism, but that they sponsored the application of German methods to the economy and social control in Japan. Nazi and fascist theory are not generally associated in the Western mind with the Japanese "economic miracle," but it is doubtful whether this could have occurred without the inspiration of these theories supporting totalitarian state control. In fact, the reform bureaucrats dominated the post-war leadership of the economic ministries, the central bank and the large business federations.

Reform bureaucrat Kishi Nobusuke, who as the most powerful official in the wartime Ministry of Munitions was the central figure in Japan's wartime industrial policy, became the dominant figure of post-war industrial policy. After a stint in Sugamo prison as a war criminal suspect (never brought to trial), Kishi became one of Japan's best-known prime ministers, then, until his death in 1987, Japan's most influential *eminence grise*.

Second only to Kishi as a shaper of post-war industrial policy was Shiina Etsusaburo, a reform bureaucrat who had the timely idea, between the surrender and the arrival of the first United States troops, of re-baptising the Ministry of Munitions so that it became the Ministry of Commerce and Industry once more. He himself became MITI minister after the war, and remained a powerful force behind the scenes, as well as one of the most prominent leaders of the LDP, until his death in 1979.

The main architects of wartime financial controls had originally come from the foreign exchange section of the Ministry of Finance. Pre-eminent among them was Sakomizu Hisatsune, who became head of the Economic Planning Agency and postal minister after the war. Many of the wartime controls over lending were coordinated in a bureau whose chief, Ichimanda Hisato, was to become governor of the Bank of Japan in 1946, a position he held for eight and a half crucial years before being appointed finance minister.

The bureaucrats survived the purges with the added advantage of being freed from their sometimes troublesome military associates. Moreover, the Occupation authorities, believing that big business had been active exponents of militant nationalism and aggression, ordered the dissolution of the *zaibatsu* conglomerates and the holding companies, which meant that the bureaucrats no longer faced rivals for power in the business world. The bureau chiefs of each ministry began to attend cabinet meetings, a practice unknown before the war. They became go-betweens between MacArthur's headquarters and government ministers, and their utterances gained significantly in weight.

When, after the war, Japanese commentators began to refer to the bureaucrats as "subcontractors of the Occupation," they missed the essential fact that the tail was wagging the dog. As Chalmers Johnson puts it: "The Occupation era, 1945-52, witnessed the highest levels of government control over the economy ever encountered in modern Japan before or since, levels that were decidedly higher than the levels attained during the Pacific War." Perhaps the biggest present bestowed on the post-war MITI bureaucrats by SCAP was the power to form cartels, an essential instrument of Japanese industrial policy.

Talkative officials have publicly acknowledged that, whereas, formally, Japan underwent a great transformation after the war, the economic system and financial controls were retained in the forms they had taken during the war. Two former Ministry of Finance bureaucrats have contrasted the two realities, the formal and the substantial, and asserted that this duality was essential in the shaping of the post-war "miracle." As they put it, the ideology of democratic equal opportunity caused an explosion of energy in favour of economic growth, while the high growth itself was achieved through the reality of strict financial controls. Writing thirty-two years after the war, they noted that the basic law governing the central bank was still the original law that had reflected the totalitarian economic purposes of the Nazi Reichsbank.

The post-war economic bureaucrats designed an industrial policy that vitalised the private sector, steering it in directions of their own choice, and fostered the growth of domestic manufacturers through a strong protectionism. This quickly became Japan's dominating—indeed, sole—major policy. The demise of the *zaibatsu* was of significance not least because it made room for the four large industrial federations that were to become post-war control centres. Pervaded by bureaucrats, each of them played a major role in the development of the System: Keidanren as overall coordinator and fund-raiser for what later became the LDP; Nikkeiren as coordinator of the anti-labour campaign; the Chamber of Commerce as the ostensible guardian, but also the controller, of smaller industries; and Keizai Doyukai as propagandist and formulator of justifications for the general course that developments were taking.

SCAP went along with plans for the formation of Keidanren on condition that it would not try to engage in economic control and would stay clear of labour relations. Two years later a way was found around the second prohibition, when several of the people who had established Keidanren helped form Nikkeiren, the headquarters of union-busting and, later, control organisation in charge of keeping wage rises significantly below productivity increases.

Among the formal aims of these federations, set forth in many public pronouncements of their early stages, was the promotion of a vigorous democracy. This is reminiscent of the advocacy of greater "individualism" by the Ad Hoc Council on Educational Reforms, whose reports implied that such an aim is best achieved by greater discipline in the schools and better instruction in what it means to be Japanese. The democracy espoused by the *zaikai* left no room for any movement representing the workers, or for socialism or indeed for any kind of political principles that might conflict with stable conservative government.

Regaining the Means of Social Control

While very kind to the economic-control bureaucrats, the Occupation authorities placed bureaucrats steeped in pre-war and wartime *social-control* methods in a frightful predicament. "Democratised" education meant the loss of a whole arsenal of indoctrination methods. Justice Ministry officials had to cope with idealists who actually believed that the law was situated above everyone, including officials. The Naimusho was broken up, and the police were reorganised. While the devastated economy warranted much economic planning and control, the new start with democracy hardly warranted a "thought police."

But, by bestowing a constitution upon Japan, General MacArthur, without realising it, did the social-control bureaucrats at least one great favour. The constitution was not wrested from the power-holders by the people. The latter, therefore, were not encouraged to believe that they had the *right* to wrest anything from the ruling elite; and the theory of ultimate benevolence could be maintained.

The main hazard to the administrators was the democratic legislature. The threat was averted thanks to a massive influx into the Diet of veterans of the disbanded Naimusho. This descent of retired bureaucrats into the pre-LDP conservative parties began shortly after the war, aided by the room made for them by the Occupation purge of wartime politicians. Some thirty elite bureaucrats joined the Liberal Party for the 1949 elections, and in subsequent elections their number grew to roughly a quarter of the Diet, providing Japan with the crucial Yoshida, Kishi, Ikeda and Sato cabinets—during whose tenure the post-war System was consolidated.

The administrators concerned with public order also made allies among the occupiers, who never understood the depth of the anti-liberalism of their "subcontractors." Among these allies was the chief of the Counter-Intelligence Corps, General Charles Willoughby. As the American in charge of labour questions remembered almost forty years later:

Willoughby was out of his depth. To him, socialism was just a station on the way to communism. Democratic socialists were not allies in the fight against the communists but subverters of the established order. . . Only Japanese conservatives could be trusted. . . For him, there was no middle ground between the conservatives and the communists.

The later Occupation period gave the social-control bureaucrats an opportunity to fend off the labour union advance. The Red Purge ousted officials with post-war "dangerous thoughts," and set the stage for the dismissal of Education Ministry officials who had cooperated too much with SCAP's democratisation efforts. Steps to remedy the "excesses of the Occupation" in other areas such as the police and anti-trust legislation completed the consolidation of post-war bureaucratic power.

Not all Japanese welcomed the retention of the wartime control bureaucrats. As one author wrote in one of the most respected of Japan's intellectual monthlies, the Tokyo Trials judged acts perpetrated by war criminals against foreigners, but did not consider those committed against the Japanese people. Men who had sent others to the front, who had deprived them of their freedom and property, who had made cruel laws, continued, he pointed out, to hold high positions in post-war cabinets. The author reminded his readers that in Germany, unlike in Japan, a general sense of justice had prevailed. The Germans themselves tried war criminals who had been acquitted at the Nuremberg Trials.

Japan's bureaucrats have always believed that their mission goes far beyond the enforcement of regulations that is the normal task of civil servants in Western nations. With or without support from their military allies, they have always been interested in social engineering, and have viewed active interference in civil society as necessary to prevent instability. The Japanese ruling elite still has an overpowering "daddy knows best" attitude, while the people have been kept under permanent political tutelage. It is this continuity through the pre-war, wartime and post-war periods, rather than the undoubted modification of elitist demeanour and the gains in personal freedom, that most significantly determines the character of the Japanese political system today.

Containing the Public

The administrators of post-war Japan have been able to create a world in which socio-political disorder is kept to a minimum. The transitional cult of submission discourages individual growth and fosters dependency. The Japanese accept a high degree of organisation and restrictions; they tolerate the way officials meddle in their lives, and do not question their permanent political tutelage. Very few can conceive of civil disobedience as legitimate political action.

Nevertheless, the administrators must remain vigilant, because the tradition established by their predecessors cannot be trusted to continue on its own. Military service no longer helps ensure discipline among young males, and the post-war family has lost most of its pre-war legal control of its members—but the enforced conformism of salaryman life is a very effective substitute.

The energy with which in the late 1980s the authorities have pursued fingerprint refusers is an example of the government bringing its might to bear on a matter that has not even the remotest potential for undermining the state. Some members of the Korean and Chinese minorities who have resided in Japan for several generations object to the rule that they must be fingerprinted for alien registration; they see this practice, which among Japanese nationals is followed only with criminals, as symbolic of the discrimination they suffer. There is no convincing reason why this antiquated method of identification should still be in use. Although the fingerprinting issue has become a diplomatic burden for the Ministry of Foreign Affairs, the officials of both the Ministry of Justice and the National Police Agency are adamant about enforcing order, and set examples by refusing to issue re-entry permits or visa renewals.

Such control for its own sake also sets an example for the Japanese people. The System would collapse if they did not take social control for granted. Whenever possible, the administrators like to combine their setting of examples with a show of benevolence. Take the case of the three 21-year-old Japanese Olympic swimmers who were caught smoking marijuana in Los Angeles in 1984. Even though they have no jurisdiction beyond Japanese borders, the Japanese prosecutors made much of the "lenient" decision not to prosecute for the reason that the young men had tried the forbidden weed only once out of curiosity. The swimmers' university was also "lenient," readmitting them after a semester during which they professed their contrition in diaries sent to the university authorities in instalments.

The Dream of a Non-Political State

As the System advances, it moves ever closer to fulfilment of the dream of a depoliticised state. In the West, too, this is an old dream. The vision of cooperation in one magnificent joint effort to improve human life and the rewards for this in the form of loving care, has inspired many social engineers and Utopians before and after Marx. Part of the dream is the familiar notion of replacing wheeling-dealing politics with unselfish and scientific government, in which the nation enjoys the benefit of advanced, technocratic expertise.

A life in which rational planning would substitute for self-seeking politics is enticing in that it promises solutions to problems that have plagued humanity throughout history. As Isaiah Berlin put it:

> Where ends are agreed, the only questions left are those of means, and these are not political but technical, that is to say capable of being settled by experts or machines like arguments between doctors or engineers. That is why those who put their faith in some immense, world-transforming phenomenon, like the final triumph of reason or the proletarian revolution, must believe that all political and moral problems can thereby be turned into technological ones.

The only question is what the planning would be for. For the Japanese System the answer to this has been clear since the Meiji period: keeping order and becoming strong. And since 1945 the administrators have, without discussing ends, consolidated, adjusted and planned for the priority of unlimited industrial expansion as if this were a self-evident good, which is indeed how they see it.

The consolidation of the System has brought great apparent stability. The question of whether the stability is more apparent than real becomes urgent only when developments that the administrators cannot cope with cause a crisis. And in 1988 it seemed that no domestic tensions could reach crisis proportions. The unacknowledged problem of legitimacy has been dealt with in an effective way, certainly more effective than before 1945. It is unlikely to become acute so long as the components of the System can prevent an authoritarian take-over by one among them. The strong tendency towards conflict is suppressed; conflict, as we have seen, is not recognised as politically acceptable.

Yet a completely depoliticised social system does not and cannot exist. The Japanese System is entirely politicised. The political functions of the businesses and business federations that form the System's solid core are conspicuous. Conglomerates do not simply exercise political influence as they do in the West; they have become integral and totally indispensable organs of the body politic. This fact, together with the unquestioning priority given by the administrators to unlimited industrial expansion, is an essential factor in the context of Japan's international relations, one that, unlike domestic tensions, could very well lead to crisis.

— 10 —

THE JAPANESE
PHOENIX

There are two main threats to the hallowed Japanese order: from Japanese and from foreigners. Both, over the past century and a half, have at times loomed large enough to frighten the ruling elite. The political events leading up to and following the Meiji Restoration can be seen as a sequence of domestic and foreign threats to established power relations, together with the reactions they provoked. For roughly six decades after that, a newly emerged bureaucracy guarded Japan against domestic disorder, using the gradually evolving surrogate religion of "national essence," as well as the military-bureaucratic institutions for social control. Since around 1955, the threat of domestic political disorder has been even more effectively dealt with through the awesome control capacities of the post-war System. But beyond the reach of these domestic measures there remained the second threat, the one from outside, a threat that by its very nature constitutes a perennial source of disquiet. The outside world simply does not lend itself to traditional Japanese techniques of control.

THE ECONOMICS OF NATIONAL SECURITY

Since a threat to their own security is automatically seen as a threat to the security of the nation, Japan's power-holders and their spokesmen have long portrayed Japan as a country particularly vulnerable to outside forces. From the Meiji period until at least the 1970s, this ever-present anxiety, sometimes latent, sometimes acute, supplied much of the energy for the effort to catch up.

Catching Up

In the half-century following the end of Japan's seclusion, the capacity of foreign powers to upset Japanese socio-political arrangements had to be countered by increasing the country's industrial and military strength. Russia and the Western states had to be made to see Japan as an equal. The most famous slogan of the Meiji period was "fukoku kyohei" ("rich country, strong military") and the response to the real or imaginary external threat was an effort to make Japan invincible. Catching up with the strongest in the world became an obsession—not just a government priority but the highest aim of all patriotic Japanese. To a degree virtually inconceivable to Westerners, many Japanese found the ultimate meaning of life, their existential lodestar, in the survival and welfare of the nation.

Catching up also meant control beyond the water surrounding Japan. In the Meiji period as well as during the Taisho democracy no Japanese with a political voice would have had it otherwise. The political parties went along with the military and the bureaucrats in their plan to make Japan a dominating power.

Success with the "strong military" part of the programme was, of course, readily demonstrable. And judging by the response of the Meiji press, expansionist goals were highly popular. The newspapers supported the Sino-Japanese and Russo-Japanese wars, as well as the insubordination of the Kwantung Army that led to the war in Manchuria and ultimately to the Pacific War. The notorious Hibiya Riot of 1905 and the ensuing confrontations between police and public in many parts of Tokyo (prompting a declaration of martial law) were protests against the terms of the Treaty of Portsmouth. In the following decades, Japanese imperialist expansion was as much in favour with the articulate public as the idea of universal suffrage.

Even so, for one segment of the elite the "rich country" part of the national mission provided an even greater inspiration. A number of Meiji period writers and officials, swept along by the vogue for Herbert Spencer and Social Darwinism spoke of a "peacetime war" among nations, stressing the necessity of economic development and seeing the military as a tool in the forceful creation of foreign markets and sources of supply.

The primary task of the Naimusho (established in 1873) in its first ten years, before Yamagata Aritomo turned it into the main headquarters of the social-control bureaucrats, was the promotion of domestic

industry. Its first minister, Okubo Toshimichi, one of the most powerful among the earliest oligarchs, despaired when he discovered on a
mission to Europe that the West was too far ahead for Japan ever to catch
up. He objected strongly to the plans for a Korean invasion on the
grounds that Japan could not afford any such adventures and should
think only of strengthening itself economically. Using 70 percent of the
newly established Naimusho's budget, Okubo helped establish government factories; merged a government marine transport firm with Mitsubishi's shipping company to eliminate United States and British
dominance in the area of transport; sent export study missions to the
West; built a trading system that bypassed foreign agents; gave financial
support to the silk, farming and other industries; and sponsored national exhibitions to propagate the advantages of fast industrialisation.

Japan has had an industrial policy ever since the early Meiji period.
Taking over enterprises, the oligarchy added to them national railway
and communications networks, and armaments, mining and shipbuild-
ing industries. As Meiji industrialisation took off, government control
over the economy became automatic, since the government either put
up the capital itself or encouraged private investors to do so by according
them protection. In practically all major industries, the Meiji government took the initiative. In the early 1880s it switched from direct
control over many factories to indirect protection, virtually giving away
what it had built. In 1881 it established a Ministry of Agriculture and
Commerce to help regulate this policy and draft the laws that for-
malised earlier transactions. An economic oligarchy came into being,
consisting of politically privileged financial houses that were beholden
to the ruling oligarchy and its bureaucratic elite. The *jinmyaku*
networks—built on kinship, marriage, bribes or friendships dating
from school—that played such a striking role in the course of Japan's
modern economic development were already functioning.

Privatisation has been a major characteristic of Japanese economic
policy. Whenever it has seemed safe to do so, the bureaucrats have
divested themselves of the bothersome task of direct management. The
custom continues, as the handling of the national railways and telecommunications in the mid-1980s indicates. The officials lose little practical
jurisdiction, while the economy gains in efficiency thanks to new
incentives, the spreading of risk and a controlled form of competition
that promotes "national selection."

Fostering Dedication

The second large catching-up campaign began in the 1950s, after post-war reconstruction had been completed, and continues today. Evincing the same single-minded dedication, it has enabled Japan to outstrip every country except the United States in economic prowess. Again, it was prompted not only, not even primarily, by what the West understands by economic motivations. The primary goal has not been to expand the choices and comforts of Japan's citizens. On the contrary, economic growth has often taken place at their expense, being directly associated with the notion of national security. And since the "strong military" part of the national mission has had to be scrapped, the economic effort has this time had to bear the entire burden.

Whereas in the Meiji period hasty industrial development was considered vital for national security, today nothing less than industrial dominance will do. That Japan's officials take this for granted is evident if one listens closely to their statements: the world must understand that they cannot allow *any* of their industries to fail in the face of foreign competition.

Most foreign observers have attested to the unquestioning dedication with which Japanese devote themselves to their tasks. Four decades after the end of the war, with national reconstruction well behind them, salarymen of the same company still exude a sense of missionary zeal. In the 1960s especially, Japanese firms gave the impression of being involved in a permanent contest. Competition was, in fact, controlled, but they were incessantly seeking to raise themselves in the business hierarchy, and top rankings within the various sectors were widely publicised. Even housewives and schoolchildren had a pretty good idea of which firm loomed largest in which field. Such publicity, and the unanimous impression given by the media (before the pollution scandals) that all this was wonderful, helped generate a phenomenal propelling force. But to be among the top firms at home was only a beginning; the race with the mighty international corporations was already well under way. In conversations with engineers and executives of the large electronic manufacturers in the mid-1970s one sensed that basically they all lived for one thing only: to catch up and outstrip IBM. Visiting the offices of Fuji Photo Film Company the day after the announcement of the "dollar shock" (resulting from Nixon's decision in 1971 to stop the convertibility of the dollar into gold, thus forcing a revaluation of the yen), I found a group of ashen-faced salarymen who explained that their prospects of catching up with and overtaking Kodak had received a set-back from which the company might never recover.

The Path to Perfection

The catching-up disposition has been such an important aspect of Japan's emergence as a major economic power that it is worth examining its ramifications in an area not directly connected with the political economy. Progress in Japan has frequently and for long periods been more immediately measurable than it has been for Westerners. At the outset of its recorded history, in the sixth century, when it was a primitive tribal society without a writing system, Japan had the momentous experience of coming into contact with T'ang China, the most sophisticated civilization on earth at the time. The adoption of cultural forms with a thoroughness rarely if ever paralleled in history established an attitude towards self-improvement that has been handed down to this day.

Characteristic of this attitude is the notion that there is a "perfect" way of doing things. In learning a skill—especially in connection with Japanese music, the traditional theatre arts, or judo, aikido, kendo and karate—the emphasis is on automatic, non-reflective repetition of what the teacher does. Mastery is reached by removal of the obstacles between the self and the perfect model, embodied by the teacher.

The idea that the student might have an inborn potential that is uniquely his own has had hardly any influence. Foreign conductors and music teachers almost uniformly remark on the great technical skill of Japanese performers, together with their relative lack of personal expression. This reflects the fact that musicians who have never studied abroad have rarely been taught that it is *they* who must interpret the music. The "perfect" way of doing anything is comparable to the rigid expectation in communal behaviour; the performer must live up to the model. According to Japanese learning methods, the skill or art has an authoritative and predetermined existence demanding subservience. There is no room for idiosyncratic variation to suit the individual practitioner.

The advantage of this approach is that it can produce great technical mastery, and a serene beauty resulting from total self-confidence. But it has drawbacks, too. Progress in a skill is measured by such narrowly defined standards that achievements not covered by these standards may well pass unnoticed. The self-consciousness that the traditional learning method generates in the earlier stages also tends to act as a brake. Since the precise manner of presentation is considered crucially important, uncountable repetitions are needed to eliminate the obstructive awareness of the self. Japanese students of traditional skills—and of modern sports—are not allowed to leave their physical movements to take care of themselves so that they can attend to what lies beyond.

I believe there is political significance in this approach to learning. Exposure to the Chinese model came so early in Japanese political development, and T'ang China represented such vastly greater sophistication, that it provided no opportunity to compare governments. The power-holders who imported the outward forms of Chinese government almost in their entirety appear to have been motivated by an awareness of a new reality that they had to live up to. I speculate that this is the origin in Japan both of the notion that there are "perfect" ways of doing things, and of the pervading sense of always falling short of these "perfect" ways.

In the nineteenth century Japan suddenly came face to face with the strength and technological marvels of the USA and European countries. This time the prevailing slogan preached that it was the material achievements of the foreigners that must be emulated, while keeping the Japanese spirit intact. And emulate the Japanese did, on a scale few other people have done before or since.

Panics, Depression and New Controls

By 1905, Japan had built up an industrial base sufficient to allow it to defeat Russia in the Russo-Japanese War (1904-5). The success of the Meiji oligarchy in stimulating economic development was followed by a further great boost for Japanese industry deriving from the First World War. This good fortune came to an end in 1920, and a chain of panics caused successive recession. In fact, the Japanese economy continued to grow fast by international standards, but this did not alter the general impression of uncertainty and disorder. Just when adjustments were having a salutary effect, the great Kanto earthquake of 1923 hit Tokyo and its environs. This was followed by deflation in 1925 and the financial crisis of 1927. Many companies, overextended because of the earlier boom, had to be rescued by government loans. The central bank had lent too much after the earthquake, and the resulting financial panic caused the collapse of thirty-seven banks and the rise to near hegemony of the five *zaibatsu* banks. All this happened against a background of increased tenant-farmer risings and other social unrest.

Disorder had, in the view of the custodians of Japan's security, reached unacceptable proportions and called for dramatic action. When this came, it marked the beginning of the end for an economic system that despite its strong bureaucratic element still resembled in many ways the *laissez-faire* economies of the West. During the Taisho Democracy period entrepreneurism had flourished, and new businesses were able to expand into large firms. Profit-making was accepted as the proper function of business. There was a labour market, and an open capital market, as well as free trade of a kind Japan has not known since, and a free inflow of foreign capital. Following the banking crisis, however, Tanaka Giichi formed a cabinet, in April 1927, that was to introduce a new approach to economic management and greater social control. He had numerous leftists arrested, and dissolved all suspect organisations. A month after the formation of the Tanaka cabinet, the minister of commerce and industry set up a deliberation council within his ministry, with the purpose of examining what was ailing the Japanese economy and what the government ought to do about it. Chalmers Johnson, the originator of the term "capitalist developmental state" (CDS), has pinpointed that development as the beginning of the industrial policy that led to post-war high growth. The economic bureaucrats started to think in terms of "industrial rationalisation" and have never stopped doing so.

The Showa depression of 1930-5, brought on by the 1929 Depression in the West, followed the many panics of the previous decade and helped bring to power the reform bureaucrats with their theories of socio-economic control based on Nazi and Italian corporatist ideas. Simultaneously, one of Japan's best-known ministers of finance, Takahashi Korekiyo, pursued an inflationary policy that was the first Japanese example of economic management of this kind. It worked, aided by stepped-up arms production. The heavy and chemical industries subsequently towed Japan out of the depression. Takahashi had always pleaded for economic rather than military expansion. For this attitude he was murdered by the super-patriots in the 26 February rebellion of 1936. This event also marked the demise of moderating forces in the face of military demands for optimum spending on the "national defence state."

The State Capitalist Laboratory

The one place relatively free from the deleterious effects of the incessant infighting among elite groups was Manchuria. Especially after the Japanese Kwantung Army had turned it into the puppet state of Manchukuo, this *de facto* colony was viewed by the military and the reformists in the bureaucracy as the ideal setting for promoting industrial schemes as an expression of the might of the empire. The Army had long been contemptuous of the large corporations, because they were interested more in profits than in working for the greater glory of the emperor. It therefore wanted to keep the *zaibatsu* out of Manchuria.

The brains behind the Manchurian Incident and other Kwantung Army operations over which Tokyo had lost all control was Colonel Ishiwara Kanji. Ishiwara, a brilliant strategist, was most closely identified with the concept of the "national defence state," and had gained attention as lecturer at the War College with his ideas about "the final war" (i.e. between Japan and the USA). He was the idol of romantic military activists. Reaching his most influential position as military economic planner in 1935, Ishiwara immediately began to draw up plans for the development of Manchuria as a base for war against the Soviet Union and for a Showa restoration—a revolution that would cleanse Japan of the elite groups that detracted from the "national essence." Neither aim was achieved; but it was Ishiwara who sketched the basic economic plans that the Kwantung Army presented to the reform bureaucrats Kishi Nobusuke and Hoshino Naoki for refinement and implementation.

Initially, the South Manchurian Railway (Mantetsu) ran a gigantic economic empire. It was transferred into Japanese hands as a result of the Russo-Japanese War and formed the vanguard of Japan's industrial and commercial penetration of China. Besides the railway, Mantetsu ran coal-mines, steel works, warehouses, electrical plants, light metal factories, banks, harbours, water transport and aircraft factories, representing some eight companies in all. It also exploited Chinese labour on a gigantic scale.

Mantetsu found it difficult, however, to raise enough capital. Thus in the key year of 1937, when all-out war with China made the full-scale exploitation of Manchuria essential, the military and reform bureaucrat planners drastically reorganised Mantetsu, separating its industrial activities from the railway and grouping them under the Manchukuo Heavy Industries Development Company. Half of the newly needed capital was to be provided by one of the so-called "new *zaibatsu*," the Nissan combine.

Nissan (the parent firm of what has today become the Nissan Motor Company and the Hitachi conglomerate) was chosen because its leader, Ayukawa Gisuke, a relative and political associate of Kishi Nobusuke, was not, in the eyes of the Army, driven by motives of mere personal gain. Ayukawa spent the next five years setting up Manchurian companies. Here again we see the importance of *jinmyaku*. Personal relationships were crucial among the reform bureaucrats, between the bureaucrats and the military and between the military and the government. Thus it was Kishi who convinced the military that his relative Ayukawa was their best choice, by arguing that he was somehow different from the money-grabbing *zaibatsu* families.

The methods of forced industrial development pioneered by the economic-control bureaucrats provided key lessons for Japan's post-war economy: a method of financing and of guaranteeing market share; and the principle of economies of scale. The task of Ayukawa's Manchukuo Heavy Industries Development Company was to establish one large manufacturing firm for each industrial sector. All these firms were then expected to develop their production capacity to the limit of their potential and at the cost of profits. They had, of course, no competitors in Manchuria.

Two years into the Pacific War, when Japan's prospects were becoming dim, the relationship between Ayukawa's Nissan combine and the Army soured, and by 1944 the failures of the Manchurian industrial experiment were more impressive then its successes.

Limits of Wartime Control

The wartime economic bureaucrats never managed to accomplish what their laws, their control associations, their Manchurian industrial arrangements and their directives to the *zaibatsu*-dominated business world envisioned. Government agencies and other power groups got in each other's way and worked at cross-purposes—a perennial Japanese problem—so that there was no efficient central control over Japan's wartime economy.

Not until after the battle of Midway in 1942 could a start be made with full industrial mobilisation for war purposes, in the form of the "enterprise readjustment movement." It involved the bureaucrats more deeply in the affairs of industrial firms than at any time since the early

Meiji period, when the government had owned those firms. And it provided another precedent for post-war industrial planning.

LEGACY OF A MOBILISED NATION

What worked haphazardly during the war worked very well after the war when, thanks to SCAP, the power of the economic bureaucrats increased considerably. Indeed, the two arrangements that have most powerfully determined Japan's post-war industrial growth are both inherited from wartime economic legislation: first, the financial relationships around which the *keiretsu* industrial groups and conglomerates emerged, and second, the neo-mercantilist trade practices. These are the two factors that have enabled post-war manufacturers to expand virtually without risk, and have shielded Japanese industries from foreign competition.

From War-Financing to Post-War Keiretsu

The foundations of the wartime financial control structure were laid years before the outbreak of the Pacific War. It was the abandonment of the gold standard in 1931 that set the stage for a new monetary approach. First, Japan's trade—hitherto relatively free—was curtailed by the Capital Outflow Prevention Law of 1932 and the Foreign Exchange Control Law of 1933. The bases for control were further consolidated by two pieces of legislation passed in 1937 against the background of a balance-of-payments crisis and the launching of full-scale warfare by Japan's Kwantung Army in China. One of them gave the Ministry of Commerce and Industry the right to slow down or stop the import or export of anything it pleased, as well as control over the use of imported raw materials. The other controlled lending for new industrial investment and gave the Ministry of Finance powers to divert money to military industries.

The first of these measures provided the basic model for the post-war Foreign Exchange and Foreign Trade Control Law, passed in 1949—which has been called MITI's single most powerful instrument for carrying out its industrial policy. The second gave MOF officials the habit, persisted in ever since, of directly guiding the banks.

In the early 1940s, the Cabinet Planning Board (CPB), tried to accomplish a more effective coordination of energies, resources and institutions as part of the "new economic order." It planned to combine the offices of minister of finance and governor of the Bank of Japan into a financial control association that would purge Japan's financial institutions of the profit motive, which was seen as greatly detrimental to the purposes of the nation. Although complete implementation of this policy was hampered by endemic infighting among bureaux in the Ministry of Finance, a president was created for post-war central-bank control over the commercial banks.

Probably the most fateful of all wartime financial arrangements, however, was introduced only about a year and a half before the defeat. This was the so-called "system of financial institutions authorised to finance munitions companies," which was intended to increase the supplies that the military machine was devouring in much greater quantities than planners had expected. The government picked the first 150 "munitions companies" to be matched with the "authorised financial institutions" that were to provide them with an immediate, unimpeded supply of funds. The authorised institutions, mainly the large *zaibatsu* banks, were backed by groups of smaller banks and other financial institutions as well as the Bank of Japan, so that they never found themselves short of money. By 1945, more than six hundred large companies were being funded in this manner, and received 97 percent of their borrowings through the designated banks. The latter dominated 70-80 percent of all lending in Japan.

This was the original model for the post-war *keiretsu* financing. The extraordinarily close relations between Japanese firms and their main bank date from the final months of the Second World War. Most large Japanese corporations are, as explained earlier, grouped together around one or another of the so-called city banks; and throughout most of the post-war period they have been unusually dependent on these banks. Whereas before the war the rate of borrowed capital hovered around 30 to 40 percent (which is comparable to post-war rates in Europe and the USA), from the late 1940s to the late 1970s major Japanese firms borrowed 80 percent or more of their capital from the city banks with which they enjoy a *keiretsu* relationship.

Heavily overloaned as they were for most of the post-war years, the banks pumping funds into the *keiretsu* became increasingly dependent on the central bank. An economist at this institution has pointed out, in a comparison with the major Western industrial powers, that "Japan is the only country where the central bank is a net lender," meaning that loans from and discounts with the central bank exceed deposits of commercial banks. This phenomenon was common enough until mid-

Meiji, but from the late 1910s until the financing of the Pacific War the big banks considered it shameful to be in debt to the central bank. In the post-war period the Bank of Japan has fought heavily with the Ministry of Finance over jurisdiction, but has had to give in on major issues. This means that ultimately MOF bureaucrats have had and (despite reports to the contrary) still have tremendous power over the development of basic industries. Wartime arrangements were reinstated in 1947 with the Temporary Interest Rate Adjustment Law, which gave MOF bureaucrats a free hand to set interest rates on loans as well as on deposits. This temporary law was still on the books in the late 1980s.

Western assessments of government-private sector cooperation in Japan have focused too narrowly on how far the bureaucracy directly subsidises industry, thus asking the wrong question. By regulating the allocation of funds, bureaucrats at the MOF and BOJ enjoy the most effective control one can have over industry.

Inherited Social-Control Supports

Besides the laws and institutions of the economic bureaucrats, the post-war legacy of wartime arrangements includes various supports that have helped to make industrial policy the grand success it has become. One essential prop is the enterprise unions, direct descendants of the Sangyo Hokokukai, the "industrial patriotic associations" which ordered labour relations for the sake of the war effort. Post-war control has in most areas become very much more sophisticated; not only have its wartime origins been forgotten, but it is generally not even recognised for what it is. Filtering information is a great deal more respectable than straight government censorship, and, as we saw earlier, post-war control over the mass media has been largely privatised, with Dentsu as the primary coordinating agency.

The man who made Dentsu great, Yoshida Hideo, could do so because he possessed one of the greatest of post-war *jinmyaku*, linked to former reform bureaucrats and other Manchurian connections. During the war, he worked with Tsukamoto Makoto, a colonel in military intelligence in Shanghai who was involved in secret political manoeuvres and the suppression of an anti-Japanese movement in colonised China. Under the premiership of Tojo Hideki, Tsukamoto was appointed section chief of the military "thought police." After the war, Yoshida made Tsukamoto a director of Dentsu. Purged politicians, businessmen and journalists were brought together by Yoshida in a club that met once a month in the Occupation years. His *jinmyaku* thus extended, he received permission to establish the first commercial radio station. Because broadcasters in Japan are at the mercy of the bureaucrats for licences, Yoshida's connections were invaluable. Dentsu's office was nicknamed the Second Mantetsu Building because of the many former Mantetsu (Manchurian Railway) executives Yoshida hired. Manchurian bureaucrats and military officers were also "rehabilitated" and trained by Yoshida for jobs either with Dentsu or in the new commercial radio and TV broadcasting companies.

The administrators repaid Yoshida for his wartime and Occupation period services by turning Dentsu into one of the great Japanese success stories. Since the 1970s, it has been the largest advertising agency in the world.

The Occupation Legacy

The opportunity to put into practice the unfulfilled designs for a centralised wartime economy and the lessons learned in Manchuria was, as we have seen, handed to the bureaucrats on a silver platter by SCAP. General MacArthur and his reformers also supplied considerable thrust to early post-war industrial policy. At first the Occupation measures against big business quite unintentionally had an opposite effect to the democratisation they were meant to accomplish. And after a communist regime had taken over China there was a shift in emphasis from democratising Japan to helping it establish a strong economy capable of withstanding a potential communist onslaught in Asia—a shift generally referred to as the "reverse course."

Dissolution and reorganisation of the *zaibatsu* holding companies not only strengthened the economic bureaucrats but also elevated bureaucratic managers to the highest positions in industry. Moreover, the scarcity of private capital immediately after the war meant that companies were almost entirely dependent on the bureaucrats for investment funds, which could be obtained through the Reconstruction Finance Bank and later the Japan Development Bank as well as the Japan Export-Import Bank.

Institutions of Forced Economic Development

Post-war reconstruction turned by imperceptible stages into an established policy of unlimited industrial expansion. Without ever debating the pros and cons of such a policy, the Diet endorsed hundreds of laws that helped to coordinate the institutions used in forced economic development. By the mid-1950s, the number of bills submitted to the Diet had increased to between 200 and 250 per year. The same pace continued until the early 1960s, when a dramatic decrease indicated that the legal apparatus sustaining high growth had been put in place.

Among the most important legal instruments supporting industrial policy was the law controlling foreign trade, which was based on that of 1937. The chief means chosen for protecting domestic industry against foreign competition were foreign currency restrictions rather than tariffs. Another important tool was the Enterprises Rationalisation Promotion Law enacted in March 1952. Together with amendments to the Special Tax Measures Law, it provided for stimulative tax exemptions, especially for exporters, and created reserve funds for developing industries. The tax measures came to be collectively known as the "capital accumulation tax system," and the preferential application of the new policies resulted in strengthening existing privileged positions.

The Japan Development Bank was set up in March 1951 and was allowed to issue its own bonds. In July 1952, the Fiscal Investment and Loan Plan was created; this "second budget," backed by Japan's vast postal savings system, was to be used totally at the bureaucrats' discretion. The Export-Import Bank, the Smaller Business Finance Corporation, the Housing Loan Corporation and the Agriculture, Forestry and Fishery Finance Corporation were also established in the early 1950s to generate a flow of funding for investment.

SCAP's contribution to economic legislation, the Anti-Monopoly Law of 14 April 1947, had been amended under the Occupation and again in 1953. It was systematically enfeebled, permitting cartels, allowing price-fixing and halting the warnings to firms with excessive economic concentration.

In the first quarter of 1949, SCAP's economic policy underwent a dramatic change with the arrival of Detroit banker Joseph Dodge, who introduced the so-called Dodge Line, a set of austerity policies designed to control runaway inflation. The Dodge phase introduced a deflationary policy that the government most probably could not have implemented by itself.

The Dodge Line was partly sabotaged almost from the beginning when the central bank ordered financial institutions to bail out firms on the verge of bankruptcy. A former bureaucrat who contributed to early post-war economic planning has pointed out that this policy was an early sign of the overloan phenomenon, and that it foreshadowed the strengthening of the control over commercial financial institutions by the Bank of Japan. SCAP ordered it stopped, and for some two years the Dodge Line slowed down the economic bureaucrats. But then, in a development of major significance for the "economic miracle," the United States began to procure supplies for the Korean War, and everyone's attention shifted to production. After only one year, 1955, in which the banks were not lending more than their deposits warranted, the policies of high growth were making full use of the overloan methods that were to allow Japanese firms to expand so rapidly.

Advantages of Trade Liberalisation

Not all measures inspired by wartime control were acceptable to the entire body of administrators. MITI lost an important battle in 1963 when its Special Measures Law for the Promotion of Designated Industries, sponsored by the Ikeda cabinet, died in the Diet because of business pressure on the LDP. The Ministry of Finance and the banking community also helped stop it, because they correctly interpreted it as an attempt at territorial expansion by the industrial bureaucrats. Moreover, the law, which aimed to empower MITI to set up formal cartels in industries that needed to be made more competitive internationally, would have been too reminiscent of the wartime bureaucratic control apparatus.

The law that MITI failed to get was drafted against a background of fear of invasion by US and European competitors. Ever since the 1930s, business had been protected against imports by foreign currency restrictions. But the administrators knew that trade liberalisation had become inevitable if Japan wanted to be accepted as a true member of the club of free-market countries. Under foreign pressure, import liberalisation, on paper at least, reached 92 percent in the summer of 1963, thus enabling Japan to attain full status in the GATT and, by joining the OECD, to become the first Asian member of the club of advanced industrial countries.

This undesired development, like others before it, was exploited with much success. The imagined threat of foreign competition acted as a tremendous spur in the industrial-machinery, chemical and car sectors, leading them to renovate their plants and rush headlong into new projects. The *keiretsu* tightened their internal relations by increasing the degree of mutual ownership.

Liberalisation, when it finally came, turned out to be virtually painless. It improved the Japanese position with regard to raw materials, and the sole important domestic victim was the coal industry. Real changes in written rules were made only in areas where Japanese industry was already internationally competitive. In sectors such as cars, computers and heavy machinery where Japan wanted to nurture infant industries a point was made of gradual liberalisation. And MITI, without a law but with much administrative guidance at its disposal, made the most of private-public cooperation.

Once the liberalisation storm had passed, there was so much of this kind of cooperation that the protectionist structures remained after their legal supports had been removed. Although on paper the liberalised areas had become free for international competition, the administrators made sure that no genuine competition from cheaper foreign products would take business away from domestic producers, relying on a variety of devices known as non-tariff barriers. When, in the face of overwhelming foreign criticism in the late 1970s and early 1980s, a programme was started to lift these non-tariff barriers, the structure that they had helped solidify stood so secure that the programme had hardly any effect on imports.

Structural Protectionism

While market forces do not ultimately dictate Japanese economic developments, the market is an important instrument used by the bureaucrats in pursuing their aims. Japanese economic intervention has recently come to be referred to as "market conforming," as distinct from the more drastic intervention in Soviet-type economies, whose planners accept no free-enterprise allies. But the market-place remains a source of uncertainty, and thus a potential problem for the administrators. A major institution for reducing such uncertainty is the distribution *keiretsu*, a web of relationships tying wholesalers and retailers in with a particular manufacturer. The distribution *keiretsu* constitute what is routinely referred to as "Japan's complicated distribution system." This is misleading. The distribution system is not complicated. It is rigged.

Wholesalers and retailers are not independent competitive units. A majority of shops retailing durable consumer goods are, in fact, comparable to the regular subcontractors of Japanese manufacturers. They are provided by the manufacturers with capital and, if necessary, technical know-how. These distribution *keiretsu* are the most effective single element for control over the Japanese market. They have greatly helped in the consolidation of Japan's oligopolies, and have been indispensable for the ubiquitous price-fixing practices. To increase the control of the largest firms, members of dealer associations are obliged to limit their stock of competing products. The distribution process has, in fact, become a marketing machine steered by manufacturers. It has greatly helped the development of Japan's consumer electronics industry.

Since tariffs and exchange controls were lifted, the distribution *keiretsu*, together with the trade associations that for the most part exclude non-Japanese members, have remained the major guarantee that Japanese manufacturers need not compete with foreigners in their home market. Consumer products not produced by members of a *keiretsu*— and this naturally includes most foreign goods—are effectively barred from the normal Japanese market, because their only route to the consumer is through specialised outlets that charge prices generally double, sometimes even quadruple, the original market value of the product.

When a major new market is at stake, such as telecommunications equipment, Japanese industries are always allowed first to consolidate their oligopolistic positions; only then are some competitive foreign products given token market shares. The pattern for this was set in 1936 when a law, designed by Kishi Nobusuke, restricted the activities of foreign car manufacturers in Japan. In the late 1920s, Ford and General Motors had begun assembling vehicles in Japan. By the mid-1930s, the two US companies supplied roughly two-thirds of the Japanese car market, much to the chagrin of the Army, which realised that Ford vehicles were more reliable than anything being made by Japanese car manufacturers with government support. Kishi's method of protecting important industries, inspired by a couple of study trips to Germany, made "authorised companies" out of Toyota and Nissan. Ford was forced to drop its plans to expand its manufacturing capacity. Life was made so difficult for both US companies that almost two years before Pearl Harbor they stopped their Japanese production ventures altogether.

The Myth of Slipping Control

At regular intervals foreign observers draw the conclusion that "Japan Inc." is being dismantled, and that the days of government supervision of industry are over. There is a widespread notion that the global economic developments of the 1980s, together with the increased sophistication of Japanese banks and corporations and the transfer of labour-intensive production to cheaper foreign labour markets, are diminishing the ability of the bureaucrats to control the private sector. Japanese officials, weary of foreign criticism about controlled trade, applaud these views and help to spread them.

Yet the loosening of controls should not be taken to mean that the System is about to crumble. It has too many institutions, habits and needs that prop it up. The idea of Japanese industry wrestling with the bureaucracy in order to escape from its grip is, quite simply, false. Whereas in the Western perspective bureaucratic meddling is automatically assumed to be abhorrent to business, elite business organisations in Japan would feel naked without the guarantee that someone is watching over them. At the level of the lower echelons, the partnership may be involuntary, but the benefits that come with it are appreciated none the less.

Maverick businessmen are not able to oppose the administrators for long. When in the summer of 1984 an enterprising oil-marketing firm tried to switch to direct imports in order to sell at lower prices—which it had every right to do, but which went against the wishes of the Ministry of International Trade and Industry as well as the Petroleum Association of Japan—the banks withdrew its credit. The following December a new law was passed, ostensibly to liberalise the import of specific oil products, but in effect restricting trade even further by closing the loophole.

The manipulations of the Ministry of Post and Telecommunications (MPT) in connection with the information-processing and communications market provide a perfect example of why the notion that the bureaucrats are losing control constitutes a basic misunderstanding of how things work in Japan. The officials concerned mapped the future of the market at various stages in the 1990s. Believing that sales would only increase from 230 billion yen in 1987 to around 560 billion in 1992, they decreed that there was room for only one new company to compete with the recently privatised Nippon Telephone and Telegraph. Officials characterised their regulations as inspired by their concern to prevent any company from getting into trouble. But from their reactions to potential foreign entrants in the Japanese telecommunications market, it became abundantly clear that they do not want genuine competition.

MAKING JAPAN INVINCIBLE

Japan lost the Pacific War, but one vision common to the nationalists of
the New Order Movement appears to have been fairly well realised. A
large segment of Japanese big business is moved by "worthier" motives
than profit-making.

Market Shares

In the metamorphosis of corporate leadership whereby the money-
grabbing entrepreneur became the bureaucratic manager, one can trace
a remarkably consistent course of development. Industry today shows
the culmination of a process that began long before the war, with the
separation of ownership and management that occurred when the
zaibatsu families hired banto, professional managers, to look after the
firms belonging to their conglomerates. The post-war apotheosis of the
manager has led to the almost complete bureaucratisation of the large
enterprises, while the disbandment of the zaibatsu by the United States
Occupation made ownership almost invisible if not totally irrelevant.
The few large firms that are still run by strong entrepreneurial leaders
are now seen as more or less peripheral to the main economy. Today, the
authentic entrepreneur, driven by the urge to become rich, is to be
found only in the small or medium-sized firms or, at most, in a few new
large firms that are regularly reminded of their subordinate station in
the zaikai pecking order.

Although this may superficially resemble developments in Western
corporations, the latter are still owned to the extent that they remain
answerable to stockholders. Since post-war Japanese firms have been
strongly discouraged from raising capital on public markets with stocks
and bonds, their dividend payments to stockholders are the lowest in
the world. In the 1970s, the leading companies listed on the first section
of the Tokyo Stock Exchange paid on average about 1.5 percent. As we
have seen, the members of a conglomerate tend to own each other. The
banks generally hold large quantities of their clients' stocks; and Japanese banks have entirely different priorities from Western stockholders.
Company presidents in Japan, instead of being bothered by major
stockholders breathing over their shoulders and forcing them to watch
the profit charts, have to worry about expansion schemes they and their
bankers have agreed on.

The shift from entrepreneur to manager has been paralleled by a shift from profit-making to expansion of the firm's market share. In the Western corporate environment the pursuit of profits and the expansion of market share are both respectable and are, of course, interrelated. What has made the post-war Japanese case special is the apparent possibility, for corporations, of ignoring profit for very long periods while pouring all their resources into expansion.

The emphasis on conquering market shares and the ability to do so at the expense of profits are relatively new. In the first third of this century, when industries were more clearly separated from the public sector, companies were driven by a need to maximise profits. But as the military-bureaucratic alliance strengthened its grip on Japan and emphasis on the "national essence" reached new heights, profit-making began to be viewed as unworthy.

Several deliberately created post-war factors forced large firms to compete for market shares, especially after the mid-1950s. The economic bureaucrats clearly demonstrate the priorities of their thinking when MITI, in the context of recession cartels, decrees capacity reduction on the basis of existing market share rather than plant efficiency. This means that firms know that their drive for a larger market share will be rewarded with a guaranteed market share. This has led to oligopoly in many fields. In most industrial sectors one will find one to three companies controlling roughly 70 percent of the market. The dominating companies agree on prices, and the pressure to conform in other areas is also great. This, in turn, promotes "order" within each industry.

Many Western appraisals of the Japanese economy refer to the cut-throat competition that is supposedly normal among corporations. It is not, but such competition as does exist is almost exclusively confined to the growth sectors of consumer industries. Occasionally a spectacular battle develops, such as the one in the motor-cycle market between Honda and Yamaha in the early 1980s, producing a proliferation of some ten to fifteen new models a month. This instance of genuine cut-throat competition (which Yamaha lost) was caused by an enormous production overcapacity arising from a sudden saturation of export markets.

The home electronics sector, where new products follow each other in quick succession, is the scene of fairly frequent battles for domestic market share involving medium-sized but fast-growing firms. More typically, however, the domestic market is a relatively stable arena that allows the Japanese corporation to concentrate on competition abroad.

In the battle for foreign market shares, Japanese managers are aided by economies of scale achieved through a solid share of the home market and high domestic earnings that often susidise the exports. Such a situation can be attained only by private understandings among firms, not by relentless competition. Large Japanese firms take very few risks. They are ensconced in a protective environment that not only shields them from foreign competitors but also fosters forms of mutual protection. It is this basis that permits them to move simultaneously into foreign markets with rock-bottom prices.

The Unbeatable Competitor on Foreign Markets

The large Japanese corporations with strong ties to industrial conglomerates are formidable competitors on foreign markets because they cannot go bankrupt and need not show any profit for a very long time. When a more or less concerted effort is made to compete with domestic manufacturers in one particular foreign market, they are basically unbeatable. This was shown by the conquest of the world markets for cameras, motorcycles, and videotape-recorders (VTRs), and by the reduction of the home market share for US machine-tool and semiconductor manufacturers to a fraction of what it was before the Japanese began to focus on it.

The VTR case offers a good illustration of the uses of economies of scale. Investments in production capacity made by Japan's seven VTR manufacturers quadrupled output between 1979 and 1981 to 9.5 million units. Two years later the figure had almost doubled, reaching a peak of 33.8 million units in 1986. The more than 13 million sets produced in 1982 represented 140 percent of world demand at the time. Such overproduction caused colossal inventories and made possible foreign sales at almost any price. Roughly five-sixths of annual production was exported. RCA and Zenith in the USA had long given up (and were pasting their brand names on Japanese-made VTRs), and Philips and Grundig, with their 700,000 units, could hardly compete seriously with the 4.9 million VTRs sent to Europe in 1982 by Japanese firms.

Foreign market shares are achieved by painstaking adjustment of prices to local supply and demand. That Japanese firms have unparalleled elasticity in this regard has been shown by the way they have hung on to US market shares despite the near doubling of the exchange rate of the yen against the dollar. Since relatively few products make up Japan's export package at any one time, Japanese industry can wage concentrated foreign sales campaigns. Their inroads, of course, are mere pinpricks compared with the overall industrial and trade statistics in the West, but at close quarters the concentrated effect is a razor-sharp sword cleaving into established US and European industries.

The experience with semiconductors and machine-tools has opened some American eyes to Japanese methods of competition. Contrary to what Japanese propaganda and overly self-critical Western commentators have suggested, the US firms in this field worked hard and were alert enough. They simply could not, even remotely, match the financing backup of the Japanese companies; and, as companies subject to the scrutiny of stockholders and boards of directors, their decisions have to be based on considerations of profitability. US entrepreneurs, to survive, need to show return on their investments. US law favours foreign firms, because it stipulates punitive action in cases of dumping only when there is clear harm to US industry. In the years that it takes to litigate a dumping case, the Japanese competitor is able to supplant the US firms.

Competitors with large Japanese firms are at an enormous disadvantage in that the latter's fortunes are much less susceptible to economic factors. Their home base has the means to grow at the expense of other human pursuits. With respect to the losses they can absorb, Japanese exporters are limited only by the other firms in their *keiretsu* and, especially, by their major banks. In industries considered essential, the lending banks can rely on the ultimate guarantee of Japan's central monetary authorities. That means that the decisions involved in lending to those who want to conquer foreign markets are not economic but political.

The Bubble That Does Not Burst

In the 1980s, other Japanese economic activities began to command international attention. In the exchange not of goods but of less tangible assets such as stocks, bonds and foreign treasury paper, Japan's firms quickly gained another formidable reputation. By the middle of the decade Japan had become the biggest creditor nation in the world, largely by investing in US treasury bonds, and serious economic periodicals were drawing proud comparisons with England in the nineteenth century, or with the USA after the Second World War. Japan's banks were overtaking the largest US and European banks in terms of assets; its four large security companies became a major international presence; foreign banks were being absorbed; and many firms were heavily investing in overseas real estate.

It was only towards the close of the previous decade that the bureaucrats had made large-scale foreign investments possible. The move came just as Japanese firms were beginning to derive high profits from their strong foreign market positions. Enhanced by the then relatively low exchange value of the yen, these profits, combined with the new freedom to explore foreign capital markets (notably by floating Eurodollar bonds), made the large firms less dependent on the banks for their capital.

By 1985, an ocean of liquidity had formed, as the banking community and monetary authorities pushed loans and encouraged corporations to increase their assets. Prices on the real-estate and stock markets began to rise sharply. This steeply raised the value of assets in general, which translated into collateral allowing corporations to borrow more heavily. By then a phenomenon called *zaiteku* — whereby manufacturers and trading firms borrow money to make more money in ways that have nothing to do with their original activities — had already altered the way many large Japanese corporations were calculating their strategies. Some manufacturers and trading companies had begun to resemble banks, except for their lack of experience and the bigger risks they took. This could not have happened on the scale that it did without the strong protective powers of the *keiretsu* relationships. And there were convincing indications that many *zaiteku* enterprises were hiding significant failings in their books.

In a Western setting these speculative activities would have brought the doom-sayers out in crowds. A few did appear in Japan, but short- and medium-term pessimists overlooked a critical factor: that the absence of a clear division between the public and private sectors, the cooperation (or collusion) among the administrators, and the ease with which economic processes can be politically controlled all add up to a situation radically different from that in the other capitalist countries.

The economy of intangibles thrives as long as the market participants have faith that the pieces of paper they exchange are backed up by actual worth. A crisis of confidence causes a stock-market crash. In the West such confidence hinges on the general performance of private enterprises. In Japan it means faith in the ability of the economic managers to keep everyone's trust in the economic apparatus going. The difference may seem subtle, but is in fact enormous.

The much publicised savings rate of the Japanese people conferred an important measure of credibility on Japanese "overloan" practices in recent decades. And when foreigners wonder about the soundness of Japanese banks, they are told about the large volume of hidden assets the banks are allowed to hold without revaluing them. But there is a curious aspect to the land and securities held in assets or collateral. According to the Economic Planning Agency, the total market value of Japanese land in fiscal 1987 was 4.1 times greater than that of all the land in the United States, which is twenty-five times the size of Japan, and has fifty-seven times more inhabitable space. Some of the land in Tokyo is priced ten or more times higher than land in Manhattan business districts. Land, in fact, has taken on a function comparable to that of gold, except of course that its value is independent of foreign market forces. Japanese specialists jokingly refer to a *tochi honi-sei*, or "land standard." As for the securities, average Japanese shares on the Tokyo stock market show a price-earnings ratio of 55.6 compared with 14.0 in New York and 12.3 in London (in January 1988). A number of explanations have been offered for this, but the simplest one is that the administrators in the banks, ministries and corporations have discovered a way of making money with money by agreeing not to spoil the party for each other.

That controls exist to make this possible was revealed in October 1987, following the stock-market crisis in New York that reverberated throughout the industrialised world but left Tokyo relatively undisturbed. Working in conjunction with the Ministry of Finance, the "big four" security firms, which form a *de facto* cartel, seem likely to keep even worse overseas crashes from doing much damage to the Tokyo stock market. In private conversation Ministry of Finance officials have been known to concede that it is easier to influence the stock market than the foreign exchange market.

The combined figure for increases in land and stock prices in 1986 exceeded the entire Gross National Product of that year by nearly 40 trillion yen. Since then land prices have climbed steeply: by an average of 96.2 percent for commercial and 89 percent for residential land in Tokyo, and of 21.7 percent in Japan as a whole, in the space of one year. All this represents a colossal amount of potential collateral for borrowing to fund further *zaiteku* and overseas investments. Before Japan's business could indulge in these expansionary practices, however, the System had to make a major adjustment.

Exploring the World's Financial Markets

Financial liberalisation loomed large in economic comment on Japan during the 1980s. The fact that it was in progress was constantly being reaffirmed by the administrators, and many statements by foreign emissaries acknowledged that it was proceeding on schedule. Here, finally, there seemed to be an area where Japan was gradually meshing with the international system.

A degree of liberalisation of financial and capital markets did indeed take place, but it was of a kind that fitted Japanese purposes, and did not significantly increase the accessibility of the Japanese market to foreign financial institutions. The Ministry of Finance bureaucrats' apparent concessions were in fact aimed, first, at bringing regulations in line with the way Japanese financial institutions were already operating, and secondly at encouraging the international emancipation of Japanese banks, security houses and insurance firms, enabling them to compete better on the money markets of the world. Until then Ministry of Finance bureaucrats had enforced a strict division of labour, with fences around the banking, securities and insurance territories, and sluices regulating the directions of the money flow, thus creating an orderly and controllable financial market during the period of high growth. But the eagerness of the financial institutions to embark on new activities was being frustrated by what many administrators had begun to agree were antiquated regulations.

In the second half of the 1980s, many foreign observers, especially those responsible for Washington's policies towards Japan, still believed that market forces would replace regulation in the financial field, but MOF guidance remains as important as it ever was. The bank-centred *keiretsu* remain bank-centred. And while the bureaucrats have not relinquished *de facto* control, partial deregulation has had the effect of fostering a new sophistication among Japanese financial institutions, as well as significantly increasing investment possibilities for the wealthy firms.

In the same period during which it was gradually discovered that Japanese speculators need not worry overmuch about a crisis of confidence, new financial powers emerged. The commercial banks were tightening their relations with the security firms. And the life insurance industry, which was becoming (thanks to Japan's ballooning pension funds) one of the strongest institutional investors on the international scene, was emerging as a third major financial force, offering what amounted to investment instruments on the domestic market. Besides being hooked up to the manufacturing-banking-trading conglomerates, the big insurers have long operated under the protection of the Ministry of Finance. This sector is dominated by a cartel-like "big three," through which it is easily monitored.

The Elusive Master-Plan

The proliferation of collusive activities inimical to free-market principles naturally makes one wonder whether all these activities might not be part of one gigantic conspiracy. The question becomes still more pertinent when one considers how collusion is rife in areas of the System not directly connected with the economy. An intense focusing on goals pursued, more often than not, without adherence to any rules and unhampered by any referee, certainly seems conspiratorial. Have the economic administrators been consciously working to create the circumstances that give them their current international power? Such questions have not been popular, partly because those who would contemplate them are too easily branded as "Yellow peril" alarmists.

There is no convincing concrete evidence for a master-plan. No conspirators, no documents have been brought to light that reveal anything of the kind. Japanese political history, I believe, is witness to the fact that political aims need not be fully conscious to be realised. Just as the omnipresent Japanist propaganda emanates not from a single agency at the centre but from the collective need of separate groups, so the efforts of these groups to guarantee their own political survival have dovetailed into what merely seems like conscious implementation of a blueprint.

It was inevitable that the post-1945 administrators should exert themselves to minimise the influence of the left, to subdue trade unionism and to reverse the "excesses" of the Occupation as soon as the Americans had left. It was entirely natural, too, that those who had experimented with establishing a "new economic order" should attempt to apply what they had learned when, after the war, they were given unprecedented scope for setting up such a new order. A tradition of reality management enabled the administrators to present their interference as democratic, so long as elections were held and there was a parliament and a seemingly free press. In view of the administrators' constant dread of disorder, it would not have been realistic to expect them to discard the institutions and habits developed before 1945 for the purpose of staving off that fear.

The Defect of the Phoenix

Although there is no convincing reason to suspect that the administrators have worked out a master-plan for industrial domination of the world, what they are doing has the same effect as if there were such a plan. The administrators see the entire world in terms of the System. Japan strives for industrial dominance because power is the only guarantee for safety; and military power is not feasible. Hence the continued voracity for foreign market shares and foreign technology.

It is essential to grasp two points with respect to this drive: First, Japan has the potential to go a very long way in achieving dominance in certain strategic industries, and could thereby make the West very dependent on it—this has already nearly happened with semiconductors. Secondly, the supposition of Western trading partners that Japan's political economy is essentially like their own provides a prime condition for achieving the administrators' international ambitions.

The wealth of Japanese firms has considerably strengthened their basis for operations on international markets. They buy foreign financial institutions and real estate, not for the sake of medium-range profits, but to pull more weight. And if land in Tokyo can be ten times as valuable as land in Manhattan in 1988, the price could be jacked twenty times should the administrators need the collateral to make their overborrowing seem respectable.

All the while, Japan's comparative advantage continues to be enhanced by other, more long-standing factors. Subcontracting, temporary employment, lower-paid female labour and early mandatory retirement still give Japanese industry the benefit of flexible and relatively low labour costs. Only one-third of the workforce has been permanently employed. After retirement, employees continue to work at much reduced salaries. Thirty-five percent of the labour force continues to work past the age of sixty-five, compared with some 10 percent in Europe. The System, moreover, continues to be structurally protectionist, shielding Japanese manufacturers from the type of competition with which the System's corporations have diminished Western firms. This factor seems certain to keep the trade imbalance between Japan and the world permanent.

It is widely believed that Western firms do not try hard enough to penetrate the Japanese market, and the administrators have been only too happy to help spread the notion of European and US business as tired and inefficient. But closer scrutiny of Japanese firms reveals that they are not less prone to bungling than are Western firms—perhaps even more so. The argument about not trying hard enough is a red herring; those who have tried extremely hard in Japan have mostly failed as dismally as those who have taken it easy. Japanese spokesmen widely advertise the fact that a number of foreign firms have been successful in their market. These firms are well known because they belong to the same small sample always mentioned in this context.

The greatest international advantage the System has enjoyed so far lies in Western misconceptions concerning the nature of the Japanese challenge. The United States has been especially vulnerable to Japan's industrial onslaught in that the US government agencies overseeing its interests have no institutional memory. Every two years or so, new sets of US officials must learn afresh that the Japanese economy does not operate in the same way as their own. Hence the continued handicap of adherence to inapplicable free-trade theories. The result has been misguided stopgap policies. Congressional pressure on the Reagan administration to cope with the Japan Problem produced a double formula to straighten the trade imbalance: a more expensive yen, and demands that Japan stimulate its domestic economy. Increased domestic demand does, indeed, make growth of the Japanese economy less dependent on exports, but there is no good reason to expect that it will lead to greater Japanese purchases of Western products. Nor has the expensive yen had the anticipated effect. It may even have worsened the West's competitive position by forcing the administrators to streamline inefficient sectors. The yen-dollar rate will have a significant effect on the Japan-USA trade balance only if the US is prepared to allow its currency to lose value and prestige even more dramatically than in 1987.

Not only did the changed dollar-yen exchange rate fail to bring the hoped-for result, it almost doubled the buying ability of Japanese investors on the US market. On top of the strength derived from Japanese financing methods, this led to a sudden surge of Japanese influence on Wall Street and other financial trading centres. A major new factor was hereby introduced, with the potential of dramatically changing Japan's relationship with the US, and with as yet uncertain, but probably important, repercussions for the West in general.

Seen in a long-term perspective, the lack of effective US and European policies towards Japan is not a true advantage to the administrators. On the contrary, their security is in danger. So far, the US has been held back by the example of the Smoot-Hawley Tariff Act of 1930, which was partly responsible for the uncontrollable protectionist chain reaction that preceded the Great Depression. But at some stage retaliatory measures seem inevitable—Congress gets the impression that Tokyo is arrogant or morally deficient. The European countries, which are equally fearful of rampant protectionism but have so far been less affected by the expansion of Japanese power, would most likely follow the US example. The European Community will have more reason for vigilance in the face of Japanese marketing aims when, in 1992, all remaining barriers among member countries are eliminated. With the West clearly unwilling to absorb the effects of any further large increase in Japan's economic might—at least if achieved in the same manner as post-war economic growth—the Japanese goal of unlimited industrial expansion has become uncertain. Restructuring is thus a vital necessity.

The phoenix has soared majestically for the entire world to see, and has drawn deserved applause and expressions of awe. But it is burdened with a defect that disorientates it. The defect is, of course, in its steering mechanism: in its inability to adopt alternative methods and aims, because of the absence of an individual or group with the power to make political decisions to shift goals. The phoenix appears stuck on a collision course.

IN THE WORLD BUT
NOT OF IT

There is a fairly widespread notion that the Japanese nation in the early 1990s is engaged in a grand debate concerning the new policies required by its international predicament and by foreign expectations. Columnists tell us that major changes are afoot, that those concerned are discussing how to import more, and that the Japanese people are waking up to the need to assume international responsibilities in keeping with their economic power.

The notion that such debates take place is wrong. It is rooted apparently in a belief that the Japanese *ought* to be discussing these things, rather than in any evidence that they are. The notion is fostered by administrators who must deal with the external world and are often desperate to suggest action in areas where they have promised results. It also accords with the general taste of the media for "Japan at the crossroads" stories. What is mistaken for national soul-searching, however, amounts to no more than the rhetorical flourishes that top administrators add to their speeches, that newspapers habitually put into their editorials and that lard the comments of English-speaking "buffers" at international panel discussions and study meetings. But the platitudinous reiteration of the need for certain changes does not imply commitment to bring them about.

THE ABSENCE OF POLITICAL CHOICE

The notion of a national debate is harmful because it lulls the observer into a false sense that shared problems are being studied and solved on the Japanese side. It also constitutes an intellectual hindrance to grasp-

ing how the System operates; it gives the impression that Japanese are
given a choice, whereas the ordinary Japanese has no idea what choosing among socio-political alternatives means.

Systematic Deprivation of Choice

The systematic deprivation of choice in practically all realms of life is
essential for keeping the System on an even keel. The Japanese have no
choice with regard to political representation: they are stuck with the
LDP. They have almost no choice in education: its major function is as a
sorting mechanism for the salaryman employment market, and the only
way to the top runs through the law department of the University of
Tokyo. Once a middle-class Japanese male has been taken on by a
company, he has as good as no alternative but to stay with that company.
The Japanese have no choice with respect to sources of news and
information: these come in the monotonous tones of a virtually fettered
press, or processed by other reality managers such as Dentsu. The
choices the market offers them as consumers do not include what the
distribution *keiretsu* do not want to distribute.

The common view of the Japanese political process assumes the
possibility of choice. It sees rulers and ruled as engaged in continuous
communication for the sake of an ever-evolving consensus. Contributing
to this consensus-forming process, are the multitude of interest groups,
academic commentators, journalists, politicians and bureaucrats whose
approval must be won for whatever is being decided. Japan's power-
holders have enthusiastically seized on this perspective, because it can
be passed off as democratic, and because it fits in nicely with the all-
important belief in the benevolence of the System.

Exhortations in the press and statements by prominent administrators seem to afford evidence that the nation is preoccupied with certain
issues. But continuous reference to the desirability of something does
not constitute a debate. This becomes clear when one looks at it closely:
everyone always seems heartily to agree with what is being said. When
the evils of the *amukudari* system and "examination hell" receive their
annual airing it is obvious that the routine exhortations have a cathartic
function, substituting, as they do, for genuine remedial action. Discussion, such as can be found in European countries and the United States,
with intellectuals and political representatives putting forward identifiable and conflicting opinions, are unknown in Japan, where nothing of
substance is debated in the proper meaning of the term.

The industrial expansion that was achieved at the cost of the environment and of housing and welfare policies and has resulted in the highest land prices in the world—all this without bringing amenities taken for granted in much of Europe and North America—was not the offspring of any kind of agreement on what is good for the people. The public was not asked to participate in the formulation of policies—was never even aware that a choice existed.

The Reverse Side of the Successful System

It is difficult to argue with success, and Japan's post-war economic success has drawn much admiration from the rest of the world. I do not mean to detract from the admirable accomplishments of the Japanese people, who have achieved a relatively safe society that can feed everyone and has only a few thousand homeless. But this book is about how the Japanese are governed. And in this last chapter I must conclude that the overall picture is rather bleak and fraught with danger.

In the eyes of the world, Japan has established itself as a rich country; yet, ironically, most Japanese think of themselves as relatively poor. The discrepancy in perception was never so strong as in the late 1980s, when currency revaluation had raised the per capita income above that of any other country, but left the buying power of Japanese salaries among the lowest in the advanced industrialised nations. As a Japanese professor teaching in New York summed it up:

> Behind a robust facade of a growing economy that is fueled by rampant speculation, about 80% of the people are bearing the burden of heavy taxes and exorbitant prices for housing, land, food, clothing and other products and services whose markets are shielded from foreign competition. The average Japanese earns about the same income as his or her American counterpart. But the Japanese must work almost five times as long to buy half a kilogram of fish, five times as long for half a kilogram of rice, nine times as long to buy half a kilogram of beef, and three times as long for four liters of gasoline.

He could have added that the privilege of using congested expressways costs a fortune, that telephone and utility rates are the most expensive in the world, that the exorbitantly priced living quarters are minuscule and that urban infrastructural problems cause as much discomfort as they did in the 1960s. Life for the average Japanese in 1988 was filled with more gadgets and much more fashion, but was not in any way more comfortable or rewarding than it was in 1968, with the one exception that the expensive yen bought cheap foreign holidays. In some ways, for instance with regard to the prospect of ever owning a place to live, life looked decidedly less promising. And these are merely the material results of how Japanese power is exercised.

Japanese education, together with indoctrination via the media and the corporations, hampers the development of liberated citizens and the self-realisation of the individual. Thus, while the System undoubtedly provides sustenance and a large measure of security to nearly all Japanese, as a form of government it is not a satisfactory substitute for a modern constitutionalist state.

Governmental Paralysis

The lack of a national debate has direct consequences for other nations. The theory of a forever evolving consensus suggests that the system is capable of producing essential policy changes. Yet the great irony of contemporary Japan is that the administrators, driven by their fear of disorder, have through a myriad of successful controls nurtured a political economy that is essentially out of control; the System as a whole is rudderless.

There have been a number of successful attempts to steer Japan towards new priorities. The one that attracted most international publicity in the late 1980s was the formation of an advisory committee under the chairmanship of the former governor of the Bank of Japan, Maekawa Haruo. The then prime minister, Nakasone, ordered the committee to present guidelines for a major restructuring of the Japanese economy that would make it less dependent on exports for its growth. What happened subsequently illustrates my point about the absence of Japanese leadership.

In the course of numerous meetings, the members of the committee, most of whom represented ministerial and other interests, picked the Maekawa Report clean of all its concrete proposals. When Nakasone saw the report, he angrily ordered it rewritten because, in his words, it did not reflect awareness of the dire international situation the Japanese economy had got into. The final version, published in April 1986, was no improvement, but Nakasone was powerless.

If all the recommendations of the Maekawa Report had been carried out, they would still have amounted to no more than a very feeble attempt to shift priorities. But even this was not to be. At almost the very moment that Nakasone was in Washington presenting the report as a token of Japanese good faith, LDP politicians said that they could not accept it. Top bureaucrats leaked their "concern" that Nakasone was misleading President Reagan. The *Nihon Keizai Shimbun* (comparable to the *Wall Street Journal*) tore the report to pieces. Finally, the Ministry of Foreign Affairs weighed in with a statement that the report did not represent Japanese policy.

The case of the Maekawa Report also illustrates the confusion of tongues that often accompanies a Japanese action. Even as Nakasone's compatriots were pulling the rug from under him, President Reagan, Secretary of State George Shultz, the *New York Times* and others were praising the breakthrough in Japanese decision-making. Under-Secretary of State for Economic Affairs Alan Wallis went so far as to call it a watershed in Japanese post-war economic thinking. The US administration, of course, desperately wanted to show the bilateral relationship in a positive light, and to demonstrate that its approach to Japan bore results. But two years after publication of the report, only a couple of points had been implemented; they were minor, and had in any case been part of earlier bureaucratic plans.

The Maekawa Committee represented one more failure to steer the System. The outside world, however, wanting to believe that Japan had a government after all, and believing that it was high time for a major restructuring, showed enthusiasm. This was seized on by the bureaucrats, who actually launched a second Maekawa Report in May 1987 because the first had made such a good impression abroad! Indeed, the chief success of the Maekawa Report has been the reaction abroad; in Japan it got no more than lip-service.

Another recent pseudo-debate concerns *kokusaika*, "internationalisation." Throughout the 1980s, the need for internationalisation was routinely stressed in thousands of newspaper editorials and tens of thousands of speeches. Numerous committees and study groups have been set up to promote it. But in Japan verbal commitment to a certain cause is often mistaken for concrete steps. The constant repetition of the term *kokusaika* creates a sense that Japan's administrators are taking action. But in fact the last thing they want to encourage is an awareness that genuine internationalisation presupposes a willingness to consider the arguments and wishes of foreigners.

AN UNCOMFORTABLE DEPENDENCE

The anomalies in Japan's relationships with other countries tend to be obscured by the unusual nature of one particular relationship. The System is extraordinarily dependent on the United States. Both parties admit that the relationship is a special one; but how very special is a point insufficiently realised by almost everybody. There is no other instance in history where one large and economically powerful nation has remained so dependent on another nation without losing its separate identity. Japan can afford to stay out of international politics, because of the shield offered by the USA. This shield signifies much more than military security and diplomatic protection. Japan could never have become a neo-mercantilist economic power without US forbearance and protection.

One must clearly distinguish between Japanese dependence on the United States and the dependence of the European countries. The West European nations have entered into this arrangement as responsible states. Their internal political arrangements do not prevent the conducting of a foreign policy apart from their alliance with the USA. If, on the other hand, Japan were to lose US indulgence it would be forced to do something in which so far it has failed regularly: conduct a foreign policy in which it can be held to account for the deals it makes.

Effective Tactics, Poor Strategy

The accomplishments of the System have been so much admired that foreigners and Japanese alike tend to overlook its inherent defects, the major one being that it has no control over itself. The success with which Japan adjusted to changes wrought by two oil crises helped obscure the failure of the administrators as a body to face up to the necessity for a much more basic restructuring. The Japanese economy is basically dependent on one market—that of the United States, which absorbs roughly 40 percent of all Japanese exports. Agriculture, heavily protected, is in worse shape than almost anywhere among the advanced industrialised economies. Industries that serve only the domestic economy are highly inefficient. Japan's relatively low standards of comfort, despite its international economic performance, indicate the presence of major structural distortions. The dispersion of power among a variety of administrator bodies, none holding ultimate responsibility, makes long-range, nationally integrated strategic planning impossible.

Circumstances have made the administrators superb tacticians but poor strategists. The parallel with the Imperial Army in China in the 1930s is fairly obvious. The Japanese military, working out of Manchuria, proved themselves to be master tacticians. But it was also clear that their actions were not guided by an overall strategic plan taking into account the world beyond China. As tacticians, MITI and Ministry of Finance bureaucrats, the banks, the business federations, the *keiretsu* companies and all the other institutions that have helped ensure social discipline and enhance Japanese productivity and export prowess have far outdone what the Japanese military achieved in China. But the overall result is that the nation faces great uncertainty with regard to its global position and, ultimately, its international economic viability.

The day-to-day tactics ensure further economic growth, allow accumulation of foreign technology and swell the paper assets propping up the impressive effort to gain control of foreign financial institutions and real estate. Dazzling as their results are, however, these tactics are not ultimately part of a grand overall strategy — unless, of course, economic conquest of the whole world is the unspoken aim of Japan's administrators. Such an aim would not, even so, constitute a credible strategy, because it could never succeed.

Mishandling of the US Relationship

It is inconceivable that a state with a government sensitive to long-term national interests could have allowed the Japan-US relationship to deteriorate to the extent that it has. Banking too heavily on US indulgence, Tokyo has badly mishandled its most important relationship — the one on which the entire edifice of its foreign relations is built. Preoccupied with their special pleading in Washington, the administrators failed to notice that Japanese actions, or inaction, were frittering away most of the considerable and genuine affection that the United States had come to have for Japan.

By the end of the 1970s, it was becoming clear that, in spite of their importance to one another, the world's two largest economic powers did not know how to cope with each other. In American eyes Japan does not play a role in the international community commensurate with its wealth. After four decades of benefits, say US critics, Japan should be willing to share in the costs of maintaining the alliance, if only for the sake of its own future security.

More specifically, the Americans think it grossly unfair that, while the Japanese have had almost completely free access to the US market, the Japanese market has not been hospitable to US competition. To say that the two sides are not speaking the same language is to understate the problem. The USA stresses that Japan itself stands to gain from free trade and open markets, but what it means by this—greater choices for the Japanese consumers—is not at all what the Japanese administrators understand by gain. A truly open market would undermine the domestic order, so how, in their eyes, could this ever be considered a gain for Japan?

The actual mechanism and extraordinary degree of Japan's dependence on the USA are but dimly understood in Washington. They are more clearly felt on the Japanese side, but the psychological burden it entails does not often permit an honest self-appraisal. Occasionally, Japanese even imply the reverse of the real situation by concluding that the USA risks losing Japan's support.

To smooth feathers ruffled by trade conflicts, the administrators tend to raise expectations in foreign governments that are not subsequently fulfilled. In the case of the USA, Tokyo's ritual arguments and empty promises convince congressmen, businessmen and other Americans only that they are being deceived.

We have seen that during the first two years of the Nakasone government the US government had expectations of effective Japanese measures. These were partly based on the personal rapport between the prime minister and the US president, the "Ron-Yasu" relationship. It was just beginning to dawn on Washington that Yasu got everything, leaving Ron nothing but a show of unanimity on military-strategic matters (which everybody took for granted anyway), when in the spring of 1985 the Senate passed by 92 votes to zero a non-binding resolution warning the president that, if he took no action with respect to trade with Japan, it would do so instead.

This sent shockwaves through Japan. But the result only demonstrated that *vis-a-vis* the outside world, the System remains politically as paralysed as ever. The administrators explain the changes in the US attitude in terms of a weakening of American economic and political power and of the supposed frustration this has brought about. Much is made of the USA having become the largest debtor nation and Japan its major creditor—in reference to the large-scale Japanese purchases of the government bonds with which Washington covers its budget deficit. The presentation of the USA as a declining power is psychologically so comforting for a once defeated nation that it tends to be overstated.

The Complication of US Politics and Ignorance

A common Japanese complaint is that it is not clear what the United States really wants. In American eyes this is ridiculous; almost every visiting American interviewed by the press hammers on the need for a more open market and reiterates that only results really count.

Even so, Japanese confusion is to some extent understandable, for official America has been sending mixed signals for a long time. In 1986, approaches were still based on the assumption that by cultivation of cordial personal ties with Japanese leaders reason could be made to prevail, and that in the end the market would straighten out any distortions. Policy measures were largely improvised on the spur of the moment, with no coherence and no consistency. For the Reagan administration just as for its predecessors, trade and the economy were considered secondary to security and strategic interests. The departments of State and Defense appear to believe that therapeutic trade sanctions would endanger the status of US bases in Japan. The possibility that Japan's industrial onslaught might, by undermining US strategic industries, actually compromise security has apparently not occurred to the US government. As one of the USA's most thoughtful negotiators with Japan put it:

Nothing in US law or tradition...anticipated the possibility of industry and trade being organised as part of an effort to achieve specific national goals rather than on the individualistic Western model...The result was a series of negotiations that never focused on the main issues but dealt with symptoms instead of causes.

Political and diplomatic considerations have done much to confuse the situation. To demonstrate success in negotiations, token concessions by Japan have been routinely presented by the US government as genuine concessions. By 1987, there had been seven market-opening packages and an action programme whose effectiveness was in doubt from the moment they were announced. Sometimes concessions extracted after much wrangling turn out upon closer scrutiny to be the same concessions obtained with great difficulty two or four years previously. I myself and a number of my colleagues have often experienced a giddy sense of unreality at the jubilation with which such measures are greeted by Washington. European spokesmen, too, have been in the habit of diplomatically praising Tokyo for insubstantial measures; but what Europe says carries not a fraction of the weight of American statements.

This process is damaging in the long run, because whenever the USA makes a fresh request for what are essentially the same concessions it is seen by many Japanese as demanding new ones. To make matters worse, the USA has sometimes asked for measures that Japan was willing to implement but that are almost totally ineffectual, such as domestic reflation through a demand package, lowering of interest rates or financial market liberalisation. Hence in the popular imagination the USA has begun to appear insatiable, demanding ever more from Japan—even though it has received almost nothing.

The Management of International Reality

Probably most detrimental to chances of solving the Japan-US conflict is the fact that the United States has permitted it to be discussed within a largely Japanese frame of reference. The administrators have gladly undertaken the management of reality in this particular realm. There exists what can best be described as a mutual understanding industry, whose Japanese practitioners take for granted that the world needs to understand Japan more than Japan needs to understand the world. Innumerable panel discussions, study meetings, lectures and symposia plead what is essentially the cause and position of the administrators. Subtle flattery ("You must teach us how to confront our dire problems!") mutes what might otherwise become critical voices.

The Western tendency for moral self-flagellation and Western intellectuals' habit of denigrating the institutions of their own country have helped shape a general perspective in which Japan is compared favourably to the West. This has been gratefully exploited by Japanese spokesmen. Panel discussions on trade problems become forums for taking foreigners to task for insufficient understanding and for not trying hard enough to break into the Japanese market. Nor should one forget the Japan apologists. As Ivan Hall wrote in the *Wall Street Journal*:

Unlike the flow of ideas between the US and Europe, the Japan-US discourse is determined largely by a small group of Japanese and American experts on each other's countries who have bridged the great linguistic and cultural gap. Ostensibly dedicated to mutual friendship, this narrow channel of scholars, journalists, and diplomats serves increasingly to skew the dialogue in Japan's favor. It does this through cultural excuses and other special pleading; by fending off critical analyses; by glossing over sensitive issues in Japan; by assuming adequate Japanese knowledge of the US; and by failing to protest Japan's restrictions on foreign academics and journalists.

The enormous propaganda potential of the System has been put to good use here. Anyone known to be involved in thinking or writing about Japan is inundated with glossy magazines and other material carrying ostensibly independent opinion that says more or less the same thing. The administrators can also take advantage of general foreign ignorance and of the quick turnover among US officials dealing with Japan.

One of the administrators' great successes is seen in the general acceptance of the postulate of "equivalent duty." The US penchant for looking at both sides of things and US defensiveness when confronted with appeals to fairness have led to agreements which include measures that the USA itself must take concurrently with those intended by Japan. Official Japanese statements urge the need for Japan to open its market further and become more responsible internationally, yet in the same breath mention the need for the USA to eliminate its budget deficit and save more. This equivalent duty tactic results in the assumption that Japan does not need to feel too bad about doing nothing so long as the USA does not do anything either, and that both sides are to blame. Any assessment of Japan that is critical can thus be dismissed as overly one-sided.

A related success is the portrayal of Japanese officials valiantly fighting on the side of the USA's free traders against a rising tide of US protectionism. Practically every statement on the bilateral relationship made by the Japanese prime minister refers to a "mutual resolve" to halt protectionist tendencies in the world. In the eyes of nearly all ordinary Japanese the danger comes from members of Congress who harbour feelings of ill will towards Japan, and from European governments that know no other way to placate their jobless. Very few are aware that the structural protectionism of the Japanese System is the major cause of the conflict to begin with.

A third and more recent success is the function that the term "bashing" has attained in Japanese manipulations of opinions. Originally used by some Americans who believe that US jealousies, frustration and even racism cause the friction with Japan, the term has been enthusiastically adopted by Japanese commentators. It tends to be automatically applied to any serious analysis of Japan's international problems that places responsibility at the feet of the administrators. The result is that many observers who wish to appear totally fair are inhibited from saying anything beyond the platitudes that most Japanese commentators can agree on.

The administrators are also unwittingly aided by US diplomats in their reality management of the relationship. The State Department and the Embassy in Tokyo have long had a tendency to echo the Japanese interpretation of bilateral problems. And even US diplomats who may not agree with their Japanese counterparts react negatively to critical analyses that their counterparts would not like to hear.

Compounding the diplomatic problem is the role of the US ambassador, who is seen less as an ambassador in the traditional sense than as a guardian watching over the relationship. In a tradition pioneered by Edwin O. Reischauer (who did much to consolidate the exploitative dependence relationship), Mike Mansfield, who was ambassador for over a decade, frequently seemed a better spokesman for Japan in Washington than the other way round. In his public statements, he tended to repeat the current Japanese line on what the USA ought to do. Mansfield had the air of being concerned, but fair and non-partisan, as if he wanted to remain above the quarrelling parties. In a representative interview, the ambassador was quoted as saying that the larger share of the responsibility for the trade problem lies with the United States. Even supposing that this were correct, such US attitudes sustain the bureaucrats of the Japanese Foreign Ministry in their belief that the conflict is essentially a public relations problem.

VICTIMISED AND ALONE

Because the world is no longer satisfied to leave relations with Japan as they are, the administrators are now called upon to act as statesmen; it is a role for which they are not equipped by training and, even more important, for which they cannot muster the necessary domestic support. Despite their supreme skills in nurturing a high-growth economy and in maintaining social control, they are—measured by what was required of them in the late 1980s—incompetent. But when the public begins to ask why other countries are so critical of Japan they can hardly concede such incompetence. An alternative explanation, that foreigners do not understand Japan, is worn out by decades of heavy duty. The single remaining explanation is that the world is actually against Japan.

This notion of a hostile world is easily accepted. It fits in with a long tradition of belief in the nation's vulnerability to unpredictable external forces. It fits in to a large extent with the psychology of many Japanese, who accept social obstacles passively. Japanese has an expression for it: *higaisha ishiki,* "victim consciousness."

Japan's War Sufferings

The general attitude towards the Pacific War is one of the best illustrations of Japanese victim consciousness. Nearly all the war films show the sufferings of the Japanese, and many young people are amazed when told that neighbouring nations suffered also at the hands of the Japanese. Atrocities committed in the occupied Asian countries tend to be ignored, and the idea that Japan was the main victim is gaining ground. The early 1950s saw anti-war films critical of the Japanese military, largely because many Japanese soldiers died. The late 1970s and early 1980s saw the appearance of the first genuinely revisionist films. Japanese soldiers are friendly, gentle, full of goodwill towards the local populations, whereas US soldiers are brutes who play football with human skulls (*Dai Nippon Teikoku*—a film that turns General Tojo into a hero). The Imperial Navy consisted of peaceful family men, trying to make the best of a difficult situation for Japan *(Rengo Kantai)*. In the film version of the fall of Singapore, the murder of five thousand Chinese is presented as motivated by guerrillas obstructing Japanese order-keeping among a local population that did not understand the good intentions of the occupiers *(Minami Jujisei)*. The end of this film shows, out of all context, a mushroom cloud—to remind us who were the really bad men in the Second World War.

Mushroom clouds, it sometimes seems, have become all but mandatory in Japanese war films. Here is victimhood in its ultimate guise: the atomic bombing of Hiroshima and Nagasaki. The belief in Japanese uniqueness has received very special support from these events: the Japanese did not just suffer, they suffered uniquely; one might even speak of national martyrdom. It has become common in Japan to consider the dropping of the atom bomb as the worst act of the war. Some even see it as the crime of the century. Older Japanese still have some sense of perspective concerning these events. A few will remember that, before Hiroshima was devastated, the generals had formed a civilian militia of 28 million men and women between fifteen and sixty years of age, who were being trained to stop the US invaders on the beaches using only bamboo spears. But a Japanese intellectual or public figure can no longer suggest that the bombs probably saved hundreds of thousands of lives. And for a week in August the nation indulges in a media-generated display of self-pity.

Sacrifice for Foreigners

The imagery of national victimhood provides a perfect frame of reference for Japan's international problems today. There is no shortage of "proof" that the international system has always obstructed Japan. One has only to remember the Asian immigration exclusion act passed by the US Congress in 1924 — still a favourite point-maker at conferences and in articles.

The sense of victimhood is nurtured by criticism from Western trading partners in connection with lopsided trade balances. The view that Japan is misunderstood carries much force because it is presented everywhere in the newspapers, the magazines and on television. It is also clear that the external world is not benevolent. It is therefore seen as crucially different from Japanese society, in which benevolence of the superior towards the subordinate is the assumption which keeps the administrators in their positions.

Japanese readily believe that adjusting the demands of the world means paying a price. The Japanese public has rarely been told that it would benefit from the greater choice and lower costs of more imported products. Many Japanese do not think the West has a case in calling Japanese trade practices unfair, because they are hardly aware that their System is not compatible with the rules of international commerce. Instead, they are told that it is the Western countries that want to change the rules in the middle of the game. It has almost become an article of faith in Japan that foreigners begrudge the Japanese the fruits of their post-war efforts. The administrators would make it appear that lazy Americans and Europeans want to force their bad habits on the thrifty, hard-working Japanese.

Even those who confirm the need for structural adjustments often assist in the campaign to portray Japan as the victim of unreasonable demands. Intellectuals may take the bureaucrats and politicians to task, but they too portray their country as the easy victim of a capricious Western world. Others praise Japan and its people for their remarkable patience in the face of "emotional American behaviour." Some respected authors see an alleged US racism at the root of the problem.

There are echoes, too, of the wartime imagery that contrasted an enfeebled USA with purposeful, dynamic and hard-working Japan. The USA is even, in all seriousness, taken to task for not appreciating the Japanese contributions to world peace.

The Administrators as Victims

If the general public has an ahistorical and apolitical view of Japan's place in the world, so, by and large, do the administrators. This is borne out by their refusal to see the conflict with the United States and other trading partners in political terms, requiring political solutions.

Here we come to an essential aspect of the Japan Problem. Japan undoubtedly exercises power in the world. The economic onslaught, apparently unstoppable by economic mechanisms, is *ipso facto* a political problem. Yet the administrators who deny that they exercise power in Japan also deny, implicitly but systematically, their exercise of power abroad. They insist that their international difficulties should be solved by economic measures taken by others, or by the workings of the market. They prefer not to see that Japan's massive export drives, and its undermining of certain industrial sectors in the USA and Europe, have political repercussions, that Europeans are beginning to seek a political solution, that the US Congress is trying to legislate one and that the reason the problem will not go away is Japanese political paralysis.

Throughout this book we have seen Japan's power-holders in charge of what is in fact a gigantic control mechanism—the System—for keeping order among ordinary Japanese. But it is clear, especially when the perspective shifts to Japan in the international context, that the administrators are also, in the final analysis, victims. They are products of the environment their predecessors created, and any debate on their situation that deviates from conventional lines is unwelcome; it is they who, tied down by their lack of imagination, are the real servants of the System. They are victims of a self-deceit inherited from their predecessors in the Tokugawa shogunate and the Meiji oligarchy: the pretense that they do not exercise power, together with the concomitant denial of any need for universally accepted rules to regulate that power, and hence the problem they have in accepting unambiguous leadership. The administrators have fostered complex personal ties that thrive on mutual aid, and their major task has been, by preventing laws and the courts from becoming the supreme regulators of society, to keep those relationships and the rules that govern them informal. They protect themselves by means of an elaborate rationale denying the forces that actually govern the System and explaining everything as a natural result of Japanese "culture." The Prussian vision of a society of perfect regimentation, and the overpowering fear of social disorder to which it is an antidote, both inherited from earlier administrators, limit their movements. They do not have the advantage, enjoyed by politicians, bureaucrats and intellectuals in most Western countries, of a political system that is to a considerable degree responsive to rational argument, to intellectual warnings and to genuine political debate. Some of them whom I know personally are horrified by the realisation that the System is, in fact, not under control.

Ultimate International Incompatibility

The denial of the true mechanisms of Japanese power, the pervasive sense of being victimised, the sense of being at once unique and misunderstood, and the absence of leadership all combine to perpetuate Japanese isolation in the world. This isolation is further aggravated by the seemingly insurmountable difficulty of fitting Japan into a larger, "legal" international framework.

The international world, especially the post-war trade system established under US auspices and sustained by such institutions as the GATT, the IMF and the OECD, operates on norms essentially different from those that make the Japanese System go round. GATT member countries do not usually arrange their relations with fellow members according to estimates of each other's power. The United States has not been intimidating Japan into an awareness of its proper position in the scheme of things. Governments may lie to each other and to their own populations, but in international dealings among non-communist trading nations there is no gap between substantial reality and formal reality remotely comparable to the institutionalised gap found in Japan. To some extent reality may be managed, but at some point foreign journalists, scholarly commentators or exasperated governments will point out the discrepancies between appearance and reality if they think these have become too great.

The Japanese System and what is left of the international free-trade system are incompatible because the latter requires adherence to rules that the administrators cannot afford to accept lest they override their own informal relations. Generally applicable rules governing the opportunities of foreign participants in Japanese society and its market would undermine and ultimately destroy the System by undermining the complex webs of *jinmyaku* and informal procedures. Deals can be made with the System, but the introduction of universal rules within the System itself is not a possible subject for such deals.

Contamination of Foreign Ways

The isolation of the System breeds attitudes that in turn intensify it and alienate the Japanese people even further from the rest of the world. Many foreign observers have seen psychological insularity as one of the main factors in Japan's international problems, and explain it with reference to cultural predilections. But Japanese isolation is encouraged by the way they are governed.

This is most clearly demonstrated by the phenomenon of the "returning youngsters" *(kikoku shijo)*—Japanese children who have received an important part of their education abroad. Except for training in engineering and other technical fields, foreign education is generally a handicap for functioning in the System. Far from being appreciated for the freshness of the experience that they bring to high schools and universities, the young returnees are often the object of teasing and bullying. The problem is so great that special schools have had to be established to remould them into acceptable Japanese. Their teachers complain that they ask too many questions. Their obvious dislike of proliferating school rules brands them as potential threats to Japanese social order. They are urged to mind their manner of walking and of laughing. Companies are not happy with job applicants who have lived abroad, worrying that their behaviour may upset the work community.

In cases where only a small number of Japanese reside in a foreign city, they demonstrate that there is nothing in their psychological make-up that prevents them from enjoying normal social relations with other peoples. It is when the expatriate community grows, and when a Japanese school is established, that their isolation becomes acute. They form exclusive Japanese clubs, or Japanese enclaves within existing local clubs, and tend, wherever possible, to move into the same town or locality. The extent of Japanese isolation from local society is incomparably greater than in communities of Americans or Europeans abroad. From private conversations with Japanese businessmen I have gathered that many feel that they cannot afford to awaken suspicion that they are picking up foreign ways, or prefer the company of foreigners.

Thus the behaviour of Japanese abroad is a consequence of pressure on them by their companies, not of some vague cultural rule.

Shall the System Last Forever?

Finally, the most important question: can the situation change? Theoretically, the answer is yes. As I have tried to demonstrate, the System's character is ultimately determined by political relationships. Nothing that is political is irreversible in the long run, especially if it is recognised for what it is. There is no good theoretical reason why the Japanese should for ever be held under political tutelage.

What might one do in an ideal situation? For a start, one would have to abolish Tokyo University. Other basic changes would have to take place in the legal and party systems. Law courses would have to be instituted in a large number of universities, and lawyers trained to give individual Japanese the means to protect themselves against the arbitrariness of the administrators. Control over the judiciary and over access to the bar would have to be taken away from the secretariat of the Supreme Court, and the artificial limitation on the number of law practitioners would have to be lifted. The schools and the media would have to work to foster individual political awareness and a sense of individual responsibility while de-emphasizing the importance of membership in companies and other organisations. All this would encourage the substitution of legal regulations for *jinmyaku* relationships, and of legally safeguarded processes for the System's informality. Any essential change for the better would also require the emergence of political parties not dependent on the porkbarrel and intent on truly representing the interests of the middle class and factory workers. This would only be a beginning, but under such conditions Japan could conceivably begin gradually to function as the constitutionalist democracy it is supposed to be. And it would move towards a solution of the problem of who, or which institution, has the right to rule.

The activities and the insights of some Japanese groups, such as the activist groups of the federation of bar associations (Nichibenren) or the alternative education reform committee of ordinary citizens, are proof that what I suggest is not asking too much, since they indicate the ability of the Japanese to be genuine citizens and to see themselves as such. Unfortunately, experience so far gives no reason for optimism. If the System is guided by any overriding, sacrosanct aim, it is its own survival, which means the survival of the administrators. This aim is mistakenly identified with the survival of Japan. The absence of political debate about national priorities, of parliamentary checks and balances, and of a legal framework for solving conflict increases risk of an intensification of Japanism. This, in turn, would be conducive to the re-emergence of extremist sentiments aimed at "saving the nation," which, as in the past, would most likely lead the nation still deeper into trouble. The Japanese System may yet go through another convulsion caused by an acute sense of confrontation with a hostile world. Such a spasm could conceivably bring to power a determined group who would plot a new course for the country, with a wholly unpredictable outcome.

The most likely possibility is that the System will muddle on, after having come to some *modus vivendi* with the Western world and the United States in particular. But this will require wise policies in the Western capitals.

The wonderful alternative of turning the System into a genuine modern constitutionalist state, and Japanese subjects into citizens, would require realignments of power akin to those of a genuine revolution.

GLOSSARY OF JAPANESE WORDS

Amakudari	post-retirement employment of bureaucrats in big business.
Burakumin	former outcasts.
Gaiatsu	pressure from outside.
Habatsu	political clique.
Honne	real intentions or motives, true meaning.
Ie	household, House.
Jinmyaku	network of special informal relations.
Juku	cramming school.
Keibatsu	family groupings through marriage.
Keiretsu	a group of corporations tied together by interlocking directorates and mutual shareholding.
Koenkai	support group for a politician, vote-collectors' organisations.
Kokutai	"national essence."
Kone	connections.
Kyoiku mama	education mother.
Naimusho	the disbanded, once very powerful Home Ministry.
Sarariiman	salaried worker.
Wa	harmony, peace.
Zaibatsu	pre-war corporate groupings around a holding company.
Zaikai	the world of big business and finance.

THE ITT
WARS

———

RAND V. ARASKOG

Condensed from *The ITT Wars*, © 1989 by Rand V. Araskog. Published by Henry Holt & Co. Printed by permission.

EDITOR'S NOTE

As a guide to the world of hostile corporate takeovers, The ITT Wars *is unique: Its author, Rand Araskog, was chairman of ITT when the company came under fire in separate raids in 1984 and 1985. His inside view of those encounters provides a gripping, detailed and valuable picture of the takeover process, complete with corporate intrigue, mysterious letters, bribes, company moles, paranoia, back-room deals and the manipulation of huge wealth.*

The first hostile bid for ITT came from Chicago financier Jay Pritzker and Denver oilman Philip Anschutz, the second from raider Irwin Jacobs. Araskog describes Pritzker and Anschutz as greedy men from wealthy families; he calls their offer a "gargantuan bribe." Essentially, he says, the raiders plan called for ITT to buy Pritzker's Hyatt Hotel chain with ITT stock, giving the raiders a large share of the company. Then Pritzker and Anschutz would buy the rest of ITT for about two-thirds of its breakup value, putting them in position to make a $3 billion profit on the deal. To lubricate the transaction, ITT's senior management would get 10 percent of the take, $300 million. Araskog's share would be $30 million.

ITT repelled the Pritzker-Anschutz assault, in spite of the fact that the company had been betrayed from within, according to Araskog. By the time the Jacobs attack came, ITT and its officers were veterans. Araskog explains how the company effectively used a series of counterattacks, including lawsuits, to fend off Jacobs and maintain its independence.

Araskog's account is not uncontroversial. Several of the people he named subsequently disputed his characterization of their roles in the battle for ITT. Nevertheless, Araskog's story of how ITT fought off the raiders is business drama of the highest form.

The ITT Wars *makes a strong case against hostile takeovers. Araskog believes they seriously undermine American business interests. As he says of his own experience with raiders: "They seemed to be motivated by the idea of playing a game, and devil take the resulting damage and disruption. It has become a most dangerous game for American publicly held corporations. All too often, companies subject to a takeover are disrupted, dismembered, downsized and hollowed out."*

A New Environment

By the time Harold Geneen stepped down in 1979 after twenty years as chairman of the board, ITT had made more than 250 acquisitions and had 2,000 working units. Revenues had gone from $800 million to $22 billion, and earnings from $30 million to $560 million. The company was the fifth largest employer in the United States, with more than 400,000 breadwinners. Geneen's methods were widely copied in other conglomerates and were taught in the nation's business schools. He was imitated, admired, and envied.

He left behind, however, a debt-laden corporation struggling to pay for its many mergers and acquisitions. Worse, the company was vulnerable to corporate raiders that might come to call. And, as business conditions changed, call they did.

In the 1980s, ITT was one of the first major American corporations subjected to a hostile bid by outside interests. The company was to be acquired and presumably dismembered: The sold-off units would pay for this exercise in financial manipulations—and, of course, provide the gross and unseemly profits for raiders.

In the next few years, we came to know some of these raiders fairly well. They were from old money and new money; sometimes they acted in an outright manner, at other times they were devious; occasionally they bluffed, occasionally they backtracked. They seemed to be motivated by the idea of playing a dangerous game, and devil take the resulting damage and disruption.

Peaceful mergers and acquisitions had long been responsible for creative growth and commercial development. In the old days, when ITT was built by Harold Geneen and Felix Rohatyn of Lazard Freres, investment banking and high finance used their power, connections, and sources of funds to build, to expand business and commerce. That was how bankers earned their fees and financiers enriched themselves.

Starting in the 1980s—in some cases earlier—the financial world turned to disinvestment. Investment bankers found that they could make even more money by tearing down and destroying what had already been built. The liquidation of companies by these hostile takeovers and leveraged buyouts threatened to undermine the structurally sound businesses that were the backbone of the economy. The basic nature of the American corporation—a business entity that had served well since its inception—was becoming a plaything in the hands of conscienceless, occasionally corrupt speculators.

Such attacks would bring profound changes across America—job losses, empty factories, community distress, and misallocation of resources. The country is only now coming to terms with those deleterious consequences. When the attack started, ITT was in the midst of its own transformation; the raids complicated that metamorphosis. Our energies were split, requiring us to fend off the raiders on the one hand while restructuring the company on the other. Either of these activities taken alone would have taxed our reserves; together, they created near exhaustion.

During this seven-year effort to save ITT, the company ran into most—if not all—of the problems and issues that defined corporate America in the 1980s: inflation, deflation, regulation, deregulation, an overvalued dollar, an undervalued dollar, an expanding economy, a recession, hostile takeover bids, demands for corporate liquidation, and officious bureaucrats.

Furthermore, there were specific problems that seemed endemic to ITT alone: alleged security breaches, extortion plots, alleged espionage in foreign subsidiaries (especially in Chile), and subtle as well as heavy-handed political pressures from foreign governments.

I was not initially concerned when I became chairman of ITT in January 1980, with takeovers, leveraged buyouts, and hostile raids, since ITT had outstanding results in my first year. Earnings had never been better. I was aware, however, that business conditions were worsening. Inflation, which had been creeping up through the seventies, reached devastating levels in the early eighties before the Federal Reserve applied the brakes and cut the money supply.

The recession of 1981-82, the worst of the postwar era, caused ITT's earnings to fall because of lower sales, lower foreign earnings due to the high value of the dollar, and high interest charges, which were particularly destructive. As a consequence of the hundreds of mergers, the company's debt was close to $5 billion—nearly half of ITT's capital.

With interest rates and inflation cresting, with the borrowing rate at 21 percent and the consumer price index rising at 14 percent per year, the debt service was extremely onerous.

One of my first long-range business plans involved reducing that debt by selling a number of companies. By the end of 1984, the corporation had divested itself of sixty-nine companies for close to $2 billion. Yet still more needed to be done to reduce the interest burden. Our goal was to lower the debt to approximately 30 percent of the company's capitalization. Hindering this goal, however, was ITT's tradition of increasing dividends. ITT was paying about one-third more in dividends than the ordinary industrial service company—a policy that became limiting for an expanding company with a goal of debt reduction. In the summer of 1984, ITT took sudden deep cuts in income and it became necessary to slash the dividend from $2.76 to $1.00—a 64 percent reduction. It was the most difficult management decision the Board of Directors ever had to make. Dividends had steadily increased, with only one interruption, for almost fifteen years. Discontinuing such a policy could prove devastating. The stock could drop in value, we might lose some institutional backing and sponsorship, the market could overreact, we might become vulnerable to the takeover and leveraged-buyout movement that had intensified over the previous year or two. Without dramatic action, however, the cash flow would only get worse, and, after all, who would have the temerity to attack a company consistently listed among the top twenty of the Fortune 500? We presumed that ITT was too large—who could swallow a behemoth?

The first week after the dividend cut the raiders came to call. We knew we were in for a serious, perhaps life-threatening fight, first from two of the wealthiest individuals in the nation, then others who wanted to buy us on the cheap. The company moved to battle stations. We could not know that inside our management we had a mole, someone who was foolishly attempting to undermine our efforts and betray us to the enemy.

— 2 —

THE "BRIBE"

The first blow in the ITT wars was struck one afternoon in October 1983. Jerry Seslowe, a clever and articulate financier specializing in venture capital and investment banking, called on DeRoy ("Pete") C. Thomas, then the chairman of the Hartford Fire Insurance Company, a wholly owned subsidiary of ITT. He had come as point man for two businessmen, Jay Pritzker and Philip Anschutz, who wanted to take ITT private.

Their interest was based on some very appealing numbers. What Pritzker and Anschutz perceived in 1983 was a cash-rich, asset-rich multinational company whose market price did not reflect its true value, then about $40 a share. Clearly, Pritzker and Anschutz saw an apparent discrepancy and a way to profit from it.

Pete Thomas briefed me after the visit. I was puzzled and concerned: How could anyone expect to buy out one of America's largest corporations? Who, other than another giant corporation, would have the audacity or the resources? What was the motivation of the offer—and was it genuine?

Jay Pritzker and Phil Anschutz were unquestionably wealthy. Pritzker, the descendant of a penniless Russian immigrant, was the son of real estate developer A. A. Pritzker. The Pritzkers owned the Marmon Group (a manufacturing conglomerate) and Braniff Airlines; held a major interest in the Hyatt Hotel chain; and also had interests in casinos and chewing tobacco. The Pritzker family, including Jay's brother Robert, had an estimated fortune of $1.5 billion. Phil Anschutz inherited a large Colorado ranch where oil was discovered. Interests in coal, uranium, real estate, and railroads also put him in the billionaires' club.

Jerry Seslowe and his associates had studied five companies as candidates for leveraged buyouts. ITT was their first choice. Seslowe's investment firm was owned by Anschutz and Pritzker, who could find corporate financing. As part of the transaction, Seslowe suggested that ITT could first acquire the Hyatt Hotel chain from Pritzker for shares in ITT, giving Pritzker a large share position in ITT before making the takeover offer. The price offered to ITT shareholders would be about $20 per share below the breakup value estimated by Pritzker and Anschutz. If they could entice shareholders with an offer over $40 per share, they might pocket a profit of $3 billion on ITT's 150 million shares of common stock, and conceivably much more. Finally, to make sure that the deal was sufficiently enticing, Seslowe also suggested that senior management would be allotted 10 percent of the return on the venture, about $300 million. My share would be $30 million—what I perceived to be a gargantuan bribe!

Pete Thomas, trained as an attorney, questioned the propriety of the deal and told Seslowe that he doubted I would be interested. He was right.

My first encounter with Jay Pritzker had taken place a year earlier, on Malcolm Forbes's yacht, the Highlander. Forbes had invited a large group of business executives and spouses to attend a West Point football game. Included in the group were Pritzker and his wife, Cindy, as well as my wife, Jessie, and we talked with the Pritzkers en route to West Point. I was impressed by his soft, friendly, pressing tone of voice, a little above a whisper when he chose. He watched intently as he talked to see the reaction of his words.

As was typical for those West Point trips on the Highlander, there were Bloody Marys in the late morning, a superb lunch, then the bus trip up to Michie Stadium. Malcolm Forbes distributed the football tickets and seated Jessie and me with the Pritzkers and himself. Throughout the game, we had opportunities to talk not just about the game but also about Chicago; about Minnesota, where Jessie and I had grown up; about ITT; and about the hotel business: the Pritzker-Hyatt chain and the ITT-Sheraton chain. It was a pleasant afternoon.

A year later, perhaps Pritzker assumed that our casual conversations had modestly paved the way for a mutual understanding. Whether it was based on the potential combination of the Hyatt and Sheraton chains, the need to build an even bigger business empire, or simply the lure of making a quick buck, Pritzker was interested in dismantling and liquidating a company to which I and thousands of employees had dedicated our careers. I was not about to let him and Anschutz "buy" me and our management team.

While Pete was conveying my reaction to Jerry Seslowe, I notified

several of the senior outside members of ITT's Board of Directors—
Dick Perkins, former chairman of the executive committee of Citicorp;
Terry Sanford, president of Duke University; Tom Keesee, executive
director of the Bessemer Fund; and Michel David-Weill, senior partner
of Lazard Freres—of what I had done. They wholeheartedly agreed
with my rejection of the offer.

Next, I brought the matter to the attention of the board's Executive
Committee at its next meeting, but I also indicated that I was not sure it
was over. I noted that we would have to proceed carefully, and the best
way to do that was to achieve a market value for ITT shares greater than
that perceived by Pritzker and Anschutz.

Making a profit on the discrepancy between true value and market
price was the raiders' advantage. Their plan was relatively simple: do a
leveraged buyout of the public stockholders with the blessings of
management—and arrange for significant financial benefits to management as well. Offer the public shareholders more than the market price
but less than a realizable value of the company after it was put on the
block. How familiar that score would become, one that would be played
over and over in the following years.

Seslowe's reaction to my response was "disappointment," but there
was no indication that he would pursue the matter further. It was only
later, through other emissaries, that the depth of his and Phil Anschutz's
interest in ITT became clear. They would shift from a friendly effort to
get management to cooperate to a high-pressure and finally an unfriendly one.

The other raider group that ITT would get to know all too well was
Irwin Jacobs and his followers. Most of Jacobs's new money came from
frightened boards of directors that bought off him and the others with
greenmail. Nevertheless, he could be dangerous, since he was capable
of amassing formidable sums to buy up stock. He never made any of the
sophisticated hypocritical noise that he was restructuring American
industry, that his was pro bono publico work. He was out for money,
pure and simple. As with other raiders, he has his own corporate vehicle
for the raids, Minstar Corporation, which has not of late proved an
overwhelming success for its public stockholders.

To keep ITT on course through the upcoming battle, I was to rely
heavily on the top management team. Cab Woodward, chief financial
officer and executive vice president, was extremely well known in the
financial community and highly thought of by commercial and investment bankers. The treasurer, who reported to Cab, was John Pfann, a

solid and loyal supporter of ITT. Howard Aibel, general counsel of the corporation, possessed an adroit and wide-ranging legal mind. He was known as "Mr. Cool." Jack Hanway, the director of administration, took an extremely hard line, but he was a loyal professional who had tremendous instinct for where the power was and what needed to be done to maintain it.

Edward ("Ned") Gerrity, senior vice president for government and public relations, was, perhaps, my closest confidant, and my only social friend among the ITT management. Although he was only eight years my senior, I thought of him as I would of my father, from another generation. Ned's deputy, Juan Cappello, was a junior member of the group. Finally, I had another powerful friend, ally, and associate in Pete Thomas, the outstanding chairman of the board of the Hartford Fire Insurance Company.

On December 23, 1983, I held a small party for these and other ITT executives on the twelfth floor of 320 Park Avenue, our headquarters in New York City. It was a jovial gathering. We were closing out the year with about the same earnings as the preceding year, but with an improved debt-equity ratio, and we shared a reasonably buoyant attitude about 1984.

At one point Ned Gerrity pulled me aside and said, "Rand, on January first you will have been chairman and chief executive officer for four full years. Like the president of the United States, you are coming to the end of your first four-year term. You must determine what you want for your second term. Think about the strong points and the weak points, and what you will do to fix them. I want to be a part of making what we have done even more successful and to work with you in every way you want to strengthen this corporation."

I was more than a little taken aback at the comparison of my tenure as CEO to a four-year term of the president of the United States. I had never thought about it that way, and I had no idea what he had in mind, but it made me uneasy.

— 3 —

STORM WARNINGS

W hen Harold Geneen came on board, the old International Telephone and Telegraph Corporation was basically a collection of overseas telephone systems and production companies with a smattering of domestic firms involved in radio, television, and appliances. The original concept of ITT—to be a foreign equivalent of American Telephone & Telegraph—had died with its founders, Sosthenes and Hernand Behn, in 1957. Indeed, the corporation floundered in the 1950s without a clear sense of purpose.

Geneen gave the company a mission to grow rapidly through the acquisition of hundreds of companies. In building ITT, he used the product asset base in Europe to acquire service and product businesses in the United States. Geneen's vision and personal energy powered the company for more than a decade of unremitting growth. The range of products was nothing less than astonishing, from Twinkies to turbines, from hydrants to hotel rooms, from radios to casualty insurance.

When Geneen retired, he left behind the greatest agglomeration of businesses ever gathered under one corporate tent. He was the conglomerateur par excellence—and Felix Rohatyn of Lazard Freres was the mergers-and-acquisitions man nonpareil. Geneen and Rohatyn's greatest strength was identifying companies that could be acquired without a fight. He believed that it was possible to nurture companies, supply them with the fertilizer of growth—cash and management expertise—and they would expand and mature. It was too costly and risky to start from scratch, especially if assets were available at a discount—far better to acquire a going concern that matched development plans. Guided by this philosophy, most of ITT's growth until 1972 was generated through external means.

These disparate entities had one main common element—a centralized staff management system. Geneen, along with other conglomerateurs of the 1960s and 1970s, had an overriding business philosophy that strong managers could manage anything, no matter how separate or incongruent.

Geneen's style became legendary, with staff meetings marked by critical quizzing of line managers. Perhaps it was his training as an accountant, but Geneen was certain that a candid, even charged exchange between him and his managers would lead to the solutions that might affect the bottom line.

His program was far from simplistic synergy, as some of his critics have charged. His purpose was to build on the needs of the second half of the twentieth century, when a service economy, he felt, would predominate. Geneen liked hard goods, but he was shrewd enough to know that some of ITT's older and more traditional fields, such as defense work, appliances, and electrical connectors, were increasingly risky and competitive. In the newer service businesses, such as financial services, insurance, hotels, and broadcasting, the risks were lower and the returns on investment higher.

ITT had acquired these businesses by using corporate paper: It issued common stock, and convertible preferred shares, to the shareholders of the acquired company in return for their equity. The number of shares ITT issued under Geneen increased tenfold, to roughly 150 million shares or their equivalent.

Along with the issuing of equity came the growth of debt. By 1979, the capitalization of the company had come close to being half debt and half equity: Not only was the corporation becoming highly leveraged, it was increasingly burdened with the servicing of that debt. In 1980, the servicing charges alone were over $600 million. To further increase cash flow problems, ITT was paying high dividends.

The cost of the mergers surfaced at the end of the 1970s when business turned down and expenses turned up. Harold Geneen never wanted to sell anything, so it was hard to break the acquisition habit even after he stepped down. Under Lyman Hamilton, Geneen's first successor as CEO, the company spent more on new acquisitions than it took in from divestitures the following year. Hamilton's ambivalent attempt to trim the company was one of the factors that set the Board of Directors against him and ended with his forced resignation.

Geneen had bet on the proposition that the economy, both here and abroad, would be subject to gradual but constant inflation. Under such conditions, it made sense to borrow, since it would always be possible to retire debts with cheaper or deflated money. When interest rates ratcheted upward in the early 1980s, this strategy backfired, making ITT debt onerous. While a little inflation enables businesses to pass rising costs on to consumers, a lot of inflation can create major problems. Moreover, the soaring dollar in the early 1980s had an adverse effect on foreign earnings. Overseas profits were extremely important to ITT, so the result was devastating when the company brought home only minidollars.

Increasingly, the financial world was looking toward a corporation's income, its cash flow, and its return on assets. ITT was in a financial box, with a collection of disparate companies—some profitable, some not, but all expensive to maintain. The future lay not in diversification, but in divestiture. ITT needed a program to focus itself on a true course if it was to regain financial strength before growing again.

As the 1980s took shape, the philosophy of corporate raiders began to sweep through the financial world: The liquidation value of companies might be greater than the sum of their parts.

This new philosophy had enormous implications for ITT and the rest of corporate America. It all started quietly and slowly on May 1, 1975, when brokerage commissions were deregulated and competition finally came to the home of capitalism, the stock exchanges. Faced with the prospects of competing, brokerage houses and investment banks searched for new kinds of business: Some brokers opened discount brokerage offices, some opened research boutiques, and some opened or expanded mergers-and-acquisitions departments.

With deregulation in the eighties, airlines, trucking, railroads, utilities, petroleum, and banking also were faced with new ground rules and new rivals. Wall Street was ready to tender advice to all these industries, suggesting ways to raise cash and spin off unwanted subsidiaries. Lowering interest rates facilitated the trend toward mergers and acquisitions, takeovers, leveraged buyouts, and hostile raids. Since it was much cheaper to buy corporate assets in the stock market or through open tender offers to private shareowners, there was little incentive to build plant and facilities from scratch.

About the only element that had remained cheap during the period of inflation from 1978 to 1982 was corporate equity, but after August 1982, even the stock market began to take off. Interest rates declined and the merger-and-acquisition race was on. Enter the years of the raider— 1983 through today.

Like most major American corporations, ITT was initially ill prepared to cope with this radically new business environment. Fortunately, we had started to unburden ITT of money-losing subsidiaries in 1979. The Rayonier Port Cartier pulp mill in Quebec was the first major holding to be spun off, reversing the trend of two decades of business acquisitions. Within a year, the remainder of Rayonier Canada properties were sold, but the U.S. properties were retained. Nevertheless, ITT was still paying out more than $1 billion in interest and dividends. Clearly, more would have to be done to reduce the debt to 30 percent of the company's capitalization—our short term strategy. Next, we pruned some dubious overseas holdings, selling more than $1 billion worth of companies in Europe between 1980 and 1983.

By the fall of 1983, we were better focused. Earnings for the year were lower than in 1980, a record year, and the much-publicized and very promising System 12 digital telecommunications switching system was at its most expensive and critical stage of development. Having been successful in Europe, its American introduction was running into towering development costs and strong competition. The Hartford and the ITT Financial Corporation were both meeting their budgets, however, and becoming the strongest income performers for the company.

— 4 —

THE WARS OF
SUCCESSION

Four years earlier, in January 1980, when I succeeded Harold Geneen as chairman, there had been a deceptive serenity in ITT, a respite from the wars of succession that had racked the company. The Board of Directors had been unhappy with Geneen's delaying tactics in searching for a successor. They had insisted on his retirement at sixty-five in 1975, but he had groomed no successor acceptable to them. The jockeying for power intensified. Indeed, Geneen was not above adding to the intrigue, with a sparkling twinkle in his eyes.

He had set up the Office of the President in 1968 to see how a number of heirs apparent performed. All power still centered on Geneen, however; the other members of the Office of the President were more staff than line executives. It was a dilatory step on Geneen's part—he had no wish to hasten his own departure.

I was promoted to the Office of the President in June 1976, along with Lyman Hamilton, then the corporation's treasurer and chief financial officer. The president's office already had two executive vice presidents and a president representing different aspects of ITT. The president, appointed in 1972, was Francis "Tim" Dunleavy, a shrewd politician and at one time the head of the company's European operations. As one observer noted, "Dunleavy was the perfect successor—for a man who had no intention of leaving."

The two executive vice presidents were Richard Bennett, an engineer with a strong background in sales, and James Lester, who had dealt with the Hartford Fire Insurance Company and overseas management activities. Though they were younger than Geneen, they were identified as adherents to his style. When Hamilton and I were added to the Office of the President, it was widely presumed that the race for Geneen's mantle was strictly between Lyman, the darling of the financial community, and me. Lyman was the odds-on choice. In the late 1960s it was assumed that Dunleavy, Bennett, or Lester would ascend to the chairmanship. The Board of Directors wanted continuity and retention of the Geneen management principles, since ITT had been extraordinarily successful through 1971 under its renowned leader.

When Geneen took command in 1959, he was not interested in acquiring other companies. For the first few years of his leadership, ITT was on a shakedown cruise—an attempt to remove all the disjointed pieces and redundancies that had accumulated like barnacles over the years, while at the same time streamlining and restructuring procedures within the component companies.

ITT had passed $1 billion in revenues the previous year, and Geneen's new management techniques had brought accolades from the media. He was beginning to look for new worlds to conquer. In fact, he established a task force to pinpoint acquisitions in 1963 and before long was on a shopping binge.

In this stage of his stewardship, no one built better or had a more adroit sense of fit and value. Once he got going, Geneen acquired companies rapidly—about one a month: Cannon in electrical connectors, Gilfillan in airport surveillance, General Controls in automatic devices, Bell & Gossett in industrial pumps, Nesbitt in ventilation, a number of companies in consumer finance and insurance, Avis in car leasing, Howard W. Sams in publishing (Bobbs-Merrill), Pennsylvania Glass Sand in raw materials for glass and filters, Levitt in housing, Continental Baking in foodstuffs. Some companies were to be a nucleus of a new division, while others complemented businesses already in hand.

Then, in the early 1970s, ITT suffered a couple of devastating black eyes—not so much for what it did as for what it was perceived to have done. In 1971, shortly after ITT's annual meeting in San Diego, overzealous company executives in the public relations department promised a substantial contribution to the City of San Diego on behalf of the Sheraton Hotel Corporation for assistance with the Republican convention there. Although this was unconnected to the settlement of an antitrust matter against the corporation for its acquisition of Hartford Fire Insurance Company, the timing of the contribution and

the settlement looked highly suspicious. ITT's irrepressible and out-
spoken Dita Beard, a member of the Washington public relations staff,
allegedly wrote a memo that made it look like there was tit for tat. The
memo reached the press and there were questions in Congress, but in
the final analysis there was no payoff, no trade-off.

The second major public relations disaster was Geneen's involvement in the Chilean imbroglio. ITT had obtained control of the Chile
Telephone Company in 1927, so the company's interest in Chile was
longstanding. By 1970, CTC's interests were valued at $153 million,
ITT's largest telephone property in South America. Indeed, it was now
the last property; all the others had been nationalized. Geneen viewed
the potential election in 1970 of socialists, communists, and splinter
left-wing groups as a threat—first in Latin America, then in lending
legitimacy to communism-by-election throughout the world.

Geneen voiced his reservations to ITT director John McCone, a
former CIA head, who in turn contacted Richard Helms, then the
director of the agency. Geneen was informed that the United States was
not backing any candidate in the Chilean election. However, a private
meeting was set up between Geneen and the head of the CIA's
clandestine services in the Western Hemisphere—for the purposes of
exchanging information. Unhappily, the official reported to his chief
that Geneen offered a "substantial fund" to the CIA. He was turned
down, the official noted, and Geneen testified he had no recollection of
the alleged offer, but it was later to haunt both Geneen and ITT.

The U.S. Government at this point began to formulate a plan
against Salvador Allende, but Geneen did not back it. It was a case of
too little too late—Allende won in October 1970, and less than a year
later, he took control of Chile Telephone without formally expropriating
it. His informal action was presumably intended to prevent ITT from
filing a claim for the value of its investment with the newly created
Overseas Private Investment Corporation (OPIC), a U.S. government
vehicle that insured ITT's investment against expropriation. Significantly, ITT's other interests in Chile, which included a telecommunications factory and two Sheraton hotels, were left untouched.

After the takeover of Chile Telephone, internal ITT memos suggesting contingency plans to forestall Allende's inauguration were
leaked to the press. Although ITT's activities and plans seemed confused and contradictory in these memos, much was made of them.
There was clearly a difference between "staff thinking" and "policy
determination," as noted later on by McCone. That is what staffs are

for, he said—"to think up alternatives, and then that is why you have bosses to make the decision."

ITT's negotiations with Allende for compensation for the telephone company takeover had been frustrating. Allende offered to pay slightly more than $12 million for the property, far from the $153 million the company was worth. Allende was no doubt scheming to let the U.S. Treasury pick up the tab through OPIC. Later, a panel of U.S. arbitrators ruled that OPIC was liable under its insurance policy. With OPIC's help, ITT settled the nationalization matter for $125 million.

The CIA connection pursued ITT for many years. Even though I knew nothing of Geneen's alleged involvement in the Chilean affair, I did know something of the CIA, since I had previously worked for the National Security Agency in Washington. In subsequent years, the CIA on three separate occasions did attempt to recruit ITT for some of its operations. And on three occasions they were turned down. The country has a right to protect its national interests, but in a democracy those activities (except in extreme, extraordinary circumstances) should be public. Every time the CIA "unofficially" came calling, I could only think of Mark Twain's cat, which sat down once on a hot stove, but never again sat down on a hot one, or, for that matter, a cold one either. We were not about to be burned again.

ITT was at a critical crossroad: The company that seemingly could do no wrong in the 1960s was now shuttling from one expose to another. San Diego and Chile were the most prominent faux pas, but there were a host of lesser events that undermined the public's confidence: the Justice Department's suits against ITT's acquisitions of Grinnel Corporation, Canteen Corporation, and Hartford Fire Insurance Company (the antitrust impasse was resolved in 1971 primarily by a consent decree that allowed acquisition of The Hartford but prohibited, without specific Department of Justice approval, any further domestic acquisition for ten years if the acquired company had assets in excess of $100 million); the IRS's announcement of its reconsideration of the 1969 tax-free merger ruling in The Hartford acquisition and its subsequent revocation in 1974; the government's refusal to pay the OPIC insurance claim over the loss of Chile Telephone Company; and a slew of derivative stockholder suits against management for alleged wrongs. All took their toll. In 1973, the price of ITT common stock hit a record high of 67⅜. As the problems multiplied and confidence ebbed, the price slid dramatically with a general fall in the market—to $12 at the end of 1974. After fourteen brilliant years from 1959 to 1973, Geneen's magic stopped working; the string of fifty-eight consecutive quarters of 10 percent profit gains ended. However, he received a new two-year employment contract, which would take him just beyond the normal retirement age of sixty-five. The fortunes of the company were fading and there was no new certain leadership in sight. Only in June 1976, when Geneen was in the final caretaker phase of his career, did the board become impatient and force him to bring in two new contenders. The directors told Geneen that they would decide which one of the two would succeed him.

Unfortunately for me, and unknown to me, the outside directors had given themselves only six months to decide between Lyman Hamilton and me. Lyman had been on the Board of Directors for several years; in June 1976, I wasn't even on the board. It was clear that a Herculean effort lay ahead if I was to have any chance.

Prior to my promotion to the Office of the President, Ned Gerrity was constantly supportive. Information on trips to the field, and the way personnel in the field reacted to me, went directly to Harold Geneen. When, as vice president in charge of the Defense Space Group, I sponsored a quality seminar, which received some newspaper attention in New Jersey, Ned Gerrity made sure that all of the favorable reviews reached Harold Geneen's desk. He made sure I was invited to all of the annual meetings from 1972 on, so I could become known to the ITT directors. He made sure he kept me in Mr. Geneen's view as much as possible, outside of the general management meetings, where I reported to Geneen and others on the status of the Defense Space Group.

The companies in my group became very strong, and Geneen placed more companies under my control. By 1974, close to twenty companies with more than $1 billion in sales reported to me in the Aerospace, Electronics, Components, and Energy Group. I had become one of the principal vice presidents and group executives of the corporation, but still one of more than thirty.

My group instituted specific policies and tight controls to avoid improper payments overseas, at a time when overseas operations of major corporations were plagued with agents' demands for excessive fees. When trouble developed for ITT in connection with sensitive payments, particularly in the telecommunications area, the ITT companies that served the Department of Defense and NASA were never involved. This did not escape the notice of Harold Geneen and the Board of Directors.

The board had grown increasingly testy about ITT's reputation for integrity. As Harold Geneen approached the age of sixty-five in early 1975, he was spending days at a time in Washington with Howard Aibel, the corporate counsel, defending himself and the corporation. There simply was inadequate time to run the sprawling company, and management deteriorated rapidly.

Prohibited from buying companies with U.S. assets in excess of $100 million, Geneen scoured Europe, buying European companies with abandon. Geneen was no longer the critical buyer of yesteryear. In one instance, both Hamilton and I recommended against a potential $15 million French acquisition, but Geneen consummated the deal because one of his European executives had "worked hard" in arranging the matter and deserved a new business. It only piled more debt on the company's balance sheet.

In addition, ITT's research and development could not keep up with the technology of the digital electronic world. ITT had been a leader in computers, it had been a leader in digital electronics, but it was now falling behind, and worst of all, did not know it.

My sympathies lay with Harold Geneen. I felt key people had let him down. He was feeling too alone, too threatened, but, until 1976, I was in no position to help, or to penetrate his own proud barriers. Many key executives feared that we were beginning to witness the unwinding of ITT as a major corporate force.

— 5 —

PASSING THE TORCH

Business transitions are always fraught with danger. Companies do not change gears easily; habits and traditions—the corporate culture—serve to keep complex organizations on track. In the mid-seventies, ITT had lost momentum: the chairman distracted by Washington political intrigue, floundering research and development, company power centers out of synch. Corporate energy seemed to diminish with each day. Perhaps it was a form of exhaustion after a decade of rapid, almost unbelievable growth. Finally, Harold Geneen was prevailed upon to revitalize the company.

On the morning of June 8, 1976, I received a phone call at my headquarters in Nutley, New Jersey, telling me to come to New York headquarters. Not expecting the call, I was not dressed for the occasion in Geneen's style—black laced shoes, black suit, white shirt, and striped tie. Geneen made it obvious that he noticed my casual attire. (I cleaned up my wardrobe and learned to like black laced shoes.) Later that week, Geneen came over to Nutley with "Tim" Dunleavy and Rich Bennett to Defense Space headquarters, where he had not been for years, to attend a briefing and to confirm that I was moving into the Office of the President.

Dunleavy, of course, was beset with disappointment, recognizing that he probably was out of the running. The competition for the CEO position was now between Lyman Hamilton and me, with Hamilton far in the lead. At forty-nine, he was also five years my senior. I was running well back in a difficult race to win.

The quasi-competition continued, but in February 1977, as I was meeting in my office one morning with Lyman, the curtain descended on my hopes. Lyman was sitting in his shirtsleeves when his secretary walked in with his jacket. A few moments later, word began to swing through the building that he had been selected to replace Harold

Geneen as chief executive officer at the end of the year. He would be named president and chief operating officer (COO) immediately. I left my office to see Geneen, stopping to comfort my loyal, red-eyed secretary, Sharon van Hook, who had worked so hard and rooted so earnestly for me.

Harold told me, his eyes glistening, that he had to choose Lyman or the board would have gone outside for his replacement. Board member Felix Rohatyn was quoted as saying Lyman was the only one who was articulate. My wife, Jessie, was stoical. "Hey, Rand," she said, "there's nothing wrong with number two in a $20 billion company."

Holding a number-two position to Lyman Hamilton did not turn out to be that easy, despite the wishes of the board, which had thought we would make a great Mr. Outside-Mr. Inside combination. I was finally elected to the board, but the appointment was a hollow victory.

Geneen stayed on as CEO until December 1977, but his relationship with Hamilton soured. On January 3, 1978, the new CEO announced new policies and a modified reorganization, as if to state, "The King is dead, long live the King." Although Lyman fought it constantly, board pressure continued to confirm me clearly as number two at ITT. I was named senior executive vice president and chief operating officer, and, most important, a member of the ITT Executive Committee.

Lyman and I agreed to a working arrangement, with great difficulty, and only after the intrusion of the Executive Committee of outside directors. At first Lyman wanted me to serve in a staff capacity, but I fought for line control and won it. I also suggested that he not leave Geneen out of key information loops, but he persisted in circumventing the chairman.

The board's confidence in Lyman declined rapidly in the spring of 1979 and dissolved completely by July 11, the day of the board meeting. I was called that morning to meet with all of the outside directors. Tension was high as I was interrogated at great length. It was fairly clear that I had broad support. After many hours of discussion, Felix Rohatyn said, "Look fellows, I've had enough. I'm in favor of going forward." That was it. Geneen then joined us. The board negotiated with Lyman for his resignation. After the board meeting, I found a message from Jessie, asking me to bring home some fresh tomatoes. Excited, I called her with the great news about my new job as CEO. She said, "Wonderful, Rand, and don't forget the tomatoes!" I hung up in amazement. But that was Jessie. Her excitement was at such a peak that

that was all she could say. When I got out of the car at home, I had forgotten the tomatoes.

The press immediately pounced on Geneen's alleged return to power and the unfair treatment of Lyman Hamilton. I sent Jack Hanway, Juan Cappello, and Jim Lester on the company plane to Brussels to request Gary Andlinger's resignation (Andlinger had been appointed head of European operations by Hamilton) and to handle the public relations aspects of the change. I wanted to replace Andlinger with Jack Guilfoyle, a seasoned ITT executive.

But the newspapers reported that Geneen had gone to Europe to fire Andlinger, saying it was a continuation of the expression of his power. Nothing could have been farther from the truth, but what bothered me most was that we knew that the reporters involved knew it was not the truth.

After replacing the ITT director of personnel, I eliminated all of the highly paid staff product line managers at ITT headquarters. One was product line manager in charge of skiing, another was in charge of researching food on the *Queen Elizabeth II*. Yet another was charged with seeing how many places in the world he could visit and still be reached by telephone.

I upgraded the technical program, and particularly the leapfrog program for digital equipment known as System 12. I increased the research budget and raised the selling prices on all of the companies ITT was planning to divest: electronic appliances and distributors, drugs, cosmetics, and food companies, principally in Europe. I reduced TV production in Europe from thirteen plants, all over the continent, to two, both in West Germany. I also closed the Rayonier Quebec pulp mill. That was not easy; it had originally been Geneen's pet project. I sent an eight-person team to Nantucket, where they spent ten hours with the vacationing Geneen, explaining my decision. He called me the next day. Before he could say anything, I said, "Hal, I couldn't pour all of the ITT you built down that sinkhole in Quebec." He responded, "Rand, I've seen all the numbers. You have to do it." And that was that.

In September, I went to Europe for business-plan reviews of our companies, feeling very much in control. We had lost no one from management whom I did not want to lose. However, there I discovered that Harold Geneen had made plans for investment projects that potentially could become directly competitive with ITT. Immediately on my return, I met with Tom Keesee, one of the senior members of the board and a close friend of Geneen's, and with Dick Perkins, telling them that I would not tolerate this. Harold would have to make a choice—continue as chairman of ITT, with its associated restrictions, or give up the chairmanship and be free to do most of the things he wanted to do. Characteristically, he chose freedom.

Effective January 1, 1980, having just turned forty-eight, I became chairman, president, and chief executive officer of ITT. My first year as chairman was the best financial year in ITT's history—with earnings of $6.20 a share. The System 12 telecommunications digital switching program was looking exceedingly strong, we had already signed a number of contracts. Things were humming.

There were, however, a few clouds on the horizon. The company was about to be hit by extraordinarily high interest rates, plus major expenditures to take people off the payroll in Europe and Latin America. These terminations would cost hundreds of millions of dollars. In addition, as a result of the socialist victory in the 1981 French elections, we were obliged in 1982 to sell our company, Compagnie Generale de Constructions Telephoniques (CGCT), for a small percentage of what we felt it was worth.

In 1981, nevertheless, performance was respectable, thanks to the results of Hartford Fire Insurance and telecommunications sales in Nigeria. In the fall of 1982, the sale of a significant part of Standard Telephones and Cables (STC) in the United Kingdom produced a substantial capital gain. That gain made 1982 also a successful year financially for ITT, sparking a dividend increase to $2.76 per share in 1982.

ITT was somewhat old-fashioned when it came to dividends. Numerous pension funds and income investors required or needed dividend income. ITT had high marks from this quarter of the investment community, since the company had raised dividends each year. In the 1960s, ITT's shares soared on growth, then faltered in the early 1970s, all the while continuing to raise dividends. But increasing dividends too much can weaken a company—a fact that was brought home to ITT in the summer of 1984. We were to learn the hard way, in the wrong environment—in the lair of the raiders.

— 6 —

THE FIRST LETTER

The siege of ITT had started in October 1983, with Jerry Seslowe's approach to Pete Thomas. Corporate Counsel Howard Aibel surveyed the scene and started to prepare our defenses against unfriendly or hostile moves. No one suspected that we would have to defend ourselves from a fifth column, an internal threat. Shortly after a birthday party for Ned Gerrity in January 1984, I received a letter from him at my home in Smoke Rise, New Jersey. In it he noted what had been accomplished in my "first term." What still needed to be done, Ned stressed, was the axing of several key executives whom I had selected to manage significant activities.

Ned no doubt felt that his long association with ITT (predating even Geneen) gave him special insight into the workings of the corporation. He had spent many years commuting to Washington, immersed in the petty plots and counterplots that passed for lobbying activities in the sixties and seventies. My first impression of him had been formed in 1967, about a year after I had joined ITT, at a management conference he had organized in Washington, D.C. The conference brought all of the ITT line general managers in the United States to see Washington and how it works. As I look back, it was in fact a glorification of Harold Geneen, Ned Gerrity, and the Washington lobbying staff. Congressmen, senators, and White House staff members participated in ITT's seminars, speeches, cocktail parties, and dinners. Gerrity, at Geneen's behest, was a top-down lobbyist—never go to the second man when you can go to the first. He had stuck out his neck for the company during the congressional hearings to ascertain ITT's role in Allende's fall in Chile. In fact, he was indicted for perjury, but the case was dismissed. So, in some ways, he felt he had paid his dues, and he probably also felt his advice should now be taken seriously.

Ned was particularly negative about Jack Guilfoyle, who had returned to the United States to run ITT telecommunications worldwide after having done a fine job running ITT Europe. Ned insisted that Jack could not handle the job and that he should go. Ned also argued that Cab Woodward was not a decision-maker and could not be entrusted with the financial affairs of the company. He attacked Howard Aibel as dishonest and disruptive, and Pete Thomas as potentially disloyal. He said Herb Knortz, ITT's executive vice president, board member, and comptroller, did not understand the business and in making a speech could clear a room more rapidly than anyone Ned knew. The only person he did not attack at the senior level was Jack Hanway. I read this all incredulously, since nothing that he had written about these executives was true. In fact, I knew it to be all to the contrary.

In the letter Ned stressed that he should be a closer confidant, that we must spend more time together away from the office at lunch discussing the company and what steps needed to be implemented. He explained that I urgently needed his advice and counsel, which I was not currently accepting. I reread the letter with dismay.

At the office, I called him in and said, "Ned, what do you expect me to do with this letter? You've run down everyone in the top management except Jack Hanway. You say that you want to help me more. Well, Ned, your job is public relations. You are not the personnel officer for the company."

Ned responded that he simply wanted to be a more significant factor, wanted to advise me more, wanted to be able to get away for lunch more to talk about these things. I said, "Ned, it is pretty hard to go off for lunch with you to talk about people that I have put into significant positions in this company. That is really not my role, nor is it yours."

"All right," he said, "if that is the way you want it." And he huffed off in a characteristic hunched-over walk. Well, so be it, I thought—another maneuver by Ned. That's over with, and now we will go on with business. That was the first letter.

In March Felix Rohatyn called to say that Harold Geneen had brought Jay Pritzker to meet him. Geneen felt they should know each other because of Jay's interest in leveraged buyouts.

Felix was puzzled. After Harold Geneen had left, Pritzker told Felix that he was in partnership with Phil Anschutz and was interested in several companies, including ITT. Felix told him that an attempt to take over ITT for a leveraged buyout would be insane, that the telecommunications part of the corporation would come apart, and that the deal would be spoiled by this likely event. Pritzker said that he was basically interested in something that would bring him a great deal of money in a short period. Felix responded that ITT was not a good answer, but that he would let me know of their conversation.

That again put me on notice that Pritzker, Seslowe and their partners had not abandoned their plans for taking ITT private. I subsequently reported the information to the ITT board. I was concerned about the Geneen relationship and asked Howard Aibel to check it out. Harold casually told Howard that Pritzker had wanted to meet Felix, and since he, Geneen, had had previous financial dealings with Pritzker, he felt it appropriate to make the introductions. "That was all there was to it, nothing sinister."

Shortly thereafter, Jessie and I and Ned and Kate Gerrity were off to Rome to attend the formal opening of the Roma, a large ITT Sheraton convention hotel midway between downtown Rome and the Leonardo da Vinci International Airport. The next day, we four were due to fly back to New York. After a morning meeting with the minister of communications, I returned to the hotel to find Ned, Kate, and Jessie waiting for me in the lobby so we could go immediately to the airport. Ned was very pale, and Kate indicated he had not been feeling well. We boarded the company plane and headed home. Ned lay on the sofa most of the way, looking gray. I was worried about him and suggested that he see a doctor upon his return, which he did. He was told to lose some weight and slow down. Ned assured me that he would try, although I knew it would not be easy for him, especially with the 1984 annual meeting coming up, at which he and his crew always played a major role.

— 7 —

THE SECOND LETTER

Within three weeks of the 1984 annual meeting in Dallas, the storm hit. A metalworkers strike in West Germany began to affect not only all of ITT's automotive and components industries, but also our major telecommunications activities. One week later, in late May, the People's Republic of China announced that it was canceling all of its log purchases from Rayonier, causing a $40 million loss for that company in 1984. Then The Hartford's problems of heavy damage claims due to inclement weather worsened. Suddenly, our ability to meet the year's goals was becoming uncertain.

John Pfann, ITT's treasurer, recommended that we take steps to stanch the outgoing tide of money. From 1979 through 1984, we had sold off $2 billion worth of companies, but almost all of that revenue had gone to pay $450 million per year in dividends, not to improve the ITT balance sheet. In his memo, Pfann suggested several possible actions, including reducing the dividend.

ITT had never reduced its dividend. In fact, dividends had increased every year until the fall of 1983. Now the thought of a cut was a wrenching one. It might result in a big drop in our stock: This would cause disappointment among our shareholders; if a dividend cut was in the company's long-term interest, it had to be considered expeditiously.

On a hot summer day, June 18, my most trusted senior staff (except Cab Woodward, who was away on a family emergency) gathered at my New Jersey home to discuss the enormous implications of my proposal—to recommend to the board of directors a drastic cut in the common-stock dividend from $2.76 to $1.00 per share.

When I raised the issue with the assembled group, I was met by dead silence and anguished expressions. Ned Gerrity just sat quietly, ashen-faced. Even John Pfann, who perhaps best understood the issue, questioned whether such drastic action was needed. But our troubles were evident. The corporation was in a cash squeeze that appeared destined to worsen.

What we did not know was that Jay Pritzker and Phil Anschutz had begun buying ITT stock at $34 and $35 a share. Before our next board meeting, they would own about 125,000 shares of ITT stock, at an average price of around $32. Two months later when Jay Pritzker disclosed this to me, I realized that if they had purchased more than 5 percent (7 million shares) of our stock at those price levels before the dividend cut, they would have had no choice but to go after ITT immediately or to take large short-term losses. The timing of our dividend cut was inadvertently opportune for them in the short term, since they were able to acquire a great deal of cheaper stock to offset their earlier purchases. In the long run, their actions were probably favorable to ITT, since their subsequent purchases helped support the price of the shares and also made their total investment in ITT profitable. Clearly, they did not have an urgent financial need to attack.

Staff at our June meeting reached a consensus. For the remainder of the meeting, while we discussed the many ramifications of the dividend cut, Ned sat quietly next to Jack Hanway on a sofa, arms crossed, staring straight ahead as though thinking about something else, very deeply. We ended the meeting around three in the afternoon.

The next day, Jim Gallagher, a tough, young former reporter who worked in our public relations department under Ned and Juan Cappello, Ned's deputy, called to tell me that the *New York Times* was planning to run an article on ITT sometime in August. We had been alerted to it and had been told that the newspaper would want interviews. The timing was good. The dividend announcement would have been made by then, if the board approved it, and any impact should have dissipated.

I then went through the painstaking business of confidential meetings with outside directors, starting on June 22, with Michel David-Weill of Lazard Freres at my office in New York. Michel listened carefully and immediately responded in the affirmative. What pleased me most was that he felt it was right to make a big cut; do it once so it would not have to be done again.

On June 26, in Washington, D.C., I met with Margita White and Bette Anderson, who had become ITT directors a few years earlier, and explained my proposal to them, asking for their concurrence. Margita White had been high up in the Ford administration, and Bette

Anderson had been a senior official in the Treasury Department in the Carter administration. Both offered complete support.

Next was Bob Schoellhorn, a relatively new director, the chairman and chief executive of the very successful Abbott Laboratories. Bob recognized the pitfalls of what I proposed to do, but voiced his support. I followed this with a breakfast meeting with Terry Sanford, president of Duke University, at the Links Club in New York, and then met with Tom Keesee, Dick Perkins, and Bill Elfers together in my office. All four of those senior directors were in full support.

There was some deep concern, particularly on Dick Perkins's part, that I personally would be in for a rough time. One of my principal supporters, Dick, had been a director while the regal founder Sosthenes Behn was chairman, had worked to bring Harold Geneen to ITT, and had been instrumental in my succeeding Lyman Hamilton. That look of pain in his eyes should have been a warning that I was underestimating what was to come.

The last outside director I talked to was Al Friedman, who had signed on when he was an investment banker with Kuhn Loeb. Al had never seemed particularly supportive. When I talked to him, it was on the basis that the directors were unanimous in their support of the dividend reduction and that I wanted him to be a part of the unanimity. He raised all the obvious questions. I told him that Michel had said basically the same things but supported the action. He shrugged his shoulders and said, "Okay, but you are in for it," and hurried out of the office.

On July 10, a new director was slated to be elected at the board meeting—Lawrence Eagleburger, president of Kissinger Associates, former undersecretary of state and former U.S. ambassador to Yugoslavia. I had asked him to come to see me just before the board luncheon at which he would be introduced to the other members. I filled him in on the proposed dividend cut, and he agreed to support me.

These meetings with the directors took place within the context of a growing danger. The afternoon I returned from Washington after speaking with Margita White and Bette Anderson, I had called Ned Gerrity to my office and told him of my dissatisfaction with our overall public relations program, and in particular with our contributions program. I was concerned about the upcoming *New York Times* article; the Times had not done a complimentary piece about ITT in years.

Fortune and *Business Week* were constantly critical and seemed to think that the ITT public relations department tried to manipulate them and tried to control news of ITT. Furthermore, we were not managing our contributions to provide the most socially responsible positions or the greatest public returns for ITT. Ned was visibly agitated. I said we should be much more cooperative with the press, allow more access to our management without the presence of the public relations staff, and substantially revamp our contributions program.

It did not occur to me then, but, in retrospect, I should have understood that the ITT contributions program was a power base for anyone occupying Gerrity's position. The date was June 26, and after that, a series of curious events occurred.

On June 28, a return call came from Leslie Wayne to Jim Gallagher, in Gerrity's department. Leslie was the *New York Times* writer assigned to the August story on ITT. Jim asked her what was going on, why had she called Bill Elfers, our director. She told Jim that she had a new deadline—Sunday, July 1. She had wanted some comments from Elfers, but he had said he did not comment about a company that he served as a director. He told her he would be happy to talk about his own venture capital company, but not about ITT.

Jim said, "I know. Bill Elfers immediately notified me about the call, and that's why I called you to find out what was going on. Your article was not supposed to appear until August." She replied, "They were going ahead with it right away." She had largely prepared it, and she said she would be glad to talk to the chief executive officer.

I was in Florida making a speech to our Abbey Life Insurance salesmen from the United Kingdom at their annual convention in Boca Raton, and would be there through Friday. Leslie told Jim that if I wanted to talk with her, it would have to be before Friday afternoon, when she would put the story to bed. Gallagher indicated that this was unfair. As an alternative, she agreed to hold a telephone interview with Cab Woodward on the afternoon of June 29.

The article, which indeed came out on Sunday, July 1, showed a negative sales curve and a generally favorable profit curve for the previous five years—information taken from the ITT annual report. Entitled "The Slumbering Giant," the article was featured with my picture on page 1 of the business section. In it were two quite damaging errors: One paragraph "revealed" that "Rand Araskog had an opportunity to sell ITT Rayonier for a very good price and turned it down." This was absolutely untrue. Second, it said that "Rand Araskog had refused to be interviewed for the article," which was also untrue.

The article dissected ITT. While it played up a high-life, corporate-style, jet-travel environment for the CEO, it stated that all was not well at the company. The article was disturbing, especially in view of the dividend question under review by the board members.

On July 2, a "second letter" arrived, dated June 27. It went to all outside directors at their homes; Dick Perkins took his copy to Jack Hanway immediately. Jack called me late that night and said he had a malicious poison-pen letter. He did not want to read it over the phone. "Who do you think wrote it, Jack?" I asked. "I don't want to say, Rand," he replied. "I want you to see it."

He had it sent to my home; I was stunned. It said the board had to get rid of Rand Araskog, going into great detail about why this should be done. But what hit the hardest was the last paragraph: "The Board of ITT must take a hard look at what's happening and why. In the end, it will be the Board who takes the blame if disaster hits ITT for it is the Board who decided on the present management and the Board who is turning its back on the problems being caused by mismanagement. You have an obligation to protect the shareholders and employees from possible shallow, face-saving moves that could adversely affect the corporation for years to come. It is time the Board took a hard look at what's happening with our society management and make decisions to stop the slide."

That expression, "You have an obligation to protect the shareholders and employees from possible shallow, face-saving moves," obviously came from someone attacking the proposal to cut the dividend. I got up after reading the letter and walked around and around, in near shock: The style of the letter was just like that of the "first letter."

Howard Aibel and Cab Woodward were equally convinced of its authorship. I decided I could not live with the continuing suspicion, so on July 9, just before a meeting of the ITT Management Policy Committee, the company's top management committee, I confronted Ned Gerrity in my office, saying, "Ned, a terrible letter has gone to the board. It attacks me in a most clever and vicious way." Then I added, "It reads just like the letter you sent me earlier this year, although now you have replaced Jack Guilfoyle with me."

Ned was white, perspiring. "I wouldn't write a letter like that. You know that. How can you think of me that way?" I replied, "Ned, it's the same style; it's the same format. It's the same theme, just the names are changed." Ned looked down, then he looked up at me—nervously, I thought—and said, "Does anyone else think I did it?" I said, "Three senior outside members of the board believe it must have been you."

Ned grew more pale, and the perspiration on his forehead had increased. He said, "I can't believe you'd ever think I would. I can't believe anyone would think I would. I love you. I love this corporation."

I waited a long time and then said, "Okay, Ned, let's put it behind us." But, I added, "Jack Hanway has a copy of the letter for you to read. You can come into the Management Policy Committee late."

He left my office and I walked into the Management Policy Committee meeting. I was astonished to see Ned come right in the other door. Jack Hanway followed a few seconds later. Ned had not bothered to go into Jack's office to see the letter. Jack, who wondered why Ned had not asked to see it, later said, "Rand, to see that letter should have been the most important thing in the world for Ned."

The next day, July 10, Larry Eagleburger and I left my office after our meeting on the dividend cut and went right to the board room, where the Executive Committee of outside directors would carry on an extensive discussion of the dividend reduction proposal. The vote of the entire board was scheduled for after lunch so that Michel David-Weill, who was in London, could be included in a conference vote on the dividend reduction. His strong "aye" came over the ocean just in advance of the other votes, and the motion carried unanimously.

If ITT management on the thirty-third floor had wondered what was delaying the directors' arrival for the board luncheon, they had suddenly had unfortunate excitement in their midst. Ned Gerrity, waiting with the others, had a heart attack. Dr. Jim Wittmer, the medical director, was summoned immediately and Ned was moved to the eleventh-floor clinic to await an ambulance. When the ITT directors arrived, Ned was being taken from the building. I was, of course, extremely shaken.

Ned had been under a doctor's care. I thought back to his illness on the plane on the return from Rome, and Dr. Wittmer gave me some details on his continuing medical problems. When Ned was in the hospital, I gave every assurance to Kate that we would do everything we could to assist her and the family. After the first three crucial days, Ned was recovering well and Kate was in good spirits. Those three days while he lay abed were among the busiest and high pressured of my life.

— 8 —

THE THIRD LETTER

When the New York market closed on Tuesday, July 10, 1984, ITT issued a press release on the dividend reduction. It was picked up by the Pacific Exchange: Our stock immediately went into a tailspin.

The next day, I was in Minneapolis attending a Dayton Hudson board meeting, but I was in constant touch with Howard Aibel and Cab Woodward. Our stock traded as low as 20⅞, with more than 9 million shares changing hands, knocking the entire market down some forty points and creating a near-record volume on the New York Stock Exchange. At 320 Park, there was fury in some of the phone calls from analysts and investors, large and small. The press was climbing all over our public relations department, where Juan Cappello was sitting in for the bedridden Ned Gerrity. To me, the overreaction of the market was incredible. Shareholders were dumping stock at large losses.

That Friday was the Hartford Fire Insurance board meeting—a hectic day. Telephone calls were coming in from investment bankers seeking participation with ITT, seeking to help, seeking to defend, offering information, seeking a position. The investment bankers were on the loose, saying that a Pritzker and Anschutz combination was buying in large amounts; that arbitrageurs were buying in all over the place. Names such as Icahn, Boesky, Jacobs, and Steinberg were thrown around. We received telephone calls from at least six investment banking houses offering to assist us.

I was in and out of the Hartford board meeting all day. After the meeting, Pete Thomas and I had a long conversation about things The Hartford could do to help itself and to help ITT overall—to participate in the defense of the corporation. He seconded the advice of John Gutfreund—stay with the program. I then talked with Howard Aibel

435

and Cab Woodward, and we agreed on a plan of action—Project Blue—
to be implemented while I was away in Europe.

To me, Project Blue was born for the purpose of keeping the blue-
and-white ITT flag flying over 320 Park Avenue. To Howard, it was "to
be prepared for something that came out of the blue." He had established an informal study group a few years earlier to explore the
corporation's options should it be subject to an unfriendly takeover
attempt. Those early precautions were now about to pay off.

Howard Aibel would lead Project Blue, with charter members
being Cab Woodward; Walter Diehl, associate general counsel; John
Navin, corporate secretary; Ralph Allen of our beleaguered investor
relations department; and Juan Cappello, sitting in for Ned Gerrity.
Howard would later add, on an ad hoc basis, representatives of outside
legal counsel and investment bankers.

That night, I flew to Rome to meet with Italian officials concerned
with ongoing discussions between FACE, ITT's large telecommunications company in Italy, and STET, the state-owned electronics company. My purpose was to protect the FACE market share in Italian
telecommunications.

While in Rome, I received the news that Pritzker and Anschutz
were still buying and that millions of shares were trading hands each
day. Juan Cappello called to say he had received a call from Jack
Anderson, the syndicated newspaper columnist, asking if I was on
vacation in Europe. Juan told Jack that I was on business in Italy, then a
few days in France, and then on to our Brussels headquarters for ITT's
European management meeting. It was very interesting to Juan, and of
course to me, that someone had tipped off Jack Anderson that I was in
Europe. And, most important, the tipster had erroneously, but perhaps
purposefully, indicated that I was on vacation. Anderson did not print
that gossip, which made me suspect that he did not trust his source.

We went from Rome to Sous-le-Vent, Michel David-Weill's estate at
Cap d'Antibes. We reviewed the situation: It was clear that we had a
whole new group of investors, that at least 25 million shares of our stock
had changed hands. Some of our long-term institutional investors
pulled out at a low price. I stayed in daily and sometimes hourly touch
with Michel and ITT headquarters in New York and Brussels.

The night I flew to Europe, largely negative letters from shareholders began to come in, criticizing ITT management in general and
me in particular. The "third letter," dated the day I left for Europe,
castigated the Board of Directors: "How could you have done what you

did and how could you support a man who headed for vacation right after cutting the dividend?"

It was incredible. I did not know it, but Jack Hanway had concluded, even at the time of the "second letter," that more than one person probably was involved in this. The new letter was briefer but equally devastating. I did not see it until my return from Europe. When I did, I was again stunned. I was no martyr, and I did not relish being burned at the stake.

ITT was about to enter something similar to a war. Arrayed before us was a variety of well-heeled, competent adversaries, and, as we would find out later, the playing field was downhill, in their favor. To make matters worse, there was trouble from within.

CONFRONTATION

The environment within the ITT headquarters building changed perceptibly in mid-July 1984. From a relaxed camaraderie among the senior staff people, a note of suspicion had crept into daily encounters. The outside assault on the corporation was almost palpable. Inside, rising tension stemmed from a sense that there was a mole within the organization—a double agent whose motives were not in the best interests of the company. As the summer wore on, an enervating and destructive mentality settled over beleaguered 320 Park Avenue.

We could have circled the wagons, but a defense was not likely to carry the battle. We had to take the fight to the enemy. Part of that offensive strategy was to explain our position to our European colleagues. Throughout the last two weeks of July 1984, I had hourly telephone communications between Europe and the United States. During my last few days in Europe, we held meetings with all of our principal European executives concerning the dividend cut. Key executives demonstrated a strong sense of loyalty to the company—extremely important because of the powerful position each one held in his own country. I took great personal strength from their positive attitudes and expressions, and returned to New York on July 26 with renewed confidence.

That confidence helped immeasurably when I walked into the twelfth-floor conference room the following morning to meet with our investment bankers and the Project Blue team. The tension in the room was electric. The looks on the faces of some of the most powerful people in New York mixed pity with excitement, mourning with anticipation. I smiled broadly at Felix Rohatyn's friendly face and said, "You all look pretty serious." Felix kindly said, "Rand, it's getting very rough out there!"

Everyone in the room—including our new counsel from Cravath, Swaine & Moore, Sam Butler, and Alan Stephenson, his partner—was extremely concerned about the company being in play. The purchases that Pritzker and Anschutz had made right up to the day we were meeting cast a heavy spell. Sam Butler did not say so then, but he thought I was a "dead man." Newspapers were heralding the takeover of ITT. Angry letters were still coming in from shareholders. We operated in a siege environment.

There was an animated, freewheeling discussion about how to handle the major shareholders. Clearly, the Goldman Sachs people— Jim Weinberg, Jeff Boisi, and two or three others were pleased at being added to the team with Lazard. While I was away, Cab Woodward and Ralph Allen had been absorbing the heat from the investment community, and Howard Aibel, Walter Diehl, and John Navin had been planning the company's defense with Sam Butler and Alan Stephenson.

ITT's meeting with the analysts from the financial community took place on July 31. Overall, it went well, considering the situation. Most of the analysts had been with us a long time. I told them we would be reducing executive personnel, that there would be no management bonuses, and that salaries would be frozen. That, perhaps, was what they most wanted to hear. Many of them were to reinstate their buy recommendations.

The meeting resulted in a great deal of press, more agitation about ITT, more interest in the company. The stock had come back up from $20 to around the $24 level. The Project Blue team was convinced that we were nevertheless in for a proxy fight.

At a defensive strategy session with Lazard and Goldman Sachs, Jon O'Herron of Lazard argued for a rising new small proxy house owned and run by one Don Carter, who frequently worked for raiders. Jon said the only time he had been involved in a losing proxy fight was when the Carter Organization was on the other side. Shortly thereafter, Howard Aibel and Walter Diehl interviewed Carter and hired him.

ITT's management day at the Conference Center in Bolton, Massachusetts, in early August was well attended. The sunny weather favored the ritual golf and tennis tournaments. Rich Bennett and Jim Lester were retiring, and after the outings we had an honorary dinner for them. Under the circumstances, morale was good and the meeting was upbeat.

The professionalism and confidence of the ITT management made me think that perhaps we should take on Jay Pritzker, head-on, before he had an opportunity to disrupt the current solidarity of ITT management. I was not certain then how to approach Pritzker in a manner that would not seem like a surrender. I began to believe that going directly to his headquarters was the most confident approach.

After we had been through our management sessions and board meetings, I called Jay Pritzker to confront him about his plans. I told him that I was planning to be in the Midwest and could drop by to see him in Chicago on August 10 if he wished.

He said, "Fine. I'm sorry I hadn't called first, but by all means come on out and we'll have lunch at our Hyatt Hotel in downtown Chicago." We agreed to meet at 12:30.

The tower suite at the Hyatt in downtown Chicago is indeed impressive, as was the ultra-courteous and attractive staff. Jay was not there yet. That day, there was an ITT story in the New York Times, which was conveniently placed on a sofa for me to read. Interestingly, there was also a story about Braniff Airlines and the problems that Jay Pritzker was having with his investment. He arrived a little late, and I suspect he was nearby and waiting to give me time to see the articles. He was friendly, with a quiet voice, and youthful for age sixty.

"Things have been pretty rough for you, haven't they? You know, we started buying the stock before the dividend cut, but not much, about 130,000 shares. We have an awful lot now. We've got 4.2 million shares, and we're in it to make some money, not as long-term investors. We think the stock is going to be put in play. We want to enjoy the ride up. Now there are several things I want to cover with you, Rand. First of all, the leveraged buyout."

I said, "Absolutely not. You brought that up before. We said no then and we say no now. I gather Seslowe is your man?" He answered, "Yes, Seslowe is my man." I countered, "You are getting bad advice."

He said, "Then how about this? You buy Hyatt from us for up to about 18 percent of your stock, so you don't need shareholder approval. Then you give us options to buy another 12 percent. In effect, we'll protect you with our 30 percent because you're going to be put in play."

I answered, "Well, I don't think so much of the idea, but I'll bring it to the attention of the board at our September meeting. But you must guarantee no more stock purchases." Surprisingly, he agreed. As I was about to leave, he said, "Say, I'd like you to talk to Phil Anschutz. I'll introduce you to him on the phone." He put in the call to Denver.

After some pleasantries, Anschutz asked me, "How did your meeting go?" "I came in here extremely negative. I am approaching neutral. Jay said you are not going to start a proxy battle or create problems but that you are in it to make some money, and I understand that. If someone else starts a fight, you'd like to join in and make some money on the other side. So, I think we should meet the next time you are in New York."

That was the end of the conversation, and, despite the invitation, I never met Phil Anschutz until after he had sold his ITT stock more than a year later. In retrospect, the day I had spent with Jay Pritzker at West Point in 1982 probably provided the basis for his agreeing to stop buying shares. No doubt he believed that I would try to work something out with him. He should have kept buying; the odds were entirely with him.

On reflection, the visit with Pritzker was both the low point and the high point in the war for ITT. Had Pritzker and Anschutz marshaled their forces and acted with alacrity, they might have won. Certainly they had the financial resources to accomplish their goals. But they were too indecisive, too cautious to launch the final assault. With ITT's stock selling in the low 20s, they had a chance for the gold ring and missed it. In fact, that visit may have saved ITT.

For the rest of August, leading up to our board meetings in September, we watched the stock hourly. Ralph Allen continued to compile letters—almost all negative—from shareholders. We were responding to all of them, putting their names on a list available only to members of Project Blue. Ned Gerrity had returned to work and took the place of Juan Cappello.

On the morning of September 10, I advised the Management Policy Committee of my reactions to Pritzker's proposals. We were recommending no interest to the board in the purchase of the Hyatt chain for 18 to 30 percent of ITT stock. Our Sheraton people felt that Hyatt was not doing as well as it had in prior periods. Moreover, there would be antitrust problems between the two hotel chains. So I told the board on September 11 that we had given careful consideration to Pritzker's suggestions and found them completely unacceptable.

The board agreed and totally rejected the idea as a form of attempted greenmail. Larry Eagleburger amused the directors by announcing that he had thought the business world would be boring after his time in the State Department. He said ITT's environment was making the State Department seem like a playground.

The day following the board meeting, I called Jay Pritzker and advised him of the board's decision. He countered by saying, "Well, then, I guess we are free to go ahead with our program."

"Jay, I don't know that I understand completely what that means. I think you are getting bad advice. ITT is a very delicate and complicated company. I think you'd be sorry to get yourself involved in the wrong way."

And he asked, "By bad advice, you mean from Seslowe?"

"Yes."

Jay was quiet and then said, "If you won't buy Hyatt, will you sell Sheraton to me?" He seemed to be backing down. I responded, "No, Sheraton is a basic part of our overall strategy. Everywhere we have major telecommunications or industrial companies, we have hotels. Our company is an integrated whole."

Jay rejoined, "I think I understand that." But he added, "Then if you ever do decide to sell, would you be sure to let us know?"

"Yes, we will," I replied. He said, "Well, all right, thank you." And that ended the conversation.

It seemed clear that Pritzker, for whatever reason—the fact that Harold Geneen would not cooperate with him, the fact that Salomon Brothers and Lazard were discouraging him, perhaps restrained by Anschutz—was diffidently standing on one foot and then the other, giving us the time we desperately needed to repair our fences with old and new investors. We continued to be utterly vulnerable, ready to fight, but without reserve forces. The quiet on the front lines prevailed.

During the first week of October, another fortuitous event occurred. I received a call from an investment banker from a small New York brokerage house, who then came to my office to advise me: "The vultures are flying over ITT again." Rumor had it that Pritzker and Anschutz had placed larger orders for additional stock in ITT, beyond the 4.2 million shares that we knew they had.

We checked and found that a large brokerage firm had probably received orders in very large volume for 100,000 share blocks of stock at up to $26¼ per share—which was very close to our stock price at the time—and that the orders probably came from Pritzker and Anschutz.

On Monday, October 8, a day prior to our board meeting, I called Jay Pritzker, who was vacationing in Barbados. I told him that an investment banker had advised me that the vultures were flying over ITT, and that those vultures were Pritzker and Anschutz. That was insulting on two counts—insulting for Pritzker and Anschutz to be called vultures, and insulting to ITT to be designated as carrion. I reported that I had insisted to this banker that the rumor was non-sense; that I was a friend of Jay Pritzker's; that there was no indication

of any animosity or aggressive takeover interest on his or Phil Anschutz's part.

Jay Pritzker immediately said, "I don't know what Phil Anschutz has
done." He stammered a little bit. "I didn't think any more stock had
been purchased." He indicated they had not attacked ITT management, nor had they expressed disagreement with it; they were simply
large stockholders. He reiterated that they were interested in making
money, and that they still thought the stock would be put into play, but
that they were not going to do it. I said I felt that as a friend I could
advise him that we should not be put in the position of having to declare
him an unwanted investor. Furthermore, I suggested that he not buy
more stock unless he was ready to declare support openly.

I went on: "You told me before that you would not be buying
additional stock, and if you are, I think you should let the world know if
you really are friendly. Otherwise, I am going to let the board know at
our meeting that you are an unfriendly investor and so advise the
public."

He insisted, "That is not the case." He seemed to be withdrawing.
We talked a bit more, exchanging pleasantries, and then I went back to
my meeting. Late that afternoon, we learned that the large orders for
additional shares at up to $26¼ probably had been canceled. Whether
or not that cancellation was directly related to my call to Jay Pritzker, I
did not know, but I believe it was.

We now seemed to have Pritzker and Anschutz off balance. Whatever their game plan, they were not executing it. We probably were
benefiting from their compelling desire to be white knights, not black
ones. To me there was no difference. On October 9, on my recommen-
dation, the board elected Ned Gerrity an executive vice president of
ITT. He was given that role ostensibly so that he could work more on
government matters and prepare Juan Cappello to be his eventual
replacement. In reality, it was a last-ditch effort to save Ned from
himself.

Ned was moved to the twelfth-floor executive office, out of his lair
on the thirty-third floor at 320 Park Avenue. The move would isolate
Ned more from his staff, give Juan a chance to take control of the ITT
press relations, and allow us to keep better tabs on the media.

ITT top management spent the second week of October at the ITT
Conference Center at Bolton, Massachusetts, reviewing the company's
technology and its future programs. At that time, I felt management
was becoming uneasy. Howard Aibel was calm, as usual, but I sensed

he was expecting another shoe to drop from some new quarter. It was again too quiet. We all sensed danger. I reflected on the last time I had been at the center, in August, one week following our management meeting, remembering a *Boston Globe* article done by Bob Metz, which was highly critical of the current management of ITT and which Howard and Juan Cappello felt had been planted.

— IO —

MORE LETTERS

W

e held a Project Blue meeting in our ITT conference room on October 17. In the midst of the proceedings, Ned Gerrity suddenly announced, "Someone is coming after us!" I asked, "Who?" He answered, "I don't know, but someone is coming after the company."

I asked him, "Who said so?" He responded, "I can't tell, but I heard it at the Westchester Country Club, and I'm sure it is true." I said, "What do you mean you can't tell us who told you?" Ned rejoined, "I promised him I wouldn't say."

We then entered into a distasteful conversation. I said, "ITT is at stake and you refuse to divulge the source of information that could be crucial to us?" He said he was sorry but that was the case.

Everyone was incredulous. A few minutes later, the meeting broke up. Shortly afterward, both Cab Woodward and Howard Aibel came to my office to express their dismay and surprise at Ned's attitude. Cab and I concluded that Pritzker and Anschutz may have found someone to front for them. We had heard the names of Irwin Jacobs and Carl Icahn, but as yet had no direct evidence of their involvement.

A little more than a week later, on October 26, the "fourth letter" was posted to board members. This letter, for the first time, was not anonymous. It was signed, "Chauncey Waddell." Also enclosed was a copy of a brief article from the *New York Post* attacking not only me, but also Bill Araskog, my son, as an employee of Lazard Freres. We soon discovered that Chauncey Waddell was no longer living, but he had had his investment offices at 437 Madison Avenue, where, curiously, ITT maintained offices and our large, top-floor meeting room.

On October 30, an ad appeared on the front page of the *New York Times* noting my fifty-third birthday. At 8:00 a.m., I received a call from Ned Gerrity telling me to be sure to look at that ad, which he and associates in the advertising department had put there. It seemed to be a gesture of friendship. That same night, my son, Bill, told me that Ned had called him that day to tell him not to worry about the *New York Post* article. Bill wondered why Ned had called his attention to the article — he was a bond trader at Lazard, not a merger-and-acquisition man.

We had been expecting shareholder proposals for inclusion in proxy material to be mailed two months prior to the annual meeting scheduled for May 1985. The deadline for such proposals was November 28, 1984. At the November board meeting, when the "Chauncey Waddell" letter was discussed, we also remarked that no company-threatening shareholder proposals were slated to be included in our proxy statement.

On November 26, I was scheduled to go to Europe for a week. Bob Metz, then on Financial News Network, called me, not the public relations department, about shareholder proposals urging dissolution/liquidation of the company. Did ITT have any comment? Within the hour a shareholder proposal arrived, calling for the liquidation of ITT. It was a form letter signed by a William Brinker. Another letter came in before I caught my flight. While I was away, three more form letters arrived from dissident shareholders on the Project Blue confidential list. Obviously, the press had been tipped off. In addition to FNN, we received inquiries that week from the *New York Times*, the *Daily News*, *Wall Street Journal*, and *Fortune*. Our response to the media was that we were not required to include this proposal in our proxy statement, because it, and the others, were technically deficient: The shareholders had not included the statement that they intended to be present at the annual meeting to make the proposal.

At that time, I did not know that Jay Pritzker's envoy, Jerry Seslowe, had been the originator of all the shareholder letters calling for the liquidation of ITT. Seslowe, Pritzker, and Anschutz had not held ITT's stock long enough, a minimum of one year, to be qualified to submit shareholder proposals themselves.

On December 4, we got a major break. Juan Cappello gave Jack Hanway documents that had been sent to Juan's home on the weekend by Bob Berrellez, a former ITT public relations executive who had been indicted with Ned Gerrity in the Chile affair. Juan had struggled with himself for forty-eight hours before turning over the documents, which implicated senior members of the ITT public relations department in a long-standing plot to destroy the company chairman and, perhaps, to put the company into play.

The documents indicated that Bill McHale, who ran ITT's regional public relations office in Florida, had requested Bob Berrellez, who had recently retired from ITT and lived in Los Angeles, to plant a long article in a West Coast newspaper that was extremely detrimental to me and the company. The highly personal attack was several columns in length.

Bob Berrellez, the apparent pawn in the Chile accusations, was solicited by Bill McHale to be a pawn again. McHale assured him that the anti-Araskog action was led by Ned Gerrity. This time, Bob's respect for Ned's deputy, Juan Cappello, and his basic allegiance to ITT kept him from joining the group. So he broke the chain and divulged the information to Juan.

A "fifth letter," signed by one Raymond Case, had been mailed on December 3 to board members. It contained essentially the same information as the press release that Berrellez had refused to plant. On Wednesday, December 5, Jack Hanway advised me of the existence of this evidence and showed me the principal documents. Jack had indeed been right that more than one person had been involved. Investigators and lawyers were already on the way to the West Coast to interview Berrellez and Florida to interview McHale.

That same day, I hosted a luncheon for Renato Altissimo, Italian Minister of Industry, who had once sold ITT a company bearing his father's name. During the pre-luncheon cocktails, Ned Gerrity put his arm around me and said, "It is going to be a good Christmas and a good year, and we are going to do just fine." Deep inside, I shuddered.

Later that same afternoon at a meeting with several Project Blue members, Ned indicated he had information that someone was buying heavily into ITT stock with takeover intentions. He provided no background. In view of the tragic news I now had, I did not press him for details. In fact, Irwin Jacobs was beginning to move on our stock, but we did not realize it until a day later when the news became public.

That same morning, Bill McHale was confronted in Florida and refused to talk, but the tape of the damaging press release was still in his IBM typewriter. He was fired for cause. Ned Gerrity was confronted in his office with the evidence by Jack Hanway and Howard Aibel. He denied any involvement. Nevertheless, he was suspended as an officer of ITT. Although I was in my office, and Ned knew it, he left 320 Park immediately, and I have not talked to him since. In January 1985 he formally retired from the corporation.

Perhaps the plot's most revealing evidence was that Jerry Seslowe had solicited proxy proposals through anonymous letters that he sent to a relatively large number of shareholders: All of them had previously written to ITT to complain of the dividend cut, and all of their names were on the secret Project Blue list.

In the rush of events, I had not had much time to reflect on Ned Gerrity's actions. My concern was always somewhat subliminal—I never wanted to believe what I knew. Suddenly a huge incubus was dispelled, and great relief settled over me. Nevertheless, it was a mixed blessing. Gerrity had been my friend, my mentor in my early days with the company. It was he who kept my name and activities within the purview of Harold Geneen. On one hand I felt I owed him, but on the other hand I felt that he owed loyalty to me and the company.

That December was probably the most anxious period in the history of ITT, and I felt that the roller coaster would never cease. No sooner had we resolved the McHale/Gerrity problem than we were faced with a powerful new threat.

On December 5 and 6, Irwin Jacobs made extensive ITT stock purchases. (He had acquired something of a reputation by salvaging assignments from flood insurers and other damaged goods—hence his nickname, "Irv the liquidator.") At the time, it was far from clear what trouble he could make. His original purchases came to light only because of the mishandling of one of his orders on December 6.

The next morning, Howard Aibel called the Securities and Exchange Commission (SEC) to brief them on events surrounding ITT. They wanted to see him that day. In fact, they had been about to call him. So Howard Aibel went down to the SEC and filled them in on everything we knew: the raiders' activities; the anonymous letters; the price swings in the stock; the liquidation proposal; the leaks to the press. It took the SEC a month to digest the incredible tale before it acted.

On January 11, 1985, the Securities and Exchange Commission began to take depositions, the first from one of the shareholders urged by Jerry Seslowe to submit an ITT liquidation proposal. I inwardly hoped it was the beginning of the unwinding of a dangerous network.

On January 7 and 8, we held our board meeting at the ITT Research Center in Shelton, Connecticut. During the board's Capital Committee meeting, ITT's divestiture of twelve industrial-products companies was approved, companies valued by ITT at $300 million to $375 million. The board also approved the sale of 50 percent of Abbey Life Insurance Company in the United Kingdom, and of ITT Publishing, Eason Oil Company, and ITT Grinnell, a total package worth $1.7 billion in cash to ITT.

Our investment bankers had strongly urged a press release on this divestiture program to counter Jacobs's thunderings and the shareholder letters. At first, I resisted, but finally I drafted a release summarizing the divestiture program, scheduled to be completed in eighteen months. The announcement went out on January 16, accidentally coincident with the day Irwin Jacobs began his next charge. He lamely remarked that our program was "too little and too late."

II

IRWIN'S CHARGE

We had done a great deal of research on Irwin Jacobs since December 6. Don Carter, head of our lead proxy firm, had worked for him in earlier takeover attempts and knew him well. If I was proud of my Minnesota farm upbringing, Irwin was equally proud of his father's burlap-bag or gunny-sack collection efforts in the same state. I could even imagine Irwin's father having called on mine in an old truck to pick up gunny sacks.

The record showed that only one CEO had driven off Jacobs. It was not completely clear whether Martin Davis of Gulf + Western had accomplished this feat by a stock repurchase plan (which may have enabled Jacobs to get out with a profit) or whether Davis had called Jacobs from his headquarters in New York, and told Jacobs to get away from Gulf + Western or "he'd be sorry." I tend to believe the latter.

On January 16, Irwin Jacobs called Don Carter from Minneapolis and offered him a million dollars to help launch a proxy fight against ITT. Jacobs said that he had gone above the 5 percent level of stock ownership and would be filing a Schedule 13D, a disclosure form required by the SEC. Don Carter told Jacobs that the Carter Organization had already been retained by ITT. Irwin Jacobs repeated the million-dollar offer, Carter refused it, and Jacobs then stated, "You know this is the end of our relationship."

I doubt Carter believed any relationship had ended. Jacobs was too practical to carry an unnecessary and impractical grudge.

The news did increase activity on the twelfth floor and the nineteenth floor (the legal department) at 320 Park Avenue. The next day, Sam Butler, our attorney from Cravath, Swaine, was called by Steve Jacobs, an attorney for Irwin Jacobs. Steve Jacobs indicated Irwin was interested in buying certain companies we were selling. When Sam asked whether Jacobs was thinking of paying in cash or in stock, he was told that Jacobs was prepared to pay cash but could use stock if that proved to be mutually advantageous. Irwin Jacobs also wanted to know whether we were interested in purchasing back the ITT stock he held. With the combination of our divestiture program and Pritzker and Gerrity sidelined, Jacobs seemed to be more conciliatory.

On Monday, January 21, top management had a meeting with Felix Rohatyn to discuss the approach made by Jacobs, and a second meeting on Wednesday with Rohatyn and Jeff Boisi of Goldman Sachs. We concluded that Howard Aibel should call Irwin Jacobs's attorney and let him know that we were not interested in selling companies for stock or buying back the stock. On the other hand, Howard could tell him that our investment bankers would provide data on ITT companies that we were prepared to sell. The attorney Howard talked to was a Mr. Lang.

Shortly thereafter, Rohatyn received a call from Lang, who indicated that Irwin Jacobs would like to receive information on O.M. Scott & Sons, our lawn-and-garden company. Arrangements were made for material to be provided. Steve Jacobs then called Howard Aibel to suggest that perhaps ITT would like to buy Jacobs's holdings of ITT stock according to a complicated formula that would produce proceeds far in excess of market value. Subsequently, Jacobs turned down O.M. Scott.

On Thursday of that same week, a man who would not identify himself—except to say that he was a securities dealer named Flynn—called John Navin, our corporate secretary, to say that Irwin Jacobs had control of 15 percent of ITT stock and had not filed a Schedule 13D. He indicated which brokerage firms held the stock—Jefferies & Company; Stephens & Co; Bear, Stearns; and a small house in New York. He would give us nothing further, and said that he would not be calling the SEC.

Carter checked out the stock and confirmed Flynn's information. There was no way of being sure that this stock was all under the control of Irwin Jacobs, but it could have been. However, almost ten days had elapsed since Irwin Jacobs had told Don Carter he had gone through 5 percent, and no 13D had been filed with the SEC.

Jacobs seemed to have launched a last-ditch attempt, perhaps even including "Flynn's" call, to get us to buy him out. Howard Aibel felt the same—that Jacobs did not have enough ITT shares to file a 13D. After all, that would have amounted to 7 million shares, with a value of a quarter of a billion dollars: no small sum. But neither had he sold out, nor had the Pritzker-Anschutz interests, so the main battle simply may have been put off for another day. On the other hand, I suspected that Irwin Jacobs had entered into an investment maze far more complicated than he had envisaged in December 1984, when he exploded into our stock, and now he was anxious to get out and to get his friends out with him. Howard Aibel called Steve Jacobs and turned down his stock-buyback proposal.

On January 25, I went to Washington to see Bud McFarlane, the national security adviser, to discuss ITT's performance on critical Department of Defense programs, particularly in regard to the hot line to Moscow and the secure telephones used by the White House and other key agencies in Washington. The next evening, I attended the Alfalfa Club dinner with Michael Blumenthal, former secretary of the Treasury under Jimmy Carter and now chairman of the Burroughs Corporation. He had also invited Bill Spoor of Pillsbury and Jim Wolfensohn, an investment adviser from New York. That dinner with Mike Blumenthal signaled the friendly termination of a merger discussion that had begun more than two months earlier between the Burroughs Corporation and ITT. Those discussions had proceeded in parallel with the large Jacobs stock purchases, the shareholder letters, the Pritzker misfortune, and the Gerrity downfall. I could not have handled anything more.

Prior to joining Mike for dinner, I read in the *New York Times* that Jacobs had made multimillion-share purchases in the stock of Phillips Petroleum, which was also under pressure from Boone Pickens of Mesa Petroleum in Texas. I thought Jacobs must have accumulated tremendous financial power to be involved in Avco, ITT, Phillips Petroleum, Castle & Cooke, Pioneer, and Tidewater—all at the same time. This man certainly could, with his associates, make a move on the huge fortress of ITT.

I reflected on the incredible leverage that junk bonds had allowed people like Jacobs, avoiding margin requirements. I thought back to the man who had had a reverse kind of leverage and power in the 1960s and early 1970s, Harold S. Geneen. Recently rumors had persisted that Ken Miller at Merrill Lynch was trying to get Geneen involved in an ITT liquidation effort—on the grounds that he had put the company together, and could do the best job of taking it apart.

Harold Geneen had been quoted in *Fortune* magazine as saying that ITT was worth $100 a share, and, of course, with the stock then trading at around $26 a share, the difference was sensational. Salomon Brothers had said our stock was worth $60 to $80 a share on a breakup basis.

And breakup was all too conceivable. ITT was fragile due to its $10 billion of overseas assets. The French had forced the sale of our remaining French telephone equipment manufacturing company, grabbing a property worth between $275 million and $375 million for a paltry $32 million. In England, the company was informed, in a gentlemanly fashion, mind you, that it would be nice if ITT sold a majority of its subsidiary, Standard Telephones and Cables (STC). We were given to understand that the future of STC would be in doubt unless we did so. STC was then almost entirely dependent upon British government orders for telecommunications equipment. Brazil was not even polite: They told us to whom to sell our subsidiary, for "one cruzeiro" and an additional amount to be paid out of future dividends, which never materialized. In Spain, officials also threatened the government orders, while burdening the company with enormous social benefit programs for the work force. Thus, the foreign exposure of the telecommunications sector due to legal and extralegal actions left ITT extremely vulnerable, but really not all that attractive to a knowledgeable liquidator.

Moreover, we knew that telecommunications could not stand alone with System 12 in its late phases of development, and that the casualty insurance business should not stand alone in the serious down business cycle. Overall, the company had integrated its investments in research and development, capital, and cash-flow support in ways that defied successful breakup of the company except under the best economic circumstances for its major business interests.

With the end of the Burroughs merger talks, our exposure was still of paramount concern. Our investment bankers continually suggested white-knight merger possibilities, while the Board of Directors considered a number of corporate restructuring possibilities to thwart the raiders. Poison-pill warrants, additional debt, and different classes of stock were all suggested, but never implemented. Larry Eagleburger commented that since he had joined the ITT board, the business community was outdoing government bureaucracy in the use of colorful euphemisms—greenmail, shark repellents, poison pills.

Two further merger candidates appeared—Wang Laboratories and Sperry. We had long considered an association with Sperry. Dick Bingham—once an employee of Kuhn Loeb, then a partner at Lehman Brothers, Kuhn Loeb, and finally the San Francisco managing partner of Shearson/Lehman—had been a close friend to ITT over the years. So when Dick called to ask if he could speak with Gerry Probst, the chairman and CEO of Sperry, about an ITT-Sperry merger possibility, I agreed.

We met at my apartment on Thursday afternoon, February 21. Dick brought Gerry as well as Vince McLean, Sperry's chief financial officer, and Joe Kroger, its executive vice president for computers. With me were Cab Woodward, Howard Aibel, Bob Smith, and Fred Gibbs. Bob Smith, our senior vice president for corporate development, was a shrewd, tough, and frequently abrasive planner and negotiator. He was also a Jekyll-and-Hyde figure. Socially, he was warm and friendly, with great one-line humor. In business, he was a bear—snarling, ridiculing, making biting comments and arrogant putdowns. But he was good; he knew what he wanted and usually got it, leaving behind bruised feelings and hurt egos.

Fred Gibbs was our computer, communications, technical expert. He had been with the Bell System, spent many years with ITT Telecommunications in Latin America, had run our communications service group, and managed our System 12 development. We relied on him for product evaluation and product fit.

We covered a lot of ground—Gerry and I alone in an adjoining room and then with the group in our library. The market price of ITT and Sperry bore a 1 to 1.3 ratio. ITT would be the survivor, I would be chairman and CEO, Probst would head the Executive Committee. When we finished, the Sperry people said they had to go off to see takeover lawyer Joe Flom, and I briefed Felix Rohatyn and Michel David-Weill. We had agreed to another meeting the next day, late afternoon, at Dick Bingham's suite at the Helmsley Palace.

Cab, Michel David-Weill, and I attended that meeting with Probst, McLean, and Kroger. Obviously Gerry had been given hard-line and not very practical advice by someone. Suddenly, they were insisting that ITT agree to at least a 2-to-1 share ratio, ITT to Sperry common stock. The companies made a good fit, but we could not agree on the ratios for exchanging shares. The Sperry people thought we were desperate for a deal due to the rumors in the marketplace, so they held out, insisting that Sperry was twice as valuable as ITT. We were vulnerable, but not desperate, so we called off the discussions. I thought it a touch ironic that Sperry and Burroughs merged to form Unisys shortly after our talks ended.

Dr. An Wang of Wang Labs showed great interest in a merger with his company—another excellent fit—with Wang Labs to be the surviving company. He offered a curious deal, trying to pass off a secondary class of stock that had limited voting powers. Clearly, it would not fly: Trying to introduce a share voting procedure and control from a company owned mainly by one person for an exchange of one class of shares in a widely held public company was virtually impossible. It would have taxed the persuasive powers of Lee Iacocca, and I knew I was no Iacocca at mesmerizing people.

Wang's grandiose proposal included a good deal of camouflage. We did not know it at the time, but his company was in a decline. Shortly after our conversations, Wang reported a precipitous drop in earnings, and his company's shares headed south with a vengeance.

Near the conclusion of these merger explorations, the pressure cooker popped safely, and ITT received a fantastic piece of good news. On March 25, 1985, the SEC finally ruled on the earlier shareholder liquidation proposals. We would not have to include them in our proxy material for the vote at the annual meeting. We were elated! But while we may have been out of the pressure cooker, we were still on the stove.

— 12 —

INTRIGUES

Georges Pebereau came to visit on April 11, 1985. Pebereau, then chairman of Compagnie Generale d'Electricite (CGE), the largest energy and electronics company in France, wished to meet privately before having lunch with me and others on a joint telecommunications project. This discussion was the first of twenty-two meetings between the two of us that would change each of our worlds and launch a new international telecommunications group.

At the private meeting, Pebereau told me that an American investment banker had tried to enlist him, together with Wisse Decker of Dutch Philips, Dr. Karlheinz Kaske of German Siemens, and Lord Weinstock of the British General Electric Company (GEC), to take over the telecommunications parts of a dismembered ITT in the event of a successful takeover campaign. Georges did not identify the parties involved, but he insisted that they had the money and capability to pick up the telecommunications portion of ITT. He had firmly declined to participate.

After Pebereau and his people had left, I talked with Howard Aibel about his disclosure. The idea of the ITT telecommunications breakup technique, the selection of the players, was too clever. I thought it had the markings of a former or current ITT insider working with Jerry Seslowe. We agreed that I should get help from Ken Corfield, the managing director of Standard Telephones and Cables, a company 35 percent owned by ITT.

I called Ken Corfield in London and asked him whether he would call Lord Weinstock and find out which U.S. investment banker was soliciting partners to cut up ITT Telecommunications. Ken called back half an hour later to say that Jerry Seslowe—Ken even spelled the name—had contacted Lord Weinstock to say there were four groups coming together: the Pritzkers; Irwin Jacobs; a Middle Eastern investment group; and a sleeper group. We knew almost certainly that the Middle East investment group was headed by an Egyptian who had previously shown interest in buying Sheraton and was a friend of Tom Pritzker, Jay's son. The sleeper could have been Walt Helmerich of Helmerich and Payne Oil Company, headquartered in Oklahoma. Walt's company had a million shares of ITT stock that had shown no appreciation, but Walt was a stated friend of mine. He would make an ideal popular leader for a takeover attempt or proxy fight.

Lord Weinstock cautioned that this group was potentially dangerous. Ken told him we would make every effort to protect him as the source of this information, but he added that we were in constant communication with the SEC on such matters. The next day, we made all of this information available to the SEC in letter form.

About the same time, Cab Woodward was called by a reporter in Minneapolis, who had been told by Irwin Jacobs that he, Jacobs, had been served with papers by the SEC asking for his files on ITT. Obviously Jacobs had fed the reporter a good deal of information. The next morning, the *Wall Street Journal* printed an article by Richard Gibson of Minneapolis and Janet Guyon of New York. The article implied that ITT had made some kind of complaint about Jacobs, who stated he was planning to speak at the ITT annual meeting. He said he represented several million shares and was concerned about the direction of the company.

In our view, the offer to speak at the annual meeting was a clever attempt to show the SEC and others how open he was being—a grandstand move that *Fortune* magazine swallowed. *Fortune* agreed to send a reporter if Jacobs would show up to speak. I was not looking forward to hearing more from the "mouth from Minneapolis," but was reconciled to his appearance.

It seemed clear that the two, three, or four groups that Seslowe had told Lord Weinstock about had engaged in extensive discussions. At some point, they could decide to come together and file a Schedule 13D. For the moment, they were acting as though the Pritzkers did not agree with Jacobs, except for their mutual dissatisfaction with the management of the company.

Preparations for the annual meeting were beginning—it was going to be newsworthy. The next important date prior to the meeting was Monday, April 22, when Moody's Investors Service would review our bond and commercial paper ratings. If ITT held its A rating, we would have taken a major step toward assuring the shareholders about the company's financial health.

Don Carter advised us that he had attended the so-called Pirates Party hosted by Drexel Burnham Lambert at the Beverly Hills Hotel. This annual party for raiders and junk-bond people had Diana Ross for entertainment and steak and lobster on the menu. There were special tables for the Pritzkers and Jacobs. Jack Stevens was there; Icahn was there; even Harold Geneen was there. All were out there rallying one another—jokes about ITT by Jacobs; a lot of conversation about a tender offer for another 20 to 30 percent of ITT by the Jacobs and Pritzker group. Carter warned us, saying, "It's ninety-five to five that you are going to get a tender offer either before or after your annual meeting for at least another 20 percent of the stock." Carter felt it was likely the offer would occur prior to the annual meeting so they could use the meeting to push their program, even though they had lost on their SEC-rejected shareholder proposal.

Then, the SEC's investigation seemed to accelerate; the Pritzkers began disavowing Jacobs and Jacobs disavowing the Pritzkers. Seslowe was talking to the newspapers about conversations with ITT. Jacobs was plugging his activities to the press. Obviously, they felt that by putting out information themselves, they could weaken any claim of conspiracy.

On Thursday, April 18, Cab Woodward and I had lunch with Fred Joseph, the chief operating officer of Drexel Burnham, who was about to become its CEO. He was the man basically responsible for establishing Drexel Burnham's near-monopoly in junk-bond investments for hostile takeovers. In Drexel's stable of a hundred investors were Carl Icahn, Ivan Boesky, Irwin Jacobs, Carl Lindner, and Saul Steinberg— people who could be expected to put up seed money in front of the junk bonds.

ITT, through the Sheraton Corporation, had commissioned Drexel Burnham several months earlier to develop a creative investment technique for building new hotels. ITT would convert several of its existing hotels into a $^{40}\!/\!_{60}$ ownership with Drexel Burnham, a partnership that would continue to build new hotels in the United States as ITT's equity in existing hotels was progressively reduced. As a result of Sheraton's relationship with Drexel Burnham, ITT established a relationship with the firm as well.

In addition, the man whose firm owned between 28 and 36 percent of Drexel Burnham, a prominent Belgian, Albert Frere, was negotiating with me for the purchase by his Bruxelles Lambert Group of about 25 percent of ITT's Bell Telephone Manufacturing (BTM) in Belgium. Because of this association, of which Fred Joseph was well aware, it seemed very unlikely to us that Drexel Burnham would try to assist any raider in a takeover of ITT.

The upshot of the meeting was that Drexel Burnham and Fred Joseph would prefer to have a normal financing and banking business with ITT rather than be involved in the junk-bond financing of a raider attempt to take the company. ITT was now doing business with all the major investment banking houses.

During our six-hour meeting with Moody's on ITT's debt ratings, we were grilled rigorously. My adrenaline was running particularly high in my two-hour presentation as lead-off speaker. Following me were Pete Thomas; Edmund M. Carpenter, executive vice president for industrial technology; and Cab Woodward. The Moody's people were far more friendly at the end of the meeting. It was also clear that they had all but made a decision to downgrade our rating. The good news was that they would not revise our rating prior to our annual meeting, only three weeks away.

In another critical step to shore up our defenses, we touched base with all of our important bankers. Cab and I met with Walter Shipley at Chemical Bank to reaffirm our relationship. Shipley made a strong statement that Chemical's board and management had adopted a firm policy not to participate in the financing of an unfriendly takeover of a client company.

ITT had significant banking relationships with Chase Manhattan, Manufacturers Hanover, Citibank, Chemical, Bankers Trust, Bank of New York, BankAmerica, Morgan Guaranty, and Irving Trust, as well as banks throughout Europe from Midland Bank in England to Deutsche Bank in the Federal Republic of Germany. We counted on our strong long-term relationships to help ensure that these banks would not support a raider organization against ITT.

The annual meeting on May 15, in Savannah, Georgia, featured the perpetual corporate gadflies, Evelyn Y. Davis and Lewis Gilbert, plus Irwin Jacobs. We later found out that two representatives were there for Pritzker and Anschutz, as well as reporters from much of the business press.

Prior to the meeting, we had a "family" dinner with the ITT directors and the Helmerichs and the Weinmanns. The latter two families had sold us Eason Oil, and each had a million shares of our stock. They had joined us in years past for these director dinners. In the course of the evening, Walt Helmerich told me that he had been contacted on numerous occasions by people purportedly representing Jacobs and Pritzker to get him to lead a move against ITT. Walt would not do that, he said, because of his confidence in the company and because of his friendship with me.

That evening I told Walt I had just learned that Pritzker and Anschutz had voted their stock against management. It originally had been voted by their broker/representatives with management, but they were now changing their votes. Their votes would be fairly obvious because the vast majority, something like 116 million out of 128 million shares accounted for, were being cast for management. I told Walt I felt they were being foolish, but so be it—the fat was in the fire.

At the annual meeting, Irwin Jacobs was sitting in about the tenth row with his attorney. Evelyn Y. Davis and Lewis Gilbert were seated right across from him. I gave a fairly long "state of the union" message, and then Gilbert and Davis traded tracks to the microphones. Jacobs obviously was getting antsy. Suddenly, he jumped up to grab a microphone, but Mrs. Davis got there at the same time and said, "Ladies first." Irwin shrugged and sat down, and I remarked, "Mr. Jacobs, now you know what I have to put up with." The room exploded in laughter, and I knew then I had him—and so did his lawyer.

Lewis Gilbert attacked Jacobs as a poor manager. I had never before appreciated Gilbert's and Davis's presence at annual meetings, but now they acted like my picadores. Jacobs finally bulled up to the microphone, said he would probably need more than the allotted five minutes, but hoped he would be forgiven. He plodded, sometimes losing his place, through a long, handwritten speech. When he finally sat down, I thought I saw two ITT managers—absentmindedly, I hope— applauding.

Jacobs got nowhere. Later, he tried to become argumentative, but I heard his lawyer tell him to sit down. He turned and snarled at him that he was going to make his point. He never did. Jacobs seemed nervous and agitated and finally wandered off to trivial matters about whether I had made certain statements to *Business Week*, the character of the statement, and the time of the statement—all rather pointless.

Evelyn Y. Davis asked whether Pritzker and Anschutz had demanded greenmail. I remember Jay's 1984 offer of Hyatt Hotels for 18 percent of ITT and options for 12 percent more. At the time, it certainly seemed like a form of greenmail. I responded, "No comment."

Near the end of the balloting, Howard Aibel informed me that the Pritzker/Anschutz votes were being changed in favor of management. The final count showed an overwhelming majority for management: 116 million out of 128 million votes, one of the largest responses by our shareholders, with about 88 percent of the shares voted.

Afterward, directors and management had a luncheon. Walt Helmerich told me that he had stepped out of the annual meeting to call Jay Pritzker to tell Jay that he was making a mistake, that he would be standing alone, that the board was united, management was united — that he ought to vote with management. Pritzker had told Walt that he would talk to Anschutz; they apparently had two or three telephone conversations. Finally, Pritzker convinced Anschutz to vote with the company.

All of the vote changes apparently did not arrive before the deadline. At the time, I told Walt, "I appreciate what you did, but I certainly hope they don't feel there is any obligation on our part, because frankly, I don't care how they voted because of the overwhelming vote we had in our favor. The only thing I wouldn't have liked was the negative publicity." Walt Helmerich said he understood; he called them entirely on his own.

We then went to the meetings. So then ended the high drama of the ITT annual meeting of 1985 in Savannah, Georgia. ITT was coming out fighting — and now on the offensive.

THE COUNTERATTACK

Jay Pritzker was extremely upset. He had learned from his representatives at our annual meeting that I had responded, "No comment," to Evelyn Y. Davis's question of whether Pritzker and Anschutz had attempted to greenmail ITT. Walt Helmerich said he tried to explain to Pritzker that this was just an answer to get rid of the question, but Pritzker was adamant. They were insulted and wanted an apology. I indicated to Walt that I had been told by our attorneys that I should respond to any question regarding greenmail with "No comment." I went on to explain the whole background of the Pritzker/Anschutz relationship, including their original attempt to get us involved in a leveraged buyout, as well as their efforts to presell our telecommunications companies in Europe.

Seemingly shocked and dismayed, Walt said he would call Pritzker to tell him he had no interest in pursuing the matter further. Pritzker had asked him to come to see me with Anschutz to make an offer for ITT. He planned to tell him that that was purposeless and that he would not join in. I appreciated his position.

Shortly thereafter, Walt called again, saying Pritzker was ready to quit hounding ITT but he still felt insulted. Walt said: "Rand, I think you should call him."

I said, "Well, if you feel that is a good idea, I will check with my legal counsel, and if they say okay, I will do so. In general, I'm averse to the idea."

Howard Aibel talked to Sam Butler at Cravath. They agreed that I should call Pritzker, so I did. I told him that I was calling to thank him for changing his vote. He told me that they had only done it because they believed Walt Helmerich had called at my request. I made it clear that Walt did it on his own. Pritzker sounded somewhat taken aback by my aggressive attitude. He went on to make some indirect offers, such as saying that Hyatt people could be helpful with ITT telecommunications in Indonesia. I explained that since ITT had been in Indonesia a long time, we knew our way around pretty well, but that we would never refuse assistance if it was proper and effective. Then came the grabber. In a very low, whispered voice, which he adopted on these special occasions, he said, "We'd like to come in and talk to you about an offer for the company."

I replied, "Fine, but as I said at the annual meeting, it will have to be for a full price. And remember, it will have to treat all shareholders equally. By the way, don't come in with that price [$38 to $40] you tried to get Helmerich to join you with. That won't even begin to fly."

Pritzker responded that he would have to think about what to do, then went on to discuss the "greenmail insult."

I countered, "I answered that question that way to be rid of the subject matter. I am surprised that you would expect an apology, in view of the activities of Seslowe with his attempts to get an improperly solicited shareholder proposal calling for liquidation of the company into our proxy material. What's more, Seslowe has been running around Europe trying to find buyers for parts of ITT. You're a major shareholder of this company, supposedly a responsible businessman. How could you allow your name to be used in that fashion? You expect an apology from me? You've got to be crazy!"

Pritzker was completely taken aback. He claimed he was unaware of the shareholder proposal and the letters until after they were reported in the press. He admitted, however, that he was aware of Seslowe's efforts.

Finally, I said, "If you and Anschutz wish to see me, you come right ahead. I will be glad to talk to you."

"I think we've talked enough," he said. "Thank you very much and good-bye."

After the annual meeting, we had a major restructuring of ITT. Two vice chairmen were appointed: Cab Woodward, for all corporate mergers and acquisitions and financial developments; and Pete Thomas, to run our service companies (Hartford, ITT Finance, Communications Operations and Information Services, Sheraton). A new president and chief operating officer, Edmund Carpenter, would be responsible for the manufacturing companies, which included industrial technology, natural resources, and telecommunications.

Soon there were more stirrings from Pritzker. Harry Gray, chairman and CEO of United Technologies, called to say that the Pritzker group had offered him $25 million to lead a takeover of ITT. They already had the financing, were ready to go forward, and had buyers for the various pieces of the company. He wanted me to know that he had turned them down. I expressed my appreciation and told Harry that we had been going through these sorts of shenanigans for several months. He told me the raiders planned to go after Bill Johnson of IC Industries or Don Kelly of Northwest Industries to replace me.

We soon learned they had also tried to enlist Walter Wriston, formerly of Citicorp; Dick Shinn, formerly of Metropolitan Life Insurance; Sandy Weill, formerly of American Express; Alexander Haig; and other prominent businessmen for a blue-ribbon board, but they had struck out, despite offering potential board members a large share of the spoils.

I called Howard Aibel's attention to the heavy "corporate establishment" content of those being sought. They seemed to have become concerned about appearances, especially in official circles. After all, ITT operated in more than eighty countries, and many of their governments were our most important customers.

The last week in September, I was in Italy as the guest of the Agnellis and other members of the Atlantic Bridge, a forum in which CEOs from both sides of the Atlantic discussed international trade between the United States and Europe. We were joined by government representatives from the United Kingdom, West Germany, France, and the United States. Telecommunications obviously was regarded as a target of opportunity by European and U.S. Government officials, and ITT's market share was the bull's-eye. I was appalled at the American trade representatives' lack of knowledge about American companies. They were supporting AT&T against another American company, ITT—to the obvious glee of our European competitors, who could only benefit by the U.S. representatives' ineptitude. The European companies had the best chance at getting some of ITT's market shares, so why not let the American trade representatives create the opening?

Several days after the trade conference, I was in Paris for meetings with former Prime Minister Raymond Barre; with Edith Cresson, the Minister of Industry and Trade; and with Georges Pebereau and Jacques Dondoux, the head of the Postes, Telephone, Telegraph (PTT). In a meeting at the Elysee Palace, I was assured by Alain Boublil, assistant to President Francois Mitterand for telecommunications affairs, that ITT was acceptable again in France and would receive favorable consideration for business relationships developed with CGE.

Prior to the October board meeting, a *New York Times* article suggested that Jay Pritzker had made efforts to solicit a blue-ribbon board for a takeover of ITT. This spurred us to load the big guns, since shareholder proposal time was again approaching.

On Friday, October 11, ITT filed suit in the New York courts against Jerry Seslowe for his shareholder liquidation proposal activities and for other efforts to manipulate our stock. The company was on the offensive and counterattacking. We would seek discovery of Pritzker's and Anschutz's records and files. Seslowe had verified each of them as principals in a letter to Richard Dieterich, one of the shareholders who had been solicited in the fall of 1984. We had turned that letter over to the SEC. We secured the assignment of the case to Dave Boies, Cravath's top trial lawyer, and we were ready for deadly serious combat.

Shortly thereafter, on October 12, a *Fortune* article repeated the *Times*'s story about Pritzker's blue-ribbon board. The article also quoted Irwin Jacobs as saying that he was sick of the whole lot of us at ITT, which did not upset any of us too much. Shortly after that article appeared in *Fortune*, Jacobs called to request a meeting with Cab Woodward. He felt there was no point in talking to me, but he never showed up for the meeting.

In any case, Cab did not want to meet with him—Cab told me it was my turn. After Jacobs's only meeting with Cab and Bob Smith in March, before the 1985 annual meeting, Jacobs had later said that he "had met ITT management and they're a bunch of dummies." Bob Smith did not care, but Cab was rather sensitive about the remark.

— 14 —

THE RAIDERS RETREAT

The war of nerves intensified in mid-October 1985. The lawsuit filed against Jerry Seslowe had brought things to a head. *Fortune* magazine was doing yet another major piece on ITT, based on Pritzker's efforts to assemble a new board. It appeared we were in for an extremely critical article—anti-ITT, antimanagement, and anti-ITT's board. It would probe the whole relationship of Anschutz, Pritzker, and Jacobs, plus their intentions toward ITT.

An analyst with Goldman Sachs informed us that he had been called by *Fortune*. He said they were doing an extensive article that looked as if it would castigate ITT and its board for failure to negotiate with Pritzker. I alerted Pritzker to the article. I felt he should know that neither of us would like it. He had been giving a consistent "no comment" to press inquiries while letting Jerry Seslowe do the singing, but Seslowe had given too much information to the magazine and created too many erroneous background details to justify a "no comment" from either ITT or Pritzker now.

Pritzker, however, felt the article was developing the way he wished, and he told me he would continue with his "no comment." Pritzker was friendly and conciliatory, which made me all the more wary of what *Fortune* was about to do.

The magazine finally told Pritzker they were going ahead without his comments, but that the piece had a good deal of coverage of him and he should take this last opportunity to talk with them. After hearing some of what *Fortune* had prepared, he thought better of his previous stance: He had a two-hour telephone conversation with the editor, much of it a conference call with both Seslowe and Pritzker on the line. After the interview, Pritzker was far more upset than we were, and he let it be known in language the editor would not repeat.

No doubt Pritzker warned Phil Anschutz about the forthcoming story. Anschutz probably had had enough of the ITT caper when the lawsuit was filed against Jerry Seslowe. If not, the news about the article probably sealed the doom of the Pritzker/Anschutz cooperation on ITT investments. Apparently they separated in late October, and Anschutz began selling his 2 million shares in the $33 to $35 price range, for a nice gain, since his purchases with Pritzker had been at an average of about $23.50 per share.

This was also a time of decision for Irwin Jacobs. Should he stay in the stock and do battle? He told Myron Magnet, lead writer on the *Fortune* article, about ITT's top managers: "I've had it up to my neck with them. Those guys are the biggest bunch of losers I ever met." Cab Woodward was right to be sensitive. He had never said anything unkind about Jacobs's bankrupt snowmobile business.

In any event, Jacobs sounded as though he was ready to surrender to the "losers." He and his group had purchased their 4.3 million shares—of which he had 1.1 million—for about $32 per share. They had held it a year at high interest rates and needed a price above $34 per share to break even. The stock was then at $32. It seemed unlikely they could make any kind of a tender offer because of the huge financing require-ment. The Seslowe lawsuit filed by ITT probably made Jacobs (not directly involved in the suit) nervous as well.

As part of our planned counterattack, we were asking injunctive relief and large damages. Among the charges were violations of the securities acts, improper proxy solicitation, insider trading, market manipulation of ITT stock, and improperly attempting to force the company to liquidate itself. We further charged that ITT had been put into play to reap enormous financial benefits at the expense of ITT, its shareholders, and the investing public.

Indeed, Jacobs had much to be nervous about. Seslowe was nothing more than a messenger boy—small potatoes. Was the suit an omen of other litigation to follow? Jacobs and his controlled corporations had been accused repeatedly of violating federal statutes and regulations. In fact, he had paid $50,000 in civil penalties, the largest penalty ever assessed by the Fed up to that time in connection with a proposed stock-redemption plan involving Mid-America Bancorporation.

Whether the Seslowe lawsuit, and the possibility of others, decided the issue is unknown, but there were signs that all the raiders might be getting out. On October 29, we heard a rumor that "Irv the liquidator" was liquidating; that he had already sold 2 million shares through Bear, Stearns to an international account (subsequently identified as Soros, a major money-management firm). Jacobs then had about 500,000 shares left, but the word was he was getting out entirely. We also heard that Phil Anschutz had reduced his position substantially and might also have as few as 500,000 shares remaining. Perhaps Pritzker had not sold in order to avoid looking afraid of the suit that had been filed against Seslowe, his financial advisor.

During that week and the closing days of the previous week, nearly 10 million shares of ITT stock changed hands. We knew that Jacobs's Minneapolis friends and Jack Stevens of Little Rock held about 4.3 million shares, and, of course, that others might be selling. On November 1, around the close of the market, Jacobs announced that he had sold out all of his ITT stock and had no further financial interest in the company.

The issue of *Fortune* carrying the article on ITT ("Is ITT Fighting Shadows or Raiders?") was dated November 11, but it came out a week or so earlier. By the time the article was published, all were gone. Myron Magnet closed his story with "Seslowe says Pritzker is now waiting to see what Irwin Jacobs, who has been rattling his sword loudly, will do. At ITT hearts are still pounding."

Who could know? Perhaps, it was the imminent magazine article—combined with the lawsuit against Seslowe and the adamant position of our managers and board—that caused other hearts to pound as they ran away from ITT.

I felt that the strategy that ITT had stuck to religiously—holding the company together, defending the company, not being willing to spin off desirable assets, not being willing to auction off pieces that were basic to the core strategies of the company—was correct.

In a free-market economy, individuals and corporation should be free to buy and sell companies if our resources are to be put to their best and most effective use. However, the major consideration for many of these takeovers has more to do with the overweening ambition of some investment houses and financiers than with business and productive efficiencies.

What makes private raids possible is the use of junk bonds—low-quality, high-interest obligations. Some institutions—such as banks, insurance companies, and pension funds, which should be in the forefront in the fight for a stable business environment—line up to buy junk bonds in order to raise their yields on their bond portfolios. But, in doing so, they lose sight of their obligation as fiduciaries to invest, and not just speculate with, their clients' funds. Their heavy participation in this area was brought home sharply after the October 1987 meltdown, when the markets for junk bonds evaporated faster than spilled tea on a hot stove. Even though the markets subsequently revived, many were hurt, deep into deep pockets. Shallow pockets collapsed.

What should the federal government do to level the playing field? The Federal Reserve took one step by ruling that investors in leveraged buyouts must obey margin regulations that require investors to put up at least 50 percent of a stock purchase. This ruling was designed to stop raiders from financing a takeover with notes issued by an intermediary shell company set up solely for the acquisition.

But more needs to be done. Regulatory agencies and Congress should consider additional measures that would slow down the torrent of takeovers:

- In order to curb rampant speculation in potential takeover candidates, require that an acquirer have all financing in hand before the public offering.
- Eliminate, reduce, or restrict the use of so-called highly confident letters issued by investment banking houses. We can be highly confident that the sun will rise tomorrow, but financial promises are on a different order of magnitude. "Highly confident" is largely in the eye of the beholder.
- To give stockholders more time for a considered judgment, extend the duration of the tender offer from twenty days to sixty or ninety days.
- Outlaw greenmail and golden parachutes. This would put necessary starch into the backbones of wavering boards and would preclude payments by crony boards of directors.
- Shorten disclosure time, when an acquirer has taken a 5 percent position in a company's stock, from ten days to one day. This would reduce the risk of underhanded or sneak attacks. Or even consider reducing the 5 percent rule to 1 or 2 percent.
- Rigorously enforce the regulations against "parking" stock—keeping shares in a third-party name to avoid disclosure.
- Mandate that an offer for more than 10 percent of a company's stock must be made to all shareholders.
- Finally, consider altering the rights of stockholders. By giving long-term investors (those holding their shares for at least one year) exclusive power to vote on stockholder proposals, the destiny of the corporation would not be at the mercy of ar-

bitrageurs and speculators. A one-year ownership requirement for voting would calm the troubled waters of corporate governance without depriving the true owners of the means for ousting incompetent or unresponsive management.

It is important not to make a blanket indictment of mergers and acquisitions: Some are clearly healthy and inject an entrepreneurial vitality. Not every corporation is a model of efficiency, productivity, and business acumen. Some deserve to be shaken up. On the other hand, the work of earlier raiders, such as James Ling, Meshulam Riklis, and Victor Posner, is hardly inspiring. Nor is the work of some present-day raiders—T. Boone Pickens, Asher Edelman, and Irwin Jacobs, not to mention Jay Pritzker.

There is reason to suspect that we may have passed the crest in hostile takeovers. Shareholders are beginning to realize that companies run by takeover artists are not only no improvement over professional management, they are frequently worse. Frank Lorenzo's Texas Air is a case in point. Eastern and Continental airlines are in worse shape—whether judged by profits, efficiency and timeliness of flights, maintenance, safety margins, or enforcement of regulatory orders. Carl Icahn has TWA leveraged up to its eyeballs with long-term liabilities nine times greater than the common equity. Moreover, the raiders are no bargains for stockholders when the target company does manage to defend itself, since it inevitably takes on heavy debt to ward off the attacker. Unocal and Southland are two examples in which the raiders not only did not enhance stockholder values, they depreciated them.

Happily, corporate raiders of late have barks worse than their bites. The situation was best summed up by Professor Warren Law of Harvard Business School, who remarked that "Most raiders haven't had the problem of demonstrating what they can do with major companies because they haven't acquired them." He suggests that if they did, they would not know what to do with them. "It would be like the (barking) dog that eventually caught the car."

At ITT, the raiders were gone; the war of nerves was finally over. Now, we could again turn our attention to building the company on a sound financial basis—and I did have a plan, whose code name became Roxane.

─ 15 ─

THE RAVISHING

ROXANE

With the exodus of the raiders, we had to get down to serious strategic work. The health of ITT was still far from optimal in the fall of 1985. Our debt servicing remained a burden, and long-term debt still was more than a third of the company's capitalization—too high. Our cash position had improved, but not yet in any dramatic way. We continued to sell off companies that no longer fitted with our business plans. Nevertheless, our exposure to foreign pressures and politics left us liable to attack or other unpleasant surprises.

If we could sell our European telecommunications manufacturing facilities to a strong European company, or possibly establish a new entity, we could reduce our foreign liabilities while bringing in substantial funds to improve our balance sheet. It would be an elegant solution to a complex problem.

Over the years, it had become apparent that ITT's telecommunications facilities were in a bind—one that was likely to get worse, not better. In many nations, telephone service was regarded as a quasi-state monopoly, like the mail and telegraph services. Furthermore, the manufacturing of telephone and switching equipment was regarded as a national patrimony, highly regulated. In the 1970s and early 1980s, swelling nationalist sentiment around the world pressured us into selling almost all of our subsidiaries, often at absurdly low prices, or accepting joint partners on highly disadvantageous terms.

Another element was the looming computerization and digitizing of telephonic networks, which was bound to make obsolete at least some parts of electromechanical systems. ITT's plants were likely to suffer.

Moreover, we also began to envision alliances of major electronic companies—AT&T and Philips, Siemens and GTE, GEC and Plessey. The competitive strength of these international combinations would be awesome indeed.

The high cost of designing software and keeping the system up to date could be offset only by attracting new customers. But while the United States had deregulated its telephone system with the AT&T consent decree, other countries were nowhere near so hospitable to foreign producers and products.

In short, there were a number of reasons to seek an alliance if ITT was to be rid of some of the problems inherent in being considered a sole foreign supplier. But while a joint venture would immediately enhance our cash flow and strengthen our balance sheet, it was fraught with danger should it fail. If negotiations were publicized, national policies might harden and governments might intervene. Other companies might enter the competition. And not the least concern was a revival of interest in breaking up ITT should the negotiations fail.

We had been having conversations with one firm—the Nixdorf Computer Company. Heinz Nixdorf and I had a meeting at the company headquarters in Paderborn, West Germany, in early December 1985, but it was unlikely we would be able to form a European majority-owned entity in telecommunications. In view of our ownership of Standard Electrik Lorenz (SEL) in West Germany, ITT could not grant a majority to Nixdorf, so the combination would have been challenged by Germany's cartel laws.

Georges Pebereau of Compagnie Generale d'Electricite and I were each modeling a telecommunications joint venture. Unknown to Pebereau, during the November 1985 ITT meetings the board approved the strategy of an ITT minority position. The joint venture would be somewhere between 51 and 70 percent CGE-owned, and CGE would have to pay cash for the ITT shares. We valued ITT's part of the joint venture at $3.3 billion to $3.9 billion, with a book value of $1.6 billion. The code name for our secret activity with CGE—"Roxane"—came from either the Morgan Stanley or the Lazard Freres office in Paris. The name was known initially to about ten people, a number that would grow ultimately to about fifty people.

The joint venture would give us back the nationalized French market and would place the new company in the strongest market position in the world. Market-share studies showed the joint venture would capture about 43 percent of the European telecommunications market and would have $12 billion of revenues, with a heavy orientation in office products in Europe and in the United States. The joint venture would be the principal worldwide telecommunications competitor with complementary markets of CGE in French West Africa, ITT in East Africa and North Africa. We had complementing strong positions in the Middle East and good distribution of products in India, China, and Australia, and other nations in the Far East. It was an excellent fit, and we all knew it.

It was an exciting possibility: Georges Pebereau and I had been gingerly leading up to the valuation of ITT's telecommunication holdings since a dinner meeting in Paris in July 1985. We had completed exhaustive studies of our telecommunications networks worldwide. I had concluded that a worst-case valuation would be $2 billion for the entire activity; an acceptable valuation, $3.3 billion; an optimal valuation, $4 billion. In 1984, all of ITT's companies together, including telecommunications, had a market value of almost $4 billion. A highly successful sale to CGE would nearly double the value of the corporation.

I met with Georges Pebereau at CGE headquarters in Paris in mid-November. That meeting turned out to be crucial. I proposed developing a joint venture in which CGE might have a majority participation. Georges sat up straight, wide-eyed behind his small rimmed glasses. Roxane was as attractive to him as to me. France would be thrust into the premier position in telecommunications. He could not sit still or contain his excitement.

I said, "You are going to have to consider a valuation of something like $3.9 billion to $4 billion for ITT's telecommunications business, so if ITT keeps 30 percent of Roxane, CGE will have to pay about $2.7 billion for 70 percent. The $2.7 billion would include the assumption of about $800 million of debt."

Georges stared at me probingly. Then he looked to the side, shrugged his shoulders, and stood up quickly to shake hands. "We have a lot to do before we seriously talk price. We are now partners."

Georges was particularly impressed by the fact that the ITT board—including Michel David-Weill, a most respected French banker—had approved French majority ownership, a majority ownership held by the French government itself.

He said, "I cannot tell any details to my Board of Directors, which represents the French government. But I assure you that the right people, of both parties, will know of our general approach. It is best for the moment not to tell them that CGE will own a majority. That might create premature waves."

I left Paris feeling we had triggered what could be the most significant transaction for ITT since Sosthenes Behn purchased AT&T's overseas telephone companies and equipment manufacturers in 1925.

During this same time period, Ed Carpenter commissioned a study by Booz Allen Hamilton to determine whether we should continue our System 12 switching investment in the shrinking United States. I felt that Georges Pebereau would have no problem with a sound decision either way.

One other avenue still remained open. It was related directly to technical and market expansion of System 12. Nixdorf was the only computer company that was effectively integrating digital data and digital communications, and I did not want to leave the Nixdorf connection unexplored. John Chluski, my representative on several ITT majority-owned companies in Europe, and I went to Paderborn to meet with Heinz Nixdorf. He discussed his company openly, and I reciprocated. It was apparent that he hoped to organize some kind of combination with ITT on a worldwide basis. On the other hand, it was equally clear that Nixdorf was not going to be involved in a business venture in Germany that he did not control. As a result, I was somewhat pessimistic about reaching an acceptable conclusion. We shook hands, agreeing only to pursue discussions in a more specific way in 1986, and John Chluski and I were once again off to Paris.

I went from Le Bourget Airport directly to a meeting with Jacques Chirac, mayor of Paris. His RPR (Rally Party of the Republic) was readying for the March 1986 elections. Seated in a high-backed, heavily stuffed chair in the mayor's palace, Chirac was tall and thin. He smoked his cigarettes in a relaxed, diffident fashion. Chirac was easy to talk to and had been well prepared by Georges Pebereau. It was a pleasure to see that 1981's negative attitude about ITT had completely dissipated, and there seemed to be a genuine wish to have us back.

John Chluski and I had a follow-up meeting with Georges Pebereau and Francois de Laage, his assistant, at our New York headquarters. We talked some about valuations, but mainly we discussed schedules and matters that would have to be attended to in early 1986. We agreed that while we could continue discussions, no final decision could be made until after the French elections in March—and, from my point of view, until after the ITT annual meeting in May.

Our goal was to continue to pursue an effective joint venture without getting to the point where public disclosure was required. Then, after the elections in France, which were expected to go to Chirac's party, we could determine a schedule of meetings, including consideration of the ITT annual meeting. Both sides knew it was essential to reach a decision by June 30, 1986. Roxane was too spectacular to remain hidden. Georges also wanted a June 30 deadline in view of an expected increase in AT&T's share of the French telecommunications market at that time. Georges and I agreed to proceed carefully and confidentially with our next meetings, scheduled for early in 1986. We each kept a list of names of people who knew Roxane.

— 16 —

DEFENSE SECRETS

We were approaching a critical decision on our North American efforts with System 12. On January 12, 1986, our consultant, Booz Allen, made its first presentation, which recommended suspension of System 12 in the United States. ITT would only obtain an unprofitable third place at best in the saturated American market, after AT&T and Northern Telecommunications. Later in January Michel David-Weill, Felix Rohatyn and I agreed that the CGE joint venture was the right one, but that Northern Telecommunications could be brought into the act. Booz Allen had suggested Northern Telecom as a possible vehicle for staying in the North American telecommunications market. They would be an alternate bidder and keep the proper pressure on CGE.

Then a major problem developed on another front. Apparently, our West German subsidiary, Standard Electrik Lorenz, was about to be notified by the German Ministry of Defense that SEL could no longer receive classified information from the United States Department of Defense. These written orders were to come from Secretary Caspar Weinberger to U.S. Ambassador Richard Burt in Bonn for transmittal to the German minister of defense.

The potential damage was monumental. Our stock was still in the mid-30s, and this incident could put our company back into play. Certainly, ITT's overall security clearance would be placed in jeopardy, if not canceled. There would be extreme financial consequences in addition to the public damage to the company. ITT again would be on the front pages of every newspaper in the Western world.

Information provided to the United States Department of Defense through a Soviet defector exposed, on the surface, a serious security leak at SEL. Our own investigation had shown no evidence that SEL was at fault, but ITT had been allowed no time with Assistant Secretary Richard Perle or Secretary Weinberger to prove it. They had made no effort to let us know that an investigation had been going on since September 1985. Our own Standard Electrik people, including Helmut Lohr, thought they had answered all of the questions successfully, and therefore they had not red-flagged the security matter to ITT headquarters in Brussels.

A meeting of the Ministry of Defense with German industrial contractors had already occurred, without SEL. We had to move quickly or competitors would have our exclusion on the front pages before we had a chance to state our case. I called Secretary Weinberger's office and told his secretary it was urgent, that I was in Brussels but I would stay right at the telephone until he returned my call.

A half hour later, Secretary Weinberger called back. I summarized: "Cap, I've been through this entire security situation relating to SEL. I am extremely concerned, as this could be devastating to ITT if your decision were to go forward. I must have an opportunity to talk to you to explain our point of view. This is the first I have heard of it. You know if you had called me down I would have given every cooperation, but your investigation has been going on completely independent of us. I believe you have information that is in many respects intended to create problems between Germany and the United States. ITT and SEL are innocent in this matter, and I will fly immediately back to meet with you."

He had listened. Then he said, "Rand, we are concerned about the way German contractors have been handling our classified information. We think some lessons need to be taught." I replied, "Yes, but this would be extremely unfair to dump this on ITT until you have heard us out."

Weinberger said, "I understand, Rand, but the order is going to stay." I asked, "When will it be released?"

He said, "By the end of next week, it should be in Germany." I replied, "Secretary Weinberger, I implore you to hold that action with the U.S. ambassador in Bonn until I can see you."

He said, "We will hold it but that does not mean it will not go forward." "I understand that, sir," I responded. "I'll be in your office whenever you say."

"Twelve o'clock Monday."

We received further briefings from our German contingent. A disclosure apparently had occurred concerning classified data, but it was a problem in another country, not an SEL violation.

At 9 a.m. on Monday, January 27, 1986, Helmut Lohr, Howard
Aibel, and a few others gathered in ITT's Washington office. We
huddled all morning to prepare our case for Secretary Weinberger.

After I greeted him at his office on the Pentagon's third floor he
responded, "Hello, Rand. I'm sorry about these circumstances, but you
understand we're going to have to make an example of somebody to
make sure that our classified information is protected by those German
contractors."

Several people were with him—Undersecretary of the Army James
R. Ambrose; Assistant Secretary Richard Perle; his legal counsel; his
military aide. Howard Aibel was with me; Helmut Lohr and the others
waited outside. We presented our story and insisted that the information
received from the Soviet defector was erroneous and that we could
refute it.

In spite of our presentation, there were staff comments that we
should be disciplined and taught a lesson. Suddenly, the one person
from whom I least expected support, Richard Perle, said, "Mr. Secretary, why don't we stop the order until I can work on this with Mr.
Araskog? There may be some things here we don't know, and I'd like to
be sure we are careful. I do agree with Mr. Araskog that this could do
severe damage to his corporation and even to our German relations. So I
would like to go slow and I would like to investigate it thoroughly and
get back to you."

Secretary Weinberger seemed surprised, and begrudgingly said,
"Well, okay, Richard, I'll put that in your hands, but I want this
resolved within two weeks, and if in two weeks I have no other answer,
we are going to go ahead and implement the order. I want you to
understand that."

Perle said he did. I think what he really understood was that
Secretary Weinberger was saving face, and that was certainly all right
with Howard and me.

Afterward, Howard and I met with Perle for several hours. He
brought in his investigative team, which obviously had been totally
convinced by the defector's information, despite the fact that it was
genuinely in error.

It took us another month to put all of this behind us, to convince
everyone that ITT and Standard Electrik Lorenz had in no way leaked
information. A leak had in fact occurred, but it had not been through
the SEL or ITT offices.

There had been nothing since the July 2, 1984, Gerrity letter that had shaken me as much as the Weinberger order. Interestingly enough, Richard Perle, who saved us from disaster, was later most courteous, even apologetic. I never heard more about the matter from Secretary Weinberger, but what could he say? After disposing of this challenge, Howard and I concluded that any raider who wanted to run ITT needed to have his head examined.

It may seem a small point in retrospect, but the raiders never fully appreciated just how delicate and complicated a corporation ITT is, with a great many government agencies monitoring its activities. Long-standing relationships facilitate the exchange of information with the regulatory bodies. If they are torn asunder by selling off component companies, business is likely to fail. An international corporation must have the kind of presence that allows for access to the highest levels of government, and these contacts are not made in a fortnight. The raiders forgot that—or perhaps they never knew it.

—— 17 ——

THE STALKING HORSE

I had reckoned on System 12 to change the fortunes of the company dramatically. Some critics said it was a bet-the-company decision, that it was reckless and a nonstarter. They were wrong; it was an outstanding achievement. In the late 1970s, the Swedish company L.M. Ericsson had had a breakthrough in digital switching that threatened to grab a significant share of ITT's European markets. We had to leapfrog their technology: It became a $1 billion priority. We created a team whose technical expertise was second to none, and our scientists created System 12—a digital switchboard with virtually unlimited capacity in voice, data, and distributed control from terminals that reduce or bypass central processing units. The modular design was easy to adopt in many foreign networks. We won virtually all the technical shoot-outs we entered, and System 12 was accepted worldwide—except in the United States.

We missed the boat in the United States because we did not anticipate the breakup of AT&T and the early opening it offered us. While we concentrated on Europe, Northern Telecommunications had moved into the U.S. market with its advanced switchboards. Regardless of our acknowledged triumphs abroad, the Baby Bell systems were hard nuts to crack, since their electronic logic and networks were basically different from our European technology.

By February 1986, it was clear that the U.S. market would not be profitable. Nevertheless, System 12 remained a highly viable switching system for the rest of the world.

I went to Nashville, Tennessee, for a Sunday meeting at the home of Ed Fitzgerald, the head of Northern Telecommunications. After I indicated ITT's serious interest in selling a majority or a minority of its telecommunications operations worldwide, we discussed the opportunities and problems that would accompany such a transaction.

Northern Telecom, a Canadian-based spinoff of Bell Canada, was a rapidly growing power in the United States. Ed felt his company was doing reasonably well penetrating Europe; it had entered Japan with more horsepower than any U.S. supplier. Overall, it was clear to both of us that we had complementary capabilities if they could be put together. They had North America and Japan and we had Europe, Africa, Latin America, and China.

The gem had been dropped in Ed Fitzgerald's hands, and he was planning to examine it carefully. I emphasized that the Northern Telecom-ITT talks had to be conducted in complete secrecy. They were aware that we were talking to CGE. Ed replied, "You bet. For our sake, too." Then he added, "Look, Rand, those Frenchmen don't pay — you know that."

We flew on to Boston, where ITT was having its February board meetings at Sheraton headquarters. The major item on the agenda was a review of System 12. Booz Allen had now confirmed their opinion, shared by our own management, that we should stop our System 12 activity in North America. Even the general manager of the System 12 activity in Raleigh, North Carolina, could not argue with the conclusions of the study. We would make the termination announcement on Thursday, February 13.

The announcement that we were stopping our System 12 activity in North America brought instant accolades from the analysts, the rating agencies, and the stock market. Cries of "What will ITT do now?" came from the business press. At the same time, we reported the results for the year.

We took a $105 million write-off for our American telecommunications effort. In March, rumors were beginning to hum around Europe, and particularly in Italy, about various international telecommunications alliances being contemplated. Siemens and GTE were supposedly joining forces, ITT was believed to be considering sales of some of its majority interests in companies in Europe. A variety of stories linked companies with ITT, but no one focused on CGE and ITT. Now Northern Telecom was out there too, also running without lights. It was working, and there were only three months to go.

After the March 16 elections in France, we reviewed the results. The new government was very positive toward Georges Pebereau and CGE. (In early 1987, CGE would be one of the first companies to be privatized.) The new government was generally aware of Pebereau's discussions with me, since we had also met with Jacques Chirac and others. As a result, they were familiar with a joint-venture plan. But Georges did not think it appropriate for me to have meetings with the new government officials until he had executed a definitive agreement. That judgment would cost Georges Pebereau his job, but surely it saved Roxane.

The next week, during our board meetings, we updated the directors on the situation in France and with Northern Telecommunications, which was showing considerable interest in buying about 70 percent of the telecommunications activities. They wanted full management control, but they had not thought through how they would hold their potential acquisition together. Europe wanted European control, and this was still a high hurdle for Northern Telecom. But their computers were whirling, working out ways to do it.

Georges Pebereau knew from Morgan Stanley that Northern Telecom was also a player, and he had advised the highest levels of the new government, in whom he had confidence, that he would be in tight competition. John Chluski had been questioned by Georges and had simply told the truth, that "several members of the ITT top management preferred Northern Telecom, but Rand Araskog strongly favored CGE."

Back in New York at the end of April, we met with Northern Telecommunications. Ed Fitzgerald brought his chief financial officer, legal personnel, and his senior vice president, Derek Davies. Cab Woodward, Bob Smith, Ed Carpenter, and Howard Aibel joined me at my apartment. During the meeting, I reached the conclusion that the only way ITT could sell to Northern Telecom was if Northern Telecom would hand us a certified check for the full purchase price for ITT telecommunications, leaving Northern Telecom to hold things together. But I did not tell them that. The European PTTs and governments, ITT's principal customers, could regard a sale of ITT's companies to another North American company as being antithetical to the principles of the EEC. Nevertheless, we wanted Northern Telecom to stay in the running, so I told Ed Fitzgerald we would have to hold everything in abeyance until after our annual meeting.

The sudden death of Heinz Nixdorf in Germany removed his corporation as a possibility for a joint venture. Klaus Luft, the new chairman, felt he first had to get his feet on the ground running the company. So we closed off that avenue and Nixdorf joined Wang, Burroughs, and Sperry as an experience in "nothing ventured, nothing gained."

— 18 —

FULL COURT PRESS

Our stalking horse was showing signs of restiveness. Ed Fitzgerald of Northern Telecommunications called my home early in June 1986 to check on the status of our talks. I assured him that he was still in the running, but we were going to reach some conclusion with CGE first.

I returned to Paris to intensify our efforts in continuous meetings at CGE headquarters with Georges Pebereau and his staff. Georges was a different man. He was on edge and his eyes darted around behind his small, round, silver-rimmed glasses. He would frequently run his hand through his thin hair, then lean far forward across the table and appeal to me. When it got to be too much for him, he would suddenly disappear and I would be given a variety of reasons for his actions. Once I was told that he was taking a subway somewhere—because he had never ridden on a subway and wanted to try it.

Back at our hotel, we would wait. Hours later his staff reported: "He became lost. After all, he had never been on a subway before." But then he would suddenly return, apparently refreshed.

The investment bankers were all active, and as of Saturday night, June 14, we were still far enough apart that I did not have information for the ITT board, which was scheduled to meet the following week in Oslo. After midnight, I laid down a final condition as to price for Georges Pebereau. If a resolution could be reached, then I would take it to the ITT Board of Directors. Otherwise, Pebereau could expect that the deal would be off and negotiations would be over.

Pebereau accepted the condition, and I took a final price to Oslo. After considerable discussion and review, the board agreed to the terms and conditions that we had negotiated, and I returned to Paris to complete the deal. In essence, we achieved a total valuation of $3.9 billion of our telecommunications business worldwide—$26 per share of ITT common stock. It consisted of 30 percent of the joint venture, worth $1.3 billion; $1.8 billion in cash; and debt transfer of $800 million. These conditions certainly met our most optimistic expectations.

We had a good deal of legal terminology still to work out, along with some unresolved matters that could affect the price. Howard Aibel took charge. We worked on Wednesday, Thursday, and Friday, but by Thursday night we were in sufficiently good shape to celebrate with a champagne party. Then we turned everything over to the attorneys for a weekend of work so we could meet again the following week for final initialing and my signature.

Finally, on June 24, working all day and into the evening, we ironed out the remaining problems and had yet another champagne party. Thinking we had everything in place, I left the next morning for Brussels, where Dan Weadock was holding management reviews with our European management. I advised the managing directors that we were about to sign a major agreement with CGE, providing for a joint venture in which CGE would take the majority. There were looks of surprise and, in some cases, dismay at the planned change in majority ownership. The managers had many questions: Helmut Lohr from Standard Electrik Lorenz, Gene Van Dyck from BTM, Miguel Canalejo from Spain, Umberto Ferroni from Italy. Finally, everyone began to acknowledge that it could be the best thing for the ITT telecommunications companies in Europe. With the level of anxiety reduced, I returned to Paris for final meetings with Georges Pebereau.

That night, I initialed and signed the agreement for ITT, then Georges Pebereau initialed it. He could not sign it until the French Government, the principal owner of CGE, had approved the contract. We expected that would be approved immediately. Georges Pebereau brought it to the attention of the Government on the evening of June 25.

After midnight that night, I was awakened at the Bristol Hotel. Michel David-Weill was calling, in deep distress—he said the French Government would not approve the agreement as written. Evidently Pebereau had not done enough to pave the way with the Minister of Industry, Alain Madelin, or with the Minister of Finance and Economy, Edouard Baladur—and, therefore, with new Prime Minister Jacques Chirac. The size of the transaction and the implications for other European countries caught them totally by surprise.

The next morning, Georges and I reconvened. He was extremely upset and walked in circles, talking to himself. The date of June 30 was on the document as a drop-dead date—both as I had initialed and signed it and as he had initialed it. He was embarrassed, but he told me that Roxane still could be saved, that the minister of industry wanted to see me right away. So on June 26, Minister of Industry Alain Madelin met with John Chluski, and Charles Goldman of Howard Aibel's staff. Madelin wanted to discuss the contract we had signed, so we went through a long explanation of the history of the negotiations, the strengths we saw in the agreement, and the benefits for CGE, for ITT, and for France.

When we were finished, Minister Madelin said they understood all this; they knew a great deal of work had gone into it, but they wanted to modify the agreement. I told him that the agreement had to stand as signed, that it had been in the works for fifteen months. If any comma were removed, if any t were uncrossed, if any i were undotted, the agreement would be null and void.

Minister Madelin seemed frustrated. Charles Goldman and John Chluski had been with me at almost all of the meetings with Georges Pebereau, and now each confirmed what I had said in French and in more detail. As a result of this absolutely firm position on our part, Minister Madelin, "I have to think about it further. I have to talk to Minister Baladur, and he would have to have some time to consider it."

We regarded the outcome as positive. Obviously, they saw the French magic in the deal and did not want to lose it. Details of the agreement hit the press in France, and then a front-page article appeared in the *New York Times*. Coverage was complimentary and highlighted the telecommunications power that France would become through this transaction. Pressure was on the French Government not to ruin the deal.

Indeed, on reflection, the price became the sticking point. The French Government would be obliged to come up with 5 billion francs, no small sum for a new government to have thrust on it without a chance to negotiate. It was as much a matter of money as it was a matter of national prestige.

That afternoon, around five in the evening, I was asked to see Minister Baladur at the Finance Ministry, together with Michel David-Weill. Baladur had worked for one of CGE's companies and was now next in line to Prime Minister Chirac. Shifting from French to English easily, Baladur again raised the issue of reopening the negotiations and I repeated everything I had said before—in a polite but absolutely firm manner. He told me they did not feel the June 30 deadline allowed sufficient time to consider the agreement. He requested an extension to the end of July. I said no, that ITT stock had climbed $1.2 billion since the details of the transaction has been leaked to the press. I reminded them that we had kept this whole matter confidential until the day we submitted the agreement to the French Government, and one day later, it was leaked to the French press and now was in the American press. Baladur's response to that was a shrug of his shoulders, saying, "Well, what did you expect?"

Eventually, I agreed to extend the termination date to July 4; Minister Baladur accepted. Then Michel and I shook hands with Baladur and departed. As we left, we noticed that Georges Pebereau's car was parked outside the building. Of course, we had suspected that Pebereau would be meeting with Baladur after we left. Baladur had good reasons, which he had not disclosed to us, for needing the extension: One involved the future of Georges Pebereau; the other concerned the financing for the huge transaction.

Flying home to the United States, I had realized that there was no way I could insist on a final decision by July 4. If I did insist, the French Government would not approve the deal. I would have to extend the deadline to July 31. Through Michel David-Weill, we communicated this to the French Government on July 1. The French then began excruciating reviews of all of the specifics of the transaction—the financial portion, the market shares, and the reaction of other countries to Roxane.

— 19 —

PARIS POLITICS

A few weekends later, Michel David-Weill called to say he had received extremely disquieting news from Paris. The new French government, which was evaluating the appointment or reappointment of the heads of government-owned major industries, including CGE, had serious reservations about reappointing Georges Pebereau.

When Minister Baladur had requested a deadline extension to July 31, I felt all the odds were in favor of approval of the agreement. Press reaction in France was favorable—proclaiming a coup for France in the worldwide telecommunications race. Disapproval could bring great political criticism, "lack-of-courage" headlines, statements that France would "miss the opportunity of the century." I figured the government could come up with the required funds, but it never occurred to me that Minister Baladur did not want to reappoint Georges Pebereau. Such a move would be a misstep that could undo Roxane, with a new man saying she was too rich or that he needed time to renegotiate her terms, which would mean no deal.

Stories had it that the French Government felt pressured by Pebereau's deal with ITT; that Georges had manipulated them; that he had not provided them with sufficient information before initialing the deal. Further, there were rumblings that a substantial cash infusion into CGE would be required to make the transaction financially sound—as much as $750 million.

Other stories indicated that Pebereau was not on the best of terms with RPR, the Chirac party, because of his loyal service as an industrial leader under the socialist government. Whatever the stories, they were upsetting. All of the work thus far had been the joint vision of myself and Georges Pebereau: I felt it would be extremely difficult for anyone else to accept the vision that we had developed.

Sunday morning, July 20, Michel David-Weill called me at my hotel in Cap d'Antibes, where I was vacationing, and asked me to come to his house. Georges Pebereau was en route to the south of France with critical news. Pebereau arrived shortly after I did. Dressed in sports attire, he seemed somewhat in disarray. He spoke rapidly in French to Michel, and even in English he spoke in a staccato. He was obviously agitated.

Georges had heard rumors about his reappointment, but whatever his fate, he wanted the joint venture to go through. He said that ITT would have to make two commitments to the French government.

I did not know it at the time, but Minister Baladur had been asked to put 5 billion French francs (more than $700 million) into CGE in order to provide a balance sheet that would allow the joint venture to go forward. This, perhaps, was the most significant cause of the Government's irritation with Pebereau—that the sum had not been specified in advance as necessary for the deal. In view of this, Baladur obviously had asked—either directly then of Pebereau or through Minister Madelin—for two concessions from ITT. The first was that we would raise no objection to CGE's CIT Alcatel's forming a joint venture with AT&T in the field of telecommunications transmission. If the AT&T-Alcatel transmission agreement were signed, presumably the French government would give AT&T the 16 percent market share previously held in France by CGCT, the former French subsidiary that ITT had given up in 1982. I insisted that the AT&T joint venture would cancel the deal. The ITT system had strong transmission capabilities—at BTM, FACE, Standard Electrica, and Standard Electrik Lorenz—and there was no way we could surrender that business to competition with another Alcatel joint venture. The two were not compatible. If Alcatel controlled the total activity, it then would favor the Alcatel-AT&T joint venture over the ITT transmission system. It would be untenable to our system house managers.

Pebereau raised his hands and exclaimed, "I am telling you that is going to be one condition and you will have to decide what to do."

Rather disgustedly I said, "What's the other?" And he replied, "It is okay for you to have 30 percent, but the French government is unwilling to have CGE entirely responsible for bringing in the other partners. ITT must take responsibility for bringing in another partner acceptable to CGE for 7 percent of the total joint venture, at $300 million minimum investment. The new investor would pay the same as Societe Generale and CTNE in Spain as they come into the joint venture."

I responded, "Georges, you and I agreed in the beginning that CGE had to buy it all and then be responsible for any resale. CGE had to redistribute the shares or ITT would not be assured of getting the total price we wanted. I will not yield."

Pebereau said, "Okay. I'm only telling you these are the two conditions. You can think about them some more."

I replied, "I'm not going to think about them at all. I've held the line from the very beginning on the things that were absolutely essential to ITT, to its board, and to its shareholders, and you can let the French government know that I will yield on neither of those points."

Georges again raised his hands, saying, "Okay, Rand, I told you, either you want this or you don't. These are two conditions that have to be met, and if they can't be met, that's it."

Sensing the tension between the two of us, Michel stepped in and became a calming catalyst. There had to be significant added tension for Pebereau, since he still had no idea what would happen to him. The rumors swirling around him in Paris and in the international press must have been rather insulting and discouraging. Yet, here he was, still trying to keep Roxane alive whether or not he was the one to have her.

The rumors, in fact, had become much more specific. An article in one of the French daily newspapers identified Pierre Suard as the likely replacement for Georges Pebereau. Suard was described as a close friend of Baladur and Chirac, a member of the party. As the head of CGE's CIT Alcatel, Suard had participated in our negotiations, but I had met him only once during negotiations and two or three times socially. He had seemed extremely negative about Roxane because of his concern that Spain represented too great a business risk.

Now, at Sous-le-Vent, Georges for the first time seemed almost pathetic. He said, "Rand, we have become friends. No matter what happens to me, don't destroy the deal." Michel and I saw him to the door. There wasn't much more for Michel and me to discuss, so I left too.

The following Tuesday, I had lunch with Georges Pebereau at CGE headquarters in Paris. He told me that he was not being reappointed chairman of CGE. The French government had decided on Pierre Suard. It was now imperative that I meet with Suard to see whether it was possible to salvage our negotiations.

Suard was waiting for me in the same conference room in which Georges Pebereau and I had met at least fifteen times. After the initial congratulations, he began our conversation with a discussion of the two French government conditions.

The first condition turned out to be perfectly acceptable to ITT. The joint venture with AT&T in transmission would be an arm of ITT/CGE's joint venture, so it would not be in competition with the system houses of ITT. Furthermore, the agreement contemplated having AT&T discontinue all transmission equipment development and manufacture in the United States. Instead, this responsibility would be handled by Alcatel in France and certain Alcatel facilities in the United States. This arrangement would in fact increase the transmission market share of the ITT/CGE joint venture.

Pierre continued, "The French government also insists that you be responsible for your 30 percent plus 7 percent more of the joint venture."

I replied, "Pierre, we would be perfectly happy to keep 37 percent and reduce the cash amount to be paid to ITT from $1.8 billion to $1.5 billion. Then we could decide to sell that 7 percent or not to sell it as we might jointly agree in the future."

Pierre said, "So, we are in agreement. I feel quite confident the French Government will approve the deal, and that the Board of Directors of CGE will approve it early next week."

I departed for the United States. Roxane was approved. The newspapers were full of the news, and on Tuesday, July 29, I returned to Paris again. We wrapped up the deal in the next two days and formed the negotiating teams to complete the final package. I was quite certain that we would be able to wrap up the deal by the end of the year.

— 20 —

COVERING ALL THE
BASES

Who would have dreamed in 1980 that seven years later, ITT would be divesting majority ownership in telecommunications—the division Harold Geneen had described as the company's heartline when he hired me. After the public disclosure of the joint venture, I called Geneen. His immediate response was, "Rand, you are doing the right thing. The situation has changed in Europe. I congratulate you."

A short time after our agreement in France, a letter from Jay Pritzker arrived at my home with the following message: "Congratulations, Rand. If I had known you were going to bite the bullet on telecommunications, I would have held on to my stock. C'est la vie. Jay."

I wrote to thank him, but I could not help recalling sitting in his Hyatt Hotel office on August 10, 1984, when he told me that life was just a game. My feelings about Jay Pritzker bordered on deep resentment. The Pritzker family fortune had been built by Jay's father in Chicago, and Jay had known nothing but great wealth. I had grown up on a Minnesota farm in the Depression days. I left that farm as a young teenager in the middle of World War II. I later went to West Point because I was excited about it, but it also relieved the financial burden on my family—three children were in college at the same time. I worked my way up the hard way, through government, Honeywell, and ITT, and I resented the idea that a guy with inherited money could walk in and destroy the career I had built—and do it with nonchalance and indifference. Perhaps for Pritzker it was nothing but a game, but my family was no game to me. It was serious business, and I resented Pritzker's intrusion into my life.

Shortly thereafter, my wife Jessie and I ran into our other nemesis, Irwin Jacobs, at a dinner dance hosted by Drexel Burnham at the Metropolitan Museum of Art. It looked like a duplicate of the West Coast "Pirates Party," with an array of the brokerage house's junk-bond customers. While I found Fred Joseph personally charming, I have grave doubts about his company's role in the leveraging of America and financing the raiders. As we were turning a gallery corner, Jessie whispered, "Hey, Rand, should we turn around? There's 'The Three Rs.'" Once upon a time, I had accused Irwin of practicing the three Rs: "Run down the management, run up the stock, and run away with the money."

I said, "No, let's say hello. We might as well cover all the bases."

We did, and we talked about Minnesota's Lake Minnetonka, about Irwin's new boat works, which he bought because he wanted better care for his yacht. We talked amiably enough and I reflected that if he had not tried to mess around with my company, I might have liked him.

Two days later, during a private luncheon with Pierre Suard, we summarized what had to be done in the next two months. We agreed that my most important task was to see that System 12 continued on its strong upward curve. Press criticism of the system had subsided, and ITT Europe headquarters personnel were confident we would deliver more System 12 switching lines around the world than would be delivered by any other supplier, including AT&T, in that time period.

Later, in Washington, I described the joint venture to top executives of the Department of Defense, whom Howard Aibel had notified prior to the July 1986 signature. We had wanted no quick rebuff, and, of course, our U.S. defense companies were not included in the transaction; they would remain exclusively within ITT.

Shortly afterward, I held meetings with Lord Keith, chairman of the board of STC in London. (Roxane included most of our 24 percent ownership in Standard Telephones and Cables of the United Kingdom.) I wanted to ensure the STC shares—which at the time were worth about $225 million—could be included in ITT's contribution to the joint venture. The transfer probably had to be approved by the Home Office of the British Ministry of Industry. Lord Keith was lukewarm to the transaction, at best, but I did not feel he would lobby to stop it.

I also gave Suard my endorsement to add Cables de Lyons, the CGE cable company, to Roxane, at a price to be agreed upon. It would make Roxane the largest cable company in the world, but would reduce ITT's ownership in the joint venture to between 34 and 35 percent.

At Victoria House in Brussels, we held the European telecommunications meeting and dinner with all of the system house managers. We discussed Roxane in exquisite detail. Each managing director reported his opinions of how the joint-venture idea was being accepted in his country, and all reports were favorable. Each country wanted assurance, however, that there would be no change in System 12. Pierre Suard was most helpful in signing letters to this effect, letters complimentary of System 12. We indeed were covering all the bases.

— 21 —

THE FINISH LINE

T he race to beat the deadline of December 31, 1986, was a deadly serious one. If we failed to finalize these global negotiations before the Tax Reform Act of 1986 came into force on January 1, 1987, ITT would lose $288 million in cash, almost $2 per share. That would have a devastating effect on our earnings, which in turn would damage the price of our stock, and possibly bring back the raiders.

Then, on Friday evening, November 15, the phone rang at our home in Smoke Rise. Jessie answered, and said, "Turn on the TV. They caught Boesky." Ivan Boesky's name was all too familiar to Jessie. I turned on the TV and the news was spilling out. Dennis Levine, an insider-trading violator charged earlier, had named names, and a big one was falling. I remember thinking that maybe this nonsense would cease. It was the beginning of the nightmare Wall Street had been building up to since the Bronfmans went after Conoco in the early 1980s. I had no pity. I only hoped that ultimately the SEC would get them all.

Near the end of November 1986, ITT had its final general management meetings in Brussels. There was some nostalgia, but our efforts were bent on ensuring that we would meet our budget for 1986 and that the plans for 1987 were in good shape. Pierre Suard canceled his appearance at dinner in the evening, so the affair was an ITT swan song.

Prior to my departure from Brussels for New York, Pierre and I met with our two public relations executives, Juan Cappello and Francoise Sampermans, to arrange the program for a joint press conference in early January in Brussels, after the final closing on Roxane. Howard Aibel had done an outstanding job conducting the incredibly complex legal negotiations; Juan Cappello was doing an equally creative job in developing a joint public relations program. We had gone from a time

494

when people thought ITT was getting out of telecommunications to a new era when ITT was organizing its major stake in the financing, policies, and operation of the joint venture.

As the closing date approached, the German cartel office 7 approved the joint venture, and approval papers were moving rapidly in Spain and Norway. Everything was on target, but in business you can never be sure—things can never go too well. We were still having trouble transferring the shares representing 24 percent ownership of STC. STC did not want them transferred, and suddenly CGE was acting as if it did not want the STC shares. Ever since Cables de Lyons had been added to the joint venture, CGE had worried about competition in undersea cable competitions with STC. Howard Aibel went to Paris to negotiate an agreement that provided we would drop to $1.25 billion from $1.5 billion in cash from CGE in exchange for keeping the STC shares, which had been put into the deal at $240 million but had a market value at the time of $260 million. It was a good deal for ITT. STC earnings were strong, and the declining dollar in relation to the pound, plus the increasing stock price, boded well for the value of the ITT holding. Ultimately, in October 1987, we sold the 24 percent interest in STC for a whopping $730 million. Our holding had tripled in value since it had been removed from the joint venture.

In those last days of December, when the 24 percent of STC stock was retained by ITT, our ownership in the joint venture went back to 37 percent. All primary shares were duly transferred. Standard Electrica's stock transferred in Spain, as did STK's in Norway. Only Taiwan, Sweden, Nigeria, two small Latin American holdings, and a small African one were put off for January transfer; $112 million was held back by CGE, with ITT's agreement, for those companies.

Pierre Suard and I felt that everything was in good shape for the end-of-year closing. On a long-distance call from Paris, he said that CGE wanted to name the new joint venture "Alcatel." They had done extensive studies and felt that this name, utilizing the name of CGE's French subsidiary, would be the best in terms of image and marketing. I concurred. I had been concerned that they would come up with something like "Duosys." I liked Alcatel, which has a nice ring in any language, has "tel" in it, and fit well with our subsidiary names, such as Alcatel Standard Electrica. Roxane was about to become history.

That was my last conversation with Pierre Suard until the deal was done. The documents were signed on December 30, 1986, in Brussels.

— 22 —

ONCE IS ENOUGH

Harold Geneen once told me, "Rand, when you get it the right way, the critics will disappear." For the moment, I felt we had it right. The fortunes of ITT had dramatically improved with the creation of Alcatel (nee Roxane). For the first time since my appointment as chairman, the corporation had a surplus of funds and a much-improved balance sheet. *Forbes* magazine selected ITT as the most improved conglomerate of 1986.

Early in January 1987, in Brussels, ABC, CNN, ESPN, and the Public Television Network conducted interviews with me to be used in conjunction with our press conference on the formation of Alcatel. More than 150 reporters gathered in the twenty-third-floor conference room in the ITT Tower on Avenue Louise. I began by explaining the background of ITT and the history of the negotiations. Then Pierre Suard took over and did a masterful job of handling a variety of questions on the future of Alcatel. ITT received broad and favorable coverage on the joint venture. The *Financial Times* called the agreement a "genuine tour de force in industrial negotiation, a breathtakingly radical piece of restructuring that would never have been pushed through without dogged determination, a touch of luck and extraordinary persistence."

In creating this significant international joint venture, there had been exchanges of stock in countries all over the world. Throughout all of this, confidentiality was maintained, and there is no evidence whatever of any insider trading. These complex, multibillion-dollar global transactions were accomplished without any individual or corporation profiting unfairly, here or abroad. Inside information was kept inside.

ITT's recent history offers a significant, simple lesson for corporate America, especially for that part of the business and financial world so in love with debt and leverage. It was, in the final analysis, the huge

496

corporate debt that precipitated ITT's time of troubles. The company was such a large, powerful, well-regarded, highly connected multinational that we had the hubris to think nothing could touch us. We were, of course, wrong. Other American corporations and the federal government are wrong, too, if they think that debt does not matter and that the good times will roll forever.

Government, business, and the public have some hard choices to make. The country can no longer afford to do everything it would wish; indeed, it can barely afford to maintain the status quo. Nor will selling off the country's patrimony and its natural assets solve our dilemma. Slipping growth and productivity, a tidal wave of imports, a debased currency—combined with a rising flood of debt and the lowest saving level in forty years—all pave the way to a lower standard of living. Unless we start to spend more of our energy and ingenuity on the basis of an industrial society, our children will certainly suffer.

ITT certainly learned that the cost of debt is a limiting factor in the health and growth of a company. We learned the lesson the hard way. And we had to avoid an unfriendly takeover in the process.

Was any benefit to the company derived from fighting the ITT wars? Well, just as my father's neighbors helped one another to thresh wheat back in the 1930s, so, too, the people of ITT banded together with a new and stronger bond to thresh the raiders. We fought when the odds were against us, and we won. ITT remains one of the most exciting companies of the twentieth century. We hope to keep the wagon train moving into the twenty-first century and not have to think about making a circle again. Once is enough.

A GREAT PLACE TO WORK

WHAT MAKES SOME EMPLOYERS SO GOOD (AND MOST SO BAD)

———

ROBERT LEVERING

Condensed from *A Great Place To Work*, © 1988 by Robert Levering
Published by Random House, Inc. Printed by permission.

EDITOR'S NOTE

Can a company treat its employees fairly, even generously, and still show healthy profits year after year? Definitely, says Robert Levering, coauthor of the bestselling The 100 Best Companies to Work for in America *and now the author of* A Great Place To Work. *He cites studies that show companies with progressive work policies generally outperform those without them. While some corporations that exploit their workers profit, there is no evidence that being a bad employer makes a company more money than being a good one.*

So, what makes a good workplace? In this study of successful management practices, Levering returns to the best of the best companies from his earlier book to find out. Through interviews with managers and employees, he discovers some startling similarities among successful working environments. He also shows how management often gets in the way of its own best interests.

Levering found the common characteristic of great workplaces to be mutual trust between employers and employees. Company policies say a great deal about this quality. On a basic level, policies represent a straightforward time-for-money contract between employers and employees. On a subtler level, they make a statement about a corporation's underlying attitude toward its workers. The best company policies bolster employees' pride in their jobs and create an environment where people work well together. In A Great Place To Work, *Levering looks at specific corporate policies that have been good for morale* and *business.*

To demonstrate how faulty management theories can create a bad workplace, Levering takes an employee's view of the ideas of four business gurus: Frederick Winslow Taylor, Elton Mayo, Peter Drucker, and Tom Peters.

Managers and employees both will find this book useful. It offers ways to evaluate the workplace and institute meaningful reforms. Perhaps most gratifying is its discovery that nice companies don't finish last. Levering notes that Sam Walton of Wal-Mart and several others interviewed for his first book are among the richest people in America: "Whether these men would like to be known as 'nice guys,' their employees consider them terrific employers. As a group, they refute the widely held belief that the only way to get rich is to exploit your employees. They have taken a lot of people with them to the top."

— I —

IN SEARCH OF A
DEFINITION

WHAT IS A GREAT PLACE

TO WORK?

Most of us can, without hesitation, answer the question "Is your company a good place to work?" We have an implicit notion about what is or is not a good workplace, but because the concept has not been considered in its own right, we don't have generally agreed upon ways to compare workplaces.

The absence of concepts to appraise companies as workplaces contrasts with the abundance of tools to assess companies as businesses. There's the notion of market share; there's the notion of sales growth, and there's the notion of profitability. We're not stuck with merely saying a company is doing well or doing poorly and giving some random facts or anecdotes to support our opinion. We have a variety of well-established devices to pinpoint how a company is performing as a business enterprise.

Not so with workplaces. About all we usually say is that a company is a good or a bad or a so-so place to work. To analyze workplaces, then, we need some concepts comparable to those used to evaluate a business's financial well-being.

Let's start with the concept of a great place to work. Here are some possible definitions:

You're paid a lot of money.

You're treated like a human being.

You do interesting work.

You get good benefits.

You're not fired at the slightest downturn.

If we were presented with a list like this and asked to define a great workplace, we'd probably say, "All of the above." On reflection, we might add a few more ideas, like working in a clean and safe environment, or being able to make suggestions or complaints without fear of reprisal.

We could easily expand our list into a hodgepodge of personnel policies, precepts about how managers should act, and descriptions of well-designed jobs. But we haven't answered the original question.

A better starting point would be to ascertain what a variety of real-life good workplaces have in common. Such an inquiry could begin by reexamining the data gathered in *The 100 Best Companies to Work for in America*. That book was, after all, the first systematic effort to describe the policies and practices of companies considered by their employees to be good places to work. Any careful reader would quickly discover, however, that there is no simple pattern uniting good workplaces.

Let me give some examples. Trammell Crow Company is a large real estate developer based in Dallas, Texas. *The 100 Best Companies to Work for in America* described the firm's exceptional profit-sharing program, which adds an extra 25 to 75 percent bonus to already substantial salaries. The offices don't have partitions, so even the top executives sit in the same bullpen area as the secretaries. That includes the founder of the firm, Trammel Crow, one of the richest men in America, worth more than $750 million, according to *Forbes*.

If we only consider Trammell Crow Company, we might conclude that these two policies—profit sharing and no executive office suites—might be two ingredients of a great place to work. Alas, it's not that simple. IBM, a company long considered a superlative employer, has no profit-sharing plan and its top executives sit in private offices. IBM, however, has had a no-layoff policy since before the Great Depression, while Trammell Crow Company has no such policy and, in fact, has laid off employees during real estate bust periods.

How about employee ownership? Workers at Publix Super Markets, the largest grocery retail chain in Florida and an entirely employee-owned operation, express an almost evangelical love for Publix, often citing the fact that they own the company as the main reason.

You would hear a different story if you talked with some of the ex-workers of Hyatt Clark, a New Jersey maker of roller bearings for automobiles. The former General Motors subsidiary slid into bankruptcy after six years as an employee-owned company. The problem: conflicts between the employee-owners and the company's management which exacerbated the already difficult problems it was having in its competitive industry.

The fact that particular policies and practices fail to define a great workplace has also frustrated human-resource professionals. They tend to think something like this: General Electric has a nifty employee savings plan; let's see if we can't do the same thing here. Over the past decade, personnel fads have included: cafeteria benefit plans, quality circles (Japanese-style work teams), employee stock ownership plans (ESOPs), and 401(k) savings plans. Some have represented genuine improvements in benefits for millions of employees. But the piecemeal approach does not get at the essence of the great workplaces. The peculiar elan of such organizations—the excitement that pervades them—is not so easily exportable. At good workplaces, the whole is greater than the sum of its policies and practices.

The question becomes: How do you explain the whole—the glue that puts policies together in a way that works?

I decided to revisit some of the *100 Best* companies to pursue that specific question. We had originally sought out lower-level employees to get their views on their employer; now I wanted to talk to the top executives and, when possible, to the founders.

From these interviews, it became clear that the quality of the workplace was something they had thought about a great deal. On one point they were united: If their companies are good workplaces, it is *not* because of any specific policies. Far more important is the nature of the *relationship* between the company and the employees.

Ewing Kauffman, chairman and founder of Kansas City-based Marion Laboratories, offers this example. During the drug firm's quarterly Marion on the Move meetings, he often hands out large bonus awards. At one meeting, for instance, he handed a production worker shares of Marion stock worth $8,000 for ten years of perfect attendance. Three other employees got stock worth $7,000, $12,000, and $15,000 for money-saving suggestions. Kauffman stresses that it's not just the fact that the company gives such bonuses that is significant. Equally important is the attitude behind the bonuses. He says: "If you do it because you want to be a father and a giver, that's not good. You don't *give* anything. They *earn* it." Kauffman is not interested in having a paternalistic father-child relationship with his employees.

Larry Quadracci, president and founder of Quad/Graphics, a Midwest printing company, makes the same point: "The systems are only as good as the attitude upon which the systems are operated." Quadracci says the fundamental attitude of his company toward employees is that "we're all in this thing together as partners for the same thing—and that is to make money. And we believe that together we're going to make more money than any of us individually can do."

Larry Quadracci offers the analogy of a marriage: "Marriages are not made in heaven, nor are jobs. Both are close, personal relationships that must be worked at daily." Quadracci's analogy makes good sense. We would not consider a good marriage to be synonymous with two people having a house, a car, two children, a dog, and three cats. We would say that a good marriage depends on how the two people relate to each other. And just as love characterizes the attitude of both parties of a good marriage, trust characterizes the attitude of both sides of a good employment relationship.

Why trust? First, employees at good workplaces constantly speak about how they "believe," "have confidence in," or "have faith in" their employers. Similarly, managers at the same companies talked about how they "can rely on," and "can depend on" their employees. There's an atmosphere of mutual trust that permeates good workplaces. Second, trust is completely lacking in bad workplaces, and appears only sporadically in workplaces considered mediocre.

When I considered trust as the defining characteristic of a good workplace, I found a straightforward handle with which to evaluate various policies and practices of a company. Let's return to the earlier example of Trammell Crow sitting in the bullpen with the secretaries and lower-level employees. Employees could consider this a reflection of the boss's distrust of them, since in the bullpen he would be able to watch and hear their every move. But that isn't how Mr. Crow's employees see it. They believe he sits in the bullpen because he respects their opinions and has nothing to hide from them. What's more, they think it shows he doesn't consider himself to be a separate breed despite his immense wealth.

A focus on the underlying relationships of the workplace does not mean that actual policies can be ignored. On the contrary, the policies are tangible manifestations of the relationships.

To cultivate a specific employee-employer relationship is to build something that really exists. It is a much different matter from what some management gurus do when they talk about trying to induce a "feeling." Techniques that manipulate people's feelings ultimately backfire unless there's a corresponding change in the reality of a relationship. Trammell Crow's employees think he respects them because he *does* respect them, not because he sits in the bullpen with everybody else. The technique makes sense for Trammell Crow because it flows naturally from his basic attitude toward employees. Employees can spot phonies. Managers who adopt the same practice only because it works at Trammell Crow Company will find it self-defeating.

Where trust exists, the employer believes the workers want to be productive and participate fully in the enterprise; employees assume the employer has their interests at heart. This trust frees employees to get a deeper sense of fulfillment from their work.

Two other kinds of relationships turn out to be nearly as important. First, there is the employee's relationship to the job itself. In the best working situation, you feel pride in what you do. It has meaning far beyond the compensation you receive. It's what employees at good workplaces mean when they say, "It's more than a job."

The other primary relationship is that among the employees, including managers. In the best working situation, you enjoy being with your co-workers. You feel part of a harmonious community, lacking in "politics," where people help each other develop and grow personally and professionally.

To sum up: From an employee viewpoint, a great workplace is one in which *you trust the people you work for, have pride in what you do, and enjoy the people you are working with.* This definition offers us a starting point for our inquiry. To get more of a flavor of good workplaces, we need to look more closely at each of the three primary workplace relationships.

— 2 —

SHOWING GOOD FAITH

NEW LANARK, PUBLIX SUPER
MARKETS, MARION LABS

Robert Owen is best known because of the utopian cooperative community he founded at New Harmony, Indiana, in the early nineteenth century. What is less known is that before setting out for America, Owen managed a textile mill in New Lanark, Scotland. At the time, it was one of the largest cotton-spinning mills in Britain, with about fifteen hundred employees.

When Owen took over the mill in 1800, he confronted a problem that has bedeviled anyone who has sought to improve the workplace: the workers were highly suspicious of their new employer's motives. As Owen put it in his autobiography: "The workpeople were systematically opposed to every change which I proposed, and did whatever they could to frustrate my object." They were convinced Owen only wanted "to squeeze as much gain out of them as possible" and "it was long before the majority of the people could be convinced that I was earnestly engaged in measures to improve their permanent condition." To convince the workers, he needed to show them he was operating in good faith—that he had no secret agenda, that his actions were in accord with his avowed intentions.

Owen's patient spadework finally paid off. In 1806 the United States placed an embargo on cotton exports to Britain. Most British mill owners simply shut down their factories and laid off the workers. But Owen believed that throwing the mill's employees out of work would have been "cruel and unjust." So he continued to pay the workers to

508

keep the mill's machinery in good working order. Owen maintained this policy for the four months the embargo lasted "without a penny being deducted from the full wages of anyone." His action cost the company seven thousand pounds in the short run, but it had a big impact. As Owen put it: "This proceeding won the confidence and the hearts of the whole population, and henceforward I had no obstructions from them in my progress of reform."

What's important to note here is the *process* through which Owen gained the confidence and trust of his work force. It reveals an *open-ended time commitment*. There are no shortcuts to gaining people's trust and confidence.

Owen instituted many reforms during his quarter century in New Lanark. He forbade corporal punishment, stopped the hiring of pauper children, reduced the working hours from fourteen hours to ten and a half hours a day, and provided a high-quality school for all children in the village. He also instituted the unheard-of practice of allowing workers the right to appeal supervisors' judgments about their job performance. Near the end of his tenure, Owen even proposed to transfer ownership of the mill to the workers. His business partners squelched this scheme, however.

Word of this model industrial community spread widely. Nearly twenty thousand people made the trek to the Scottish lowlands to see the mill. Included among the visitors were British nobility and politicians, ambassadors from many countries, even Grand Duke Nicholas of Russia. Many visitors remarked on the mill's unusual esprit.

Unfortunately, relations also began to slip during the final years of Owen's management. His growing fame and involvement in various social reform movements led him to take long trips away from the mill. As a result, he became an increasingly remote figure to his employees. One New Lanark visitor remarked in 1819: "(Owen) has as little direct intercourse with the inhabitants of his colony as a general has with his soldiers." A few years later, Owen sought to increase the workers' contribution to the employee sick fund, set up by him but supposedly administered by the workers. A group of them wrote a letter to Owen's business partners, complaining:

> We view it as a grievance of considerable magnitude to be compelled by Mr. Owen to adopt what measures soever he may be pleased to suggest on matters that entirely belong to us. Such a course of procedure is most repugnant to our minds as men, and

degrading to our characters as freeborn sons of a highly favoured Britain.

This episode demonstrates a final important lesson that can be drawn from the story of this Scottish mill: Employment relationships involve *constant communication*. Owen's reforms may have generated a reservoir of goodwill among the workers, but such a reservoir runs dry if everyday human contact is neglected.

PUBLIX SUPER MARKETS:
"THEY DIDN'T HAVE TO DO THAT"

Constant communication is the byword at Publix Super Markets, whose three hundred-plus stores are located in Florida. The quality of the company's interaction with its fifty-one thousand employees has impressed several observers. Several years ago, respected pollster and social analyst Daniel Yankelovich wrote:

> Publix Super Markets, Inc., is a remarkable operation. The people who work there are the most highly motivated people I have ever seen in a large organization. I admit I have seen people as highly motivated in a very small family organization. But . . . Publix is now a very large organization, and to see people with that quality of motivation is really outstanding.

In early 1985, I attended a banquet at a hotel in Jacksonville celebrating the opening of Publix's Store 263 and honoring the forty-seven new employees. As they do for every store's opening, the company's top dozen corporate officers traveled to the banquet from the Lakeland headquarters (two hundred miles away).

The banquet had the earmarks of an old-fashioned revival meeting. Executives and managers from other Publix stores rose to give testimonials—all variations of the same gospel: "I started with this company at the bottom, just like you, and after years of hard work, I've been able to get ahead in my career. You can, too, because Publix is a land of opportunity for anyone who works hard. This is a company that cares about you."

Between testimonials, the emcee for the banquet engaged the new employees in a trivia quiz: "How large is Store 263?" Someone answered, "Thirty-eight thousand square feet." "Where does the name Publix come from?" Another employee raised his hand and explained that it was the name of a now-defunct movie theater chain. "Who owns Publix?" Everyone in the crowd answered at once: "We do!" The emcee congratulated them and proceeded to explain that all Publix share-holders are employees, and that after one year's service, new employees would be granted stock.

The high point of the evening came when George W. Jenkins stood up to speak. Wearing a bright green sports jacket emblazoned with Publix logos, the seventy-seven-year-old company founder sprinkled his talk with numerous anecdotes about the good old days, and a sermonette on "getting along with other people." Referring to himself as "an old groceryman who loves to talk shop," Jenkins noted that Publix was now Florida's largest supermarket chain, selling more than $3 billion a year worth of groceries. But he also observed that "It's harder to stay on top than to get there because everyone's trying to pull you down. So we don't want to get complacent." He gave an upbeat assessment of the valuable contribution he expected from the new people, and told them: "Starting tomorrow, Publix will be a little better or not quite as good, depending on you."

By the end of the evening, the energy and enthusiasm were almost palpable. The excitement continued the next morning. Long before Store 263 opened its doors, the chain's top executives (including Jenkins and company president Mark Hollis) were all there, helping in the bakery, adjusting rows of cans on the shelves. When the first customers came through the doors, the executives were still there, even doing such menial tasks as bagging groceries and carrying them out to customers' cars.

At first glance, this banquet and store opening may appear to be like a sports pep rally. From an employee viewpoint, it is difficult to look at pep rally-style events without some cynicism. For one thing, there is typically an air of unreality about them. You hear "Our team is the best in the world" even when the team has lost the last ten games. For another, pep rallies appear to be a blatantly manipulative technique. The principal rule seems to be: Tell people whatever will make them feel good. Then they'll work harder so we (the company) will make more money.

But much more was going on than just a typical pep rally. We need also to consider the *context* of the banquet—in this case, *the overall relationship between the company and the employees.* On the one hand, the employees were certainly turned on by the event. It was pretty heady to have the founder, president, and other top executives of a large company welcome you in person to the enterprise and then work alongside you during your first day on the job. That kind of attention is bound to make people feel special.

But Publix officials also made a series of *promises* and *implied commitments* to new employees. They promised a "career, not just a job." They said the new employees would be "owners" of the company. And they said that the employees were now part of the "Publix family," where they would be cared for as people, not just as cashiers or meat cutters. So it would be an error to conclude that employees were only turned on because executives made a two-hundred-mile trek from corporate headquarters, ate a chicken dinner with the troops, and then rolled up their sleeves to tidy up shelves and bag groceries. Employees were more impressed by the implications for their own future. The company had gone out of its way to pledge an extraordinary relationship with them.

There is, of course, a down side to any promise or commitment. By welcoming employees into the "Publix family" with open arms, the company was raising expectations about the employment relationship— far beyond what workers could hope for at most workplaces. If the reality of work life at Publix didn't match the eloquent talk, Store 263 might turn out to be an even worse place to work than had Publix's officials stayed away altogether.

Publix's leaders have, of course, been around long enough to be fully aware of these dangers. Founder Jenkins, for instance, won't commit the company to a no-layoff policy because he's not sure the company can always provide jobs. He has seen too many big chains lose their shirts to think it can't happen to Publix. But, not only are Publix's leaders extremely careful about making commitments, they are also conscientious about keeping the ones they do make. Hollis speaks frankly about the problem: "I think (the relationship with employees) could change on us very quickly if we suddenly stopped visiting the stores so frequently." New store openings have averaged two a month for the past few years, and Jenkins, Hollis, and other senior executives personally attend every one. What's more, all of them visit every store in the chain once every two years. And these executive visits are not just a brief ceremonial walk through the store followed by a long, closed-door session in the manager's office poring over the profit-and-loss statements. The executives make it a point to talk personally to employees. And employees say it's not unusual for company executives to do tasks like bagging groceries if the store is busy.

Like the opening-night banquets, frequent executive visits could be construed as a great technique because it appears to lift employee morale. But again, to draw such a conclusion would be to view the technique outside the context of the company's relationship with employees.

One final point: When doing his study of Publix, Daniel Yankelovich found it significant that employees frequently stated: "They didn't have to do that." (It was a phrase, incidentally, I also heard repeatedly at other good workplaces.) Yankelovich observed that employees typically made this statement after they remarked on an unusual benefit or an unexpected gesture by a manager. One example was an employee whose manager had thrown a Christmas party for the store's employees. She told the interviewer:

> He (the manager) is doing it on his own. Now, that is the sort of thing that makes you feel appreciated, and he really does notice that we do good work. He didn't have to do that.

These voluntary acts also have the effect of personalizing the workplace. They indicate that the management recognizes the employees as human beings, not as easily replaceable cashiers and stock clerks. Indeed, Yankelovich reported that the most common single comment he heard from Publix employees was that they felt treated "like a person, not like a number."

As we have seen, Publix often goes beyond what is customary. Publix's top executives don't have to appear in person at every store's opening. Publix's top executives don't have to show up and work alongside employees in the stores. But they do. And because they take the risk inherent in going beyond the traditional employee-employer relationship, they open the possibility of developing a fuller, more trusting relationship.

Granted, a thin line separates this pattern of action from paternalistic acts that have the effect of stifling people. The paternalistic employer, as we shall discuss later, often gives employees unexpected gifts, whether or not they are deserved. At Publix, the management gives no gifts. As in the instance of the manager's throwing a Christmas party, Publix managers express appreciation for something the employees have done. So rather than feeling suffocated by these gestures, employees feel that they are based on something that is genuinely deserved but not normally recognized. The focus is on the employees and their contribution, not on the management as giver.

MARION LABS: AN "UNCOMMON COMPANY"

At Marion Labs, employees refer to the company as "uncommon" and to those who work there as "uncommon people." The term uncommon is also applied to certain benefits. For instance, during the summer months, employees are permitted to take Friday afternoons off (with pay). So those days are called uncommon Fridays. If production meets certain goals, employees are given an additional week of paid vacation between Christmas and New Year's Day. That's called uncommon winter.

Headquartered in Kansas City, Marion Labs manufactures and sells prescription drugs. The two thousand employees (who refer to each other as associates) have other reasons to consider Marion uncommon. Marion has a no-layoff policy and a profit-sharing plan. Marion has a generous suggestion-award program, distributing some ten thousand shares of stock annually among those with the best suggestions. And Marion is one of the very few companies in America that offer stock options to all employees.

A principle constantly repeated at Marion is: "Those who produce shall share in the results." This sounds like a reasonable principle for any organization to follow. But Ewing Kauffman, Marion's founder, knows from bitter personal experience how rarely it is practiced in corporate America. He explains why he left his previous company, where he was a drug salesman:

> I worked for another pharmaceutical company and was paid no salary, no expenses, just straight commission. The second year, I made more money than the president. So they cut my commission rate. I stayed and built it back up so that I again made more money than the president. This time they cut up the territories to cut my income. So I quit and started Marion Laboratories (in 1950). That experience left me with a firm resolve that I would never do that to my people. I was also smart enough to figure out from mathematical formulas that the more money they made, the more money the company would make. So we would share. They would share in the results. And we

extended it to everybody—manufacturing, packaging—not only salesmen, but throughout the company.

Kauffman's experiences also led him to the second principle that forms the basis for Marion's relationship with its associates. It is a secularized version of the Golden Rule: "Treat others—whether customers, suppliers, or other Marion associates—the same as you would want to be treated . . . as an individual, with integrity, trust, and honesty."

While the first principle can be seen clearly in various personnel policies, the second is translated into what Kauffman calls the "little things"—the way everybody treats each other. These little things include such practices as:

Acceptance of honest mistakes:

One middle manager tells the story of how he made a serious error of judgment that cost the company nearly a hundred thousand dollars. At the time, he had only been with the company for a year. He was called into a meeting with three senior executives. At the beginning of the meeting, the manager was "as nervous as a cat on a hot tin roof and as white as a piece of paper." But the three executives kept telling him to relax, and they spent the next hour going over the details of the mistake. Finally Gerald Holder, a senior vice-president, asked the manager, "Do you know how it happened? What you would do different? How would you prevent it from happening again?" When the manager indicated that he understood, Holder told him, "Congratulations, the chances of that happening again are minimal, aren't they?"

This does not mean that Marion never fires anyone. On the contrary, Marion executives insist they do not tolerate mediocrity. But they make a sharp distinction between employees who consistently fail to meet agreed-upon expectations and employees who make honest errors of judgment. Fred Lyons, Marion's president, makes the point this way:

> We tell people: "Feel free to make mistakes. If you're not making mistakes, you're not doing anything. Just don't make the same one twice."

Criticize up, praise down:

Ewing Kauffman has long had a saying that he repeats to everybody, especially to managers: "Don't bitch, complain, or criticize on your same level or down because all it does is hurt morale and lower you in the estimation of your fellow people. Instead, make complaints up the ladder, because it's the only way to get action." By making his views known so widely, Kauffman puts company managers on notice that they must always be willing to listen to complaints and take action to rectify problems.

At the same time, Kauffman preaches that it's important to give credit where it is due. He thinks this is particularly difficult for most middle managers. Often when a subordinate comes up with a useful idea and tells it to his or her manager, the manager will pass the idea along to his superior without acknowledging the source. In the short run, the middle manager thinks he looks good in the eyes of his superior. But in the long run, the subordinate will stop passing along good ideas. Worse, this kind of behavior fosters backstabbing.

Kauffman explains that this is a difficult pattern to break since it is so common to act in our own short-run interest. So he encourages managers to acknowledge the contributions of others. When a manager presents an idea and credits it to a subordinate, Kauffman makes it a point to contact the subordinate directly to compliment him or her. Kauffman says the subordinate's first reaction is: "Boy, the old man praised me." Then he or she thinks: "My boss told Mr. K. that I thought it up. He didn't take credit for himself. Don't I have a wonderful boss!"

Share information broadly:

Four times a year, the entire company attends the Marion on the Move meeting. Two things stick in my mind about the meeting I attended. First, the good-natured fun. Second, the candor with which executives spoke about the company's financial condition and the competitive problems they faced. Company president Fred Lyons says: "We are pretty open. If we have a vulnerability, it's the fact that we're too open with each other. But that's okay. We take that chance. But we keep a very open communication and we share a lot of things that I think in many companies would be considered confidential."

While Marion's distinctive personnel policies may be considered the flesh and bones of its relationship with employees, these "little things" give lifeblood to the relationship. For it is through the little things that the company's management demonstrates its *respect for people as thinking, feeling human beings*. Because management shows respect to associates, the associates show respect toward both the management and each other. The respect people feel toward each other is why the term *associates* seems an accurate description of the relationship among people at Marion. It doesn't have the feel of a label imposed by management to paper over an exploitative or paternalistic setup.

The "little things"—which seem like commonsense notions of how people should relate to each other in organizations—all foster an environment where a more trusting relationship can flourish.

THE GOOD–FAITH PRINCIPLE

Trust does not exist naturally in the workplace. Where it does take root and grow, it requires constant attention and care. Part of the reason for this is that human beings naturally question the motives of others. We are all afraid of being taken advantage of. So we are very careful about whom we trust. Managements of good workplaces acknowledge that everyone inevitably has doubts about the company's credibility. Rather than ignore this natural skepticism, they act in ways that allow employees to make up their own minds about the company's trustworthiness.

In this chapter, we've seen examples of companies that have shown the ability to gain and (at least for two of them) maintain the confidence of employees. How these managements demonstrate their trustworthiness can be summed up as follows:

- *Patience and consistency:* Developing confidence doesn't flow from the results-oriented approach that dominates much of American management thinking. Trust is not amenable to quick fixes that can be reflected on quarterly income statements. Managers at good workplaces implement their policies and practices with great care and deliberateness.
- *Openness and accessibility:* When there's a free flow of information, employees can learn for themselves what the management is up to, and they can raise questions directly with those in authority.
- *Willingness to go beyond the conventional relationship with employees:* When a company does more than it has to do for employees, the employees feel free to do more than they have to for the company.
- *Delivering on promises:* While high-sounding promises may generate enthusiasm and excitement, they also increase expectations. When people don't do what they say they will, it undermines trust.

- *Sharing the rewards of mutual effort equitably:* Management can use very sophisticated human-relations-oriented techniques to obscure inequities in the sharing of rewards. For a while, these techniques may fool employees. But eventually, employees will become disillusioned.

These five points have one quality in common. They all demonstrate the company is acting in good faith. Employees can look at these traits to assure themselves about the company's motives and intentions.

By being patient and consistent, open and accessible, a company's management makes it easy for employees to evaluate the company's actions for themselves. We might formulate this as the *good-faith principle*. It means earning trust by continually demonstrating respect for the employees' right to question the company's actions. By acting in good faith, the company can demonstrate that it is not trying to manipulate people into doing something against their own interest. This has an incalculable effect on how people relate to each other.

— 3 —

REDESIGNING JOBS

NORTHWESTERN MUTUAL LIFE

In 1910, a symbolic milestone was passed when census data revealed that blue-collar workers exceeded farm workers for the first time in U.S. history. But the industrial age was short-lived, soon overshadowed by the information age and an economy based on services rather than manufacturing. As a result, the overwhelming majority of Americans now go to work at an office instead of a factory. The 1970 census disclosed that clerical workers had become the largest single occupational group in the country. This group is often referred to as pink-collar workers because it is so overwhelmingly female, accounting for one third of the women but only 6 percent of the men in the work force.

This dramatic shift has not, however, been accomplished by an equally dramatic change in management thinking about work. In fact, many companies have simply applied Frederick Taylor's scientific-management approach (the subject of a later chapter) to the office. In adapting time-and-motion-study techniques, some zealous adherents of the scientific-management gospel resorted to mechanical devices to monitor clerical work. Early examples included typewriters with keystroke-counting attachments and clock-driven time stamps to record when clerks received and completed batches of work. Scientific managers could then use such information to subdivide work into discrete tasks and prescribe the "one best way" for clerical workers to do their jobs. The goal was to make the office as efficient as an assembly line.

DIVIDEND DOTTERS AND COMPUTERS

Like factory workers, many clerical workers repeat the same task all day long. Before computers were commonplace, for example, life-insurance companies had the job of dividend dotter. To determine the annual dividend, one worker performed a complicated calculation on a manual calculator and entered the figure in pencil on a card. The card then went to another worker, the dividend dotter, who conducted the entire calculation again. If the dividend dotter arrived at the same answer, she or he would place a red dot next to the original figure.

At one time, Northwestern Mutual Life Insurance Company had a dozen dividend dotters. Computers have made that job, as well as manual calculating machines, obsolete. But the introduction of computers did not eradicate the legacy of Frederick Taylor. The new technology often meant more, not less, specialization and assembly-line-style working conditions. For instance, Northwestern Mutual once employed twenty workers who did nothing but handle address changes. By 1982, however, that job specialty had been eliminated. How Northwestern Mutual transformed its clerical work is the story to which we now turn.

The story begins in 1979, when company executives noticed an increase in complaints from both agents and policy owners about the quality of service rendered by the Milwaukee home office. Officials first commissioned a management-consulting firm (Roy Walters & Associates) to study the problem. The study concluded that the solution lay in reorganizing the work flow rather than merely adding more staff. At this point, company officials made a crucial decision—to include the workers who were directly involved in the reorganization.

The first step was to inform everyone of the problem. Executives conducted meetings with the approximately 550 clerical workers in two departments, new business and policy owners services. They detailed the nature of the complaints and described the consultant's findings. They outlined the mechanism for change—task forces to look at every aspect of the work flow, including each job and each step in the process. Eighteen task forces were set up to survey issues like technology, training, communications, and systems. Each task force included upper management, middle management, and clerical staffers.

From the outset, company officials emphasized that the goals were to improve service and to increase productivity. They explicitly assured everyone both in writing and verbally that productivity improvements would not result in anyone being laid off. They also invited officials of the Office and Professional Employees Union to the first general meeting to hear firsthand the presentation made to employees. The union has represented clerical workers in Northwestern Mutual's home office since 1935. Robert Ninneman, the senior vice-president who oversaw the reorganization, says that inviting the union leaders to the initial meeting was important, "to give them a feeling for what we wanted to accomplish. They recognized that we were operating in good faith, and they went along with the change." As evidence of union support, not one union grievance was filed, though hundreds of jobs were affected.

The lack of union grievances is all the more remarkable when you consider how much the workers' jobs were changed. In the policy owners services department, there were about sixty different job classifications for only two hundred workers. As on an assembly-line-production setup, each worker performed clearly defined tasks. In addition to the workers who only entered address changes, others only handled changes in the frequency of premium payments, while still others only made substitutions in policy beneficiaries, and so on. Under the old system, three different clerks had to handle a letter requesting three different changes in the policy, with each making the required entries before passing the file along.

There was a rationale for the old system: efficiency. Clerks who only entered address changes could become extremely fast at that operation. What's more, the company didn't have to spend much time in training, and workers could be easily replaced if they became sick or quit. On the down side, the task forces discovered that many of the customers' complaints could be traced to the fact that several clerks handled the typical piece of correspondence, increasing the chances for delays. Worse, nobody felt any overall responsibility for how quickly the letter was serviced. It's no wonder. After all, the Taylor-style system placed distinct limits on each worker's responsibility. The situation corresponded to a frequent criticism of conventionally organized auto-assembly plants. Individual workers don't assume responsibility for the quality of the car because jobs are sharply defined to preclude any sense of the whole.

The task forces met this problem head on. After considerable study, they reduced the sixty different job classifications in the policy owners services department to six. The byword of the reorganization was one-stop service. As a result, only one clerk, not three, was needed for a letter requesting changes in a policy's premium-payments schedule, beneficiaries, and addresses. Greatly expanding the workers' jobs required extensive retraining—35,000 classroom hours for two hundred employees.

The reorganization greatly expanded employees' responsibilities in another way. The task forces divided the country into four geographic regions. Clerical workers, now called service representatives, were not only assigned to a region, but to specific agencies within the region. Service representatives, who previously only related to stacks of paper and their computer terminals, began communicating directly with agency-office staffs. The company also encouraged face-to-face meetings between the home-office clerks and their local counterparts, often paying for service representatives to visit local offices.

The reorganization accomplished the basic business goal of improving service. Complaints were sharply reduced. Efficiency improved markedly. In the new business department, 82 percent of applications for insurance were handled within five working days as opposed to 52 percent previously. And productivity increased, too. The company increased the value of its insurance policies by 50 percent between 1982 and 1984 but only had to increase the new business staff by 7 percent.

On a personal level, most employees felt much better about their jobs, but this reaction was not universal. Some of the clerical workers simply didn't want the increased responsibility. Ninneman describes how the company dealt with this group:

> We had a handful, as might be expected, who were much more comfortable doing the relatively simple job, with a narrow dimension to it. In those cases, we literally tried to redesign something that would fit what they wanted to do and what they could feel comfortable with. There was a little shuffling of personnel from department to department. We ended up with a little pool of people that didn't quite fit, but they eventually got placed somewhere in the company. So we kept our commitment, and everybody felt very good about it.

Employees also generally felt good that the company expressed appreciation to the troops involved in the process. Northwestern held a series of thank-you luncheons for employees in the executive dining rooms. And about a third of the employees were promoted (with higher pay) because of the increased responsibilities they had assumed.

ENRICHING JOBS

People familiar with contemporary personnel trends might categorize the reorganization at Northwestern Mutual Life as job enrichment. This technique was popularized by Frederick Herzberg, a management theorist in the Elton Mayo human-relations tradition (discussed in a later chapter). Herzberg's theory was first put forth in his 1959 book *The Motivation to Work*. In it, Herzberg identifies five factors that can make a job satisfying: achievement, recognition, the work itself, responsibility, and advancement. People feel motivated to work harder when they can achieve something tangible in doing their job, get recognized for their work, feel the work itself is interesting, and so on. So instead of concentrating on factors like pay and working conditions that don't have much impact on motivating people, Herzberg argues that managers should focus on enriching workers' jobs (making the work more interesting, increasing workers' sense of responsibility and achievement, etc.). In that way, workers would both be happier and work harder.

The Northwestern Mutual clerical workers undeniably had their jobs enriched. But as we shall see, what happened there differed in several important respects from the classic job-enrichment program. Fortunately, it is possible to compare the Northwestern Mutual experience with a job-enrichment program that occurred at nearly the same time at another Midwestern insurance company. In her 1977 book, *Pink Collar Workers*, Louise Kapp Howe devotes a chapter to a large Chicago-based insurance company that had recently implemented a typical job-enrichment program.

The Chicago insurance company (which Howe did not identify) was considered an enlightened employer. It offered good benefits—medical and life insurance, a pension, a stock-investment plan, a tuition-refund program, and "the assorted we're-all-one-big-family activities: travel clubs, picnics, baseball games, bowling teams, holiday parties, a company newspaper." In this environment, the company's job-enrichment program fit in perfectly. According to the personnel officer in charge, the program was based on three principles: that workers "want to do a complete job and not an isolated task," that they need "regular feedback on their performance," and that "they want to participate in decisions about how the work is done, instead of simply being ordered from above." The personnel officer described to Howe how the company implemented a "job-enrichment" program in one department:

In group claims we took a large office of eighty clerical workers and broke them into smaller units of ten each. Now each clerk is handling the records of individual customers from beginning to end, instead of just fragmented pieces of the job.

At first glance, the personnel officer's description may make it appear that what happened at the Chicago company was identical to the reorganization at Northwestern Mutual. At both companies, there had been clerks who only performed address changes. After the reorganizations, those same workers handled a variety of items. At both companies, the employees' jobs were expanded to give them greater responsibility.

But the similarities stop there. According to Howe, the clerical workers in the Chicago company felt that, at best, their jobs had improved only marginally. Some employees thought there was no improvement, and some thought it made their jobs worse. And it made no dents whatsoever in their underlying suspicions toward the company, which they referred to as Big Daddy. Even the personnel officer responsible for the job-enrichment program admitted that it had not succeeded, using his own four objectives for the program: to increase worker happiness, reduce absenteeism, decrease turnover, and increase productivity. He could not give any evidence whatsoever of improvements in any of the four areas.

To account for the resounding success of the Northwestern Mutual reorganization and the apparent failure of the job-enrichment program at Howe's Chicago insurance company, we have to explore the basic differences between the two stories. For one thing, we should recall the assurances Northwestern Mutual made at the outset both to the union and to the clerical workers that nobody would lose her job. By contrast, the workers at the Chicago insurer had been hearing rumors for months that the company was thinking of moving to the suburbs. (Several months after Howe's interviews, she reported that the rumors were well founded. The insurer had indeed decided to move its headquarters to a suburban community more than an hour away from Chicago, forcing many of the clerical workers to leave the company.) In this atmosphere, it is easy to see why workers would not see the point in enriching a job that might soon be eliminated.

Northwestern Mutual was unionized, and the Chicago firm was not. Whatever else is true about unions, they do provide a mechanism for protecting employees' rights. Another significant difference was that

Northwestern Mutual gave promotions and pay increases to at least a third of the workers. At the Chicago company, the clerical workers may have had their jobs "enriched," but not their pocketbooks. When Howe asked the personnel officer whether workers got any more money or promotions, he answered: "No, those are separate issues; important issues to be sure, but separate from what we're talking about here — which is improving the job itself."

The personnel officer revealed an assumption common throughout the business world, the notion that the workplace is made up of several distinct parts and that employee morale can be improved by simply tinkering with each part individually. Sometimes employees need more pay; other times, a new pension plan or health-care benefit; still other times, enriched jobs.

What's rarely recognized is that the workplace is a *system of interdependent relationships*. The quality of a workplace involves three distinct but overlapping relationships — with the company, with the job, and with other employees. How people feel about the workplace depends on all three of those relationships. In the case of the Chicago insurer, the employee's relationship with his or her job may have improved somewhat because of the job-enrichment program. But because the company did nothing to assure people about their security, the gnawing distrust of the company's intentions continued to fester (and for good reason).

Northwestern Mutual employees did not have this distrust of the company's motives. It wasn't just because of the assurances of job security, either. The company demonstrated its good faith by involving employees in the reorganization process itself. According to all involved, many of the changes derived directly from suggestions made by the clerical workers themselves. The reorganization was not imposed from above. Northwestern Mutual's employees talk proudly about being responsible for the changes. This contrasts sharply with what took place in Chicago. Despite the rhetoric about giving workers the right to "participate in decisions," the Chicago company was offering only a phony form of participation. The company had already decided that an enriched job was one where workers did "a complete job and not an isolated task." Like a doctor who prescribes a pill whether or not you need it, the company decided that people were going to do more fulfilling, self-actualizing jobs because that was going to make them happier.

THE HAPPINESS PARADOX

The problem is that not everyone fits the Herzberg (or any other) psychological model. Howe interviewed one employee who complained that the job-enrichment staff treated employees as if they were "all alike," not allowing for the fact that some like to work at a different pace and in different ways.

This *recognition of individual differences* is one of the key reasons why the Northwestern Mutual experience worked. During the task-force process, the company respected what individual workers had to offer. And when the changes were implemented, the company tried to do everything possible to help each individual fit in.

This leads us to the most fundamental contrast between the two episodes. The Chicago insurer claimed that the principal objective of the job-enrichment program was to increase worker happiness. The company assumed that if the employees were happier, they would be absent less often, stay with the company longer, and work harder. At Northwestern Mutual, worker happiness was not on the agenda. Improved service was the primary objective, and increased productivity was secondary. The irony is that Northwestern Mutual was more successful at achieving worker happiness than was the Chicago insurance company. How can we explain this paradox?

In the first place, it wasn't really true that the primary objective of the Chicago job-enrichment effort was worker happiness. The top management presumably bought the underlying thesis of all motivational management techniques—that self-actualized workers will be more highly motivated and will work harder. So job enrichment is a means to higher productivity; it is not an end in and of itself. As Howe discovered, workers at the Chicago company immediately saw through the rhetoric and understood the real goals of job enrichment.

Northwestern Mutual, on the other hand, told people honestly from the outset what it intended to do—and why. It wanted people to work smarter, if not harder. It wanted them to engage their minds and share their knowledge to help improve service. This straightforward approach helps explain why employees there felt better about the changes.

According to some management theorists, employees will feel more committed to a change if they are allowed to participate in the process. That may be true psychologically, for some people. But again, this idea assumes that the goal is to make employees happy—and ultimately more productive.

These management theorists miss the whole point. Northwestern Mutual *did* not involve employees in redesigning their own jobs to raise their morale and level of motivation. They did it because it made sense. The company genuinely believed employees had significant contributions to make. And their ideas did make a difference. The employees helped to design jobs for themselves that, for the most part, made the best use of their aptitudes, skills, and interests. Employee participation may have helped morale, but it wasn't the higher morale that led to more satisfying jobs. It was the substance of employee participation—their suggestions and ideas—that led to the creation of more challenging and satisfying jobs. Because much management literature is fixated on the psychological impact of worker involvement, it tends to ignore the actual content of that involvement.

Given the opportunity, workers will redesign their jobs, not only to make them more productive, but more satisfying as well. At least that's what happened at Northwestern Mutual Life.

There's another way of viewing this point. Northwestern Mutual's management acknowledged from the outset that the employees could help solve a problem, so it treated them as partners. And it did so in a democratic fashion—giving employees full information and the ability to have an impact on issues that directly affected them. It was through a *democratic partnership* that Northwestern Mutual reorganized its clerical work. Had it gone the path of the Chicago firm, it's doubtful it would have either solved its service problems or had a happy workforce. Honesty goes a long way.

— 4 —

PROMOTING FAIRNESS

FEDERAL EXPRESS, TEKTRONIX

W e generally accept as a given the contrast between our time at work and the rest of our lives. Once you enter the office or factory, you lose many of the rights you enjoy as a citizen. There's no process for challenging—or changing—bad decisions made by the authorities. There's no mechanism to vote for people to represent you in decision-making bodies. There's no Freedom of Information Act to help you discover what is going on behind closed doors. There's no presumption of innocence or trial by peers.

We take for granted that such rights don't apply to the workplace partly because most of us have never seen examples to the contrary. There are, however, some remarkable companies that have made a serious attempt to incorporate some of the ideals of political democracy to promote fairness in the workplace.

TRIAL BY ONE'S PEERS

"COMPANY POLICY PROHIBITS INTIMIDATION." So read the headline in an issue of Federal Express's monthly newspaper, distributed to all of the overnight-delivery company's fifty thousand employees. What followed was this story:

> Jason Alan had been called into a meeting with two super-visors. One proceeded to berate Alan for poor work performance. The discussion became heated. Alan stood up and said he was

528

going to talk with his personnel representative. One of the supervisors told him to sit down and finish the discussion. Alan refused and left the office. The next day Alan's supervisor gave him a warning letter for insubordination and put a copy in Alan's personnel file.

The story may sound typical of what happens every day. An employee refuses to follow an order and gets reprimanded. No big deal, right? Not at Federal Express. Alan filed a complaint through the company's grievance machinery, and a board of review overturned the management decision. According to the article: "The board's rationale was that Alan had been put in an intimidating environment—two managers against one employee." Ted Sartoian, the executive who oversees the grievance process, was quoted as saying: "Federal Express employees have the right to work in an environment free of intimidation. The autocratic manager who rides roughshod over employees is not tolerated at Federal Express."

The newspaper article is just the tip of the iceberg at Federal Express. The company has what is probably the most fully developed system for handling employee grievances. Its Guaranteed Fair Treatment (GFT) procedure has received rave notices from Alan Westin, senior professor of law at Columbia University and nationally recognized expert in constitutional law. Federal Express's GFT procedure consists of five steps:

1. Discussion of the problem with immediate supervisor.
2. Review by the supervisor's manager.
3. Review by the senior vice-president of the division. He or she can uphold or overturn the previous management decision or initiate a board of review.
4. Establishment of a board of review consisting of five voting members. The nonvoting chairman of the board picks three members from a list of six nominated by the employee. The employee selects the other two members from a list of four employees nominated by the chairman. Decisions of the board of review are binding on the company as well as on the employee.
5. Review by the appeals board, made up of the firm's chief executive officer, chief operating officer, and senior vice-president of personnel. It decides whether to grant a board of

review if it was denied in Step 3 by the division's senior vice-president.

Note that the employee making the complaint can nominate people from his own work area, so the majority of the board of review can literally be his friends. But based on his experiences in the Marine Corps in Vietnam, Federal Express's founder, Fred Smith, argues that an employee's peers don't automatically vote for their co-workers. "People who are professional and do their job well don't brook laggards. Contrary to the great myth that the work ethic is dead, people are very anxious to do a good job."

Professor Westin finds the peer-review aspect of the GFT process important for two reasons: First, "employee participation helps achieve better results over the long course by building employee experiences and attitudes into the decision-making process." At the same time, "having employee participation usually makes rules unfavorable to the complainant more acceptable, and earns more general employee trust in the system than one entirely presided over by management members." According to Westin's in-depth study of the system, more than 80 percent of the employees rated it as fair as or fairer than the criminal and civil courts or a union grievance system.

It's not just the involvement that makes this system work. The review by the appeals board symbolizes the top management's commitment to the process. Every Tuesday morning, Fred Smith, Federal Express's founder and chief executive officer, Jim Barksdale, the executive vice-president, and Jim Perkins, the top personnel officer, sit down in corporate headquarters in Memphis to review between three and a dozen GFT's that have worked their way up the system. They usually spend a full morning on the cases.

According to Professor Westin, this commitment is crucial:

Given the inevitable conflicts between employee fair treatment and hard-driving managers and executives "getting things done," it will always take the prestige of the CEO—or a top executive enjoying the CEO's full confidence—and occasional intervention by that executive, to protect the system from favoritism or the "management-team instinct." Also, only the CEO or other top executive can ensure that the visible and invisible reward system that spurs managers on is geared to recognize allegiance to the fair procedure system, and to punish the occasional abuse of it by managers.

When Federal Express instituted GFT, company founder Smith wanted to make sure employees understood that the company was serious about it. Smith insisted that plaques outlining the GFT procedure be placed in all work areas throughout the company—some eight hundred plaques. The plaques are made of metal and wood, costing nearly a hundred dollars apiece. And Sartoian remembers the final touch—four metal rivets: "Fred Smith told me, 'I want rivets put in there so that people think that this is solid, in the wall, that it ain't going anywhere.'" And the company backs up the process with money—an estimated $2 million a year to administer the GFT, *about seventy dollars per employee per year.*

Fred Smith once told a group of Federal Express managers that he considers the GFT "the glue that holds this company together." Smith's metaphor has wider applicability. Fairness is the glue that holds a good workplace together. When employees perceive that the management makes a sincere effort to be fair in compensation, benefits, promotions, and in coping with disputes with supervisors, they are more likely to extend their trust in other areas. Fair treatment affects every aspect of the workplace.

FREEDOM OF SPEECH, FREEDOM OF PRESS

Tektronix publishes one of the few weekly newspapers for employees in corporate America. But it's not the weekly frequency that makes *Tekweek* so unusual. It's published without any censorship from the management.

Anyone familiar with company newsletters can immediately see the difference. Most are bland or promotional. Not so *Tekweek*, where employees often directly challenge management decisions. For instance, there's a regular feature, "Employees Are Asking." The questions are followed by responses from management. One *Tekweek* column in 1987 had the following question: "When things are as tight as they seem to be, why is (the instrument division) spending $100,000 to move a group or groups to a new location in the same building?" The vice-president of the division gave a detailed response, arguing that the move would reduce leasing costs by $39,000 to $52,000 a year, make the work areas more efficient, and improve the appearance for visiting customers. This kind of exchange is commonplace at Tek, as the company is universally called. Managers know they are living in a goldfish bowl.

The openness at Tek can be traced to its history. Founded in Portland, Oregon, in 1946, Tek is the world's largest manufacturer of oscilloscopes used for measuring electronic instruments, making it a *Fortune* 500 company, with some twenty-thousand employees. Its founders, Jack Murdock and Howard Vollum, were intrigued with the concept of industrial democracy. Tek instituted a profit-sharing plan during its second year of business and still pays out 35 percent of its net profits to employees.

Murdock was also impressed with a participatory-management system, called multiple management, at McCormick Company, the Baltimore spice company. At Tek, the idea of employee participation has been translated into what is known as the area-rep program. Employees elect a representative from their work groups (one area rep for about every forty employees). Once a month, each work group is granted forty minutes of paid company time for the area-rep activity. Generally speaking, reps use the time to learn more about the company. They may visit another Tek facility or invite a senior official to talk about a specific subject. On a monthly basis, the approximately three hundred area reps get together for a forum on a topic of interest, such as compensation. Employees give questions for their reps to ask the executives who speak at such forums. The highlight of the year is the area-rep meeting addressed by the president. He delivers a State of Tektronix speech and then opens himself to questions. As might be expected, the gloves are off during the question-and-answer period. The tougher questions and the president's answers are reported in full in the next issue of *Tekweek*.

Tek's president, Earl Wantland, acknowledges that the freewheeling atmosphere can be uncomfortable for management:

> Anxiety is a natural part of the human creature. But it's important to deal with people honestly and openly about issues and give them some opportunity to express their positions. It's also important to give people a chance to adapt to whatever the new norms are likely to be rather than for changes to come in as completely arbitrary actions, with no common courtesy at all in terms of the impact on the individual.

Wantland points out that management is uncomfortable with the free flow of ideas for another reason:

> A lot of people, especially folks that aren't very secure, have a tendency to restrict the flow of knowledge, because it is a power source. And if you keep the people uninformed, you keep them vulnerable and insecure and therefore not very aggressive, and with an unwillingness to question what's going on.

Information is a source of power in any organization. When managers restrict its flow, they enlarge their power at the expense of those under them. However, this creates serious problems for the organization, because people need information in order to make intelligent decisions. Unless you prefer an organization of automatons, the more knowledge people have, the better will be their individual work and the more productive will be their collective efforts.

Restricting information goes hand in hand with a more rigid, hierarchical approach to doing business. People in the hierarchy jealously guard their information and apportion it a little at a time. They may feel that nobody down the line can be trusted to make the right decision because truth resides only in the loftier ranks. Such thinking is dangerously self-defeating, according to Wantland:

> In general, the highly planned, highly structured, hierarchical approach to business doesn't work. Each person, no matter where they are in the hierarchy, only knows so much, and that's not near enough. If you push everything through a hierarchy, you're going to be missing important elements of what it is that you're dealing with, because of the natural filtering process that goes on whenever information is passed along. Some people have skills in management, but that doesn't make them the most knowledgeable person about any particular issue that comes up. So it's very important that we have an open enough atmosphere here so that we can bring knowledge to whatever issues we are dealing with—and to let the information flow in a fairly free and fluid form.

Wantland is arguing that the free flow makes sense strictly on business grounds. But it also makes sense in terms of workplace relationships. The way information is handled affects any community. If you don't know what's going on, rumors can fly, and it's hard to contribute fully and enthusiastically. When information gets distorted, people begin to mistrust each other, and once credibility is undermined, cooperation suffers. In short, without the free flow of information, people can't work together as well as when everyone has the chance to make an informed contribution.

Ultimately, the value of democratic forms like freedom of speech or trial by one's peers is that they make for a better community. Democratic forms make sense because a democratic society makes for a better way to live.

Robert Dahl, the respected political scientist, recently wrote a book arguing that the disparity between an undemocratic workplace and a democratic society is no longer tenable. He writes:

> *If* democracy is justified in governing the state, then it must *also* be justified in governing economic enterprises; and to say that it is *not* justified in governing economic enterprises is to imply that it is not justified in governing the state.

If nobody should be treated as a second-class citizen in society at large, why should anyone be accorded second-class status during a large part of his or her waking hours? A good workplace takes this argument to heart.

— 5 —

SCIENTIFIC MANAGER

FREDERICK WINSLOW TAYLOR

Most of us have worked in places where the boss contends that it's his job to do the mental work while the employees do the physical or routine work. Gordon Forward, the president of Chaparral Steel, once summed up the idea perfectly: "Most companies assume you should check your brains every morning at the factory door."

If you've ever wondered where that idea came from, meet Frederick Winslow Taylor, the father of scientific management. Other Taylor legacies include efficiency experts, time-and-motion studies, standardized work procedures, planning departments, and the piece-rate wage based on established standards—"paying men, not positions."

Taylor's techniques were ideally suited to mass production. Taylor made several visits to the infant automobile industry in Detroit. In 1909, he delivered a four-hour lecture to Packard's management, which soon proclaimed itself "Taylorized." And Henry Ford's right-hand man, James Couzens, came under Taylor's influence. He helped put the principles of scientific management into practice at the world's first moving assembly line, which opened in Highland Park, Michigan, in 1913. Taylor also served as a consultant to other major companies, including Du Pont and General Electric, which helped spread the gospel of scientific management throughout American industry. Time-and-motion studies continue to be used widely. United Parcel Service, for instance, employs over a thousand efficiency experts who track UPS drivers' movements with stopwatches.

More than just his techniques have filtered through to the present day. Taylor's philosophy is almost universally accepted in practice, if not in theory, by managers throughout the world. Indeed, as Peter F. Drucker once wrote: "(Scientific management) may well be the most powerful as well as the most lasting contribution America has made to Western thought since the Federalist Papers." Taylor's contribution has not been limited to capitalist countries, either. Lenin urged Soviet industrial managers to study scientific management:

> The possibility of building socialism depends exactly upon our success in combining the Soviet power and Soviet organization of administration with the up-to-date achievements of capitalism. We must organize in Russia the study and teaching of the Taylor system and systematically try it out and adapt it to our ends.

Most people who've written about management have been consultants or business-school professors. Few of them have actually been workers or managers. Frederick Taylor was both. Born in 1858 into a middle-class family in Philadelphia, he passed up a chance to attend Harvard and went to work as an apprentice patternmaker in a machine shop. He rose through the ranks from day laborer to journeyman machinist to gang boss to foreman and finally to chief engineer of the Midvale Steel Company. In his managerial positions, Taylor began his experiments to bolster efficiency and formulated principles of the "task system," later known as "scientific management."

Taylor has two distinct sides to his personality. On the one hand, he had a wide range of interests outside of work. He was a terrific tennis player. He had a good sense of humor. In Frank Barkley Copley's biography, there's a priceless photo of Taylor in the costume of a woman; he played her part in an amateur play. This engaging, social side of Taylor helps explain how he spread his ideas so effectively and acquired so many disciples.

But Frederick Taylor also hated imprecision. A childhood friend, who later became an artist, recalled:

> Fred was always a bit of a crank in the opinion of our boyhood band, and we were inclined to rebel sometimes from the strict rules and exact formulas to which he insisted that all our games must be subjected . . . Even a game of croquet was a source of study and careful analysis with Fred, who worked out carefully

the angles of the various strokes, the force of impact and the advantages and disadvantages of the understroke, the overstroke, etc.

Biographer Copley traces this aspect of Taylor's personality to his Puritan and Quaker forebears. Wherever it came from, Taylor always strove for perfection. Above all, he couldn't stand to waste time or energy, and he thought it unforgivable for anyone else to do so, either. Loafing on the job, or soldiering, as it was then known, was to Taylor "the greatest evil with which the working-people of both England and America are now afflicted." His entire career was devoted to rooting out soldiering from the industrial scene.

Why do people loaf on the job? Taylor believed it stemmed from "the natural instinct and tendency of men to take it easy." This inherent laziness is compounded when you get a group of workers together. They invariably pressure more energetic workers to slow down. What's worse, they engage in "systematic soldiering . . . with the deliberate object of keeping their employers ignorant of how fast work can be done. So universal is soldiering for this purpose that hardly a competent workman can be found in a large establishment . . . who does not devote a considerable part of his time to studying just how slow he can work and still convince his employer that he is going at a good pace." Taylor spoke from experience. He had worked alongside other machinists at Midvale for a number of years.

How do you get people to work harder? When first promoted to management as a gang boss, Taylor thought he could easily induce his former associates to move faster. He estimated that they had set the machines to produce only one third of their potential. So he tried a variety of tactics—from verbal persuasion to "discharging or lowering the wages of the more stubborn men." After three years, output increased; it even doubled in some instances. But Taylor's hard-nosed techniques had provoked a "war" between the workers and the management. This was altogether unsatisfactory. As Taylor later wrote: "For any right-minded man, this success is in no sense a recompense for the bitter relations which (a manager) is forced to maintain with all those around him. Life which is one continuous struggle with other men is hardly worth living."

Taylor wanted a method that would both increase output *and* lead to the "harmonious cooperation between the workmen and the management." That goal is worth noting because it has often been under the guise of bettering the conditions of workers that some of the worst abuses have been perpetrated.

Taylor's system had several features. First, management must analyze each task. Taylor knew that when a manager tells someone he is working too slowly, the worker is likely to retort, "No, I'm working as fast as I can." How can management counter that response? Science. The scientific manager subjects every task in the workplace to dispassionate scientific inquiry to eliminate any dispute about whether someone is goofing off. "Every single act of the workman can be reduced to a science," Taylor insisted.

One of Taylor's examples was shoveling coal. Based on his studies at Bethlehem Steel, Taylor concluded that "a first-class man would do his biggest day's work with a shovel load of about 21 pounds." Not 18 or 24 pounds per shovelful, but 21 pounds. To arrive at conclusions about "the science of shoveling," Taylor's people "conducted thousands of stopwatch observations . . . to study just how quickly a laborer . . . can push his shovel into the pile of materials then draw it out properly." These time-and-motion studies determine the "one best way" to shovel coal or perform any other task, thereby "substituting exact scientific knowledge for opinions or the old rule-of-thumb of individual knowledge."

With this information, the entire workplace could be organized scientifically. The planning department, as the "brains" of the operation, directed every aspect of the work. Workers were taught how to do their work scientifically. A single foreman was replaced by a half dozen or more managers, whom Taylor called "teachers." In one machine shop, Taylor created seven different slots to oversee the workers. In this scheme, the "inspector" explains the quality that is expected; the "gang boss" elucidates on the quickest motions; the "speed boss" makes sure the machine runs at the proper rate; the "repair boss" takes care of the machine; the "time clerk" keeps track of output for piece-rate payment; the "route clerk" coordinates the flow of materials to and from the worker; and finally, "in case a workman gets into any trouble with any of his various bosses, the 'disciplinarian' interviews him."

To hear Taylor or any of his army of disciples talk about its virtues, scientific management was the best friend the American industrial worker ever had. The scientific organization of the workplace frees the worker to concentrate on improving his efficiency. To overcome any worker resistance, Taylor preached that new piece-rate standards must be set so that workers would be paid substantially *higher wages* than before, even double or triple. The company could afford paying more because the improved efficiency meant it would incur much *lower total labor costs*. Besides getting more money, workers in a Taylor-run plant received elaborate training, proper tools, and the best possible physical working conditions. What more could anybody ask?

If the work relationship was merely a one-for-one market exchange, like buying a loaf of bread, scientific management would have made a nirvana out of thousands of American workplaces. Instead, its impact has been disastrous. Scientific management is rooted in distrust. Taylorism assumes that workers are naturally lazy and that they will sabotage efforts to increase productivity. Taylor designed his system to make that impossible. It makes a frontal assault on the worker's main source of power—his knowledge. As Taylor wrote in his classic essay *The Principles of Scientific Management:*

> . . . traditional knowledge may be said to be the principal asset or possession of every tradesman . . . Foremen and superintendents know, better than any one else, that their own knowledge and personal skills fall far short of the combined knowledge and dexterity of all the workmen under them.

Because the workers can't be trusted, scientific management tries to wrest control of their knowledge. Industrial engineers don't use stopwatches and other techniques merely to establish an objective scientific standard; they aim to steal what Taylor frankly acknowledges as the employee's "principal asset." Once it possesses enough know-how about the specifics of each task, management can exert absolute control over the workplace. Taylor summed it up clearly:

> It is only through *enforced* standardization of methods, *enforced* adoption of the best implements and working conditions, and *enforced* cooperation that this faster work can be assured. And the duty of enforcing the adoption of standards and of enforcing this cooperation rests with the *management* alone.

All of Taylor's talk about creating a "harmonious" relationship between management and the employees aside, scientific managers may have to bare their fists if they don't get voluntary cooperation. Once cooperation has been "enforced," the division between planners and doers can be made permanent. As Taylor put it: "One type of man is needed to plan ahead and an entirely different type to execute the work." In short, the manager provides the brains, the worker provides the brawn. This conception of management has dominated the workplace since Taylor's day.

Over the years, Frederick Taylor and scientific management have had their share of critics. Some have singled out several of Taylor's anecdotes in which he refers to workers as "mentally sluggish," "stupid," or like an "ox." Though Taylor did indeed use those phrases, he did not say that workers were inherently stupid. Quite the reverse. As we've seen, Taylor realized that workers had brains and a considerable amount of knowledge. He objected to workers' using their intelligence against management instead of for it. So Taylor devised a system to neutralize the power of employee intelligence and make it irrelevant to how work was accomplished. Under scientific management, an employee not only doesn't have to think—he's not supposed to. His thinking is to be done by the new cadre of managers ("teachers"). The replaceable worker—comparable to a machine part—is what scientific management attempted to achieve.

Scientific management had an especially devastating impact on employee pride. Without a feeling of control over your work, it's almost impossible to take much satisfaction in what you do. Taylor's system took away more than the employee's knowledge ("his principal asset") about how to do a job. It took away pride of workmanship.

This point can best be illustrated by listening to comments from workers with some firsthand experience of Taylorism. The year was 1911. The place was the Watertown Arsenal near Boston. Not long after some Taylor-trained industrial engineers came into the arsenal, the machine-shop molders staged a wildcat walkout. The molders returned to work after a week, and Taylor's disciples continued their time-and-motion analysis. In itself, the event was insignificant. But because it occurred at a federal installation, the government sent investigators to study the situation. As a result, we have transcripts of interviews with the molders. A central complaint revolved around the destruction of self-esteem.

A molder named Isaac Goosetray told investigators: "It will make an inferior class of workmen, for the simple reason that when a man is speeded up too much he will slight his work and the consequence will be in a short time from now that . . . we will have an inferior class of workmen."

James A. Mackean, who worked in the arsenal's machine shop,

echoed this concern: "They can give us certain speeds and feeds in figures; but they cannot show us how to do the work better by any system than we know now. They can show us how to do it faster, but not better."

Mackean's remark sums up another key problem with scientific management. It does offer the possibility of improving productivity. But what about quality? One industry that has taken scientific management to heart is the American auto industry. Problems with poor quality in American automobiles can be traced at least in part to this Taylor legacy of removing the responsibility for quality from the worker. Japanese car makers, by contrast, have long placed responsibility for quality in the hands of the workers through the mechanism of work teams or quality circles.

Some Japanese even blame Taylorism more generally for America's industrial problems. Konosuke Matsushita, founder of Japan's largest electronics firm, Panasonic, once told a group of Western industrialists:

> We Japanese are going to win and the industrial West is going to lose out. There is nothing much you can do about it because the reasons for failure are within yourselves. Your firms are built on the Frederick Taylor model where the bosses do the thinking and the workers wield the screwdrivers. You are convinced deep down that this is the right way to run a business.

Matsushita's observation has merit. The Taylor system has had an enormous appeal to managers the world over. It gives them a superior status and has helped create many of the managerial positions. After all, more managers—a lot more managers—were needed to operate a plant scientifically.

Since this new class of managers benefited from Taylorism, it follows that they would be threatened by a system that trusts the employees. That is precisely what has happened. In the late 1970s and early 1980s, a number of American companies instituted quality circles and other participatory-management techniques, largely in response to the desire to emulate the successful Japanese. In 1986, *Fortune* published an article about the experience:

> It was really beautiful. Hourlies and supervisors, pencil pushers and clock punchers, all gathered around the corporate foundry to forge a new relationship based on the idea that workers

could play an active part in management . . . The new way entailed asking employees how their work might be improved and then letting them improve it, often in work teams or so-called quality circles. The initial results were (impressive): A study of 101 industrial companies found that the participatively managed among them outscored the others on 13 of 14 financial measures.

Based on such results, we should have expected that every company in the land would have eagerly signed up. Here was the obvious answer to boosting America's competitive edge. But no, just the opposite occurred. *Fortune* quoted one business-school dean as saying: "The problem with participative management is that it works." About 75 percent of the programs installed during the early 1980s were scratched by 1986. Why? According to *Fortune*, the opposition came not from the workers but from:

> . . . management, upper, middle, and lower. The concept was banished to the shop floor and, even if it flourished there, was never permitted to creep higher. Jump on the quality circle bandwagon? Sure. Takers were everywhere. But change the behavior of managers or the organizational structure? Not this decade, thanks.

As the *Fortune* article demonstrates, you can't de-Taylorize a workplace without displacing the people whose jobs depend on acting as the employees' "brains." A later chapter, on Preston Trucking, shows how one company rooted out the scientific-management thinking and replaced it with a philosophy based on the assumption that the individual employee knows how to do his or her job best. Fully one quarter of the managers left the company as a direct result of that transformation. (Preston has meanwhile performed better than many of its competitors.)

One final point. Taylor argued that soldiering stems from natural laziness. Yet his own account contradicts that analysis. Consider the machinists at Midvale Steel Company before Taylor instituted his task system of management. Taylor acknowledged that the machinists didn't just sit around all day doing nothing. They spent time and energy figuring out how to keep production levels down. Taylor's rhetoric places the blame on worker laziness, but the intent of his system is to redirect the energies of the workers—to get them to cooperate with management rather than to subvert production. Taylor didn't try to figure out how to "motivate" his workers. He assumed that workers were already motivated, but that they were motivated toward the wrong goals.

If laziness doesn't explain soldiering, what does? A more likely cause can be found in working conditions since the onset of the Industrial Revolution. Workers lost the feeling of being connected to the product they made or the service they rendered. As skilled craftsmen or farmers, they had a direct relationship with their own work. They used their tools to create something. In the factory setting, and especially under scientific management, the worker became a tool in the hands of others. As Taylor himself stated: "In the past man has been first; in the future the system must be first." If loafing on the job is seen in this light, its solutions lie in removing the sources of the alienation.

Taylorism undermines every aspect of a great workplace. It's antithetical to building trust, it's fatal to employees' feeling pride in their own work, and it's destructive to creating genuine harmony in the organization. His successors have been unable to root out Taylor's legacy because, as we shall see, they share some of his assumptions even as they abhor some of Taylorism's excesses.

— 6 —

PSYCHOLOGICAL
MANAGER

ELTON MAYO

Police investigators often work in pairs. One adopts the tough-guy stance while the other plays the part of the nice guy. One relentlessly hammers away at his quarry; the other offers understanding and consideration.

This same duality can be seen in many organizations. Most companies not only have nice guys; they have an entire department in which they reside—the personnel department, now often called the human-resources department. This nice-guy approach to management didn't just happen. Its roots can be traced to the 1930s and an industrial psychologist named Elton Mayo. How Mayo's human-relations movement came to occupy such a prominent place in American management is an ironic story of the tough guys creating the nice guys.

Frederick Taylor's scientific-management had suggested an engineering solution to the people problem of industry. Management need only conduct detailed analyses of tasks to eliminate the troublesome "human element" from the workplace. Employees could then be manipulated with the proper mixture of wages and discipline, just as their machines could be adjusted to deliver peak performance.

But even well-organized and well-intentioned employees get tired. They get bored. Their minds wander and productivity suffers. Ironically, fatigue and monotony became a greater problem with the spread of the scientific-management system.

Since the engineering approach had offered a solution to soldiering, surely it could solve these new "human" problems, too. At least that's what Taylor's disciples believed. Factory managers sponsored studies to figure out how to solve the problems of fatigue and monotony in the workplace. One of these studies had the surprising result of challenging scientific management itself.

THE HAWTHORNE DISCOVERIES

Research engineers of Western Electric Company (AT&T) launched the study in question in 1923 at its sprawling Hawthorne Works plant near Chicago. They wanted to know whether worker productivity would be affected by changes in lighting. So they increased or decreased the lighting in several different departments. After months of study, they found no obvious correlation between lighting and work output. Sometimes people worked better when the room was dimly lit, sometimes worse.

The engineers then turned to other factors, such as the effect of rest breaks and changes in piece rates. They picked five young women and built a special test room adjacent to a large work area for the experiment. By isolating the workers, they sought to minimize variables and make the study more scientific. The women performed their usual job—assembling telephone relays that consisted of thirty-five separate pieces secured by four machine screws. It generally took about one minute to assemble each relay. The women normally worked a forty-eight-hour week, including a half day on Saturday, without any rest breaks. The researchers wanted to know about fatigue. For instance, did rest periods in the morning and afternoon make the workers feel less tired and improve their output? Every few weeks for two years (1927-1929), they made changes in the women's work day and piece rates, and studied the effects of those variations in both worker morale and productivity.

No one anticipated the results: The workers' productivity improved almost regardless of which changes were instituted.

How could such results be explained? Baffled, the research engineers turned to Elton Mayo, head of Harvard Business School's new industrial research department.

THE AUSTRALIAN "DOCTOR"

Mayo came from a family of doctors in South Australia and everyone assumed that he would continue the tradition. But Mayo flunked or dropped out of three medical schools before finally getting a degree in philosophy in 1904. The degree enabled him to teach, and he spent the rest of his career affiliated with universities, first in Australia, later at the Wharton School of Business, and then at Harvard.

Mayo never fit comfortably into the narrow specialization of the academic world, and never got a Ph.D. Nevertheless, he had enormous personal effect on people. His biographer, Richard C. S. Trahair, writes: "When he entered a room he gave the impression that an important person had arrived. On the street in good weather he wore a brimmed hat with a colorful band, carried a cane, sported a handkerchief up his sleeve, and walked with a jaunty swagger that used the full length of his slim body." A brilliant conversationalist and a lecturer who could spellbind audiences, Mayo loved theorizing on a wide variety of topics. He saw himself as a healer and a therapist. Despite the fact that he never completed medical school, he was referred to as "Dr. Mayo." Mayo never did anything to disabuse people of the notion and even had a set of doctor's scales in his business school office.

Shortly after arriving in America in 1922, Mayo got himself an invitation to speak on medical psychology—a hot lecture-circuit topic of the day. His talk impressed an associate of John D. Rockefeller, Jr. Interested in seeing whether Mayo's ideas could be applied to industry, Rockefeller agreed to fund studies of workers at some factories in Philadelphia.

It was through his association with Rockefeller that Mayo became known to Western Electric executives. They invited him to come to Chicago and consult with them about their studies. Never at a loss for a theory, Mayo offered a radical interpretation. He contended that the changes that had been introduced—the variations in rest pauses and piece rates—were only "minor matters" compared with the profound change in the work environment brought about by isolating the women in the test room. In particular, Mayo singled out the role of the sympathetic "observer," who didn't act like a typical plant supervisor. This is what is often referred to as The Hawthorne Effect, a familiar term in the lexicon of social science. It means that behavior may improve because of the attention people receive from being singled out for study rather than because of the test changes themselves. More important, Mayo stressed that the test room was not merely six individual workers. They constituted a social grouping with a life of its own. To Mayo, the test room itself was "a new industrial milieu, a milieu in which (the workers') own self-determination and their social well-being ranked first and the work was incidental."

Mayo suggested that the discovery of the social milieu in the workplace should be studied further, and Western Electric launched what may well be the largest industrial study in history. To learn more about supervisory practices and improve the quality of supervision, Western Electric interviewed more than twenty-one thousand Hawthorne workers between 1928 and 1930. Thirty full-time researchers were employed. Mayo helped orient them in nondirective interview techniques, which let the workers talk freely about whatever subjects interested them. The interviews typically lasted one and a half hours.

The extensive interviewing project prompted one last experiment. This time the researchers decided simply to observe the social dynamics of the bank-wiring department, where fourteen men assembled telephone terminals. Unlike the procedure followed in studying the five women relay-assembly workers, researchers did not alter the bank-wiring workers' normal routine. The only difference was the existence of an observer. He mostly sat in a corner and took notes. Though the men initially viewed him with suspicion, the observer was soon accepted. The study lasted for six months, until May 1932, when the men were laid off because of the Depression.

What the Hawthorne researchers discovered would not have surprised Frederick Taylor. They saw that the bank-wiring workers intentionally restricted their output; that is, engaged in soldiering. The work group had an elaborate social dynamic. A worker who produced more than the group's informal standard was called a rate buster and was subject to severe social pressures. Anyone who produced less, a chiseler. The workers also singled out as a squealer anyone who told a supervisor anything that could reflect badly on a co-worker. In short, the bank-wiring room was a sociologist's dream—and an industrial supervisor's nightmare.

The results of all three phases of the Hawthorne experiment also created a nightmare for the theory of scientific management. According to Mayo and his disciples, the Hawthorne study proved conclusively that merely changing the physical conditions of work won't even touch the underlying psychological and social problems that cause people to be less than fully productive. Any effort to improve productivity had to start with an understanding of both human nature and the nature of social organizations. The workplace is full of human beings, not machines, as Frederick Taylor would lead us to believe. It takes the sensibility of a humanist to understand and to deal with workers.

The Hawthorne experiments shook up the engineering-management establishment of the day. As historian David F. Noble wrote:

> The discoveries of Mayo and his colleagues were startling and constituted a revolution in management thought; needless to say, the engineers who had conceived the original project had hardly suspected anything of the kind . . . The Hawthorne experience called into question many of the basic assumptions of scientific management, gave impetus to the infant applied sciences of industrial psychology and sociology, ushered in the new field of "human relations," and provided management educators with a wealth of case-study material.

Mayo left the laborious task of writing up details of the experiments entirely in the hands of his proteges Fritz Roethlisberger and Thomas North Whitehead (son of Alfred, the famous philosopher). Instead, he lectured widely and wrote two short volumes (*The Human Problems of an Industrial Civilization* and *The Social Problems of an Industrial Civilization*) to put forth his interpretations of Hawthorne to a wider audience.

What Mayo actually says in those books defies easy categorization. He was an eclectic thinker who drew freely from various fields—anthropology, psychology, sociology, political science, and philosophy. His analysis of the Hawthorne interview program, for instance, provoked a lengthy discussion of psychologist Pierre Janet's theory about obsessives. His ruminations about the cause of poor morale in the workplace led him to write for pages about sociologist Emile Durkheim's concept of anomie. Mayo's protege Fritz Roethlisberger explains:

> Mayo was not a systematic thinker. Although he stated his ideas vigorously, he never stated them rigorously. His accomplishments are best seen in the context of face-to-face relationships. His chief products were the people that he influenced and

helped to develop. Even the ideas that he developed in books were more often in the nature of seeds to be cultivated in the field than of rigorous hypotheses to be tested in the laboratory.

The seeds Elton Mayo planted have borne fruit in the form of a wide variety of management practices, from psychological testing and attitude surveys to job-enrichment programs and management training in human-relations skills. More important than the specific human-relations techniques, however, has been the widespread managerial acceptance of Mayo's basic humanistic premises. For instance, managers commonly assume the need to apply psychological techniques to get employees to perform more efficiently.

At first glance, Mayo's message may appear like one that should be applauded by employees. His humanism certainly offers a welcome antidote to Taylor's lack of compassion. It's also hard to argue with someone who recognizes your *human* qualities rather than only your skills. Unfortunately, the human-relations approach to the workplace also contains a serious flaw. The perception that workers are patients and managers are therapists undermines the building of a great workplace.

WORKERS AS PATIENTS

Richard C. S. Trahair writes that Mayo saw himself as "a healer of disease in industrial society." Of course, the main sufferers from the disease are industrial workers. Mayo states this explicitly in his books. Using data from the Hawthorne interviews, Mayo wrote that the workers' statements about their working conditions and their supervisors were totally unreliable. Two workers with identical jobs under the same supervisor could give wildly different descriptions of their work situation. Citing the theories of various psychologists, particularly Pierre Janet, Mayo speculated that the workers exhibited an "obsessive response" to their work environment. Mayo did not believe that all workers were crazy and would be better off in asylums. But he did believe that they suffered from a mild form of mental illness that affected their productivity. That's why they gave such distorted accounts of their work and were often unhappy with their jobs.

According to Mayo, talking out problems through a nondirective counseling session called an interview helped workers overcome their obsessions. He writes:

One woman worker, for example, discovered for herself during an interview that her dislike of a certain supervisor was based upon a fancied resemblance to a detested stepfather. Small wonder that the same supervisor had warned the interviewer that she was "difficult to handle." But the discovery by the worker that her dislike was wholly irrational eased the situation considerably.

According to the researchers: "It was evident that the complaints of this type of person could not be taken seriously as criticisms of company policies or conditions." On the contrary, in Mayo's opinion, Western Electric was "committed to justice and humanity in its dealings with workers."

What we see here is a clear example of the human-relations approach in action. Viewing the workplace through the prism of a therapist, the industrial manager tends to see all problems as personal problems. The appropriate solution invariably requires the individual worker to adjust to the company. But how accurate is Mayo's view of the workplace? We need look no further than the case Mayo himself cites. The full transcript of the interview with the worker reveals that the woman might not have been so irrational after all.

In the transcript the worker contrasts the disliked supervisor with her previous one, who "says little jokes and makes you feel good." Her current boss, on the other hand, is "kind of mean-like. He's so mean-looking . . . He talks (mean), too." According to the worker, the supervisor criticizes employees harshly whenever a mistake is made, and he often harasses them with petty demands. She claims that other supervisors aren't so abusive. Most important, she insists that her feelings are shared by the other workers: "They all feel the same; they haven't much use for him. It seems like he just likes to hurt people. He just wants you to know that he's the boss."

On the basis of the interview, the worker appears to have had lots of sound reasons for disliking her supervisor. If anything, there appear to be ample grounds for arguing that her supervisor needed to change his behavior toward subordinates. But that wasn't even considered an option. Mayo places the entire burden on the employee, and the employee alone, to adjust to what appears to be a pretty bad situation.

The supervisor clearly believed that the interview would straighten out the worker. The technique, in other words, might have been portrayed to the workers as a purely neutral one, but the management wanted the workers interviewed because it might help with their problem cases.

This example illustrates the deception at the core of the human-relations approach. Beneath the guise of making people feel better lurks the real goal: increasing productivity. Daniel Bell, a Harvard sociology professor, reviewed the work of Elton Mayo and the subsequent human-relations movement in his 1956 essay, "Work and Its Discontents." According to Bell:

> The ends of the enterprise remain, but the methods have shifted, and the older modes of overt coercion are now replaced by psychological persuasion. The tough brutal foreman, raucously giving orders, gives way to the mellowed voice of the "human relations oriented" supervisor.

Certainly improving productivity is a desirable goal for an industrial enterprise. And anyone would prefer a mellow-voiced supervisor to a brutal boss. But when matters are not communicated in an above-board way, it undermines trust.

While Elton Mayo himself didn't come up with other techniques besides the interview, the human-relations movement he spawned continues to develop them: psychological testing, sensitivity training, job-enrichment programs, to name just a few. These management styles all view the workplace from a psychologist's perspective. Subsequent management theorists have had more sophisticated theories of human nature than Mayo's rather crude view of obsessives and industrial maladjustment. For instance, one of those who have followed the trail blazed by Mayo is Abraham Maslow, a popular humanistic psychologist. Maslow developed a sophisticated model of human nature called the hierarchy of needs. Maslow argued that once people meet their basic survival needs they have a need for self-actualization. Two popular management styles are explicitly grounded in Maslow's model—Frederick Herzberg's job-enrichment program (discussed earlier) and Douglas McGregor's Theory Y (which was the basis for sensitivity training and organizational development). A more recent exponent of the psychological approach to management is Tom Peters, whom we will discuss shortly.

SPONTANEOUS COOPERATION
WITHOUT CONFLICT

Advocates of the human-relations approach invariably suggest that reliance on humanistic managerial techniques eliminates conflicts between management and labor. Instead of two warring factions, Mayo envisioned a workplace characterized by "spontaneous cooperation," where everybody would work together harmoniously.

The vision of a workplace of cooperative workers has great appeal. But it assumes a fundamental unity of interest between the individual and the organization. What happens, however, if you think your supervisor is treating you unfairly? Or if you don't agree with your humane supervisor about how to do a task? Or if you think the company is paying you too little money? By trying to reduce such complaints to individual psychological problems, the human-relations approach implies that it's possible to achieve cooperation merely by making changes in the minds of the employees rather than in the policies and practices of the company. In this sense, Mayo's concept of spontaneous cooperation echoes that of Frederick Taylor's call for cooperation. Both assume that management alone will dictate the terms. That employees might have legitimate interests is simply not part of Mayo's theory.

Mayo's view also lacks a theory for handling conflicts in the workplace. The human-relations specialists who've followed in Mayo's footsteps have discovered that they simply have to step aside when major conflicts develop. That's one explanation for why personnel (or human-resource) departments usually get relegated to the background in organizations. The human-relations movement can make people feel better, but it doesn't offer much besides psychological persuasion and exhortation if the employees aren't responsive. For all its shortcomings, scientific management provides specific suggestions about how to deal with uncooperative (soldiering) employees. Taylor's approach sets standards and has mechanisms for enforcement—or, as Taylor put it, "enforced cooperation."

Perhaps the deficiencies in the human-relations approach could be overlooked if that approach was shown to be a powerful tool in raising productivity. But there is strong evidence that refutes the underlying assumption of the human-relations movement that happier workers are more productive. The eminent industrial psychologist Victor Vroom surveyed twenty different studies that attempted to see what relationship, if any, existed between job satisfaction and work performance.

His conclusion: "There is no simple relationship between job satisfaction and job performance." Sometimes happier workers produced more; sometimes they didn't.

How do we explain this finding? One explanation is that many of the human-relations-style techniques don't affect structural changes in the workplace. They often concern only how supervisors relate to their subordinates. For that reason, workers often consider these techniques to be mere window dressing, if not by-products of a manipulative management. Employees may appreciate being treated better, but it may not result in work getting done more efficiently.

Does that mean that productivity requires an authoritarian management style like Frederick Taylor's? Not if we look closely at the research Vroom and others have conducted. Vroom, for instance, has noted that when employees have more say over their jobs, they are often more productive. As we saw in the chapter on Northwestern Mutual Life, when employees are accepted as full partners in the work process, they often work more efficiently.

It is ironic that Vroom's conclusion was entirely consistent with Mayo's research at Hawthorne. In explaining the change in the environment of the test room of the relay-assembly workers, Mayo wrote what could have been used as a terrific example of building trust in the workplace:

> There had been a remarkable change of mental attitude in the group . . . At first shy and uneasy, silent and perhaps somewhat suspicious of the Company's intention, later their attitude is marked by confidence and candor. Before every change of programme, the group is consulted. Their comments are listened to and discussed; sometimes their objections are allowed to negative (overrule) a suggestion. The group unquestionably develops a sense of participation in the critical determination and becomes something of a social unit. This developing social unity is illustrated by the entertainment of each other in their respective homes.

Mayo could have used such examples from the Hawthorne experiments to argue for greater employee democracy and participation in decision making. But Mayo had a lifelong aversion to worker participation. It had overtones of socialism and of the trade unionism he'd opposed in Australia. According to Richard C. S. Trahair: "Mayo preferred the American approach, which did not allow economic areas to be debased by the modern developments in democracy."

Instead, Mayo placed his hope in a managerial elite. Throughout his career, he voiced the highest regard for industrial managers, but he held that they needed training. One of the biggest contributions of Mayo and his followers was the field of management training, especially in the area of human relations. Mayo saw it as crucial that managers develop a clinical approach toward workers. Unlike the "irrational" employees he oversees, "the administrator of the future must be able to understand the human-social facts for what they actually are, unfettered by his own emotion or prejudice . . . We do not lack an able administrative elite, but the elite of the several civilized powers is at present insufficiently posted in the biological and social facts involved in social organization and control."

The key word here is *elite*. Like Taylor before him and Peter Drucker to follow, Mayo helped provide the vision for a distinct managerial class. This enlightened managerial elite would have two sets of skills. One involves the finely honed administrative skills allowing managers to make all business decisions on their own without input from employees. This is the Taylor legacy. The second encompasses the human-relations skills necessary to induce the "irrational" employees to go along with management's decisions—and feel satisfied with the arrangement to boot. This is Mayo's contribution. What comes through loud and clear from an employee viewpoint is the idea that management is an elite, whether the individual managers portray themselves as tough guys or nice guys.

— 7 —

PROFESSIONAL MANAGER

PETER F. DRUCKER

I t's not unusual to hear a young person say that his or her vocational goal is to be a manager. We take that idea for granted largely because we generally consider management to be a profession, somewhat like medicine or law. As for other professions, you can go to a professional-training school where the discipline of management is taught and degrees are offered. About fifty thousand people a year receive an MBA in the United States. Of course, you don't need an MBA to practice management, but still, we accept as commonplace the notion that someone can be a professional manager.

If any one person can be said to be responsible for the wide acceptance of the professional manager, it's Peter F. Drucker. Born in Vienna in 1909, Drucker is the son of a former high government official in Austria who founded the Salzburg international music festival. Educated in Germany, Drucker fled the Nazis and settled in the United States in 1937. Two years later, his first book, *The End of Economic Man*, appeared. Since then he has written almost two dozen books (including two novels) and hundreds of articles on economics, politics, social trends, and management. He also taught management at New York University for more than twenty years and has been a management consultant to dozens of major corporations throughout the world.

In assessing his own influence, Drucker can't be accused of modesty. He calls himself the "man who *discovered* management." He credits the acceptance of his ideas with saving "a dying Ford Motor Company;"

with revitalizing Sears, Roebuck after the Second World War; and with getting General Electric to adopt a "decentralization policy"—a policy that, in Drucker's words, "probably had more impact on industrial structure around the world than any other move by a major company in the post-World War II period." Then, of course, there are the Japanese, whose success in the postwar years can be traced to their adoption of Drucker's ideas—at least according to Drucker. In Japan, he writes, "I am credited with substantial responsibility for the emergence of the country as a major economic power . . ."

One of Drucker's most widely accepted notions is management by objectives, commonly referred to as MBO. In its simplest form, it means that managers ought to define goals and base their activities on them. According to Drucker:

> Each manager, from the "big boss" down to the production foreman or the chief clerk, needs clearly spelled-out objectives. These objectives should lay out what performance the man's own managerial unit is supposed to produce. They should lay out what contribution he and his unit are expected to make to help other units obtain their objectives. Finally, they should spell out what contribution the manager can expect from other units toward the attainment of his own objectives.

When Drucker penned those words in 1954 in *The Practice of Management*, he thought American managers were overly concerned with process. Auto-company managers, for instance, got so involved in the process of making cars—in the details of design and workmanship— that they lost sight of the overall objectives of the corporation. Such managers might build great cars, but the company itself could go out of business because the managers ignored other goals, like making a profit.

Considered in isolation, it's hard to fault the management-by-objectives idea. It sounds like common sense. What it has come to mean when put into effect is another matter. As John J. Tarrant points out in his biography of Drucker:

> In practice . . . we often see the concept of management by objectives translated totally into a formulation that might be called "bottom-line management," or management by results. More and more an upper-echelon executive holds himself aloof from what is going on beneath him. He figures that his respon-

sibility lies in hiring somebody to do a job, telling him the "bottom-line" results that are expected, and then rewarding the subordinate if he delivers or firing him if he does not deliver.

This translates into a lot of pressure on lower-level managers. If all that matters are results, who is going to be concerned with the quality of the workplace? It's doubtful that the harried supervisor trying to attain his objectives is going to worry much about gaining the trust and confidence of individual employees.

In *The Practice of Management*, Drucker writes: "It is not the business of the enterprise to create happiness but to sell and make shoes. Nor can the worker be happy in the abstract." The implication is that the effective executive shouldn't bother trying to "create happiness." It's not his job. The manager is to focus on the economic objectives of the organization. Employees "must be definitely subordinate to the claim of economic performance: profitability and productivity."

It would be misleading to imply that Drucker himself urged managers to grind up employees. He writes persuasively about the importance of treating workers as "resources," not merely as "costs." Nevertheless, it is easy to see how the hard-nosed, bottom-line, results-only managers draw much inspiration from Drucker.

On the other hand, there are a lot of good, even brilliant, insights in Drucker's thinking. His critique of Mayo and the human-resources movement in his book *Management: Tasks, Responsibilities, Practices* is devastating:

> They use terms like "self-fulfillment," "creativity," and "the whole man." But what they talk and write about is control through psychological manipulation . . . Psychological despotism should have tremendous attraction for managers. It promises them that they can continue to behave as they have always done. All they need is to acquire a new vocabulary.

And he suggests that the key issue overlooked by human-relations managers is that the "work relationship has to be based on mutual respect . . ." What makes Drucker frustrating, however, is that such insights aren't coupled with any understanding of the workplace from the employee viewpoint. For instance, a common Druckerism is : "The basic task of management is to make people productive."

Drucker's sympathies are totally with the manager in the employee-manager equation. And the thrust of his work has been to create a managerial elite capable of running business enterprises effectively. In the Drucker universe—reflected in practice by thousands of organizations throughout the land—employees are second-class citizens. Drucker's devotees may protest such a harsh judgment, since he has written countless perceptive comments about avoidable problems created by authoritarian managers. And he has written approvingly of such managerial techniques as IBM's job-enlargement and job-security policies. Yet Drucker insists managers must always make clear who is boss.

Drucker made explicit his top-down bias in his utopian book, *The New Society*, published in 1950. In it he wrote:

> The rank-and-file job holders—whether of production, technical or clerical jobs—obviously cannot be given authority and responsibility for decisions regarding the enterprise's business . . . The very definition of these jobs is that they take orders rather than give them.

Part of the reason why Drucker-style professional managers operate in a hierarchical fashion can be traced to Drucker's basic political outlook. He genuinely believes that society needs a managerial elite—a distinct class of people to run a complex society of organizations. But Drucker has always posited a much higher mission for corporate executives: They are the torchbearers of a Western civilization almost destroyed by the nightmare of Nazism and the scourge of Marxism. As Drucker once put it: "Management, its competence, its integrity and its performance will be decisive both to the United States and to the free world in the decades ahead."

A problem is that professional managers have become all-purpose managers. In Drucker's view, there isn't much difference between the manager of a commercial airline, a bank, an automobile plant, a hospital, or a computer manufacturer. The economy is suffering from these all-purpose managers jumping from industry to industry. Improving the quality of automobiles isn't something we can expect from a job-hopping MBA spending a few years in the auto industry before taking a better-paying job with a computer firm. The corps of all-purpose professional managers also has a deleterious effect on employee morale. As a breed apart, the professional managers not only block off possibilities for advancement for the nonprofessionals below, but they often tend to act like know-it-alls in areas where they are in fact know-nothings.

One further note. It's consistent with Drucker's goal-oriented approach that contemporary business-management schools are increasingly churning out specialists in finance. Finance is, after all, the ultimate managerial abstraction. These managers don't have to know anything about particular industries. They merely need to know how to manipulate a business in such a way that the numbers look good in the short run.

— 8 —

EVANGELICAL
MANAGER

TOM PETERS

A few years ago *Business Week* published a chart listing twenty different crazes that have captivated American managers since the Second World War. A few, like matrix management and zero-based budgeting, have little direct bearing on the workplace. But most of them are devoted to improving employee productivity, such as one-minute managing, Theory Y (participative management), Theory Z (quality circles), and management by walking around (excellence). Others have enriched no one but the management consultants who implemented them.

Most business fads on the *Business Week* list have come and gone without attracting the notice of the general public. Not so with excellence, first promulgated in the 1982 book *In Search of Excellence*, which has sold more than five million copies. Besides making the book's coauthor, Tom Peters, a millionaire at age forty, the book helped catapult Peters to a celebrity status rarely associated with management consultants. Peters is a perpetual motion machine, on the road over forty weeks a year making some two hundred fifty speeches, sometimes as many as three in one day. He writes a weekly nationally syndicated newspaper column and has appeared on several nationally televised public-television specials.

Peters earned a reputation for flamboyance at the staid management-consulting firm of McKinsey & Company. He occasionally showed up for work in khaki shorts and a T-shirt at the San Francisco office, where he met his coauthor, Robert H. Waterman, Jr. This behavior is unheard of for a $250,000-a-year McKinsey consultant. It is also not what one would expect from someone with a civil engineering degree from an Ivy League university (Cornell) and both an MBA and a Ph.D. in business from Stanford University. But such eccentricities would not surprise anyone who has ever heard Tom Peters speak. He peppers his sermons with dozens of anecdotes, works up a sweat stalking back and forth across the stage, and often shouts himself hoarse. Peters charges $15,000 for a two-hour speech and is reportedly the world's most highly paid speaker, earning about $1.5 million annually in fees.

Despite Peters' show-biz antics on stage, he is quite capable of holding his own with the sharpest of business-school academics. He has taught at the Stanford Business School and authored articles in academic journals. But Tom Peters doesn't pretend to be a seminal thinker like Frederick Taylor, Elton Mayo, or Peter F. Drucker. He calls himself an interpreter, a popularizer of management thinking. Peters once declared: "There's absolutely nothing new whatsoever between *(In Search of Excellence's)* covers. It was a translation of ideas and material that had been around for up to fifty years. All it added was brilliant timing and packaging."

GOOD NEWS FROM AMERICA

The timing was indeed perfect. In 1982 the country was in the midst of a recession, with unemployment hovering around 10 percent. Many of the unemployed were auto, steel, and textile workers recently displaced because of imports from Japan and other foreign countries. There was a widespread feeling that we were beginning to see the end of American industrial dominance. Many people also believed that American corporations had become overly bureaucratic, stodgy, and out of touch. A sign of the times was the previous year's most discussed business book, William Ouchi's *Theory Z*, which advocated that American business adopt Japanese management practices. As Tom Peters later said: "American industry was ready for a little positive news."

Peters and Waterman had just the ticket. In some ways, their "upbeat message" paralleled the optimistic 1980 campaign oratory of Ronald Reagan, who promised to restore pride to the country after its international humiliations. Both proclaimed solutions to America's problems through a return to basic American values. In the book's introduction, Peters and Waterman declare:

There is good news from America. Good management practice today is not resident only in Japan. But, more important, the good news comes from treating people decently and asking them to shine, and from producing things that work . . . Hierarchy and three-piece suits give way to first names, shirt-sleeves, hoopla, and project-based flexibility . . . Even management's job becomes more fun. Instead of brain games in the sterile ivory tower, it's shaping values and reinforcing through coaching and evangelism in the field—with the workers and in support of the cherished product.

Peters and Waterman based their "good news" on what they found at America's most successful companies. They picked forty-three companies that were both innovative and had performed well financially over the previous two decades: " . . . the companies were not truly excellent unless their financial performance supported their halo of esteem."

The forty-three excellent companies had eight attributes in common, spelled out in chapter titles that have since become part of the American management lexicon: "A Bias for Action;" "Close to the Customer;" "Autonomy and Entrepreneurship;" "Productivity Through People;" "Hands On;" "Value-Driven;" "Stick to the Knitting;" "Simple Form;" "Lean Staff;" and "Simultaneous Loose-Tight Properties." Excellent management means staying in close touch with employees and customers. The shorthand name for the style they advocated was "management by wandering around."

Not ones to shy away from hyperbole, Peters and Waterman insisted that "management practices in the excellent companies aren't just different. They set conventional management wisdom on its ear." They claim that conventional management has been hostage to the "rational model," which the authors see as "a direct descendant of Frederick Taylor's school of scientific management." Peters' and Waterman's theories can save managers from falling into the rationalist trap:

What our framework has really done is to remind the world of professional managers that "soft is hard." It has enabled us to say, in effect, "All that stuff you have been dismissing for so long as the intractable, irrational, intuitive, informal organization can be managed."

Like Elton Mayo, the starting point for the Peters and Waterman view of human nature is that "people are not very rational . . . man is the ultimate study in conflict and paradox." First on their list of inherent contradictions is that "all of us are self-centered, suckers for a bit of praise, and generally like to think of ourselves as winners." At the same time, "none of us is really as good as he or she would like to think."

Peters and Waterman see this insight as the basis for organizational strategy:

> We all think we're tops. We're exuberantly, wildly irrational about ourselves. And that has sweeping implications for organizing . . . The lesson the excellent companies have to teach is that there is no reason why we can't design systems that continually reinforce this notion; most of their people are made to feel that they are winners . . . Their systems make extraordinary use of nonmonetary incentives. They are full of hoopla . . .
>
> Researchers studying motivation find that the prime factor is simply the self-perception among motivated subjects that they are in fact doing well. Whether they are or not by any absolute standard doesn't seem to matter much.

Step back and reflect for a moment about what's being said here. People are irrational "suckers" who don't want to face reality. So organizations ought to develop policies that make them feel like winners even if they aren't. All that's important is how people *feel* about themselves. So companies should have frequent celebratory events full of "hoopla."

Another example. According to Peters and Waterman:

> . . . the excellent companies appear to take advantage of yet another very human need—the need one has to control one's destiny. At the same time that we are almost too willing to yield to institutions that give us meaning and thus a sense of security, we also want self-determination. With equal vehemence, *we simultaneously seek self-determination and security*. That is certainly irrational.

Peters and Waterman have raised here a fundamental workplace issue—perhaps the most important one from the standpoint of em-

ployees. Individuals always give up some control over their lives when working in an organization. Employees can never be entirely free to do what they want to do, since no organization can afford a do-your-own-thing approach. This is a genuine and ongoing problem, not one that any organization (or society) has ever solved once and for all.

Because Peters and Waterman see this issue in strictly psychological terms, we should not be surprised that they offer a psychological solution:

> Psychologists study the need for self-determination in a field called "illusion of control." Stated simply, its findings indicate that if people think they have even modest personal control over their destinies, they will persist at tasks . . . They will do better at them. They will become more committed to them . . . The fact, again, that we *think* we have a *bit* more discretion leads to *much* greater commitment.

Giving lower echelons in the organization more responsibility is certainly laudable, as we saw in the story about Northwestern Mutual Life. This is an important part of a great workplace. But when we look more closely at the Peters-Waterman push-authority-far-down-the-line prescription, we discover that there's a catch. Based on psychological principles, they are saying that if you give people a little control over their job, the tension between the organization and the individual—between "self-determination and security"—can be eradicated. Whether the increased control people are given over their jobs is real or merely illusory doesn't matter.

MOTIVATION OR MANIPULATION?

For the moment, let's assume that a company's management can successfully motivate workers by pursuing policies based on these psychological insights and theories. Peters and Waterman seem to think that's true, and they're not alone. Management consultants and business-school professors have been preaching variations of the same gospel for a half century now. And for almost a half century, the philosophy of motivational management has had its critics, mostly those who charge it with being manipulative.

What is meant by the term *manipulative?* In a recent article, moral

philosopher Raymond S. Pfeiffer offers a definition based on the work of various psychologists, social critics, and philosophers:

> To manipulate someone, such writers broadly agree, involves a subtle influence on that person's actions, beliefs, desires, feelings, or values, which in turn inhibits rational deliberation. It may involve the falsification or omission of information, or it may involve a play on one's nonrational impulses. But it is widely characterized by an element of subtle and often deceptive persuasiveness.

Using that definition, excellence management appears to qualify. Peters and his coauthors seem to revel in what Pfeiffer would call "a play on one's nonrational impulses." To them, motivation means finding the right irrational buttons to push. Techniques that play on people's psychological needs (such as their need to be winners, or to feel control over their destiny) create a subtle yet irresistible pressure on people to do as the management wants.

And consider the actual meaning of some of the terms Peters and Waterman use approvingly in their book. My dictionary defines *hoopla* as "something—as utterances—designed to bewilder or confuse;" and *sucker* as "a person easily cheated or deceived." Or we could note their sympathetic discussion of *illusion of control*. Peters and Waterman make no attempt to disguise the use of deceptive techniques. They celebrate it.

INTEGRITY VERSUS DEMOCRACY

The real problem with deceptiveness is that it clouds rational thinking. As Pfeiffer puts it, "Motivation management does not assist workers to arrive at a motivated state as the result of a wholly free, fully informed, open, rational, analytic, or critical approach to the issues."

The antidote to manipulation is democracy. Democracy in this context does not mean that everybody in a company should have an equal vote on whether to buy more pencils. Rather, it's the notion that people should have some say in issues that affect them, like the process to redesign work at Northwestern Mutual Life. It means they should have forums for the free exchange of information, ideas, opinions (and criticisms), like the employee newspaper at Tektronix. It means they should have mechanisms that assure due process in cases where they feel

their rights have been violated, such as the Guaranteed Fair Treatment procedure at Federal Express. Such companies have explicit policies and procedures that speak to the employee concern about manipulation in the workplace. Without democratic institutions, citizens have no legitimate process to fight tyrants. By the same token, without democratic institutions in the workplace, employees have no recourse against being manipulated by well-meaning managers.

Organizations have every right to want their employees to be motivated. But employees have every right to make up their own minds about the level of commitment they wish to make to their organizations (over and above the minimal requirements of a job). The rights of the two parties are not necessarily inconsistent, but they do need to be balanced.

A Peters disciple (of which there are many) could, of course, challenge this argument. Even if there are manipulative aspects of the excellence concepts, the little deceptions and tricks played on employees to get them motivated aren't exactly major transgressions. Besides, the intentions of the Peters-style managers are good. If there is a little unavoidable manipulation involved, it's for a wholly justifiable cause—one that benefits both employees and the company.

This justification assumes that the interests of the employee and the company are the same. That is, after all, the biggest selling point of the whole idea of excellence. It proclaims that excellent companies are not only successful financially but offer consumers high-quality products and employees a good working environment. There is no need to worry about manipulation, since employees benefit when the company succeeds.

THE BOTTOM LINE

But is this claim valid? Do the employees' interests and the company's interests always coincide? One way to assess this claim is to look at how Peters defines the company's interests. On this point, Peters and his coauthors have been absolutely crystal clear. The bottom line of excellence *is* the conventional bottom line—profitability. The excellent companies weren't picked because of the quality of their products, nor because they were good workplaces. It was only *after* the coauthors had selected companies that demonstrated financial prowess that they looked for common attributes, including workplace practices. In a review of *In Search of Excellence* in the *Harvard Business Review*, Daniel

Carroll noted that it was ironic that the same "authors, who leave no doubt about their abhorrence of the rational model, with its numerative determinism, seem to use exactly that to select excellent companies."

To point this out is not to suggest that making money is a bad objective. Nor is it to suggest that seeking profitability is inconsistent with a good workplace. Indeed, as we argue later, companies that are good workplaces often are much more profitable than their competitors. But the relationship between workplace practices and a firm's financial performance is extremely complicated. Carroll's *Harvard Business Review* article pointed out that Peters and Waterman failed to acknowledge that technology, finances, government policy, raw materials, and other factors can also affect a company's financial viability. What's important to note here is that if your eyes are fixed on one goal—in this case, profitability—it colors everything else you observe.

Consider McDonald's, the world's biggest fast-food chain. McDonald's has consistently grown larger and more profitable over the past three decades. That's why it was cited repeatedly in *In Search of Excellence*. Peters and Waterman also single out McDonald's as one of seven firms to profile in their chapter on people management. The authors quote a former colleague: "You know, one of the things that strikes me most about McDonald's is their people orientation. During the seven years I was at McKinsey, I never saw a client that seemed to care so much about its people."

You won't, however, hear such rave reviews of McDonald's by talking to those working behind the counters or in the kitchens— McDonald's entry-level employees, who often earn the minimum wage. They express their feelings about their employer by leaving it in droves. One hundred percent-a-year turnover rates are common at McDonald's restaurants throughout the land.

The employee perspective is simply ignored by most people writing about business, including Peters and his coauthors. They talk about employees a lot and create elaborate psychological theories about what makes them tick, but rarely do they consider the world from the employees' viewpoint. Everything gets reduced to the issue of productivity, including the problem of employee morale. McDonald's founder, Ray Kroc, one of Peters' corporate heroes, is quoted admiringly as saying: "A well-run restaurant is like a winning baseball team, it makes the most of every crew member's talent and takes advantage of every split-second opportunity to speed up service." The dreaded rationalist Frederick Taylor would have loved Ray Kroc.

PEOPLE FIRST

What about companies that are both financially successful and good workplaces? Let's take a look at IBM, a company that has been both highly successful and generally thought of as a good workplace, especially by the overwhelming majority of people working there. It's one of the excellent companies. At one point Peters and Waterman introduce a passage about IBM with the following exhortation:

> Treat people as adults. Treat them as partners; treat them with dignity; treat them with respect. Treat *them*—not capital spending and automation—as the primary source of productivity gains.

The authors then go on to quote Thomas J. Watson, Jr., who once wrote that IBM considers "respect for the individual" the most important single belief to the company and how that belief was "bone-deep" in his father. Both Watson and his father had been chairman of IBM.

Peters and Waterman did not, however, continue to quote Watson who, in the same book, stated explicitly: "As businessmen we think in terms of profits, but people continue to rank first." That Watson asserts that people "rank first" demonstrates something that distinguishes good workplaces: the explicit recognition that people do matter *as* people. But it's only when organizations have to choose between "people" and profitability that we discover whether this belief is "bone-deep" or merely suntan lotion for balmy days. It doesn't have any meaning to say that you "respect that individual" if you do so only at your convenience.

This is an absolutely crucial distinction in understanding what makes for a good workplace. IBM has on several occasions in its long history refused to lay people off in difficult times. It did so because it really does put people first, even when it may mean some short-term financial problems. IBM executives might argue that in the long run, the no-layoff policy has potential financial benefit by maintaining employee morale. But that's beside the point to those whose vision is fixated on profits and productivity.

Wall Street pundits are not alone in decrying the short-term effects of IBM's no-layoff policy. So, ironically, is Tom Peters. In his third book, published five years after the first, he proclaims an "end of the era of sustainable excellence." Because the world is changing so rapidly, "There are no excellent companies . . . No company is safe. IBM is

declared dead in 1979, the best of the best in 1982, and dead again in 1986."

It appears that the fixation with the bottom line has actually led Peters to a betrayal of what a lot of people thought excellence was all about in the first place. But excellence, at least to the originators of the craze, meant exactly what they said it meant: financial success. The idea may have been trumpeted as iconoclastic, populist, and revolutionary. But it ultimately appears to embrace (or co-opt) precisely the sort of thinking it claimed to be rejecting. IBM hasn't changed. Peters, however, has apparently given up on IBM. It's not that IBM has abandoned its own principles—or even the Peters-Waterman eight attributes of excellent companies. IBM is no longer excellent because it only made $4.8 billion in net profits in 1986, down from $6.5 billion the previous year, thereby being only the second most profitable company in American instead of number one.

Sure, times are tough today. But they've been tough before and will be tough as long as people try to make a buck in business. What Peters appears to be saying is that because times are tough, there are no lasting principles, no enduring ideas—only techniques that may work (which he calls "prescriptions") for those facing troubled times.

Many of his techniques, looked at in isolation, may represent substantial improvements in the workplace. But if the techniques are only aimed at increasing efficiency, the heart and soul of a good workplace is still missing. As suggested throughout this book, a good workplace is not merely a collection of progressive practices and policies. A good workplace is defined by the type of *relationship* that grows from a company's policies and practices.

EVANGELISTIC MANAGEMENT

One final point. When assessing a management theory's impact on the workplace, it's always a good idea to look at the nature of the relationship projected between the manager and employee. In Taylor's case, we could say the relationship is that of thinker and doer. In Mayo's, doctor and patient. In Drucker's, superior and subordinate. In the case of Tom Peters, a close approximation would be that of evangelist and convert.

This analogy seems appropriate for several reasons. Tom Peters not only talks explicitly of the need for "evangelism" in relations with workers, but it's part and parcel of his speaking and writing styles. His

second book, *A Passion for Excellence*, coauthored with Nancy Austin, even concludes with what sounds like an altar call:

> When you have a true passion for excellence, and when you act on it, you will stand straighter. You will look people in the eye. You will see things happen. You will see heroes created, watch ideas unfold and take shape. You'll walk with a springier step. You'll have something to fight for, to care about, to share, scary as it is, with other people. There will be times when you swing from dedicated to obsessed. We don't pretend that it's easy. It takes real courage to step out and stake your claim. But we think the renewed sense of purpose, of making a difference, of recovered self-respect, is well worth the price of admission.

The manager with this "passion for excellence" is, above all, supposed to instill the same sense of purpose and, as Peters puts it repeatedly, "meaning" in the employees. The theoretical basis for this, according to Peters and Waterman, is the concept of a "transforming" leader developed by political scientist James MacGregor Burns. Unlike the rational and bureaucratic "transactional" leader, the "transforming" leader is charismatic. According to Peters, "He is concerned with the tricks of the pedagogue, the mentor, the linguist—the more successfully to become the value shaper, the exemplar, the maker of meanings . . . He is both calling forth and exemplifying the urge for transcendence that unites us all."

Like the evangelist, the transforming leader has a gospel to preach— a "cherished product," in this case—and he seeks to convert the uncommitted, to motivate employees to higher and higher levels of productivity. He not only has to get employees to do their work, but he has to help them in the spiritual quest for meaning in their lives. This burden takes its toll. And Tom Peters and Nancy Austin are the first to acknowledge it:

> We are frequently asked if it is possible to "have it all"—a full and satisfying personal life and a full and satisfying, hard-working professional one. Our answer is: No. The price of excellence is time, energy, attention and focus, at the very same time that energy, attention and focus could have gone toward enjoying your daughter's soccer game. Excellence is a high-cost item.

Since the excellent manager is constantly trying to instill the same "passion" in employees, they too may discover that the "meaning" they have achieved for their lives is also a "high-cost item." In the end, an "excellent" workplace is a workplace of workaholics. Because the interests of the organization are paramount, there is no provision for the individual who won't give his or her all to the company. There is, of course, nothing wrong with individuals *willingly* and *rationally* agreeing to work as hard as possible. But employees' rights as individuals must be protected to make sure that they don't get trampled over by the organization—or by charismatic leaders.

Like other management gurus, Peters ultimately promotes a managerial elite. It is not the kind suggested by Frederick Taylor or Peter Drucker, who saw a distinct class running organizations. Peters' manager is a modern variation of Mayo's "administrator of the future," who is to apply the skills of a social scientist to the organization. The Peters' transforming leader uses the "tricks of the pedagogue, the mentor, the linguist" to become the "value shaper, the exemplar, the maker of meanings." But where Mayo's administrator was "unfettered by his own emotion or prejudice," Peters' leader is emotional, prone to work in shirtsleeves while wandering around inspiring the troops. As with the Taylor-Drucker rationalist-style managerial class, the Mayo-Peters human-relations-style managerial class sets itself apart as the embodiment of the will of the organization. In neither school of thinking is there room for a genuine partnership with employees.

— 9 —

CAN A BAD
WORKPLACE BECOME
GOOD?

PRESTON TRUCKING

Good workplaces are typically new companies. Employees of newly formed companies frequently describe a "familylike" atmosphere. They not only talk about the thrill of building a company from scratch; they also say they feel they are treated like human beings.

After the honeymoon phase, however, the feeling that nobody cares replaces a new company's family feeling. The attitude that it's just a job replaces the perception that people are working together toward some important goals. Office politics replace the feeling that everybody is in the same boat and having fun.

Size is a common culprit. When more employees are taken on, the personal touch gets lost. The founder, who used to know the names of each employee's children, doesn't even recognize the newest employees. As the operation becomes more complex, professional managers appear with their bags of human-relations techniques that supplant the informal ways of doing things. Bureaucratic structures appear; memos replace conversations.

There are exceptions to this pattern. Most of *The 100 Best Companies to Work for in America* have long since passed through the start-up or entrepreneurial stage. Yet in almost every instance, the founder instilled

It was like the bad guys and the good guys. They were the bad guys 'cause they were company. They had the right to discipline us, and we knew it.

The atmosphere in 1978 at other terminals was similar to Philadelphia's. After the incident in Detroit, Preston commissioned a management-consulting group (Behavioral Systems, Inc., of Atlanta, led by clinical psychologist Aubrey Daniels and former football star Fran Tarkenton) to conduct a survey at the Detroit and York, Pennsylvania, terminals. The survey showed that morale was equally low at both places. For every one good comment about the company, there were forty critical ones.

The company then asked its consultants to train managers and supervisors. The consultants taught a system they dubbed performance management. To an outsider, this system may appear rather crude. It is based on decidedly unfashionable behaviorist psychological theory. (Think of Pavlov's dog or Skinner's rats.) The idea is that you can alter people's behavior by rewarding actions you approve (positive reinforcement) and punishing those you disapprove (negative reinforcement). The consultants simplified the theory even more by prescribing the following: Preston's managers should find and praise four acts that an employee does correctly for every one action that they criticize.

On the face of it, this four-to-one positive reinforcement sounds blatantly manipulative. Going from being kicked in the butt all the time to being patted on the back could make anyone suspicious. Certainly it doesn't sound like the sort of thing that could fool Teamsters dock workers and truck drivers.

Yet it worked. From Storck's viewpoint, the management stopped "hassling (the men) every day for little things." When a worker did something that was considered a serious discipline problem—like coming in late repeatedly—the Philadelphia terminal managers asked Storck, as the shop steward, to help resolve the issue. Almost overnight, the level of grievances filed by workers decreased to almost nothing.

This 180-degree turnabout didn't come across as manipulative. Why? Employees cite two reasons. First, manipulation implies secret or ulterior motives. It's extremely hard to accuse anyone of being manipulative if he puts all his cards on the table. Preston's management had *no hidden agendas*. It told everyone exactly what it was doing. And there was no mystery about why the company was using the technique. Preston's managers told of the challenge facing the company from deregulation and openly proclaimed productivity as their objective.

More important, manipulation often suggests getting another person to do something differently. In this case, employees were not being asked to change; managers and supervisors were. In the context of Preston's labor-management war, the positive-reinforcement technique had the effect of unilateral disarmament.

To emphasize its commitment to the new management style, the company's top executives distributed a "mission statement." This statement may have the distinction of being the only corporate philosophy statement in America to quote the German philosopher and poet Goethe:

PRESTON PEOPLE
MAKE THE DIFFERENCE

Success is People Working Together

Preston's most important asset is people, not tractors, trailers, terminals, or management systems. The following quotation from the German philosopher Goethe summarizes our regard for people, "Treat people as though they were what they ought to be and you help them become what they are capable of being." This means that *Preston People* must be regarded as partners rather than as adversaries.

The person doing the job knows more about it than anyone else. It is the responsibility of managers to ask for suggestions, to listen to possible solutions to specific problems, and to help implement productive change. Each employee has unlimited possibilities. Good managers have the ability to recognize and unleash the potential for better performance. Managers have no more important responsibility than to develop our people and continually create a better, more productive environment. At Preston improvement is always possible and is continually sought.

Every Preston employee deserves to be treated with respect. Each group of employees must understand what is important for its success and how it contributes to the progress of the Company. Supervisors are expected to hold regular meetings which will accomplish this objective. Employees are encouraged to ask any question which will give them better information about their jobs, benefits, the Company, or the performance of their groups. The better informed each employee is about his job and how it relates to other jobs, the greater will be the opportunities for making the organization more effective . . .

Managers are to be fair, firm, and positive in correcting substandard performance and inappropriate behavior. Discipline such as firing or time off without pay is employed only as a last resort for flagrant violations of ethical standards or work rules which have been clearly communicated. In all areas where correction is needed, managers must first counsel the subordinate about his actions and obtain a commitment for constructive change. The manager must ask what he can do to help the employee bring about the needed improvement . . .

Although managers observe and rectify errors, it is just as important that they give credit when a job is being done properly. No healthy work environment should have more negative comments than positive ones. The obligation of managers and supervisors is to create an atmosphere wherein employees constantly gain more knowledge and are able to participate in setting challenging goals to achieve outstanding results.

To sum up, Preston's management approached its employees with the following proposal: Let's make a deal. Instead of working at cross-purposes, why don't we work jointly on a common project—keeping Preston Trucking afloat. We'll assume you know best how things should be run, so we will let you run them. All we want from you is to do your work in the best way you know how.

It would be fair to say that this newly defined relationship between employees and management was based on *respect*—a key ingredient of trust. When you respect someone, you communicate two things: first, that you recognize limits to what you will require of the other person, and second, that you acknowledge that the other person has something valuable to contribute. Preston's message to its employees conveyed both of these elements of respect. The company placed limits on its behavior toward employees and it acknowledged the importance of employee knowledge: "The person doing the job knows more about it than anyone else." We should now look at the specific techniques Preston used to tap into that know-how.

WE RAN THE SHOW OUT THERE

In a true partnership, each partner has some say in the business. This was the message the company conveyed when it proposed that people become "partners rather than adversaries." By asking employees to assume more responsibility, Preston, in effect, voluntarily gave up some of its prerogatives. All managers and supervisors were required to hold regular meetings with their employees. At these sessions, employees suggested ways of improving their jobs and the company's efficiency. But it wasn't the meetings that made the difference. It was that the company acted on the suggestions.

Richie Storck explained the process:

> We started having meetings, company meetings, with super-visors and the men, and they started getting more input. They started asking, "What can we do to change things?" And then the men started seeing maybe they really do care about our concerns and our ideas. I mean, we got some good, smart guys out there. There's not any cowards on that dock. They know their business. They know what they're doing.
>
> They started listening to us, our suggestions, as before they didn't. Then they started more or less leaving us alone, and we more or less ran the show out there. If we had a problem, we took it to the supervisor. Everybody gave a little bit. We talked about things. Like faith. Just leave the guys alone, they'll do the job. Now there's quite a few Saturday and Sunday nights the super-visor will be late or something, we have men come in and open the doors up and start working with nobody supervising.

The company went beyond listening to and implementing employee suggestions. An important corollary to the idea of partnership is sharing information. The company set forth the policy in the mission statement: "The better informed each employee is about his job and how it relates to other jobs, the greater will be the opportunities for making the organization more effective."

The company told employees that they could have access to any information that was also available to the management. Memos and reports are freely shared with all employees. There are no secrets permitted. This further reduced the power gulf between management and employees.

LAUGHINGSTOCK OF THE INDUSTRY

Anyone familiar with American management will immediately recognize the basic technique Preston adopted. It employed a variation of quality circles—a technique of Japanese management that became a fad at many American businesses in the early 1980s. This is a technique of participatory management that numerous business-school theorists have advocated over the past quarter century. An MIT industrial psychologist named Douglas McGregor framed the concept with his distinction between Theory X and Theory Y managers. Theory X managers believe employees are fundamentally lazy and must be prodded to work harder. Theory Y managers believe that employees want to be productive, so they need only a good "atmosphere" or "managerial climate" to flourish.

In one important respect, Preston varied from Theory Y philosophy as spelled out in McGregor's classic book, *The Human Side of Enterprise*. McGregor saw participation as "a special case of delegation" and, hence, a technique that maintains the basic status quo in workplace power relationships. Preston's executives knew from the outset that the name of the game is power. They knew there was no way employees could achieve more control over their work without real trade-offs taking place. It could not be merely a form of delegation, because the supervisors actually had to give up some authority for the process to work.

Everyone at Preston agrees that managers did in fact lose authority because of the changes. Managers had to learn to live, in the words of one Preston executive, "with their egos at their ankles." Bosses couldn't be absolute bosses anymore. The result: About 25 percent of Preston's managers left the company *because of* the change in managerial philosophy. One regional manager told a corporate vice-president that he was resigning so that he would no longer have to be associated with "the laughingstock of the industry."

The management exodus underscored that what happened at Preston was genuinely different from what happened to most experiments in participatory management. Even where the efforts were less ambitious than at Preston, managerial opposition usually stopped the programs cold. *Fortune* ran a major article in 1986 describing how most participatory-management programs installed in the early 1980s had been scratched because the top executives had succumbed to opposition from middle managers. There's no theory of management that proposes reducing the manager's power. Management theorists from the time of Frederick Taylor have shared the aim of increasing, not decreasing, managerial control over the workplace. Even the proponents of Theory Y have a blind spot when it comes to power. Calls for "empowerment" of workers by the Theory Y-style managers often have a hollow ring because they don't address the trade-off essential to any real empowerment. More power to the workers means less power to the managers. That's just how power works.

To be consistent with the new relationships, the company began calling employees associates and supervisors coordinators. Other companies (J. C. Penney, Wal-Mart Stores) refer to employees as associates. It implies the sort of partnership that Preston was trying to build.

The term *coordinator* is Preston's own attempt to cope with the altered status of supervisors. It's a term that reflects their new role within the company. The separate managerial class, with its unchallenged authority over the workplace, has no role at the new Preston. Coordinators organize things so that work done by one part of the organization can be used effectively by another part, or they connect the work done by the organization to the outside world. Their role is *not* to supervise the work of others in the usual sense of the term. As Preston employees like to reiterate: "The person doing the job knows more about it than anybody else."

WE TOOK CHANCES WITH PEOPLE

As Preston's employees gained more confidence that the company's management was sincerely interested in their efforts, they gave more of themselves to their work. This was especially apparent among Preston's city drivers, who pick up freight from various customers and bring it back to the local terminal, where it is sorted and put on long-distance trucks. As these drivers became more comfortable with the new Preston, they often volunteered to solicit more business. Soon, they were being called driver-salespersons, making Preston's drivers the only ones in the industry who actually helped make sales. At other trucking companies, salespeople make the sales calls, while drivers simply pick up and deliver freight. It's the old brain-versus-brawn distinction. Trusting Teamsters drivers to *talk* directly with customers was the sort of change that made Preston the industry's laughingstock in the eyes of some detractors.

But it's hard to quarrel with results. Larry Regosch has dozens of stories about the new system's paying off. As Philadelphia terminal manager (and Richie Storck's boss), Regosch says he used to ride workers as much as any other manager in the company—a fact Storck and others will testify to. But he has become an ardent supporter of the new style. He says that the changes meant "we took chances with people."

Regosch's favorite example is what happened at American Honda, which is the Philadelphia terminal's largest account. John Wilson, the Teamsters driver on the route, learned from the American Honda traffic manager that there had been an increase in damaged-freight claims. So Wilson went to Regosch and said: "I feel if I'm given the proper equipment, I could reduce the damages at Honda." At the time, Wilson loaded all the Honda freight (mostly car parts) into one trailer and drove it to the terminal, where it was off-loaded and reloaded on trucks bound for different locations. Wilson suggested that Preston park *four* different trailers at Honda every day. Each trailer would only be loaded with freight slated for a specific destination. Because of the reduced handling, Wilson argued, there would be less of a chance of damage.

The terminal manager agreed with Wilson's plan and agreed to put four trailers at the distributor's warehouse. Honda was so pleased with the results that it began giving more of its business to Preston. In the first year, Preston's Honda account doubled in revenues, and it increased by another 50 percent the following year. By early 1988, Preston was using a dozen trailers daily—all because it was willing to take a risk on one of its drivers' suggestions.

We could, of course, take a cynical look at this story and say: These drivers have been tricked into working as salesmen, but they are not getting any commissions or other benefits for their extra labor. I asked Richie Storck, the Teamsters steward, whether Preston's employees weren't simply getting more work for the same money. He answered indignantly:

> Would you rather drive home and feel whipped, and feel that you'd been through hell that day? Or would you rather get the personal satisfaction when you went home that you did something to help the company and your fellow men by getting more freight? That's why other outfits went out of business, because they just did their eight hours' work and went home. They had no concern for the company.

Employees have not only received psychological rewards from their additional efforts. In 1984, Preston introduced a Scanlon bonus plan, through which employees share directly in the results of their higher productivity. It was the first and, as of this writing, only trucker to have such a program.

It would be unfair to end our consideration of Preston giving the impression that all problems have been resolved. As Storck explained:

> It's one big happy family. But I know the (terminal manager) is a company man, and he knows I am a union man. We may have different views about different situations, like a man and a wife. But if another major truck company in the city says, "Let's go after Preston's freight," then all of a sudden, we're one. Then it's not a union and a company anymore, it's Preston, and we'll go get 'em.

Storck insists, in other words, that he hasn't been tricked at all. His current attitude is that instead of being a hired hand—an employee— he's now a *partner* in the business. Rather than the management's having sole responsibility for whether the firm keeps in operation, Storck feels he shares that responsibility with everyone else, including the management. He sees himself on a more equal plane with them.

Among Preston employees there is a newfound sense of pride in themselves and their company. If you refer to them as employees, however, you may find yourself corrected. They are *associates* now, you are told. Aside from the increased pride in themselves and their company, Preston associates feel that a great side benefit of the changes is the relaxed atmosphere. Not only is the relationship with the company better and the relationship with the job improved, so is the relationship of employees with each other.

— 10 —

THE ROLE MODEL THAT CRASHED

PEOPLE EXPRESS

People Express was probably the most elaborate (and certainly the most highly publicized) attempt at corporate democracy in the modern era. It was launched with the noblest of intentions. Donald Calvin Burr, the airline's president, once said: "The single predominant reason that I cared about starting a new company was to try and develop a better way for people to work together." He named the company *People Express* to underscore the firm's commitment to a people-oriented management philosophy.

The company's people philosophy was translated into policies aimed at transforming employees into "owner-managers." There were no supervisors, secretaries, or vice-presidents at People Express. All employees were given the title of manager, and performed a variety of jobs. Most were customer service managers, who rotated monthly, weekly, or even daily among jobs—in the air as flight attendants, at the airports as ticket agents, or behind the scenes in the accounting or scheduling departments. They were guaranteed lifetime job security. They shared in the profits, and they all owned a minimum of a hundred shares of the airline's stock. The airline trumpeted this fact in one of its newspaper ads: "When you fly People Express, an owner is never more than a few steps away."

People Express used its unconventional management philosophy as its primary recruiting tool. One of its recruiting ads heralded: "People Express is growing fast because we put people first!"

583

The pitch worked. When People Express interviewers showed up, thousands of applicants turned out. According to *Inc.* magazine: "As hokey as the term may sound, the so-called people structure has the drawing power of last call at a Saturday night beer blast."

Once on board, People Express employees entered an intensive five-week, six-day-a-week (without pay) training program. The highlight came when company president Don Burr addressed them. Those who saw him in action portrayed Burr as an "evangelist" who preached his "new management" gospel with "messianic zeal." *New York Times Magazine* writer Sara Rimer attended a 1984 training session. She wrote:

> Burr never misses an indoctrination session. He cracks jokes. He preaches, sometimes taking *Star Wars*, his favorite film, as his text for a sermon on the forces of good and evil in the business world. And he inevitably ends with his own vision of People Express: The Good Company. "You're not a commodity," he told the recruits . . . "You're not a beaten-down worker. You're a manager. You're an owner."

After two hours under his spell, one of the employees "practically floated out of the room." He told the reporter: "I think the man's a wizard. This is the opportunity I've been waiting for all my life. This is my road to self-actualization."

That comment typified the employees' reaction to their first taste of life inside People Express. It's no wonder that the former head of competitor New York Air said, "Don Burr is a motivational genius." Ten- and twelve-hour days were the norm. This translated into high productivity. People Express operated with about fifty employees per airplane, about half the industry average. Not only did People Express expect its "manager-owners" to work hard, it also expected them to work cheap. In 1986, for instance, the firm paid its workers an average of $28,200, compared with the industry average of $43,200. (They were paid more on average, however, than the employees of Continental Airlines.)

The highly productive and relatively cheap labor force helped fuel People Express's phenomenal growth. By some measure, it was the fastest-growing company in American business history, shooting from zero to more than $1 billion in revenue in less then five years. It became the biggest carrier serving the New York metropolitan area from its headquarters at Newark Airport. With its purchase of the ailing Frontier Airlines in late 1985, it became the nation's fifth largest airline. But its expansion was costly. Too costly. Buying the nearly bankrupt Frontier Airlines drained People Express. Burr agreed to sell the entire airline to Texas Air, which merged it into the company's Continental Airlines subsidiary on February 1, 1987.

Because People Express's management style was so highly publicized, many people were quick to conclude that the airline's demise proves that corporate democracy doesn't work. This may be unfair. Strong arguments could be made that, if anything, People Express's labor policies helped prolong, rather than interfered with, the company's survival. At any rate, People Express failed as a business. Why it failed is a topic that will undoubtedly be discussed for years to come in many business schools.

Our concern is with People Express as a place to work. To gain more insight into the dynamics of work life at People Express, I talked at length with numerous employees during two trips to the airline's headquarters in Newark. My last visit came during the final week of the airline's existence as an independent entity. For the most part, the employees still believed in the ideals that had attracted them to the airline, but almost all were bitter about what had happened. They talked of feeling "ripped off," "betrayed," "lied to," and "manipulated." They stressed that these feelings surfaced on a large scale *before* the airline flew into the financial turbulence that caused it to be sold. The financial problems only exacerbated the already serious morale problems. In short, the reality of People Express as a workplace did not correspond to the rhetoric about corporate democracy.

THE START-UP SYNDROME

Part of what happened at People Express has occurred at countless other companies. There's an infectious excitement about being involved in launching a company. The early years were exciting times for People Express employees. They felt like winners, and they could see tangible results from their hard work.

But working for a start-up can have a darker side as well. Many employees worked long, uncompensated hours, since the airline was almost always understaffed. This wreaked havoc on personal lives. As managing officer Lori Dubose told researchers for a Harvard Business School case study in 1982: "And start-up team members—oh my God, they've got ulcers, high blood pressure, allergies, a divorce . . . it's one thing after another . . . We've all been physically run down."

How an employer deals with the human strains of its start-up phase indicates a great deal about the kind of relationship it intends to have with employees over the long run. Some employers don't even see it as a problem. They may, in fact, perpetuate a start-up environment indefinitely because of the benefits of running a company with employees who are so swept up in the excitement of the enterprise that they work long — often uncompensated — hours. So the question becomes: Is the company operating in a start-up mode for legitimate business reasons? Or does the start-up style mask an exploitative relationship? If so, trust between the company and employees becomes impossible.

In the perpetual start-up environment, employees are often deceived because they are given so much responsibility. The responsibility is good, but the employer doesn't reward employees for their above-and-beyond-the-call-of-duty efforts. The company takes their hard work for granted.

People Express showed signs of being addicted to this start-up syndrome. Its cross-utilization and job-rotation policies certainly helped maintain a kind of electric tension. These policies fostered a constant crisis atmosphere because the frequent changes of assignments made developing routines impossible. Don Burr himself told the Harvard researchers:

> Now there are a lot of people who argue that you ought to slow down and take stock and that everything would be a whole lot nicer and easier and all that: I don't believe that. People get more fatigued and stressed when they don't have a lot to do. I really believe that, and I think I have tested it. I think it's obvious as hell and I feel pretty strongly about it.

Burr also argued that the short-run stresses were unfortunate, but that overwhelming benefits would accrue to everyone from the rapid-expansion plan. But the long-term employees I interviewed felt Burr got hooked on bigness for its own sake and lost sight of the airline's original goals. Burr himself gave credence to that view when, in late 1985, he justified the airline's constant expansion:

> Leadership is not pandering to what people say they need. It's defining what the hell people need. It's not saying, "Oh, yeah,

you want another candy bar? Here. Rot your teeth." That's not what builds empires . . . All I want to do is win.

Burr's justifications sound similar to the language of other CEOs, who make no pretense of trying to create a good working environment. There appears to have been a clear conflict between Burr's winning-is-everything attitude and his espousal of humane management. At many companies, the top management doesn't suggest that it has any goal for the organization besides fattening the bottom line and creating a bigger enterprise. But People Express appeared to be different, and many (if not most) employees signed up because of the eloquence about its enlightened management style. They placed their trust in the organization. When they saw that things were not different, they felt betrayed.

WHAT'S WRONG WITH BEING A SECRETARY?

In a column he prepared for *The Wall Street Journal* in 1985, Donald Burr wrote:

Every worker at People Express is a manager . . . No one has a secretary at People Express. We run a company that will do about $600 million in volume without having one secretary. I answer my own phone and I hand write my own letters. Needless to say, I don't write much.

At first blush, Burr sounds like a working-class hero. Not only did People Express have no secretaries, but because of the cross-utilization/job-rotation policy, no employees could find themselves in a boring, repetitive job.

Let's step back and ask: What is the matter with being a secretary? Thousands of secretaries love their jobs. They feel they are making a meaningful contribution to the organizations they work for. It is not the *job* of being a secretary that's fundamentally wrong. It's frequently the servile *relationship* with their bosses that many secretaries find objectionable. By publicizing its lack of secretaries, People Express was trying to say that it had no menial jobs. In proclaiming that every employee is a manager, the company was saying: You're not just a flight attendant or a ticket agent, you're a *manager*.

But what's so great about everybody being a manager? Sure, it's important to feel you have some control over your own work, that you don't have to be bossed around by some nincompoop. But non-managerial tasks are important, too. The trouble with People Express's setup was its underlying bias: that only managers do significant work in this world. There was unspoken contempt for those who do the humdrum tasks. As the employees quickly learned, running an airline is comprised of lots of prosaic tasks. At first, calling everybody a manager and moving employees around at an almost frenetic pace obscured the mundane aspects of ticketing passengers and serving them coffee. The constant movement seemed like fun. When the novelty wore off, however, employees were still ticketing passengers and serving them coffee. Only it wasn't quite as challenging as it had been at first.

Nevertheless, employees insist that People Express was a "fun" place to work, even in its last weeks of operation. Many of them claimed that what made working there fun was *not* the job-rotation system; it was their relationships with other employees. Job-rotation allowed people to "keep up with" other employees, as several of them put it. And the cross-utilization policy contributed to a lack of social and political hierarchy. Employees reported a genuine camaraderie within the organization. In other words, the job-rotation system may have failed in its ostensible purpose of improving employees' relationships with their jobs, but it helped create better relationships among the employees themselves.

In terms of the basic workplace relationships, then, People Express gets high marks for creating a sense of community. It gets only mixed reviews for the employees' relationships to their jobs. Employees were so much a part of the team effort that their sense of pride depended on how the team was doing. When People Express was doing well, they felt good about their jobs. When the firm began to stumble, there was little for them to be proud of individually. Because their sense of accomplishment was wrapped up in the fortunes of the enterprise, they took the company's failures quite personally. This added to the bitterness.

TRUST AT WORK

THE DIFFERENCE BETWEEN
COMMODITY AND GIFT
INTERACTIONS

During the Iran-contra hearings in the summer of 1987, Secretary of State George Schultz told of an incident early in his Washington career when his mentor told him that to get along in the capital Schultz should always remember that "trust is the coin of the realm."

The same might be said of workplaces. Without trust, the workplace can easily become dehumanized. Employees feel like robots. But with trust, workplace relationships can flourish. People feel more pride in what they do and achieve deeper enjoyment from relationships with others with whom they work.

Despite trust's importance, it has rarely been addressed as such by those writing about the workplace. So the following discussion puts us into largely uncharted territory.

BUILDING THE TRUST RESERVOIR

Trust doesn't just happen. It's the product of what has happened within the workplace over time. In this regard, trust in workplace relationships is no different from trust in personal relationships. We're all familiar with this process. If somebody fails to return a book we've loaned them, our level of trust in that person may be affected. Similarly, if we tell someone a secret and that person respects our confidence, our level of trust in that person may increase.

One way of describing this phenomenon is in terms of a *trust reservoir*. Consider the following illustration. Before the radical transformation at Preston Trucking, the company commissioned a consulting firm to conduct a survey. At the York, Pennsylvania, terminal an employee offered this assessment of the typical career pattern of a Preston employee:

> First, the new employee starts out eager to please and a hard worker. Second, after his probationary period, he continues to be an industrious worker. Third, after a time the lack of any praise, or even opinion of his work, and the negative attitudes of his fellow veteran employees who've already gone through the same thing, takes its toll, and he begins to slack off. He forms the opinion that if the company doesn't give a damn, why should he. Fourth, by this time he has reached the crossroads. He can (a) revamp his performance and try to influence the company by his positive attitude, or (b) just put in his time and no more than that. Unfortunately, (b) is too often the common choice because (a) never seems to do any good.

The feelings expressed by the Preston employee are familiar indeed. The most common reaction to the erosion of one's trust reservoir is *cynical* emotional withdrawal. Sometimes workers react by striking back. Union-organizing drives, for instance, can typically be traced to the erosion of trust. Workers assert that they can no longer rely on the employer to look after their best interests, and turn to the union for protection.

In his most recent book, *Tales of a New America*, Robert B. Reich describes what happens when trust breaks down:

> Commercial dealings are hedged about by ever more elaborate contracts. There is a proliferation of work rules, codes, and standards to be followed. Requirements and expectations are well documented in advance; enforcement procedures are minutely delineated.

Besides pushing relationships toward a more formal mode, the erosion of trust can be seen as the root of various other pathologies—such as higher levels of stress and lower productivity.

Let's consider the opposite process, when trust reservoirs are augmented. That's what happened at Preston Trucking in the years after the interview cited earlier. It's also what happens in great workplaces. In fact, the constant replenishing of trust reservoirs is the single most distinguishing characteristic of great workplaces. Employees recognize that the company cares about them and respects them. This recognition makes them commit themselves to the relationship and to their work for the company. At the same time, the company sees that the risks it has taken (its willingness to reward and recognize work, the willingness to give more control to the employees) have met its expectations. This makes the company willing to extend itself even more. These kinds of interactions build the trust reservoirs that can help the relationship survive the difficult times that any company (or relationship) goes through because of outside pressures.

GIFTS AND COMMODITIES

How do great workplaces build up trust reservoirs? To answer that question we need to look more closely at the nature of interactions that build trust. Because of certain kinds of interactions, employees of better workplaces often talk about feeling that they have "more than a job" and are part of a "family" or "partnership." At the same time, other interactions are not unlike what happens in other companies: employees put in hours on the job and take home paychecks. Looking at a good workplace from the viewpoint of employees, it's as if they participate in two distinct types of interactions—one familiar to any workplace and another that is peculiarly related to good workplaces. Put another way, it's as if employees are operating on two different levels simultaneously.

Not long ago I came across a book that helped me appreciate what makes good workplaces tick. In *The Gift*, poet and essayist Lewis Hyde explains the place of creativity in our market-oriented society. Hyde puts forth the idea that a work of art is a gift rather than a commodity. Works of art exist in two parallel economies—the market economy and the gift economy. In the market economy of supply and demand, a painting may be sold for thousands of dollars. But the painting also has a separate life as a gift:

That art that matters to us—which moves the heart, or revives the soul, or delights the senses, or offers courage for the living, however we choose to describe the experience—that work is received by us as a gift is received. Even if we have paid a fee at the door of a museum or concert hall, when we are touched by a work of art something comes to us which has nothing to do with the price . . .

Anthropologists have written extensively about the customs and mores of the gift economy, which predates money or even barter. In the typical gift exchange, acceptance of a gift obliges the recipient to certain implied duties. The recipient may be obliged to give a gift in return; or the obligation may only be to express appreciation or goodwill to the gift giver. In all cases, a distinct social bond is created. As Hyde puts it: "It is the cardinal difference between gift and commodity exchange that a gift establishes a feeling-bond between two people, while the sale of a commodity leaves no necessary connection." *Both sides recognize that whenever a gift is given, the giver is giving part of himself.*

While reading Hyde, I was struck by the similarities between what happens in great workplaces and his description of a gift economy. Interactions between company and employees are acted out according to implicit rules somewhat like the unstated rules of gift exchanges. When the Preston driver, described in an earlier chapter, offered to take over the American Honda account, he did so as if he were offering the company a gift—his creative work. It was not a tit-for-tat offer where the worker was saying he would do more work if he received more money. The company recognized the nature of his suggestion and responded appropriately. His manager not only gave the driver the appropriate equipment, but he expressed appreciation in a variety of ways for the gift that had been offered.

The analogy of the gift economy strikes a resonant chord for another important reason: *Human work is not just a commodity.* What struck the Preston workers most strongly about the company's transformation was that the management no longer treated them as if they offered only a commodity—time on the job. Before the changes, the company related to the workers purely in terms of a simple time-for-money exchange. Much of that exchange was spelled out in detail in the Teamsters' contract between the two sides. But work cannot be so carefully circumscribed. It encompasses individual initiative and creativity. When people work, as opposed to merely laboring for money, they are offering part of their individual essence, part of what distinguishes them as human beings.

Note, however, that it is precisely its giftlike nature which allows an insensitive employer to ignore it. A gift can be refused. If a company refuses to accept the work freely offered by its employees, it is entirely free to do so. Indeed, generations of management ideology have blinded employers to anything but the commodity aspect of work. The Preston worker at the York terminal quoted earlier described what it is like for an employee to have his work gift ignored by the employer. What makes good workplaces special is that the company recognizes giftlike exchanges with employees and actively cultivates them.

This distinction between commoditylike and giftlike work helps us to understand the two levels of interactions at great workplaces. The exchange of gift work is *not* a substitute for the straightforward agreement between a company and an employee to do a certain job for a specified amount of pay, that is, a commodity exchange. Rather, gift work coexists with that. Commoditylike and giftlike exchanges of work represent two different aspects of work life.

We could briefly sketch some of the major differences between these two types of workplace interaction:

In commodity interactions, both sides give up something to receive something else roughly equivalent in value. The worker gives up forty hours of work and receives a weekly paycheck in return. By contrast, giftlike exchanges are more complicated because they rely on trust. One side gives up something without having a guarantee about what, if anything, it will receive in return.

Another significant difference: If something goes wrong in a commoditylike exchange, adjustments can be made based on the terms of the original exchange. If an employee is an hour late, his or her paycheck can be docked by an hour. But if someone violates trust, the other party may consider itself betrayed—a highly charged term.

Part of the reason for the feeling of betrayal is that trust occurs within the context of open-ended relationships. This presents another sharp distinction with commodity exchanges. Both parties in the commodity exchange have other options: the employer can always hire other workers, and the workers can quit and go elsewhere. Giftlike interactions suggest, on the other hand, an ongoing relationship.

There is one other significant difference between gift and commodity exchanges. In a commodity transaction, the terms for the exchange are generally available to all. The hourly wage will be available to anyone willing to do the job. This is part of the employment relationship at any workplace, good or bad. An exchange involving trust is different. The terms can vary completely depending on who is involved and what is at stake. A trust interaction is highly personalized.

The highly personalized nature of trust is more clearly understood if we compare the dynamics of a commodity exchange with the dynamics of a gift exchange. In the commodity exchange the rules of the game are clear: both sides give up as little as possible while trying to extract the maximum value. Classic economic theory is based on the assumption that everyone plays this game of enlightened self-interest. Adam Smith, among others, claimed that the greatest good for all comes from everyone's following his or her self-interest.

Giftlike interactions dictate a different set of rules. They are not competitive with each side trying to maximize itself at the other's expense. Rather, each side is willing to give up something because it trusts that the other will recognize its sacrifice as a gift toward building something in common, a better relationship. And because the better relationship is founded on trust, trust is the basic currency of giftlike interactions, just as money is the fundamental medium of exchange in commoditylike interactions.

These dynamics have special relevance to the workplace. Trust heightens the ability of people to cooperate with each other. Achieving the cooperation of the workers has, of course, been an objective of management for generations, since the days of Frederick Taylor. But many management theorists, especially those espousing various motivational techniques, try to get the employees to give up part of themselves for the common good without sacrificing any management power. The fact that only one side is playing according to the rules of the gift-type exchange is why motivational techniques are often viewed with such distrust by employees. Both sides have to participate in gift-type interactions for genuine cooperation to exist.

MAKING WORK INTO A COMMODITY

Economists and management theorists have generally ignored giftlike work (as opposed to time-for-money labor) as a valid subject of study. This helps explain the lack of concepts to appraise companies as workplaces rather than as businesses. Even the most enlightened management theorists place their motivational techniques squarely within the context of financial success. The financial bottom line remains the only bottom line. The interactions between the company and the employees are evaluated solely in terms of a cost-benefit analysis. Hence the workplace is ultimately seen through the accountant's prism, reducing the employee's contribution to an interchangeable commodity.

There is, of course, some merit in evaluating workplaces according to financial and productivity yardsticks. Commodity exchanges represent *one* reality of the workplace. People do spend time on the job in exchange for money. But the commodity-type labor exchange is not the *only* reality. Great workplaces have distinctive patterns of interaction. The maintenance and growth of trust between the employer and employees is a central concept. So is the need for pride in one's job and the sense of enjoyment of the relationships with others. The elements of trust, pride or fun cannot be produced through a simple tit-for-tat, commodity-type exchange. Such qualities can only be nurtured through giftlike interactions that bring out what is most distinctively human in both sides of the employment relationship.

— 12 —

WHAT MAKES SOME
WORKPLACES SO GOOD

"Deople are our most important asset." Organizations throughout the land welcome newly hired employees with variations
of this slogan. Orientation sessions and employee handbooks
convey the same message: "This company values you as a person." "You
are important to this company." Unfortunately, such sentiments often
bear little resemblance to reality. Employees at many companies correctly conclude that such platitudes have been lifted from a business-
school textbook on human relations.

To complicate matters, genuinely good employers greet their new
employees with similar declarations. Advanced Micro Devices has long
used the slogan, "People first, products and profits will follow." IBM's
employee handbook proclaims that "respect for the individual" is the
first tenet of its business. And Publix Super Markets has plastered its
stores with banners saying, "Publix People Make the Difference."

The problem is that almost all organizations would like to convince
employees that they care about their people. Many companies sincerely
intend to create a good place to work, but as time passes, the pressures of
the marketplace open a gap between a company's good intentions and
the reality of work life.

The best way to judge a place to work is to visit the company and
talk with employees, but this is not always practical. Another approach
is to look at a company's personnel policies and practices and see what
they say about the nature of the workplace relationships. Policies and
practices operate on two distinct levels. On the base-line level, which
we are calling the commodity level, policies represent a straightforward
time-for-money agreement. But any policy simultaneously makes a

statement on the trust level about the company's underlying attitudes. Our focus is on the trust level. Some policies broadcast a message that undermines trust, while others build up trust by acknowledging the giftlike aspect of human work. Great places to work are characterized by the latter.

Let's look at some policies to see how evaluating workplaces by this method works:

TERMS OF EMPLOYMENT

There are two elements of the basic workplace exchange—time and money. Time is what employees have to give. By taking a job, they give the company the bulk of their waking hours and much of their productive energy. All leisure activities must be shoehorned into the rest of the day or into their days off. Employees also give a great deal of themselves to the job, whether or not they fully intend to.

On the most elementary level, good workplaces make sure to hold up the company's end of the time-for-money exchange by establishing wage-and-benefits compensation that is considered fair. Most good workplaces have a reputation for paying well. But building trust isn't determined by the size of paychecks alone, though paying well can go a long way to making people feel that their personal sacrifices are appreciated. What's important is that the company is making an honest attempt to pay as much as it can afford. It's difficult for employees to feel that theirs is a good place to work if the company appears to be taking financial advantage of them. Unfairness in the basic time-for-money exchange poisons the trust reservoir.

Good workplaces also see that the employees' commitment of time requires more than decent wages and benefits. Many good workplaces also make a commitment of their own—job security. Nearly a third of the *100 Best* companies, for instance, have no-layoff policies or state explicitly that they will attempt to maintain full employment unless, as Federal Express's Fred Smith puts it, the company is "at death's door." A no-layoff policy makes a powerful statement on the trust level. It says that the company considers that it has a *relationship* with employees, not merely an agreement to pay them for the time they spend on the job. It says that the relationship is a serious one—like a marriage rather than a one-night stand.

One reason a no-layoff policy helps build trust is that it implies that the company is willing to impose a burden on itself for the sake of its relationship with employees. At Hallmark Cards, J. D. Goodwin, a plant manager in Kansas City, explains, "Our attitude is that when we have a downturn, it's the managers who have a problem. It shouldn't be an employee problem." This is not merely rhetoric, either. During the recession of 1981-82, Hallmark loaned about six hundred production employees to other departments to do a variety of jobs (such as repainting) and even had a crew of workers do community volunteer work, for which they were paid by Hallmark. The company spent a total of $10 million to maintain jobs for its surplus workers until business picked up again.

A no-layoff policy also communicates that everyone in the company is considered important, not just those at the top. H. B. Fuller, a Minnesota-based glue maker, has a job-security policy that makes this point dramatically. Everyone who has been working at the company for at least two years will be affected equally by any reductions at a particular plant. During the 1982 recession, for instance, everyone at a vacuum-cleaning division was cut back to a four-day work week, including the vice-president of the division.

THE JOB

Work involves more than spending a prescribed number of hours at a company. It implies doing certain tasks, doing a job. There are three kinds of job-related policies we shall look at: *how* and *when* jobs are to be done and *who* is to do them.

How jobs are to be done:

When we work on a job, we generally want to accomplish something in the process and to feel proud of our work. People generally put more effort into their jobs than the minimum that is absolutely required. Good workplaces recognize this as being, in effect, a gift to the company. They acknowledge this gift by accepting it. That is, good workplaces provide ways for people to assume an increasing share of *responsibility* for their own work.

In Northwestern Mutual Life and Preston Trucking, we saw how two companies engaged in this process of increasing employee responsibility for how to do their jobs. We noted how at Preston the company adopted as its unofficial slogan, "The person doing the job knows more about it than anybody else." Both companies employed participative-management techniques as ways to accept increased employee responsibility—a job-enrichment-style program at Northwestern, quality circles at Preston. But participative-management techniques by themselves may only affect the commodity level of the workplace relationships.

For one thing, such techniques can be seen as thinly disguised efforts to undermine employees' job security. Or they may be perceived as a means of forestalling unionization or undermining an already existing union. At both Northwestern and Preston Trucking, the managements went out of their way to involve the unions in the process. By doing so, they made it easier for employees to believe the company when it said its objective was productivity.

Participative-management programs often broadcast conflicting messages precisely because they are, in general, creations of management consultants steeped in psychological theories. Such psychologically-based techniques proceed from the assumption workers would work harder if only they were happier. There's nothing wrong, of course, with employees being happy. But as we saw in the case of the Chicago insurer, it is extremely difficult to convince people that there is not an ulterior motive to making them happy through more enriched jobs or having regular work discussion groups. That suspicion can destroy the very morale the programs are supposed to improve.

What distinguished good workplaces is the openness and honesty about the real motivations of such productivity techniques as quality circles (used at Preston Trucking) or job enrichment (used at Northwestern Mutual Life). Employees understand that the actual objectives correspond to the stated ones. On that basis, trust is possible. Similarly, good workplaces don't shy away from the political implications of greater employee responsibility either. A decision now left to the employee may be one that would, previously, have been made by someone higher up.

One final point. There is no way to increase employee responsibility without some increase in risk. That's why at Marion Labs the company stresses that management must be willing to accept honest mistakes. If employees are not given the opportunity to fail, to make mistakes, they probably don't have any genuine responsibility. Because increased responsibility involves risk, it taps directly into the dynamics of trust.

When work is to be done:

A good example of a policy that acknowledges the desire to do a good job is flextime. Flextime gives employees choices about their working schedule. Employees who work eight-hour shifts can arrive between seven and nine o'clock in the morning and leave between three and five in the afternoon. Viewed as part of the time-for-money exchange, flextime doesn't change the employees' agreement to put in their eight hours a day. But on the trust level, flextime makes an important statement: It says we, the company, trust you, the employees, to determine when to do the job. It demonstrates respect toward the employees' desire to do a good job, while at the same time finding the best hours to work their shift from the viewpoint of their personal lives.

Who does the job:

Good workplaces assume that a firm's growth is due largely to the efforts of the people working there. So they have policies and practices that offer those people the opportunity to grow with the enterprise.

For this reason, promotion from within is gospel at virtually all good workplaces. Unlike firms where the best jobs are open to outsiders, most good workplaces make a strong point of trying to hire from within first. Many have job-posting systems, where openings are announced within the company before any outsiders are even considered. When Delta Air Lines needed two staff writers for the company newspaper, the editor assumed that he would have to hire outsiders. He was surprised, therefore, when nearly a hundred Delta workers applied, eighteen with journalism degrees, and ten with prior broadcast or newspaper experience. Because the company assumed that its own employees were its main resource, it was able to uncover a lot of hidden talent. At the same time, such a policy lets employees feel that they are considered capable of growth and are recognized as more than a ticket agent, a stewardess, or whatever job slot they happen to occupy.

WORKPLACE RULES

In accepting a job, an employee puts himself at the mercy of the company in a variety of ways. He can be ordered to do unpleasant tasks. He can be promoted or demoted without explanation. He can be intimidated. He can be fired or laid off without warning. Rights Americans enjoy as citizens simply do not exist as employees. For instance, the Bill of Rights protects free speech, prohibits unreasonable search and seizure, and provides for due process and trial by one's peers. Yet companies throughout the country routinely violate these same rights. Employees can be penalized for speaking their minds. Management can search employees' desks without anyone blinking an eye. Employees can be required to submit to urine tests for drugs, and are routinely fired without warning. A federal study entitled *Work in America* put it this way:

> The United States must resolve a contradiction in our nation—between democracy in society and authoritarianism in the workplace.

Unions can make individual employees less likely to be singled out for abuse, but they can do little to prevent employers from behaving badly toward all employees as a group. There are laws regarding minimum wages, overtime pay, and discrimination, and there are far more stringent health and safety codes in effect today than a half century ago. But for most day-to-day problems, the law offers little comfort.

Good workplaces recognize the vulnerability of employees and go to great lengths to provide safeguards to assure fairness. This requires addressing two major problems: the huge imbalance of power of the organization over the individual employee, and the proclivity for management to be treated as first-class citizens and other employees as second-class citizens at best. Good workplaces typically have a variety of practices that reduce class distinctions. Few of the companies we visited while researching *The 100 Best Companies to Work for in America* had executive dining rooms. If they did, the executive dining rooms usually had a clearly understood function of being a place to dine certain customers.

Good workplaces also eliminate other perks of a privileged class. Some firms, like Marion Labs, extend this to benefits. For instance, all Marion employees get stock options, a benefit usually reserved only for top executives. At Advanced Micro Devices there are no executive parking lots. When its flamboyant founder Jerry Sanders arrives to work late, he has to park his Rolls-Royce in the outer parking lot and walk just like any other latecomer.

Countering the imbalance of power between the organization and the individual requires *extending rights* to employees. When a company guarantees rights, it places limitations on its own power. That is why policies which extend employees' rights go a long way toward building trust. Rights show good faith on the part of the organization by directly addressing the problem of employee vulnerability.

Here are examples of the kinds of rights that characterize many good workplaces:

Right to due process:

The most basic right is that of appealing decisions that the employee considers unfair. Federal Express's Guaranteed Fair Treatment procedure shows how such a policy helps to build trust among employees. Not only is the GFT an elaborate grievance procedure, but the final decision might be handed down after a trial by one's peers. The GFT also underscores the fact that all employees are equal citizens because it is also used by management employees when they feel they have been unfairly treated.

Right to full and accurate information:

Federal Express employees also have the right to information. A company policy enables any employee to see any piece of information with only three exceptions: other employees' personnel records, plans that could be used by competitors, and sensitive financial data that the Securities and Exchange Commission does not permit to be distributed prematurely. So, for instance, if a courier wants to know how his wage compares with that of drivers for competitors, he would be able to ask for and be shown wage surveys and comparable scales at United Parcel Service and Emery. A policy of no secrets does much to build trust if for no other reason than it can help stop rumors that erode people's confidence in each other.

Most good workplaces also have elaborate communications systems that provide ongoing information about all aspects of the company. Information isn't restricted to the highly sanitized version of reality often seen in glossy company magazines. Federal Express's Fred Smith insists that approach is hopelessly out of step with the times:

> You are dealing with a very sophisticated work force today. They may not all be highly educated formally, but they can tell you about the federal deficit, about the Japanese, about the MX missile. Even if they get all their news from TV, they see all kinds of issues discussed there—corruption, abortion. So, to have a corporate publication that mambie-pambies around . . . is not going to have any credibility at all with employees. You ought to talk about it when we get crummy letters from customers or that

there are terrible wrecks involving our vans or that somebody gets caught by the FBI. You ought to put the news in there.

Some good workplaces demystify the usually sacred issue of compensation. Security Pacific Bank, headquartered in Los Angeles, hands each new employee a card that lists the salary ranges for each of the thirty pay grades within the company. Making this kind of information available helps put every employee on the same footing. Some make more money than others, but at least those who make less have the same right to information as those who make more.

Right to free speech:

The freedom of speech enjoyed by the Tektronix employee newspaper, discussed earlier, is a good example of this right in action. Tek employees not only have the right to their own opinions on work issues, but they also have the right to broadcast those opinions without fear of retribution. The company newspaper isn't the only vehicle for expressing opinions. Tek's area representative system enables employees to ask questions about anything from anyone in the company, including the president.

Tandem Computers takes a high-tech approach to free speech with regular companywide gatherings using an inhouse TV satellite network that links Tandem offices and plants throughout the country. Employees not only hear the latest information directly from the top officers of the company, they can also ask questions during these sessions. The company never edits what is said in these TV meetings.

Right not to be part of the family/team:

Employees at most good workplaces say they feel their company has an atmosphere like that of a family or a team. However, this can translate into social pressure to conform. It can be one of the worst ways in which an organization can tyrannize the vulnerable individual. Good workplaces often have a tolerant attitude toward the loners and eccentrics. As one Tektronix employee explained: "I feel I can be me here." In this sense, good workplaces are very much like real families in that people don't have to do anything or prove anything to be part of it.

A tolerant attitude toward individual differences also means that good workplaces accept those who want to have no more than a commodity-type exchange with the company. Donald Hall, chairman of Hallmark Cards, one of the most familylike companies in America, states emphatically that "there has to be a place for those who only want to put in their eight hours a day and go home. There has to be a place for those who don't want to be part of the family."

Like other rights, the right not to be part of the family or team represents a risk. A company's management may prefer a workplace of workaholics but, as we saw from the example of People Express, such an environment exacts a tremendous toll on the human beings who work there. A good place to work is, above all, a place where people thrive. People cannot thrive unless they have some say in how much they wish to contribute.

A STAKE IN SUCCESS

Good workplaces recognize that compensation alone does not adequately recognize the contribution people make. Acknowledging that employees are central to a firm's success, they make sure that employees have a genuine stake in the enterprise so they can share the rewards of their joint endeavors. This is accomplished largely, but not entirely, through sharing profits and/or ownership.

Sharing rewards:

More than half of the firms listed in *The 100 Best Companies to Work for in America* have profit-sharing plans. On the commodity level, profit sharing could be considered as only a means of compensation. On the trust level, however, profit sharing has an entirely separate meaning. By paying part of its profits directly to employees, a company is saying that employees are valuable enough to the enterprise to share rewards of the firm's success.

Like participative-management techniques, profit-sharing or other incentive techniques are not panaceas. They are subject to a wide variety of interpretations by employees. Many firms, for instance, see profit sharing as merely another device to bolster productivity. If increased productivity is the sole reason for profit sharing, the policy suggests little more than a direct commodity exchange: Work harder and you will get more money.

At good workplaces, the company makes clear that increasing productivity is only part of the reason for profit sharing. It's instructive to look back at one of the first known profit-sharing plans. Edme-Jean Leclaire owned a painting company in Paris when he began sharing profits with employees in 1842. By 1882 the firm's one thousand

workers were receiving annual profit-sharing bonuses equal to 22 percent of their wages. Leclaire argued that because of profit sharing:

> (The workers) are no longer mere journeymen who act like
> machines and quit their work before the clock has sounded its last
> stroke. All have become partners working on their own account:
> in virtue of this, nothing in the workshop ought to be indifferent
> to them—all attend to the preservation of the tools and materials
> as if they are the special keepers of them.

It is this sense of feeling a part of the company that sharing the
rewards of success brings out. At Tektronix, which gives employees 35
percent of all corporate profits, profit sharing is absolutely fundamental
in terms of the company's relationship with employees. As Earl Wantland, Tek's president, explains:

> Profit sharing (means) that the employee should be considered
> more than an eight-hour-a-day person. An employee should have
> other real, tangible relationships with the industrial enterprise.
> So we have structured our profit sharing so that the employees as
> a group benefit to the equivalent extent as the shareholders as a
> group, in terms of our margin and our performance. That way
> employees have a real stake. We structure our salaries so that
> profit sharing is an integral part of the pay at Tektronix. So
> employees have the opportunity to earn more if we collectively
> are more productive.

Sharing ownership:

A high percentage of good workplaces offer some form of employee
ownership. They range from 100 percent employee-owned companies
like Publix Super Markets and Quad/Graphics to firms that have a
sizable percentage of employee ownership, like Lowe's Companies and
Hallmark Cards, where between a quarter and a third of the company is
owned by employees, to companies where only a small percentage of
the firm is employee owned, like Preston Trucking. In some firms,
employee ownership is considered as merely another benefit, but most
good workplaces stress another dimension to ownership: employees are
not just working for someone else; they are working for themselves.

Sharing recognition:

Profit sharing and sharing ownership aren't the only ways of sharing rewards. One of the most critical forms of reward is recognition. Whether someone is adequately recognized can play a critical role in the building—or destroying—of trust. When employees start working for a company, they are generally willing to extend themselves, to show how much of a contribution they can make. Unless this trust is reciprocated by recognition of their extra effort, employees often feel hurt, even betrayed, and retreat into themselves.

Most good workplaces seem to have dozens of formal and informal ways of recognizing people's work efforts. One Delta employee said that what he likes most about the company is that you are always acknowledged for doing good work. He says people feel that they are working in a "climate of approval."

— 13 —

Spotting Bad Workplaces

FROM EXPLOITATION TO PATERNALISM

Unfortunately, most workplaces that employees are likely to encounter have policies and practices that undermine trust. There are, of course, a wide variety of bad workplaces. What follows are four of the most familiar patterns of bad workplaces.

EXPLOITATIVE

The exploitative workplace can be defined as one in which the employer systematically takes unfair advantage of the employees. Using terms from the previous chapter, employees of such firms have few or no rights, are given tasks without responsibility, and don't share in the rewards of the enterprise.

Injustice most distinguishes the exploitative workplace from other types of workplace. The employer often believes he can act with impunity and rule by whim. This can lead to despotism or tyranny—to the workplace as jungle. There is complete disregard for employee health and safety and a divide-and-conquer policy toward employees.

MECHANICAL

The assembly line is the best-known symbol of industrial civilization. It represents the triumph of the machine over people, the system over the individual. It is also the paradigm of the mechanical workplace.

Charles R. Walker and Robert H. Guest spent two years talking with workers on an automobile assembly line. Published in 1952, *The Man on the Assembly Line* remains the classic study of the subject. The workers paint a depressing picture:

> "The assembly line is no place to work, I can tell you. There is nothing more discouraging than having a barrel beside you with 10,000 bolts in it and using them all up. Then you get a barrel with another 10,000 bolts, and you know every one of those 10,000 bolts has to be picked up and put in exactly the same place as the last 10,000 bolts."

> "The worst is the pressure. It's like on a dog sled. As soon as the whistle blows, they yell, 'Mush,' and away you go producing cars."

> "You cannot get quality and quantity. That's my big worry about the place. I don't like it. I always like to be proud of my work. But I can't be on this job very much. Everybody is working under too much pressure for speed and 'get it out.' "

These quotes illustrate the problems most often cited about assembly-line work: it's boring, repetitious, mindless, pressured. Walker and Guest point out, however, that the most psychologically disturbing result of assembly-line work is "the sense of becoming depersonalized." Workers described themselves as feeling like "robots," "a cog in the wheel," "one of the machines," "interchangeable." There is no room for individuality, no room for the qualities that make people people and not robots.

Many big financial institutions have organized clerical work as if it were part of an assembly line. And the mechanical workplace can be seen in bureaucratically organized institutions as well. In *Contested Terrain: The Transformation of the Workplace in the Twentieth Century*, economist Richard Edwards describes how managements of modern corporations exercise power. Instead of relying on authoritarian supervisors, they develop systems:

Bureaucratic control is embedded in the social and organizational structure of the firm and is built into job categories, work rules, promotion procedures, discipline, wage scales, definitions of responsibilities, and the like. Bureaucratic control establishes the impersonal force of "company rules" or "company policy" as the basis for control.

From the employee viewpoint, there is little difference between working on an assembly line or for an organization that operates through bureaucratic control. The individual is subordinated to the system to such an extent that he or she feels like a mere appendage to the process — a part of the machine. The feelings of depersonalization are the outcome in either instance.

ENTREPRENEURIAL

Nothing is done by the book in entrepreneurial workplaces, which most often exist in newer companies led by a strong, even charismatic, leader. The leader often preaches a gospel of flexibility, of change, of creativity, of challenge. These companies display a special social dimension as well. The entrepreneurial workplace often appears to be one big happy family. Employees feel that everybody is "in it together." People are not compartmentalized into job slots, so everybody pitches in together to do the work.

Appealing? You bet it is. There's much to be said for entrepreneurial workplaces. Employees often get a tremendous amount of genuine responsibility. They are not merely assigned tasks as in the mechanical workplace, but they may fully participate in a major project, as at People Express, the prototypical entrepreneurial workplace. And just as the entrepreneurial workplace does not put individuals into predetermined job slots, it tends to avoid hierarchical relationships.

Behind the glittering facade is another reality. Although employees are given considerable responsibility for their work, they rarely have any rights. As in exploitative workplaces, justice in the entrepreneurial workplace is based on whim rather than any clearly established rules. Why? The gospel of flexibility. Establishing rights, such as due process, ties management's hands.

There's another, more insidious, reason why managements of entrepreneurial workplaces avoid tying their own hands. *They* benefit from the employees' long hours of work. Those who aren't willing to maintain the grueling pace can find themselves subjected to ostracism from the happy family.

A good place to work makes specific provisions for people *not* to participate in the great big happy family. From an employee perspective, this is a fundamental issue of fairness. It's simply not fair for an entrepreneurial-style workplace to demand that work be the only thing in people's lives.

PATERNALISTIC

There are two main elements of paternalism, both of which distort workplace relationships:

1. Control through gifts:

Gift giving is the most obvious characteristic of paternalistic employers. They shower benefits on their employees, many more than employees may expect. This may appear similar to what occurs in good places to work. For good employers may also offer employees more than they could expect from other jobs. But paternalistic gift giving has an entirely different motivation. The paternalistic gift giver seeks control. A famous magazine magnate, known in his day as a paternalistic employer, was once quoted as saying: "Spoil them! Like spoiled children they'll grouse about you all the time and jump the moment you call."

This technique often works. Because of the paternalistic employer's overwhelming generosity, employees incur a debt they cannot ever repay. Usually they just let themselves be controlled because the paternalistic employer does, after all, meet their security needs. *Often,* however, the resentment turns into rage. Workers lash out at the paternalistic employer with even more anger than they do against the exploitative employer because the stifling paternalistic environment is such an affront to people's dignity.

2. Shielding from reality:

Douglas Strain, founder of Electro Scientific Instruments, says that paternalistic employers tend "to shield or protect people from the vicissitudes of the world." He thinks management has no business trying to play this role. Richard Sennett calls paternalism "false love." In his book *Authority,* Sennett says that the paternalistic employer tries to appear to his employees as a loving father. But, he writes, "the essential quality of nurturance is denied."

That is the key difference between a good workplace and a merely paternalistic one. In a good workplace, the respect and care shown employees help them grow for their own benefit as well as for the benefit of the company. In the paternalistic workplace, the paternalistic care stultifies personal growth. The irony is that in the long run, it also stifles the company.

— 14 —

DO NICE COMPANIES
FINISH LAST?

What about the bottom line? That's the inevitable question that anyone advocating a better working environment must face. People in business want to know the effect of a good environment on the firm's profitability. They ask: Great workplaces may be terrific for the people working there, but don't the owners get shortchanged?

Underlying this question is a skepticism about anything that might detract from the unbridled quest for profit. In a great workplace, importance is attached to means as well as to ends. The welfare of employees is not compromised to achieve ever higher profitability. In this respect, a great workplace collides with the dominant business ethos. Our culture assumes that business and morality don't mix. In the rough-and-tumble business world, it's thought that those who relentlessly pursue their own self-interest are winners; those who don't are losers. As baseball manager Leo Durocher put it, "Nice guys finish last."

But how valid is the presumption that good employers jeopardize the financial viability of their enterprises? Is it true that success shines only on the greedy?

NICE GUYS VERSUS TOUGH GUYS

There are plenty of well-known examples of avaricious individuals who've succeeded in business. J. Paul Getty was purportedly the richest man on earth at the time of his death in 1976. Numerous anecdotes reveal the oil billionaire's ungenerous spirit. He installed pay phones for guests at his fabulous English estate. He thought nothing of pitting his sons against each other in vicious games, ultimately driving one of them to narcotics addiction and another to suicide. When the wife of one of his sons once complained, "Your lawyers are killing my husband," Getty reputedly told the lawyers: "Keep killing my son."

American business history is replete with characters like J. Paul Getty, John D. Rockefeller (who forced his own brother into bankruptcy), and Jay Gould (the railroad entrepreneur who was referred to by his contemporaries as "the most hated man in America," "a despicable worm," and "the worst man on earth since the beginning of the Christian era"). There are many contemporary examples as well.

However, when researching America's best workplaces, I was struck with how frequently companies considered good employers were founded by people who had become extremely wealthy. Out of curiosity, I placed a *Forbes* 400 list alongside a list of the firms picked for *The 100 Best Companies to Work for in America*. Among the *Forbes* 400 are sixty-five individuals or families whose fortunes come from having founded or run one of twenty-one companies listed among the *100 Best*. The companies are: Anheuser-Busch, Trammell Crow, Dayton Hudson, Digital Equipment, Walt Disney, Du Pont, Federal Express, Hallmark Cards, H. J. Heinz, Hewlett-Packard, Intel, Johnson & Johnson, Johnson Wax, Knight-Ridder, Levi Strauss, Marion Laboratories, 3M, Nordstrom, Tektronix, Wal-Mart Stores, and Weyerhaeuser.

Seven men interviewed for *The 100 Best Companies* or this book show up on the 1987 *Forbes* 400 list. They are:

- Sam Walton, reputedly the richest man in America, head of Wal-Mart Stores (net worth: $8.5 billion)
- David Packard, ranked as the fourth richest American, founder of Hewlett-Packard (net worth: $2.8 billion)
- Ewing Kauffman, founder of Marion Labs drug company and co-owner of the Kansas City Royals baseball team (net worth: $1.3 billion)
- Trammell Crow, who leads the largest real estate firm in the country (net worth: $600 million)
- Donald Hall, chairman of Hallmark Cards (net worth: $450 million)
- Fred Smith, founder of Federal Express (net worth: $295 million)

- John Weinberg, chairman of Goldman Sachs (net worth: $225 million)

Whether these men would like to be known as "nice guys," their employees consider them terrific employers. As a group, they refute the widely held belief that the only way to get rich is to exploit your employees. They have taken a lot of people with them while going to the top. Their employees have not only benefited financially, but many of them report that their lives have been enriched from the working environment they have enjoyed. Without exception, these employers ascribe their success largely to their people-oriented philosophies.

RESOLVING A CONTRADICTION

We have then a contradiction. On the one hand, there's a widespread belief that the only way to get rich is to take advantage of other people. On the other hand, there are many examples of people who worked their way into the ranks of the superrich while being generous employers.

How can we explain this discrepancy? A partial answer comes from looking at how good employers behave in other aspects of their businesses. Some of the best employers are also ferocious competitors. Retail clerks may find Wal-Mart a terrific company to work for, but executives at K mart or Sears probably consider Sam Walton anything but nice. They would see him as a tough-minded competitor who's bent on becoming the largest retailer in America within the next decade.

In the marketplace, a firm (or an individual) is expected to compete aggressively because it's the nature of the market exchanges for each party to try to get the most while giving up the least. This can be done without being unfair or violating the rules of the marketplace game. It's a far different matter, however, when aggressive behavior is carried out within the company. As explained earlier, a great workplace requires relationships built on trust rather than pure self-interest. By nature, trust interactions are nonaggressive and sharing, requiring a different mode of behavior from marketplace exchanges.

On the other hand, ethical considerations have their place in marketplace transactions. Few policies destroy employee morale more quickly than a cavalier attitude toward business ethics. Several good employers I have visited place tremendous stress on the importance of integrity and fairness in competing with other firms.

It's not only in the marketplace that good employers can be tough. They can also be very demanding on their own employees. Hallmark Cards, which has long had a no-layoff policy, fires nonperformers. It considers workers who don't pull their own weight as endangering the ability of the company to guarantee job security in economically depressed times. Good employers communicate clearly to their employees that the company is not a sugar daddy. Any trust interaction involves expectations. And good employers often have very high expectations of employees.

STUDIES, STUDIES, STUDIES

So far we have explored some of the reasons why people are skeptical about the financial viability of good workplaces. But we have skirted the question raised at the beginning of this chapter: What about the bottom line? How do good workplaces stack up?

That question puzzled Patrick McVeigh, a stock analyst at Franklin Research & Development, a Boston-based private money manager. Shortly after the publication of *The 100 Best Companies to Work for in America* in 1984, he made some comparisons between a broad sampling of other companies (the Standard & Poor 500) and the *100 Best* companies (the seventy firms with publicly traded stock). McVeigh measured the two groups of companies using two conventional financial yardsticks—growth in profits (in terms of earnings per share) and increase in the price of stock.

The results were spectacular. Over the previous decade, the *100 Best* companies outperformed the S&P 500 by a wide margin. The *100 Best* companies were more than twice as profitable as the average for the S&P 500; and their stock prices grew at nearly three times the rate of the others.

A year and a half later, stockbrokers Theodore A. Brown and Thomas Van Dyck conducted a similar study for Dean Witter Reynolds. In a booklet entitled, "Socially Responsible Investing: The Financial and Socio/Economic Issues," Brown and Van Dyck analyzed the financial performance of the *100 Best* companies using a technical criterion familiar to serious investors—average compounded total return on investment. Over the five-year period from 1981 to 1985, the publicly traded *100 Best* companies earned investors a substantial 17.69 percent more money than investors in the S&P 500 companies. Brown and Van Dyck asserted:

The evidence is strong that companies that treat their workers well benefit on the bottom line. The prudent investor can no longer ignore the quality of the workplace as an investment issue.

These two surveys are not unique. The extensive literature on this subject overwhelmingly supports the notion that a great workplace is typically a more productive one. By using the *100 Best* list of good workplaces, the Franklin Research and Dean Witter analysts used a broad characterization of good workplaces. Other researchers have defined their criteria more narrowly. They've tried to determine the effect of such practices as employee stock ownership, participatory management, and profit sharing on productivity or profitability. The following three studies illustrate recent research along these lines:

- A 1985 study of 101 industrial firms found that those employing participative-management techniques outscored other firms on 13 of the 14 *Value Line Investors Survey* measurements, including financial strength, earnings per share, average annual earnings yield, and net profit. (The only measure on which these firms did not beat the *Value Line* average was "earnings predictability.") This survey also indicated that companies with participative-management techniques showed lower employee turnover, absenteeism, and grievances than other firms. What's more, S. Andrew Carson, the financial researcher and business-school professor who conducted the survey, concluded: "Overall, the study clearly showed that the more participatory the firm, the higher its level of financial and behavioral success."
- In 1986, the National Center for Employee Ownership (NCEO) released its study of forty-five companies with ESOPs (employee stock ownership plans) to determine what effect employee ownership had on performance. Compared with firms in their industries without ESOP plans, the ESOP companies grew on average 7.1 percent faster in terms of sales and 6.5 percent faster per year in number of employees. The same study also revealed that the ESOP firms experienced significantly higher rates of growth after the introduction of employee ownership than before. According to NCEO's projections, over a ten-year period "the ESOP companies would generate 46 percent more jobs and 40 percent higher sales growth than the

companies would have experienced without employee ownership."

- In 1982, the New York Stock Exchange surveyed a sample of companies with more than a hundred employees to determine the effect of a variety of human-resource programs, ranging from formal training, profit sharing, and quality circles to employee attitude surveys, suggestion systems, and flexible work hours. New York Stock Exchange economists William C. Freund and Eugene Epstein asked firms to evaluate the impact of these programs. More than three quarters of the 1,158 firms reported that the programs were successful in improving productivity and lowering costs. (None of the firms reported that the programs were unsuccessful; most of the remainder suggested that it was "too early to evaluate" the results of such programs.)

Other studies could be cited, such as the Work in America Institute analysis of more than two hundred studies on worker-productivity experiments conducted between 1971 and 1981, or a recent book entitled *The Schuster Report: The Proven Connection Between People and Profits* (John Wiley & Sons) based on a survey of 592 large industrial and service companies. The evidence consistently shows that companies with progressive employment practices *tend* to do better than competitors without similar policies. The research does not prove that good employers *always* perform better. Nor does it indicate that companies that exploit their workers never profit. But it does demonstrate that, in general, the better employers enjoy more financial success than their competitors. I could find no study that could be used to argue the opposite viewpoint—that bad employers perform better financially than good employers.

CHICKEN OR THE EGG?

Before we accept as definitive the conclusion that there is a positive link between good workplace practices and financial success, we should address the chicken-or-the-egg question: Which came first, good employment practices or financial success? Perhaps the studies merely show that successful companies can afford to be generous to their employees, that good workplace practices are a by-product of profitability. Therefore, employers should keep their eyes fixed on the bottom line. If the company succeeds well enough, it can afford the luxury of treating its people better.

This argument has serious problems. For one thing, it ignores that two of the studies cited above, by the NCEO and the New York Stock Exchange, explicitly pinpointed the effect of the introduction of certain techniques. They clearly showed that the more progressive practices *preceded* the improved financial performance.

It's also been my observation of the *100 Best* companies that good employment practices were explicit goals of the company from the outset. (Preston Trucking was one of the few exceptions.) Being founded with high ideals about creating a good working environment does not, of course, distinguish good workplaces. Many other companies have been founded with similar ideals but gave up when the going got rough. What makes good employers good is that they avoid compromising their people during difficult times.

Similarly, I can think of no examples of firms that became good employers *after* achieving financial success. As a company prospers, it may have more to share with employees. But if sharing the spoils of success has not been a pattern before prosperity strikes, it is highly unlikely to become the policy afterward.

At the same time, it's undeniable that being successful is a terrific morale booster. Everybody likes being number one. There's nothing wrong with trying to be the best or the biggest or the most profitable unless you use questionable means to achieve those goals. Having high competitive goals can be a major factor in eradicating the traditional gulf between management and employees. But everybody does have to have a genuine stake in the outcome. Otherwise, attempts to boost team spirit and morale will backfire because they will be correctly perceived as yet another manipulative technique.

Perhaps we can explain the success of good workplaces in a straightforward way. Good workplaces are defined by having a high degree of trust in the workplace relationships. In general, we can assume that where the level of trust is high, people cooperate better than where it is low. So good workplaces will have an edge since cooperation is the name of the game in complex businesses. With hundreds or thousands of people doing many different but interrelated tasks, it matters a great deal how well people are able to coordinate their activities.

Doug Strain, founder of Electro Scientific Instruments, a *100 Best* company, gives this example of how trust improves cooperation:

We were very fortunate in our beginnings because the four of us founders had known each other for years and had gone through school together. We just trusted one another. That releases a lot of energy to apply to tasks rather than wondering, for instance, whether if you go off on a long trip that you'll come back and find out somebody has stabbed you in the back or killed the project or done something without letting you know about it. Not having to watch that sort of thing really releases a lot of energy for the work.

It takes a while to evolve that sort of thing. That is, trust isn't built up overnight. You really have to watch yourself all the time to be sure that you've explained your motivation for doing things and make sure you put yourself in the other person's shoes. But once trust happens, it just seems to me that there's just so much more energy released for the important things. I think trust is the real grease that makes an organization run.

Obviously, trust is not a cure-all for every organizational ill. Even a well-coordinated company can't survive selling obsolete products as, for instance, the horse carriage makers learned after the turn of the century. But trust does, as Strain suggests, provide an awfully good grease.

A final caveat must be inserted, however. Just because good work-places tend to be more productive and profitable does not mean that good employers are primarily motivated to treat their people well in order to improve profitability. Ewing Kauffman, founder of Marion Labs, offers an interesting perspective on this point. He told a gathering of company employees:

> Don't be ashamed to say that we are profitable. Hold your head high and your chest out and say, "We're the best in the industry, with more sales and more profits per associate than any other company." Be proud of it. Glory in it!

He then went on to say that the more important question was: "Does your company have a heart?" His answer, of course, was a resounding yes: Marion's products help humanity; it shares its success with its employees; it has a sense of corporate responsibility.

As far as Ewing Kauffman is concerned, there is no conflict between being profitable and being a good employer. He's saying that prof-itability isn't the only, or even the most important, criterion by which the firm should be judged. Profits have their place. Without profits, a private enterprise will die. But a firm's bottom line isn't how we should ultimately judge the enterprise. We need to eat in order to live. It's a far different matter to say that we should live in order to eat.

What's more important about a great workplace is that profits are not something to be achieved at the expense of the people responsible for creating them. A great workplace suggests that it's possible to achieve success while *enriching* the lives of the people who work there. The growth they achieve through more trusting relationships also helps the firm grow and prosper. And because fairness is a fundamental characteristic of a great workplace, a highly profitable good workplace literally enriches its employees, too. This is not merely a utopian vision. It's already a working reality at good workplaces throughout the land.

— 15 —

TOWARD A NEW
WORKPLACE ETHIC

Work is so central to our lives that it is how we typically identify ourselves ("I'm an engineer"; "I'm a cashier"). Work defines our role in society. It determines our level of income and hence our standard of living. All this is obvious, but more than our social identity is determined by our work. How we work, the quality of the workplace, also affects our personal lives.

The state of our personal health, for example, can be affected by our work. There are up to 100,000 deaths and 340,000 disabilities each year resulting from work-related diseases. One government agency estimated that 2.3 million workers in such industries as mining, foundry work, ceramics, and plastic manufacturing risk contracting a lung disease called silicosis.

Work affects our mental health as well. Here is an excerpt from a recent report by the National Institute for Occupational Safety and Health:

> There is increasing evidence that an unsatisfactory work environment may contribute to psychological disorders. Studies have shown that factors contributing to an unsatisfactory work environment may include work overload, lack of control over one's work, nonsupportive supervisors or co-workers, limited job opportunities, role ambiguity or conflict, rotating shiftwork, and machine-paced work.

As we've seen repeatedly throughout this book, good workplaces address most of these pathological problems. The issue of increasing employees' control over their own work, for instance, is a key issue in creating a better employee relationship with his or her job.

It's worth noting that the question of executive stress has been a popular subject among psychologists and others for years. The image projected has been of the hard-driving executive whose health gets destroyed by the terrible pressures of his or her job. This is a real problem that has affected many individuals. But what has been almost universally ignored is the terrible toll workplace stress has placed on the people who work underneath the hard-driving executives. Four studies conducted among more than five thousand Swedish and American men disclosed that the lower tenth of workers, measured in terms of their ability to control their own jobs, were five times more likely to develop heart disease than the top tenth of the workplace hierarchy, who had the greatest control over their own jobs. According to one of the researchers, Dr. Robert Karasek of Columbia University, the health risk of low job control is "roughly the same order of magnitude as smoking or an elevated serum cholesterol level."

Throughout this book, we've seen that the bad workplaces subscribe to the notion, held by society at large, that serving employees cannot be a principal purpose of an enterprise. At best, people are seen as a means to an end, the end being higher productivity or higher profitability. By contrast, the underlying message of good workplaces is that a company does not have to sacrifice its people for the good of the enterprise. In a profound sense, good workplaces declare that the people working for a company *are* the enterprise, and their needs should not always be subordinated to other goals of the organization.

Robert Greenleaf, a former management educator for AT&T, made an eloquent plea for a new workplace ethic in his volume, *Servant Leadership*, published a decade ago. He wrote that "work, all work, exists as much for the enrichment of the life of the worker as it does for the service of the one who pays for it." If this assumption was genuinely accepted by business at large, Greenleaf says:

> When a business manager who is fully committed to this ethic is asked, "What are you in business for?" the answer may be: *"I am in the business of growing people*—people who are stronger, healthier, more autonomous, more self-reliant, more competent. Incidentally, we also make and sell for a profit things that people want to buy so we can pay for all this. We play that game hard and well and we are successful by the usual standards, but that is really incidental . . ."

Does this sound farfetched? Impractical? Absolutely not. Several years ago, Milton Moskowitz, Michael Katz, and I coauthored a book entitled *The Computer Entrepreneurs*, composed of profiles of sixty-five men and women who founded companies that were part of the then-infant personal-computer industry. Because most of them had recently founded their companies, it was easy to explore with them their motivations for becoming entrepreneurs. What we heard is no surprise to anyone who has talked to entrepreneurs. They started their companies because they were frustrated in their previous jobs. Either they had ideas that they couldn't get their previous employers to go along with, or they simply couldn't tolerate the working atmosphere. Almost unanimously they wanted to create a new company where they would be able to grow and do work that was meaningful to them. Many of them sincerely wanted the same for their employees as well. Sure, they hoped they would get rich. But that wasn't their underlying reason for creating the company. They wanted a place to work that was fulfilling and meaningful.

Our society is in many ways at an economic crossroads. The 1987 stock market crash, the mergers and takeover binge, the mind-boggling trade deficits with Japan, West Germany, and other countries—these events point to a new era for the United States. The post-World War II era of America as the biggest and most important economic power on earth is coming to a close. There will be those who refuse to face this reality and say that only if we can improve productivity, can we regain our competitive edge. Unfortunately, calls for higher productivity have usually been translated into prescriptions that mangle people in the workplace. Such calls solidify the notion that the only thing that matters is more, faster, bigger.

Instead of falling back on old reflexes because of this crisis, we should use this opportunity to engage in a major rethinking, not just about where we're going but about how we expect to get there. One of the strongest messages of good workplaces is that being biggest is not as important as being best. Instead of being the world's biggest producer, our face to the world could be that of being the best producer. Being the best means not just producing the best quality. We could be the best producer in the ways in which we produce things. We could become known as the place where all people at all levels are treated decently because work is seen as an end in and of itself. The workplace, in this vision, becomes a place for people, not for people who feel like robots.